Planning for Retirement Needs

Huebner School Series   *Walt J. Woerheide, Editor*

Huebner School Series

Planning for Retirement Needs
Fifth Edition

David A. Littell
Kenn Beam Tacchino

The American College/*Bryn Mawr, Pennsylvania*

This publication is designed to provide accurate and authoritative information about the subject covered. While every precaution has been taken in the preparation of this material, the editor and The American College assume no liability for damages resulting from the use of the information contained in this publication. The American College is not engaged in rendering legal, accounting, or other professional advice. If legal or other expert advice is required, the services of an appropriate professional should be sought.

Library of Congress Catalog Card Number 2001135188
ISBN 1-57996-039-1

Printed in the United States of America

Contents

You will notice when reading this book that some of the indexed numbers are for 2002 and some are for 2001. At the time of publication, the indexed numbers for 2002 were not generally available. However, many of the pension limits for 2002 were changed by the Economic Growth and Tax Relief Reconciliation Act of 2001. This book does reflect the changes made by that law—and these numbers appear as the limits for 2002. As soon as available, the remaining 2002 indexed numbers will be posted at http://www.amercoll.edu/coursepages/hs326/hs326.asp

Preface

This book represents a radical departure from traditional pension literature by focusing primarily on the practical application of the retirement material in a financial services practice. To this end it includes a feature titled "Your Financial Services Practice" as well as a shorter counterpart called the "Planning Note." In addition, the book is replete with examples and case studies intended to demonstrate how the pension concepts apply in real-world situations. This new practitioner-oriented approach came about for a variety of reasons, perhaps the most important of which is that student feedback indicated a need for change in this direction.

This book is geared to those with little or no experience in the retirement field. The material focuses on the basics that a financial services professional needs to know and deals sparingly with the retirement concepts that are not germane. For example, stock plans are not discussed in great detail because they are not a part of the typical financial services professional's practice. In addition, the amount of detail on any given topic depends on the topic's relevance to our audience. Determining the appropriate plan for the small business is covered in great detail, for example, whereas the question of which funding method the actuary should choose to fund a plan is covered only briefly. In other words, areas such as funding methods and stock plans are discussed in the context of how they apply to the financial services professional. While the material is applicable to the large-, medium-, and small-plan markets, the emphasis is on the small-plan market, where the financial services professional does most of his or her business.

Almost all general statements that one can make about pension material are subject to qualification or exception. If the qualifying remark or exception is of significant magnitude, we have put it into the text as a parenthetical expression. If the qualifying statement or exception would serve to confuse the larger issue, however, we have omitted it so that you won't get caught up in the minutia and miss the major point.

It is our sincere hope that this practitioner-oriented approach will speak to your interests and provide both a practical and educational treatment of retirement planning for the business and the business owner as well as for the individual. For those interested in learning more about the topics discussed in other course materials and books prepared by The American College, related courses include the following:

- HS 341 *Selected Retirement Planning Topics*, which goes deeper into qualified and other tax-advantaged retirement plans, focusing on advanced design issues, relevant topics not discussed in depth in this book, and issues relevant to those involved in the ongoing operation of retirement plans.
- HS 336 *Financial Decision Making at Retirement,* which goes deeper into the topic of individual retirement planning. In addition to a discussion of determining financial needs and identifying sources of retirement income, this course provides an in-depth look at important issues facing retirees, including the taxation of pension benefits, providing for medical coverage in retirement, and housing issues facing the retiree.

The authors would like to acknowledge the help of many individuals who were instrumental in the development of current/former editions of this textbook.

- Current and former faculty members who participated in the drafting of of this text including William J. Ruckstuhl, Edward E. Graves, and Robert J. Doyle.
- Practitioners in the retirement planning field including Gerald Levinson, Prentice Hall, Inc.; Joseph P. Garner, Paul Paleologopoulos, and Ken Switzer, all of Massachusetts Mutual Life Insurance Company; and Gary Lyons, who acted more like a coauthor than an adviser.
- Our fellow faculty members at The American College, especially Burton T. Beam, Jr., Ted Kurlowicz, and John J. McFadden.
- Educators outside The American College including Robert W. Cooper, PhD, Drake University, and George Rejda, PhD, University of Nebraska.
- The College's editorial staff, especially Renée Heron for manuscript editing.
- The College's production staff, especially Susan Doherty and Evelyn Rice for their production assistance.

About the Authors

David A. Littell, JD, is a professor of taxation at The American College. A native of Chicago, David holds a BA in Psychology from Northwestern University and a JD from the Boston University School of Law. At The American College he is responsible for course development in pension and retirement planning. He is a member of the Pennsylvania Bar and the Delaware County Bar Association. He was previously an attorney with Saul, Ewing, Remick & Saul, and Paul Tanker & Associates, both Philadelphia-based firms.

Kenn B. Tacchino, JD, LLM, is a consultant to The American College and a professor of taxation at Widener University. He is also editor of *The Journal of Financial Service Professionals*. He received his BA from Muhlenberg College, his law degree (JD) from Western New England Law School, and his LLM from Widener University School of Law. Kenn is a member of the American Bar Association and National Council on Aging. He previously worked for Massachusetts Mutual Life Insurance Company and Prentice-Hall.

Planning for Retirement Needs

1

Pension and Retirement Planning Overview

Learning Objectives

An understanding of the material in this chapter should enable the student to

1-1. Describe the extent of and opportunities in the retirement planning field.

1-2. Identify why tax-advantaged retirement plans are positive for employees.

1-3. Identify why the tax-advantaged retirement plans are good for employers.

1-4. Indicate why business owners are interested in qualified plans.

Chapter Outline

THE ALLURE OF THE RETIREMENT MARKET

Retirement planning continues to be an important marketplace for the financial services professional. Public consciousness regarding the need for retirement planning has never been higher. The baby boom generation is marching toward retirement age; and pension benefits are more visible to consumers as employers promote the advantages of employee involvement in 401(k) and 403(b) plans. But, this is only part of the story. The retirement market is where the money is; almost $8 trillion in assets was owned by private retirement plans in 1998—even more if you add federal, state, and local government plans.[1] Also, Americans are aging. As of the year 2000, one out of every eight Americans was over age 65 and, by the year 2025, that figure will increase to one out of five. Considering these demographics, the potential for the growth of the retirement market is nothing short of tremendous.

For financial services professionals, the retirement market offers many attractive and lucrative opportunities to serve clients including

- setting up qualified plans or other tax-advantaged retirement plans for corporations and other for-profit business entities (chapters 3–5)
- setting up retirement programs for nonprofit organizations (chapter 6)
- modifying existing retirement programs to maximize tax-shelter potential, either by changing the existing plan or by instituting multiple plans (chapters 3–6)
- supplementing existing retirement programs with 401(k) plans (chapter 5)
- updating existing plans to conform with legislative changes (chapters 7–10)
- updating existing plans to conform with changing organizational needs (chapters 7–10)
- designing retirement programs that meet the owner-employee's tax and savings objectives (chapters 7–10)
- advising clients about investment strategies that are appropriate for retirement programs (chapters 11–12)

- selling investment products that are appropriate for retirement programs (chapters 11–12)
- planning for the purchase of life insurance in tax-sheltered plans (chapters 10 and 12)
- setting up nonqualified plans for executives (chapters 15–16)
- selling IRAs and Roth IRAs to clients (chapters 17–18)
- planning for a client's retirement (chapters 19–24)
- planning for the best disposition of a client's retirement benefits (chapters 25–26)

Many financial services professionals choose to specialize in pensions. Others, however, complement their existing practice by providing one or more of these services under the umbrella of comprehensive financial planning. Whether you choose to specialize or offer one or more of these services to clients as part of a comprehensive package, the information in this book should open up a world of opportunity.

WHAT YOU WILL FIND IN THIS BOOK

This book is intended to be an introduction to two major areas. Part 1 discusses advising businesses and nonprofit organizations with regard to the choice and maintenance of an appropriate retirement plan. Part 2 provides an introduction to individual retirement planning. The marriage of these two topics reflects the current state of the pension field. As the field has matured, selling retirement plans as tax shelters or as employee benefits is not enough. With the popularity of 401(k) and 403(b) plans, which allow for employee pretax contributions, employees are more involved than ever in ensuring their own retirement security. Employers often look to their pension advisers to help educate their employees about retirement planning. Employee education also helps employees better understand and appreciate the retirement benefits provided by the employer. The pension adviser helps the business owner choose an appropriate retirement plan and must be able to help the owner determine his or her retirement needs.

Even the financial adviser who works as a retirement planner, but not directly with pension planning, must still have a great deal of knowledge of the pension area. He or she needs to be able to evaluate clients' pension benefits and understand the tax treatment of those benefits.

Part 1 begins with an overview (chapters 1–2) of the types of plans available, the tax implications, and the strengths and weaknesses of various choices. Chapters 3–6 discuss the various types of plans available for both for-profit businesses and nonprofit entities. Then, chapters 7–10 address specific plan design issues such as designing the benefit formula, plan eligibility, vesting provisions, participant loans, and plan distributions. After that is a discussion of the funding of retirement plans (chapters 11–12) and administrative issues involved in establishing, maintaining, and terminating plans (chapters 13–14). Chapters 15 and 16 introduce nonqualified plans, which are generally used to provide additional benefits for executives. The final two chapters of part 1 discuss the one type of tax-advantaged retirement savings vehicle available for individuals—IRAs.

Part 2 begins with a discussion of the need for individual retirement planning and a review of the types of relevant issues facing various types of clients. Following that is a discussion of determining an individual's financial needs in retirement and identifying sources of retirement income. Once needs and available income are identified, the next step is determining any income shortfall and choosing an appropriate investment strategy for saving additional amounts. The final topic in part 2 relates to an important issue facing retirees: how to plan for the distribution of pension assets held in qualified plans and other tax-advantaged retirement vehicles.

THE UNIVERSE OF RETIREMENT PLANNING VEHICLES

Part 1 focuses on an introduction to the world of employer- and individually sponsored retirement vehicles. Entering this world means exposure to a new vocabulary. Learning and remembering this terminology is facilitated by the organization and categorization of the material. You will find that many plans share similar features and only occasionally have differences. Throughout the book there are charts and tables to help you remember the material.

Tax-Advantaged Plans of Private Employers

tax-advantaged retirement plans

qualified plans

One way to organize this discussion is to look at the types *of tax-advantaged retirement plans* that can be sponsored by for-profit and nonprofit employers. Most of these are employer-sponsored plans that are referred to as *qualified plans*. Qualified plans are those plans subject to Code Sec. 401(a) and include defined-benefit pension plans, cash-balance plans, money-purchase pension plans, target-benefit plans, profit-sharing plans, 401(k) plans, stock bonus plans, and ESOPs.

All qualified plans are subject to a number of basic requirements, and each type of plan has its own special characteristics. Two other types of tax-advantaged plans available to for-profit entities are referred to as SEPs (simplified employee pensions) and SIMPLEs (savings incentive match plans for employees). These tax-advantaged plans make up the bulk of the retirement market because of their tax advantages, business applications, and special appeal to the business owner. Tax-exempt entities can also sponsor qualified plans, SEPs, and SIMPLEs. In addition, public school systems and those nonprofit organizations qualifying for Code Sec. 501(c)(3) tax-exempt status can sponsor 403(b) plans that are also referred to as tax-sheltered annuities.

Universe of Qualified Plans

- Defined-benefit pension plan
- Cash-balance pension plan
- Money-purchase pension plan
- Target-benefit pension plan

- Profit-sharing plan
- 401(k) plan
- Stock bonus plan
- ESOP (employee stock ownership plan)

All the employer-sponsored tax-advantaged plans share some characteristics. First, all are employer-sponsored plans that provide for deferred compensation. The compensation may be part of an employee's salary that is held for retirement (as in a salary reduction 401(k) plan, SIMPLE, or 403(b) plan), a share of the profits (as in a profit-sharing plan), an employer-provided amount equal to a percentage of salary (as in a money-purchase plan), or the promise of a monthly salary substitute after retirement (as in a defined-benefit plan). In all tax-advantaged plans the sponsor is required to make contributions to a trust or an insurance contract or, in the

---

Other Tax-Advantaged Plans Available to Private Employers

- SEPs (simplified employee pensions)
- SIMPLEs (savings incentive match plans for employees)
- 403(b) plans (limited to 501(c)(3) organizations)

---

case of a SEP or SIMPLE, an IRA account. Such amounts are held and invested and distributed only at a later time according to the rules applicable to that plan.

What makes tax-advantaged retirement plans special is that the employer gets to take a tax deduction at the time contributions are made to the plan, even though employees do not have to pay income tax until benefits are paid to them. Under the normal rules that apply to the taxation of compensation, the employer is eligible for a tax deduction only at the time employees are determined to have taxable income. For example, in a nonqualified plan for executives, the taxation of compensation can be deferred, but only at the cost of deferring the employer's deduction until the time taxes are paid. The normal taxation rules are like a seesaw—the employer on one end can be elevated (receive a tax deduction) only if the employee at the other end is touching the ground (paying taxes). Conversely, the employee can be elevated (avoid paying taxes) only if the employer is on the ground (not receiving a tax deduction). These "laws of tax physics" are suspended, however, if the employer is willing to satisfy the requirements of one of the tax-advantaged retirement plans.

Tax-advantaged Plan Attributes

- Employer deduction with contribution
- No tax on trust account
- Employee taxed on benefits distributed
- Ability to roll distributions into other tax-deferred plans
- Pure insurance portion of death benefit not taxable

A second unique tax advantage is that income on assets held in a trust or an insurance product is not taxed. Retirement investments earn interest and appreciate without being subject to taxation in the year any gain occurs. (This same principle applies to the cash value buildup of life insurance.) Although such amounts are not taxed at this level, income is taxed as it is paid out as part of an employee's benefits.

A third advantage has to do with taxation of distributions. As we have discussed, benefits are not taxed until they are distributed from the plan. In addition, in most cases, distributions can be rolled over into other tax-advantaged plans, further delaying the payment of income taxes. Also, death benefits paid from the proceeds of a life insurance contract are excludible from income to the extent of the pure insurance amount paid (the difference between the policy's face amount and its cash value). In addition, certain distributions from qualified plans (but not SEPs, SIMPLEs, or 403(b) plans) may be eligible for special tax treatment. Such treatment includes the following:

- *Forward averaging*—Although special averaging has generally been repealed, 10-year forward averaging continues to be available to qualified-plan participants born before January 1, 1936 who receive a lump-sum distribution. In some cases, forward averaging results in a lower effective tax rate (in exchange for taking the entire amount into income in one year).

- *Capital-gains treatment*—Another grandfathered tax rule allows individuals born before 1936 to treat the portion of a lump-sum distribution attributable to pre-1974 plan participation as capital gain subject to a grandfathered tax rate of 20 percent.

- *Deferral of gain on unrealized appreciation*—A recipient of a lump-sum distribution may elect to defer paying tax on the net unrealized appreciation in the employer securities that are distributed. If the distribution is not a lump-sum distribution, unrealized appreciation is excludible only to the extent that the appreciation is attributable to nondeductible employee contributions.

In exchange for these tax advantages, the law imposes—as you will see throughout part 1—a large number of requirements. Although the rules are different for each type of plan, there are many similarities. Before we get into the details, it is helpful to get a feeling for what types of requirements are involved.

- *Broad employee participation*—In order for the owners and managers to participate in the tax benefits, the plan must cover a significant number of rank-and-file employees.
- *Vesting*—To make sure that employees who leave prior to the plan's normal retirement age receive some benefits, an employee must be vested in some benefits after he or she has reached a specified number of years of employment. Some types of plans require immediate vesting.
- *Employee communications*—All plans must describe to employees what the terms and conditions of the plan are and to what benefits a participant will be entitled.
- *Nondiscrimination*—All plans have rules regarding the relationship between the level of benefits provided for highly compensated employees and the level of benefits provided to the rank and file.
- *Prefunded*—As has already been mentioned, all plans require that assets be contributed to a funding vehicle—once assets are in the plan they are no longer owned by the employer sponsoring the plan. These assets can be used only to pay plan benefits.
- *Plan document*—Plans need to be stated clearly in writing.

Nonqualified Plans

nonqualified plans

Another very different type of employer-sponsored retirement planning vehicle is the *nonqualified plan.* Most use this term to describe deferred-compensation plans other than the tax-advantaged plans described above. Nonqualified plans differ in almost every way from their tax-advantaged counterparts. Unlike the tax-advantaged plans, nonqualified plans are generally for only a few key people. There are few design restrictions regarding the benefit structure, vesting requirements, or coverage. In most cases, nonqualified plans do not have separate assets. The employer either pays benefits out of general corporate assets or sets up a side account. Sometimes a trust is set up, but assets must be available to pay the claims of creditors in order to avoid current taxation.

In exchange for the added flexibility in plan design, the tax rules are not as kind to a nonqualified plan. A plan can generally be designed to defer the payment of income taxes by the employee until benefits are paid out; but the employer's tax deduction is deferred to the time of payout as well. This is a disincentive to the corporation, because cash payments or qualified plan contributions for the executive would be currently deductible. Because the loss of the tax deduction does not have an impact on nonprofit or governmental entities, Congress has established special limits on the amount of deferred compensation to employees of such entities under Code Sec. 457. Another difference between tax-advantaged and nonqualified plans is that benefits are not as secure. With a nonqualified arrangement, if the entity has financial difficulty, any money set aside to pay benefits can generally be attached by creditors.

Nonqualified Plans

- Can limit to executives
- Few design restrictions
- Employer deduction matched to employee income
- Limited benefit security for participants

IRAs

individual retirement account

The final type of plan discussed in part 1 is the *individual retirement account* (IRA). As its name implies, this type of plan is generally established not by the employer but by individuals. Although part 1 focuses mostly on employer-sponsored plans, an understanding of the IRA and the newer Roth IRA is crucial to this discussion. At times, a business owner or employee will be faced with the choice of participating in a company-sponsored plan or establishing an IRA or Roth IRA. Also, in some cases, an individual can choose to participate in both. Understanding the connection between employer sponsored plans and IRAs is crucial for the following reasons:

1. Most working individuals will still have some IRA options. Many will have the option of making a $3,000 contribution (for 2002) to a Roth IRA, and some will have the option of choosing instead to make a deductible contribution to a traditional IRA.
2. The IRA is the funding vehicle for the employer-sponsored SEP and SIMPLE. This means that most rules applicable to IRAs will apply to those plans as well.

3. A significant portion of qualified plan and 403(b) benefits that are paid to terminated employees is rolled over into IRAs. Once the money is in a traditional IRA, many individuals will also have the option to convert to a Roth IRA.

HOW TAX-ADVANTAGED PLANS BENEFIT EMPLOYEES

Tax-advantaged retirement plans make up the bulk of the retirement planning market because of the significant benefits to employees, employers, and business owners. Tax-sheltered plans play a significant role in the retirement security of American workers. Today, almost two-thirds of those nearing retirement age are covered by a pension plan.[2] Along with Social Security and individual savings, employer-provided pensions have a significant impact on the retirement security of Americans.

In addition, today employer-provided savings plans—such as the 401(k) plan and the SIMPLE—help employees save even more for retirement, by providing an easy payroll deduction savings vehicle with significant tax advantages for the employee. Savings plans have significantly changed the retirement planning landscape. 401(k) plans have virtually blasted their way onto the scene. Since they were established in 1978, they have grown to the extent that today one of four employees covered by a qualified plan participates in a 401(k) plan. Looking just at large and midsize employers, the percentage is much higher.

Case Study: Saving on a Pretax versus an After-tax Basis

To demonstrate how saving on a tax-deferred basis affects retirement accumulations, let's take the example of Bob Bluecollar and William Whitecollar. Bob Bluecollar (aged 40) earns $25,000 annually and has a 15 percent marginal federal tax rate. William Whitecollar (aged 40) earns $150,000 and has a 36 percent marginal federal tax rate. Both Bluecollar's and Whitecollar's employers offer them the opportunity to receive an additional $5,000 annually in cash or have that amount contributed to a 401(k) plan on a pretax basis. All invested money earns a 10 percent rate of return.

Under the qualified plan, both Bluecollar and Whitecollar will save $5,500 by the end of the first year:

Amount contributed	$5,000
plus 10 percent interest	500
Amount saved after one year	$5,500

If Bluecollar and Whitecollar invested the cash they received for retirement (individual savings approach), they would have less saved. The culprit would be the individual taxes that Bluecollar (15 percent) and Whitecollar (36 percent) would have to pay on the cash and interest earnings:

	Bluecollar	Whitecollar
Amount of bonus	$5,000.00	$ 5,000.00
minus individual taxes	750.00	1,800.00
Amount actually saved	4,250.00	3,200.00
plus 10 percent interest	425.00	320.00
Subtotal	4,675.00	3,520.00
minus taxes on interest earned	64.00	115.20
Amount saved after one year	$4,611.00	$3,404.80

Table 1-1 shows the growth of retirement savings for both employees from ages 40 to 65 using both methods. The figures reflect the amount of retirement savings if the funds are distributed to the employees at one time and are taxed at their normal marginal tax rate (15 percent for Bluecollar and 36 percent for Whitecollar).[3] Note that the savings for Bluecollar and Whitecollar under a qualified plan would be significant even after taxes have been paid. By age 65, Bluecollar's qualified plan would have accumulated $97,015 more than his individual savings. For Whitecollar, the qualified approach would have yielded $148,509 more than individual savings. Not only is the qualified plan a more effective way to save, but also, as the figures indicate, the higher the employee's tax bracket, the greater the tax and retirement savings when a qualified plan is used. This special appeal to highly paid employees is what fuels sales and can be considered a critical advantage of qualified plans.

TABLE 1-1
After-tax Comparison of Retirement Savings Methods*

Participant	Qualified	Individual Savings
Bluecollar at age 65 Whitecollar at age 65	$459,772 $346,181	$362,757 $197,672

*Certain underlying assumptions were made that may affect the actual amount received. The assumptions do not, however, significantly affect the disparity between the savings methods.

A Penny Saved—More Than a Penny Earned?

Another way to look at the savings opportunities in a tax-advantaged plan is simply to look at the advantages of orderly savings over a long period of time—or the time value of money. Here, qualified plans don't really have an advantage over other types of savings, except for the ease of saving on a payroll deduction basis. Economists tell us that if we save over a period of time, our savings will increase due to the "opportunity cost" (that is, the gain obtained by investing as opposed to spending). In other words, by squirreling away money over time and forsaking the current use of that money we can ensure that the amount will increase through accumulated interest. Interest can be viewed as a way of quantifying the opportunity cost accruing to a person who waits to receive money. In the previous example, in the qualified plan Bluecollar accumulated after-tax earnings in the amount of $334,772.

After-tax lump sum received at age 65	$459,772
minus total amount invested	(125,000)
After-tax interest accumulation	$334,772

Note that the amount Bluecollar has at age 65 is over three times the original investment. As you might expect, the combination of time value and qualified tax advantages is particularly suited to meeting the retirement-savings goal. Through the use of the qualified plan, Bluecollar and Whitecollar have "purchased" some significantly enhanced retirement security.

YOUR FINANCIAL SERVICES PRACTICE: TRANSLATING TAX CONCEPTS

The extra retirement savings available under a qualified plan can perhaps best be explained to your client by using the concept of an interest-free loan. Explain to the client that by forgoing immediate taxation on amounts put into and earned by a qualified plan, the Internal Revenue Service is, in effect, making an interest-free loan to the plan participants to help them accumulate retirement savings. The amount of this "loan" for an individual in the 38 percent federal, state, and local tax bracket is 38 cents for every dollar saved and for every dollar of interest earned (in other words, the amount of the tax). To put it another way, if participants had to use after-tax dollars to save for retirement, they would have only 62 cents for every dollar saved and every dollar earned. The duration of this "interest-free loan" lasts until retirement distributions are received. For distributions paid out under a life annuity, this means that the "interest-free loan" lasts, in part, until the employee's death. Almost everyone should understand this loan analogy—especially if they have an appreciation for time-value-of-money concepts.

WHY EMPLOYERS NEED TAX-ADVANTAGED RETIREMENT PLANS

In addition to meeting the retirement needs of employees, what other incentives prompt employers to implement a retirement program? Unlike participation in the public retirement program—Social Security—participation in a tax-advantaged or nonqualified retirement program is voluntary. And, administrative and funding costs represent a major expenditure (up to 10 percent of payroll for most medium-sized and large firms and even higher for firms where tax shelter is the primary objective). So, what is the bottom-line payoff for these employers?

The payoff comes in the way retirement plans solve a number of operational problems. Although these solutions don't show up on the balance sheet, the following are key ingredients in a company's fiscal success:

- attraction and retention of employees
- avoidance or appeasement of unions
- employee motivation
- graceful transition in turning over the workforce
- social responsibility
- retirement saving as part of successful compensation planning

Attraction and Retention of Employees

Managers contend that the compelling reason for the salary levels and other employee benefits they offer is local and industry standards. The same logic holds true for private pension programs. In other words, if the local pay scale calls for X amount in salary to attract and retain employees, it also calls for a certain level of retirement benefits. Further, if industry standards in insurance, for example, call for a certain level of commissions, they also call for a certain level of retirement benefits. Employers who ignore what the competition is doing with their retirement programs soon become noncompetitive.

By meeting competitive standards, retirement programs play a special role in attracting and retaining key employees. An attractive retirement program has a special appeal for employees whose current income needs are being satisfied. Those employees whose skill and knowledge are at such a level as to command a high salary are particularly interested in a qualified plan as a means of sheltering their earnings from taxes. These highly compensated employees are usually desired by both an employer and a competitor, and the right retirement plan may be the deciding factor in determining what employment opportunity is best.

Retirement plans also attract older employees who are not in the relatively rare position of being highly marketable. For example, many capable employees have flocked to federal and state government jobs—even though the salary levels are not equal to those in the private sector—because of their attractive retirement benefits (for example, up to 75 percent of final salary) and their unique plan design (early retirement after 20 years of service).

Perhaps the most important role of retirement plans is not to attract but to retain employees. If they are well designed and correctly implemented, retirement plans can be a primary reason for staying with a particular company. Benefit formulas can be structured to account for service, and benefits can be vested in such a way as to make it economically desirable for employees to remain instead of going to a competitor. In this age of job-hopping and multiple careers, a soundly structured pension program can be the employer's best recourse against the loss of experienced personnel.

Avoidance or Appeasement of Unions

In 1948, the courts determined that pensions constitute wages and are a condition of employment and, therefore, are negotiable for collective-bargaining purposes (*Inland Steel Company v. National Labor Relations Board,* 170 F.2d 247). Since then retirement plans and unions have developed a special relationship.

On one hand, retirement plans have been used to stifle or limit the growth of a union movement. The implementation of a retirement system or the embellishment of an existing system is believed by some managers to be a viable method of forestalling the establishment of a union. While federal law prohibits employers from "union busting," it does not prohibit the employer from competing with unions in trying to meet employee needs. What better way to demonstrate that the employer is looking out for the best interests of the employee than to establish a system of retirement benefits?

On the other hand, in unionized companies, retirement benefits and other elements of plan design are always one of the hottest bargaining chips. In these companies, private retirement plans have become a necessary way of life rather than an option. In addition, the laws for and design of some union retirement plans (collectively bargained plans in which more than one employer is required to contribute) have evolved differently from the laws for nonunion plans. (The laws for the so-called *multiemployer pension plans* are beyond the scope of this book and will not be covered. For more information see Internal Revenue Code Sec. 414(f).)

Employee Motivation

Employee motivation is another reason employers need private retirement plans. Numerous studies have shown that profit-sharing plans and stock ownership plans increase employee identification with the corporation and provide an incentive to increase productivity. A highly visible retirement plan can do wonders for employee morale, improve workers' attitudes toward authority in the work environment, and may be the best management tool available for turning the corner on important projects or getting through crucial times.

Graceful Transition in Turning over the Workforce

superannuated employees

Employers face a common problem dealing with the employees who outlast their usefulness. Such employees have been there "forever" and are highly compensated, but productivity does not warrant the high salary. These employees are sometimes called *superannuated employees*. Because it is not considered valid business practice to dismiss long-time employees who are not economically productive (for whatever reason) and because personal affection and respect may keep an employer from demoting these employees, an alternative solution is necessary. The alternative is the proper use of the pension plan. With sound plan structure, early retirement can be made attractive. In addition, "golden handshakes"—special packages that make early retirement even sweeter—can be offered. If handled properly, a potentially uncomfortable situation can be turned into a mutually beneficial solution through the use of the private retirement program.

Social Responsibility

Some employers ask for private retirement programs because of their social desirability. These employers want to provide economic security for retired workers despite the lower profit margin that will result. Traditionally, the retired worker could rely on Social Security and private savings as well as a company pension. These employers, however, feel a need to beef up the company pension because they fear for the future existence of Social Security (at least in its current state), and they recognize that we have become a society of spenders and not savers. What's more, the needs of the aged are creeping more and more into the social consciousness, and these employers feel obliged to do their part by instituting forced savings through a retirement program.

Less altruistically, few employers want former employees to be destitute after retirement. Companies often go to painstaking lengths to be known as a good place to work, and fear of negative public relations stemming from the perception that the employer did not "take care of " employees can stimulate a social conscience.

Retirement Saving as Part of Successful Compensation Planning

One question often raised by clients is: Why not pay retirement benefits out as current compensation and let employees fend for themselves when it comes to saving for retirement? After all, the funds used to provide for retirement and the funds used to pay salary are both part of the same compensation package. Enlightened employers, however, feel that by committing a certain part of salary for retirement purposes they not only allow their employees to benefit from the aforementioned tax advantages of a qualified plan, but also provide employees with the most effective compensation package possible. In other words, they are providing a system that meets their employees' financial security needs for both today and tomorrow in the most tax-efficient manner available.

WHY BUSINESS OWNERS NEED TAX-ADVANTAGED RETIREMENT PLANS

Business owners have special needs and concerns when it comes to planning for their retirement and running their business. These include the following:

- tax sheltering as much income as possible
- solving liquidity problems that occur at retirement or death
- sheltering their assets from legal liability and bankruptcy
- avoiding taxes on excess accumulated earnings

Tax Shelter for Business Owners

Qualified plans and other tax-advantaged plans represent one of the best tax shelters available. We have already shown how much more an employee can save for retirement on a pretax versus an after-tax basis. It is important to remember that in the small business environment employers are also employees. Owners of closely held businesses, members of professional corporations, partners, and the self-employed frequently set up retirement plans with the tax sheltering of personal income as their primary motivation. These markets are comprised of upscale clients who often ask to get the most possible tax savings from the qualified-plan tax shelter (and, consequently, make the biggest contributions toward their retirement). Retirement plans are one of the few tax shelters still remaining today. They are also attractive because the rules are clear (making the degree of tax risk quite low) and this is one tax shelter that is not likely to go away.

Note that when the business owner compares saving for retirement through a tax-sheltered vehicle versus after-tax savings, the comparison is not quite the same as for the average employee. The owner may look at required contributions for other employees in the qualified environment as a drain on his or her own savings account. If, for example, only 50 percent of the contribution to the plan is for the benefit of the owner, the owner may feel that he or she is better off taking the entire contribution amount, paying taxes, and saving outside the plan. This is a legitimate concern and may stop some business owners from establishing a plan. However, when working with these types of clients, be sure to fully consider the following:

- The reality is that in almost all cases the contributions for the other employees have some value to the business. If contributions to the plan are not made, the employer may end up having to pay additional cash benefits to employees. Also, some of the other reasons for establishing a plan (discussed above) will come into play, such as employee attraction and retention.
- If the contributions do have some value to the owner, then when making the mathematical comparison of the qualified plan versus after-tax savings, consider quantifying that value. Take, for example, the small business owner with $50,000 to save. If the amount is contributed to a qualified plan, assume that he or she will get $30,000 and other employees will get the other $20,000. If the owner feels that the contribution for the employees has a value to the business of $10,000, then compare a $40,000 contribution to the plan versus $40,000 saved in an after-tax environment.
- An experienced pension professional may be able to come up with creative ways to limit contributions for other employees. In today's pension environment there are some viable options.

Liquidity Concerns

In addition to appealing to business owners as a stable tax shelter, qualified plans are appealing because they solve liquidity problems that often occur at retirement or death. Small business owners typically have a difficult time building business or personal liquidity. They are self-achievers and often feel psychologically compelled to reinvest money in their "baby." A common profile for the business owner is an individual who initially finds success by investing in himself or herself and the business and who continues to do so throughout his or her lifetime. Because his or her "money personality" tends to be more that of a spender than of a saver, the savings that occur through a qualified plan may represent the business owner's only cash available at retirement or death. Thus, the qualified plan (along with, for example, a buy-sell agreement) may be essential to the continuation of the business after death or retirement.

Financial Security Concerns

A third reason that business owners are well served with a tax-advantaged retirement plan is that the plan may provide them with some financial security in the event that their business fails. Federal pension law generally forbids the assignment or alienation of pension benefits. Federal bankruptcy law, however, does not specifically exempt pension assets from the bankrupt estate. For many years, the courts disagreed on this issue. The issue was finally settled by the United States Supreme Court in the case of *Patterson v. Shumate* (112 S. Ct. 1662 (1992)). The court granted extremely broad protection for assets held in retirement plans subject to the protection of ERISA—declaring that such benefits would be excluded from the bankrupt estate. *Patterson* protection seems quite secure for amounts held in qualified plans except in one case. Plans that cover only the business owner and his or her spouse are not subject to ERISA and, therefore, may not be eligible for *Patterson* protection. It is possible, however, for state law to expand protection to such plans. Similarly, whether IRAs are eligible for protection is a matter of state law.

Patterson protection is great news for the small business owner who can protect himself or herself from financial ruin (in case of business failure) by accumulating assets in a qualified plan. This is also good news for the financial services consultant, who now has one more reason to convince the employer to establish a retirement plan. As noted above, the law is still evolving in this area and, if bankruptcy protection is a critical concern for the owner, he or she should seek legal advice.

Accumulated Earnings Tax Concerns

accumulated earnings

Qualified plan contributions sometimes provide one other advantage to the small corporation—lowering the business's exposure to the *accumulated earnings* tax. This tax is essentially a penalty tax for C corporations that attempt to reduce shareholders' tax burden by accumulating earnings instead of paying them out to the shareholders. The tax rate on improper accumulations is 39.6 percent of accumulations that exceed $250,000 ($150,000 for a personal services corporation). Any amounts contributed to a qualified plan will reduce the exposure to the accumulated earnings tax. (For a discussion of the accumulated earnings tax, see Code Secs. 531 through 537).

CHAPTER REVIEW

Answers to the review questions and the self-test questions start on page 673.

Key Terms

tax-advantaged retirement plans   individual retirement account
qualified plans   superannuated employees
nonqualified plans   accumulated earnings tax

Review Questions

1-1. What opportunities to serve the business and the business owner are available to financial services professionals practicing in the retirement market?

1-2. Why is it important to discuss individual retirement planning when reviewing the types of retirement plans available to private employers?

1-3. Name all the qualified plans as well as the other tax-advantaged retirement plans.

1-4. What are the similarities among all tax-advantaged plans, and what makes qualified plans different from the other tax-advantaged plans?

1-5. From the employee's perspective, what are the tax advantages of participating in a qualified plan?

1-6. Scopes is the owner of Monkey Business, Inc., a small business that trains monkeys for work in films. Scopes would like to save $15,000 a year for retirement. Scopes pays federal and state taxes at the 36 percent marginal rate.
   a. Will Scopes save more for retirement under a qualified plan or by taking the $15,000 as extra income and investing it on his own? Why?
   b. Calculate the amount that Scopes will have saved after one year under the qualified plan and individual savings approaches, assuming the amount saved earns 10 percent interest.

1-7. Why is the ability to use a qualified plan analogous to an interest-free loan from the government?

1-8. RAMCO is a relatively small nonunionized company with 60 "younger" employees. RAMCO is in the competitive computer software market and will soon face a major project of updating its technology to be competitive with the new generation of computers. How can a qualified plan help RAMCO?

1-9. What special personal needs does a qualified plan serve for the owner of the business?

Self-Test Questions

T   F   1-1. With the growth of 401(k) and 403(b) plans, individual retirement planning has become an integral part of corporate retirement planning.

T   F   1-2. A SEP is a qualified retirement plan.

T   F   1-3. Distributions from a 403(b) plan are eligible for 10-year forward averaging.

T   F   1-4. In order to avoid current taxation of earnings, tax-advantaged retirement plan funds must be invested in tax-sheltered investments, such as life insurance and municipal bonds.

T   F   1-5. Participants in a tax-advantaged plan can generally delay paying taxes at termination of employment by rolling the benefit into another tax-advantaged plan or IRA.

T   F   1-6. A strength of tax-advantaged retirement plans is that the plan can include highly compensated employees and exclude the rank and file.

T   F   1-7. Qualified plans are more popular than nonqualified plans because they qualify for special tax advantages that are not available to nonqualified plans.

T   F   1-8. The higher the employee's tax bracket, the greater the tax savings using a qualified plan.

T   F   1-9. A qualified plan is the most tax-efficient way to save for retirement.

T   F   1-10. Retirement plans play a key role in making a company competitive in the marketplace because they help the employer to attract and retain younger employees.

T   F   1-11. If it is well designed and correctly implemented, the retirement plan can be an enticement for an employee to stay employed with the company.

T   F   1-12. Pensions are often negotiated in labor contracts because they constitute wages and are a condition of employment that is subject to the collective-bargaining process.

T   F   1-13. Retirement plans can provide for a graceful transition in the workforce by allowing for early retirement and providing "golden handshakes" to older nonproductive employees.

T   F   1-14. Qualified and other tax-advantaged retirement plans represent one of the best tax shelters available for business owners.

T F 1-15. Funds in a qualified plan may be protected in bankruptcy proceedings.

T F 1-16. Contributions to a qualified plan can reduce the small business's exposure to the accumulated earnings tax.

Notes

1. 1999 Life Insurance Fact Book Update, Council of Life Insurance, 1999.
2. General Accounting Office report of Aug. 5, 1996.
3. Most taxpayers continue after retirement to take advantage of additional tax-deferred growth by withdrawing funds over time as they are needed. However, in this example to come up with a snapshot comparison tax was calculated at 65 (which underestimates the value of the tax deferral). To compensate, we have used the taxpayer's normal marginal tax rate—which is not technically accurate because the additional income would put both taxpayers in the highest 39.6 percent bracket.

The Retirement Field

Learning Objectives

An understanding of the material in this chapter should enable the student to

---

2-1. Describe the legislative environment for qualified retirement plans.

2-2. Describe the regulatory environment for qualified retirement plans.

2-3. Identify the professionals and organizations that comprise the retirement field.

2-4. Identify the various sources of information used by financial services professionals practicing in the retirement field.

Chapter Outline

Success in finding clients, planning for clients, and servicing clients starts with an understanding of the boundaries, players, and equipment involved in the retirement field. The retirement field's boundaries are the rules set up by federal legislation and government agencies; the players include your clients, potential clients, support-service companies, and even the inner workings of your own organization; and the equipment is the information sources that are available to provide answers when experience fails to provide them. This chapter will take you on a tour of the retirement field and introduce you to the regulatory environment, pension players, and information sources that will become an integral part of your financial services practice.

Because the multifaceted pension industry is largely an outgrowth of the regulatory process, we will explore this complex area first (including the relationship between the financial services professional and the industry-shaping laws) and review the functions of the regulatory agencies. Then, we will discuss the pension prospects—who is involved and to what extent—and the service and financial organizations that serve them, with special emphasis on the insurance industry. We will end by reviewing the sources for pension information—those that provide answers to a client's questions and those that analyze current trends and put pensions in perspective.

THE LEGISLATIVE ENVIRONMENT

Employee Retirement Income Security Act (ERISA)

The passage of the *Employee Retirement Income Security Act (ERISA)* in 1974 marked the beginning of the current retirement-plan era. ERISA represented an intensified commitment by the federal government to oversee the retirement market (especially plans that cover nonhighly compensated employees). Leery of broken retirement promises and plans being used as tax shelters for the wealthy, the federal government decided to protect the retirement interests of all plan participants and implemented ERISA to establish equitable standards and curtail perceived abuses. The text of ERISA has become the pensioner's bible. ERISA's commandments forbid discrimination in favor of the prohibited group (highly compensated employees), restrictive vesting schedules that keep longtime participants from receiving benefits, and inadequate plan funding, which leads to bankrupt plans. In addition, ERISA requires reporting and disclosure of information about retirement plans to the Internal Revenue Service (IRS), the Department of Labor (DOL), the Pension Benefit Guaranty Corporation (PBGC), and plan participants. In fact, ERISA forces information to be widely disseminated, thereby causing such administrative nightmares that it has become affectionately known as the "full employment in pensions act."

ERISA is composed of four sections known as *titles*. The purpose of the first title is to protect an employee's right to collect benefits. To accomplish this, title I requires employers to report plan information to the federal government and disclose information to participants (reporting and disclosure rules), restricts unlimited employer discretion regarding vesting and plan participation (employers cannot discriminatorily choose whom to cover), implements plan funding standards (employers must set aside sufficient assets to fulfill retirement promises), and lists fiduciary responsibilities (the responsibilities and liabilities of those in charge). Title II amends the Internal Revenue Code, setting forth the necessary requirements for special tax treatment (the plan qualification rules); these requirements are covered in detail in chapters 7 through 10. Title III creates the regulatory and administrative framework necessary for ERISA's ongoing implementation. Responsibilities are divided between the Internal Revenue Service and the Department of Labor, with the IRS having primary jurisdiction for much of the initial and operational administration of pension plans. Title IV establishes the Pension Benefit Guaranty Corporation, an agency that insures pension benefits. The PBGC collects premiums from covered plans (defined-benefit plans only; defined-contribution plans are not insured) and insures a minimum level of benefits for employees if the plan is terminated with insufficient funds.

Four Titles of ERISA

- *Title I*—Amends the labor law to ensure the employee's right to collect promised benefits

- *Title II*— Amends the Internal Revenue Code to condition tax benefits on meeting certain minimum standards

- *Title III*— Creates a regulatory framework for ongoing implementation

- *Title IV*—Establishes the Pension Benefit Guaranty Corporation to insure benefit payments from defined-benefit pension plans

---

The enforcement strategies provided by ERISA are interesting. To enforce title I of ERISA, plan participants, the Department of Labor, and plan fiduciaries can sue to force the payment of appropriate benefits and to require plan representatives to fulfill their jobs. Also, to encourage compliance, errant plan officials can be held personally liable for losses to the plan, fined for certain errors, and in some cases even held criminally liable. It is interesting to note that courts have generally interpreted the enforcement provisions of ERISA to prohibit monetary punitive damages for ERISA claims. Even though ERISA does provide for the award of attorney's fees, the inability to receive punitive damages has probably limited the number of private suits under ERISA over the years.

The strategy for encouraging compliance under the Internal Revenue Code is quite different. Here, both the plan sponsor and the plan participants enjoy special tax treatment in exchange for compliance with the law. Failure to comply can allow the IRS to take away the plan's tax-advantaged status. Because this penalty can harm participants (who are not responsible for ensuring plan compliance), plan disqualification is rarely enforced. In lieu of this terminal penalty, the IRS often negotiates a monetary penalty (payable by the sponsor) and requires that the employer fix any plan defects.[1] Disqualification is not the sole punishment contemplated under the Code. Some plan defects result, not in plan disqualification, but in a penalty tax. Examples of this will be seen throughout the text.

Unfortunately (or fortunately, depending upon your perspective), ERISA was just the beginning of what has seemed like an endless stream of legislation further regulating private pension plans. From 1974 until today the only constant has been change. There have been many law changes during this period with the most recent being the Economic Growth and Tax Relief Reconciliation Act of 2001. (For those interested in a detailed description of the changes over the years, see appendix 1.) For the newcomer to the pension field, the presentation in the appendix may seem overwhelming and confusing. Therefore, an overview of some of the major areas of congressional involvement and a description of the legislative trends over the years appear below.

- *Taxation of pension benefits*—At the time of ERISA, pension benefits were subject to many significant income and estate tax benefits. Over the years, one by one, the special tax advantages have been repealed. For example, at one time, pension benefits were not subject to estate taxes at all. Today, all pension assets that remain after the death of the participant are included in the taxable estate. Similarly, many of the special income tax rules have been repealed and in most cases pension income is treated as any other ordinary income (although some rules have been grandfathered and others have been repealed prospectively).

- *IRAs*—Over the years, IRA rules have swayed with the political breeze. At the time of ERISA, deductible IRA contributions were limited, then IRAs were opened up to virtually everyone, and then, once again, deductible contributions are limited to those who do not participate in an employer-sponsored retirement plan or have relatively low income. We have had some expansion in the last few years with the introduction of the Roth IRA and now with an increase in the maximum contribution limits.

- *Maximum deductible contributions*—Through the eighties and nineties, the trend was to lower the maximum deductible contribution for highly compensated employees. This was done to raise tax revenue, and maybe also out of a perception that plans inappropriately benefited the highly compensated. Contributions were limited by lowering the maximum allowable contribution for each employee, freezing cost-of-living adjustments on contribution limits; limiting the amount of compensation that can be taken into account; imposing limits on employee contributions; and aggregating plans. This trend had a significant impact on executive compensation and benefit planning, making supplemental executive nonqualified deferred-compensation plans a more and more important part of the retirement planning package. In 2001, there was a significant departure from this trend, with increases in allowable contributions for each participant, an increase in the compensation cap, and an increase in the maximum deductible contributions. These changes were intended to increase retirement savings and to encourage small businesses to establish retirement plans.

- *Limiting tax deferral*—Tax revenue is also lost the longer pension assets remain in a tax-deferred environment. To speed up the taxation of benefits, Code Section 401(a)(9) was introduced in 1986, requiring that distributions from all tax-sheltered plans begin at age 70 1/2 (or, in some cases at actual retirement, if later). These minimum-distribution rules have an impact on any retiree receiving qualified plan, 403(b), or IRA distributions.

- *Parity*—Over the years, the trend has been toward giving all types of business entities equal access to retirement plan vehicles. With a few minor exceptions, today C corporations, S corporations, sole proprietorships, partnerships, and even limited liability companies (LLCs) are all on the same footing.

- *Plans of small businesses*—Apparently, based on the perception that retirement plans of small businesses have treated rank-and-file employees unfairly, today a special set of rules, referred to as the *top-heavy requirements,* applies to the plans of many small businesses. These rules require special minimum contribution and vesting requirements for certain top-heavy plans. Again, the law change in 2001 changed this trend somewhat, simplifying the top-heavy rules and giving the owner the opportunity to accumulate more in a retirement plan.

- *Affiliation requirements*—To ensure that businesses cannot avoid pension coverage requirements by operating separate entities, and to eliminate "double dipping" under the maximum deduction rules, over the years Congress has enacted a series of complex rules requiring the aggregation of related employers. These rules have successfully eliminated loopholes and at the same time have complicated matters for both multinational corporations operating multiple divisions and for the small entrepreneur involved in several businesses.

- *Funding*—ERISA imposed minimum funding requirements for defined-benefit pension plans, and established the Pension Benefit Guaranty Corporation (PBGC). This organization ensures that employees in privately sponsored defined-benefit plans will receive at least some of the benefits promised by the plan. For over 20 years, the PBGC ran deficits that reached $2.9 billion in 1993. In response, a number of law changes have required both larger employer contributions and higher

PBGC premiums. As a result, as of the end of 2000, the PBGC recorded its fifth consecutive year-end surplus.

- *Employee Stock Ownership Plans (ESOPs)*—To encourage employee stock ownership, in 1981 the Economic Recovery Tax Act (ERTA) provided for a new type of retirement plan vehicle with numerous special tax advantages referred to as an ESOP. Today, some of these provisions have been repealed, but ESOPs still provide significant tax advantages, as well as a mechanism for a plan to purchase stock on a leveraged basis—providing a viable buyer for the small business owner looking to sell or retire. In fact, ESOP coverage was expanded by the 1996 Act that allowed an S corporation to sponsor an ESOP.

- *Simplification*—One legislative trend that had been consistent from the time of ERISA until 1996 was that each new law made the pension world more complex. Interestingly, in 1996, we had true pension simplification. The changes are modest, but hopefully future legislation will continue in this direction. Provisions include simplifying the definition of highly compensated employees, simplifying the distribution rules, and eliminating several complex aggregation requirements. This new law also introduced the SIMPLE, a savings plan alternative to the 401(k) plan with fewer administrative requirements. The 2001 tax law contained additional simplification provisions, making plans (especially 401(k) plans) easier to administer.

REGULATORY AGENCIES

Legislation makes up only part of the regulatory picture. The other part, the administration of the qualified-plan system (and, to a lesser extent, the nonqualified-plan system), is carried out by the Internal Revenue Service, the department that is required to interpret the laws, explain legal fine points, and oversee the day-to-day operations of retirement plans.

The Internal Revenue Service

The IRS plays the most prominent role of all the bureaucratic agencies.

IRS Regulatory Responsibility

- Qualification letter program
- Audit existing plans
- Interpret legislation

Initial Plan Qualification

In order for an employer to receive favorable tax treatment, the pension plan must meet the qualification requirements. Plan sponsors may, and usually do, request an IRS advance determination that the plan meets those requirements. Employers send in the plan and appropriate forms requesting IRS approval; the IRS agent checks the plan to see if it meets the guidelines (over time the IRS has developed elaborate rules regarding what provisions may and may not be included); and, if necessary, the IRS and employer enter into negotiations over points at issue. If the plan meets IRS standards, a favorable advance-determination letter—which assures the employer that the plan is qualified and that the first year's contributions will be deductible—is issued. Although the program is voluntary, most employers take advantage of getting "preapproval" that plan contributions are eligible for special tax treatment.

YOUR FINANCIAL SERVICES PRACTICE:
NEW LEGISLATION AS A MARKETING OPPORTUNITY

The constant legislative changes that occur in the retirement area (some might call it overregulation) affect the financial services professional in many ways.

- Continual plan review is necessary to determine what impact the new legislation will have on corporate retirement goals.
- Plans must be updated to reflect law changes.
- Clients rely on additional communication and explanation because pension law becomes increasingly complex and detailed.
- Continued education becomes necessary to keep up with the new laws.

One side effect of this constant federal legislation is the opportunity for financial services professionals to perform a detailed review of the plan and corporate retirement goals. Without legislative change and subsequent plan amendment, employers might ignore their plans, and the plans could become stale and outdated. The financial services professional should capitalize on the opportunity created by legislative change and help the business owner evaluate new retirement goals and strategies.

A second side effect of federal legislation is the need to consider the impact on highly compensated employees. Some of the changes have resulted in the need for secondary nonqualified plans to supplement their retirement Income.

Ongoing Auditing

The IRS monitors retirement plans after initial qualification through periodic planned audits. The purpose of IRS surveillance is to make sure that changes in facts or circumstances have not affected plan qualification and that plans are used as retirement vehicles rather than as a tax shelter for the prohibited group. Plans chosen for audit are selected from information supplied in the annual 5500 filings, which includes the type and structure of the plan, plan assets, plan liabilities, plan income, and plan funding. In addition, information regarding plan changes, actuarial methods, and distributions to participants and their beneficiaries is required.

In recent years, the IRS has developed another ongoing enforcement strategy that encourages employers to step forward voluntarily when plan problems are discovered. In exchange for voluntary compliance, the employer is subject to much smaller penalties—usually a set fee—instead of the much larger penalties that could occur if the IRS found the problem upon plan audit. There are actually a number of different programs that have been coordinated under the Employee Plans Compliance Resolution System (EPCRS). These programs encourage voluntary correction of problems and, in many cases, reward employers for taking reasonable steps in keeping their plans in compliance with the law. *Financial planning practice:* Because the IRS program rewards quality administration, service providers can now tell potential clients how their "quality" services can help to keep the client out of trouble.

Interpretation

One of the major responsibilities of the IRS is to issue numerous communications that further explain the existing laws of the Internal Revenue Code. These communications include the following:

final regulations

- *Final regulations* explain and interpret the various sections of the Internal Revenue Code and deal with legal fine points that are not specifically addressed in the Code. Final regulations are legally enforceable, and the Internal Revenue Service is bound by them. They are originally published in the *Internal Revenue Bulletin* and the *Federal Register* and are later bound together with other regulations in a set of *Internal Revenue Regulations*. Final regulations can also be found in many of the loose-leaf services (discussed later).

proposed regulations

- *Proposed regulations* are sometimes issued right after major legislation to give guidance to practitioners on complex provisions of new laws. Unlike final regulations, proposed regulations will have no legal force or effect unless they specifically state that they can be relied upon by taxpayers. Still, they are an indication of the IRS's current thinking and are widely followed. Proposed regulations can be changed before they are finalized—often as the result of negative feedback at public hearings.

temporary regulations

- *Temporary regulations* may be issued as an alternative to final regulations, or can be issued simultaneously with proposed regulations. They are binding until they are superseded or withdrawn. This allows individual and corporate taxpayers to rely on the regulations without fear of incurring a Sec. 6661 penalty for substantially understating income tax liability, a protection that is not available to proposed regulations. A great deal of time can pass between the time a regulation is proposed and when it becomes final, and temporary regulations are relied on heavily in the interim.

revenue rulings

- *Revenue rulings* are the IRS's interpretations of the provisions of the Internal Revenue Code and regulations as they apply to factual situations that taxpayers have presented. Revenue rulings are replete with valuable examples that clarify complex legal issues and may be used as precedents, thus giving you and your clients a sense of security if you are venturing into an area to which the rulings apply.

private-letter rulings

- *Private-letter rulings* interpret the law in light of a specific set of circumstances and indicate whether the IRS believes the action to be acceptable. Private letter rulings address only the specific facts presented to the IRS and, because of this, a taxpayer cannot rely upon guidance provided. Still, they are an important form of guidance, since they address real-life cases that might be similar to your client's situation. (*Planning Note:* If the IRS's position regarding a situation your client is entering into is unclear, you should recommend that the client consider getting a private-letter ruling. For a fee, the IRS will issue a ruling that will be binding in the client's situation.)

- *Publications* include general reviews of retirement topics provided by the IRS. Using understandable terms (no legalese), these publications cover a variety of topics. (*Planning Note:* Publications are written to provide a general overview of the tax law on certain topics. The publications on Keogh plans and qualified retirement plans make good mailers for your clients.)

The Department of Labor (DOL)

Through its Office of Pension and Welfare Benefit Plans (OPWBP), the DOL is heavily involved in the pension arena.

DOL Regulatory Responsibility

- Protect participants through enforcement of the reporting and disclosure rules
- Police the investment of plan assets
- Interpret legislation

Reporting and Disclosure Rules

The first duty of the DOL is to ensure compliance with the reporting and disclosure rules. The most important disclosure requirement is that the plan provide summary plan descriptions (SPDs) to participants. Failure to comply with this or other reporting and disclosure requirements can result in fines and, in some egregious cases, imprisonment.

Prohibited Transactions

A second duty of the DOL is to oversee plan investments. To assure that no self-dealing or conflict of interest is involved, ERISA provides that plans cannot have certain dealings with parties who have close relationships with the plan or the company (referred to as parties in interest). Such behavior is referred to as a prohibited transaction. (The responsibility for overseeing prohibited transactions is shared by the IRS, and a separate but similar set of rules for prohibited transactions is also part of the tax law. What constitutes a prohibited transaction is quite complex and will be discussed further in chapter 12.) For now, understand that the goal of the rules is to keep the interests of the plan separate from the interests of the sponsoring entity, and to ensure that no persons benefit unduly because of their close relationship to the plan. Also note that the statutory scheme prohibits a broad range of behaviors and then carves out a number of statutory exemptions and gives the DOL the authority to issue others.

Fiduciaries

fiduciary

In conjunction with its responsibility to monitor plan investments, the DOL governs the actions of those in charge of running the retirement plans—fiduciaries. A *fiduciary* is a person or corporation that exercises any discretionary authority or control over the management of the plan or plan assets, renders investment advice for a fee, or has any discretionary authority or responsibility in the administration of the plan. Every plan has at least one named fiduciary who is responsible and accountable for operating the plan. Fiduciaries (named or otherwise) invest plan assets (subject to the rules on prohibited transactions), see that plan documents conform to the law, administer plans, and make major decisions regarding plan operation.

The Department of Labor has the means to ensure that fiduciaries uphold their responsibilities; it may sue plan fiduciaries and require a restitution to the plan for any losses resulting from breach of fiduciary duty. (In addition, under the tax provisions overseen by the IRS, a fiduciary may be responsible for excise taxes for violation of the prohibited-transaction provisions.) In doing its job of overseeing the fiduciary responsibility rules and the prohibited-transaction rules, the DOL (and, in a subordinate role, the IRS) acts like a police officer on the beat, carefully checking to see that the laws protecting plan participants are not broken.

Interpretation

As we have just seen, like the Internal Revenue Service, the DOL issues numerous communications that create pension rules and explain existing laws. Many of these items parallel IRS publications. The DOL issues final regulations, temporary regulations, and proposed regulations, which perform the same functions as their IRS counterparts. In addition, the DOL issues advisory opinions that are similar to the private-letter rulings issued by the IRS. As with IRS private letter rulings, your clients can inquire about the acceptability of their acts or transactions, and only the parties actually involved can safely rely on the opinion. Owing to the DOL's unique responsibilities, not all of its communications are similar to those of the IRS. The DOL issues important communications called *prohibited-transaction exemptions* (PTEs). These exemptions can either be on a class basis (for example, "All banks with FDIC insurance are exempt from . . . .") or on a particular transaction basis. (*Planning Note:* The prohibited-transaction exemption is an avenue your client can travel to get approval before taking an investment action that falls into the prohibited-transaction gray area. For example, if your client is a party in interest, he or she can get an exemption from the restrictions on prohibited transactions by applying for a PTE.)

Pension Benefit Guaranty Corporation (PBGC)

Pension Benefit Guaranty Corporation (PBGC)

The PBGC was established under title IV of ERISA as a quasi-governmental corporation. Both the IRS and the Department of Labor are involved to a certain extent with the PBGC, because the Board of Directors includes the Secretaries of Labor, Treasury, and Commerce. Even though the organization, as a quasi-governmental agency, has access to federal government resources, the federal government is not generally liable for any of the obligations or liabilities of the Corporation. This is meaningful, because the PBGC's primary responsibility is to insure participants in and beneficiaries of employee benefit plans against the loss of benefits arising from complete or partial termination of the plan. PBGC insurance coverage applies to most defined-benefit plans of private employers (defined-benefit plans of professional services organizations such as physicians, dentists, attorneys, and accountants who have 25 or fewer active participants are exempt from PBGC coverage). The program does not apply to any defined-contribution plans.

PBGC Regulatory Responsibility

- Administer insurance program for defined-benefit plans
- Oversee termination of covered plans
- Interpret legislation

The PBGC operates by collecting compulsory premiums, which are $19 per participant per plan year (more if the plan is underfunded). For such premiums, the PBGC guarantees to pay certain benefits promised under the plan, in the event that the plan has insufficient assets. The guaranteed benefits are subject to a specified ceiling that is adjusted annually and is currently about $3,200 per month.

TABLE 2-1 Review of the Regulatory Environment for Qualified Plans		
IRS	DOL	PBGC
Initial plan qualification Ongoing auditing through 5500 forms Legal interpretation	Summary plan descriptions Oversee fiduciaries and plan investments Legal interpretation	Insure defined-benefit plans Oversee plan fund solvency Legal interpretation

In conjunction with its duty to insure benefit payments, the PBGC has the power to investigate anyone who has violated or is about to violate any of the plan termination insurance provisions. It can also initiate a lawsuit in federal court for the enforcement of the provisions of title IV. To help the PBGC identify problems, certain events that would indicate that the plan is in financial difficulty must be reported to the PBGC.

The PBGC has another enforcement tool. If a PBGC investigation reveals that a plan is not funded according to legal standards, or that the plan is unable to meet its benefit payments, or if there is a possible long-run loss that will get out of hand unless the plan is terminated, the PBGC may require the plan to be involuntarily terminated to help cut PBGC losses. The PBGC can also cut its losses by tapping up to 30 percent of the net worth of employers whose plans have terminated, leaving the PBGC liable for payments.

Another function of the PBGC is overseeing plan terminations initiated by the plan sponsor. Today (see chapter 14), an employer can terminate a defined-benefit plan covered by the PBGC insurance program only in limited circumstances. Essentially, the plan must either have sufficient assets to pay all benefits (referred to as a voluntary termination), or the company must virtually be facing liquidation (called a distress termination). When the employer terminates such a plan, it is required to give advance notification to employees and submit the proper forms to the PBGC.

As is the case with the IRS and the DOL's Office of Pension and Welfare Benefit Plans, the PBGC issues various communications that serve as sources of information for the financial services professional: PBGC regulations, news releases, opinion letters, publications, and multiemployer bulletins.

PENSIONS: PROFESSIONALS AND ORGANIZATIONS

While the impact of the regulatory environment on the retirement market is great, these federal laws and agencies are nonetheless only the rules and umpires. Employers sponsoring pension plans plus the expanding service and investment industry are the pension professionals and organizations. Together they are responsible for almost 700,000 private pension plans covering more than 67 million participants, as well as numerous plans and participants in the public sector.[2]

Benefit Associations and Designation Programs

In addition to The American College's CLU, ChFC, and REBC designations and the College's Master of Science in Financial Services with its pension certificate track, several other associations are prominent in the benefits community. These include the following:

- The American Society of Pension Actuaries (ASPA) is an organization for those involved with the consulting, administrative, and design aspects of pension and employee benefit plans. ASPA members include Fellows of the Society of Pension Actuaries (FSPA) and Certified Pension Consultants (CPC). ASPA can be contacted at (703) 516-9300.
- The Association of Private Pension and Welfare Plans (APPWP) is the business community's lobbying arm for pensions and employee benefit plans. APPWP can be contacted at (202) 289-6700.
- The Employee Benefits Research Institute (EBRI) is the research arm of the pension and employee benefit community. EBRI can be reached at (202) 659-0670.
- The International Foundation of Employee Benefit Plans is an organization for those involved with benefit consulting and the like. This organization is a cosponsor of the Certified Employee Benefit Specialist (CEBS) designation. The International Foundation of Employee Benefit Plans can be contacted at (262) 786-6710.
- The National Institute of Pension Administrators Educational Foundation, Inc. (NIPA) sponsors the Accredited Pension Administrator (APA) designation. NIPA can be reached at (312) 245-1085.
- The National Tax Sheltered Annuity Association (NTSAA) is a relatively new organization representing the interests of those in the 403(b) tax-sheltered annuity marketplace. They can be reached at (800) 543-0152.
- Other groups that focus on specific portions of the pension market include the ESOP Association, (202) 293-2971, and the Profit Sharing /401(k) Council of America, (312) 441-8550.

Plan Sponsors

Retirement plan sponsors constitute one of the most important financial markets today. And because demographics indicate an aging population, which means increased savings for retirement, the plan sponsors' market is possibly *the* most important financial market of tomorrow. Currently, only about 50 percent of employers have adopted retirement plans. Those who do adopt plans spend, on average, 6 percent of their payroll on qualified-plan premiums and pension payments. This figure, however, is much higher in the small plan market.

Sponsors of retirement plans include corporations, partnerships, and self-employed individuals. If a partnership, limited liability company (which is taxed as a partnership) or self-employed individual sponsors a qualified retirement plan, that plan is sometimes known as a Keogh plan. At one time, the rules for Keogh plans and regular corporate qualified plans differed dramatically because the owner of an unincorporated business, even though he or she performs substantial services for the business, is not technically an employee of the business but is instead referred to as a self-employed person. Over time, however, the differences between corporate plans and Keogh plans have been almost eliminated. (The differences that remain are in chapter 3.)

Prospects—The Candidates for Pensions

Pension prospects range from business owners and professional corporations needing relief from income tax problems to larger organizations looking to satisfy organizational objectives through retirement plans. Every business owner, whether motivated by tax savings, competitiveness, or a sense of moral obligation to the employees, can be shown the need for a retirement system. The best prospects, however, will be

- businesses where the owner is an active employee interested in tax savings, such as professional corporations, sole proprietorships, and closely held businesses
- large corporations operating in a competitive labor market
- companies and service organizations—large, small, or individually run—that are just turning the corner on financial success
- institutions such as public schools, colleges, hospitals, and charitable organizations
- recently unionized employers or employers staving off union organization
- corporations with one type of retirement plan who may need a supplemental program—a 401(k) arrangement, for example

**YOUR FINANCIAL SERVICES PRACTICE:
RETIREMENT PROSPECTING**

Prospecting techniques in the retirement market differ from those in the personal selling market. While prospecting in the retirement market does include the traditional methods of direct mail, preapproach letters combined with phone calls for appointments, and the use of existing clients as referred leads, other unique methods are available. These include (1) developing accountants and attorneys—professionals who are in touch with the financial ability of the employers to provide retirement benefits—into centers of influence, (2) creating working relationships with banks interested in some trust business that complements pension insurance sales, (3) obtaining pension consultants or actuarial firms as referral sources, (4) working with casualty and insurance brokers in the commercial and industrial market whose clients are probably also pension prospects, and (5) purchasing lists of pension prospects in your area. Dunn & Bradstreet, (800) 526-0651, publishes the ERISA redbook, which contains information reported on the annual form 5500 reports filed by each plan sponsor in a specific geographic region. Judy Diamond Associates, Inc., (800) 231-0669, offers a number of similar listings, as well as lists of small businesses that do not currently have retirement plans.

Service and Financial Groups

The pension market is replete with organizations offering to design and implement plans; provide consulting, record-keeping, legal, and actuarial services; furnish employee communications; and oversee plan administration. In short, those in charge of pensions can easily farm out the entire process to *third-party administrators (TPAs)*. The same is true regarding the management of the pension plan assets. For those plan administrators who would rather do some or all of their work in-house, there are a variety of computer services, many offered by small, specialized companies.

third-party administrators (TPAs)

The organizations that provide plan services include consulting houses, actuarial firms, insurance companies, administrative consultants, and software companies. In the financial market, there are trust companies, commercial banks, investment houses, asset-management groups, and insurance companies. The major service and financial groups have no particular areas of concentration, but rather offer a myriad of services. For example, consulting houses do not just do consulting and plan installation and administration, they may also offer computer services and investment facilities. Computer software companies may offer consulting services as well as creating software.

master and prototype plans

Many financial services organizations sponsor *master and prototype plans*, standardized plans approved and qualified in concept by the Internal Revenue Service, which are then adopted by their customer organizations. The master and prototype plans offer an employer fewer choices in plan design and, thus, can be installed very easily. The use of a master or prototype simplifies the task for the financial services professional by setting up an easily understood framework to work with, known as the *adoption agreement*. The adoption agreement resembles a smorgasbord in many ways—for example, you choose one out of five benefit formulas, one out of three vesting tables, and so on—which simplifies the plan design process and saves time.

INFORMATION

Where do you turn when you need to answer a client's question or find out about the latest law or idea? What sources and references offer necessary information to a pension practitioner? The resources you can call on include primary sources, books, periodicals, loose-leaf services, on-line databases, and software packages. The following is an analysis of the major items that should be considered for inclusion in your pension library.

Primary Sources and Other Invaluable Resources

primary sources

The most reliable and important sources of information are, of course, the *primary sources*: texts of the laws, the Internal Revenue Code, the example-laden regulations, and many of the numerous agency interpretations. Unlike secondary sources such as books and periodicals, primary sources can be relied on by the practitioner as an accurate and legally enforceable representation of a situation.

Although not binding—like primary sources—the IRS and Department of Labor both have publications that explain, usually in plain English, the various rules and regulations. Many of these publications are well written, provide additional guidance on the agency's interpretation of the law, and, best of all, they are free! The IRS has especially good publications on IRAs and the taxation of pension distributions.

A final invaluable source for learning about Congress's meaning of a particular law is to look at the law's statutory history. Generally, the most meaningful of these documents are the committee reports of the Senate, House of Representatives, and Conference Committee (where differences between provisions in the House of Representatives and Senate bills are resolved). Also, with tax legislation, oftentimes the joint committee on taxation prepares a report,

blue book

which is known as the *blue book* (available from most loose-leaf services). These are highly regarded in the tax community as understandable resources that explain the legislative intent behind the law.

These primary sources can be found in many places, as discussed below. Today, in many ways the easiest way to access most of this material is to go directly to the government web sites discussed below.

Books

Several outstanding books in the pension field provide in-depth overviews of pensions and retirement plans. These include

- Allen, Melone, Rosenbloom, and Vanderhei, *Pension Planning* (a thorough and well-regarded treatment)
- Beam and McFadden, *Employee Benefits* (another good overview of the employee benefits field)
- Canan, *Qualified Retirement and Other Employee Benefit Plans* (comprehensive coverage of the legal requirements)
- Bennett, et al., *Taxation of Distributions from Qualified Plans* (a comprehensive and technical treatment of the income and estate tax consequences of qualified plans)
- *The Pension Answer Book Series* (The first edition covered the whole pension field; now, there is a whole series of specialty books covering such topics as 401(k) plans, 403(b) plans, plan investments, and plan distributions.)
- A yearly reference book, such as *Tax Facts* (published by National Underwriter, Cincinnati, Ohio), is also an important addition to any pension library.

Periodicals

There are innumerable periodicals reporting on every angle of pensions and retirement. The employee benefit side of pensions is covered in *Employee Benefits Plan Review* (which contains an excellent listing of benefit-plan service companies) and *Benefits Quarterly* (loaded with perceptive articles). From the investment side of pensions, there are *Pension World* (targeted to plan sponsors and investment managers) and *Pensions and Investment Age* (the newspaper of corporate and institutional investing). The insurance side of pensions is represented by the *Journal of Financial Services Professionals* and *Life Insurance Selling* (the annual reports on pensions are full of good ideas).

Loose-leaf Services

Loose-leaf services are publications that describe the legal and administrative framework of pensions in an up-to-date manner. The term *loose-leaf* refers to the fact that individual pages can be constantly revised to reflect recent happenings and then mailed out to subscribers to replace current pages in a loose-leaf binder. Information about retirement plans, laws, and related areas is always available and current. Commonly used loose-leaf services are the *BNA Pension Reporter* (published by the Bureau of National Affairs, Washington, D.C.), *Pension Plan Guide* (Commerce Clearing House, Chicago, IL), *EBPR*

Research Reports (Charles D. Spencer and Associates, Chicago, IL), and RIA (this service contains pension document forms from Corbel & Company, Jacksonville, FL). Most of these services also provide a weekly bulletin reporting the latest news about retirement plans to keep readers current and informed.

Each of the services and report bulletins mentioned above has its own special appeal: the BNA service provides a thorough and insightful weekly bulletin but lacks significant reference volumes; the CCH service provides large volumes of printed source material (revenue rulings and the like) and thorough report bulletins; the RIA service is similar to CCH, with the added strength of the Corbel plan documents; while the EBPR service provides much statistical data. Most pension practitioners have access to more than one service, and those interested in all forms of employee benefits are enthusiastic about the BNA service.

Commercial Electronic Resources

Today, many of the periodicals and loose-leaf services are now also available on CD-ROM and/or through the Internet. For example, on the Internet, CCH Access and RIA Checkpoint allow access to pension services as well as a wide array of other products offered by these companies.

Because the world is changing so fast, check with the major publishers to see what is currently available. Publishers include Tax Analysts (800) 955-2444, BNA (800) 372-0133, CCH (800) 835-5224, RIA (800) 431-2057, Charles D. Spencer (800) 555-5490, Warren Gorham & Lamont (800) 950-1210, and Panel Publishers (800) 234-1660.

Two different types of commercial electronic resources are also worth considering, ABI/INFORM and Lexis/Nexis. ABI/INFORM links up with leading businesses and management publications and summarizes articles for a quick reference. A controlled vocabulary lets you search for all the information on a specific pension term (for example, 401(k) plans) and lists the various article titles relating to that term. Lexis/Nexis is basically a law library that provides considerable source material. Each service is targeted for a different type of subscriber—ABI/INFORM for business and insurance, and Lexis/Nexis for the legal profession.

Surfing the Net

In addition to the commercial sources just mentioned, there is a rich array of information available on the Internet. Of interest to those in the employee benefit field are the following:

- *Department of Labor*
  www.dol.gov
  This site includes a summary of laws and regulations governed by the DOL. It also includes the full text of bills and statutes. It is an in-depth resource for free access to primary source materials.
- *U.S. Government Printing Office*
  www.access.gpo.gov
  In this site, you can search the Federal Register for the full text of agency regulations or the U.S. Code for laws.
- *International Foundation of Employee Benefit Plans*
  www.ifebp.org
  Here you will find information about the organization and available services, as well as the latest industry news.
- *Benefits Link*
  www.benefitslink.com
  This is another source for bills and regulations laws, as well as U.S. Supreme Court Decisions relating to employee benefits.
- *IRS*
  www.irs.gov
  This site contains tax regulations and IRS publications and forms.
- *Employee Benefit Research Institute*
  www.ebri.org
  Here you will find many useful statistics and studies. This site also has links to other employee benefit web sites.

Every day, a massive amount of new information becomes available on the Internet. See The American College's Course Pages/Updates for HS 326 for an up-to-date link list at www.amercoll.edu/coursepg/hs326. Also, consider using a search engine such as Yahoo or AltaVista to locate

- web pages for the organizations and publishing companies discussed in this chapter
- news groups that cover related topics
- advertisements for other service providers in the benefits area

Software

A wide variety of software packages that enable financial services practitioners to do their jobs more efficiently are available from insurance companies and pension vendors. Software packages are available for client illustrations, pension administration, portfolio management, form preparation, and plan document preparation, as well as for number crunching in a variety of other areas.

Insurance company home offices and other financial institutions have their own software. In addition to the packages available from your own home office, there are a few vendors that you should become familiar with because of their prominence in the industry. For example, Corbel & Company is well known for its document preparation services. For a modest fee, Corbel will take the information you have gathered on its fact finder and create plans and summary plan descriptions for your client. (*Planning Note:* For agents who do not have access to their company's prototype plans, acquaintance with Corbel's product is strongly recommended.) Another service provided by Corbel is PENTABS, which is software that completes the IRS's required 5500 family of forms.

CHAPTER REVIEW

Answers to the review questions and the self-test questions start on page 673.

Key Terms

Employee Retirement Income Security Act (ERISA)	fiduciary
final regulations	Pension Benefit Guaranty Corporation (PBGC)
proposed regulations	third-party administrators (TPAs)
temporary regulations	master and prototype plans
revenue rulings	primary sources
private-letter rulings	blue book

Review Questions

2-1. What were the major reforms instituted by the Employee Retirement Income Security Act of 1974 (ERISA)?

2-2. What have been the post-ERISA legislative trends with regard to the following areas?
a. maximum deductible contributions
b. limiting tax deferral
c. parity between various business entities
d. funding
e. simplification

2-3. What effect does new legislation in the retirement area have on the financial services professional?

2-4. What is the role of the Internal Revenue Service with regard to the retirement market?

2-5. Your client, Dr. Sandra Scalpel, would like to fund her qualified money-purchase plan using 50 percent of her retirement account to purchase universal life insurance. As the rule currently stands, the IRS allows 50 percent of the account balance to be used to purchase whole life insurance and only 25 percent of the account to be used to purchase term insurance. The IRS has informally indicated that universal life policies are subject to the 25 percent (not the 50 percent) funding limitation. No regulations or other formal guidance is dispositive on this issue. What can be done to solve this uncertainty in the law that would enable Dr. Scalpel to use 50 percent of her retirement account to purchase universal life insurance?

2-6. What is the role of the Department of Labor in the pension process?

2-7. What are the types of organizations involved in providing consulting and investment services to retirement plans?

2-8. What resources are available to assist the financial services professional with technical research and to help the financial services professional keep abreast of changes in the pension field?

Self-Test Questions

T   F   2-1. Title IV of ERISA requires employers to report plan information to the federal government and disclose information to participants.

T   F   2-2. Since ERISA, the law has been changed to provide for special rules for small "top-heavy" plans.

T   F   2-3. Recent legislative changes have somewhat simplified the pension law.

T   F   2-4. Employers must secure a favorable advance-determination letter in order to take a deduction for contributions made to a qualified plan.

T   F   2-5. Regulations are the IRS's precedent-setting interpretations of the provisions of the Internal Revenue Code as they apply to factual situations facing clients.

T   F   2-6. The summary plan description is intended to explain clearly the plan provisions to participants.

T   F   2-7. Failure to comply with the reporting and disclosure requirements of ERISA can result in criminal penalties, including fine and imprisonment.

T   F   2-8. Every plan has at least one named fiduciary who is responsible and accountable for operating the plan.

T   F   2-9. The DOL issues advisory opinions that are similar to the private-letter rulings offered by the IRS.

T   F   2-10. The defined-benefit plan of a professional-service employer with 15 employees must be covered by PBGC insurance.

T   F   2-11. The qualified-plan rules for Keogh plans and regular corporate plans are dramatically different.

T   F   2-12. Individually designed plans are easier for financial services professionals to use than master and prototype plans.

T   F   2-13. The most reliable and important sources of information are primary sources, such as the texts of laws and the Internal Revenue Code.

T	F	2-14.	Loose-leaf services are updated annually.
T	F	2-15.	Software packages are available for client illustrations, pension administration, portfolio management, and form and document preparation.

Notes

1. The IRS currently has a several formal programs for substituting plan disqualification with a monetary penalty. The programs can apply upon an IRS audit, or can be voluntarily entered into by employers who discover that qualification violations have occurred.
2. Based on Department of Labor abstract of 1996 Form 5500 Annual Reports.

3

Preliminary Concerns

Learning Objectives

An understanding of the material in this chapter should enable the student to

---

3-1. Describe both the importance of and a method for identifying a business client's needs and objectives in selecting a qualified plan.

3-2. Compare qualified plans to other tax-advantaged retirement plans.

3-3. Compare defined-benefit and defined-contribution plans.

3-4. Compare pension and profit-sharing plans.

3-5. Identify the Keogh plan market and calculate the maximum allowable deduction under a defined-contribution Keogh plan.

Chapter Outline

One of the most promising and lucrative opportunities in the retirement market is the chance to design a client's retirement program. Financial services professionals who act as consultants in this area provide a valuable service that not only leads to the sale of retirement-plan products but also to the investment of their client's retirement assets. Furthermore, financial services professionals who bring technical expertise to the retirement-decision process gain the confidence of clients and may be entrusted with sales opportunities in other areas of the business. Conversely, financial services professionals who desire only to manage plan assets or sell investment products find themselves at a competitive disadvantage if they cannot offer the technical expertise expected.

For these reasons, it is essential that financial services professionals learn how to select the most appropriate retirement plan or plans for their clients. The study of this process starts with the selection of the most appropriate tax-advantaged plan for your client (chapters 3–6). After a thorough discussion of the rules that affect plan choices, design, investment, and administration, we will discuss supplemental nonqualified plans (chapters 15 and 16) for executives.

In order to choose the best retirement plan, you will need to identify the client's needs and objectives, understand the various plan options, and match the client's needs and objectives with the proper tax-advantaged retirement plan or plans.

IDENTIFYING NEEDS AND OBJECTIVES

When advising a client on retirement-plan choices, your initial step is to focus the client on the important issues he or she faces, both personally and professionally. In addition, you need to discern the organization's needs and objectives that are relevant to plan selection. The device used to accomplish these steps is a pension planning fact finder (see pp. 62–66 at the end of this chapter). This seven-step fact finder gives you one perspective on the task, however, other choices in fact finding may work better for you. In any case, you should use this fact finder or an alternative to

- guide the client toward focusing on important issues
- gather the information necessary for you to make insightful recommendations
- provide a systematic approach for solving the client's retirement puzzle
- serve as a due diligence checklist that will ensure the selection of the most appropriate plan
- record your dealings with the client for liability protection

UNDERSTANDING THE FACT FINDER

Step 1 of the fact finder helps you to identify organizational needs, the foundation for proper plan choice. The important comparative analysis that is started in step 2 (involving the interplay between these factors) requires additional discussion with the client to establish the relative desirability of each objective. For example, when an employer has the multiple objectives of attracting and retaining key employees, avoiding an annual financial commitment to fund the plan, and providing tax shelter for top executives, you must gauge what need is most important and to what degree the other needs will have to be subordinated in order to choose the best plan for your client.

Step 3 lists the primary and secondary reasons for establishing the plan, and is a culmination of steps 1 and 2. It forces your client to set priorities on the motives for establishing the plan. Motives can be disparate even in similarly structured organizations, but several generalizations about motives can be made:

- Large organizations typically want to meet the needs of the business while getting the most for the employees out of a given expenditure.
- Small organizations, such as closely held businesses, are particularly concerned with providing tax shelter and extensive retirement benefits to owners and key employees.
- Some organizations, large and small, desire to adequately provide for rank-and-file employees; others want to favor the key employees and will only grudgingly meet the minimum statutory requirements for other employees; and still others fall somewhere between these two polar viewpoints.
- Some organizations establish plans to attract and retain key employees or to motivate employees, and they want the most cost-effective system to meet those goals.
- Some organizations are interested in resolving problems with older, unproductive employees and in creating a graceful transition out of the workforce.
- In today's world, more and more employers want to form a retirement savings partnership with employees and want employer contributions to primarily match employee contributions.

The first three steps provide some insight into the type of plan to be chosen. Steps 4 and 5 (discussing cost objectives and cash flow) are, however, perhaps the most important determinants of the type of plan the client will adopt. The price tag the client can comfortably live with is sometimes a product of the client's objectives (what he or she wants to provide) and sometimes a product of the economics of the situation (what he or she can afford). Often what clients can afford will vary according to what they want and what they consider a cost-effective price. When considering cost objectives, the organization's ability to make the economic commitment year in and year out should be carefully studied. Some industries have fluctuating profits that ebb and flow with certain uncontrollable economic conditions, while others are fairly stable. In other words, it is not just a question of how much, but also how consistently a certain payment level can be maintained or how much flexibility is needed in order to meet benefit commitments. Carefully examine the following issues before deciding on a price range:

- annual variations in profits
- future cash needs for capital expansion
- potential changes in the prospect's industry over the next 5 years
- the length of time until the principals retire
- the tax-shelter needs of owner-employees

Step 6 (distinguishing between personal and organizational goals) helps you to better understand the priorities laid out in step 3 and the cost objectives laid out in step 4 by differentiating between the personal needs of the client and corporate objectives. The client's personal needs are of the utmost importance in the small-plan market and should be given every consideration. In medium-sized plans, however, equal weight should be given to the organization's goals and the needs of the principals. As a general rule, the larger the plan, the more important the organizational goals.

Step 7 (analyzing the company's census) is perhaps the most important step in the fact-finding process. A thorough understanding of the ages and salary levels of the people who will be covered by the plan is essential for making the correct plan choice and in establishing the best possible plan design. For example, if all the members of the firm are "older" (by pension standards over age 45), then it may be desirable to put in a defined-benefit plan that accounts for past service (discussed later). If, however, salary levels are low and employees are young, a more basic plan, such as a simplified employee pension plan, may be desirable. The last question in step 7 is also crucial. Under the plan rules, certain related employers have to be aggregated for purposes of determining whether a plan satisfies coverage requirements. The rules are quite complex; therefore, it is best to simply ask some broad questions that will elicit a description about the relationships so that a qualified individual can analyze for aggregation issues.

YOUR FINANCIAL SERVICES PRACTICE:
INFORMATION GATHERING

The pension planning fact finder is just the jumping-off point in your quest to identify your client's needs and objectives. The initial interview should be followed by open communication lines that allow the client's concerns to be more clearly developed over time. The following points typify what can happen in this intervening time:

- Frequently, the person you speak with will not correctly represent the desires of the entire body of authority within the organization. The company will need time to sort out its collective feelings and come up with a response. Try not to get involved in the infighting that may occur, and try to remain as diplomatic and neutral as possible.
- The company's attorney or accountant should be brought into the process in the early stages. A common problem is that the attorney or accountant may resent playing the subordinate role (even though he or she may know little about pension plans). Once again, the solution is diplomacy.

CHOOSING BETWEEN A QUALIFIED PLAN AND THE OTHER TAX-SHELTERED OPTIONS

Chapters 4 and 5 discuss the various types of qualified plans. Chapter 6 addresses those tax-advantaged plans that are not categorized as qualified plans. For the for-profit employer, the other types of plans available include the SEP and the SIMPLE. The nonprofit employer that is a 501(c)(3) organization also has the option to sponsor a 403(b) tax-sheltered annuity plan.

As we have already begun to discuss (and as described in detail in later chapters), establishing and maintaining a qualified plan requires a significant amount of documentation, government reporting, and employee communication. For the small business, these requirements can be quite onerous. SEPs and SIMPLEs are intended to provide the small business with some less complicated options. Plan documents are less complicated, and there are fewer IRS reporting requirements. Simplicity translates into lower administrative expenses and less time spent operating the plan. However, in exchange for simplicity is a rigidity in plan design. These plans have less flexibility than qualified plans in most regards. The important differences include

- *Coverage.* While the qualified plan rules provide significant flexibility in the number and makeup of the employees covered by the plan, the SEP and SIMPLE eligibility requirements are set in stone.

- *Vesting.* Contributions must be fully and immediately vested in the contributions to SEPs and SIMPLEs, while qualified plans can have a vesting schedule.
- *Contributions.* In some cases in a qualified plan, benefits or contributions can be different for different classes of employees. This is not the case in SEPs and SIMPLEs, where all participants must receive essentially the same level of benefits.
- *Maximum contributions.* In most regards, the limits are lower for SEPs and SIMPLEs than for qualified plans.

The SEP is the appropriate plan option when the employer is going to fund all of the plan benefits. In a SEP, as in a profit-sharing plan, the employer can make contributions annually (or more often) on a discretionary basis. When the employer wants to allow employees the opportunity to make additional contributions on a pretax basis (making it similar to a 401(k) plan), then the SIMPLE is the appropriate choice.

The 403(b) tax-sheltered annuity is a unique retirement planning vehicle. Only tax-exempt 501(c)(3) organizations and public school systems are allowed to sponsor such plans. At one time, there were relatively few rules governing these plans. However, over time, the situation has evolved, and more and more of the rules that apply to qualified plans now apply to 403(b) plans, too. One type of plan that still operates quite differently from the way that a qualified plan does is the 403(b) plan that involves only employee pretax contributions. This type of plan will not be subject to many of the requirements of ERISA (as long as certain requirements are met). With this type of arrangement, the employer has little involvement; the service provider works directly with the employees. When the employer makes contributions to a 403(b) plan, then the plan operates very much like a qualified plan. (The distinctions between the plans are covered further in chapter 6.)

CHOOSING BETWEEN A DEFINED-BENEFIT AND A DEFINED-CONTRIBUTION PLAN

Assuming that the employer is going to choose from among the qualified plan options, the first consideration is whether the employer wants a plan of the defined-benefit or defined-contribution type. All qualified plans fall into one of those two categories and each category represents a different philosophy of retirement planning. This philosophy is reflected in the

defined-benefit plan   definition of each term. A *defined-benefit plan* is a plan that specifies the benefits each employee receives at retirement. In most plans, the benefit is stated as a percentage of preretirement salary, which is payable for the participant's remaining life. Under a defined-benefit plan, the contributions required by the employer vary depending upon what is needed to pay the promised benefit, and the amount of annual funding is determined each year by the plan's actuary.

In many ways, the defined-benefit plan looks like an insurance solution to the retirement problem. The risk that is being insured is the loss of income due to the inability to work any longer. Another risk is that an individual will outlive his or her money in retirement. The traditional defined-benefit plan addresses both of these issues. The amount of the benefit is tied to what will be lost—employment income. To address the issue of longevity, in the traditional plan, the benefit is payable for the retired employee's entire life. It is interesting to note that this plan design is due in part to the fact that the first defined-benefit plans were funded with insurance products, although today many "self-fund" the promised benefits.

defined-contribution plan

A *defined-contribution plan,* on the other hand, is a type of plan in which employer contributions are allocated to the account of individual employees. This approach is similar to a personal savings approach in which an individual opens up a bank account and makes regular contributions, and the account grows based on the rate of investment return. Because of this approach, defined-contribution plans are sometimes called *individual account plans.* One way to look at these dissimilar approaches is to say that defined-benefit plans provide a fixed predetermined benefit that has an uncertain cost to the employer, whereas defined-contribution plans have a predetermined cost to the employer and provide a variable benefit to employees (based upon the rate of return).

All qualified plans fall into either the defined-benefit or the defined-contribution category. The names of the various qualified plans and the categories into which they fall are listed below. Note, however, that two types of plans are referred to as *hybrid plans*. First is the *cash-balance plan*, which is a defined-benefit plan that has some of the characteristics of a plan using the defined-contribution approach. Second is the *target-benefit plan,* which is a defined-contribution plan that has some of the characteristics of a defined-benefit plan. These distinctions will become more clear in the next two chapters, where the plans are discussed in more detail. Also note that the SEP, the SIMPLE, and the 403(b) tax-sheltered annuity plan all use a defined-contribution approach and share the same strengths and limitations of other defined-contribution plans (in comparison to the defined-benefit approach).

Qualified Plan Categories

Defined-Benefit Plans	Defined-Contribution Plans
• Defined-benefit pension plan • Cash-balance pension plan	• Money-purchase pension plan • Target-benefit pension plan • Profit-sharing plan • 401(k) plan • Stock bonus plan • ESOP

Rule Differences

Because of their vastly different nature, there are a number of important rule differences that apply to defined-benefit and defined-contribution plans. First is how the maximum benefit rules of Code Sec. 415 apply. In defined-benefit plans, the rules limit the maximum yearly benefit allowed, which is the lesser of 100 percent of the highest 3-year average compensation or $160,000 (as indexed in 2002) payable at age 65. In a defined-contribution plan, the maximum contribution each year is limited. The rule is that the maximum contribution for any participant for the year (called *annual additions*) is the lesser of $40,000 (indexed for 2002) or 100 percent of salary. Annual additions include all employer contributions, employee contributions (of any type), and forfeitures that are allocated to the participant's account.

As mentioned in chapter two, the PBGC insurance program guarantees certain benefit payments from most privately sponsored defined benefit plans (with the exception of plans with fewer than 25 participants sponsored by professional services organizations). In a defined-benefit plan the amount of assets will never exactly match the promised benefits, and the PBGC program is there to provide assistance if the company is in financial trouble and the plan does not have sufficient assets to pay the promised benefits. This program does not cover defined-contribution plans since the plan's assets always match the promised benefits owed to participants.

Another important rule difference is that defined-benefit plans are subject to a special coverage provision referred to as the minimum participation rule, which is discussed in detail in chapter 7. Defined-contribution plans are not subject to this rule.

A final distinction is the way the maximum deductible contribution is calculated. In defined-contribution plans, the maximum deductible contribution is 25 percent of aggregate compensation of all covered participants. In a defined-benefit plan, the limit is based on actuarial calculations and is not limited to a specific percentage of compensation.

TABLE 3-1
Rule Differences

Defined-Benefit Plans	Defined-Contribution Plans
Law specifies the maximum allowable benefit payable from the plan—lesser of 100% of salary or $160,000 per year	Law specifies the maximum allowable annual contributions—the lesser of 100 percent of salary or $40,000
Generally subject to the PBGC insurance program	Not subject to the PBGC insurance program
Must satisfy the minimum participation rule of Code Sec. 401(a)(26)	Not subject to the minimum participation rule
Deductible contribution based on actuarial calculations	Deductible contribution limited to 25% of aggregate compensation

Comparing the Defined-Benefit and Defined-Contribution Approach

Because defined-benefit plans typically describe benefits as a percentage of final-average compensation, benefits can be geared to replace a specified percentage of salary for the long service employee. Also, defined-benefit plans can provide benefits based on past service (that is, years worked before the plan was initiated), while defined-contribution plans cannot. This means that benefits can accumulate more quickly for the older employee in a defined-benefit plan. Such plans reward those employees who continue employment until retirement, because benefits are usually tied to both length of service and final income.

In defined-benefit plans, the burden of providing an adequate retirement income is placed solely on the employer, because the employer promises to fund the plan sufficiently to pay promised benefits. This means that the risk of the investment experience is on the employer and contributions will increase if investment experience is worse than expected and will be reduced if performance is better than expected. Even though the employer is responsible to make required contributions it is important to note that there is generally some funding flexibility in defined-benefit plans. There is typically some range (as determined with the help of an actuary)—from the required minimum to the maximum allowable deductible contribution.

Also, defined-benefit plans generally provide for a built-in "preretirement" inflation factor by gearing benefit payments to salary levels received just prior to retirement. Defined-benefit plans, however, generally do not increase automatically for inflation occurring after retirement—although it is not unusual for an employer to provide periodic ad hoc benefit increases for retirees. This makes the defined-benefit plan unique, because defined-contribution plans can not imitate this inflation protection.

Tying benefits to final-average salary does have one down side. When a participant changes jobs, the benefit can be reduced significantly because of the loss of the highest years of salary in the calculation. This means that the benefit is not as portable as in a defined-contribution plan where benefits accrue more ratably over the years. This lack of portability ties the employee to the employer, which has a benefit for the employer offering the defined-benefit plan.

For these reasons, employers looking to 1) maximize benefits for older workers, 2) give long-term employees (including key people) a secure and specified retirement income, and 3) tie employees to the company through the benefit program will be interested in the defined-benefit plan. Still, the defined-benefit plan is only an option if the company is in the financial position and competitive posture to be able to meet the financial obligation of maintaining this type of plan.

Plans in the defined-contribution category are significantly different. From the perspective of both the employer and the employee, such plans look and feel more like deferred-compensation plans. A specified amount is set aside for the employee's benefit, which is paid out at termination of employment (as long as the participant is "vested") or, in some cases, even earlier.

This means that defined contribution plans do not provide a retirement benefit that is closely tied to the individual's retirement needs—as in a defined-benefit plan. It's not to say that defined-contribution plans will not provide adequate retirement income; it is just much harder to pinpoint the benefit. Also, in a very real way, the employee is at more risk, because the benefit is tied to the plan's investment return. In other words, if stock market prices fall drastically, it is the employee who must worry in a defined-contribution plan but the employer who must worry in a defined-benefit plan.

With a defined-contribution plan, the employer's cost is determinable and will not vary with the plan's investment return. Also, these plans cost less to administer.

Employees can more easily follow the growth of their benefits with a defined-contribution plan and can more readily appreciate the value of the cost of the plan to the employer. Defined-contribution plans may also allow employees to direct the investments in their individual accounts. As well, the participant's benefit is stated as a single account balance and lump-sum distributions are generally allowed—which is not always the case in a defined-benefit plan.

This account balance is more portable should an employee switch jobs. The lump-sum value can be rolled over to an IRA or to the new employer's plan. Because the benefit grows with annual contributions and investment experience, a participant is not penalized by changing employers as can be the case with a defined-benefit plan.

Easily determinable costs appeal to employers whose financial positions dictate caution (typically organizations with volatile cash flow). What's more, key employees tend to feel more comfortable about individual accounts that they invest, portable benefits, and the lump-sum distributions traditionally offered under defined-contribution plans. As a result of this employer and key-employee appeal, defined-contribution plans have become a hot ticket for financial services professionals in the pension field.

TABLE 3-2
Types of Plans Compared

Defined-Benefit Plans	Defined-Contribution Plans
Defines the benefit	Defines the employer's contribution
Contributions not attributed to specified employees	All contributions allocated to individual employee accounts
Employer assumes risk of preretirement inflation, investment performance, and adequacy of retirement income	Employee assumes risk of preretirement inflation, investment performance, and adequacy of retirement income
Can provide benefits based on past service	Cannot provide benefits for past service
Costly to administer	Lower administrative costs
Can be difficult to communicate both the amount of benefits and the value of the benefit (amount it costs the employer)	Easy to communicate the amount of employer contributions and the "bank-account" type benefit.
Unpredictable costs	Predictable costs

The Realities of the Marketplace Today

A look at the contrast between the defined-benefit and the defined-contribution approach would not be complete without a discussion of the realities of today's marketplace. Even though the defined-benefit approach still has the strengths that have been mentioned, very few small businesses today are interested in establishing or maintaining this type of plan. Back in the mid-1980s, defined-benefit plans were quite popular in the small plan market, because often the maximum contribution to the defined-benefit plan (on behalf of the business owner) was substantially larger than to a defined-contribution plan. This afforded the middle-aged business owner the opportunity to both save on taxes and quickly accumulate a significant retirement benefit.

However, the trend began to change with the Tax Reform Act of 1986. This act made changes that lowered maximum contributions and increased the complexities of maintaining a defined-benefit plan. Many small plans were terminated and few new ones were established. For example, in 1991, 10,064 defined-benefit plans were terminated and only 370 new plans were started. The Department of Labor's Abstract of 1996 Form 5500 reports showed a continued downward trend in the number of defined-benefit plans, with an 8 percent decrease from 69,500 in 1995 to 63,700 in 1996. For the same year, the number of defined-contribution plans increased one percent from 623,900 in 1995 to 632,600 in 1996. Specifically, 401(k) plans increased by 15 percent to 230,800, while non-401(k) defined-contribution plans decreased 5 percent to 401,800.

This does not mean, however, that defined-benefit plans are not an important part of the retirement planning landscape. Many midsize and large companies still maintain defined-benefit plans and, overall, defined-benefit plans still cover 40 million employees in the private sector. In the small plan marketplace, the pension industry has begun to recognize that defined-benefit plans could play an important role for the older business owner who has not accumulated enough for retirement, has a strong cash flow, and who is looking for a significant tax shelter. With the number of aging baby boomers today, we may see more defined-benefit plans in the first decade of the new millennium.

Nevertheless, defined-contribution products have become the bread-and-butter sale for those who deal in qualified deferred compensation. The defined-contribution approach appears to appeal both to senior managers—who are looking for simplicity and contribution certainty—and to employees—who like that they can more easily understand the plan and appreciate that benefits are more portable.

Multiple Plans—Combining Defined-Benefit and Defined-Contribution Plans

Defined-benefit plans and defined-contribution plans are not mutually exclusive, and two or more plans can be set up for any one employer. If defined-benefit and defined-contribution plans are used together, restrictions apply to the overall deduction limits and, more important, to the maximum benefits that can be provided for individual participants.

Today, a combination defined-benefit and defined-contribution plan is typically used in a larger company to provide a comprehensive benefits package. As discussed earlier, an individual participating in a defined-contribution plan (or plans) may receive an allocation (counting all defined-contribution plans) of the lesser of 100 percent of pay or $40,000 (for 2002). And an individual participating in a defined-benefit plan (or plans) may receive a maximum annual benefit of the lesser of 100 percent of salary or $160,000.

A defined-benefit/defined-contribution combination may be appropriate in the small plan marketplace as well, when the business owner is looking to maximize benefits and deductible contributions. Theoretically, a plan sponsor could contribute $40,000 on behalf of the owner to a defined-contribution plan and fund the maximum allowable benefit in a defined-benefit plan for the owner as well. In practice, this may be quite beneficial in some cases, but it is also quite complex. The plans would have both satisfy all the coverage and nondiscrimination rules, as well as satisfy the maximum deductible contribution limits, too. In other cases, the employer will be able to accomplish the same objective with a single defined-benefit plan—a much simpler arrangement.

CHOOSING BETWEEN A PENSION PLAN AND A PROFIT-SHARING PLAN

All qualified plans fall into either the defined-benefit or defined-contribution categories. Similarly, all plans are also classified as either pension plans or profit-sharing plans. As you can see in the chart below, both types of defined-benefit plans, along with target-benefit and money-purchase plans, are categorized as pension plans. All other defined-contribution plans are profit-sharing plans.

Qualified Plan Categories

Pension Plans	Profit-Sharing Plans
• Defined-benefit pension plan	• Profit-sharing plan
• Cash-balance pension plan	• 401(k) plan
• Money-purchase pension plan	• Stock bonus plan
• Target-benefit pension plan	• ESOP

pension plan category
profit-sharing
  category

The most important difference between a plan in the *pension plan* category and one in the *profit-sharing* category concerns the employer's commitment to the plan. Under a pension plan, the organization is legally required to make annual payments to the plan, because the main purpose of the plan is to provide a retirement benefit. Under a profit-sharing-type plan, however, an organization is not required to make annual contributions. The reasoning here seems to be that profit-sharing plans are not necessarily intended to provide retirement benefits as much as to provide a sharing of profits on a tax-deferred basis.

Consistent with this rationale, the law generally provides that profit-sharing-type plans may be written to allow distributions during employment, while pension plans cannot make distributions until the participant terminates employment. The law allows a profit-sharing-type plan to make in-service distributions on amounts that have accumulated in the plan for a stated number of years. The IRS has interpreted this to mean that distributions can be made on contributions that were made to the plan 2 or more years ago. Also, anyone who has 5 years of plan participation can receive a distribution of his or her entire account balance. In-service distributions can also be made after a stated event, such as a financial hardship. Note that one type of profit-sharing plan, the 401(k) plan, is subject to special, more restrictive in-service withdrawal constraints (discussed in chapter 5).

A final distinction between pension and profit-sharing plans concerns the ability of these plans to invest in company stock. Plans in the pension category can invest only up to 10 percent of plan assets in employer stock. Plans in the profit-sharing category, on the other hand, have no restrictions; all plan assets can be used to purchase employer stock (although this is seldom the case). See table 3-3 for a summary of plan differences.

TABLE 3-3
Differences between Pension and Profit-Sharing Plans

Characteristic	Pension Plan	Profit-Sharing Plan
Employer commitment to annual funding	Yes	No
Withdrawal flexibility for employees	None	After 2 years
Investment in company stock	Limited to 10%	Unlimited

KEOGH PLANS

Keogh plans

In addition to categorizing plans either as defined-benefit or defined-contribution, or as pension or profit-sharing, qualified plans are categorized by the type of business organization they serve. Today, all types of businesses choose from among the same group of qualified plans. Historically, that was not always true. At one time, plans for, partnerships and self-employeds were governed by separate statutory provisions, and plans for such organizations were referred to as *Keogh plans*. Unfortunately, the name still sticks—generally creating more confusion than information. Today, a sole proprietor does not establish a Keogh plan; he or she establishes a profit-sharing, defined-benefit, or other plan from the array of tax-advantaged retirement plans. And, except as described below, the rules for sole proprietorships and partnerships are entirely the same as for corporate entities, and the same considerations regarding plan choice and plan design apply.

There is, however, one remaining distinction between plans of sole proprietorships and partnerships[1] and corporate plans: The self-employed person's contribution or benefit is based on net earnings instead of salary. This creates some complications because net earnings can be determined only after taking into account all appropriate business deductions, including the deduction for the retirement contribution—thus, the amount of net earnings and the amount of the deduction are dependent on each other.

If a defined-benefit plan is used, an actuary is needed to straighten out the confusion and to determine the plan contribution amount itself. However, if a defined-contribution plan is used, it will be necessary to calculate the maximum deduction for the client (see the work sheet in table 3-4).

This means that a sole proprietor or partner with a profit-sharing plan or money-purchase pension plan can only contribute 20 percent of compensation (not 25 percent of compensation as with a corporate plan). Further complicating matters is the fact that self-employed individuals get a deduction for income tax purposes equal to one-half of their Social Security self-employment tax on their federal tax return. In addition, when calculating the contribution, the maximum compensation that can be used is $200,000 (as indexed in 2002). (See chapter 8 for a discussion of the compensation cap.) Fortunately, these complications can be eliminated if you follow the formula in table 3-4.

TABLE 3-4
Keogh Deduction Work Sheet

Step I: Self-employed person's work sheet

1. Plan contribution as a decimal (for example, 25% would be 0.25) _____
2. Rate in Line 1 plus 1, shown as a decimal (for example, 0.25 plus 1 would be 1.25) _____
3. Divide Line 1 by Line 2. This is the self-employed contribution rate. (For example, 0.25 ÷ 1.25 = .20) _____

Step II: Figure the deduction

1. Enter the self-employed contribution rate from Line 3 of Step I.
2. Enter the amount of net earnings that the business owner has from Schedule C (Form 1040) or Schedule F (Form 1040). _____
3. Enter the deduction for self-employment tax from the front page of Form 1040. $_____
4. Subtract Line 3 from Line 2 and enter the amount. $_____
5. Multiply Line 4 by Line 1. This is the amount that may be deducted by the business owner.* $_____

$_____

*Note that this amount cannot exceed $40,000.

ADDITIONAL PRELIMINARY CONCERNS

Before we study the menu of qualified plans, it should be noted that choosing the best retirement plan is not as simple as picking one type of plan from the menu. The design of the plan must also be considered in order to make the proper plan choice. This is because qualified plans are principally differentiated by only one design feature—their benefit formulas. The many other design choices, however, also affect your plan choice. To put it another way, plan choice is a function of plan design, and plan design is a function of plan choice.

The plan-design details that help you to make a more informed decision are presented in chapters 7 through 10.

***Example*:**   The professional corporation of Davis and Wickstrom is primarily interested in providing tax-sheltered savings for key employees and minimizing costs attributable to rank-and-file employees. Davis and Wickstrom ask you to help choose the best retirement plan for them. A defined-benefit plan designed with a benefit formula that is integrated with Social Security, and with restrictive eligibility and vesting provisions, is most probably the preferable choice. But if you had only considered the menu of retirement plans without considering the design features, you might have chosen a 401(k) plan instead. At first blush, the 401(k) seems to be a likely fit because it allows tax-sheltered savings for key employees and minimizes costs attributable to the rank and file. On closer inspection, however, you'll see that 401(k) plans may not provide enough tax shelter for the principals because such plans must be designed to meet a special nondiscrimination test known as the *actual deferral percentage test*. (See chapter 5.)

A second consideration when choosing a qualified plan is the makeup of the entire benefits package. For example, if there is a nonqualified plan for key employees, the choice of a qualified plan for all employees should be dovetailed with the nonqualified plan to reach the desired result. When group life and group disability plans are involved, other considerations arise. As a general rule, the choice of a retirement plan should reflect the fact that it is only one part of a benefits package. Special care should be taken to ensure that benefits are not duplicated under the different employee benefit plans.

PENSION PLANNING FACT FINDER

Client's Name   _____

Address   _____

Client's Name   _____

Address   _____

_____

_____

_____

_____

Phone Number   _____

_____

Key Contacts   Name   _____

Title   _____   Phone No._____

Name   _____

Title   _____   Phone No._____

Name   _____

Title   _____   Phone No._____

Client's Attorney   _____   Phone No._____

Client's Accountant   _____   Phone No._____

Employer Identification Number   _____

Fiscal Year   _____

Accounting Method (circle one)
   Cash
   Accrual

Business Structure (circle one)
   C Corp.
   S Corp.
   Municipal Corp.
   Partnership
   Sole Proprietorship
   Exempt Organization
   Professional Corp.
   Government Agency

State of Incorporation or Domicile   _____

Date of Incorporation or Establishment   _____

Were there any predecessor entities? (circle one)   Yes   No

Affiliated Companies

   Name   _____   Name   _____

   Address   _____   Address   _____

     _____   _____

   Phone No.   _____   Phone No.   _____

Step 1: Set retirement priorities.

Listed below are some typical concerns that organizations have when instituting a retirement program. Grade each of these concerns by scoring 1 for very valuable, 2 for valuable, 3 for moderately valuable, and 4 for least valuable.

1. To what extent is it important to use a qualified plan as a tax shelter for owner-employees and key employees? [1] [2] [3] [4]
2. To what extent is it important to maximize benefits for long-service employees by including service prior to the inception of the plan? [1] [2] [3] [4]
3. To what extent is it important to place the risk of investing plan assets with the employee? [1] [2] [3] [4]
4. To what extent is it important to institute a plan that is easily communicated to employees? [1] [2] [3] [4]
5. To what extent is it important to institute a plan that is administratively convenient? [1] [2] [3] [4]
6. To what extent is it important to institute a plan that has predictable costs? [1] [2] [3] [4]
7. To what extent is it important to avoid an annual financial commitment? [1] [2] [3] [4]
8. To what extent is it important to allow employees (including owner-employees) to withdraw funds? [1] [2] [3] [4]
9. To what extent is it important to minimize plan costs by limiting benefits for lower-paid employees? [1] [2] [3] [4]
10. To what extent is it important to create a market for employer stock? [1] [2] [3] [4]
11. To what extent is it important to leverage the purchase of employer stock? [1] [2] [3] [4]
12. To what extent is it important to attract key employees? [1] [2] [3] [4]
13. To what extent is it important to retain experienced personnel? [1] [2] [3] [4]
14. To what extent is it important to motivate the workforce? [1] [2] [3] [4]
15. To what extent is it important to deal with superannuated employees? [1] [2] [3] [4]
16. To what extent is it important to give participants the opportunity to save additional amounts on a pretax basis? [1] [2] [3] [4]
17. To what extent is it important that employer contributions be made only for employees who elect to contribute? [1] [2] [3] [4]
18. To what extent is it important that benefits for those who terminate prior to retirement be portable? [1] [2] [3] [4]

Step 2: Discuss with the client the interplay between various factors in step 1. For example:

	Yes	No
1. Does the desire to provide tax shelter for owner-employees and key employees outweigh the need to cut costs attributable to lower-paid employees?	[Y]	[N]
2. Does the desire to provide tax shelter for owner-employees and key employees outweigh the need to have an easily communicated and administratively convenient plan?	[Y]	[N]
3. Does the need to provide tax shelter for owner-employees and key employees outweigh the need to have predictable costs and payment flexibility?	[Y]	[N]
4. Is it more important to retain employees than to attract employees?	[Y]	[N]
5. Is it more important to motivate employees than to attract or retain them?	[Y]	[N]
6. Is it more important to provide an adequate retirement standard of living than to cut plan costs?	[Y]	[N]
7. Is it more important to provide an adequate retirement standard of living than to have predictable costs?	[Y]	[N]
8. Is it more important to provide an adequate standard of living during retirement than to avoid an annual commitment to funding the plan?	[Y]	[N]
9. Is it more important to provide an adequate standard of living during retirement than to allow employees (including owner-employees) to withdraw funds?	[Y]	[N]
10. Is it more important to provide an adequate standard of living during retirement than to have administrative convenience and an easily communicated plan?	[Y]	[N]
11. Is it more important that contributions go only to employees who elect to participate than to provide retirement benefits to all workers?	[Y]	[N]

Additional Comments

Step 3: List the primary reason(s) for establishing the plan and the secondary reason(s) for establishing the plan.

Primary   1.

               2.

               3.

Secondary   1.

               2.

               3.

Step 4: Discuss the employer's cost objectives. Discuss the price range that is desired both now and in the future.

Step 5: (A)   What are the current and future cash-flow situations

           (1) for the company

           (2) for the industry in general

       (B)   Attach balance sheets from the last 3 years.

       (C)   Attach appropriate profit and loss statements.

Step 6: Distinguish between the personal needs that the plan will satisfy for the principals and the organizational goals that are sought.

Step 7: Analyze the company's census (list of employees).

1. What percentage of employees can be expected to turn over before retirement?
   _____% leave before they complete one year of service
   _____% leave between their first and second years of service
   _____% leave between their second and third years of service
   _____% leave between their third and fourth years of service
   _____% leave between their fourth and fifth years of service
   _____% leave between their fifth and sixth years of service
   _____% leave between their sixth and seventh years of service
   _____% leave with more than seven years of service
   _____% are "lifers" with the company

2. What groups of employees exist?
   _____salaried employees
   _____hourly paid employees
   _____collective-bargaining unit employees
   _____leased employees

3. To what extent are part-time employees used?
   _____part-time employees are used
   _____no part-time employees are used
   _____part-time employees work less than 500 hours
   _____part-time employees work between 500 and 999 hours
   _____part-time employees work 1000 or more hours

4. How many offices (profit centers) are there?
   _____number of different locations

5. What benefit programs do chief competitors offer?

6. Attach employee census.

7. Attach other group benefit plans.

8. Identify other related employers and the relationship to this one. The list should include any entities with interrelated ownership and other entities that work together with this one to produce a product. Describe in detail the chain of ownership and how the entities work together.

CHAPTER REVIEW

Answers to the review questions and the self-test questions start on page 673.

Key Terms

defined-benefit plan
defined-contribution plan
pension plan category

profit-sharing plan category
Keogh plan

Review Questions

3-1.   June Jones is thinking of installing a retirement plan for her budding flower business. June has indicated that she knows nothing about retirement plans and would like to speak with her financial adviser on the issue. What steps should the adviser take to help June focus on the important issues facing both her and the business and to gather the appropriate information that would enable the adviser to make recommendations?

3-2.   What are two typical stumbling blocks that financial services professionals face when helping to plan a client's retirement program?

3-3.   Sam Doyle, owner of Doyle's Furniture, Inc., has requested a qualified plan that (1) provides an adequate pension for his employees, regardless of what the stock market does, (2) takes care of employees who have been with him for a long time, (3) provides a pension that reflects his employees' salaries at retirement, and (4) ties his long-service employees to the company. Should Doyle's Furniture, Inc., use a defined-benefit or a defined-contribution plan? Explain.

3-4.   What advantages are available to the employer under a defined-contribution plan?

3-5.   Indicate whether the following statements describe a defined-benefit plan or a defined-contribution plan:

  a.   Benefits accrue based on all years of salary.
  b.   Benefit costs are less predictable.
  c.   Administrative costs are lower.
  d.   Plan assets are allocated to individual accounts for each participant.
  e.   The maximum annual addition for an employee is the lesser of 100 percent of salary or $40,000.
  f.   It can provide benefits based on past service.

3-6.   Under what circumstances is it desirable to use a combination defined-benefit plan and defined-contribution plan?

3-7. What are three basic differences between plans that fall into the pension family and plans that fall into the profit-sharing family?

3-8. Faye is a sole proprietor with a qualified profit-sharing plan that enables her to contribute 25 percent of earned income. Faye's net earnings from schedule C are $100,000. Faye's deduction for one-half of her self-employment tax is $6,434 for 2002. What is the maximum deduction that Faye is allowed to take under her profit-sharing plan for 2002?

Self-Test Questions

T   F   3-1. Financial services professionals who have technical expertise about qualified plans have a competitive advantage when it comes time to determine who will manage plan assets or who will sell investment products to the plan.

T   F   3-2. When it comes to providing a retirement plan, closely held businesses are particularly concerned with providing maximum benefits for rank-and-file employees.

T   F   3-3. Helping a client set a price range for his or her qualified plan involves compromise—balancing the benefits that the owner wants to provide with his or her ability to afford the price tag.

T   F   3-4. A thorough understanding of the ages and salary levels of employees who will be covered by the plan is essential to making the correct plan choice.

T   F   3-5. SEPs and SIMPLEs will generally cost less to maintain than a qualified plan, but in exchange the employer will have fewer design options.

T   F   3-6. A 403(b) plan is a retirement plan available to all types of corporate entities.

T   F   3-7. Under a defined-benefit plan, the contributions required by the employer vary depending upon what is needed to pay the promised benefit, and the amount of annual funding is determined each year by the plan's actuary.

T   F   3-8. The maximum yearly benefit allowed under a defined-benefit plan is the lesser of 100 percent of salary and $40,000.

T   F   3-9. In defined-contribution plans, employees are clear how much "deferred compensation" they are receiving, although they are not sure what the ultimate benefit will be from the plan.

T   F   3-10. Defined-benefit plans tend to provide more retirement income for long-service employees than defined-contribution plans because defined-benefit plans can fund for past service and defined-contribution plans cannot.

T   F   3-11. Defined-contribution plans can gear their benefit payments to salary levels used just prior to retirement.

T   F   3-12.   Plans from the defined-contribution category have easily determinable costs, which appeals to employers whose financial position dictates caution.

T   F   3-13.   Under a defined-contribution plan, the employer bears the risk of preretirement inflation.

T   F   3-14.   Under plans from the defined-benefit category, the employer bears the risk of investment performance.

T   F   3-15.   Today, a combination defined-benefit and defined-contribution plan is typically used in a larger company to provide a comprehensive benefits package.

T   F   3-16.   Under a profit-sharing plan, an organization is committed to making annual payments to the plan.

T   F   3-17.   Plans from the pension category can invest up to 25 percent of their assets in employer stock.

T   F   3-18.   A Keogh plan is a qualified plan that is sponsored by a partnership or self-employed individual.

T   F   3-19.   Keogh plans have a special rule for calculating the maximum contribution for the self-employed owner.

Note

1. Note that limited-liability companies that are taxed as partnerships will be subject to the same limitations as those that apply to partnerships.

4

Defined-Benefit, Cash-Balance, Target-Benefit, and Money-Purchase Pension Plans

---

Learning Objectives

An understanding of the material in this chapter should enable the student to

---

4-1. Explain the various types of defined-benefit formulas.

4-2. Describe the advantages and disadvantages of a cash-balance plan.

4-3. Describe the advantages and disadvantages of a money-purchase plan.

4-4. Describe the advantages and disadvantages of a target-benefit plan.

Chapter Outline

In order to help your client choose the best retirement plan, you first need to examine the menu of tax-advantaged plans. In the next two chapters we will preview the full range of qualified plans, and in chapter 6 we will discuss SEPs, SIMPLEs, and 403(b) plans. We will assess each plan's strengths and weaknesses, focus on the objectives that each plan serves for your client, and discuss the typical candidates for each type of plan.

The various types of qualified plans are, in part, explained by the characteristics of the categories they fall under (defined-benefit versus defined-contribution, and pension versus profit-sharing) and, in part, by their benefit or contribution formula. In chapter 3, you learned a significant amount about each type of category, as you learned how each plan was categorized. The one remaining piece of the puzzle is the plan's benefit or contribution formula. Let's take a closer look at the various types of retirement plans and their benefit (contribution) formulas.

DEFINED-BENEFIT PENSION PLANS

A defined-benefit pension plan falls within both the defined-benefit and pension categories. Knowing this means you already know that defined-benefit plans have the following characteristics:

- The maximum benefit that a person can receive each year is $160,000, as indexed for 2002.
- Assets are not allocated to individual accounts.
- The employer assumes responsibility for preretirement inflation, income adequacy, and investment results.
- The benefit formula can be designed to consider past service.
- The older business owner can provide the maximum tax-shelter potential available under a qualified plan.
- They are more costly to administer than defined-contribution plans, because, among other things, they require the services of an actuary.
- The benefit formula and value of the benefit may be more difficult to communicate than in defined-contribution plans.
- The employer's future costs are not precisely known.
- Annual employer contributions are required.
- Participants may not take in-service withdrawals.
- Investment in the sponsoring company's stock is limited to 10 percent of the plan's assets.

Let's take a closer look at defined-benefit pension plans from a design standpoint by examining the various types of benefit formulas that are used.

The Unit-Benefit Formula

unit-benefit formula

The most frequently used defined-benefit formula is the *unit-benefit formula* (also known as the percentage-of-earnings-per-year-of-service formula). This formula uses both service and salary in determining the participant's pension benefit. A unit-benefit formula might read this way: "Each plan participant will receive a monthly pension commencing at normal retirement date and paid in the form of a life annuity equal to 1.5 percent of final-average monthly salary multiplied by years of service. Service is limited to a maximum of 30 years."

Example: Larry Novenstern is retiring after 25 years of service with his employer. Larry's final-average monthly salary is $5,000. To determine Larry's benefit, multiply 1.5 percent by the $5,000 final-average monthly salary by 25 (the number of years of service). Larry's monthly retirement benefit will be equal to $1,875 paid in the form of a life annuity. (Note that if a different distribution option is chosen, the benefit will be the actuarial equivalent of the life annuity.)

The unit-benefit formula is the most frequently used benefit formula because it best serves a variety of employer goals.

- The goal of retaining and rewarding experienced personnel is achieved because the pension benefit is based, in part, on the years of service an employee works for an employer.
- The goal of rewarding owner-employees and key employees is achieved because the pension benefit is based, in part, on salary, which is higher for owner-employees and key employees.
- The goal of providing the desired income-replacement ratio can be achieved through proper design of the benefit formula. The *income-replacement ratio* represents the amount of an employee's gross income that will be replaced under the retirement plan. Employers believe that there is no need to replace 100 percent of an employee's final-average salary in order to provide the desired standard of living at retirement for several reasons:

    income-replacement ratio

    − Social Security benefits and private savings will fund part of the needed retirement benefit.

- The preretirement standard of living can be maintained at retirement on a lower income because the employee pays less in taxes in the retirement years (such as no Social Security taxes).
- The preretirement standard of living can be maintained at retirement on a lower income because the employee has reduced living expenses (no work-related expenses such as transportation and clothing; self-supporting children; paid-up home mortgage; and so on).

For these reasons, employers generally choose an income replacement of between 40 and 60 percent of final-average salary for employees who have spent their career with the employer, and something less for employees who have not spent as long with the employer.

Example: The Cooper Corporation would like to provide a 60 percent income-replacement ratio for long-service employees and would like to provide a proportionately reduced income-replacement ratio for shorter-service employees. In order to accomplish these goals, the Cooper Corporation should choose a benefit formula that reads: "Each plan participant will receive a monthly pension commencing at normal retirement date and paid in the form of a life annuity equal to 2 percent of final-average monthly salary multiplied by years of service. Service is limited to a maximum of 30 years."

Under this benefit formula, the long-service employees will be provided with a 60 percent income-replacement ratio, and employees with fewer than 30 years of service will be provided with an equitably reduced income-replacement ratio. In addition, by placing the years-of-service cap at 30 years, the Cooper Corporation will never have to fund for benefits higher than 60 percent of average monthly salary.

Through the use of this benefit formula, the Cooper Corporation has achieved several goals:

- The goal of providing for a graceful transition in the workforce is achieved because the use of a years-of-service cap (in the example above, 30 years) discourages employment beyond the stated period. If the employer desires a more rapid turnover of older employees, a lower service cap can be used. If the employer wants to retain experienced personnel, however, a longer service cap may be used, or the employer may choose not to cap service at all.

- The goal of providing the most cost-effective defined-benefit plan possible is achieved because the unit-benefit formula is more cost-effective than other types of defined-benefit formulas. Cost-effectiveness can be defined in this case as getting the most value for each pension dollar by achieving employer goals at the least possible cost. To the extent permitted by law, the employer can reward employees with long service and/or high compensation and avoid paying disproportionate benefits for other employees.

The reason unit-benefit formulas are the most cost-effective means of spending defined-benefit dollars can be best understood by examining the alternative defined-benefit formulas.

Elements of the Unit-Benefit Formula

Compensation	Base pay, taxable income, or some other nondiscriminatory definition
Final-average compensation	Typically takes the average of the highest 3–5 years of compensation
Service	Can count years of participation or years of service, even service prior to the plan set-up
Form of benefit	Typically a life annuity, or a life annuity with period certain
Normal retirement age	Typically 65 but can be age 62 or younger

Other Defined-Benefit Formulas

flat-percentage-of-earnings formula

Under an alternative defined-benefit formula called the *flat-percentage-of-earnings formula* (on IRS forms, called a fixed-benefit formula), the benefit is related solely to salary and does not reflect an employee's service.

Example: Such a benefit formula may read: "Each plan participant will receive a monthly pension benefit equal to 40 percent of the final-average monthly salary commencing at normal retirement date and paid in the form of a life annuity."

This formula is generally not cost-effective, however, because it provides a disproportionate benefit to employees hired later in their careers, which is costly to fund. At one time, these formulas were quite popular with small businesses when the owner was significantly older than the rank-and-file employees. The owner could accrue a full benefit over a short period of time while benefits for other employees accrued over a much longer period of time. Realizing that this was discriminatory, the IRS passed regulations that now require a flat-percentage-of-earnings formula to have a 25-year minimum period of service in order for the participants to receive the full benefits promised. For those with less than 25 years of service, the benefit will be proportionately reduced.

Example: Use the 40 percent retirement benefit from the previous example and apply a pro rata reduction for those with less than 25 years of service. If Debbie had final-average compensation of $100,000 and 10 years of service, her benefit would be $16,000 (40 percent of $100,000 multiplied by 10/25).

---

flat-amount-per-year-of-service formula

A second alternative to the unit-benefit formula is a formula that relates the pension benefit solely to service but does not reflect an employee's salary. This type of formula, called a *flat-amount-per-year-of-service formula,* might read: "Each plan participant will receive a monthly pension benefit commencing at normal retirement date and paid in the form of a life annuity equal to $10 for every year worked."

Flat-amount-per-year-of-service formulas are relatively uncommon except in union-negotiated plans. When used in union plans, a flat-amount-per-year-of-service formula may relate the benefit to the actual hours a participant worked. For example, participants working 1,000 hours might receive half as much as participants working 2,000 hours.

flat-amount formula

A third alternative to the unit-benefit formula is the *flat-amount formula* (on IRS forms the flat-amount formula is called a flat-benefit formula). The flat-amount formula provides the same monthly benefit for each participant. This type of formula treats all employees alike and does not account fordifferences in earnings and service. A flat-amount formula might read: "Each plan participant will receive a $200-a-month pension benefit commencing at normal retirement date and paid in the form of a life annuity." As with the flat-amount-per-year-of-service formula, this type of formula is found primarily in union plans. (See table 4-1 for examples of the four types of benefit formulas.)

Formula	Example
Unit-benefit Flat-percentage of-earnings Flat-amount-per-year of service Flat-amount	2% of FAC* times years of service 50% of FAC* $ 30 per month times years of service $450 per month
*Final-average compensation	

TABLE 4-1
Defined-Benefit Plan Formulas *

Elements of the Benefit Formula

Now, let's turn our attention from the defined-benefit formulas themselves to the major elements that constitute them. If a plan has a unit-benefit formula, that formula commonly will read as follows:

Example: A participant will be entitled to a life annuity beginning at the normal retirement age in the amount of 1.5 percent of final-average compensation times years of service. Normal retirement age is the later of age 65 or 5 years of plan participation.

Each of the factors in this benefit formula affects the ultimate value of the benefit. The factors include the definition of compensation under the plan, the definition of years of service, the form of benefit, and the age at which benefits can begin. Each of these factors is discussed more fully below.

The Definition of Compensation

One of the most important elements of the defined-benefit formula is the amount of compensation used in the benefit formula. This is a function of both the definition of compensation and the definition of "average" (or final-average) compensation. The most comprehensive definition of compensation includes all wages that are included in taxable income, plus any pretax salary deferrals under a 401(k) plan (or 403(b)) or SIMPLE. A less comprehensive definition can be selected but must undergo scrutiny under rules that prohibit discrimination in favor of the highly compensated employees. As a way to keep plan costs both predictable and under control, many employers choose base salary as the definition of compensation—excluding any extra pay such as bonuses, overtime, or commissions. Under the nondiscrimination rules, this definition would be a problem only if the rank-and-file employees received significant additional pay while the highly compensated did not.

final-average compensation

Just as meaningful is how *final-average compensation* is defined. Benefits could simply be based on the participant's final year (or highest year) of compensation—but this, too, could result in both higher and more unpredictable plan costs. It is more common to choose a definition such as the average of the final 3 (or 5) years' salary, or the average of the highest 3 (or 5) years' consecutive salary. Averaging the highest few years of salary serves the dual purpose of leveling off any abnormal years of compensation while providing a benefit that is tied to the individual's highest salary (providing preretirement inflation protection).

career-average compensation

In the past, plans sometimes based benefits on the individual's entire salary history. This type of formula is referred to as a *career-average compensation* benefit formula. This formula worked in one of two ways. One way was to have the benefit based on average compensation—looking at the individual's entire salary history. The other way was to have the formula provide a benefit such as one percent of the current year's salary plus one percent of the next year's salary, and so on. In this way, the benefit was an accumulation of the benefits earned for each year of service. Today, this type of formula is rare. If the employer really wants a plan that provides benefits based on career-average salary, a defined-contribution plan is generally chosen.

As with all types of qualified plans, compensation is capped at $200,000 (as indexed for 2002), meaning that compensation used for a particular year in the formula can not exceed that year's compensation cap.

Service

past service

Another important element of the defined-benefit formula is the definition of service. What's unique to the defined-benefit approach is the ability to account for *past service*—service with the employer prior to the inception of the plan. Providing for past service is particularly important to clients who are setting up a new plan for the benefit of long-service employees. If past service is not accounted for, these employees will find that their retirement benefits are inadequate. Another important reason to account for past service is to maximize the tax-shelter potential of the plan for owner-employees and key employees. A benefit formula that fully accounts for past service provides a bias toward these employees because they frequently are the ones who have the most past service.

Past service can be accounted for wholly or partially. In other words, the plan can provide for all service prior to the inception of the plan (for example, 2 percent times final 3 years' average salary times *all* service with the employer) or can provide a downgraded benefit (or no benefit) for service prior to the inception of the plan. A benefit formula with a downgraded past-service benefit might read: "Two percent times final 3 years' average salary times all service with the employer after the plan's inception date plus one percent times final 3 years' average salary times all service with the employer prior to the plan's inception date."

Form of Benefit

**normal form of
benefit payment**

In a defined-benefit plan, the *normal form of benefit payment* is an essential characteristic of the plan benefit. The most common normal form of payment is a life annuity (meaning that payments continue only for as long as the participant lives). However, some plans will use a different normal form, such as a life annuity with a certain period of payments (typically 5 to 10 years)—meaning that the benefit will be payable for the longer of either life or the specified time period.

The normal form of payment has a direct impact on the value of the benefit. For example, a life annuity with 10-year certain payments of $1,000 a month is more valuable than a straight life annuity of $1,000 a month. This is significant when participants have the option to receive the benefit in other forms, because the optional forms of payment are almost always the actuarial equivalent of the normal form of payment. For example, if the life annuity with 10-year certain payments were converted to a single-sum benefit, the participant would receive more than if the conversion were based on the straight life annuity. (If this concept seems confusing, the discussion in chapter 26 regarding forms of payment should help to clarify.)

Finally, note that providing a benefit as a life annuity is very different from a defined-contribution plan, where the benefit is based on the account balance. With a defined-contribution plan, if the participant elects to receive a life annuity, the amount of the benefit payment will be based on the annuity that can be "purchased" with the single-sum amount. Another way of saying this is that in the defined-contribution plan, the normal form of payment is a single-sum amount.

Normal Retirement Age

Because defined-benefit plans generally provide benefits in the form of a life annuity, another factor that directly affects the value of the benefit is the date at which benefits can begin. The earlier the retirement age, the longer the payout period and the more valuable (and costly) the benefit. (This subject is discussed more in chapter 9.)

Candidates for This Type of Plan

Unlike defined-contribution plans, defined-benefit plans can be designed to ensure that benefits replace a specified portion of the participant's preretirement income. But this type of plan comes with a fairly high price tag. Although there may be mitigating factors, such as integration of the plans with Social Security (see integration, chapter 8) and lower costs owing to better-than-expected investment return, defined-benefit plans remain expensive to fund. Also, the actuarial calculations involved make them costly to administer.

For the older business owner, the defined-benefit pension plan is a way to shelter larger amounts than can generally be contributed to a defined-contribution plan. This is because the time to fund for the benefit is short and the annual contributions required to fund the plan will be more significant. At the same time, the older business owner can create a significant retirement benefit over a short period of time, because past service can be factored into the retirement computation.

The Fact Finder

Candidates for defined-benefit pension plans fill out step 1 of the fact finder (see chapter 3) by grading as "very valuable" the following:

- To what extent is it important to use a qualified plan as a tax shelter for owner-employees and key employees?
- To what extent is it important to maximize benefits for long-service employees by including service prior to the inception of the plan?

Candidates for a defined-benefit pension plan frequently grade as "least valuable" these goals:

- placing the investment risk with the employee
- avoiding an annual financial commitment
- instituting a plan that has predictable costs
- instituting a plan that is administratively convenient
- instituting a plan that is easily communicated to employees

In addition, defined-benefit pension plan candidates fill out step 2 of the fact finder by answering "yes" to these questions: Is it more important to provide an adequate retirement standard of living than to cut plan costs? Is it more important to provide an adequate retirement standard of living than to have predictable costs? Is it more important to provide an adequate standard of living during retirement than to have administrative convenience and an easily communicated plan?

YOUR FINANCIAL SERVICES PRACTICE:
GETTING MORE OUT OF
DEFINED-BENEFIT PLANS FOR LITTLE OR NO COST

Surprisingly, many large- and medium-sized organizations find that employee enthusiasm about the firm's defined-benefit plan is low. However, because of the relative complexity of the defined-benefit plan, employees will not appreciate the plan without significant communication. Ways to improve the employee's appreciation of the plan would be to

- issue frequent and informative benefit statements
- rework the summary plan description (see chapter 13)
- set up periodic meetings to review benefits
- demonstrate how favorably an employee's defined-benefit plan compares with other retirement plans
- provide more general retirement planning seminars
- publicize the percentage of employee payroll used to fund the defined-benefit plan and the approximate cost of funding each participant's benefit

---

CASH-BALANCE PENSION PLANS

The cash-balance concept is a relatively new idea in pension plan design, with the first plan introduced in 1984. In its short history, it has been used primarily by large, and in some cases midsize, corporations as an alternative to the traditional defined-benefit plan. In fact, most of the cash-balance plans in existence today started as traditional plans that were later amended. The cash-balance plan is generally motivated by two factors: the selection of a benefit design that employees can easily understand and appreciate, and as a cost-savings measure.

cash-balance plan

The *cash-balance plan* is a defined-benefit plan that is designed to look like a defined-contribution plan. As a defined-benefit plan, it has some level of funding flexibility and is subject to minimum funding requirements and the PBGC insurance program. At the same time, the defined-contribution-like design means it is easier to explain the benefit formula and the plan will provide a more portable benefit for today's mobile workforce.

The heart of the cash-balance plan is the benefit structure. As in the defined-contribution plan, the benefit is stated as an account balance that increases with contributions and investment experience. However, in a cash-balance plan the account is fictitious. Contributions are a bookkeeping credit only—no actual contributions are allocated to participants' accounts.

Investment credits are also hypothetical and are based either upon a rate specified in the plan or on an external index. To the participants, however, this plan looks like a traditional defined-contribution "account balance" plan. When an employee terminates, the benefit payout is based upon the value of the participant's account. A cash-balance formula might appear as in the following example:

Example: The participant is entitled to a single-sum benefit that is based on a credit of 5 percent of compensation each year. The credited amounts will accumulate with interest. Interest will be credited annually using the 30-year treasury rate on that date. Actual investment experience will not affect the value of the benefit.

The cash-balance benefit can be used as the sole benefit structure under the plan, or as an add-on to a preexisting, more traditional defined-benefit plan formula. The sponsor can design any contribution credit formula that will meet its goals, as long as it is clearly defined in the plan document and satisfies nondiscrimination rules and other legal requirements. Most typically, the contribution credit is stated as a percentage of the individual's current year's pay (for example, 5 percent of salary), or as a formula that considers both salary and years of service to reward those with longer service. For example, a formula can assign credits of 3 percent of salary for those with less than 5 years of service, 6 percent for those with 10 or more years of service, and 9 percent for 20-year veterans. Credits given for investment experience can be stated as a fixed, predetermined rate, a floating rate (based on some external index outside the control of the employer), or a combination of a fixed and floating rate, such as the rate of one-year Treasury bills. The contribution and interest credits can be treated as made annually or more often, if the employer prefers. Also, because this is a defined-benefit plan, contribution and interest credits can be made for past years of service.

From the employer's perspective, this plan is still a defined-benefit plan. Contributions are required in the amount necessary to satisfy the minimum funding requirements. Under these rules, the employer has a degree of flexibility in determining the required contribution. Also, as in any defined-benefit plan, the employer is ultimately responsible for making contributions necessary to pay promised benefits—meaning that the sponsor is "on the hook" for the plan's investment experience. If trust assets earn a higher rate of return, then expected future contributions are reduced, and vice versa.

From the employee's perspective, the cash-balance design looks mostly like a defined-contribution plan. The only similarity to the defined-benefit approach is that benefits are guaranteed by the PBGC and are not affected adversely by downturns in the market. In all other ways, the cash-balance plan mirrors the strengths and weaknesses of the defined-contribution plan. Benefits accrue (depending upon the formula) more evenly over the participant's career, meaning that benefits are not lost if the employee decides to change jobs. A cash-balance plan, like a defined-contribution plan, is easy to communicate. The contribution and interest credits are both easy to follow and may be more appreciated than a traditional defined-benefit plan. Similarly, the cash-balance plan does not have many of the strengths of the traditional defined-benefit approach. Benefits do not replace a specified percentage of preretirement income, and because benefits are not based on final salary, the benefit is not inflation adjusted up to the time benefits begin.

Advantages and Disadvantages

The fact that the cash-balance plan looks like a defined-contribution plan makes the plan easier for participants to understand. But the more interesting question is, looking at the plan as a defined-contribution substitute, does it offer anything that a defined-contribution plan does not? The answer is yes. A cash-balance plan formula can establish credits for past service; in some circumstances, this is a big advantage over the defined-contribution plan. However, looking at the plan from the participant's perspective, the real thing (a true defined-contribution plan) is probably better than the imitation. In an account plan, assets are generally invested with a long-term investment horizon. Participants sharing in the investment experience of a long-term stock-oriented portfolio will usually be better off than if they are credited with a small but steady rate of return. Also, the PBGC guarantee is not really meaningful. The PBGC does not guarantee all benefits, and an employee could lose out if the company folds at a time when the plan has insufficient assets. On the other hand, in a defined-contribution plan, benefits are fully funded at all times and are outside the reach of the employer's creditors.

But, this leads us to the real point of the cash-balance concept: It is not driven solely by employee concerns but in conjunction with the employer's needs and objectives. At least up to this point in time, almost all cash-balance plans in existence today are converted traditional defined-benefit plans. There are two main driving forces: cost savings and a decision that the defined-contribution philosophy makes more sense for the company. The employer may feel that the defined-benefit plan is underappreciated and that the defined-contribution approach will be better received by the employees.

Candidates for This Type of Plan

As described above, so far, the typical candidate for the cash-balance plan is the midsize or large company that has a well-funded defined-benefit plan and that is looking to both save on benefit costs into the future and change to a defined-contribution approach. Prior to the cash-balance concept, the employer looking to save on costs would amend the traditional benefit formula—either lowering or freezing future benefit accruals. However, this would alarm plan participants as they saw their benefits being reduced. Under the cash-balance alternative, the old defined-benefit promise is frozen at the current accrued benefit level and the benefit is stated as its single-sum equivalent. Benefits accruing after the change simply increase the total account balance. With the right cash-balance formula, employees might actually welcome the change in benefit structure, while the employer saves money.

YOUR FINANCIAL SERVICES PRACTICE:
CASH-BALANCE PLANS RECEIVE BAD PUBLICITY

In the last few years, several large employers converting traditional defined-benefit plans to cash-balance plans have received some bad publicity. There are two primary issues: 1) a lack of communication—employees didn't understand the change and 2) older employees weren't fully informed that their overall benefits would be lower than they were under the old plan. This means that employees who have heard of the cash-balance controversy may be wary of this plan design. In response, employers generally need to carefully consider grandfathering provisions for older employees. Congress has also responded and beginning in 2002 ERISA will require full disclosure to participants of any plan amendment that reduces future benefit accruals.

However, this is not magic. The new benefit structure cannot be cheaper and remain as good. Generally, older long-service employees are hurt the most in the transition. To protect this group, some employers grandfather the old benefit formula for older employees or give them a larger annual credit under the new formula. The employer could also decide to put some of the savings into another plan, such as making a matching contribution to a 401(k) plan. In this way, the employer sends the message that retirement security is now going to be a joint effort between the employer and employees.

This same employer with the overfunded defined-benefit plan could instead terminate the plan and establish a true defined-contribution plan. However, there are several reasons that amending the plan into a cash-balance plan is more appealing:

- While the employer would not be able to effectively use any excess in the defined-benefit plan to fund the defined-contribution plan, this can be accomplished seamlessly with the cash-balance approach.
- In the future, benefits in the cash-balance plan could be increased both for current and past service. This would be prohibited in a defined-contribution plan.
- The defined-contribution plan lacks the funding flexibility of the cash-balance plan.
- Unlike the cash-balance plan, in a defined-contribution plan, future employer contributions are not reduced by stronger-than-expected investment performance.

For all of these reasons, the cash-balance plan is a terrific solution to this one specific situation. Expect more large and midsize companies to continue to explore the possibility of changing to the cash-balance approach.

Finally, it is not yet clear whether cash-balance plans will become popular as a new plan alternative. For the smaller employer looking for a new retirement plan, the cash-balance approach has all the headaches of a defined-benefit plan: PBGC premiums, large administrative costs, and an annual required contribution. The cash-balance option has more funding flexibility than a traditional money-purchase or target-benefit plan, but it also has much less flexibility than the discretionary profit-sharing or profit-sharing 401(k) plan. The cash-balance plan does have one major advantage over other defined-contribution plans—the maximum contribution on behalf of the owner can exceed $40,000 in some cases. For this reason, some actuarial firms are starting to install cash-balance plans for small businesses.

MONEY-PURCHASE PENSION PLANS

A money-purchase pension plan falls within both the defined-contribution and pension categories. Knowing this means you already know that money-purchase pension plans have the following characteristics:

- The maximum annual contribution that an employee can receive is the lesser of 100 percent of salary or $40,000.
- Participants in the plan have individual accounts that are similar to bank accounts.
- The employee assumes the risk of preretirement inflation, investment performance, and adequacy of retirement income.
- The plan cannot provide for past service.
- Administrative costs are relatively low.

- The plan is easily communicated to employees.
- The plan has predictable employer costs.
- The employer is required to fund the plan annually.
- Employees are restricted from having in-service withdrawals.
- The employer can deduct up to 25 percent of compensation.
- Investments in company stock are limited to 10 percent of the plan's assets.

money-purchase pension plan

Under a *money-purchase pension plan*, the company's annual contributions are based on a percentage of each participant's compensation. For example, the money-purchase contribution formula may provide that annual contributions will equal 10 percent of compensation for each participant (if Karen Lamb earns $40,000, the annual contribution placed in her account is $4,000). Money-purchase plan benefits for each employee are the amounts that can be provided by the sums contributed to the employee's individual account plus investment earnings. For example, if Karen Lamb worked for 20 years and her salary remained at $40,000, at retirement she would have $80,000 plus accumulated interest of $58,876 (assuming a 5 percent annual rate) in her account. The term *money-purchase* arose because the participant's account is traditionally used to purchase an annuity that provides monthly retirement benefits.

The maximum annual limit that can be tax sheltered under a money-purchase plan is 25 percent of total covered compensation. This deduction limit is now the same as for profit-sharing plans. Without the advantage of funding flexibility that the profit-sharing plan has, money-purchase plans are used to provide a fixed contribution and, therefore, gives the sense to employees that it is a substantial and permanent retirement plan. Typically, these organizations provide between 3 and 12 percent of compensation as the annual contribution. Self-employed people provide another market for money-purchase plans (they like the money-purchase plan's simplicity). For example, a self-employed person may express a desire to tax-shelter 15 percent of his or her earned income for retirement.

Money-purchase pension plans can be likened to the station wagons of the retirement fleet because of their dependable annual contributions and simple, basic design. The major advantages of money-purchase pension plans are the predictable costs for the employer (since contributions are based on employee compensation, the employer contribution is basically a percentage of payroll), administrative ease, and understandability for the employees. Corporate objectives, such as competitiveness, attraction, and retention of key employees, can be met within the money-purchase framework without being prohibitively expensive for the employer.

Advantages and Disadvantages

One major drawback of a money-purchase plan is that contributions are based on the participant's salary for each year of his or her career, rather than on the salary at retirement. Given a stable inflationary environment, this may not have a negative impact on the adequacy of retirement income. If inflation spirals in the years prior to retirement, however, the chances of achieving an adequate income-replacement ratio are diminished. Take, for example, someone who earned an average middle-class income and whose career spanned the 1950s, 1960s, and 1970s. In 1950, this person earned $2,000 and received a 10 percent money-purchase contribution of $200. In 1960, the employee earned $12,000 and received a 10 percent money-purchase contribution of $1,200. In 1970, the employee earned $24,000 and received a $2,400 contribution. During the 1970s, double-digit inflation hit, and salary levels increased to account for the increased cost of living. If the participant retired in 1980, he or she would be at a disadvantage because only part of the plan contributions would account for the inflationary period right before retirement. What's more, most of the annual contributions would be based on deflated salaries that accrued before the inflationary spiral. In other words, if a final-average defined-benefit plan were used, the employer would have to make significant contributions to account for an increased final-average salary assumption owing to higher inflation.

A second drawback is the inability to provide an adequate retirement program for older participants. Those who enter money-purchase pension plans later in their careers have less time to accumulate sufficient assets.

Money-purchase pension plans can work, however, given the right set of circumstances.

Example 1:   New employee Bill Nelson is 55 years old and has no other retirement funds except Social Security. Nelson earns $50,000 annually and plans to retire at age 65. The money-purchase pension formula calls for 10 percent of salary to be deposited in Nelson's account each year. The account earns 10 percent interest. Under this accumulation scheme, Nelson will have $79,687 at age 65. Even after combining this with Social Security, Nelson's income will not be adequate to continue his preretirement standard of living.

Example 2:   New employee Gloria Benson is 35 years old and has no other retirement funds except Social Security. Benson earns $50,000 annually and plans to retire at age 65. The money-purchase formula calls for 10 percent of salary to be deposited in Benson's account each year. The account earns 10 percent interest. Under this accumulation scheme, $1,355,122 will be amassed at retirement. Combined with Social Security, Benson's income will be adequate during the retirement years to maintain the proper standard of living.

Candidates for This Type of Plan

Candidates for money-purchase plans are businesses with

- a steady cash flow
- young, well-paid key employees
- a stable workforce (low turnover)
- the need for easily communicated employee benefits

Money-purchase candidates disclose on the fact finder that it is less important to provide an adequate retirement standard of living than to have predictable costs, and that it is more important to have administrative convenience and an easily communicated plan than to provide an adequate retirement standard of living.

TARGET-BENEFIT PENSION PLANS

target-benefit pension plan

A cousin to the money-purchase pension plan, the *target-benefit pension plan* falls within both the defined-contribution and pension categories. Because of this, it shares many of the characteristics of the money-purchase pension plan, including the following:

- The maximum annual contribution that an employee can receive is the lesser of $40,000 or 25 percent of salary.
- Participants in the plan have individual accounts that are similar to bank accounts.
- The employee assumes the risk of preretirement inflation, investment performance, and adequacy of retirement income.
- Administrative costs are relatively low.

- It has predictable employer costs.
- The employer is required to fund the plan annually.
- Employees are restricted from having in-service withdrawals.
- The employer can deduct up to the full amount available under the Sec. 415 limits.
- Investments in company stock are limited to 10 percent of the plan's assets.

Target-benefit pension plans are, however, a unique form of defined-contribution plan because they include some of the features associated with traditional defined-benefit plans. One of these features is that a defined-benefit formula is used to determine the annual contribution. An actuary determines the amount of funds needed for a level annual contribution by using actuarial and interest assumptions in conjunction with the benefit formula. The organization's level annual contribution will not change in subsequent years except to reflect new plan participants and increases in the compensation of existing plan participants. For the sake of convenience and simplicity, the plan is often equipped with a chart indicating contribution levels, and the further use of an actuary after the plan's inception is seldom needed (see figure 4-1).

FIGURE 4-1
Target-Benefit Pension Plans

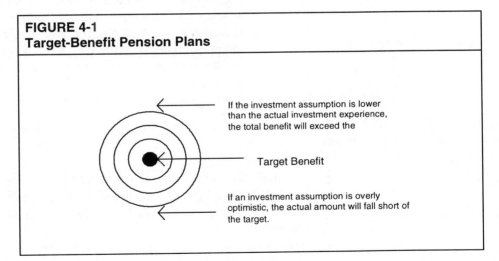

If the investment assumption is lower than the actual investment experience, the total benefit will exceed the

Target Benefit

If an investment assumption is overly optimistic, the actual amount will fall short of the target.

Once the plan has been established, the employer hopes to provide a specific benefit (the target) at retirement. However, the employer does not guarantee that the targeted benefit will be paid. The investment risk falls on the participants, and an amount less than or greater than the target may be available, depending on the actual interest. (*Planning Note:* Under most target-benefit plans, the employee directly participates in the investment return on his or her account balance. If your client desires, however, you can structure the plan to provide a floor of benefits for participants regardless of poor investment return.)

Example: The Ma and Pa Diner has a target-benefit plan for its five employees: Ma Kettle (aged 58), Pa Kettle (aged 60), Wanda Waitress (aged 28), and Wendy Waitress (aged 26). The benefit formula in the plan provides for 3 percent of final-average salary multiplied by years of service. At the inception of the plan, the actuary takes into account final-average salary assumptions, age, mortality, interest earnings, and other assumptions in order to project the annual level contribution for each participant. Because of the comparatively advanced ages of Ma and Pa Kettle, their annual contribution is likely to be very high (particularly since the plan was just recently adopted). But because Wanda and Wendy Waitress are relatively young, and there are many years to accumulate interest and to fund for the benefit, their annual contributions will be relatively low. At retirement, the benefits for any employee may be lower or higher than the targeted amount, due in part to the investment performance of the employee's account.

Employers that are good candidates for target-benefit plans are businesses that have

- an employee census that shows a mix of employees that includes older owners and younger rank-and-file employees
- recent economic success and the likelihood that the success will continue
- older, well-paid owner-employees and key employees
- a desire to have a defined-benefit plan without a pocketbook to match their desire

Advantages and Disadvantages

Target-benefit pension plans are uniquely suited for older owner-employees who are initiating a retirement program. Typically, these types of owner-employees have put off retirement programs because money was tight in the early years. They have now reached a stage of fiscal maturity, and the 50- to 55-year-old owner-employee has started to think about tax shelters and retirement. The benefit formula in a target-benefit pension plan requires contributions for older employees that will be larger because there is less time to fund for the target benefit.

Target-benefit pension plans can be thought of as the sports cars of the retirement fleet—they provide for the speedy accumulation of substantial retirement benefits for older employees. They also offer the added inducement of big tax deductions just when they are needed for the owner-employer. While target-benefit plans may be slightly more expensive to administer than other types of defined-contribution plans, generally the tax shelter, and not the higher cost, is the client's chief concern.

Target-benefit plans have several disadvantages, as well. They do not provide the same level of security as the defined-benefit plan and, at the same time, lose some of the simplicity of the defined-contribution approach. More specifically, the disadvantages include the following:

- Unlike the defined-benefit plan, the participant is not promised a specified benefit. Even though the plan can target a benefit, the actual benefit will be more or less, depending upon the performance of plan assets.
- The benefit formula is more difficult to understand than in a traditional money-purchase pension plan. The annual contribution is based on the amount needed under an actuarial cost method to fund a targeted benefit amount. This is a difficult concept to communicate.
- Rank-and-file employees may have difficulty understanding why two workers with the same wages and years of service but who are of different ages will be entitled to different contributions under the plan.
- In most cases, the plan is established with the goal of allocating the lion's share of the contribution to the business owner. The contribution for even one older nonhighly compensated employee can be so high that it can defeat this goal. Therefore, this plan design is not appropriate when either the owner is young, or the company has one or more older rank-and-file employees.

Target-Benefit Plans in the Marketplace Today

Currently, the target-benefit plan is somewhat out of vogue. Enthusiasm for this type of plan has waned with the advent of age-weighted and cross-tested profit-sharing plans (discussed in the next chapter). The primary reason for this waning interest is that almost the same objectives can be met with those plans without the employer having to commit to annual required contributions. As you will understand better after reading about those plans, the age-weighted plan is really quite similar to the target-benefit concept, while the cross-tested plan is even more flexible.

TABLE 4-2 Hybrid Plans: Mirrors of Each Other	
Target- benefit Pension Plan	**Cash-balance Pension Plan**
Defined-contribution plan	Defined-benefit plan
Not subject to PBGC	Subject to PBGC
Participant entitled to vested account balance	Participant entitled to promised benefit, regardless of actual plan assets
Feels like a defined-benefit plan because contributions target a monthly benefit at retirement	Feels like a defined-contribution plan because promised benefit is based on an accumulated hypothetical account balance
Contribution is fixed based on the contribution formula	Contribution is variable based on the actuarial determination

CHAPTER REVIEW

Answers to the review questions and the self-test questions start on page 673.

Key Terms

unit-benefit formula
income-replacement ratio
flat-percentage-of-earnings formula
flat-amount-per-year-of-service
   formula
flat-amount formula
final-average compensation

career-average compensation
past service
normal form of benefit payment
cash-balance plan
money-purchase pension plan
target-benefit pension plan

Review Questions

4-1. Ralph Camdon, the owner of a local tour bus company, would like a defined-benefit plan that helps to retain and reward experienced personnel, that rewards owner-employees and key employees who have high salaries, and that provides an income-replacement ratio of 60 percent for "career" employees.

    a. What type of benefit formula should Ralph use in his plan? Explain.

    b. Give an example of how the benefit formula should be written.

4-2. In what situations are flat-amount-per-year-of-service formulas typically used?

4-3. Describe a flat-amount formula.

4-4. a. Explain how the definitions of *compensation* and *final-average compensation* affect the participant's benefit.

    b. If the normal form of benefit is a life annuity, does this have the same value as if the normal form of benefit is a life annuity with 10-year certain payments?

    c. Does a life annuity payable at a normal retirement age of 65 have the same value as a life annuity payable at age 62?

4-5. Why would an employer choose to account for past service in the defined-benefit plan?

4-6. Bill Crosby owns a small sporting goods manufacturing plant. He is instituting a defined-benefit plan for his business, which has been in existence for 15 years without any plan. Bill would like to have a competitive benefit formula to attract key people to his plant. He would also like to provide a past-service benefit for employees who have been there over the years, but he doesn't feel he can afford as lucrative a past-service benefit as his future-service benefit. What options does Bill have?

4-7. Explain the following about cash-balance plans:

    a. Is the cash-balance plan a defined-benefit or defined-contribution type of plan?

    b. What makes the cash-balance benefit formula different from a traditional defined-benefit plan?

    c. Why are employers with well-funded traditional defined-benefit plans choosing to amend them into cash-balance plans?

4-8. What are the major advantages and disadvantages of a money-purchase plan?

4-9. Dr. Debbie Dwyer runs her own veterinary clinic, Pet Care, Inc. Dr. Dwyer is 56 years old and has never set up a qualified plan for her practice. (She was formerly a housewife until she went to veterinary school at age 45.) Dr. Dwyer has two younger employees whom she would like to include in a retirement plan, but she can't afford to pay too much. In fact, Dr. Dwyer can afford to save only 20 percent of her $100,000 salary. What type of pension plan should Dr. Dwyer adopt? Explain.

4-10. Indicate what type of plan you would recommend in each of the following situations:

  a. Candidate Able has a business that has a steady cash flow, young well-paid key employees, and a low turnover rate. Able's objectives are to adopt a plan that has predictable costs, has a significant benefit, is administratively convenient, and is easily communicated to employees.

  b. Candidate Baker has been maintaining a traditional defined-benefit plan. His employees don't seem to understand the plan and apparently would prefer the defined-contribution approach. The defined-benefit plan is currently well funded, and Baker has indicated his desire to lower or eliminate contributions over the next few years.

  c. Candidate Charley has indicated that the following objectives are very important: (1) maximizing benefits for older owner-employees and key employees, (2) using a qualified plan as a tax shelter for owner-employees and key employees, (3) maximizing benefits for older employees, (4) maximizing benefits for long-service employees, and (5) providing an adequate retirement income to owner-employees, key employees, and rank-and-file employees.

Self-Test Questions

T   F   4-1. Employers typically provide an income-replacement ratio equal to 100 percent of an employee's final-average salary.

T   F   4-2. If the employer desires a more rapid turnover of older employees, the plan's benefit formula should contain a years-of-service cap.

T   F   4-3. Under a flat-percentage-of-earnings formula the benefit relates solely to service.

T   F   4-4. To satisfy nondiscrimination rules, flat-percentage-of-earnings formulas generally have to reduce benefits for participants with fewer than 25 years of service.

T   F   4-5. A plan that defines compensation as base compensation will not have a problem under the nondiscrimination rules if the only additional pay is to rank-and-file employees for overtime.

T   F   4-6. An important reason to account for past service is to maximize the tax-shelter potential of the plan for long-service owner-employees and key employees.

T   F   4-7. Past service is often ignored in the small plan market.

T   F   4-8.   A participant who receives a life annuity benefit of $2,000 a month beginning at age 65 has received a more valuable benefit than the participant who received a $2,000 life annuity beginning at age 62.

T   F   4-9.   When accounting for past service, the plan can be designed to either provide for all service prior to the inception of the plan or provide a downgraded benefit for service prior to the inception of the plan.

T   F   4-10. Candidates for a defined-benefit plan typically have the objective of instituting a plan that has predictable costs.

T   F   4-11. Candidates for a defined-benefit plan indicate that the desire to provide an adequate standard of living in retirement outweighs the need to have an easily communicated and administratively convenient plan.

T   F   4-12. A cash-balance plan is a form of defined-contribution plan.

T   F   4-13. Most cash-balance plans started as traditional defined-benefit plans that were amended into cash-balance plans.

T   F   4-14. Under a money-purchase plan, the company's annual contributions are mandatory and are based on each participant's compensation.

T   F   4-15. The maximum annual contribution for a particular employee under a money-purchase plan is $160,000 per year.

T   F   4-16. One major drawback to a money-purchase plan is that participants are not protected if inflation spirals just before retirement age.

T   F   4-17. Money-purchase plan candidates typically have the objectives of instituting a plan that has predictable costs and that is easily communicated to employees.

T   F   4-18. A target-benefit plan is a form of defined-contribution plan.

T   F   4-19. Under a target-benefit plan, the employer bears the investment risk and gets the benefit of the investment return.

T   F   4-20. Under a target-benefit plan, the employer guarantees that the employee's benefit will be the target amount or greater.

T   F   4-21. Target-benefit plans best serve young, highly paid professionals who are looking to maximize benefits.

T   F   4-22. Interest in the target-benefit plans has waned because today's employers can meet the same objectives with an age-weighted or cross-tested profit-sharing plan.

Profit-Sharing Plans, 401(k) Plans, Stock Bonus Plans, and ESOPs

Learning Objectives

An understanding of the material in this chapter should enable the student to

5-1. Describe the requirements for the profit-sharing continuation and allocation formulas.

5-2. Identify the various employer objectives that are served by using a profit-sharing plan.

5-3. Explain the characteristics of a 401(k) cash or deferred plan.

5-4. Explain the special rules and requirements that apply to 401(k) cash or deferred plans.

5-5. Describe the planning purposes for which a stock bonus plan and employee stock-option plan can be used.

Chapter Outline

Let's turn our attention to some qualified plans that aren't necessarily intended to provide a pension at retirement. Unlike the pension plans discussed in chapter 4, profit-sharing plans, 401(k) plans, stock bonus plans, and employee stock ownership plans (ESOPs) are often designed to distribute organizational earnings on a tax-sheltered basis with only a partial regard to meeting retirement needs. Historically, these plans have been considered more of a tax shelter for deferred income than a retirement system that will provide an adequate pension in the retirement years. More recently, however, these plans have become intimately involved with the employer's decision to meet the need for an adequate pension in the following ways:

- They have become part of a comprehensive retirement package that combines these plans with other plans to fund for retirement needs.
- They have become "pensionlike" in their actual application. (For example, regular reoccurring substantial contributions, even if the employer has no profits.)

PROFIT-SHARING PLANS IN GENERAL

A profit-sharing plan is a defined-contribution plan that also falls within the profit-sharing category. (*Planning Note:* Don't be confused by the fact that profit sharing is both a category of plan and a type of plan.) Before we begin to discuss the specifics of this plan, we already know the following:

- Employer contributions are discretionary.
- The plan can allow for in-service withdrawals.
- The plan can conceivably invest up to 100 percent of the plan's assets in the sponsoring company's stock.
- The maximum annual contribution that an employee can receive is the lesser of 100 percent of salary or $40,000.
- Participants in the plan have individual accounts that are similar to bank accounts.
- The employee assumes the risk of preretirement inflation, investment performance, and adequacy of retirement income.

- The plan cannot provide for past service.
- Administrative costs are relatively low.
- The plan is easily communicated to employees.
- The employer can deduct up to 25 percent of compensation.

There are two parts to the contribution formula in a profit-sharing plan. One relates to how much the company contributes to the plan and the other relates to how the contribution is allocated among the participants. Let's take a closer look.

Contributions

From the employer's perspective, one of the primary strengths of the profit-sharing plan is that the employer can make contributions on a discretionary basis. In addition, since 1987, an employer can make a contribution to a plan whether or not there are actually profits. There is one limit, however, contributions must be "substantial and recurring" over the years, or the IRS could determine that the plan has been terminated. The result of this is that all participants become fully vested. (See chapter 14 for a further discussion of this issue.)

Most plans are written today specifying that the board of directors make the decision each year as to whether to make contributions or how much to contribute. Whether a company actually contributes more in a good financial year is a business decision. However, if the employer is trying to use the plan as a way to motivate participants, there should be a clear relationship between the company's performance and contributions made to the plan.

Another way to address the issue of employee motivation is to write the plan to require a specified contribution. One way to do this is to state the required contribution as a specified percentage of profits or some other objective formula stated in the plan. This approach is appropriate when the employer wants employees to feel that they have a clear and determinable stake in the performance of the company. Another way is to stipulate that a certain percentage of each participant's salary will be contributed each year. For example, the company will contribute 10 percent of a participant's compensation. This type of contribution requirement allows the employer to use the profit-sharing plan in the same manner as a money-purchase pension plan, in which the corporate goal is typically to provide an adequate pension benefit, not to provide a vehicle for employees to share in company profits.

YOUR FINANCIAL SERVICES PRACTICE:
GETTING THE MOST MILEAGE OUT OF THE PLAN

Employers never enjoy spending money on retirement benefits that employees don't appreciate. Because a profit-sharing plan typically does not require a specified employer contribution, it may be difficult to get employees to appreciate the value of the plan. To get the most out of the plan, the employer should consider taking the following steps:

- Clearly communicate the amount of the contribution and how it was derived.
- Make regular and reoccurring contributions, if at all possible.
- Provide clear and comprehensive benefit statements.
- Identify circumstances that would result in larger employer contributions.

Allocation Formulas

The heart of a profit-sharing plan is the method of allocating the employer contribution among the participants. This formula must be definite and predetermined. Historically, the most common allocation formula has been one that allocates the total contribution so that each participant receives a contribution that is the same percentage of compensation, for example, 3 percent or 5 percent. This allocation formula in the plan document would read something like this:

> "Employer contributions made for the year will be allocated, as of the last day of each plan year, to each participant's account in the proportion that the participant's compensation bears to the total compensation of all eligible participants for the plan year."

Under this type of allocation formula, if, for example, the employer contributed $10,000, total payroll was $100,000, and Alexander earned $25,000, he would have an allocation of $2,500 ($10,000 x $25,000/$100,000). If Barbara earned $30,000, her allocation would be $3,000 ($10,000 x $30,000/$100,000). As you can see, the employer contributed 10 percent of payroll and each participant received an allocation of 10 percent of his or her compensation.

This allocation formula has been popular, in part, because it is clear that it satisfies the requirement of Code Sec. 401(a)(4), which requires that contributions or benefits cannot discriminate in favor of the highly compensated employees. Other ways to allocate contributions include integration with Social Security and newer methods such as age-weighting and cross-testing. (All of these allocation methods are discussed fully in chapter 8). As you will see, these allocation formulas add a whole new dimension to the profit-sharing plan, allowing this simple, versatile plan to be used to skew the contributions to older (and, not coincidentally, more highly compensated) business owners. As well, allocation formulas can be designed to meet any number of other compensation objectives.

YOUR FINANCIAL SERVICES PRACTICE:
SWITCHING INVESTMENT CARRIERS

Frequently, when you are prospecting in the retirement field, you will encounter the existence of an established plan that is invested with a competitor. The emergence of new ideas, like cross-testing or age-weighting, can be a useful weapon in fighting the uphill battle of converting already-spoken-for assets. Even if the new design does not fit the needs of these prospective clients, at the very least you will be regarded as someone who is in touch with current trends and who is on the cutting edge of your profession. Future dealings can stem from this favorable impression.

Advantages of a Profit-Sharing Plan to the Business and Business Owner

Even though the profit-sharing plan does not provide the most secure benefit to employees, it is an extremely flexible vehicle that is a very popular choice. Here are some of the organizational objectives these plans serve:

discretionary contributions

- *allowing discretionary contributions*—The plan can be designed with no predetermined formula so that the employer has the option of not making contributions in a given year (for example, the plan may provide that contributions, if any, will be determined annually by the board of directors).
- *permitting withdrawal flexibility*—Plans can be designed to allow employees to withdraw funds from participant accounts as early as 2 years after they were contributed by the employer.
- *controlling benefit costs*—Organizations find that adopting a profit-sharing plan is a fiscally responsible move. The organization will not be saddled with cash-flow problems caused by mandatory contributions. Flexibility is especially important for employers with fluctuating profits.
- *improving productivity*—Another cost advantage is profit sharing's correlation to productivity. Many believe these plans help to increase employee identification with the employer and provide an incentive to employees. This increased productivity can be viewed as a way to maximize the cost-effectiveness of the employer's

contributions. The old saying "You have to spend more to get more" applies here, however.

- *providing legal discrimination in favor of older owner-employees*— The profit-sharing plan can be set up to give (allocate) the majority of the profits to older, high-salaried owner-employees. When used in this manner, the profit-sharing plan makes an excellent tax shelter for the older business owner. This approach also lowers contributions for rank-and-file employees (see chapter 8).

Disadvantages of a Profit-Sharing Plan to the Business and Business Owner

A profit-sharing plan is extremely versatile, and is an excellent vehicle for the small business. As compared to other types of plans there are a few disadvantages. The primary one is that rank-and-file employees might perceive the plan as a hollow benefit if discretionary contributions are not made or if the lion's share of profits goes to the business owner. As discussed above, this problem can be limited through good communication with employees.

Profit Sharing Plans: A Summary of the Rules

- **Contributions**—discretionary unless otherwise specified in the plan
- **Allocation formula**—must have a definite and predetermined formula for allocating the contribution among participants. Allocating based on compensation or integration with Social Security is common, with other formulas possible so long as the plan can satisfy a nondiscrimination test.
- **In-service withdrawals**—if allowed by the plan, benefits can be distributed to active participants as long as the participants have met the plan's conditions.
- **Maximum contribution**—like other defined contribution plans the maximum contribution is 25 percent of the payroll of all participants.
- **Employer securities**—like other profit-sharing type plans, the plan can invest more than 10% of plan assets in employer securities.
- **Other provisions**—subject to eligibility and vesting requirements that apply to qualified plans

---

Candidates for Profit-Sharing Plans

With the incredible versatility of the profit-sharing plan, a large number of companies are candidates for profit-sharing plans. These include businesses with

- cash-flow problems
- less economic stability (for example, new businesses and capital-intensive businesses)
- young, well-paid key employees
- no desire to ensure the adequacy of an employee's retirement income

Candidates for profit-sharing plans fill out the fact finder by typically grading as "very valuable" the following:

- placing the investment risk on the employee
- avoiding an annual financial commitment
- allowing employees (including owner-employees) to withdraw funds. (If this is the case, design the plan to allow withdrawals after 2 years; if this is not the case, a profit-sharing plan may still be desired but withdrawal restrictions should be incorporated.)
- motivating the workforce

Candidates for a profit-sharing plan typically grade these goals as "least valuable":

- maximizing benefits for long-service employees by accounting for past service
- providing a specified replacement ratio

Profit-sharing candidates typically answer "yes" to the fact finder question: Is it more important to motivate employees than to attract or retain them? And they typically answer "no" to these fact finder questions: Is it more important to provide an adequate retirement standard of living than to allow employees (including owner-employees) to withdraw funds? Is it more important to provide an adequate retirement standard of living than to have predictable costs?

Candidates for a profit-sharing plan usually put contribution flexibility at the head of their priority list, usually opt for a low income-replacement ratio, and typically come from an organization or industry with an unstable cash-flow history.

YOUR FINANCIAL SERVICES PRACTICE:
LIFE INSURANCE AND PROFIT-SHARING PLANS

Profit-sharing plans have a unique need that can be met through the purchase of life insurance. In addition to using life insurance to fund participants' accounts (discussed in chapter 12), life insurance can be purchased on the client's key people (owner-employees, key employees, and officers) as a general asset of the profit-sharing trust. The profit-sharing trust is permitted to make this purchase because it has an insurable interest in the client's key people. This insurable interest stems from the fact that company profits are generally required to fund the profit-sharing trust and that these people are primarily responsible for these company profits. Here's how it works:

- Insurance contracts are purchased out of unallocated assets given to the trust by the organization.
- The insurance contracts are owned by the trust, which pays the premiums and is also the named beneficiary.
- Because the contracts are not allocated to participant accounts, the percentage limitation applied under the incidental death benefit rules (see chapter 10) is not applicable.
- Upon the death of the insured, the insurance proceeds are paid to the trust and are then typically allocated among participants on the basis of the account balance of each participant.

With the flexibility in allocation formulas available today, profit-sharing candidates also include those businesses interested in providing a lion's share of the benefits for the key employees while minimizing the cost of benefits for the rank-and-file employee. This can be done quite effectively using the age-weighted and cross-tested allocation formulas discussed briefly above and in more depth in chapter 8. At one time, employers with this goal looked either to the defined-benefit plan or the target-benefit plan. Today, the profit-sharing plan allows for similar skewing of the contribution to the targeted group while maintaining the flexibility of the profit-sharing plan.

YOUR FINANCIAL SERVICES PRACTICE:
PROFIT-SHARING PLANS BECOME EVEN MORE FLEXIBLE

By increasing the maximum deductible contribution limit in profit-sharing plans from 15 percent to 25 percent of compensation, the Economic Growth and Tax Relief Reconciliation Act of 2001 eliminates the need for small employers to maintain two defined-contribution plans. Before the law change, a common strategy for the sole proprietor or small business owner was to establish a 10 percent money-purchase plan and a profit-sharing plan. This strategy provided the owner the opportunity to contribute up to 25 percent of compensation while retaining some contribution flexibility. Now this objective can be accomplished within the single more flexible profit-sharing plan. Small businesses that have been maintaining two plans might consider consolidation in order to limit administrative costs.

CASH OR DEFERRED ARRANGEMENTS—401(K) PLANS

cash or deferred arrangement (CODA)

An option that is available under a profit-sharing plan (or a stock bonus plan, which is discussed next) is the *cash or deferred arrangement (CODA)*. When the CODA option is part of a profit-sharing or stock bonus plan, that plan is usually referred to as a 401(k) plan. (401(k) is the section number in the Internal Revenue Code that outlines CODAs.) A 401(k) plan allows plan participants the opportunity to defer taxation on a portion of regular salary or bonuses simply by electing to have such amounts contributed to the plan instead of receiving them in cash. Participants enjoy abundant tax savings. For example, if Simms is in the 28 percent marginal tax bracket and elects to reduce his salary by $6,000, he will save $1,680 in taxes. That's like having Uncle Sam as a contributing partner in Simms's retirement savings. What's more, the money Simms puts in the plan earns tax-deferred interest until retirement. If Simms encounters financial problems, he may decrease his future contributions or discontinue contributions altogether simply by changing his salary reduction agreement (the form that authorizes the employer to reduce the salary and make plan contributions in the amount of the reduction).

Today almost all large private employers and many midsize companies sponsor such plans (often in addition to sponsoring more traditional plans such as a defined-benefit or money-purchase pension plan). The plan is starting to expand into the small plan market as well, and today it is the most popular new plan to install.

401(k) Plan Design

Remember that a 401(k) plan is a profit-sharing (or occasionally a stock bonus) plan that contains a salary deferral (401(k)) feature. This means that, in addition to the salary deferral feature, the plan can contain a traditional profit-sharing feature, an employer matching contribution feature, or both. The plan may even allow for employee after-tax contributions. This means that the plan can be as simple as a *stand-alone plan* (salary deferrals only), or as complex as a plan that allows pretax and after-tax employee contributions, employer matching contributions, and employer profit-sharing contributions.

stand-alone plan

YOUR FINANCIAL SERVICES PRACTICE:
401(k) PLANS FOR NONPROFIT ORGANIZATIONS

Beginning in 1997, nonprofit organizations became eligible to sponsor 401(k) plans. This option may not be that important for 501(c)(3) organizations that can select the 403(b) plan (see chapter 6), but it is important for other types of nonprofit organizations that previously did not have the opportunity to sponsor any tax-advantaged plan that allows for pretax salary deferrals. These organizations could be a good niche 401(k) market.

A stand-alone plan (a plan allowing only pretax salary deferrals) can be used by an organization that cannot afford a comprehensive retirement program. The stand-alone plan can be expanded and enhanced in the future as the financial strength of the sponsor grows. It can also be established as a supplement to other retirement plans.

The employer that wants to combine salary deferrals with additional employer contributions to the same plan can choose how to spend those dollars—as matching or as profit-sharing contributions. A common practice today is to choose a *matching contribution* feature in which the plan sponsor agrees to match employee savings to a certain extent. For example, the sponsor might agree to contribute fifty cents to the plan for each dollar that the employee saves, up to the first 6 percent of compensation that the participant saves. In this example, the maximum employer match is 3 percent of compensation.

matching contribution

Both the matching percentage and the maximum match must be carefully chosen to meet the employer's objectives and budget. The primary reason for the match is to stimulate plan participation through the offer of an instant return on the participant's savings. Another goal is to create a retirement planning partnership between the employer and the participants. Under this philosophy, an employer is committed to contribute toward an employee's funds for retirement, but only if the employee is willing to save for retirement. Finally, the feature can act as a profit-sharing incentive.

To meet specific employer objectives, the design of the matching contribution can be as straightforward as described above, or more complex—such as a graded formula in which the matching contribution rate varies for different levels of salary deferrals. Under a typical graded formula, the employer contributes fifty cents for each dollar saved by the plan participant, up to 4 percent of covered earnings, plus twenty-five cents for each dollar saved over 4 percent, but not more than 6 percent of covered, earnings. Matching contributions can also be made on a discretionary basis. Because the uncertainty of the employer's contribution might discourage plan participation, it is more common to provide a small, guaranteed matching contribution, which can be made larger at the discretion of the employer.

A profit-sharing feature in a 401(k) plan works the same way as in a traditional profit-sharing plan. Contributions are made for eligible participants, regardless of whether they make salary deferral contributions. When the 401(k) plan is the only plan sponsored by the employer, it is not uncommon—in a good year—for the sponsor to make both matching contributions and profit-sharing-type contributions.

YOUR FINANCIAL SERVICES PRACTICE:
401(k) PLANS FOR THE SMALL BUSINESS

Even with the popularity of 401(k) plans, only a minimal portion of small businesses sponsor them—meaning that there is still a lot of opportunity for the financial services professional. Open doors to new clients with the following points:

- Administration costs are often lower today than before because many organizations have designed simplified "cookie cutter" type packages.
- If the sponsor already has a profit-sharing plan, point out that a 401(k) feature can be added to that plan, a second plan is not needed. This is especially true after the Economic Growth and Tax Relief Reconciliation Act of 2001 because the deduction limits have gone for profit-sharing and 401(k) plans.
- With low unemployment, in our economy, a small employer with a state-of-the-art 401(k) plan can better compete for, and retain, employees.
- The opportunity to design a 401(k) plan to include a safe harbor contribution that eliminates the need for nondiscrimination or top-heavy testing makes it much easier for a small employer to maintain a 401(k) plan today.
- A 401(k) feature combined with an age-weighted or cross-tested profit-sharing plan could allow the business owner to maximize his or her own contribution and lower the cost of benefits for rank-and-file employees.
- If the employer likes the salary deferral concept but still feels that the plan is too complex, they should consider the SIMPLE IRA (discussed in chapter 6).

Also note that a 401(k) plan can include employee after-tax contributions in addition to employee pretax salary deferrals. This feature is not that common, but is occasionally included—primarily because employees like the withdrawal flexibility of after-tax contributions. These contributions do not have to be subject to the withdrawal restrictions that apply to pretax contributions (as discussed below). This feature is common in older plans that were converted from after-tax thrift plans. In this case, some employees are more secure with the old way of doing things.

Note that when a plan has more than just salary deferrals, it must have separate bookkeeping accounts for each type of contribution. This requirement is due, in part, to the fact that the accounts attributable to employer matching and profit-sharing contributions are subject to the same rules that apply to a traditional profit-sharing plan, while the salary deferral account is subject to the special rules described below.

Salary Deferral Limitations

The heart of the 401(k) plan is the salary deferral feature. The amount of elective deferrals can never exceed a specified limit. For 2002, the limit is $11,000. Under the Economic Growth and Tax Relief Reconciliation Act of 2001, the limit goes up to $12,000 in 2003, $13,000 in 2004, $14,000 in 2005, and $15,000 in 2006. After 2006, the maximum dollar amount will increase for inflation in increments of $500.

In addition, under the new law, the maximum salary deferral is increased for those individuals who have attained age 50 by the end of the current year. For 2002, the additional allowable contribution is $1,000. The additional amount becomes $2,000 for 2003, $3,000 for 2004, $4,000 for 2005, and $5,000 for 2006. Table 5-1 below shows the maximum contribution, including the new catch-up election, over the next several years.

TABLE 5-1
Scheduled Increases to the Maximum Salary Deferral Amount

Year	Maximum for all participants	Participants over 50	Total for those over 50
2002	$11,000	$1,000	$12,000
2003	$12,000	$2,000	$14,000
2004	$13,000	$3,000	$16,000
2005	$14,000	$4,000	$18,000
2006	$15,000	$5,000	$20,000

It is important to understand that this maximum salary deferral limit to a 401(k) plan applies to the individual. This means that all salary deferral contributions made by that the individual to any 401(k) plan, Code Sec. 403(b) annuity, simplified employee pension (SEP), or savings incentive match plan for employees (SIMPLE) will be treated as one plan under the rules. This is even true for an individual working for a number of unrelated employers.

***Example*:**   Ina Thrifty, age 52, is a doctor doing research for Drug Co., which maintains a 401(k) plan. For 2002, Ina plans to make the maximum $12,000 salary deferral contribution ($11,000 plus the $1,000 catch-up). Ina is also in a group medical practice (which is unrelated to Drug Co.). The practice also has a 401(k) plan. Unfortunately, Ina can not make any salary deferral contributions to that plan, because the maximum deferral limit applies to all plans in which she participates.

Special Rules That Apply to 401(k) Salary Deferrals

The 401(k) salary deferral part of the profit-sharing plan is subject to a number of special rules:

- 401(k) salary reductions are immediately 100 percent vested and cannot be forfeited.
- In-service withdrawals are to be made only if an individual has attained age 59 1/2 or has a financial hardship.
- An extra nondiscrimination test called the *actual deferral percentage (ADP) test* applies to salary deferral amounts (discussed later in this chapter).

Vesting

Technically, amounts contributed to the plan under a salary deferral election are considered employer contributions—even though they are made at the election of the participant. Still, such amounts are treated somewhat differently from how other employer contributions are treated. Normally, employer contributions can be subject to a vesting schedule, meaning that if the employee leaves before working for a designated period of time, some or all benefits are forfeited (as discussed further in chapter 9). The portion of the participant's account that is made up of employee salary deferrals (and investment experience thereon) must be nonforfeitable at all times. In other words, employee salary deferral contributions to a 401(k) plan are always 100 percent vested. This makes sense, because participants were entitled to receive such amounts at the time they elected to make the salary deferral. When the plan has employer profit-sharing accounts, such accounts can be subject to a vesting schedule under the normal rules. Beginning in 2002, employer matching contributions are subject to more accelerated vesting rules. (These will be discussed more fully in chapter 9.)

In-service Withdrawals

A regular profit-sharing plan can allow employees the option of withdrawing the entire account upon 5 years of plan participation or withdrawing contributions 2 years after they are made. However, under a 401(k) plan, withdrawals from the salary deferral election account are restricted.[1] The plan must provide that no distributions from the salary deferral account will be made before separation from service unless either the employee has attained age 59 1/2 or has incurred a financial hardship (referred to as a hardship withdrawal). A *financial hardship* is defined as a financial need that is "necessary in light of immediate and heavy financial needs of an employee" and no other resources can be reasonably available to meet this need.

financial hardship

So plan administrators do not have to make difficult hardship determinations on a case-by-case basis, the regulations provide a safe harbor method for determining hardship. Under the safe harbor rules, the following specific circumstances constitute hardships:

- medical expenses
- purchase of a principal residence for the participant
- payment of tuition for postsecondary education for a participant or his or her spouse, children, or dependents
- payment of amounts necessary to prevent the eviction of the participant from his or her principal residence or from foreclosure on his or her mortgage

The rules also provide a safe harbor method for determining whether "other resources are reasonably available to meet the need." An employee will be deemed to lack "other reasonable resources" if the following conditions are met:

- The employee must obtain all distributions other than hardship distributions and all nontaxable loans available under all plans maintained by the employer.
- The plan must provide that the employee's elective deferral contributions and nondeductible contributions will be suspended for 6 months after the distribution.

Example:	Employee Adams makes elective contributions from January 2001 to June 2001. In June 2001, Adams takes a hardship distribution from the plan. Adams cannot make elective deferral contributions to his 401(k) plan until January 2002 (the 6-month waiting period).

Most employers choose to adopt both safe harbor provisions so that they are not in the position to have to examine an employee's financial condition. A plan does not have to allow for hardship withdrawals, and some employers choose instead to allow loans, because loans can be made without tax consequences.

Actual Deferral Percentage Test

actual deferral percentage (ADP) test

401(k) plans are subject to a special nondiscrimination test known as the *actual deferral percentage (ADP) test,* which

- ensures that higher-paid employees don't use the 401(k) plan to stockpile contributions that otherwise would have produced needed tax revenue
- forces employers to design the 401(k) plan so it attracts participation by lower-paid employees by making the amount that higher-paid people can tax-shelter conditional on the amount that the lower-paid employees actually tax-shelter

In order to pass the actual deferral percentage (ADP) test, one of two requirements must be satisfied:

- *the 125 percent requirement*—Under this requirement, the average of the actual deferral percentages (ADPs) for highly compensated employees for the current year cannot be more than 125 percent of the average ADPs for nonhighly compensated employees in the previous year.
- *the 200 percent/2 percent difference requirement*—Under this requirement, the average of the ADPs for highly compensated employees for the current year cannot be more than 200 percent of the average ADPs for nonhighly compensated employees in the previous year and the difference between the deferral percentages for the two groups cannot be more than 2 percent.

highly compensated employees (HCEs)

The first step in performing the ADP test is determining the *highly compensated employees.* The highly compensated employees include

- individuals who are 5 percent owners during the current or previous year and
- individuals who earned over the earnings limit in the preceding year. In 2000 and 2001, the earnings limit is $85,000. (The employer can elect to limit this group to employees whose compensation puts them in the top 20 percent of payroll.)

The second step is determining the ADP for each employee eligible to participate in the plan. The ADP is simply the individual's salary deferral amounts for the year divided by compensation earned for the year. The final step is determining the average for the nonhighly compensated group for the previous year. Remember that all participants eligible to make salary deferrals are included, meaning that those who do not make salary deferrals have ADPs of zero.

TABLE 5-2
Maximum ADP Limits for Highly Compensated Employees

ADP of Nonhighly Compensated Group	ADP Limit
1%	2%
2%	4%
3%	5%
4%	6%
5%	7%
6%	8%
7%	9%
8%	10%
9%	11.25%
10%	12.50%
11%	13.75%
12%	15%
13%	16.25%
14%	17.50%
15%	18.75%
16%	20%

Once the average of the ADPs for the nonhighly compensated employees for the prior year is determined, the maximum average of the ADPs for the highly compensated employees for the current year can be determined. In general, if the ADP for the nonhighly compensated group is less than 2 percent, the 200 percent limit applies. If the ADP for the nonhighly compensated group is at least 2 percent and not more than 8 percent, the 2 percent spread limit applies. If the ADP for the nonhighly compensated group is 9 percent or more, the 125 percent limit applies (see table 5-2).

Case Study: Medical Group Professional Corporation

Now that we have laid out the rules, let's examine the application of the ADP test in a case. The Medical Group Professional Corporation has a 401(k) plan and wants to know what the maximum deferral percentage for the highly compensated employees will be for 2002. At the end of 2001, the census data are as follows:

	Salary	Percentage Contributed
Dr. Ben Casey (CEO/75% owner)	$60,000	8%
Dr. Roberta Stone (V.P./25% owner)	60,000	8%
Dr. Mel Practice	99,000	6%
Dr. Frank Burns (treasurer)	20,000	5%
Dr. Ruth Rosenhauser	86,000	8%
Dr. Julius Miller	40,000	8%
Nancy Doe	40,000	5%
Joe Jones	25,000	5%
Sally Crowe	25,000	5%
Jack Dixon	20,000	5%

The first step in the ADP test is to determine who falls into the highly compensated group and who is not a member of that group.

- Dr. Ben Casey and Dr. Roberta Stone are highly compensated employees because they are more-than-5-percent owners.
- Dr. Mel Practice and Dr. Ruth Rosenhauser are highly compensated employees because they receive annual compensation in excess of $85,000 (in year 2001) and are members of the top-paid group (the top 20 percent of the employer's payroll).
- Dr. Frank Burns, Dr. Julius Miller, Nancy Doe, Joe Jones, Sally Crowe, and Jack Dixon are not highly compensated employees.

The second step necessary to perform the ADP test is to determine the deferral percentage for the nonhighly compensated group.

Nonhighly Compensated	
Dr. Frank Burns	5.0%
Dr. Julius Miller	8.0%
Nancy Doe	5.0%
Joe Jones	5.0%
Sally Crowe	5.0%
Jack Dixon	5.0%
Average % Deferred	5.5%

This means that in 2002, the maximum average ADP for the highly compensated group will be 7.5 percent. (As discussed above, if the deferral percentage for the nonhighly compensated employee group is between 2 and 8 percent, the allowable spread is 2 percent.) Looking at the 2001 data, the average of the ADPs for the highly compensated is on track.

Highly
Compensated

Dr. Ben Casey	8.0%
Dr. Roberta Stone	8.0%
Dr. Mel Practice	6.0%
Dr. Ruth Rosenhauser	8.0%

Average Percent Deferred   7.5%

Satisfying the ADP Test

The Small Business Job Protection Act of 1996 greatly simplified 401(k) testing by allowing employers to pass the ADP test using the nonhighly compensated deferral percentage from the previous year. This change means that the employer knows the maximum deferral percentage for the highly compensated group at the beginning of the plan year and can appropriate limit contributions by the highly compensated so that the test is satisfied. The law went further and provided for other relief from the rigors of the ADP test. The following are all provisions that a 401(k) plan sponsor will want to consider when planning strategies to satisfy the test.

Current Year Testing—Prior to the Small Business Job Protection Act, the maximum ADP for the highly compensated employees was determined by looking at the ADP percentage for the nonhighly compensated employees for the current year. Under the law, employers can elect the old method of performing the test. Occasionally, current year testing provides a better result for an employer than the new "lookback" testing. This may be particularly true in the first year of plan operation. In the first year, the ADP for the nonhighly compensated group (under lookback testing) is deemed to be 3 percent. If the employer elects instead to use current year testing, the actual ADP for the nonhighly compensated group may be substantially higher, allowing larger contributions by the highly compensated. (Note that if an employer elects current year testing it can only change the election in limited circumstances.[2])

401(k) SIMPLE—As described more fully in chapter 6, an employer can establish a plan called a SIMPLE funded with IRA accounts. An employer can instead elect an amendment adopting essentially the same rigid design restrictions within the 401(k) plan. The result is relief from the ADP test and top-heavy testing (described in chapter 10). This option has not been popular, however, because an employer willing to adopt theses design restrictions would prefer the SIMPLE IRA, because it is a plan that is much easier to maintain. A much better option for the sponsor wanting the flexibility of the 401(k) plan is the 401(k) safe-harbor design.

401(k) Safe Harbor—401(k) plans can also avoid the ADP test by satisfying a safe harbor requirement. Under the 401(k) safe harbor, the ADP test is not required if the employer makes at least a 100 percent matching contribution on the first 3 percent of salary deferred and 50 percent of the next 2 percent of salary deferred.[3] As an alternative, the employer can make a nonelective contribution of 3 percent of compensation for all eligible participants (regardless of whether they make salary deferral elections or not). In addition, contributions must be fully vested and subject to the hardship withdrawal restrictions that apply to salary deferral accounts.

This rule is fairly flexible and even allows the employer to satisfy the safe harbor contribution with contributions to another plan. This safe harbor option can be quite useful to the 401(k) sponsor. It is more flexible than the 401(k) SIMPLE because it doesn't cap employer contributions and allows employees to defer up to $11,000 (for 2002) each year. The decision to elect the safe harbor can also be made on a year-to-year basis. The major considerations for the 401(k) sponsor considering the safe harbor will be the following:

- Is the sponsor willing to make contributions that are 100 percent vested at all times?
- How does the safe harbor contribution compare to the current level of employer contributions?
- Are the goals of the highly compensated employees being thwarted by failure to satisfy the ADP and ACP (actual contribution percentage; a discussion follows) tests?

Correcting excess contributions—In addition to these options, the law also continues to give plans the option to correct a failure of the ADP test after the year ends. There are a number of complex correction methods that create another safety net for satisfying the ADP test.

Other 401(k) Plan Issues and Requirements

Plans with Matching Contributions

actual contribution percentage test (ACP)

If a 401(k) plan has matching contributions or after-tax employee contributions (or both), the plan generally must satisfy another nondiscrimination test referred to as the *actual contribution percentage test (ACP)*. This test operates in essentially the same manner as the ADP test. In many cases, the results of the ACP test are essentially the same as those for the ADP test. (The details of the test are discussed in detail in chapter 8.) However, the ACP test can become more problematic if the matching contribution is complex—for example, employees with more than 10 years of service receive a 100 percent match while other employees receive a 50 percent match. On the practical side, the ADP and ACP tests mean that the highly compensated must be aware of the possibility that their contributions may be limited, and that the plan design must involve the input of the plan administrator or someone very familiar with the operation of these rules.

Cafeteria Plans

A popular use of 401(k) plans is to include them as one of the benefits available under a cafeteria plan. The 401(k) plan is the only type of qualified plan that can be part of a cafeteria plan. The term *cafeteria plan* stems from the fact that these plans allow employees to pick from a menu of benefit choices. More specifically, the benefit dollars in a cafeteria plan are flexible. This means that employees can take them in cash; allocate them to pay for certain welfare benefits (such as life insurance, health insurance, or child care); place them in a 40l(k) plan; or do a combination of any of these three. To the extent that an employee elects to spend benefit dollars on tax-advantaged benefits like a 401(k) plan, there is no current taxation. For this reason, employees may wish to contribute to 401(k) plans in lieu of other benefits available in the cafeteria plan (such as group life insurance in excess of $50,000) that are taxable.

Other Employee Benefit Plans

Many employee benefit plans (including pension plans, group life insurance, and disability insurance) calculate benefits based upon the participant's compensation. For example, in a group life insurance plan, the employee's beneficiaries may be entitled to a benefit of two times compensation. When an employer installs a 401(k) plan, benefits under other plans may be reduced if salary reduction elections reduce the definition of compensation under those plans. Unless the employer is exceptionally concerned about costs, it will not want to reduce the definition of compensation, because this indirectly penalizes employees for making salary deferrals. Sometimes the employer forgets to review the impact of the salary deferrals on other employee benefits, and benefits are accidentally reduced. The adviser should be sure to discuss this issue with the employer at the time the plan is installed.

Note that salary deferral elections do not adversely affect Social Security benefits. Salary deferrals are considered wages for calculating benefits (as well as for determining Social Security taxes).

Additional Design Considerations

Because 401(k) plans only succeed when employees elect to make salary deferrals, many 401(k) plans encourage employee participation through matching contributions, employee investment direction, participant loan programs, and hardship withdrawals. While these features are discussed in other parts of this book, it is helpful to understand how they tie specifically into the 401(k) plan environment.

- *Matching contributions*—Most 401(k) plans contain some sort of matching employer contributions to encourage employee participation. A common formula is a 50 percent match up to 6 percent of compensation deferred.
- *Employee investment direction*—Because employees perceive salary deferrals as "their own money," most 401(k) plans now give participants the right to direct the investment of at least the salary deferral account. This trend is extremely widespread, and it is rare to find a 401(k) plan that is designed otherwise.
- *Participant loans*—Employees may be reluctant to make salary deferrals unless they can access funds in case of an emergency. Participant loan programs are quite common in 401(k) plans because they allow at least limited access without tax consequences.
- *Hardship withdrawals*—Another way for employees to access funds is through hardship withdrawals. Most 401(k) plans allow either loans or hardship withdrawals, and in some cases both options.

401(k) Plans: Contribution Limits

- **Salary deferral limit**—salary deferral contributions made at the election of the participant are limited to $11,000 in 2002. The limit is increased to $12,000 for participants over age 50. Note that this limit applies to all salary deferral plans (including SIMPLEs and 403(b) plans) that a participant contributes to, even with an unrelated employer.
- **Maximum allocation**—as with other defined contribution plans, the maximum allocation to a single participant counting all types of contributions can not exceed $40,000 (in 2002). If the individual participates in other defined contributions sponsored by the same (or related) employer, then both plans are aggregated in determining the $40,000 limit.
- **Employer deduction limit**—The employer's deductible contribution is limited to 25 percent of all covered payroll. This limit will rarely effect an individual participant, since it is an aggregate limit. Also, salary deferral contributions are not counted when determining the 25 percent limit.

(continued)

- **Nondiscrimination tests**—The nondiscrimination tests that apply to salary deferral contributions (the ADP test) and to matching employer contributions (ACP test) can in some cases result in lowering the allowable contribution for one or more highly compensated employees. These tests have no impact on the nonhighly compensated employees. There is a special 25 percent penalty tax in first 2 years of participation.

STOCK BONUS PLANS AND EMPLOYEE STOCK OWNERSHIP PLANS (ESOPs)

Stock bonus plans and ESOPs are variations of profit-sharing plans and are, therefore, similar in many ways:

stock bonus plans

- *Stock bonus plans,* ESOPs, and profit-sharing plans are all defined-contribution plans and all fall into the profit-sharing (not pension) category.
- Contributions need not be fixed and need not be made every year.
- The allocation formulas used under a profit-sharing plan may be used under either a stock bonus plan or an ESOP.
- The amount of deductible employer contributions allowed (25 percent) is the same for all three types of plans.
- Contributions for all three types of plans are usually, but are not legally required to be, based on profits.

Stock bonus plans and ESOPs differ from profit-sharing plans, however, in three important ways:

- Both stock bonus plans and ESOPs typically invest plan assets primarily in the employer's stock (in fact, an ESOP is required to invest primarily in employer stock). Profit-sharing plans, on the other hand, are usually structured to diversify investments and do not concentrate investments in employer stock (even though they are legally permitted to do so).
- Both stock bonus plans and ESOPs are chosen because they provide a market for employer stock. This, in turn, generates capital for the corporation and is a method to finance a company's growth. Profit-sharing plans, however, are not viewed as a way to finance company operations but are more concerned with providing tax-favored deferred compensation that can be used for retirement purposes.

- Stock bonus plans and ESOPs allow distributions to participants in the form of employer stock. Profit-sharing plans generally do not. This creates a distinct advantage for participants in a stock bonus plan or an ESOP, because they receive a tax break inasmuch as the unrealized appreciation (gain in value) is not taxed until the stock is sold. (See chapter 25 for a complete discussion of this rule.)

Stock Bonus Plans

Technically, a stock bonus plan is a plan that allows distributions in employer stock. Some or all of the plan's investments can be held in employer stock from time to time. Stock bonus plans have recently given way in popularity to ESOPs, however, because ESOPs allow the plan to borrow to purchase the securities. If this feature is not needed, the stock bonus plan may still be the right choice because it is subject to fewer legal restrictions. Let's take a closer look at ESOPs.

Employee Stock Ownership Plans

leveraged ESOP

ESOPs enjoy the same advantages as stock bonus plans and offer an extra advantage to your clients—they can be used to allow the employer to borrow in order to provide contributions. (When an ESOP is used for this function it is also known as a *leveraged ESOP.*) Under this technique, known as leveraging, the plan trustee acquires a loan from the bank and uses the borrowed funds to purchase employer stock. Generally, the employer guarantees repayment of the loan, and the purchased stock is held as collateral. The result is that the plan receives the full proceeds of the bank loan immediately and pays the loan off with the employer's tax-deductible contributions to the ESOP. The collateralized stock is placed in a suspense account. The employer makes annual (deductible) contributions to the plan, which are used to pay back the bank. As the loan is paid off, the stock is released from the suspense account.

Reasons Candidates Choose Stock Bonus Plans and ESOPs

One major advantage of stock bonus plans and ESOPs is that they give employees a stake in the company through stock ownership. This neatly fits most employers' goals of employee motivation and retention. A second major advantage is the previously mentioned delayed taxation of gain on stock distributions. Enhanced cash flow is a third advantage. Cash flow is enhanced because the employer makes a cashless contribution to the retirement plan. A fourth—and perhaps most important—advantage of stock ownership plans is that they help to create a market for employer stock. This is especially important if the organization's stock is not publicly traded. And, the leveraging advantage associated with ESOPs is also enticing for organizations.

The major disadvantage of stock ownership plans is the possibility of the employer's stock falling drastically in value and, therefore, cutting the availability of retirement funds. Without any diversity of investment, participants are exposed to potential disaster. There is, however, some relief available for ESOP participants. The law requires that once an ESOP participant attains age 55 and completes at least 10 years of participation, the participant may elect (between the ages of 55 and 60) to diversify the retirement benefit by moving up to 50 percent of his or her account balance into other investments. (For more information, see Code Sec. 401 (a)(28).)

A second disadvantage of stock ownership plans is that if the stock is not readily tradable on an established market, the employer is required to offer a repurchase option (also known as a put option). This option must be available for a minimum of 60 days following the distribution of the stock and, if the option is not exercised in that period, for an additional 60-day period in the following year. The repurchase option creates administrative and cash-flow problems for employers.

Candidates for ESOPs and stock bonus plans are similar to candidates for profit-sharing plans and generally fill out the fact finder in a similar manner. But, unlike the typical profit-sharing candidate, ESOP and stock bonus plan candidates rate as "very valuable" fact finder item 10—creating a market for employer stock. Also, ESOP candidates rate as "very valuable" fact finder item 11—leveraging the purchase of employer stock.

YOUR FINANCIAL SERVICES PRACTICE:
LIFE INSURANCE AND ESOPs

Special arrangements must be made in advance for the corporation to buy back stock from a terminated employee or from a deceased employee's estate without creating a cash-flow crunch. Typically, this is accomplished through the sale of life insurance to the ESOP. For example, the ESOP could purchase life insurance on the lives of its principal employees. At the death of any one of these employees, the life insurance proceeds are used to buy back the stock transferred from the deceased employee's estate.

CASE STUDY: BAKER MANUFACTURING, INC.

Bill Baker is the president of Baker Manufacturing, Inc., a firm that produces parts for personal computers. Baker Manufacturing has a defined-benefit pension plan for its 40 employees. Bill wants to improve rank-and-file productivity and morale. Business is excellent, but to meet increased sales orders, Bill needs to get more out of his employees. To make matters worse, two of Bill's experienced line workers have just left to work for a competitor. In addition, several of Bill's people have approached him regarding tax-sheltering part of their salary (Bill is also interested). Bill would like to do something extra, but cash flow is a problem. He feels he may need to hold onto profits in case the never-ending new generations of computers require different manufacturing equipment. How would an ESOP help to solve Bill's problems? Would a 401(k) plan offer a solution?

An employee stock ownership plan (ESOP) would be helpful in solving Bill's problems because it would allow him to do something extra without creating cash-flow problems because his ESOP would be leveraged. In addition, employee morale would be improved by the extra benefit provided. Employees would be encouraged not to leave because of their ties to the company's fortunes through the stock itself and the amount of stock contributions, which are based on company profits. And, because company profits would be more important to the employees than ever, productivity would likely increase. Bill and his executives could also enjoy the tax advantages of taking distributions of highly productive company stock when they terminate.

TABLE 5-3
Qualified Plan Scorecard

PENSION	**PROFIT-SHARING**
Defined-benefit	Profit-sharing
Cash-balance	Stock bonus
Target-benefit	ESOP
Money-purchase	401(k)
KEOGH	**DEFINED-CONTRIBUTION**
Defined-benefit	Target-benefit
Cash-balance	Money-purchase
Target-benefit	Profit-sharing
Money-purchase	Stock bonus
Profit-sharing	ESOP
401(k)	401(k)
CORPORATE	**DEFINED-BENEFIT**
Defined-benefit	Defined-benefit
Cash-balance	Cash-balance
Target-benefit	
Money-purchase	
Profit-sharing	
Stock bonus	
ESOP	
401(k)	

A cash or deferred arrangement (401(k) plan) would also be helpful because it would provide something extra for only a minor cost. The executives who wanted to shelter income from taxes would have the opportunity to convert some of their salary into pretax savings (up to the $11,000 maximum in 2002). If Bill provides a matching contribution, the organization's cost would rise slightly, but the paybacks would be increased productivity, better morale, and retention of employees.

CHAPTER REVIEW

Answers to the review questions and the self-test questions start on page 673.

Key Terms

discretionary contributions	highly compensated employees
cash or deferred arrangement	(HCEs)
(CODA)	actual contribution percentage
stand-alone plan	test (ACP)
matching contribution	stock bonus plans
financial hardship	leveraged ESOP
actual deferral percentage (ADP)	
test	

Review Questions

5-1. Umbrella, Inc. is a business whose cash flow literally fluctuates with the weather. Umbrella, Inc. would like a qualified plan, despite its erratic cash flow. In addition, the owners of this small business would like to be able to withdraw their funds if they decide to expand the business. What type of qualified plan should Umbrella, Inc. have? Explain.

5-2. Describe the concern about the discretionary nature of the profit-sharing plan and the strategies necessary to ensure that the plan is successful.

5-3. What is an allocation formula?

5-4. Accountants, Inc. has decided to adopt a profit-sharing plan that allocates profits in excess of $10,000 to participants by the ratio that the compensation for a participant bears to the compensation of all participants. Anne with $100,000 in compensation, Bob with $70,000 in compensation, and Cassie with $30,000 in compensation are the plan's only participants. How much will be contributed to each participant's account if Accountants, Inc. has a $30,000 profit?

5-5. John Zark, a sole proprietor, would like to set up a retirement program that both maximizes tax deductions up to a 100 percent of salary or $40,000 limit (as indexed for 2002) and affords him the opportunity to skip contributions in a given year. What plan or plans would you recommend for John?

5-6. How can life insurance be used by a profit-sharing trust to protect plan participants from an economic downturn in the event of the death of a key profit maker?

5-7. What is the maximum salary deferral in a 401(k) plan?

5-8. Describe the four types of contributions that can be made to a 401(k) plan.

5-9. Under what circumstances may withdrawals be made from a 401(k) plan?

5-10. ABCO, Inc. has adopted a 401(k) plan whose participants, their compensation, and their percentage contributed are as follows:

Eligible Employee	Compensation	2001 Percentage of Compensation Contributed
Abner Anderson (CEO/75% owner)	$100,000	8%
Barbara Bellows (VP/25% owner)	80,000	8%
Cindy Clark (sec/treasurer)	60,000	5%
Don Davidson	40,000	5%
Ellen Ewer	30,000	9%
Frank Fern	20,000	5%
Gary Grant	20,000	5%

In 2002, what will be the maximum deferral percentage for highly compensated employees under the actual deferral percentage test? Explain.

5-11. Describe other ways that can be used to help satisfy the ADP test.

5-12. Describe the advantage ESOPs have with regard to borrowing to fund the plan.

5-13. Why does an employer who has an ESOP want to consider having life insurance on key executives in the plan?

Self-Test Questions

T   F   5-1. A profit-sharing plan can be set up to provide for discretionary employer contributions.

T   F   5-2. Employers can set a cap on the amount of profits that will be contributed to a profit-sharing plan.

T   F   5-3. Profit-sharing plans can be designed to allow employees to withdraw funds from participant accounts as early as 2 years after they were contributed by the employer.

T   F   5-4. If a profit-sharing plan is used, the organization's deduction for contributions to the plan is limited to 25 percent of aggregate participant payroll.

T   F   5-5. In most plans, the board of directors is given the discretion whether or not to make contributions each year.

T   F   5-6. The employer must have current or accumulated profits in order to make contributions to a profit-sharing plan.

T   F   5-7. Integration with Social Security, age-weighting, and cross-testing are all allocation approaches that can be used to skew the employer's contribution to the older, more highly compensated employees.

T   F   5-8. Piggybacking a profit-sharing plan with a money-purchase plan is no longer necessary, because the maximum deductible contribution has been raised to 25 percent of compensation.

T   F   5-9. Under a 401(k) plan, an employee may make salary reduction contributions of up to $40,000.

T   F   5-10. An IRA is a better tax-advantaged savings option than the 401(k) plan for most employees.

T   F   5-11. In addition to salary deferrals, an employer can make both matching contributions and profit-sharing contributions to a 401(k) plan, or neither contribution to the plan.

T   F   5-12. Employer matching contributions can be fixed or can be made on a discretionary basis.

T   F   5-13.   Employee salary deferral contributions to a 401(k) plan are always 100 percent vested.

T   F   5-14.   Withdrawals can be made from a 401(k) salary deferral account after participants have been in the plan for 2 years.

T   F   5-15.   A financial hardship is said to occur if the employee has to pay college tuition.

T   F   5-16.   In 2001 and in 2002, Sally owns 2 percent of the employer's stock and earns $65,000. Sally will be considered a highly compensated employee for purposes of the actual deferral percentage test for 2002.

T   F   5-17.   A popular use of the 401(k) plan is to include it as one of the benefits available under a cafeteria plan.

T   F   5-18.   Salary reductions made under a 401(k) plan will reduce the amount of Social Security taxes that are owed.

T   F   5-19.   Stock bonus plans and ESOPs are defined-contribution-type plans.

T   F   5-20.   One of the advantages of receiving a distribution in stock from a stock bonus plan or an ESOP is that the unrealized appreciation is not taxed until the stock is sold.

T   F   5-21.   Under the technique known as leveraging, the employer borrows funds from the participants' ESOP account to pay future contributions to the plan.

T   F   5-22.   It is prudent for a corporation with an ESOP to buy life insurance on the lives of its key employees so the ESOP can buy back stock from the key employees' estates.

T   F   5-23.   A candidate for an ESOP is similar to a candidate for a profit-sharing plan except that a candidate for an ESOP would like to create a market for employer stock and/or leverage the purchase of employer stock.

Notes

1. Note that, similar to the vesting rules, the participant's profit-sharing and matching contribution accounts can be subject to the normal withdrawal rules that apply to profit-sharing plans.
2 IRS Notice 98-1.

3. The rules actually allow the matching formula to be stated in a different way as long as resulting contributions equal the contributions under the basic matching formula. Also, the rate of matching contribution for any highly compensated employee cannot exceed the rate for any nonhighly compensated employee. This provision would prohibit a formula that gave a larger match for individuals with long service if even one highly compensated employee received the larger contribution.

6

SEPs, SIMPLEs, and 403(b) Plans

Learning Objectives

An understanding of the material in this chapter should enable the student to

---

6-1. Describe a simplified employee pension (SEP) plan and identify its unique features, its similarity to an IRA, and the rules it has in common with qualified plans.

6-2. Describe the SIMPLE plan and discuss when its use would be appropriate.

6-3. Identify the market in which 403(b) plans can be used.

6-4. Describe a 403(b) plan with regard to how it can be funded, the applicable legal requirements, and the determination of an individual's maximum contribution.

Chapter Outline

In this chapter, we explore three types of tax-advantaged retirement plans that are not qualified plans covered under Code Sec. 401(a). What is meaningful about these plans is that each has its own unique set of rules. Who can sponsor each type of plan, how much can be contributed, who must participate, vesting provisions, and how contributions are allocated are different from these aspects of qualified plans—and different from each other. You will also see that in some instances, some of the qualified plan rules do apply.

To determine whether the SEP, the SIMPLE, or the 403(b) plan is more appropriate for your client than any of the qualified plan alternatives, this chapter fully explores each type of plan and compares them to qualified plans. At times, the comparisons might be somewhat confusing because at this point in the book you are not yet familiar with all of the rules that apply to qualified plans. Previous chapters have introduced you to the types of qualified plans available, and chapters 7 through 9 will flesh out eligibility, vesting, and limits on contribution formulas, as well as other issues. You may find it helpful to review this chapter for a second time after finishing chapter 9.

SEPs

simplified employee pension (SEP)

A *simplified employee pension (SEP)* is a retirement plan that uses an individual retirement account (IRA) or an individual retirement annuity (IRA annuity) as the receptacle for contributions. As its name implies, this type of plan is simpler than a qualified retirement plan, making it, in many cases, attractive to the small business owner.

The documentation, reporting, and disclosure requirements are less cumbersome than for a qualified plan. Trust accounting is also eliminated, because separate IRAs are established for each participant and all contributions are made directly to each participant's IRA. Because contributions must be nonforfeitable, the participant's benefit at any time is simply the IRA account balance.

The SEP is often a good choice for the small business because of the reduced administrative tasks and expenses. However, the SEP still has its complications, and the prospective sponsor needs to go in with a clear understanding of the ongoing responsibilities of maintaining such a plan. Also note that there is a tradeoff under the tax rules: in exchange for simplicity is the loss of flexibility. For example, under a SEP, all employees meeting specified requirements must be covered under the plan; the allocation formula may not contain an age-weighting factor (unlike the profit-sharing plans, discussed in chapter 5); and benefits must be fully vested at all times. These requirements are reviewed in more depth below.

Characteristics of the SEP

From a design perspective, the SEP is quite similar to the profit-sharing plan. The employer may, on a discretionary basis, make contributions, which are allocated to participants' accounts. The plan may also allow employees to make pretax salary deferrals, like in a 401(k) plan—except that the nondiscrimination requirements are even stricter than for a 401(k) plan.

Technically, SEPs are subject to the rules contained in IRC Sec. 408(k)—in contrast to qualified plans, which are subject to IRC Sec. 401(a) and related provisions. IRC 408(k) provides some requirements that are unique to SEPs, borrows some of the qualified plan requirements, and states that the investment and distribution provisions for IRAs also apply to SEPs. To learn these rules, it is helpful to group them in these categories.

Requirements Unique to SEPs

Coverage Requirements. SEPs are subject to a very different set of participation requirements from those for qualified retirement plans. The rules require that contributions be made for all employees who have met all three of the following requirements:

- attained age 21
- performed services for the employer for at least 3 of the immediately preceding 5 years
- received a minimum of $450 of compensation for the year (indexed limit for 2001)

From a planning perspective, this set of requirements means that the employer can exclude employees with less than 3 years of service but must cover all employees—including part-time employees earning more than $450—who have 3 or more years of service. For the employer with numerous short-term employees, this requirement is significantly preferable to the qualified plan rules. On the other hand, the employer with a number of long-term part-time employees may not be satisfied with the coverage provisions of the SEP.

The 3-year requirement can also cause problems for companies with related subsidiary companies and for small groups of individuals who own two or more companies. If, in either case, the affiliation constitutes a "controlled group of corporations,"[1] the employees of all the related companies must all be covered under the same plan. This rule generally eliminates the SEP as a viable alternative in the larger corporate setting. The most dangerous problem is that a small employer who is unaware of this rule will establish a plan for one company and forget to cover employees in related companies.

Contribution and Allocation Formula. The SEP is generally designed to mirror a profit-sharing plan—that is, company contributions are made on a discretionary basis, although the plan can require specified employer contributions. What makes the SEP different from the profit-sharing plan is that contributions *must* be allocated to participants in a way that provides a benefit as a level percentage of compensation. (For example, all employees receive an allocation of 5 percent of compensation.) This limits the use of the SEP in two regards. First, if the plan has employee pretax contributions (salary reduction simplified employee pension, or SARSEP), the employer may not encourage employee contributions by providing matching contributions. Second, the allocation formula cannot use cross-testing (discussed in chapter 8) to skew contributions to the older employees. The only exception to the level-percentage-of-compensation rule is that the allocation formula may be integrated with Social Security in the same manner as in other defined-contribution plans. This provides highly compensated employees with contributions that are slightly larger (as a percentage of pay) than those for the rank-and-file employees.

Vesting. All contributions to a SEP, either by the employer directly or as an employee contribution (by deferral election), must be immediately and 100 percent vested. From the employer's perspective, this requirement is more onerous than for qualified plans, but remember that employees can be excluded from the plan until they have completed 3 years of employment.

Employee Elective Deferrals. Before 1997, an employer could establish a SEP that allowed employees the opportunity to make pretax contributions in the same way as in a 401(k) plan. This type of salary reduction SEP is often referred to as a SARSEP. The Small Business Job Protection Act of 1996 replaced the SARSEP with the SIMPLE and after 1996 no new SARSEPs can be established. However, SARSEPs in operation on December 31, 1996 can continue to be indefinitely maintained under the old rules. Therefore, it is still important to understand how they work.

In a SARSEP, the maximum employee contribution is the same as in the 401(k)—$11,000 for 2002—and this amount can be contributed as long as the maximum deductible contribution and maximum allocation rules described below are satisfied. The SARSEP salary deferral feature is subject to several requirements that do not apply to 401(k) plans, each of which makes the plan less attractive than a 401(k) plan:

- Only an employer with 25 or fewer employees can sponsor a SARSEP.
- At least 50 percent of all eligible employees must participate in the SARSEP.
- The employer may not make matching contributions to encourage employees to contribute to the plan.

Like the 401(k) plan, the SARSEP must satisfy a mathematical nondiscrimination test. The test is similar to, but more stringent than, the 401(k) test. Under this test, the deferral percentage for *any* highly compensated employee (HCE) cannot exceed 125 percent of the average deferral percentage of the nonhighly compensated group. For example, if the average deferral for the nonhighly compensated group is 5 percent, no HCE can contribute more than 6.25 percent of compensation.

Timing of Distribution. Participants must be given the opportunity to withdraw the account balance at any time. This is entirely different from the situation with qualified pension plans, which do not allow distributions until termination of employment, and from qualified profit-sharing plans, in which the employer can choose whether or not to allow in-service withdrawals.

Documentation and Reporting. The supporting plan document is much simpler than with a qualified plan. The IRS supplies a form document—Form 5305(SEP) for plans with employer contributions only and Form 5305A(SEP) for plans that allow employee pretax contributions. Service providers, such as banks and insurance companies, may also sponsor a SEP prototype document and receive IRS approval. If the IRS form or the prototype document is used, the plan does not have to file Form 5500 annually as long as participants receive (1) either a copy of the plan or a summary of the plan, (2) some general information about SEPs, and (3) annual notice of contributions made on their behalf. When working with SEPs, note that these alternative document and disclosure requirements must be followed exactly or the plan sponsor will be required to file annual Form 5500 reports and meet all other ERISA disclosure requirements.

Qualified Plan Rules That Apply to SEPs

Maximum Contribution and Allocation Limits. The maximum employer contribution to the SEP is the same as for a profit-sharing plan, that is, 25 percent of the compensation of all employees eligible to participate in the plan. All profit-sharing plans and SEPs sponsored by the same company are aggregated under this rule. The maximum amount that can be allocated to each participant from employer and employee contributions is the lesser of 100 percent of compensation or $40,000 (indexed for 2002)—the same as for other defined-contribution-type plans. Similarly, the $200,000 compensation cap (as indexed in 2002) that applies to qualified plans also applies to SEPs.

Top-heavy Rules. The same rules that apply to qualified plans apply to SEPs. Although most SEPs will be top-heavy (benefits for key employees will generally equal or exceed 60 percent of total benefits), the top-heavy rules do not have much effect on the SEP. SEPs are already required to have 100 percent immediate vesting, and the minimum contribution requirement for nonkey employees does not have much effect because of the special nondiscrimination rules that apply.

IRA Rules That Apply to SEPs

Investment Restrictions. Because contributions are held in IRA accounts, the limitations that apply to individually sponsored IRAs also apply to SEPs. These rules prohibit investment in life insurance and in collectibles (except for U.S. government gold coins). Similarly, loans cannot be made from a SEP.

Taxation of Distributions. Distributions are taxed in the same way as distributions from IRAs. Distributions are treated as ordinary income and are not eligible for special lump-sum averaging. The penalties for early withdrawals and large distributions apply (as they do with qualified plans). Most distributions can also be rolled over to avoid current taxation, but only to other IRAs.[2]

SEP Candidates

Candidates for SEPs fill out the pension planning fact finder by grading as "very valuable" the items about avoiding an annual financial commitment and instituting a plan that is administratively convenient. SEP candidates say "no" to the following questions in step 2 of the fact finder: Is it more important to provide an adequate retirement standard of living than to avoid an annual commitment? Is it more important to provide an adequate retirement standard of living than to have administrative convenience and an easily communicated plan?

SEP: A Summary of the Rules

- **Employer contributions**—similar to a profit-sharing plan, contributions are discretionary with a maximum deductible contribution of 25 percent of compensation.
- **Allocations**—must allocate based on compensation or integrated with Social Security
- **Eligibility**—must cover all employees age 21 with 3 years earning $450 or more (as indexed in 2001) in the last 5 years.
- **Vesting**—full and immediate vesting required
- **Withdrawal restrictions**—Withdrawals can be made at any time.
- **Investment restrictions**— like other IRAs, can not invest in life insurance or most collectibles
- **Salary deferral contributions**—not allowed except in grandfathered SARSEP started before 1997.
- **Taxation**—like other IRA's, subject to ordinary income tax upon distribution

The SEP is a good choice for the small employer with these goals in mind. The coverage rules are easier to work with than those for a qualified plan; shorter-term employees (less than 3 years) can be excluded from the plan, eliminating cost and administrative burdens. However, the SEP is not the right approach when the employer has many long-term part-time employees, because they will have to be covered under the plan. The lack of flexibility in the coverage and vesting requirements also eliminates larger employers as SEP candidates.

YOUR FINANCIAL SERVICES PRACTICE: OPPORTUNITIES IN THE SEP MARKETPLACE

The financial services professional who can offer the employer a SEP in addition to offering investment services has a real business opportunity. Take, for example, the business owner who has been frustrated by the complexity and expense of maintaining a qualified plan. He or she may be swayed to change vendors if you can offer a superior investment product and at the same time reduce headaches and administrative expense with the SEP approach.

Any employer considering a profit-sharing plan should also consider a SEP, because the maximum deduction limits (25 percent of compensation) and the ability to make discretionary employer contributions are the same. Assuming the coverage requirements discussed above do not cause any problems, the SEP is usually the better choice. However, the profit-sharing plan should be chosen when the employer wants a more aggressive, age-weighted or cross-tested allocation formula that skews contributions to the older, more highly compensated employees.

SIMPLEs

savings incentive match plan for employees (SIMPLE)

Beginning in 1997, employers had a new plan option available, referred to as the *savings incentive match plan for employees (SIMPLE)*.

Plan Requirements

Like SEPs and SARSEPs, the SIMPLE plan is funded with individual retirement accounts, which means that the following requirements apply to the SIMPLE:

- Participants must be fully vested in all benefits at all times.
- Assets cannot be invested in life insurance or collectibles.
- No participant loans are allowed.

Eligible Employers

Any type of business entity can establish a SIMPLE; however, the business cannot have more than 100 employees (only counting those employees who earned $5,000 or more of compensation). If the employer grows beyond the 100-employee limit, the law does allow the employer to sponsor the plan for an additional 2-year grace period. Also note that to be eligible, the sponsoring employer cannot maintain any other qualified plan, 403(b), or SEP at the same time it maintains the SIMPLE.

Salary Deferral Contributions

In a SIMPLE, all eligible employees have the opportunity to make elective pretax contributions of up to $7,000 (indexed for 2002). Under the Economic Growth and Tax Relief Reconciliation Act of 2001, the maximum contribution limit is scheduled to increase in future years. In 2003, the limit is $8,000, $9,000 in 2004 and $10,000 in 2005. After that, the $10,000 dollar limit is indexed in $500 increments.

As with the 401(k) plan, participants who have attained age 50 before the end of the year can make additional contributions to a SIMPLE. For 2002 the additional amount is $500, $1,000 for 2003, $1,500 for 2004, $2,000 for 2005, and $2,500 for 2006 and thereafter. Table 6-1 below summarizes the maximum salary deferral amounts over the next several years.

TABLE 6-1
Scheduled Increases to the SIMPLE Salary Deferral Amount

Year	Maximum for all participants	Participants over 50	Total for those over 50
2002	$7,000	$500	$7,500
2003	$8,000	$1,000	$9,000
2004	$9,000	$1,500	$10,500
2005	$10,000	$2,000	$12,000
2006	$10,000	$2,500	$12,500

Employer Contributions

Unlike the 401(k) plan (or the old SARSEP), there is no nondiscrimination testing, meaning that highly compensated employees can make contributions without regard to the salary deferral elections of the nonhighly compensated employees.

However, in exchange, the SIMPLE has a mandatory employer contribution requirement. This contribution can be made in one of two ways:

1. The employer can make a dollar-for-dollar matching contribution on the first 3 percent of compensation that the individual elects to defer, or
2. The employer can make a 2 percent nonelective contribution for all eligible employees.

If the employer elects the matching contribution, there is one other option. Periodically, the employer can elect a lower match as long as

- the matching contribution is not less than one percent of compensation
- participants are notified of the lower contribution within a reasonable time before the 60-day election period before the beginning of the year

The employer can elect the lower percentage for up to 2 years in any 5-year period, which can even include the first 2 years that the plan is in force.

The employer contribution amount just described is both the minimum required and the maximum employer contribution allowed. In other words, if the employer elects the matching contribution, 3 percent is the maximum match, and nonelective contributions are not allowed. If the employer elects the nonelective contributions, then the 2 percent contribution is the maximum, and matching contributions are not allowed.

Maximum Total Contributions

Whether a SIMPLE is an appropriate plan for an employer depends in part on whether the maximum that can be contributed for the business owner is enough to satisfy the owner's objective. Unfortunately, determining this is a bit complicated over the next several years as the maximum contribution is scheduled to increase. Another complicating factor, is the ability of those over age 50 to contribute an additional amount.

If we are going to calculate this amount we need to know the year and whether the participant is over age 50. The maximum amount that can be contributed for and individual who has not attained age 50 for 2002 is the maximum salary deferral amount ($7,000 for 2002) plus the 3 percent matching contribution. In 2002, the maximum is $14,000 as long as the employee earns over $233,000 of compensation or more (3 percent of $233,000 is approximately $7,000[3]). For the individual earning less, the maximum matching contribution is limited by the 3 percent rule. Table 6-2 shows the maximum contribution for an individual earning $150,000 and $300,000. Because the maximum contribution level is scheduled to increase through 2005, the table shows the maximum for 2002 through 2005. Note that the table does not take into consideration the catch-up election for those over age 50.

Table 6-2
Maximum SIMPLE Contribution

Year	Salary	Maximum Salary Deferral	Matching Contribution	Total Contribution
2002	$150,000	$ 7,000	$ 4,500	$ 11,500
2002	$300,000	$ 7,000	$ 7,000	$ 14,000
2003	$150,000	$ 8,000	$ 4,500	$ 12,500
2003	$300,000	$ 8,000	$ 8,000	$ 16,000
2004	$150,000	$ 9,000	$ 4,500	$ 13,500
2004	$300,000	$ 9,000	$ 9,000	$ 18,000
2005	$150,000	$ 10,000	$ 4,500	$ 14,500
2005	$300,000	$ 10,000	$ 10,000	$ 20,000

Eligibility Requirements

The SIMPLE has eligibility requirements that are different from both the SEP and the qualified plan. The plan must cover any employee who earned $5,000 in any two previous years and is reasonably expected to earn $5,000 again in the current year. Employees subject to a collectively bargained agreement can be excluded. Eligible employees must be given the right to make the salary deferral and receive either an employer matching or nonelective contribution. For determining eligibility, compensation is essentially taxable income plus pretax salary deferrals. For a self-employed person, compensation is net earnings (not reduced by salary deferral elections). SIMPLEs can be maintained only on a calendar-year basis, and all employees become eligible to participate as of January 1.

Plan Operations

The sponsoring employer must notify participants that they have the 60-day election period just prior to the calendar year to make a salary deferral election or modify a previous election for the following year. The employee who does make a salary deferral election must be given the option to stop making deferrals at any time during the year. The sponsor can require that the participant wait until the following year to elect back in, or may have a more liberal election modification provision—for example, allowing participants to modify their election at any time.

Every year, prior to the 60-day election period, the trustee must prepare and the employer must distribute a summary plan description (SPD) that includes employer-identifying data, a description of eligibility under the plan, benefits provided, terms of the salary election, and description of the procedures for and effects (tax results) of making a withdrawal. Also, 30 days after the calendar year ends, the trustee must give participants a statement of the year's activity and the closing account balance.[4]

YOUR FINANCIAL SERVICES PRACTICE:
MARKETING SIMPLES

Some financial services professionals choose not to get involved in selling the highly technical qualified plan. These professionals may still want to consider marketing the SIMPLE. With no annual reporting, individual IRA accounts, and no distribution paperwork, the SIMPLE poses little time-consuming administration. With a SIMPLE, the professional is likely to establish a direct relationship with all the participants, providing an ever-expanding group of individual clients.

The clear and precise disclosure requirements are accompanied by clear penalties for failure to comply. The trustee is fined $50 a day for late distribution of participant statements or the annual summary plan description. The employer is fined $50 a day for late notification to participants of their right to make salary deferral elections.[5] The disclosure requirements and penalty system were probably deemed necessary, because there is no direct incentive for the employer to encourage SIMPLE participation (unlike the 401(k) plan, in which highly compensated contribution levels are tied to nonhighly compensated contributions under the ADP nondiscrimination test).

Like SEPs, the plan cannot put any limitations on participant withdrawals. This means that participants have access to funds at any time to spend them or roll them over into another IRA. To discourage participants from spending their SIMPLE accounts, a special new tax rule assesses a 25 percent penalty tax (in addition to ordinary income taxes) for amounts withdrawn within 2 years of the date of participation. Other early withdrawals may be subject to the special 10 percent excise tax discussed in chapter 23.

Administrative costs for a SIMPLE should be quite low. At the present time, no annual reporting with the IRS or DOL is required. Also, unlike the 401(k) plan, no ADP test or other nondiscrimination tests must be performed.

Candidates for the SIMPLE

The candidate for the SIMPLE will be the employer looking for a plan that allows participants the right to make pretax contributions and who wants to develop a plan that creates a retirement planning partnership between the employer and employee. The candidate must have 100 or fewer employers and also be looking for a plan with the lowest possible administrative hassle and cost.

The employer considering the SIMPLE will be choosing between the 401(k) plan and the SIMPLE. Feature by feature, the advantage almost always goes to the 401(k) plan. 401(k) plans are better for maximizing contributions and skewing employer contributions to a targeted group of employees—which are typically two common goals of small plan sponsors. In addition, a 401(k) plan is much more flexible. The plan can be limited to part of the workforce as long as the minimum coverage requirements are met, and matching and profit-sharing contributions can be designed to meet a variety of goals. Finally, employer contributions can increase or decrease over time.

This is not to say, however, that the SIMPLE IRA is not a good retirement plan. It is most likely to appeal to the employer that has never maintained a plan before who is looking for a low-cost plan with few administrative headaches. With little expense, the employer can have a plan that looks to the employees just like a 401(k) plan. Other reasons that a small business would choose the SIMPLE over the 401(k) plan include:

- The employer expects that it could not satisfy the 401(k) nondiscrimination test. For example, there are many employers (such as retailers) that consist of a young transitory work force that is not very interested in contributing to a plan and a stable manager group definitely interested in contributing. Unlike a 401(k) plan, with the SIMPLE, if the rank-and-file employees decline participation, the managers can still contribute.

- Because the SIMPLE is cheaper to maintain, it is generally the better choice if the employer is not concerned about the design constraints of the plan.

SIMPLE: A Summary of the Rules

- **Limits on sponsorship**—any type of employer as long as there is no other plan and 100 or fewer employers
- **Salary deferral contributions**—eligible participants can defer $7,000 (in 2002)
- **Employer contributions**—sponsor must contribute *either* a specified matching *or* nonelective contribution
- **Employer contributions**—nondiscretionary like profit-sharing plans
- **Eligibility**—must cover all employees with 2 years of $5,000 or more of compensation
- **Vesting**—full and immediate vesting required
- **Withdrawal restrictions**—Eligible for withdrawal at any time, but subject to special 25 percent penalty tax in first 2 years of participation
- **Investment restrictions**— like other IRAs, can not invest in life insurance or most collectibles
- **Taxation**—like other IRA's, subject to ordinary income tax upon distribution

---

- There are several other advantages that the SIMPLE has over the 401(k) plan regarding the IRA funding vehicle. Participants can withdraw their funds at any time. If money is withdrawn to pay educational expenses, the 10 percent early withdrawal penalty tax will not apply. Also, an employer can terminate the plan quite simply, without having to be concerned about making distributions from the trust.

403(b) PLANS

Overview

403(b) plan

The plans we have studied up to this point are not limited to any particular type of industry. For the most part, they are available to any organization. In contrast to other retirement plans, a *403(b) plan* can be sold only to tax-exempt organizations and public schools. Despite these limitations,

403(b) plans represent a separate and lucrative opportunity for financial services professionals, particularly those who sell annuity products. A 403(b) plan, which is also referred to as a tax-sheltered annuity (TSA) or a tax-deferred annuity (TDA), is similar to a 401(k) plan. Like the 401(k) plan, the 403(b) plan

- permits an employee to defer tax on income by allowing before-tax contributions to be made to the employee's individual account
- allows deferrals in the form of a salary reduction that is chosen by the employee or a retirement payment that is made by the employer
- can be used in conjunction with, or in lieu of, most other retirement plans

However, 403(b) plans are distinguishable from 401(k) plans both in the market they serve and in their makeup. In this section, we will discuss the distinct market that 403(b) plans serve and analyze the fundamental makeup of a 403(b) plan.

Eligible Sponsors

Sec. 501(c)(3) organizations

A 403(b) program can only be sponsored by either *Sec. 501(c)(3) organizations* (employers that are exempt from tax under Code Sec. 501(c)(3)) or educational institutions of a state or political subdivision of a state. Tax-exempt organizations under Code Sec. 501(c)(3) include entities organized and operated exclusively for religious, charitable, scientific, public safety testing, literary, or educational purposes. A state or local government or any of its agencies or instrumentalities can be a qualified employer, but only with regard to employees who perform (or have performed) service, directly or indirectly, for an educational organization. An educational organization is defined as one that maintains a regular faculty and curriculum and has a regularly enrolled body of students in attendance at the place where its educational activities are conducted.

YOUR FINANCIAL SERVICES PRACTICE: COMPLIANCE PROBLEMS

Believe it or not, one of the most common 403(b) compliance problems is an ineligible entity adopting a plan. Apparently, a significant number of nonprofit organizations that have not filed for tax-free status under Code Sec. 501(c)(3) have adopted 403(b) plans. When working with a nonprofit organization, ask to see its IRS determination letter regarding its tax status. Do not set up a 403(b) plan unless the client can produce the IRS document confirming this tax status.

Employee Status

Contributions to a 403(b) annuity plan can only be made on behalf of individuals who are current, former, or retired employees of an eligible employer. This includes an employee at any level but does not include independent contractors. The determination of whether an individual is self-employed may be difficult, especially in the case of hospital-based physicians. Clergy members are generally considered self-employed for purposes of applying Social Security taxes, but are considered employees for purposes of 403(b) plan participation. In other cases, if the employer pays Social Security taxes, an employee-employer relationship probably exists; if Social Security taxes are not paid, the necessary relationship generally does not exist.

Funding Vehicles

Funding a 403(b) annuity plan can be done either by purchasing an annuity contract from an insurance company or by purchasing shares in a mutual fund. Neither the Code nor the Regulations define what type of annuity contracts can be provided. Therefore, contracts with a wide variety of features may be used; they may be single-premium or annual-premium, provide for fixed variable annuity payments, begin immediately or provide deferred payments, and either include or omit a refund provision. Annuity contracts may also contain incidental life insurance protection. The term *incidental* has essentially the same meaning as in the qualified plan context (see chapter 10 for more detail). The other funding alternative is contributions to custodial accounts invested in regulated investment company stock, whether or not shares are redeemable—more commonly referred to as a mutual fund.

Even though there is some flexibility in the investment vehicles, there is certainly less flexibility than in qualified retirement plans. In qualified plans, assets can be invested directly in stocks, bonds, money instruments, or even more exotic investment alternatives. This distinction is probably less important than it first seems, because 403(b) plans are most similar to 401(k) plans. Most 401(k) plans provide individual investment direction, giving participants the option to choose between a number of mutual funds or annuity options. Some 401(k) plans, however, actually offer individual brokerage accounts, which would not be allowed in a 403(b) plan.

Written Document Requirement

Regardless of whether the 403(b) program is subject to ERISA, the funding vehicles—either annuities or mutual funds—must be purchased by the employer subject to a 403(b) program. In addition, if the plan is subject to ERISA (see below) the plan will have to be in writing. The written document must contain the following information:

- designation of a named fiduciary
- procedure for establishing and carrying out a funding policy
- procedure allocating responsibilities for the operation and administration of the program
- procedure for amending the plan
- basis upon which benefits will be paid

An employer, insurance company, or custodian sponsoring a tax-sheltered annuity program is not required to obtain IRS approval of the form of the annuity contract, custodial agreement, or retirement plan. In fact, the opinion letter and determination letter processes available to qualified plans are not available for Sec. 403(b) annuities. However, because failure to satisfy Sec. 403(b) would cause contributions to be treated as taxable income to participants, occasionally employers seek private letter rulings approving the form of document under Sec. 403(b).

Nonforfeitable and Nontransferable

An employee's rights under the contract must be *nonforfeitable*. In the context of an annuity contract, this has a slightly different meaning than full vesting under a qualified plan with a vesting schedule. It does not appear that joint ownership with the employer with clear vesting rules would be prohibited. However, a vesting provision is rare because of the impact it would have on the calculation of the exclusion ratio.

As a practical matter, ownership ordinarily is vested solely in the employee, thus leaving him or her free of any restrictions or problems that might arise by virtue of insolvency or change of employer management. As sole owner of the contract, the employee is free to exercise any of his or her contractual rights—subject, of course, to restrictions on transferability. Thus, where an insurance company product is involved, the employee may be free to elect a reduced paid-up annuity, to exchange the contract for a reduced annuity with an earlier maturity date, to surrender the contract, or to borrow against its cash value from the insurer.

The contract also must be *nontransferable*. This generally means that the contract cannot be assigned, discounted, pledged as collateral for a loan or as security, or sold to anyone other than the insurance company. However, an assignment can be made to the insurance company as collateral for a loan.

Loans from a 403(b) annuity to a participant are allowed to the same extent as under qualified plans (see chapter 9).

YOUR FINANCIAL SERVICES PRACTICE:
THE ANNUITY CONTRACT

In many ways, the 403(b) contract is more similar to an IRA account than to a pension trust. When employees leave, they can leave benefits in the account, or even transfer them to a 403(b) account with another vendor. Unlike the pension trust, the account can continue as a 403(b) account without the intervention of a plan sponsor. For a terminating employee, this is meaningful primarily for one reason: participant loans. If the 403(b) account is rolled over into an IRA, then loans become unavailable.

Employee Elections to Defer Salary

Tax-sheltered annuity contracts must be purchased by an eligible employer, however, the premiums paid by the employer may either constitute additional compensation for the employee or may be indirectly paid by the employee as a reduction in salary. Amounts contributed under salary reduction are excludible from gross income (for federal tax purposes).

Plans that offer salary deferral contributions must offer the opportunity to all employees (regardless of age or service), unless such employees are covered under another salary deferral type plan.[6] In addition, the employer may not require a minimum contribution level beyond a de minimis contribution of $200.

The agreement to defer salary must be legally binding and irrevocable for amounts earned while the agreement is in effect. An individual can change the election prospectively during the year (as often as the plan allows) or end the agreement for amounts not yet earned.

If a Code Sec. 403(b) annuity plan only contains salary deferral contributions, the plan is extremely simple to operate because it is generally not subject to ERISA and is subject to few tax rules that require ongoing compliance. In a salary deferral only plan, it is typical for vendors to solicit employee participation directly with little involvement of the sponsor.

**YOUR FINANCIAL SERVICES PRACTICE:
TAX ACT OF 2001 REPEALS THE EXCLUSION ALLOWANCE**

One of the major administrative complexities of the 403(b) plan has been determining the maximum allowable contribution under the exclusion allowance rule. Beginning in 2002, the exclusion allowance has been repealed and contributions are now simply limited by the same dollar limitation that applies to 401(k) plans and total contributions (including salary deferrals and employer contributions) can not exceed the lesser of 100 percent of salary or $40,000. This makes the 403(b) vehicle even more attractive to employers with fewer administrative hassles for the employer, employee, and the financial services professional.

Employer Contributions

Employers may use 403(b) plans as a means of providing additional retirement benefits for their employees. Including employer contributions drastically changes the nature of the plan, subjecting it to ERISA and placing additional fiduciary responsibility on the plan sponsor. Also, a significant number of additional tax rules—which make the 403(b) plan more like a qualified plan—will apply.

As in a 401(k) plan, employer contributions can be made as matching contributions based on employee elections to deter compensation.

Another alternative is to make contributions on a nonelective basis, as in a profit-sharing plan or money-purchase pension plan. Typically, such plans provide contributions as a uniform percentage of compensation; however, some flexibility is available in determining the allocation formula. When employer contributions are made, the nondiscrimination requirements of Code Sec. 401(a)(4) will apply to the amount allocated to such contributions.

The following briefly describe the additional rules that apply to a 403(b) plan when the plan contains employer contributions other than salary deferrals.

- *Coverage requirements:* the employer contribution feature has to satisfy the provisions of Code Sec. 410(b) (discussed in chapter 7).
- *Matching contributions*: must satisfy the average deferral percentage (ACP) test that applies to 401(k) plans (discussed in chapter 8).
- *Nonelective employer contributions*: the allocation of employer contributions must satisfy the nondiscrimination requirements of Code Sec. 401(a)(4) (discussed in chapter 8).
- *Timing of contributions*: employee salary deferral contributions must be contributed by the 15th day of the month following the month that the employee would have otherwise received the contribution.

Employer contributions can be made up to the due date of the employer's tax return (plus extensions) for the tax year ending with or within the plan year.

- *Joint-and-survivor requirements:* the plan will be subject to the qualified joint-and-survivor rules. The plan may, however, be eligible for the exception that applies to profit-sharing plans (see chapter 10).

Maximum Deferral Limit

The maximum salary reduction contribution made by an individual is subject to the same dollar limitations that apply to 401(k) plans (discussed in chapter 5). For 2002, the dollar limit is $11,000. Under the Economic Growth and Tax Relief Reconciliation Act of 2001, the limit goes up to $12,000 in 2003, $13,000 in 2004, $14,000 in 2005, and $15,000 in 2006. Also, as with the 401(k) plan, additional contributions can be made by individuals who have attained age 50 by the end of the current year. For 2002, the additional allowable contribution is $1,000. The additional amount becomes $2,000 for 2003, $3,000 for 2004, $4,000 for 2005, and $5,000 for 2006.

Also remember that the dollar limit applies to all contributions made by the individual to any 403(b) plan, 401(k) plan, simplified employee pension (SEP), or savings incentive match plan for employees (SIMPLE). This is true even if the individual is covered by plans of unrelated employers. For example, a 40-year-old participant deferring $6,000 in a 403(b) plan for 2002 would only be able to defer a maximum of $5,000 under a 401(k) arrangement for 2002.

On top of the normal limit (including the additional contribution allowed by participants over age 50) another special "catch-up" election applies to 403(b) plans. Individuals who have completed at least 15 years of service with most eligible sponsors[7] are eligible for the catch-up election. The otherwise applicable limit ($11,000 for 2002) is increased for such eligible individuals by the smallest of the following amounts:

- $3,000 (which makes the limit $14,000 for 2002)
- $15,000, reduced by increases to the regular limit the individual was allowed during earlier years because of this rule
- $5,000 times the number of years of service for the organization, minus the total elective deferrals made under the plan for the individual during earlier years

Code Sec. 415 Limitations

The Code Sec. 415 limitations that apply to qualified defined-contribution plans also apply to Code Sec. 403(b) annuity plans. The annual amount that can be credited to a participant's account, including employer contributions, employee contributions, and forfeitures, cannot exceed the lesser of 100 percent of the employee's compensation from the employer or $40,000 (indexed for 2002).

Distributions

Similar to 401(k) plans, 403(b) plan benefits are generally distributed at the time of termination of employment. In a plan funded with annuity contracts, salary deferral contributions can only be withdrawn in-service if the participant has attained age 59 ½ or suffers a financial hardship. When the plan is funded with mutual fund custodial accounts, then the in-service withdrawal restrictions apply to all types of contributions. Distributions are generally subject to ordinary income tax treatment and the 10 percent early withdrawal Sec. 72(t) penalty tax (discussed in chapter 25).

CHAPTER REVIEW

Answers to the review questions and the self-test questions start on page 673.
For additional review, see case studies in Appendix 9.

Key Terms

simplified employee pension (SEP)	403(b) plan
savings incentive match plan for employees (SIMPLE)	Sec. 501(c)(3) organizations

Review Questions

6-1.   Describe a simplified employee pension (SEP) plan's similarities to the qualified plan and IRA, as well as the SEP's unique design characteristics.

6-2.   What are the major advantages and disadvantages of a SEP?

6-3.   In the following situations, identify whether a SEP is appropriate and, if not, what other type of plan should the sponsor consider.

a.   Candidate Growthco, Inc. has indicated that it would like to have the option to avoid contributions in certain plan years. Growthco wants to motivate employees, but it is hesitant to use stock ownership as an incentive because the owners want to control all stock.

    b. Candidate Smallco, Inc. has five employees and has indicated that it would like to institute a plan that is administratively convenient and allows the company to skip contributions.

    c. Candidate TAMCO, Inc. would like to provide a plan that encourages participants to save for their own retirement and that allows for discretionary employer contributions. TAMCO would like to accomplish this objective in the most tax-efficient manner.

    d. The owner of candidate Transition, Inc. would like to retire and sell the company to the employees. Transition, Inc. employees do not have sufficient funds to purchase the stock outright.

6-4. Technology, Inc. maintains a SEP. Determine whether the following employees are eligible for the plan as of January 1, 2002.

    a. Sally, aged 45, was hired August 15, 1999 on a full-time basis. Sally earns $55,000 a year.

    b. Rich works part-time on an on-and-off basis. He earned $3,000 in 1998, nothing in 1999, $2,500 in 2000, and $1,500 in 2001.

6-5. Describe the major characteristics of the SIMPLE plan.

6-6. What are the contribution options that the employer has?

6-7. What employers are most likely to choose the SIMPLE?

6-8. Identify the market in which 403(b) plans can be used.

6-9. The benefits administrator of Mercy Hospital has asked you to determine which of the following employees are eligible to participate in the hospital's 403(b) plan. List all eligible employees.

    a. Dr. Smith, who heads up the hospital's radiology department and is a full-time employee of the hospital

    b. Dr. Jones, who has admitting privileges at the hospital and is considered an independent contractor

    c. Gary Green, who is called in by the hospital every summer to clean out the boilers

    d. Joy Cheerful, who works part-time (500 hours per year) distributing magazines to patients

6-10. a. List the two methods that can be used to fund a 403(b) plan.

     b. How can insurance protection be provided under both of these methods?

6-11. What is the difference between a 403(b) plan that contains only salary deferral contributions versus one that has additional employer contributions?

Self-Test Questions

T   F   6-1.   A simplified employee pension plan is a retirement plan that uses an individual retirement account or an individual retirement annuity as the receptacle for contributions.

T   F   6-2.   Employers are allowed to discriminate in a simplified employee pension plan with regard to contributions that can be made to highly compensated employees.

T   F   6-3.   A SEP is a popular plan design choice for large corporations.

T   F   6-4.   All amounts contributed to a simplified employee pension plan are immediately 100 percent vested in the participant.

T   F   6-5.   Today, employers can establish a salary reduction SEP.

T   F   6-6.   A simplified employee pension plan cannot contain a loan provision.

T   F   6-7.   A candidate that has a large number of part-time employees should choose a simplified employee pension plan because a SEP can be designed to exclude part-time employees.

T   F   6-8.   A SIMPLE can allow participants to borrow from the plan.

T   F   6-9.   An employer can sponsor both a SIMPLE and a money-purchase pension.

T   F   6-10.   The employer can make both the 3 percent matching contribution and the 2 percent nonelective contribution to the SIMPLE.

T   F   6-11.   The employer who has few rank-and-file employees interested in participating in the plan should consider the SIMPLE over the 401(k) plan.

T   F   6-12.   All those who receive payment for services from a qualified tax-exempt organization or public school are considered eligible employees for purposes of making contributions to the organization's 403(b) plan.

T   F   6-13.   A 403(b) plan can only be funded with an annuity contract or a mutual fund.

T   F   6-14.   Contributions to a mutual fund custodial account under a 403(b) plan can be used to purchase insurance if the insurance has no cash value, if it is incidental, and if the cost is included in the employee's gross income.

T   F   6-15.   All employees willing to defer $200 or more generally have to be eligible to make salary deferrals under a 403(b).

T   F   6-16.   403(b) plans that contain employer contributions must satisfy ERISA requirements and meet coverage and nondiscrimination requirements that apply to qualified plans.

T   F   6-17.   A 403(b) plan cannot be designed to permit participant loans.

T   F   6-18.   The same salary deferral dollar limit that applies to 401(k) plans applies to 403(b) plans as well.

T   F   6-19.   If an employee participates in a 401(k) plan or a SEP, the salary reduction contributions under those plans are aggregated with 403(b) deferrals when applying the $11,000 limit (as indexed for 2002) on salary deferrals.

Notes

1. The determination of whether a controlled group of corporations exists is governed by IRC Secs. 414(b) and (c). The area is quite complex, but as a rule of thumb, a controlled group exists when one company owns 80 percent or more of another corporation or the same five or fewer individuals have controlling interest in two or more businesses. The rules also apply to partnerships and sole proprietorships. In the small business setting, a common example would be one individual owning two separate businesses.
2. Only installment payments or a part of a minimum required distribution may not be rolled over.
3. Note that 408(p)(2)(iii) does not apply the $200,000 (indexed for 2002) compensation cap for purposes of determining the 3 percent matching contribution. However, for the employer that elects the 2 percent nonelective contribution in lieu of the match, the $200,000 compensation cap does apply. This means that the maximum nonelective contribution would be $4,000 (2 percent of $200,000).
4. Code Sec. 408(l).
5. Code Sec. 6693(c)(1).
6. Including a Code Sec. 457 plan, a Code Sec. 401(k) plan, SIMPLE, or another Code Sec. 403(b) annuity plan.

7

Coverage, Eligibility, and Participation Rules

Learning Objectives

An understanding of the material in this chapter should enable the student to

---

7-1. Describe the planning tools used in the plan-design process.

7-2. Explain the coverage requirements applicable to qualified plans.

7-3. Describe the aggregation rules that apply for testing coverage.

7-4. Describe the plan participation rules, and identify the various factors that planners consider when choosing eligibility and participation provisions.

Chapter Outline

Perhaps the most challenging assignment in the retirement field is advising a client about how his or her plan should be designed. In order to design a plan effectively, the financial services professional must

- acquire an expertise about the qualification rules
- ascertain the client's objectives
- choose plan provisions that meet the qualification rules and accomplish employer objectives

In addition, both the client's objectives and the qualification rules are constantly evolving and require financial services professionals to monitor client needs and know the latest laws and regulations. In this chapter and the next three chapters, we will define and explore the various plan-design features. The emphasis will be on the qualification rules that apply to qualified plans and the ways plan design can be used to meet your client's objectives. The last part of the chapter will review the different rules that apply to other tax-sheltered plans. Let's start, however, with a brief overview of the plan-design process.

THE PLAN-DESIGN PROCESS

The first step toward effective plan design has already been taken. The fact finder that you set up to choose the best retirement plan can also be used to help you design the plan properly. However, designing a plan is dictated not only by the client's objectives but also by the laws and regulations regarding plan qualification. In other words, picking the specific provisions that will constitute the client's plan consists of weighing what the Internal Revenue Code permits against the client's objectives and pocketbook. Take as an example the first design feature we consider below—which employees should be eligible for the plan. The coverage rules are quite complex. In this case, complexity allows a great deal of freedom in plan design, but also requires intimate knowledge of the boundaries of the law.

The plan-design process is simplified for insurance agents and other financial services professionals by the use of master and prototype plan documents. With these documents most of the plan language is standardized, and the employer has limited design alternatives, which are contained in a **adoption agreement** document referred to as the *adoption agreement*. The adoption-agreement approach helps the adviser by organizing the design process. The document is relatively simple to follow, because it lists the various design features and provides several alternatives under each one (for example, the various vesting schedules and the alternative design choices available for early, normal, and deferred retirement). Employers (with your help) then pick from the menu of options that is provided.

The adoption agreement simplifies plan design by directing and limiting available design options, but it also locks out from consideration some important but nonstandard design choices that might meet a unique employer need. Generally, if employers desire this specialized treatment they should pay the additional fees to have an attorney, consulting firm, or insurance company home office design the plan (called an individually designed plan). On the other hand, employers willing to buy an "off-the-rack" plan probably can save on fees and yet meet their goals and objectives through the use of the standard design options contained in your company's adoption agreement.

You can see that to properly advise the client, the adviser needs to have an in-depth understanding of the rules. Knowing the options in the adoption agreement is not enough. The adviser must be able to know the limits of the law, so the client will be able to decide when it is time to establish a plan that does not fall within the prototype options.

**YOUR FINANCIAL SERVICES PRACTICE:
EFFECTIVE PLAN DESIGN**

As a rule of thumb, any design decision you make in one area of the adoption agreement should be consistent with design decisions you make in other areas of the adoption agreement. In other words, one strategy in designing an effective plan is to ask yourself: Does each design decision consistently support the employer's objectives? For example, if the desire to limit costs attributable to short-service employees motivated the employer to choose the most restrictive age and service requirements offered in the adoption agreement, the same employer objective should also generate a restrictive vesting schedule and a benefit formula that rewards service. This approach to plan design will ensure a design that is correct and complete. However, remember the words of Alfred North Whitehead: "Seek simplicity and distrust it." There may be reasons to stray from design consistency to meet a unique employer objective.

COVERAGE REQUIREMENTS

The first major design decision facing you and your client is deciding what employees to cover under the retirement plan. This decision is directed by extensive and complicated laws and regulations. As a payback for providing valuable tax advantages for qualified plans (and consequently losing revenue), the legislature requires that retirement plans must cover a broad spectrum of employees and not just a group of highly compensated employees (who are defined by statute).

The Definition of a Highly Compensated Employee

Understanding the coverage requirements begins with identifying the employees that are considered highly compensated employees (HCE). We first encountered the highly compensated group when discussing the 401(k) actual deferral percentage test. As you may recall, highly compensated employees include individuals who are 5 percent owners during the current or previous year and individuals who earned $85,000 (as indexed in 2001) in the preceding year. Under the second category, the employer can elect to limit the group to only those individuals whose earnings put them in the top 20 percent of all employees. Note that the applicable indexed limit is based on the year the salary is earned. For example, for determining HCE status for 2002, look back to compensation earned in 2001 and the applicable limit for that year ($85,000 for 2001).

The 410(b) Rule

Sec. 410(b) of the Internal Revenue Code specifies who must be covered under a qualified plan. The rules are meaningful any time the employer decides not to cover all employees under the plan. The employer may want to exclude one class of workers, such as hourly employees, or employees who are part-time or have short service. In other cases, the employer will want to set up two or more plans, each covering a different group of employees. Essentially, a plan can cover any portion of the workforce, as long as it satisfies one of three tests under Sec. 410(b): the percentage test, the ratio test, or the average-benefit-percentage test.

When performing any of these tests, note that certain classes of employees can always be excluded from testing. These include collectively bargained employees, employees who have worked less than one year, certain part-time employees (working less than 1,000 hours per year), and employees younger than age 21 (discussed in more detail later in this chapter). These employees will be referred to as *excludable employees.* Essentially this means a plan can always exclude those employees defined as excludable, as well as any additional employees as allowed under one of the three coverage tests.

Also be aware that when testing a 401(k) plan, an individual eligible to make a salary deferral election will be considered a participant in the plan, regardless of whether he or she makes the election to make a salary deferral. For other plans, this is not the case. Subject to several exceptions, a participant must actually receive a contribution (or benefit accrual in a defined-benefit plan) in order to be considered a participant for that year.

percentage test

The Percentage Test

A plan will satisfy Sec. 410(b) if it benefits at least 70 percent of employees who are not highly compensated employees. As just described, employees who are not eligible for participation in the plan because they don't meet the age and service requirements or who are covered by a collective-bargaining agreement (discussed later in the chapter) are not counted for purposes of this test.

Example: The law firm of Block, Meyers, and Andrews has 24 employees. Because 4 of these employees work part-time and have not met the minimum-service requirements for participation in the plan (discussed later in the chapter), the percentage test would apply only to the remaining 20 employees. Of these employees, 12 fall within the statutory definition of highly compensated and 8 do not. Six of the 8 employees who are not highly compensated belong to the Manhattan office (the one covered by the plan) and 2 belong to the Teaneck, New Jersey, office (which does not have a plan). Under the percentage test, the plan must benefit at least 70 percent of the 8 employees who are not highly compensated (note that employees from both offices are counted). That is, 6 employees (6 out of 8 is 75 percent) must be benefited. Because the law firm's Manhattan plan benefits 6 of the nonhighly compensated employees, the plan passes the percentage test.

ratio test

The Ratio Test

The ratio test requires a plan to benefit a percentage of nonhighly compensated employees equal to 70 percent of the percentage of highly compensated employees benefited under the plan. Again, employees who are not eligible for participation in the plan because they do not meet the age and service requirements or are covered by a collective-bargaining agreement are not counted for purposes of the ratio test.

Example: The Thunder Company has 120 employees on its payroll. Because 20 of these have not yet met the minimum age and service requirements of the plan, the ratio test would apply to only 100 employees. Thirty of the remaining employees are highly compensated, and 15 of 30 highly compensated employees actually participate in the plan (the additional 15 are part of a separate group that does not have a plan). Seventy of the remaining employees are nonhighly compensated, and 40 of 70 nonhighly compensated employees participate in the plan (the additional 30 are part of the separate group that does not have a plan).

Because 50 percent (15 out of 30) of the highly compensated employees participate in the plan, the ratio test requires that at least 35 percent of the nonhighly compensated employees (70% x 50% = 35%) must benefit under the plan. In other words, at least 25 (35% x 70 = 24.5) nonhighly compensated employees must benefit under the plan. Because Thunder Company has 40 nonhighly compensated employees benefiting under the plan, the plan satisfies the ratio test.

Average-Benefit Test

Another way to satisfy the minimum-coverage requirements is to satisfy the average-benefits test. This is actually a very complex analysis that has three separate parts. Here we will summarize these rules and when they are generally applied, but will not get into all the details.

The first requirement under the average-benefits test is that the plan has to cover employees who represent a *reasonable classification of employees*—which means that the eligibility requirements (specifying who qualifies for participation and who does not) must use some objective means of classification, such as job classification, nature of compensation (salaried or hourly), or geographic location. The second part of the test is a very complex percentage test. Suffice it to say that the percentage of nonhighly compensated employees required to be covered under this section will generally be quite small. The third part of the test is the *average-benefit-percentage test*. This portion is satisfied if the average-benefit percentage for nonhighly compensated employees is at least 70 percent of the average-benefit percentage of the highly compensated employees. This requirement

average-benefit-percentage test

is different from the others in that it counts benefits earned in any qualified plan sponsored by the employer.

In operation, note that the administrator will test the plan under the less complicated percentage and ratio tests before tackling the more complex average-percentage test. Understand that the reason for this test is to provide relief for the larger employer that wants to cover most employees under some qualified plan, but chooses to cover them under two or more separate plans. The employer might want to do this because it has different geographic locations or has workers with very different types of jobs. Although the math is complex, the bottom line is that the employer can generally have such an arrangement as long as, overall, the benefits for nonhighly compensated employees under all the plans are at least 70 percent of the benefits provided to the highly compensated under all the plans.

For the small employer sponsoring one plan, the average-benefit test will not result in lower required participation than the ratio test. All the nonhighly compensated employees who are excluded from the plan are counted as having zero benefits when determining whether the average-percentage test has been satisfied. In other words, the small employer sponsoring one plan will have to satisfy the percentage or ratio test. The average-benefits test will be of no help.

Three Minimum-Coverage Tests

- *Percentage test*—the plan covers at least 70 percent of the nonhighly compensated employees
- *Ratio test*— the percentage of nonhighly compensated employees covered is at least 70 percent of the percentage of HCEs covered under the plan
- *Average-benefits test*— the group covered represents a reasonable classification, a complex minimum percentage test is satisfied, and the benefits of nonhighly compensated employees average at least 70 percent of the benefits provided to HCEs looking at all retirement plans of the sponsor

---

Separate Lines of Business

separate lines of business

If an employer has *separate lines of business,* the 410(b) tests may be applied separately in each line of business. In order to qualify for this favorable treatment, the separate lines of business must be operated for bona fide business reasons and must have at least 50 employees. The IRS has issued complex regulations for determining whether a separate line of business exists. Because of the difficulty of demonstrating compliance, most employers will look to the separate-line-of-business rules only as a last resort—when looking for ways to ensure that each plan meets the coverage requirements.

The 401(a)(26) Minimum-Participation Rule

401(a)(26) minimum-
participation
rule

Defined-benefit plans must satisfy a second coverage requirement under Code Sec. 401(a)(26) referred to as the *minimum-participation rule.* Under this rule, an employer's plan will not be qualified unless it covers (1) 50 employees or (2) 40 percent of the employer's employees, *whichever is lesser.* However, a special rule applies when there are two employees; in this case, both employees must be covered.

This rule does not count employees who are not eligible because of the age and service requirements or who are part of a group covered by a collective-bargaining agreement. The effect of this rule is that employers with more than 125 employees cannot maintain a plan covering fewer than 50 participants, and if the employer has fewer than 125 employees, then the 40 percent limit applies. The result is that smaller employers will be limited to a maximum of two separate plans (in order to meet the 40 percent rule).

Apparently, the justification to have an additional eligibility requirement for defined-benefit plans is that Congress is concerned that small employers would establish defined-benefit plans that only covered the owners of company and would cover other employees under a separate defined contribution with less value. The minimum-participation requirement eliminates this possibility.

Aggregation Rules

To avoid the coverage requirements, some employers try to segregate their management employees from the rank-and-file employees by creating a related or subsidiary corporation. To close this loophole, the Code contains what are referred to as the *controlled group rules* that require aggregation of employers that have a sufficient amount of common ownership, and the *affiliated service groups rules* for other situations in which related businesses work together to provide goods or services to the public. When either aggregation rule applies, the employers are treated as one employer for virtually all the qualified plan rules. Both rules apply to both corporations and "trades and businesses," including partnerships, proprietorships, estates, and trusts. Regulations provide guidance for determining ownership interests in these kinds of entities.

A third type of affiliation relates to situations where individuals are "leased" on a long-term, full-time basis. In some cases, such individuals will be treated as working for the recipient for purposes of the coverage requirements. Each of these rules is covered more fully below.

Controlled Group Rules

controlled groups

There are three types of *controlled groups:* parent-subsidiary, brother-sister, and combined groups. A parent-subsidiary controlled group exists whenever one entity (referred to as the *parent company*) owns at least 80 percent of one (or more) of the other entities. Additional entities may be brought into the group if a chain of common ownership exists. Other entities included in the chain must be at least 80 percent owned by one or more (in combination) of the other entities within the chain.

Example: Corporation A owns 80 percent of Corporations B and C, and Corporations B and C each own 40 percent of Corporation D. Because Corporation D is 80 percent owned by entities within the group, Corporation D is part of the parent-subsidiary controlled group that includes all four corporations.

A brother-sister controlled group exists whenever the same five (or fewer) owners of two or more entities own 80 percent or more of each entity, and more than 50 percent of each entity when counting only *identical ownership*. Identical ownership is tested by counting each person's ownership to the extent that it is identical in each entity. For example, if an individual owns 10 percent of Corporation A and 20 percent of Corporation B, he or she has a 10 percent identical ownership interest with respect to each corporation. The identical ownership interests of each of the five (or fewer) individuals is added together to determine whether the 50 percent test has been satisfied, as shown in table 7-1 for these shareholders.

TABLE 7-1
IDENTICAL OWNERSHIP

Shareholder	Corporation X	Corporation Y	Identical Ownership
Joe	20%	12%	12%
Sally	60%	14%	14%
Ralph	20%	74%	20%
Total	100%	100%	46%

Under these assumed facts, the 80 percent ownership test has been met, because three individuals who have ownership in each entity own 100 percent of both businesses. However, the 50 percent identical ownership interest test has not been satisfied (only 46 percent identical ownership). Therefore, this group does not constitute a controlled group.

When determining an individual's ownership interest under the brother-sister controlled group rules, attribution rules require that stock owned by spouses (with one narrow exception) and children under age 21 must be treated as owned by the individual. When a person owns more than 50 percent of an entity, he or she is deemed to own any interest owned in that entity by his or her adult children, grandchildren, parents, and grandparents, as well.

The last type of controlled group is the combined group under common control. A combined group exists if an entity is both a common parent in a parent-subsidiary group and a member of a brother-sister group. If this is the case, the two related controlled groups are treated as one controlled group.

Types of Controlled Groups

- Parent-subsidiary
- Brother-sister
- Combined

Affiliated Service Group Rules

affiliated service group

In 1980, Congress enacted the first *affiliated service group* rules. Small business corporations had managed to divide management and the rank-and-file into separate entities and avoid the controlled group rules. The rules have been expanded several times over the years to address new avoidance schemes. Today, the law is quite complex, and the details are beyond the scope of this book. However, when working with clients, there are several threshold issues that help advisers to identify when affiliation problems might be present. Except for management services affiliation (discussed below), affiliated groups exist only when all three of the following elements are present:

- when two or more business entities work together to provide one service or product to the public
- when at least one of the entities is a service organization, which is an organization for which capital is not a material income-producing factor. Organizations in the fields of health, law, engineering, actuarial science, consulting, and insurance are automatically deemed service organizations.
- when at least some common ownership exists between the two entities

---

**YOUR FINANCIAL SERVICES PRACTICE:
AVOIDING HIDDEN AGGREGATION PROBLEMS**

One common problem the financial services professional faces when setting up a retirement plan is finding out important information at the last minute or after the fact. For example, an employer who is interested in setting up a plan for the ABC Company may also own the XYZ Company but fail to give you this important information. Because it is possible that the employees of both ABC and XYZ must be considered for the purposes of the coverage requirements, it is important to question the employer about additional holdings, other key employees' additional holdings, and the corporation's additional holdings. (See question 8 in Step 7 in the fact finder in chapter 3.) In the small-company context, the minimum-coverage rules are unforgiving, and an employer who misses a controlled group issue may very well end up with one or more disqualified plans. This is a complex area of the law, and the role of the pension advisor should be to identify affiliation issues and then encourage the client to pursue a final determination from a qualified tax attorney.

The affiliation rules come into play regularly in the medical world, where there are partnerships between doctors and hospitals providing services in outpatient clinics, MRI testing centers, and other cooperative medical centers. In these cases, there must be a careful analysis to see if the MRI testing center, for example, is affiliated with the doctor's medical practice or with the hospital.

Management services affiliation is defined by a much broader rule, which essentially prohibits an executive of any size company from separating himself or herself from the company for the purpose of establishing his or her own retirement plan.

The Leasing of Employees

Instead of hiring employees directly, a business may lease employees from a third party for a number of legitimate reasons. Unfortunately, at one time, leasing of employees was also used as a way to circumvent the minimum-coverage requirements. The employer would lease rank-and-file employees and then exclude them from plan eligibility. Code Sec. 414 (n) was enacted to eliminate such practices by requiring that individuals leased on a full-time, ongoing basis would be treated as employees for purposes of the coverage requirements.

leased employee

A *leased employee* is a person who provides services to the recipient and meets all three of the following requirements:

- The services are provided pursuant to an agreement between the recipient and a leasing organization.

- The services are provided on a substantially full-time basis for a period of at least one year.
- The individual's services are performed under the primary direction or control of the service recipient.

Under the regulations, an individual need not be an employee of a leasing organization. The leasing relationship can exist directly with the leased employee, which means that a self-employed individual can be treated as a leased employee. Services are deemed to be substantially full-time for a year if the individual is credited with 1,500 or more hours of services (this number is reduced if employees generally work fewer than 40 hours a week). Legislative history indicates that the "primary direction or control" test is determined considering whether the recipient of the leased employee's services has control of where, when, and how services are performed; the order in which they are performed; who performs them; and whether the leased employee is directly supervised. This same legislative history indicates that clerical workers are generally considered within primary direction and control, while self-employed professionals such as attorneys, accountants, computer programmers, and the like are not.

Even if an individual is a leased employee under the above conditions, he or she will not be treated as an employee of the recipient if leased employees constitute no more than 20 percent of the recipient's nonhighly compensated workforce and the leasing entity maintains a safe harbor plan. A safe harbor plan must be a money-purchase plan with a nonintegrated contribution rate of at least 10 percent of compensation, and must provide for immediate eligibility and 100 percent immediate vesting.

The objective of the leased employee rule is to ensure that a company cannot avoid covering a large number of employees by leasing them versus hiring them directly. On the other hand, if the employer leases only a few individuals, the minimum-coverage rules have enough latitude to allow the leased employees to be excluded from the qualified plan—or, in the alternative, the leased individuals can be ignored if the leasing organization maintains a safe harbor qualified plan. In this way, the leased employee rules work fairly well to eliminate abusive situations without penalizing the average employer. In general, the most annoying requirement for employers is that businesses that receive nonemployee services are required to keep records to demonstrate whether individuals are technically considered leased employees. An employer may be exempted from the record-keeping requirement, but only if all three of the following conditions are satisfied:

- All of the recipient's qualified plans must specifically state that leased employees are not eligible to participate.
- No qualified plan of the recipient can be top-heavy.

- The number of leased persons providing services to the recipient during the plan year must be less than 5 percent of the number of employees (excluding leased persons and HCEs) covered by the recipient's qualified plans.

A final note: the controlled group rules, affiliated service rules, and leased employee rules were written to eliminate most situations where entities were artificially separated so a qualified plan would cover only some of the employees. Be careful when looking at any arrangement that "smells bad." The rules are fairly comprehensive—most such schemes are prohibited. This is one area of the law where if it looks too good to be true, it probably is!

EMPLOYEES THE PLAN SHOULD COVER

We have seen some of the key rules that dictate whom a plan *must* cover.

- Plans cannot be used exclusively to tax-shelter income for highly compensated employees.
- To discourage this use, and to encourage a national policy of private retirement coverage, the coverage tests ensure that rank-and-file employees are sufficiently included.

But beyond this lies the question of whom the plan *should* cover. While it is true that most clients with smaller organizations will be trying to maximize tax advantages for themselves as opposed to providing coverage for rank-and-file employees, there is a case to be made for covering these employees. It is not an idealistic plea for the underdog or merely an opportunity to increase commissions; it is plain common sense that employers in small firms often overlook. First, an employee who is not covered by the plan resents second-class status and will eventually seek employment elsewhere. Even if the employer spent only 40 work-hours training that individual, 80 work-hours have been lost because the training process must be repeated with the new replacement. The cycle is also apt to repeat itself several times. What's more, the most important asset a small business can have is the experienced rank-and-file employee. There is little room for inexperienced and unproductive or counterproductive people in any organization, and—especially in small businesses—retirement plans go a long way toward coaxing employees to remain long enough to become experienced, productive workers. The second reason to cover the rank and file in a small business is to encourage loyalty and team spirit. For small businesses, it is crucial that their employees not only be experienced but also committed to the welfare of the business. The result is that the principal reason to encourage a retirement umbrella covering all employees is that the business is best served by this arrangement and that it *is* cost-effective to include nonkey employees.

OPTIONS AVAILABLE UNDER THE PLAN COVERAGE RULES

In spite of such legislative roadblocks as Secs. 410(b)(1) and 401(a)(26), as well as the aggregation rules and your good advice, many employers (especially small employers) still desire to provide retirement benefits for owners and key employees only, and to avoid the expense of providing benefits for the rank-and-file employees. If this is how your clients feel, relief is available in the following forms:

- gaps under the coverage requirements
- coverage of employees in comparable plans
- certain plan-design features to delay the participation of employees for as long as possible (discussed later in this chapter)
- nonqualified deferred compensation (see chapters 15 and 16)

Gaps in the Coverage Requirements

The coverage rules allow the employer to save costs by excluding a portion of the workforce. To summarize, the rules allow the following employees to be excluded:

- All employees who have not satisfied minimum age and service requirements or are subject to a collective bargaining agreement (often referred to as "excludables") can be excluded without issue.
- If the plan covers all of the highly compensated employees, an additional 30 percent of the (nonexcludable) nonhighly compensated employees can be excluded.
- Any HCE can be excluded from coverage.

Example: Loophole, Inc. has 10 employees (who are not excludables). Two are highly compensated and 8 are not. If the employer establishes a defined-contribution plan that covers one highly compensated employee, only 35 percent, or 3, of the nonhighly compensated employees have to be covered. This is because, under the ratio test, 70 percent of the percentage of highly compensated employees covered (50 percent), equals 35 percent.

In addition, if the plan does exclude some of the highly compensated, fewer nonhighly compensated employees have to be covered under the plan.

As you can see, the ratio test allows the exclusion of a significant number of rank-and-file employees when some of the highly compensated employees are excluded from the plan. This rule can be effective for small businesses when some of the highly compensated are not interested in participating in the plan because they are very young, very old, or not interested for other reasons.

One important limitation applies to the rules described above. The Age Discrimination in Employment Act (ADEA) prohibits discrimination against individuals aged 40 and older. To avoid problems under this act (and possibly other state laws), a plan provision excluding a group of employees from a qualified plan should be based on a reasonable (and real) job classification. For example, the plan may exclude hourly employees, secretaries, associate attorneys, or other job classification. It is a good idea to seek the advice of a labor or employment lawyer when addressing this specific issue.

Coverage of Employees in Comparable Plans

As described above, each plan sponsored by the employer must satisfy the Sec. 410(b) minimum-coverage requirements. Also, defined-benefit plans must satisfy the requirements of Sec. 401(a)(26). There are several meaningful exceptions to these rules. First, if the employer excludes all highly compensated employees, the plan can cover any group of nonhighly compensated employees, without regard to either coverage rule. This rule allows for tremendous design freedom. This approach could be used by an employer that decided to provide retirement benefits for executives through a nonqualified arrangement, and wanted a qualified plan for only a small portion of the nonhighly compensated workforce.

Another option under Sec. 410(b) is to aggregate two plans for purposes of testing whether the coverage requirements are met. Under this option, if the employer wishes to establish two plans for separate groups of employees, and the plans will not meet the coverage requirements on their own, they can generally be aggregated and tested together, as long as the total benefits provided (looking at the plans as one) do not discriminate in favor of the highly compensated. How this works will be more clear after reading the next chapter, which explains the nondiscrimination requirements. Note, however, that the aggregation rules do not apply to the Sec. 401(a)(26) minimum-participation rule. In other words, a defined-benefit plan (that covers at least one highly compensated employee) will always have to cover the lesser of 50 employees or 40 percent of the workforce.

In total, you can see that the coverage rules are quite flexible, especially in the case of an employer that wishes to have numerous plans that cover different groups of employees. There are a number of ways to demonstrate compliance with the coverage rules in this case. And, as described above, even the employer that wants to have a single plan that excludes some employees will have more freedom to do so than you might first suspect.

WHEN SHOULD PARTICIPATION BEGIN?

Once you and your client have decided the employees that should and must be covered, the next step is to decide when an employee's participation should begin. In general, participation can be delayed for certain employees on the basis of their ages and their years of service with the company.

There are several reasons to delay participation as long as legally possible. For one thing, employees do not start earning benefits until they become plan participants (except in defined-benefit plans, which may count service with the employer prior to the participation date for benefit purposes), and by delaying participation, the client's organization can save retirement dollars attributable to turnover. A second cost-saving feature of delayed participation involves the administrative and record-keeping duties associated with tracking employees who leave. Because turnover is highest for employees in their first few years of employment and for younger employees, it makes sense from an administrative standpoint to delay their participation in the plan. Besides, if the retirement plan is funded with individual insurance policies, the employer loses out on funds that provide death benefits and the commissions paid for benefits for employees who leave (the front-end load).

There are, on the other hand, some good reasons to begin participation immediately. These include maximizing contributions for employees by not delaying coverage and attracting specialized employees by making the plan highly competitive. These specialized employees (such as a computer whiz or a high-powered salesperson) usually possess highly desired skills or profit-making ability, and any delay in participation may make the plan's benefit package less desirable to them.

If your client's circumstances warrant immediate participation, then the plan should be designed appropriately. But even under such circumstances, the client must still adhere to the statutory participation rules. In general, any employee who is not excluded from the plan based upon employment classification must become a participant no later than the first entry date after the employee meets the age and service requirements of the plan. The maximum age and service requirements are age 21 and one year of service **21-and-one rule** (commonly referred to as the *21-and-one rule),* so after an employee becomes 21 and has garnered one year of service, he or she is entitled to join the plan on the next plan entry date.

The 2-Year/100 Percent Rule

**2-year/100 percent
rule**

One exception applies to the general 21-and-one rule—a special provision that allows up to a 2-year service requirement if the employee is immediately 100 percent vested upon becoming a participant (called the *2-year/100 percent rule*). This method is desirable if the company's vesting schedules are already as liberal as the 2-year/100 percent schedule and your client desires to delay participation as long as possible. If your client wants a more restrictive vesting schedule and also desires to delay participation, however, you will have to determine which carries more weight—the maximum-service requirement or the restrictive vesting schedules.

Entry Date

The last choice associated with when plan participation must and should begin is the selection of an entry date for employees to become participants in the plan. An employee who meets the minimum age and service requirements of the plan, and who is otherwise eligible to participate in the plan, must be allowed to participate no later than the earlier of (1) the first day of the first plan year beginning after the date the employee met the age and service requirements or (2) the date 6 months after these conditions are met. In other words, entry dates can delay participation up to 6 months after the 21-and-one or 2-year/100 percent hurdles are jumped. For clients who desire to delay participation as long as possible, semiannual entry dates should be set up, typically January 1 and July 1. This way, the employer will stretch out the preparticipation period as long as possible. Other typical entry dates include the anniversary date of the plan (this can be used only if the age requirement is not more than 20 1/2 and the service requirement is 6 months or less), quarterly entry dates, monthly entry dates, and daily entry dates.

Determining Service

The term *year of service* has a special meaning for purposes of meeting the one-year-of-service or 2-years-of-service eligibility requirements. An employee who works 1,000 hours during the initial 12-month period after being employed will earn a year of service. For example, Larry is hired on October 5, 2000. If Larry has worked at least 1,000 hours or more by October 4, 2001, he has acquired a year of service. Note that Larry does not receive a year of service after he worked his 1,000th hour but on his first anniversary of employment.

YOUR FINANCIAL SERVICES PRACTICE:
THE ELIGIBILITY AND PARTICIPATION RULES IN A SAMPLE ADOPTION AGREEMENT

The following sample illustrates how the rules might appear in a typical adoption agreement (note that terms whose first letter is capitalized are defined in the plan):

Section B: Eligibility (refers to Section 2 of the plan)

(1) The Age and Service requirements for participation in the Plan are

    (a) Attainment of age ___ (not to exceed 21)

    (b) Completion of ___ Year(s) of Service (not to exceed one year, unless the Plan provides Full and Immediate Vesting (Section G). (If the Plan provides for Full and Immediate Vesting, it is not to exceed 2 years.)

(2) The Plan's Entry Date will be (check one)

    ( ) daily
    ( ) the Friday in any calendar week
    ( ) the first day of any calendar month
    ( ) quarterly (Jan. 1, April 1, July 1, Oct. 1)
    ( ) semiannually (Jan. 1, July 1)
    ( ) annually (Jan. 1) (Note: If the entry date is annually then the Age requirement in Section B(1)(a) cannot exceed 20 1/2 and the Service requirement in Section B(1)(b) cannot be more than 6 months.)

(3) Hours of Service shall be determined on the basis of the method selected below. The method selected shall be applied to all Employees covered under the Plan. (Check one)

    ( ) On the basis of actual hours for which an Employee is paid or entitled to payment.
    ( ) On the basis of days worked. An Employee shall be credited with 10 Hours of Service if under Section 19 of the Plan such Employee would be credited with at least one Hour of Service during the day.
    ( ) On the basis of weeks worked. An Employee shall be credited with 45 Hours of Service if under Section 19 of the Plan such Employee would be credited with at least one Hour of Service during the week.
    ( ) On the basis of semimonthly payroll periods. An Employee shall be credited with 95 Hours of Service if under Section 19 of the Plan such Employee would be credited with at least one Hour of Service during the semimonthly payroll period.
    ( ) On the basis of months worked. An Employee shall be credited with 190 Hours of Service if under Section 19 of the Plan such Employee would be credited with at least one Hour of Service during the month.

The phrase *an hour of service* also has a special meaning; it includes not only the hours an employee works, but also any hours for which an employee is entitled to be paid, such as vacations, holidays, and illness time. One way to compute the hours for purposes of the 1,000-hour requirement is to count each hour an employee works for which he or she is entitled to be paid (the standard-hours counting method).

Because the standard-hours counting method can be administratively cumbersome, the IRC permits some alternative counting methods—called equivalencies—to be used. However, in choosing an equivalency, the employer will pay a premium of extra hours for using this administratively convenient system. Therefore, another aspect of plan design is helping your client choose the best alternative. The equivalencies include the following:

- The elapsed-time method, which does not look at the hours of service worked because service is measured from date of employment to date of severance. For example, if Barbara starts working on January 18, she would have one year of service on the following January 18 regardless of how many hours she actually worked.

- The hours-worked-including-overtime method, which looks at the actual hours worked including overtime but excluding nonworked hours such as vacation, holidays, and sick time. If this test is used, an employee needs to work only 870 hours to earn a year of service.

- The hours-worked-excluding-overtime method, which looks at the actual hours worked excluding overtime, vacations, holidays, and sick time. If this is used, an employee needs only 750 hours for a year of service.

- The time-period or pay-period method, which looks at the days, weeks, semimonthly pay periods, months, or shifts actually worked by the employee and applies the following equivalencies:
  - a credit of 10 hours of service per day if the employee worked one hour in any day
  - a credit of 45 hours of service per week if the employee worked one hour in any week
  - a credit of 95 hours of service for semimonthly pay period if the employee worked one hour in any pay period
  - a credit of 190 hours per month if the employee worked one hour in any month
  - a credit of the number of hours per shift if the employee worked one hour in any shift

- The equivalencies-based-on-earnings method, which calculates the hours worked on the basis of the employee's earnings. For example, if the employee is paid hourly, the equivalency can be determined by dividing the employee's total earnings by the hourly wage. (If the hourly wage changed over a period, the employer should look at the actual hourly wage, or the lowest hourly wage during the period, or the lowest hourly wage paid to employees in the same or similar job classification during that period.) If the employee's earnings are not based on hourly rates, the hourly rate is calculated by translating the employee's salary into an hourly rate—for example, by dividing annual salary by a 40-hour week or 8-hour day.

The choice of an equivalency boils down to two disparate considerations. The first is administrative convenience. By coordinating the hours of service with payroll's records, the employer may be able to use an existing computer or accounting system and eliminate duplication of work efforts. The second and more important concern when choosing an hour-of-service definition is to permanently exclude part-time employees from the plan. This can result in substantial savings for your client. What's more, it will not prejudice your client when the coverage rules are applied because part-time employees (with less than 1,000 hours of service) are generally not counted for purposes of the 401(a)(4), 410(b)(1), or 401(a)(26) tests. If your client's desire is to exclude part-time employees, as is usually the case, then it is likely that the standard-hours counting method should be used in lieu of any equivalency (note that all equivalency methods generously define the hours used). To make sure that part-time employees do not slip in under these rules—complicating administration of the plan—the employer may want to establish a policy limiting the number of hours part-time employees can work.

CASE STUDY: THE MATTHEW MATT MANUFACTURING COMPANY

The Matthew Matt Manufacturing Company, makers of wrestling mats, employs 75 full-time employees and 15 part-time employees. Matthew Matt is establishing a qualified plan and is trying to determine the appropriate eligibility and participation provisions. He desires to minimize costs, encourage rank-and-file employees to stay (experienced mat makers are hard to find), and exclude the part-time employees from the plan. In addition, Matthew tells you that a competitive wrestling mat company is forming in the area. The relevant questions the financial services professional must address are these:

- Should participation be delayed and, if so, for how long?
- What definition of hour of service should be used?
- What entry date should be used?

In answer to the first question, Matthew Matt should delay participation as a cost-saving measure. When a plan is installed in an existing business, however, the employer must take into account the service already acquired (preplan service) for eligibility purposes. In this case, to placate employees who might jump to the competitor, the plan will count preplan service.

How long Matthew delays participation—which could be for one or 2 years, the statutory maximums—would depend on his decision about vesting and his perception of the competitive threat.

Since Matthew wants to exclude part-time employees to the full extent possible, the company will choose the most restrictive method for determining whether the 1,000-hours-of-service requirement has been met. This is generally the standard-hours counting method. However, if Matthew uses his part-time employees seasonally (for 2 months during wrestling season) and needs them for overtime during that period, then the most restrictive method might be the hours-worked-excluding-overtime method. This method looks at the actual hours worked and excludes overtime, the Christmas holidays (which fall in wrestling season), sick time, and the like.

When choosing an entry date, considerations such as administrative convenience and employee morale also come into play. Because employee morale is most important in light of the threat of competition, it will probably be desirable to choose a less restrictive entry date that matches administrative pay practices—monthly, for example.

OTHER TAX-SHELTERED RETIREMENT PLANS

While the eligibility and participation requirements for qualified plans are quite flexible, this is not the case for SEPs and SIMPLEs. The rules here are rather rigid. The same eligibility requirements that apply to qualified plans apply to 403(b) plans, as well as an additional requirement that applies to salary deferral elections. Also note that the aggregation rules discussed in this chapter apply when performing the coverage tests for 403(b) plans, SEPs, and SIMPLEs.

SEPs

As described in chapter 6, any individual (not subject to a collective bargaining agreement) who is aged 21 and has earned $450 (2001 indexed amount) in 3 of the 5 previous plan years must be a participant as of the first day of the following plan year. Take, for example, an individual who meets the $450 requirement in 1998, 1999, and 2000 and works for a company that maintains a SEP on a calendar-year basis. That person must become a participant as of January 1, 2001.

Under these inflexible requirements, all long-term employees—even part-timers—must be covered under the plan. This causes problems for larger employers that may want to establish separate plans for different groups of employees and employers with a significant number of part-time employees. Finally, note that nothing in the SEP rules stops an employer from establishing less restrictive eligibility requirements.

SIMPLEs

Similar to the SEP, SIMPLEs have totally inflexible coverage requirements. The rules, however, are different from both the qualified plan and the SEP requirements. The SIMPLE must cover any employee (including those under age 21) who earned $5,000 in two previous calendar years and is reasonably expected to earn $5,000 again in the current year. Employees subject to a collectively bargained agreement can be excluded. SIMPLEs can be maintained only on a calendar-year basis. And all employees become eligible to participate as of the January 1 after they have earned $5,000 in two prior years. Essentially, SEPs have a 3-year wait, while SIMPLEs have a 2-year waiting period.

403(b) Plans

If a 403(b) plan includes employer contributions (that are not related to a salary reduction agreement), the plan must satisfy the 410(b) requirement discussed earlier in this chapter. An additional coverage rule applies to 403(b) plan salary deferral elections. Essentially, any employee who can contribute $200 or more must be given the option to make a salary deferral election. Exceptions are made for employees who normally work fewer than 20 hours per week and employees eligible to make salary deferral elections to other types of plans, including 401(k) and 457 plans.

CHAPTER REVIEW

Answers to the review questions and the self-test questions start on page 673.

Key Terms

adoption agreement
percentage test
ratio test
average-benefit-percentage test
separate lines of business

401(a) (26) minimum-participation
   rule
controlled groups
affiliated service group
leased employee
21-and-one rule
2-year/100 percent rule

Review Questions

7-1.   List two planning tools that can be used in the plan-design process.

7-2.   Which of the following employees of the Off the Books Company (a business accounting computer software firm) are considered highly compensated employees in 2002?

	2001 Salary
Al Abernathy (96% stock owner/president)	$110,000
Becky Brooks (4% stock owner/vice president)	102,000
Charlie Carr (secretary)	87,000
Dick Dawson (treasurer)	60,000
Ellen Elko	30,000
Fran Forcey	25,000
Greg Gillespie	25,000
Hanna Hill	20,000
Isabel Ingram	20,000
James Jordan	20,000

7-3.   Describe the three ways to satisfy the minimum-coverage requirements of IRC Sec. 410(b).

7-4.   What does the separate-line-of-business rule allow an employer to do, and what are the basic requirements necessary to satisfy the separate-line-of-business rules?

7-5.   Explain the 401(a)(26) nondiscrimination rule, and describe the types of plans that are subject to this rule.

7-6.   What happens when two companies are treated as one under the controlled group or affiliated service group rules?

7-7.   Does an individual who is considered a leased employee have to be covered by the recipient company's retirement plan?

7-8.   In addition to their involvement in the Off the Books Company, Al Abernathy and Becky Brooks (see question 7–2) are 50 percent co-owners and the only employees of By the Numbers, Inc., a consulting firm that advises companies about their accounting systems. Answer the following questions about the treatment of these businesses under the nondiscrimination rules:
   a.   Will Off the Books and By the Numbers be aggregated for purposes of the nondiscrimination tests?
   b.   Assuming that Off the Books has a defined-benefit plan that covers all of its 10 employees and that By the Numbers has no plan, will the Off the Books plan pass the 410(b) nondiscrimination requirements?

  c. Assuming that By the Numbers has a defined-benefit plan that covers its two employees and Off the Books does not have a plan, will the By the Numbers plan pass the 410(b) nondiscrimination requirements?

  d. What impact does the separate-line-of-business exception have on the answer in part (c) above?

7-9. Dr. Ebenezer Smith would like to cover the minimum amount of employees in his office's qualified plan. What factors should be brought to his attention regarding the effects of avoiding coverage of rank-and-file employees?

7-10. Discuss the opportunities available for limiting participation under a qualified plan.

7-11. The B&W architectural firm is thinking of amending its qualified plan.

  a. List the pros and cons of delaying participation in the plan for as long as possible.

  b. If the B&W firm chooses to have an entry date that occurs only once annually (January 1), what are the maximum age and service requirements that can be used?

7-12. a. What are the various methods that can be used to count hours of service in a qualified plan?

  b. What are the design considerations underlying the selection of an hour-of-service provision?

7-13. Describe the coverage rules that apply to SEPs, SIMPLEs, and 403(b) plans.

Self-Test Questions

T F 7-1. In order to pick the best provisions for a client's plan, the planner must balance what the Internal Revenue Code permits with the client's objectives and pocketbook.

T F 7-2. An adoption agreement is a standardized plan approved and qualified by the Internal Revenue Service.

T F 7-3. It is important to check to make sure that each design decision supports the employer's objectives.

T F 7-4. All employees who were 5 percent owners in the current or prior year are highly compensated employees.

T F 7-5. In order to pass the 410(b) nondiscrimination requirement, an employer must pass the percentage test, the ratio test, and the average-benefits-percentage test.

T F 7-6. The ratio test requires a plan to benefit a percentage of nonhighly compensated employees that is at least 56 percent of the percentage of highly compensated employees benefited under the plan.

T   F   7-7.   The average-benefits coverage test is designed to allow large employers that cover employees under a number of different plans to more easily satisfy the coverage requirements.

T   F   7-8.   If an employer has separate lines of business, the 410(b) tests may be applied separately in each line of business, providing the businesses are operated for bona fide business reasons and have at least 50 employees.

T   F   7-9.   The 401(a)(26) rule applies only to defined-benefit plans.

T   F   7-10.   If two companies are part of an affiliated service group, both companies are treated as one for purposes of the various qualified plan rules.

T   F   7-11.   A parent-subsidiary controlled group exists if the parent company owns 80 percent of the subsidiary.

T   F   7-12.   One way employers can avoid the 410(b) coverage test is by segregating their management employees from rank-and-file employees in a separate related or subsidiary corporation.

T   F   7-13.   An individual who satisfies the definition of leased employee must be covered under the recipient company's qualified plan.

T   F   7-14.   One reason small businesses should cover all rank-and-file employees under their plans is to encourage loyalty and team spirit within their organizations.

T   F   7-15.   When considering the minimum-coverage requirements, the employer has to be just as careful when excluding highly compensated employees as when excluding nonhighly compensated employees.

T   F   7-16.   An employer can cut plan costs by delaying an employee's participation in the plan for as long as legally possible.

T   F   7-17.   The maximum age to which plan participation can be delayed is age 25.

T   F   7-18.   An employee cannot be made to wait more than one year before being eligible to participate in the plan.

T   F   7-19.   The employer can choose an entry date that, in effect, can force an employee to wait an additional 6 months after the age and service requirements are met.

T   F   7-20.   An employee will be considered to have a year of service upon working 1,000 hours for the employer.

T   F   7-21.   Under the standard-hours counting method, the employer must count each hour an employee works and each hour for which an employee is entitled to be paid in order to determine how many hours of service an employee has.

T   F   7-22.   Employees with fewer than 1,000 hours of service can be excluded from the plan.

T F 7-23. If employer A and employer B are part of a controlled group, a SEP can generally be established for the employees of employer A and exclude employer B.

T F 7-24. A SIMPLE must cover any employee who earned $5,000 in any 2 previous calendar years and is expected to earn $5,000 in the current year.

Designing Benefit Formulas and Employee Contributions

Learning Objectives

An understanding of the material in this chapter should enable the student to

8-1. Identify the rules relating to the service and compensation that can be considered in a plan's benefit formula.

8-2. Explain the strategies for satisfying the nondiscrimination rules for defined-contribution plans, as well as SEPs, SIMPLEs, and 403(b) annuity plans.

8-3. Explain the strategies for satisfying the nondiscrimination rules for defined-benefit plans.

8-4. Discuss the past and current role of voluntary employee after-tax contributions and describe the nondiscrimination rules that apply to these types of contributions.

Chapter Outline

PRELIMINARY CONCERNS

When designing the benefit structure in a qualified plan or 403(b) plan, the rules provide for a substantial degree of discretion. The primary limitation is Code Sec. 401(a)(4), which provides that benefits cannot discriminate in favor of highly compensated employees. In this context, the definition of highly compensated is the same as described in previous chapters. In this chapter, we will review the nondiscrimination rules and explore their boundaries.

First, we will give an overview of the nondiscrimination rules. Next, we will review some concepts relevant to a discussion of nondiscrimination, and then discuss the specific impact on defined-contribution and defined-benefit plans. Finally, we will compare these rules to the allocation rules that apply to SEPs and SIMPLEs.

Nondiscrimination Rules

Sec. 401(a)(4) nondiscrimination rule

All qualified plans (and 403(b) plans) must be designed to satisfy the *Sec. 401(a)(4) nondiscrimination rule* that a plan cannot discriminate in favor of highly compensated employees (HCEs) with regard to benefits or contributions. The requirements are satisfied if either the contributions or the benefits are nondiscriminatory. Under the statutory language, a plan will be deemed nondiscriminatory if contributions or benefits bear a uniform relationship to compensation. For instance, if in a defined-contribution plan contributions are allocated so that all participants receive a contribution of 3 percent of the current year's total compensation, the plan is not discriminatory. If the plan is a defined-benefit plan, and each participant earns an accrued benefit of 2 percent of compensation for the current year of service, the plan will also be deemed nondiscriminatory.

The more interesting question is to what extent the plan can deviate from the uniform percentage of compensation rule without being considered discriminatory. Ever since the enactment of ERISA, one form of discrimination has been allowed: the plan can have benefits that integrate with Social Security. Essentially, this allows a plan to discriminate in favor of the highly compensated employees to make up for the fact that the Social Security system discriminates against them. However, for many years it was unclear what else could be done, since no regulations clarified the general statutory language. Due to the lack of guidance, designing any other type of formula was risky. Since 1993, when the IRS issued almost 200 pages of final regulations, the situation has changed drastically. The regulations were quite helpful, because they

- establish objective criteria for determining whether a plan violates the nondiscrimination requirement
- clarify that a plan can demonstrate it is not discriminatory by showing that its contributions or benefits are not discriminatory
- establish several safe harbor methods for determining whether the plan satisfies the nondiscrimination standards
- create general tests for testing a plan that chooses not to adopt one of the design safe harbors

Now, with regulations that contain clear, objective rules a plan can determine at any time whether or not it is in compliance with the nondiscrimination standards, and if the employer is willing to do some testing, the plan design can really be quite creative.

After reviewing some preliminary issues, we will more fully discuss exactly what these regulations allow defined-contribution and defined-benefit plans to do.

Accrued Benefits

One key concept under the nondiscrimination rules is that discrimination is tested based on the benefit provided for that year, not the overall benefit provided under the plan. When discussing the total benefit that a participant has earned under a plan up to the present time, this amount is referred to as the participant's *accrued benefit*. This is in contrast to describing the benefit that is expected to be paid out if the participant continues in employment until normal retirement age, which is referred to as the *projected benefit*. The amount earned for the current year is simply referred to as the accrued benefit for the year.

In a defined-contribution plan, the participant's accrued benefit at any point is the participant's present account balance. The accrual for the specific year is the amount contributed to the plan on the employee's behalf for that year.

In a defined-benefit plan, the concept is the same. The accrued benefit is the benefit earned to date, using current salary and years of service. The accrued benefit earned for the year is the additional benefit that has been earned based upon the current year's salary and service.

A number of complex rules apply to the way benefits accrue under a plan. This is due to the fact that before ERISA was enacted, a participant

accrued benefit

projected benefit

would often be entitled to no benefit until he or she hit normal retirement age after, say, 30 years of employment. In this case, the entire benefit was essentially earned in the final year. This was called backloading the benefit. ERISA imposed rules to prohibit backloading. For example, under the rules, a plan's benefit formula could not be written to say that an individual earns a benefit of one percent of final average compensation times years of service for the first 10 years of service and 2 percent of final average compensation for service in excess of 10 years. This would be a prohibited backloading.

Permissible methods of determining a participant's accrued benefit are complex and are well understood by pension actuaries working with defined-benefit plans. However, we will simply discuss the most predominant method of accruing benefits today. If you were to see a benefit accrual method that was different, you might want to discuss the issue with the plan's actuary.

As discussed in chapter 4, the most common benefit formula in a defined-benefit plan today is the unit-benefit formula. In most cases, under this formula, the accrued benefit is determined by applying the formula based on the current salary and service.

Example:	The Average Corporation has a retirement benefit formula of 1.5 percent of final average compensation times years of service. Normal retirement age is 65. Joe started employment at age 30. At age 40, after 10 years of service, Joe's accrued benefit is 15 percent of his final average compensation—based on his salary history to date. He has accrued a benefit of 1.5 percent of final average compensation for the current year. His projected retirement benefit is 45 percent of final average compensation, because he will have earned 30 years of service if he continues working until normal retirement age.

Calculating Service

In chapter 4, we began to discuss the implications of the definition of service for purposes of determining the participant's benefit in a defined-benefit plan. There is one additional concern that is important to consider. Similar to the eligibility and vesting rules, there are minimum service requirements for determining whether the participant is entitled to earn a year of service under the plan. In a defined-benefit plan, a participant is not typically credited with a year of service if he or she has 1,000 hours of service (as is the requirement with the eligibility and vesting rules). In a defined-benefit plan, a year of service can be defined for benefit purposes in a variety of ways, as long as the definition of a year of service

- is applied on a reasonable and consistent basis
- does not require more hours of service than are customarily rendered during a work year in the industry involved
- accrues benefits for less than full-time service on at least a pro rata basis
- gives participants with 1,000 hours at least a partial year of service (For certain industries that customarily work for seasonal or nontraditional years, 1,000 hours must garner a full year of service.)

This last requirement means that unlike the rules that apply to eligibility and vesting, the plan can actually require up to 2,000 hours of service before a full benefit is accrued.

In a defined-contribution plan, contributions must be made for participants who earn 1,000 hours of service for the year. This means an individual can become eligible to participate, receive an allocation for one year, and, if he or she then goes part-time, may not be eligible for contributions in subsequent years. There is an exception. Participants who terminate employment before the last day of the year can be excluded from receiving a contribution for the year, even if they have earned 1,000 hours of service. However, if such persons are excluded, they are also not considered participants under the minimum-coverage requirements. Therefore, having a last-day requirement means the employer could have trouble passing the coverage tests if a significant number of employees terminate employment before the end of the year.

In either a defined-contribution or a defined-benefit plan, hours of service may be determined by using the standard-hours counting method (each hour actually worked is counted, plus hours for which the employee is entitled to be paid, such as vacations and holidays) or by using one of the equivalency methods discussed earlier. The definition of hour of service for contribution or benefit purposes can be different from the definitions used for eligibility or vesting purposes.

Compensation for Benefit-Formula Purposes

When looking at the plan's benefit or contribution formula, benefits are based, in part, on how compensation is defined in the plan. The definition of compensation can include or exclude overtime, bonuses, and other nonrecurring compensation. In the small-plan market, the plan should be designed with a liberal definition of compensation in order to maximize the amount of contributions or benefits (tax shelter) that can be made. In larger, nonintegrated plans, employers typically ask you to use the definition of compensation that best suits the company's goals. If a restrictive definition is chosen, the definition will have to satisfy IRS nondiscrimination regulations. For example, if executives are the only employees who receive bonuses and rank-and-file employees are the only ones who work overtime, a definition of compensation that includes bonuses but not overtime will be considered discriminatory. Many plans choose an inclusive definition of compensation to avoid the nondiscrimination issue.

A second rule relating to compensation is that the annual compensation considered in the benefit or contribution formula is limited to a maximum amount. In 2002, compensation is capped at $200,000.

***Example*:**	George Gotchya earns $300,000 in 2002. He notices that the company is contributing 10% of compensation for all participants in 2002 to the Company's profit-sharing plan. When he looks at his benefit statement he sees that only $20,000 has been allocated to his account. When he asks the benefit department about this, they let him know that under the law compensation can not exceed the compensation cap of $200,000 (as indexed for 2002).

Amending Benefit Formulas

The process of plan amendment is typically thought of in conjunction with changes mandated by legislative reform and changes necessitated by unforeseen business developments. Some employers may also want to gradually increase benefits for a variety of reasons, including the following:

- A gradual benefit upgrade may satisfy the employer's benefit objective of consistently improving the employee benefits package. Some employers feel that periodic movement in the employee benefits package is necessary in order to retain employees.
- Employers may be skeptical of funding unknown plan costs and may desire to ease into the plan commitment slowly.
- An employer with erratic cash flow may set up a manageable benefit formula that will gradually be increased as cash flow stabilizes, as opposed to adopting a discretionary profit-sharing plan.

The primary legal restriction on plan amendments is the anti-cutback rule. Essentially, the rule provides that benefits that have already accrued cannot be taken away from the participant. Several years ago, the anti-cutback rules were expanded to include other aspects of the participant's benefit, such as the form of benefit payment. Congress considered the form of payment to be an essential part of the benefit promise. For example, if the plan allows benefits to be paid as a life annuity or as a single sum, the plan cannot be amended to take away the single-sum form of payment.

The anti-cutback rules do not, however, prohibit amending the benefit formula on a prospective basis. This applies both to the actual benefit formula and the form of payments.

DEFINED-CONTRIBUTION PLANS

The nondiscrimination rules apply (with the exception of the target-benefit plan) in essentially the same manner for all types of defined-contribution plans. First, we will discuss three major allocation approaches that are currently used: contributions as a level percentage of compensation, integration with Social Security, and cross-testing. Then, we will apply these concepts to specific types of plans.

Level Percentage of Compensation

As mentioned above, the nondiscrimination regulations offer several methods for determining whether the plan satisfies the nondiscrimination rules. One method is to satisfy a safe harbor test that is completely design based. That is, if the plan design fits within the specified safe harbor design, the plan will be deemed to satisfy the nondiscrimination test. To satisfy the basic defined-contribution plan design safe harbor, the plan must

- have a uniform normal retirement age and vesting schedule applicable to all employees, and
- group all employer contributions and forfeitures for the plan year under a single, uniform formula that allocates the same percentage of compensation or the same dollar amount to every participant

This formula is often chosen. In larger companies, a plan that provides the same benefits to everyone is easy to administer and explain. If larger benefits are to be provided for the executives, they are provided in a nonqualified environment. Small employers also choose this approach, sometimes for the same reason and other times simply because this allocation formula is offered as an option in a prototype plan, and the owner (and unfortunately sometimes the adviser) does not fully understand other options. In today's qualified plan environment, the small employer should, even in a simple profit-sharing plan, be making an informed choice between the level percentage of pay, *integration with Social Security,* and cross-testing methods.

integration with Social Security

Integration with Social Security

Nondiscrimination regulations also provide that the benefit structure can be integrated with Social Security. Under this approach, the employer essentially gets to make larger contributions for those individuals who earn more than the taxable wage base. This is allowed because under the Social Security system, the employer does not make contributions (pay taxes) on earnings in excess of the wage base. In this way, Social Security actually discriminates against the highly compensated. This disparity can be made up, to a degree, under a qualified plan using the methods described below.

Both money-purchase and profit-sharing plans can use this method, although if an employer sponsors both types of plans only one plan can have a fully integrated formula. If a defined-contribution plan formula is integrated with Social Security, contributions may be higher (as a percentage of compensation) for those employees who earn more than a *specified integration level*. If the integration level is set at the current taxable wage base ($80,400 for 2001), HCEs may receive up to 5.7 percent of compensation in excess of the taxable wage base, as long as the employer makes contributions equaling at least 5.7 percent of total compensation.

specified integration level

Example:　　Justin, Inc. establishes a money-purchase pension plan that provides for a contribution of 5.7 percent of compensation plus 5.7 percent of compensation in excess of the taxable wage base. Justin, the owner, earns $200,000. The contribution made on his behalf for 2002 is $18,217. This is 5.7 percent of $200,000 (the maximum allowable compensation for 2002) ($11,400) plus 5.7 percent of ($200,000 minus $80,400)[1], which equals $6,817.

If the employer cannot afford to contribute at least 5.7 percent of compensation across the board, the maximum disparity will be reduced. Under the rules, the integrated portion cannot exceed the contribution that is based on total compensation. This means that if 4 percent is contributed based on total salary, an additional 4 percent can be contributed based on compensation in excess of the integration level.

Under the rules, the integration level cannot exceed the taxable wage base. The integration level can be lower, but this generally reduces the maximum disparity allowed. Table 8-1 shows the required reductions. The reason for the reduction is to remove the advantage of setting the integration level just above the compensation level of the highest rank-and-file employee.

***Example*:**   Bakery, Inc. rank-and-file workers earn a maximum of $30,000. The owner, Mr. Crueler, earns more than $200,000 (the 2002 compensation cap). He might want to consider setting the level at $30,000 (instead of the taxable wage base) to maximize the integrated contribution on his own behalf.

Even though the required reductions are supposed to take away the advantage of lowering the integration level, it may be worth running the numbers to see what happens in a particular situation. Let's look at our example above. Because $30,000 is between 20 percent and 80 percent of the taxable wage base, the maximum disparity is reduced to 4.3 percent. Comparing the two integration levels, the maximum integrated portion using the $30,000 integration level is $7,130 ($200,000 – $30,000 x 4.3 percent), while the maximum integrated portion using the taxable wage base is $6,817 ($200,000 – $80,400 x 5.7 percent). In this case, there is only a several $100 difference and it is probably not worth choosing the lower integration level. Also, next year, rank-and-file employees' salaries might go up and the integration level would need to be changed. In most cases, the "game is not worth the hunt," and the integration level should simply be set at the then-current taxable wage base.

TABLE 8-1
Maximum Integration Disparity Using Different Integration Levels

Integration Level	Maximum Disparity Allowed
Taxable Wage Base (TWB)	5.7%
Below the TWB but at least 80% of the TWB	5.4%
Below 80% of the TWB but at least 20% of the TWB.	4.3%
Below 20% of the TWB	5.7%*

*Note that the maximum disparity bounces back to 5.7 percent with a very low integration level. This is because, at very low levels, the rank-and-file employees will also be receiving a contribution based on salary above the integration level.

Choosing the Integrated Formula

An integrated formula is an appropriate method for skewing contributions toward the highly compensated employees. However, the maximum excess amount that a highly compensated employee can get is only about $6,800 (5.7 percent of the maximum compensation, $200,000 less the taxable wage base). This means if the business owner wants a full allocation of $40,000 (approximately $33,000 more), other employees would have to get almost 17 percent of compensation.

Today, if the business owner's goal is maximizing disparity, he or she should consider the cross-tested allocation formula described below. However, as you will see, these are complex plans that have some extra administrative costs. As an alternative, the integrated plan provides some disparity without much complication. A plan may be adopted using a standardized prototype plan document. This means that the inexpensive standardized plans sponsored by many insurance companies and other service providers can be adopted at little expense. Also, a plan can be designed to fit within the safe harbor, ensuring ongoing satisfaction of the nondiscrimination regulations without annual testing.

The compensation cap has created another reason for using an integrated formula. Some small business owners are perfectly happy to establish a plan that allocates the same percentage of compensation for each participant (such as 3, 4, or 5 percent of compensation). However, today, if the owner earns more than the $200,000 (indexed for 2002) compensation cap, the contribution on behalf of the owner with this type of formula will actually result in a smaller amount (as a percentage of pay) than for other employees.

Example: Mr. Nice Guy wants to contribute 5 percent of compensation for each employee. If he earns $250,000, the contribution on his behalf will actually be 4 percent of compensation! That is because 5 percent of $200,000 (indexed for 2002) equals a contribution of only $10,000 for the owner. A $10,000 contribution is only 4 percent of $250,000.

For this reason, the same business owner might consider the integrated formula simply to make up for the loss associated with the compensation cap.

Cross-testing

If the employer does not want to use a contribution or allocation formula that fits within one of the design safe harbors, virtually any other formula can be adopted as long as, on an annual basis, the plan can demonstrate compliance with the general nondiscrimination test. This can be done in one of two ways: either by testing contributions made to the plan on behalf of each participant or testing benefits that can be provided from contributions and forfeitures made for the year. Testing benefits in a defined-contribution plan is referred to as *cross-testing*. It requires converting allocations into equivalent life annuity benefit amounts using the methodology described in the regulations. Once these allocations have been converted, the general test is then performed, using benefit accrual rates based on those annuity amounts expressed as a percentage of compensation.

cross-testing

In the most practical terms, the regulations allow discrimination in favor of older workers because it takes a larger contribution to buy a specific benefit for an older worker than it does to buy the same benefit for a younger worker. This is a powerful concept, and the regulations are quite flexible. An employer that decides to go the cross-testing route must understand the following:

- *Mathematical test*—On an annual basis the administrator must perform a test to demonstrate compliance with the nondiscrimination rules.
- *Retroactive compliance*—Even if the test is not satisfied, the plan can be amended, increasing benefits for the nonhighly compensated employees, to the extent necessary to satisfy the test.
- *Additional expense*—Plan documents, IRS determination letters, and annual administration will be somewhat higher for a cross-tested plan.
- *Minimum contribution*—In most cases, when cross-testing is used, the regulations require a 5 percent minimum contribution for rank-and-file employees.

The simplest method to satisfy the general test is to allocate the contributions and forfeitures in such a way that, after conversion to a defined-benefit accrual, the rate of accrual is the same for each participant. In this way, the general nondiscrimination test will always be satisfied, without further testing. This type of allocation formula is referred to as an *age-weighted formula.*

age-weighted formula

- Example:
  - Consider a plan with three participants. Susan, aged 50, earns $150,000 per year. Her employees, Ralph and Paula, ages 35 and 28 respectively, each earn $30,000 per year. Also, assume the employer wants to contribute the maximum deductible contribution of $31,500 (15% x $210,000 total compensation). Use the following steps to determine the appropriate allocation formula that will result in a uniform benefit accrual for each participant:
  - First, determine how much would have to be contributed for the year to provide a monthly benefit at age 65 equal to one percent of each participant's compensation. One percent of Susan's $150,000 annual ($12,500 monthly) compensation is $125. One percent of Ralph's and Paula's $30,000 annual ($2,500 monthly) compensation is $25.
  - Next, assume it costs $95.38 (see table 8-2) at age 65 to provide a benefit of $1 per month payable for life. Susan would then need $125 x $95.38 = $11,922; Ralph and Paula each would need $25 x $95.38 = $2,384 at age 65 to provide a benefit of one percent of their pay.
  - Assuming plan assets earn 8.5 percent, a single contribution of $3,506 today would accumulate after 15 years to the $11,922 Susan would need at age 65 ($11,922 x .2941; see table 8-3). Similarly, a single contribution of $206 today would accumulate after 30 years to the $2,384 Ralph will need at age 65, and a single contribution of $117 today would accumulate after 37 years to the $2,384 Paula will need at age 65.
  - Under the age-weighted profit-sharing plan, the actual contribution is discretionary. That contributed will be allocated to participants in proportion to the $3,506, $206, and $117 amounts calculated above. Susan receives 91.82 percent of the total contribution, Ralph receives 5.40 percent of the contribution, and Paula receives the remaining 2.78 percent of the contribution.
  - In this example, if an age-weighted allocation method were adopted, the maximum deductible contribution would be $31,500 (15 percent of the $210,000 covered payroll). Table 8-4 shows how this $31,500 contribution is allocated under an age-weighted profit-sharing plan.

Table 8-2
Annuity Purchase Factors

1984 UP Mortality Table 8.5% Interest

Age	Amount to Purchase $1 Monthly Annuity	Age	Amount to Purchase $1 Monthly Annuity
55	$115.0104	63	$99.7222
56	113.3069	64	97.5720
57	111.5413	65	95.3829
58	109.7158	66	93.1640
59	107.8336	67	90.9263
60	105.8896	68	88.6669
61	103.8869	69	86.3737
62	101.8294	70	84.0346

Table 8-3
Discount Factor

8.5% Interest

Years before Retirement Age	Discount Factor	Years before Retirement Age	Discount Factor
1	0.921659	23	0.153150
2	0.849455	24	0.141152
3	0.782908	25	0.130094
4	0.721574	26	0.119902
5	0.665045	27	0.110509
6	0.612945	28	0.101851
7	0.564926	29	0.093872
8	0.520669	30	0.086518
9	0.479880	31	0.079740
10	0.442285	32	0.073493
11	0.407636	33	0.067736
12	0.375702	34	0.062429
13	0.346269	35	0.057539
14	0.319142	36	0.053031
15	0.294140	37	0.048876
16	0.271097	38	0.045047
17	0.249859	39	0.041518
18	0.230285	40	0.038266
19	0.212244	41	0.035268
20	0.195616	42	0.032505
21	0.180292	43	0.029959
22	0.166167	44	0.027612

TABLE 8-4
Age-Weighted Allocation Method

Name	Age	Monthly Earnings	1% Monthly Annuity	Single Sum at 65	Present Value	Allocation Percentage	Allocation of $31,500
Susan	50	$12,500	$125	$11,922	$3,506	91.57%	$28,884
Ralph	35	2,500	25	2,384	206	5.39	1,697
Paula	28	2,500	25	2,384	117	3.04	959

As you can see in the example, with the right census and appropriate employee communications, the age-weighted profit-sharing plan can be an excellent choice. It has all of the advantages of the profit-sharing plan, and can result in substantial skewing of the employer's contribution to the key employee(s). In most cases, the plan will pass the annual nondiscrimination test without actual testing, although the plan design will not technically satisfy one of the design safe harbors.

The major problem with the age-weighted formula is that it is contingent upon having the perfect employee census. In the previous example, the approach works because the NHCEs are substantially younger than the HCE. Even a single older employee can destroy the intended result. In addition, age weighting is hard to explain, and might cause employee dissatisfaction. In the example above, Paula might have difficulty understanding why Ralph is entitled to a $1,697 allocation, while she receives only $959, because they each earn the same salary. And, under revised regulations for 2002, that Paula would actually have to receive a minimum 5 percent allocation, instead of the 3 percent, is a result of the age-weighted allocation.

For these reasons, the age-weighted allocation has not become very popular. Also, the more the pension industry has grown to understand the general nondiscrimination test, the opportunities it provides have become more clear. When working with the general nondiscrimination test, the employer can essentially start with any plan allocation formula—which is then tested against the general nondiscrimination test. This design approach is much more satisfying, because the employer can first create a design that meets its goals, and then analyze whether the design satisfies the test.

For the small employer, this might mean allocating $40,000 (the maximum allocation under the 415 limits in 2002) to the highly compensated, and 5 percent of compensation to all other employees (the minimum allocation prescribed under the proposed regulations). Once the objective has been determined, projected contributions are then translated into an accrued benefit for each employee, which is tested under the general nondiscrimination test. If the plan passes, then the design can be adopted. If not, then the contribution level for the nonhighly compensated can be raised, or the contribution for the owners can be lowered, until the test is satisfied.

The actual mechanics of cross-testing are quite complex, and are beyond the scope of this book. However, note that the following objectives can generally be accomplished with a cross-tested plan:

- *Skewing contributions*—When the average age of the business' owners is 10 years or more older than the nonhighly compensated employees, cross-testing will allow the plan to establish an allocation formula in which the owners receive the maximum $40,000 allocation allowable under IRC Sec. 415 (indexed in 2002), while the rank-and-file employees receive substantially less— typically 5 percent of compensation.
- *Older nonhighly compensated employees*—Unlike age-weighting, cross-testing works even with several older nonhighly compensated employees—as long as the average age of the owners is somewhat greater than the average age of the nonhighly compensated.
- *Design flexibility*—One other substantial advantage is the incredible design flexibility allowed under the general test. Often an employer will want to make a larger contribution for a specific group of employees (for example, longer service employees or salespersons). Before these regulations, an employer had little flexibility. Now the opportunities for creative plan designs that meet a number of planning objectives are almost limitless. For example, the employer may decide to contribute 5 percent of pay for new employees, 6 percent for employees with 5 or more years of service, and 7 percent for employees with 10 or more years of service.

Any employer considering a plan with a cross-tested allocation formula must be advised of certain disadvantages. The plan will need to be tested for discrimination on an annual basis. Gathering accurate employee data, especially age information, can be a daunting task. Preliminary testing (at the beginning of the year) and final testing will have to be performed. The plan design may have to change on an annual basis if census data or employee salaries change. For example, the plan may satisfy the rules in year one with a 5 percent allocation for NHCEs, while the next year a 6 percent allocation may be required. A design change must be accompanied by a properly timed plan amendment. A plan sponsor will need to adopt an individually designed plan and will have to request an IRS determination letter under the general nondiscrimination test with a minimum $1,250 filing fee.

**YOUR FINANCIAL SERVICES PRACTICE
IRS RECONSIDERS NONDISCRIMINATION REGULATIONS**

As we go to press, the IRS has issued new proposed regulations that would modify the current final nondiscrimination regulations. The rules are proposed (not finalized) and do not become effective until plan years beginning after January 1, 2002. For a number of years, the IRS has criticized the use of cross-testing to provide what the IRS considers unfair disparity between the benefits of rank-and-file employees and the owners. Under the proposed regulations, a defined-contribution plan can continue to use the cross-testing approach, but, in most cases, the plan must now provide a minimum contribution of 5 percent of compensation for the nonhighly compensated employees.

Each of these disadvantages ultimately relates to one element: additional cost. The prospective client should be given a clear picture of just what to expect in additional fees. The additional costs will not stop the employer if the savings under the cross-tested plan (compared to an age-weighted or integrated plan) are substantial.

Types of Plans and Nondiscrimination Approaches

Now that we have looked at the nondiscrimination rules in general, let's take a look at the types of choices employers commonly make with specific types of plans.

Profit-Sharing Plans

Profit-sharing plans are designed using all three approaches. Today, almost all employers that have been interested in age-weighting or cross-testing have chosen the versatile profit-sharing plan. Discretionary contributions, in-service withdrawals, and the ability to circumvent the qualified joint and survivor annuity rules (see chapter 10) are meaningful qualities for the small business owner in today's business environment.

401(k) Plans

Remember that 401(k) plans are profit-sharing plans. If the 401(k) plan has a profit-sharing type contribution, an allocation could be designed that takes advantage of the cross-testing flexibility. Nondiscrimination testing can be confusing in a 401(k) plan because of the different types of contributions allowed and the nondiscrimination rules that apply to different types of contributions. Let's review:

- *Employee salary deferral contributions*—Nondiscrimination is tested solely through the ADP test (see chapter 5). The 401(a)(4) rules do not apply.
- *Employer matching contributions*—Nondiscrimination is tested solely through the ACP test (which is discussed later in this chapter). The 401(a)(4) rules do not apply.
- *Employee after-tax contributions*—Nondiscrimination is tested solely through the ACP test.
- *Employer profit-sharing contributions*—Only these types of contributions must satisfy the nondiscrimination rules of 401(a)(4) discussed in this section.

403(b) Plans

403(b) plans, like 401(k) plans, must be analyzed feature by feature. 403(b) plans are subject to the following discrimination requirements:

- *Employee salary deferral contributions*—Unlike in the 401(k) plan, salary deferrals in a 403(b) plan are not subject to any nondiscrimination requirements.
- *Employer matching contributions*—If the 403(b) plan has a matching contribution, these contributions *do* have to satisfy the ACP test (which is discussed later in this chapter). The 401(a)(4) rules do not apply.
- *Employer nonelective contributions*—If the 403(b) plan has an employer contribution for all eligible employees, these types of contributions must satisfy the nondiscrimination rules of 401(a)(4) discussed in this section. Like profit-sharing plans, the 403(b) plan can use either of the design safe harbors: level percentage of compensation or integrated with Social Security. The allocation formula also can take advantage of the cross-testing or age-weighted approaches.

Money-Purchase Pension Plans

Even though money-purchase pension plans can take advantage of cross-testing, most employers choosing this allocation approach have chosen profit-sharing plans—where contributions are discretionary. Money-purchase plans more typically contain contributions that are a level percentage of compensation or that are integrated with Social Security.

Target-Benefit Pension Plans

The contribution formula established under a target-benefit plan could be tested under the general nondiscrimination test. However, the regulations provide a separate design safe harbor for such plans, and employers establishing such a plan will probably want to take advantage of the design safe harbor.

Several threshold issues determine whether a target plan is suited for a particular employer. First, a target plan, like the age-weighted profit-sharing plan, will not work with even a single older NHCE. Second, because the target plan is a pension plan, the employer must be willing to commit to a timely annual contribution. And unlike a defined-benefit plan, the annual contribution is a fixed amount. Finally, the employer must be willing to live with pension plan requirements (including no in-service distributions and the qualified joint and survivor annuity requirements).

Because today an age-weighted profit-sharing plan could be designed to give similar results as in the target-benefit plan, the employer is more likely to choose either the age-weighted or more flexible cross-tested profit-sharing plan. Most employers today are simply not willing to make a commitment to a fixed annual contribution. And for those few who are willing to commit to annual contributions, a defined-benefit plan is often the better choice, due to the flexibility of annual contributions and the ability (in the right circumstances) for the employer to contribute more on the key employee's behalf than in a defined-contribution plan.

SEPs

As you learned in chapter 6, the contribution to a SEP must either be allocated as a level percentage of compensation or integrated with Social Security (in the manner described above). The SEP cannot use a cross-tested or age-weighted allocation formula.

SIMPLEs

Contributions to a SIMPLE are subject to even more rigid rules. If the employer makes a profit-sharing type contribution, all eligible participants must receive 2 percent of compensation. If instead, the employer makes a matching contribution, the match is fixed as a dollar-for-dollar match, up to the first 3 percent of compensation deferred.

DEFINED-BENEFIT PLANS

The nondiscrimination rules provide design safe harbors for plans that provide level benefits and those that integrate with Social Security. Again, if the employer wants to establish a plan that does not fit within the safe harbor, the formula can be defined in any way, as long as the plan can demonstrate nondiscrimination on an annual basis. Each of these three alternatives is discussed below.

Uniform Percentage of Compensation

There are actually three design-based safe harbors under the regulations. For all three, the plan must have the same benefit formula (and form of payment) for all participants and a uniform retirement age. Most important, the benefit formula must provide, at the normal retirement age—for all participants with the same years of service—either the same dollar benefit or the same percentage of average annual compensation. Also, the plan cannot require mandatory employee contributions.

All of the following designs can satisfy the safe harbors:

- *Unit credit plans*—As long as the above requirements are met, the plan can use a standard unit credit plan that accrues the benefit each year based on the plan's benefit formula.
- *Fractional accruals*—A unit-benefit formula or a flat percentage of pay (with a 25-years-of-service requirement) that accrues benefits using the fractional accrual method can also satisfy the design safe harbor.
- *Fully insured plans*—As long as the above requirements are met and the plan satisfies the definition of a fully insured plan under Code Sec. 412(I), the plan satisfies the nondiscrimination requirements.

In addition, any of these approaches will still satisfy the design safe harbor if the plan is integrated with Social Security as described below.

Integration with Social Security

Similar to the defined-contribution plan, the defined-benefit formula can be designed to provide a greater percentage of benefits for highly paid employees than for rank-and-file employees. Even though the rules are conceptually similar to defined-contribution plans, the integration-level approach for defined-benefit plans applies somewhat differently.

The rules also allow for an integration approach in which a benefit is described and then a portion of an individual's Social Security benefit is subtracted from the total (referred to as *offset integration*). At one time, this was the most common integration approach in defined-benefit plans. However, under current law, this approach rarely works as well as the integration-level approach and is, therefore, not used very often. This approach, therefore, will not be discussed here.

Defined-benefit plans that use the integration-level approach are called *excess plans* (or *stepped-up plans*). Here's how an excess plan works:

- The plan has a specified integration level, which is tied to compensation.
- The benefit formula can provide the participant an additional benefit for compensation earned above the integration level.
- The additional or "excess" benefit cannot exceed either of the following limits:
  - The excess benefit percentage cannot be more than 0.75 percent of compensation for each year of service and an excess benefit can only be provided on a maximum of 35 years of service, meaning that the maximum excess benefit can not exceed 26.25 percent of compensation.
  - In no case can the additional benefit provided based on compensation in excess of the integration level exceed the benefit provided based on total compensation.

covered compensation

The integration level in a defined-benefit plan is almost always *covered compensation,* which is the average of the taxable wages for the individual participant using the 35-year period ending with the year that the employee reaches his or her Social Security retirement age. Table 8-5 provides a portion of a covered compensation table for 2001. The concept of covered compensation is confusing for two reasons. First, as you can see in the table, covered compensation is different for participants of different ages, because the average of taxable wage bases depends on the years worked. Older workers will have lower covered compensation levels than younger workers, because the taxable wage bases over their final 35 years of work are lower than those for younger workers using more current years. Second, every year the table for covered compensation changes as cost-of-living increases apply. This means that the covered compensation amount keeps increasing as an individual gets older. Also, note that to satisfy the integration rules, the plan must define final-average compensation as at least the 3 highest years of compensation.

Example: The ABC Corporation has a defined-benefit plan with an integrated benefit formula. The formula provides participants with an annual benefit of one percent of final average compensation (defined as the average of the highest 3 years of compensation) plus an additional .5 percent of compensation earned in excess of an individual's covered compensation. The additional integrated portion of the benefit is capped at 35 years of service. This benefit formula complies with the integration rules. The excess benefit does not exceed .75 percent per year of service and the excess is only provided on the first 35 years of benefit service. Let's calculate a benefit for Joe who retires at age 65 in 2001 with 30 years of benefit service and a final average salary of $55,000. Joe's covered compensation is $37,212. Joe's benefit is ($55,000 x .30) + ($23,872 x .15) = $19,168.20.

Table 8-5
2001 Covered Compensation

Calendar Year of Birth	Calendar Year of Social Security Retirement Age	1998 Covered Compensation
1935	2000	$35,100
1936	2001	37,212
1937	2002	39,312
1938	2004	43,464
1939	2005	45,540
1940	2006	47,616
1941	2007	49,656
1942	2008	51,648
1943	2009	53,568
1944	2010	55,452
1945	2011	57,312
1946	2012	59,148
1947	2013	60,936
1948	2014	62,580

Other Plan-Design Alternatives

If the employer with a defined-benefit plan wants to establish a benefit formula that does not satisfy any of the safe harbor designs, the plan will have to satisfy the general nondiscrimination tests. Two types of plans are likely to have plan designs that do not satisfy the safe harbors. The first group includes plans that historically have had nonconforming benefit formulas. In other words, the sponsor adopted a formula in the past that does not today satisfy the nondiscrimination safe harbors. If the plan is still meeting the objectives of both the employer and employees, the sponsor may choose not to bring the formula into compliance, but instead to go through the testing process.

The second group will be employers that choose to provide different benefit levels for different groups of employees in one plan. The employer might, for example, want to provide different benefit levels for employees of certain classes, in different geographic locations, or in different subsidiaries. The employer here has two choices: either establish one plan with different benefit levels and go through annual testing, or establish separate plans for each group. Here, each plan will have to satisfy the minimum-coverage requirements of Code Sec. 410(b). Under the law, either approach will generally work, meaning that the employer will make the decision based upon its own goals and objectives and not on the legal limitations.

VOLUNTARY EMPLOYEE CONTRIBUTIONS

Today, in most cases, qualified plan benefits are funded by employer contributions with the exception of pretax elective salary deferral contributions that participants make to 401(k) plans, 403(b) plans and SIMPLEs. However, qualified plans are technically allowed to provide for another type of contribution, the *voluntary after-tax employee contribution*.

voluntary after-tax employee contribution

Prior to 1987, this feature was quite common in qualified plans because up to 10 percent of compensation could be contributed by any employee without having to consider any of the other contribution limits, and without regard to which employees elected to make contributions. This feature was often used primarily by the business owner and other highly compensated employees.

Beginning in 1987, however, many of these provisions were eliminated due to new nondiscrimination requirements and a new rule requiring that all such contributions count against the maximum annual contribution limit (the lesser of 100 percent or $40,000 as indexed for 2002) for defined-contribution plans. Because of this, most plans eliminated contributions after 1986, however, many plans still have contributions that were made prior to this date. This is important to note when dealing with a client who is receiving a pension distribution. The principal amount of employee contributions is treated as basis, and is not subject to income tax. Earnings are subject to the same taxation rules that apply to other pension distributions.

The only place where after-tax contributions are still found is in 401(k) plans, where employees are sometimes given the opportunity to make contributions on a pretax or after-tax basis. Some employees prefer the after-tax contributions because they can be withdrawn more easily than pretax contributions, which are subject to the special withdrawal requirements discussed in chapter 5.

Nondiscrimination Requirements for Employee Contributions and Employer Matching Contributions

Plans that provide for voluntary employee after-tax contributions must satisfy a nondiscrimination test that is similar to the actual deferral percentage (ADP) test called the *actual contribution percentage* (ACP) test. This test considers after-tax contributions along with matching employer contribution. Under the ACP test, instead of comparing the salary deferrals—as a percentage of compensation—we are comparing the matching and after-tax contributions as a percentage of compensation.

In operation, the test is virtually the same as the ADP test. In order to pass the ACP nondiscrimination test for employer matching contributions and employee contributions, one of two requirements must be satisfied:

1. *The 1.25 requirement.* Under this requirement, the contribution percentage for all highly compensated employees for the current year cannot be more than 125 percent of the contribution percentage for nonhighly compensated employees for the previous year.
2. *The 200 percent/2 percent difference requirement.* Under this requirement, the contribution percentage for highly compensated employees for the current year cannot be more than 200 percent of the contribution percentage (in the previous year) for nonhighly compensated employees, and the difference between the two groups must be 2 percent or less.

Note: For purposes of the nondiscrimination tests, the term *highly compensated employee* is defined as described under the ADP test in chapter 5.

Table 5-2 (see chapter 5) can be used to determine the maximum contribution percentage limits for highly compensated employees. For example, if the contribution percentage is 6 percent of compensation for nonhighly compensated employees, then the highly compensated employees can have an 8 percent contribution percentage.

CHAPTER REVIEW

Answers to the review questions and the self-test questions start on page 673.

Key Terms

Sec. 401(a)(4) nondiscrimination rule

accrued benefit

projected benefit

integration with Social Security

specified integration level

cross-testing

age-weighted formula

covered compensation

voluntary after-tax employee contribution

Review Questions

8-1. Does allocating 3 percent of compensation to each participant in a profit-sharing plan satisfy the 401(a)(4) nondiscrimination requirements?

8-2. Answer the following questions regarding accrued benefits:
   a. What does the term *accrued benefit* mean in a defined-contribution plan?
   b. What does the term *accrued benefit* mean in a defined-benefit plan?
   c. What does the term *projected benefit* mean in a defined-benefit plan?

8-3. In a defined-benefit plan, what is the maximum number of hours of service an employer can require in order to credit a participant with a full year of service for benefit purposes? If the maximum number of hours is required, what happens if the participant earns only 1,000 hours of service?

8-4. Describe the compensation cap and its impact on the benefits of highly compensated employees.

8-5. Answer the following questions regarding Social Security integration in defined-contribution plans:
   a. If the employer contributes 8 percent of total compensation for each participant, how much more can be contributed for employees who earn more than the taxable wage base (assuming this is the integration level)?
   b. If the employer contributes 3 percent of total compensation for each participant, how much more can be contributed for employees who earn more than the taxable wage base (assuming this is the integration level)?
   c. If the employer contributes 8 percent of total compensation for each participant, how much more can be contributed for employees who earn more than $70,000 (assuming this is the integration level)?

8-6. Describe what cross-testing is and how it can be used to get a larger percentage of the employer's contribution to the older, highly compensated employees.

8-7.   What is the major limitation with an age-weighted contribution formula?

8-8.   What are the strengths and limitations of the cross-tested formula?

8-9.   What type of defined-contribution plan is most often used with the age-weighted or cross-tested contribution formula?

8-10.   Describe the nondiscrimination requirements that apply to 401(k) plans.

8-11.   Describe the types of allocation formulas that can be contained in a SEP.

8-12.   Weese has a final average salary of $50,000 and has worked for the employer for 20 years. Weese's covered compensation is $24,000, and the plan's benefit formula provides for one percent of final-average compensation plus .75 percent of final-average salary multiplied by years of service (limited to 35 years of service). Does the plan satisfy the integration rules, and what is Weese's benefit under the plan?

8-13.   Explain the nondiscrimination requirements for employer matching contributions and employee contributions.

Self-Test Questions

T   F   8-1.   Code Sec. 401(a)(4) requires that the plan cannot discriminate in favor of highly compensated employees with regard to benefits or contributions provided under the plan.

T   F   8-2.   Under current law, the plan sponsor has little assurance whether the plan's contribution or benefit formula satisfies the 401(a)(4) nondiscrimination requirement.

T   F   8-3.   In a defined-benefit plan, an individual's accrued benefit at any time is the promised benefit at that time based on compensation and service as of that date.

T   F   8-4.   A plan's definition of compensation can generally include or exclude overtime, bonuses, and other nonrecurring compensation.

T   F   8-5.   If employee Able earns $300,000 and is a participant in a money-purchase plan that pays an annual benefit of 10 percent of salary, employee Able's annual addition to his participant account is $30,000.

T   F   8-6.   Once the plan's benefit formula is in place, it cannot be amended unless the plan is terminated.

T   F   8-7.   A defined-contribution plan that provides for a contribution for each employee in the amount of 4 percent of compensation plus 5.7 percent of compensation in excess of the taxable wage satisfies the Social Security safe harbor provisions.

T   F   8-8. In order to take advantage of the maximum disparity of 5.7 percent, a defined-contribution plan must either set the integration level at the current year's taxable wage base or a set number that is less than 20 percent of the taxable wage base.

T   F   8-9. Choosing an integrated formula in a defined-contribution plan allows the owner to receive the lion's share of the contribution.

T   F   8-10. A SEP can have a cross-tested allocation formula.

T   F   8-11. The most common integration level in a defined-benefit plan is covered compensation, which refers to the average of the participant's taxable wage bases for the 35-year period ending with the year the individual attains the Social Security retirement age.

T   F   8-12. Employer matching contributions and employee after-tax contributions are subject to a nondiscrimination test similar to the actual deferral percentage test used for 401(k) plans.

NOTES

1. In this example, if the plan is integrated at the taxable wage base, the 2002 wage base should be used in the calculation. At the time of this writing, this number was not yet available.

9

Helping Clients Choose the Best Loan, Vesting, and Retirement-Age Provisions

---

Learning Objectives

An understanding of the material in this chapter should enable the student to

9-1. Describe the legal requirements pertaining to a loan provision and the desirability of incorporating a loan provision into a client's plan.

9-2. Explain the vesting requirements applicable to qualified and other tax-advantaged plans.

9-3. Identify the design considerations associated with choosing normal, early, and deferred retirement provisions.

Chapter Outline

Three of the most important decisions in designing a plan are:

- deciding whether the plan should permit loans
- choosing the plan's vesting schedules
- choosing the plan's retirement-age provisions

Decisions in these areas significantly affect the makeup of the plan's participants, the makeup of the employer's work force, and the employer's costs.

PLAN LOANS

Most types of retirement plans may have provisions that allow participants the opportunity to borrow from the plan. Loans allow participants the ability to access funds without tax consequences. However, loans also add administrative expense and may undermine retirement planning objectives. The decision whether or not to have a loan provision depends upon the type of plan, plan objectives, and the legal restrictions upon plan loans. An informed decision must address the following two important concerns:

- Are plan loans appropriate?
- What legal restrictions will apply?

Are Plan Loans Appropriate for Your Clients?

The Advantages and Disadvantages of Plan Loans

The primary reason to include a loan provision in the plan is so employees (including executives and business owners to the extent legally permitted) can enjoy the current beneficial use of their retirement savings. In other words, a loan provision in a qualified plan provides the best of both worlds—tax shelter for plan contributions and access to sheltered funds when the need arises without causing a taxable distribution.

There is another side to the story, however. Several good reasons for *not* allowing plan loans also exist. First, a loan provision in the plan may be inconsistent with the employer's objective of providing retirement security. Funds used to repay plan loans are often taken from funds that would have been retirement savings. This might create an unwanted dependence on the employer's plan as the sole source of retirement funds, especially when loans are taken by employees who are close to retirement. Second, loan provisions are labor-intensive and costly to administer. They are especially troublesome from an administrative point of view in dealing with the default of a loan. Employers typically do not relish being put in the untenable position of being a credit agency or hounding their employees for payment. What's more, if a loan is defaulted, serious consequences abound, such as the following:

- There is an immediate tax liability to the participant, because the defaulted loan is treated as a current distribution.
- The participant may incur a 10 percent penalty if the distribution occurs prior to age 59 1/2.

Despite their pitfalls, loan provisions are very popular for the following reasons:

- Business owners are eligible for plan loans to the same extent as other employees.
- Administrative problems with plan loans can be minimized by using a program that would only permit loans under a stipulated number of circumstances, such as for college education payments, purchase of a home, or demonstrated financial hardship.
- Administrative problems can also be mitigated by placing a $1,000 minimum on the amount of any loan, thus eliminating pesky small loans.
- Problems with loan defaults can be eliminated if the employer requires payroll deduction for loan repayments and requires complete repayment upon termination of employment. If the participant defaults, benefits payable are reduced by the outstanding balance (resulting in a taxable distribution of the amount of default).

Types of Plans

The degree to which a loan provision is considered desirable depends in part on the type of plan involved. Clients who have a 401(k) plan or 403(b) plan should strongly consider a loan provision. In these plans it can be difficult to get the enrollment necessary to pass the actual deferral percentage test, if participants are concerned that elective deferrals will be locked up until retirement. However, by "unlocking" plan funds through a loan provision, an employer may be able to entice the required participation to satisfy the applicable tests.

Sometimes loan provisions are considered for pension plans of the defined-contribution type. Because pension plans are prohibited from making in-service withdrawals—that is, distributing funds prior to death, disability, termination of employment, or retirement—a loan provision allows "use" of plan assets during employment. However, pension plans of the defined-benefit type seldom contain a loan provision. First, calculating the maximum loan amount requires an actuarial calculation, increasing administrative expenses. Second, a loan provision undermines the concern for retirement security, usually the number one reason for adopting the plan.

For profit-sharing plans the consideration is somewhat different. Because a profit-sharing plan may be designed to allow in-service withdrawals, a loan provision is not necessary to provide employees access to plan benefits during employment. However, loans do provide for the use of funds on a tax-free basis.

Employee stock ownership plans (ESOPs) generally do not have loan provisions because plan assets are required to be "primarily invested in employer securities" meaning that the plan will not have sufficient cash investments to support a loan provision. For the same reason, stock bonus plans that are heavily invested in employer securities should not have a loan provision.

Finally, note that plan loans are prohibited in SEPs, SIMPLEs, and IRAs. Table 9-1 summarizes the applicable rules.

Legal Parameters for Plan Loans

Plans designed to permit loans must adhere to certain requirements that govern the availability, amount, duration, interest, security, and repayment of the loan.

Loan Availability

As was previously stated, your client can choose to include the option for plan loans or to exclude the option altogether. If plan loans are made available, however, they must be available to all participants on a reasonably equivalent basis and must not be available to highly compensated employees in an amount greater than the amount made available to other employees. In addition, loans must

- be adequately secured
- be made in accordance with specific plan provisions
- bear a reasonable (market) rate of interest

Almost all plans use the participant's accrued benefit as security. Other security can be appropriate, but most plans will not want to get into this because of the administrative complexities. If the participant defaults on the loan, the benefit will be reduced in the amount of the outstanding principal

TABLE 9-1
Desirability of Plan Loans

Plan	Consideration
401(k) plan	A loan provision entices participation so that the actual deferral percentage test can be passed.
403(b) plan	A loan provision entices participation so that the 401(m) test can be passed.
Contributory plan	A loan provision entices participation so that the 401(m) test and 410(b) nondiscrimination tests can be passed.
Pension plans (money-purchase, target-benefit and cash-balance)	A loan provision can get around the restriction against in-service withdrawals.
Pension plans (defined-benefit)	Loan provisions are not frequently available because calculating the maximum loan amount requires an actuarial calculation.
Profit-sharing plan	A loan provision is less crucial, because in-service withdrawals are allowed. However, the loan does provide for tax-free access.
Defined-benefit plan	Although a loan provision can be useful (see pension plan), it is often forsaken because of administrative problems.
ESOP	A loan provision is seldom used because of the requirement that the plan be invested primarily in employer stock and because the plan often lacks the cash to loan to participants.
Stock bonus plan	A loan provision is a problem if the plan lacks cash to support the program.
SEP	No loans are permitted.
SIMPLE	No loans are permitted.
IRA	No loans are permitted.

(and accrued interest). If this happens, the participant now has a taxable distribution subject to ordinary income tax and the 10 percent early distribution excise tax, if the participant has not attained age 59 1/2 (see chapter 25).

YOUR FINANCIAL SERVICES PRACTICE: PLAN LOANS

Some financial services professionals use loan provisions to overcome the employer's common objection about locking up retirement funds. In some cases, this may eliminate the final hurdle to a sale. On the other hand, some financial services professionals are not fond of plan loans because loans take potential investment funds away from the asset pool. The decision is, of course, up to the plan sponsor, who will probably not be as concerned with depleting the asset pool.

Another issue that comes up with loans is that in plans subject to the qualified joint and survivor annuity requirements (see chapter 10), both spouses must sign off on the loan. This is because a loan default can reduce the participant's benefit, which affects the spousal rights to that benefit as well.

Restrictions on Amounts and Repayments

In addition to rules on loan availability, there are limits on the amount each participant can borrow. The limit is $50,000 or one-half of the vested account balance, whichever is less. Under the tax rules, a participant may borrow up to $10,000 even if this amount is more than one-half of the vested benefit. For example, a person with a vested benefit of $13,000 could still borrow up to $10,000. However, in practice, employers do not allow loans in excess of the 50 percent limit, because DOL regulations would require security other than the participant's vested account balance—which would be complex to administer.

A participant's loan must be repayable by its terms within 5 years. The one exception to the 5-year rule is if a loan is used to acquire a participant's principal residence. In this case, a reasonable repayment schedule (presumably over the life of any mortgage involved) will suffice. Another important factor concerning the 5-year rule is that "sham" repayments are not allowed. Before 1987, the 5-year rule was subject to frequent abuse. Participants would repay the loan on the last possible date and take out the loan again immediately after repayment. For this reason, the rules were designed so that the $50,000 limit is reduced by the highest outstanding loan balance during the one-year period ending the day before the loan date. The rules were also changed to add a restriction that requires level amortization of loan repayments of principal and interest being made at least quarterly.

Example: Bill Smith borrows $50,000 from his qualified plan and pays off the loan on a level amortization basis over 5 years ($10,000 annually). At the end of 5 years when the loan is repaid, Bill wants to take out another loan. The maximum amount available for this second loan is $40,000 (the $50,000 limit minus $10,000 paid back in the prior year).

Interest on a plan loan will be treated as consumer interest that is not deductible by the employee as an itemized deduction unless the loan is secured by a principal residence. Because plans generally do not want to make loans on this basis, the tax deduction is rarely available. Note that even if a plan wanted to allow them, such loans are specifically prohibited in situations where the loan is (1) made to a key employee, as defined by the Code's rules for top-heavy plans (see chapter 10) or (2) made in a 401(k) or 403(b) plan.

VESTING

Determining a plan's vesting schedule is another important and difficult planning decision. This is partly because of the common misconception that retirement benefits are a form of deferred wages owned by the employee. This misconception is fostered by the fact that benefits are usually related to salary levels. The fact is, however, that retirement benefits are not a deferred wage but rather a wage-related benefit that is contingent on the employee's ability to meet the requirements of the vesting schedule.

Understanding the Vesting System

The vesting concept is perhaps best understood in light of its history. Before the passage of the Employee Retirement Income Security Act (ERISA) in 1974, it was accepted practice in some companies to offer retirement benefits only to employees who retired from the company after completing long periods of service (for example, 30 years). The result was a system that ignored the retirement needs of many, bound others in an unwanted fashion to their company, and shortchanged employees whose service was long but not long enough. Partly as a result of a television documentary and subsequent congressional hearings that publicized horror stories of long-service employees left penniless during retirement, Congress recognized the injustices of this situation and enacted ERISA, which ensured that employees would receive some retirement benefits if they terminated employment prior to reaching normal retirement age. ERISA established rules for determining how much service is required before benefits become nonforfeitable. These rules were called *vesting schedules*. Subsequent to ERISA the rules have been changed several times, each law providing less and less required service before full vesting occurs.

Vesting Schedules

An employer is required to choose a vesting schedule that is at least as favorable as one of two statutory schedules: the 5-year cliff vesting or the 3-through-7-year graded vesting. Note, as described further in chapter 10, that a plan that is considered top-heavy must actually adopt a vesting schedule that meets even more rigid requirements.

The 5-year cliff vesting is a schedule under which an employee who terminates employment prior to the completion of 5 years of service will be entitled to no benefit (zero percent vested). After 5 years of service, the employee becomes fully entitled to (100 percent vested in) the benefit that has accrued on his or her behalf. Five-year cliff vesting is easy to remember if you visualize an employee climbing a cliff for 5 years and finally becoming entitled to the benefits upon reaching the top. The cliff vesting schedule is as follows:

5-Year Cliff Vesting

Years of Service	Percentage Vested
0–4	0
5 or more	100

The other statutory vesting schedule, known as the 3-through-7-year graded schedule, requires no vesting until the third year of service has been completed; at that point the vested portion of the accrued benefit increases 20 percent for each year served.

3-through-7-Year Graded Vesting

Years of Service	Percentage Vested
0–2	0
3	20
4	40
5	60
6	80
7 or more	100

While these two schedules constitute the legally mandated requirements, more liberal vesting schedules can be employed if desired. For example, an employer could establish a 2-year cliff vesting schedule or a 4-year graded schedule, where the participant earned an additional 25 percent vesting for each year of service.

When examining the issue of vesting, it is important to note that the vesting schedules just described apply primarily in the case of an individual who terminates employment (on a voluntary or involuntary basis) prior to reaching a plan's normal retirement age—or some other stated event that triggers a benefit under the plan. Under the law, an individual who reaches the plan's normal retirement age must become 100 percent vested regardless of the number of years of service earned.

***Example*:**   If Don Fields starts working for the Bonanza Company at age 62 and the Bonanza plan has 5-year cliff vesting and a normal retirement age of 65, Don must be 100 percent vested at the plan's normal retirement age of 65 in spite of the fact that he is not entitled to anything under the vesting schedule.

Also, it is typical for a plan to fully vest participants—regardless of the years of service performed—at attainment of an early retirement age, upon disability, or at death. These decisions are voluntary, and are based on the plan's objectives (discussed in chapter 10).

Another important consideration is that the participant's benefit attributable to employee after-tax contributions or employee pretax salary deferral elections in a 401(k) plan must be 100 percent vested at all times. This rule applies both to contributions and to investment experience thereon. For this reason, any plan that has either type of employee contributions must keep separate accounts for employer and such employee contributions.

In today's pension environment, there are numerous other situations where benefits must be fully vested at all times. All of them are summarized below. As you can see, Congress keeps whittling away at the vesting restrictions. This is probably because anything less than full and immediate vesting limits benefit "portability"—an important concern to a mobile workforce that changes jobs frequently.

- *SEPs and SIMPLEs*—Contributions to a SEP or SIMPLE must be fully vested at all times (chapter 6).
- *403(b) plans*—Employer contributions to a 403(b) plan are generally fully vested. Such amounts could technically be subject to a vesting

schedule, but because of the operation of the exclusion ratio, it is impractical to do so (chapter 6).

- *Plan termination*—Benefits must become fully vested upon a full or partial plan termination (chapter 14).
- *Safe harbor 401(k) plans*—Contributions to a 401(k) SIMPLE and contributions made to satisfy the 401(k) safe harbor provisions must be fully vested (chapter 5).
- *Two-year eligibility rule*—In exchange for the ability to exclude employees for 2 years (instead of one), contributions must be fully vested (chapter 7).

In addition, the vesting schedules discussed above must be modified in two situations. First if the plan is top-heavy (discussed in chapter 10) the plan has to use a vesting schedule that is as favorable as 3-year cliff vesting (fully vested after 3 years) or a 6-year graded vesting schedule. Under the 6-year schedule the participant must earn 20 percent vesting after 2 years of service and an additional 20 percent for each additional year of service (fully vested after 6 years).

The same vesting schedules that are used for top-heavy vesting must also be used for employer matching contributions in 401(k) plans as well.

Example: Bunny, Inc. maintains a 401(k) plan that has employee salary deferrals, employer matching contributions and employer profit-sharing contributions. Salary deferrals must be fully vested at all times. The employer wants to use cliff vesting for the employer matching and profit-sharing contributions. The matching contribution account must fully vest participants after 3 years of service. If the plan is not top-heavy, the profit-sharing account can use 5-year cliff vesting.

Choosing the Most Appropriate Vesting Schedule

The various vesting schedule choices and their exceptions obviously have design implications you must consider in helping your clients make the best choice. The most important vesting design question is whether an employer should choose a restrictive schedule (using the maximum wait allowed) or a liberal vesting schedule.

To the employer, the major advantage of choosing a restrictive vesting schedule is that it may be able to cut costs attributable to employee turnover.

forfeiture

reallocated forfeiture

When employees terminate employment prior to being fully vested, the nonvested portion of the accrued benefit (referred to as a *forfeiture*) can be used to reduce future employer contributions. For example, if five employees terminate employment with the National Furniture Company, each with a $4,000 forfeited benefit, National's contribution for next year is reduced by $20,000. The employer also has the choice in any defined-contribution plan to use forfeitures as an additional contribution for remaining employees (in pension parlance, this is referred to as *reallocated forfeitures*). Reallocated forfeitures do not result in a direct cost savings, but they do allow the employer the opportunity to provide bigger benefits for long-term highly compensated employees—at no extra cost. (*Planning Note:* Forfeitures that are reallocated to employees are added to other contributions, and the aggregate amount cannot exceed the 25 percent or $35,000 limit. If the plan's benefit formula is already designed to reach this limit, then forfeitures should not be reallocated.)

Another advantage of choosing a restrictive vesting schedule is that it helps retain employees. Many employees are convinced that it is economically desirable to delay a job change until they become fully vested (this may not always be the case in reality) and, consequently, stick it out at a company until the vesting requirements are fulfilled. When employers have spent time training employees and having them become acclimated, a restrictive vesting schedule that encourages employees to stay around after they have reached a productive level may pay back the organization for the time it invested.

In contrast to these reasons for adopting a restrictive schedule, there are some good reasons to adopt a more liberal schedule or to have immediate and full vesting:

- to foster employee morale
- to remain competitive in attracting employees
- to meet the design needs of the small employer who desires few encumbrances to participation for the "employee family"

Additional Vesting Rules

The choice of a vesting schedule is only the first in a series of vesting-design choices. The vesting schedule raises several questions that need to be answered through plan design:

- Does the adoption of one of the legally required vesting schedules (or a less restrictive version) guarantee that the plan does not discriminate in the vesting area?

- What years of service must be counted for vesting-schedule purposes?
- What happens if an employee leaves employment and then returns?

**YOUR FINANCIAL SERVICES PRACTICE:
CUTTING COSTS FOR CLIENTS THROUGH PRUDENT
VESTING DESIGN**

More often then not, clients in the small-plan market are concerned about lowering plan costs attributable to rank-and-file employees. One way to painlessly accomplish this objective is to carefully consider the client's turnover pattern before setting a vesting schedule. The fact finder (chapter 3) provides a series of questions addressing employee turnover (or expected turnover). For example, if a high employee turnover is expected between 5 and 7 years of service, then a graded schedule (as opposed to a cliff schedule) may save the employer money. Conversely, if turnover is expected to occur between 3 and 5 years of service, then a 5-year cliff schedule is preferable to a graded schedule that begins partially vesting people after 3 years of service. In any case, it is prudent to look closely at the pattern of turnover that exists and design the vesting schedule accordingly.

Vesting and Discrimination

Usually the inclusion of one of the required vesting schedules (or a less restrictive schedule) guarantees that the plan will meet IRS standards. There is, however, an exception: a plan cannot in practice have a pattern of abuse that discriminates in favor of highly compensated employees. For example, a plan could have a discriminatory turnover rate if the company made a practice of firing employees before their benefits were vested. If this happened, the IRS would disqualify the plan because of its discriminatory vesting application. As a planner, you should advise the employer to use self-restraint in its personnel practices—in other words, make sure the company polices itself before the IRS has to do it.

Vesting-Service Considerations

As we've seen, vesting schedules rely exclusively on years of service to determine an employee's vested benefit. The years of service that are counted for vesting purposes include years in which the employee has 1,000 or more hours of service. Hours of service can be determined by using the standard-hours counting method (each hour actually worked is counted plus hours for which an employee is entitled to be paid, such as vacations and holidays) or by using any one of the equivalency methods discussed in chapter 7. If this sounds familiar, it should; the 1,000-hour rule and definition for years of service were used for eligibility purposes and in the benefit formula, and many of the same issues (exclusion of part-time employees, administrative convenience) discussed under eligibility and benefit formulas arise here, too.

It would seem likely that the same methods of counting years and hours of service should be used for eligibility, benefits, and vesting, but this is not always the case. In other words, the plan's definition section can be designed to include different definitions for years of service and hours of service. One instance when this would be appropriate is if the employer wants immediate eligibility (to make the plan competitive) but restrictive vesting (to cut costs and encourage employee retention). In this case, a liberal definition for year of service and hour of service may be employed for eligibility purposes, while a restrictive definition is used for vesting purposes.

If the employer's goal is to delay an employee's receipt of benefits for cost or other reasons, the definitions of year of service and hour of service should be appropriately restrictive (use the full 1,000 hours and the most restrictive definition for hour of service, which is typically the standard-hours counting method). One other difference between counting service for eligibility and vesting is that vesting service can be measured for all years based on the plan year. Remember that the first year of eligibility service must be measured from the hire date. Many plans will choose the plan year definition for administrative simplicity. Also, for the individual hired in the second half of the plan year, it could mean one less year of service.

In addition to designing these definitions, you can design the plan to exclude certain years of service:

- Years of service earned prior to age 18 can be excluded. (Generally, it's a good idea to exclude vesting service prior to age 18, because turnover is higher among younger employees, and the employer could save on future expenditures because of forfeitures.)

Example: Checkout clerk Alice White has a year of service for each year from age 16 through age 21, at which time she terminates. If the employer's plan is designed to count vesting service prior to age 18, Alice meets the plan's 5-year cliff vesting schedule, having had 6 years of service (16, 17, 18, 19, 20, 21). But if the plan is designed so that only service after age 18 is counted, Alice is not vested because she has only 4 years of service (18, 19, 20, 21). (Note that Alice meets the definition for eligibility most commonly used: one year of service and attainment of age 21.)

- Years of service before the plan went into effect can be excluded.
- Certain years of service prior to a break in service can be excluded (discussed below).

There are, however, circumstances where the plan cannot be designed to cut service for vesting purposes:

- Service prior to eligibility (past age 18) will be counted even if the employee was not a participant in the plan.
- Service for a different component of the employer, even though the employee was not covered by the plan, must be counted. For example, Sally Jerkins is a 15-year member of the Oakland office, which does not have a pension plan. Her company transfers her to the San Diego office, which does have one. Sally will be 100 percent vested when she transfers to San Diego under the plan's cliff vesting schedule because of her 15 years of service.
- Service with any member of a controlled group of corporations, with a commonly controlled business, or with an affiliated service group must be counted for vesting purposes. For example, George Gray is a 15-year employee of Modern Kitchens, which is under a controlled group with Total Home Concepts. Modern Kitchens has no plan; Total Home has one. When George is hired by Total Home, his years of service from Modern Kitchens will apply for vesting purposes.
- Service with a predecessor employer if the successor employer maintains the predecessor's plan must be counted. In other words, if an employee's company changes hands and the new owners maintain the same plan, service with the old owner counts for vesting purposes.

Breaks in Service

In some limited circumstances, the rules allow a plan to disregard certain years of vesting service during which a participant has had sporadic employment. The employer establishing the plan can take advantage of these rules or choose to disregard them.

For any of the rules to apply, the participant must first incur a break in service. A *break in service* is a year (using the same measuring period used for determining vesting) in which the individual does not complete more than 500 hours of service. If there is a break in service, there are three rules that may be applicable. Under the first rule, prebreak service may be disregarded until an individual is reemployed and completes a full year of

break in service

service. For administrative purposes, this is probably a good idea, in case the reemployment does not last.

The second and most useful rule applies only to defined-contribution plans. Under this rule, if an individual has five consecutive breaks in service, the nonvested portion of the benefit earned prior to the break can be permanently forfeited.

Example: Ralph terminates employment with a $2,000 account balance. He is 50 percent vested and so he is eligible to receive a benefit of $1,000. He returns to the same employer 7 years later. Regardless of how much postbreak service he earns, Ralph cannot earn back the $1,000 benefit that he forfeited.

Most defined-contribution plans should consider adopting this provision. Otherwise, it is possible to have to make up contributions (or hold the forfeitures in a separate account) virtually forever.

YOUR FINANCIAL SERVICES PRACTICE:
WHEN TO REALLOCATE FORFEITURES

If a defined-contribution plan is drafted to reallocate forfeitures to the remaining employees, a decision has to be made as to when the forfeitures will occur. One option is to wait until the participant has been gone for 5 years (five one-year breaks in service). This option ensures that the contributions are still available if a terminated employee returns to service and earns the right to such amounts. When the plan does not allow the distribution of benefits before the normal retirement date, the employer should always elect this option. However, if the employer allows immediate payment at termination of employment, the employer may wish to allocate forfeitures on the valuation date immediately following termination. This eliminates both the administrative expense and the confusion involved in maintaining many small accounts for terminated employees. This option makes sense if terminated employees generally do not return to service. If this option is elected, the employer must understand that additional contributions might have to be made when terminees return to service within 5 years.

Under the third rule, prebreak and postbreak service do not have to be aggregated for an individual who is zero percent vested and who then incurs five consecutive one-year breaks in service. This rule is not adopted as regularly as the others because it adds administrative complexity and rarely applies. The employer who has a revolving workforce might want to consider adopting this vesting requirement.

RETIREMENT AGES

Choosing the plan's retirement age should be motivated primarily by business reasons, not tax or plan cost considerations. The employer should carefully consider at what age it wants to encourage employees to retire. The employer has to be concerned about the orderly retirement of older, highly compensated employees, while it does not want to inadvertently encourage its older, more experienced employees to leave and go to competitors. Such issues determine the success or failure of an organization and are much more important than plan cost or tax considerations.

Effective plan design concerning retirement age boils down to the following four questions:

- What should the normal retirement age be?
- Should there be early retirement, and if so, when should it start?
- Should early retirement be subsidized?
- What provisions should be made for deferred retirement?

Normal Retirement Age

normal retirement age

When you are designing the retirement plan, you typically define a *normal retirement age*—that is, the age specified in the plan at which the employee has the right to retire. The term *right to retire* means that the employee can retire without the employer's consent and will receive his or her full benefit under the plan. In general, an employer and his or her adviser can choose any age up to 65 as the normal retirement age. Age 65 is typically chosen as the plan's normal retirement age because that is the age at which a retiree (currently) can receive unreduced Social Security benefits. Age 62 is another common choice for normal retirement because that is the earliest age at which a retiring worker can receive reduced Social Security benefits. In addition, some retirement ages are set by industry standards. For example, a relatively young age can be chosen if it is the age at which employees customarily retire, such as in professional sports. Finally, some government plans do not link normal retirement to any particular age but take into account only years of service. For example, a plan can be structured to have the normal retirement age after 25 years of service.

Under certain circumstances, the normal retirement age can be greater than 65. This usually occurs in new defined-benefit plans that have a number of older employees, which makes the start-up funding cost prohibitive, or in existing plans that frequently hire people 55 or older. In these cases, the employer should take advantage of an exception to the general rule: For an employee who commences participation in the plan within 5 years of the plan's normal retirement age, the plan can delay actual retirement until the employee's fifth anniversary. For example, a 62-year-old hiree can have a normal retirement age of 67, not 65 as is the case for other employees in the plan.

(*Planning Note:* If life insurance is used in part or in whole to fund the plan, then this post-65 normal-retirement-age provision should be strongly considered. In effect, it takes time for cash values to accumulate in the policies, and these exceptions stall retirement so that accumulation can occur.)

Early Retirement

An employer can choose to provide retirement benefits earlier than normal retirement age. As with the choice of normal retirement age, the pension tail should not wag the business dog when the employer makes this decision. Typical early retirement ages are 55, 60, and 62. Effective design of a plan offering early retirement should take into account the practices of the employer's competitors.

Sometimes (especially in defined-benefit plans) age is not the only determinant of early retirement; rather, both age and service dictate the early retirement age. One typical early-retirement provision requires age 55 and 10 years of service (in pension parlance, this is known as 55 and 10). The service requirement is valuable for employers who would like to assure themselves of enough time to fund the benefit (for example, when life insurance is used to fund the plan). So if cash flow is a problem, a years-of-service requirement is desirable.

If the employer's industry is prone to have superannuated employees or if the industry requires certain physical skills that employees may lack later in their careers, an early-retirement option is probably a good idea. In addition, the early-retirement option serves the business purposes of allowing for a graceful change in management and attracting key employees who consider early retirement a valuable lifestyle choice. Under certain circumstances, early retirement may not be a desirable option. If the employer fears that certain key employees will take a job with a competitor in order to acquire a second pension check or, if a majority of the organization's business skills and knowledge are centered in a few key people whose loss would devastate the organization, early retirement is probably not a good idea.

The early-retirement benefit can either be subsidized or nonsubsidized. If it is subsidized, the actuarial reductions for early retirement (that is, the percentage reductions taken from the normal-retirement-age benefit to reflect the longer payout period) do not reflect the true cost of providing the benefit, and the difference represents an increased employer cost. For small plans whose owner-employees are looking for tax savings, a subsidized early-retirement program will garner bigger deductions and should be strongly considered as a planning alternative. For medium-sized and large plans, some subsidy may be called for—if, for example, the employer desires to eliminate older employees—but a substantial subsidy can be prohibitively expensive.

Employers who want to offer early retirement (say for competitive reasons), but are not delighted with the prospect of losing experienced employees, should consider nonsubsidized early retirement. If early retirement is not subsidized, the actuarial reduction will reflect as closely as possible the true experience of the early-retirement costs.

Deferred Retirement

A plan should always be designed to accommodate the possibility of deferred retirement—retirement after the normal retirement age. For one thing, the Federal Age Discrimination in Employment Act prohibits

---

**YOUR FINANCIAL SERVICES PRACTICE:
THE RETIREMENT-AGE RULES IN A SAMPLE
ADOPTION AGREEMENT**

Regardless of what the employer chooses regarding early, normal, and deferred retirement, these decisions are reflected in the plan's definition section, which contains detailed descriptions of the terms *early retirement, normal retirement,* and *deferred retirement,* and it often spells out the actuarial reductions attributable to early retirement. In addition to containing choices regarding the plan's definition section, the adoption agreement also contains sections for choosing early, normal, and deferred retirement provisions.

The following sample illustrates how the early retirement age sections might appear in a typical adoption agreement:

Section T: Early Retirement Age (refers to Section 20 of the Plan)

(1) Retirement Prior to Normal Retirement Age (Section S) (check one)

    ( )   will not be permitted
    ( )   will be permitted upon attaining age ___ and completing ___ years of
        ( )   service
        ( )   participation

---

involuntary retirement (except for some executives and employees in high policy-making positions). For another thing, it is desirable from a business standpoint to make provisions that allow, or even encourage, productive employees to remain on the team. In addition, the employer must continue to make contributions in a defined-contribution plan if a deferred retirement is chosen. In a defined-benefit plan, benefits cannot stop accruing at a specified age; however, the plan can contain a maximum number of years of service for determining benefits under the plan. For example, the benefit formula could be stated as two percent of final average compensation times years of service, with service limited to 30 years.

CHAPTER REVIEW

Answers to the review questions and the self-test questions start on page 673.

Key Terms

vesting schedules
forfeitures
reallocated forfeitures

break in service
normal retirement age

Review Questions

9-1. What are the advantages and disadvantages of designing a plan to include a loan provision?

9-2. To what extent does the type of plan involved affect planning for a loan provision in
    a. 401(k) plans
    b. 403(b) plans
    c. contributory plans
    d. defined-contribution type pension plans
    e. profit-sharing plans
    f. defined-benefit plans
    g. stock plans
    h. SEPs and SIMPLEs

9-3. How can a loan provision help a financial services professional to overcome the client's objection that plan funds are being "locked up"?

9-4. The New City Heating Supply Company (an S corporation) has a qualified money-purchase plan that allows employees to take loans up to the maximum legal limit. What is the maximum loan that can be taken by the following employees?

Employee	Vested Account Balance	Percentage of Corporate Ownership
a. Mary Woods	$ 17,000	0
b. Peter Muhlenberg	$160,000	0
c. Donna Dickenson	$200,000	50

9-5.   Which of the following sets of vesting schedules can be used in a qualified plan (other than 401(k) matching contributions or top-heavy plans)?

a. | Years of service | Percentage vested |
     |---|---|
     | 09–10 | 0% |
     | 10 | 100 |

b. | Years of service | Percentage vested |
     |---|---|
     | 1 | 50% |
     | 2 | 60 |
     | 3 | 70 |
     | 4 | 80 |
     | 5 | 90 |
     | 6 | 100 |

c. | Years of service | Percentage vested |
     |---|---|
     | 0–4 | 0% |
     | 5 | 50 |
     | 6 | 100 |

9-6.   What is the special vesting rule that applies to matching contributions on 401(k) plans?

9-7.   a.   Under what conditions should an employer choose a restrictive vesting schedule for the plan?
       b.   Under what conditions should the employer choose a liberal vesting schedule for the plan?

9-8.   Identify the following periods of service that must be included and those that can be excluded for vesting purposes:
       a.   service prior to eligibility earned by a 20-year-old participant
       b.   service earned by a 16-year-old employee
       c.   service for a subsidiary of the employer, even though the subsidiary did not have a qualified plan
       d.   service with a predecessor employer if the successor employer maintains the predecessor's plan
       e.   years of service before the effective date of the plan

9-9.   Identify the three break-in-service rules that may allow the employer to disregard prior service for vesting purposes.

9-10. When should a past-65 normal retirement age be considered?

9-11. What are the advantages and disadvantages of
       a.   including an early retirement provision in a plan
       b.   subsidizing an early retirement benefit

9-12.   Discuss the deferred-retirement requirements.

Self-Test Questions

T   F   9-1.   If a plan loan is defaulted, the participant is subject to income tax and the 10 percent early distribution tax if the distribution occurs prior to age 59 1/2.

T   F   9-2.   Business owners of a C corporation are ineligible to take plan loans.

T   F   9-3.   A 401(k) plan may not have a loan provision.

T   F   9-4.   No loans are permitted from simplified employee pension (SEP) plans.

T   F   9-5.   Plan administrators can allow owner-employees to have sweetheart rates on their loans.

T   F   9-6.   The law permits a participant with a $24,000 account balance to take a loan of $12,000 from the plan.

T   F   9-7.   A participant's loan must be repayable by its terms within 5 years unless the loan is used to acquire a participant's principal residence.

T   F   9-8.   The vesting schedule is a plan design feature that specifies how much service is required before benefits become nonforteitable.

T   F   9-9.   Over the years, the law has been changed to extend the period for which a participant can be forced to wait before being fully vested in his or her retirement funds.

T   F   9-10.   Under a 5-year cliff vesting schedule, an employee is not entitled to retirement benefits until 5 years after he or she has left the service of the employer.

T   F   9-11.   Under a graded vesting schedule, the employee must be at least 60 percent vested after 5 years of service.

T   F   9-12.   Regardless of the vesting schedule that is chosen, a participant must be 100 percent vested at the plan's normal retirement age.

T   F   9-13.   Salary deferrals under a 401(k) plan can be subject to a vesting schedule.

T   F   9-14.   Forfeitures used to reduce future employer costs are known as reallocated forfeitures.

T   F   9-15.   Forfeitures that are reallocated to participant accounts can allow the participant to exceed the 100 percent of salary or $40,000 maximum defined-contribution limit.

T   F   9-16.   By using one of the required vesting schedules (or a more liberal version), an employer is guaranteed that it will meet IRS standards for vesting purposes.

T   F   9-17.   Years of service earned prior to age 18 can be excluded for vesting purposes.

T   F   9-18.   A one-year break in service will occur if an employee has fewer than 1,000 hours of service in a year.

T   F   9-19.   In a defined-contribution plan, if a participant has five consecutive breaks in service, the nonvested portion of the benefit earned prior to the break can be permanently forfeited.

T   F   9-20.   The choice of a retirement age should not be made solely for tax or cost reasons but should be motivated primarily by personnel and other business priorities.

T   F   9-21.   The normal retirement age is the age specified in the plan at which the employee can retire without the employer's consent and receive full benefits under the plan.

T   F   9-22.   A plan's normal retirement age can never be greater than age 65.

T   F   9-23.   An employer who chooses to include a service requirement for early retirement cannot require more than 10 years of service by the employee.

T   F   9-24.   If an early retirement benefit is subsidized, the actuarial reductions that are used do not reflect the true cost of providing the benefit, and the difference represents an increased employer cost.

T   F   9-25.   An employee can be mandatorily retired at age 70.

T   F   9-26.   The employer must generally allow benefits to continue accruing in a defined-benefit plan or must continue to make contributions in a defined-contribution plan if a deferred retirement is chosen.

Death and Disability Benefits; Top-Heavy Rules

Learning Objectives

An understanding of the material in this chapter should enable the student to

10-1. Explain the incidental-death-benefit rules for qualified plans with regard to

   a.   the amount of insurance that can be provided
   b.   the maximum preretirement death benefit available
   c.   the maximum postretirement death benefit available

10-2. Describe the qualified preretirement survivor annuity, the automatic joint and survivor annuity, and the PS 58 rule.

10-3. Explain how disability benefits can be provided under a qualified retirement plan.

10-4. Explain the purpose of the top-heavy rules, and describe the additional restrictions that apply to a top-heavy plan.

Chapter Outline

The primary purpose of a qualified retirement plan is to provide retirement benefits to employees. The retirement plan, however, can be used to meet the insurance needs of participants by providing both death and disability coverage in the preretirement period.

INCIDENTAL RULES FOR DEATH BENEFITS

Death benefits under a retirement plan must be "incidental" because Uncle Sam is providing tax advantages to the qualified plan for retirement needs, not insurance needs. The word *incidental,* however, may be somewhat of a misnomer. The term has a special meaning that is defined through a series of revenue rulings. As a result of these rulings, a fairly substantial "incidental" death benefit can be provided through the use of life insurance in a qualified plan.

The maximum death benefit that can be provided under the incidental rules is not specifically stated. Instead, a plan will be deemed to meet the incidental death-benefit requirement if it passes either of two tests: the 25 percent test or the 100-to-1 ratio test.

The rules described below apply to qualified plans and 403(b) plans, which are allowed to invest in life insurance. The rules do not apply to SEPs and SIMPLEs because these types of plans cannot have life insurance.

The 25 Percent Test

In order to determine whether life insurance is an incidental benefit provided by the plan, the cost of providing the life insurance is compared to the cost of providing all benefits. When this method is used, the total cost of the life insurance that is provided cannot exceed a specified percentage of the total cost of the benefit. You might assume that under the 25 percent test the maximum percentage of total benefits used to provide life insurance cannot exceed 25 percent, but this assumption is only half right. The 25 percent test is actually a misnomer, for it is really two tests: a 25 percent test and a 50 percent test, depending on what type of life insurance protection is involved. If term insurance or universal life is involved, the aggregate premiums paid for the policy cannot exceed 25 percent of the participant's total benefit. If a whole life policy other than universal life is used, however, the aggregate premiums paid for the whole life policy cannot exceed 50 percent of the participant's total benefit, *and* the entire value of the life contract must be converted into cash or periodic income at or before retirement. The reason for the increase from 25 to 50 percent (and the need for the conversion into cash) is that about half of the premiums paid under a whole life policy represent pure insurance protection, and the other half represent the investment element of the policy.

Example: Tim Rivers has a $100,000 account balance. If he uses universal life or term insurance, the aggregate premiums that can be used to pay for Tim's life insurance total a maximum of $25,000. If he has another form of whole life policy, the aggregate premiums that can be used to pay for his life insurance total a maximum of $50,000.

The 100-to-1 Ratio Test

The 100-to-1 ratio test does not look at the amount of insurance bought but concentrates on the death benefit offered. Under this safe harbor test, the death benefit is limited to a maximum of 100 times the expected monthly benefit or, if greater, the reserve for the pension benefit. For example, if the expected monthly benefit is $1,500, then the total death benefit could be $150,000 or the reserve (at the date of death) if greater. The 100-to-1 ratio test was derived from the death benefit that is provided under a retirement-income contract. Retirement-income contracts are individual life products issued by insurance companies that are used to fund qualified plans (see chapter 12). As you might suspect, the 100-to-1 ratio test is best suited to a defined-benefit pension plan because the expected monthly benefit is easily determined. However, the test can be applied to any type of pension or profit-sharing plan.

Exceptions

The 25 percent test and the 100-to-1 ratio test are subject to certain exceptions. The following are the most important exceptions to these incidental-death-benefit rules:

- The incidental limitations do not apply to life insurance bought with nondeductible voluntary employee contributions.
- The incidental limitations do not apply to profit-sharing plans under certain conditions. If the profit-sharing plan permits in-service withdrawals (for example, after 2 years) and if life insurance is purchased with funds that could be withdrawn, there is no incidental limit on the amount of these funds that can be used to purchase life insurance. In other words, the incidental limitation applies only to

funds in a profit-sharing plan that have not accumulated under the plan long enough to be distributed. If the profit-sharing plan does not permit withdrawals, however, the incidental rules will apply to all funds.

• The IRS treats universal life insurance as term insurance for purposes of the 25 percent rule, even though universal life is a form of whole life coverage that is otherwise subject to the 50 percent exception.

YOUR FINANCIAL SERVICES PRACTICE:
PROVIDING DEATH BENEFITS IN QUALIFIED PLANS

Even though the incidental rules limit the death benefits that can be provided, the financial services professional retains a good deal of discretion when designing the retirement plan's death benefit with respect to the benefit level and funding method. When designing a plan for the small employer or the professional corporation, you must keep in mind that the insurance needs of the principal individuals (business owners, key employees) will govern the death-benefit design. In the medium-sized or large organization, the employees' insurance needs will be harder, if not impossible, to determine. In this situation, the retirement plan's insurance benefit and other group life benefits will be decided by competition and other market factors.

When funding the plan's death benefit, you can choose either individual life insurance (as is usually the case with smaller employers) or a cash distribution made from plan assets (for example, a distribution of the account balance in a defined-contribution plan). The choice of the death-benefit funding vehicle usually dovetails with the decision about what plan funding vehicle is most appropriate. (Using qualified-plan funds to satisfy personal insurance needs will be discussed more thoroughly in chapter 12.)

---

split-funded plan

• A *split-funded plan* is a plan that is funded with both individual life insurance policies and a side fund (see chapter 12). In a split-funded plan, the 100-to-1 ratio can be exceeded if the life insurance policy does not provide a death benefit in excess of the 100-to-1 ratio and the amount of the death benefit is limited to the total of (1) the reserve under the policy and (2) the participant's account in the side fund.

Example: Under this approach, the death benefit will be considered incidental for an expected monthly benefit of $1,500 if the reserve is $140,000 and the side fund is $70,000 (total $210,000), even though the 100-to-1 ratio is exceeded.

Incidental Rule for Postretirement Death Benefits

We have been looking at limitations on the amount of death benefits that can be provided if a participant dies *prior* to retirement. But, there are also limitations on the amount of death benefits that can be provided *after* retirement. These rules come into play when the annuity form that is chosen provides a substantial death benefit, such as a joint and survivor annuity or a 20-year stipulated annuity. The details are somewhat complex and are discussed in depth in chapter 25. At this point, simply understand that the objective of the rule is to ensure that participants cannot defer taxation of a significant portion of their benefits until after they die. For example, if a participant aged 75 elects a 100 percent survivor annuity option and the contingent beneficiary is a 25-year-old granddaughter, a larger portion of the retirement benefit will actually be paid to the granddaughter than to the participant. To prohibit this result, the rules, as they apply to this example, would limit the survivor annuity percentage that the granddaughter can receive. The incidental-death-benefit rule generally does not apply when the beneficiary is the spouse.

MANDATORY DEATH BENEFITS: QPSA AND AUTOMATIC J&S

If we think of the incidental rules as placing a ceiling on death benefits in a qualified plan, the additional death-benefit rules can be thought of as a floor under the incidental ceiling. There are two applicable rules that construct the death-benefit floor. Implementing them depends on the retirement status of a given participant. Before retirement, the plan must provide a spousal benefit called a qualified preretirement survivor annuity (QPSA). After retirement, the plan must protect the participant's spouse by requiring that the normal form of distribution from the retirement plan for a married participant must be a joint and survivor annuity (sometimes referred to as an automatic J&S). The legislative motive behind both of these rules is to protect the spouse's right to a piece of the participant's retirement income.

qualified pre-retirement survivor annuity (QPSA)

The *qualified preretirement survivor annuity (QPSA)* (pronounced "quip-sa") is defined differently for defined-benefit and defined-contribution plans. In both cases, however, the QPSA is required to be provided only for married participants who were married for one year before the participant's death (plans sometimes waive the one-year requirement for administrative convenience). For a defined-benefit plan, the amount of the survivor annuity is basically equal to the amount that would have been paid under the qualified joint and survivor annuity (below). To determine this amount, the plan administrator assumes that the participant retired the day before death, or if the participant was not yet able to retire, left the company the day prior to death, survived until the plan's earliest retirement age, and then retired with an immediate joint and survivor annuity. For a defined-contribution plan, the qualified preretirement survivor annuity is an annuity for the life of the surviving spouse that is at least actuarially equivalent to 50 percent of the vested account balance of the participant as of the date of death.

The QPSA need not be an employer-sponsored benefit; the employer has the choice of requiring employee contributions to fund this benefit or, conversely, reducing the normal benefit actuarially. If the second choice is the case, the employee generally has the option of electing out any time after age 35. A written confirmation of the spouse's consent to the election out is required. If the employer decides to fund the QPSA, an election out is not necessary, and the employer will save the administrative headache of accounting for employee contributions, judging the validity of spousal consent forms, and risking the potential litigation associated with a spousal consent mistake.

qualified joint and survivor annuity (QJSA)

The *qualified joint and survivor annuity (QJSA)* must be the normal form of benefit distribution offered to a married participant at retirement. As with the QPSA, the participant can elect out of the benefit with spousal consent. The election out (which is common) must be made during a 90-day period prior to the annuity's starting date. The rationale for this short period is to prevent the employee from making a premature choice regarding what form of distribution to take from the retirement plan.

In addition, plans of the profit-sharing type (including profit-sharing plans, stock bonus plans, ESOPs, and 401(k) plans) are not required to provide the QJSA and QPSA benefits if certain criteria are met. Most advisers encourage employers to take advantage of this exception in order to simplify plan administration. In order to qualify for the exception, the plan must not allow any life annuity options, and must not accept direct transfers of plan benefits from other plans subject to the QJSA requirements. Finally, the plan must provide that if a married participant dies prior to retirement, the spouse must be entitled to receive 100 percent of the participant's plan benefit (the spouse can waive the benefit).

THE PS 58 RULE

PS 58 rule

As discussed in chapter 1, employees are generally not taxed on the benefits promised from, or the contributions made to, a qualified plan. Taxation occurs at the time benefits are received. The one exception is when life insurance is purchased in a plan to provide death benefits. In this case, the current cost of the "pure insurance" protection is subject to taxation under the *PS 58 rule*. The cost attributable to this pure life protection will be the lower of the actual cost as provided by the carrier or the rates supplied by the so-called PS 58 table (see table 10-1).

TABLE 10-1
PS 58 Rates—One-Year Term Premiums for $1,000 of Life Insurance Protection*

Age	Premium	Age	Premium	Age	Premium
15	$1.27	37	$ 3.63	59	$ 19.08
16	1.38	38	3.87	60	20.73
17	1.48	39	4.14	61	22.53
18	1.52	40	4.42	62	24.50
19	1.56	41	4.73	63	26.63
20	1.61	42	5.07	64	28.98
21	1.67	43	5.44	65	31.51
22	1.73	44	5.85	66	34.28
23	1.79	45	6.30	67	37.31
24	1.86	46	6.78	68	40.59
25	1.93	47	7.32	69	44.17
26	2.02	48	7.89	70	48.06
27	2.11	49	8.53	71	52.29
28	2.20	50	9.22	72	56.89
29	2.31	51	9.97	73	61.89
30	2.43	52	10.79	74	67.33
31	2.57	53	11.69	75	73.23
32	2.70	54	12.67	76	79.63
33	2.86	55	13.74	77	86.57
34	3.02	56	14.91	78	94.09
35	3.21	57	16.18	79	102.23
36	3.41	58	17.56	80	111.04
				81	120.57

*These rates are used in computing the cost of pure life insurance protection that is taxable to the employee under qualified pension and profit-sharing plans. The rate at the insured's attained age is applied to the excess of the amount payable at death over the cash value of the policy at the end of the year.

If there is any good coming out of the PS 58 rule, it is that the PS 58 costs an employee pays (along with any employee after-tax contributions or employer contributions on which the employee has paid tax) are considered part of an employee's cost basis. When the employee takes retirement distributions from the plan, he or she will not be required to pay taxes on the portion of the distribution attributable to cost basis. In other words, the pure life insurance protection will not be taxed twice.

For a self-employed person with a Keogh plan, or a 5 percent owner in an S corporation, however, the rules are applied differently. The portion of employer contribution that is allocable to the cost of pure insurance protection for the self-employed individual is treated as a nondeductible contribution. Also, at the time of payment, PS 58 costs are not recovered tax-free by the business owner.

THE IMPLICATIONS OF DEATH-BENEFIT DESIGN

There are innumerable reasons to include life insurance in an employee benefits package, including competitiveness, attraction and retention of employees, and other advantages for the business owner. By including life insurance protection in a benefit package, business owners are able to (1) receive favorable group rates for themselves and their employees, (2) shift a nondeductible personal expense to the company, and (3) if necessary, gain favorable underwriting for ratable or uninsurable individuals (which potentially means life insurance protection without physical exams or medical questions).

What this boils down to is that the most important question facing the financial services professional is not whether death benefits should be provided, but rather what vehicle should provide them. Is it in the employer's best interest to provide the majority of death benefits in a group insurance plan or in a retirement plan? What system will provide the lowest employee and employer cost for the desired benefit level?

Many employers choose to provide the death benefits outside of the qualified plan. One reason is that the benefit structure, especially in defined-benefit plans, does not provide an appropriate amount of insurance. In defined-benefit plans, the death benefit is tied to the participant's benefit (for example, 100 times the monthly retirement benefit). This means the death benefit would be quite small in the early years, when the participant may need the insurance protection the most. Insurance in a defined-contribution plan poses a different problem. Premiums are taken from the participant's account and can have the impact of reducing the ultimate retirement benefits provided. There are also tax reasons employers choose to provide death benefits outside the qualified plan. First, the applicable Sec. 79 table 1 tax rates for group plans are lower than the PS 58 costs applicable to retirement plans. Also, Sec. 79 provides a $50,000 exemption (the premiums paid for the first $50,000 of term insurance covering an employee are not taxable), which further eases the tax bite. Finally, the tax treatment of insurance proceeds is more favorable outside of the plan, where in most cases the entire death benefit is not taxable.

For these reasons, most mid-size and large organizations provide death benefits outside of the qualified plan. For small organizations, however, providing the death benefit in the qualified plan may be more administratively convenient, be better serviced by the life agent, and do double duty for the retirement dollar by offering a tax-favored way of providing permanent life insurance. Small business owners also sometimes use qualified plan assets to purchase life insurance for estate planning purposes. If the individual has a life insurance need, the most available assets to pay the premiums may well be in the qualified plan. One popular planning device is to purchase a second-to-die life insurance policy in a profit-sharing plan (pension plans cannot hold second-to-die policies). This is, however, a very complicated subject (outside the scope of this text), and it is even unclear what the IRS's position is on this matter.

DISABILITY BENEFITS

Designing a plan to include disability benefits is similar to designing one to include death benefits in the retirement plan. It is not a question of their inclusion in an employee benefit program but rather where these benefits belong. Most large companies that maintain separate long-term disability plans do not provide disability income benefits in their retirement program. If there is an existing disability income program, the financial services professional needs to be concerned only with the coordination of the retirement plan and the disability income plan. For example, is the retirement plan designed to provide adequate benefits after the long-term disability income benefits stop? This can be a problem if the retirement benefit is based on service and service is cut short because of disability. One way that retirement plans can be designed to deal with this problem is by stipulating that service for benefit purposes continues to accrue if disability occurs.

***Example*:**	In a defined-benefit plan where the benefit at normal retirement age will be equal to 2 percent multiplied by years of service multiplied by final salary, the plan can stipulate that service will be earned during each year of disability.

Another way retirement plans are able to overcome the lack-of-service problem is to immediately vest participants 100 percent in their accrued benefit or account balance if disability occurs.

Sometimes an employer has a separate disability plan in addition to a retirement plan that provides disability benefits. In this case, you as the planner must coordinate your client's retirement and disability benefits so there is no duplication of coverage.

A third possibility is for the employer to set up a retirement plan that provides all the disability benefits. If disability benefits are provided in the retirement plan, as is the case with many small plans, benefits can take several forms. They can be

- a distribution of a 100-percent-vested accrued benefit or account balance
- a distribution from a defined-benefit plan plus a plan-paid subsidy
- provided by disability insurance purchased under the plan

No matter what form the disability benefit takes, there are two additional decisions about plan design that must be made when the retirement plan either totally or fully provides the disability benefit. First, the plan must contain a definition of *disability*. Typically, the disability definition for a retirement plan is fairly restrictive. If a restrictive definition is desired, disability is said to occur when the Social Security disability definition is met. This makes the plan administrator's job easy—a painless verification is possible, and the Social Security people do all the work. If your client desires a more liberal definition of disability, you should remember to include standards for determination and verification. (*Planning Note:* One easy way to include standards for determination and verification is to purchase disability insurance and let the insurance policy definition and claims office make the determination.)

Second, consider whether or not the retirement plan's disability benefit should have age and service requirements. Reasons to include these requirements are to permit enough time for your client to properly fund the benefit and to reward only long-service employees with the benefit. In addition, if there are age and service provisions, the question of whether the disability was attributable to a preexisting condition is also sidestepped. The main reason for *not* having age and service requirements for disability is the negative impression it can create among employees.

TOP-HEAVY RULES

In chapter 1, it was implied that retirement plans were a tug-of-war. On one side of the rope are the government regulations regarding eligibility, coverage, and vesting. On the other side, pulling equally hard, are financial services professionals looking to gain tax-shelter and retirement protection for their business-owner clients without over-spending for the rank and file. The government's intervention stems from a spread-the-wealth philosophy and the desire to get the most for their money when it comes to allowing tax advantages for retirement plans.

The anchor of the government's tug-of-war team is the top-heavy rules, aimed specifically at small employers such as professional corporations and closely held businesses. The rationale for the strict scrutiny of small organizations is that employers and owners of these organizations are more prone to the temptation to shape the organization's retirement plan primarily to shelter taxes for themselves and key employees. As financial services professionals would be the first to attest, the government's suspicion is well founded. (Clients that fall into the small-plan category are almost invariably interested in tax shelter first and retirement needs second.)

The top-heavy rules are so inclusive that many financial services professionals design smaller plans according to top-heavy specifications without even bothering to take the traditional tack of designing plans according to regular pension rules and then adding contingency provisions in case the plan is or becomes top-heavy. As we shall see, under the rules for determining top-heaviness, this is a realistic approach for most small plans because they seldom can be anything *but* top-heavy.

When Is a Plan Top-Heavy?

A defined-contribution plan is top-heavy if more than 60 percent of the total amount in the accounts of all employees is allotted to key employees. Because defined-benefit plans use an accrued benefit instead of account balance, a defined-benefit plan is top-heavy if more than 60 percent of the present value of the entire amount of the plan's accrued benefits is set aside for key employees. In other words, if key employees have more than 60 percent of the retirement pie, the plan is considered top-heavy.

The top-heavy test is applied once a year (on the last day of the preceding plan year). The date the test will be performed is specified in the plan (under the definitions section) and is called the plan's determination date. Computer software is available for performing top-heavy testing, or if you prefer, a consulting or computer firm can conduct the test. Also, there are a number of small software companies that have a telephone link to computers that perform the test under a user-fee arrangement. For a small defined-contribution plan, however, the test can be performed without assistance in a short amount of time.

The top-heavy test is detailed and replete with exceptions. For this reason, an employer is fortunate to have access to such resources as consulting houses and computer software. Close scrutiny of the top-heavy rules is desirable from a planning standpoint, however, because understanding coupled with effective personnel decisions and plan design may enable the plan to escape top-heavy status.

The top-heavy test requires answers to the following questions:

key employee

- *Who is a key employee?* An individual is a key employee if at any time during the prior year he or she has been any of the following:
  - an officer receiving annual compensation in excess of $130,000 (as indexed for 2002). If there are 30 or fewer employees, no more than three officers are treated as key employees. If there are 31 to 500 employees, no more than 10 percent of the employees are treated as officers. And, if there are more than 500 employees, no more than 50 officers are key employees.
  - a person who owns more than 5 percent of the company
  - a person who is more than a one percent owner with annual compensation of more than $150,000

- *Which employers will be treated as single employers for purposes of the top-heavy test?* Separate plans of related employers are generally aggregated for purposes of top-heavy testing. There is required aggregation of an employer's multiple plans with every plan that covers a key employee or that allows a key-employee plan to meet the applicable nondiscrimination and minimum-participation standards.

Permissive aggregation—that is, picking and choosing whom to group together—is also possible. Planners can use permissive aggregation if the hourly plan (a nonkey-employee plan) is not needed to help the key-employee plan satisfy the nondiscrimination and minimum-participation requirements but is needed to prevent top-heaviness. In other words, if a plan covering key employees is top-heavy and permissive aggregation would avert top-heavy status, it is desirable to use these rules.

Example: The National Paper Company maintains both a salaried-only plan, which covers some key employees, and a separate plan for hourly paid employees, none of whom is a key employee. If the salaried-only plan independently satisfies the nondiscrimination and minimum-participation rules (chapter 7), it is not aggregated and is tested independently for top-heaviness. However, if the salaried-only plan satisfies nondiscrimination and minimum-participation requirements only when considered together with the hourly plan, a required aggregation results. If the required aggregation group is top-heavy, then each plan in the group is top-heavy. If the group is not top-heavy, however, then neither plan is top-heavy.

Top-Heavy Provisions

Almost all plan documents must contain top-heavy language. The plan document must specify that if the plan is or ever becomes top-heavy, certain special rules (described below) will become effective. Larger plans (covering over 100 employees) are rarely top-heavy, and top-heavy contingency language is included in the boilerplate language of the plan. However, most small plans (covering 25 or fewer employees) will be top-heavy. Therefore, these plans should be designed to automatically comply with the special top-heavy provisions. In fact, many prototype plans are drafted in this manner.

Whether or not the plan is designed to satisfy the top-heavy requirements or contingency top-heavy provisions are included, you must ensure that the plan design, or contingency provisions, meets the following top-heavy requirements:

- special vesting rules
- minimum benefits for nonkey employees
- a special limit for situations where both a defined-benefit and a defined-contribution plan are present

If these rules are met, a top-heavy plan will continue to remain qualified.

Special Top-Heavy Vesting Schedules

The top-heavy vesting schedules are similar to the schedules that were discussed earlier, only more liberal for the employee. The schedules are

1. The top-heavy version of the 5-year-cliff schedule is a 3-year/100 percent cliff schedule. (In other words, an employee must be 100 percent vested after 3 years of service.)

2. The top-heavy version of the 3-through-7 graded schedule is a 6-year graded schedule that increases the vested percentage 20 percent for each year of service after the first year. Either of these top-heavy schedules can be chosen regardless of the non-top-heavy schedule used.

6-Year Graded Schedule

Years of Service	Percentage Vested
0–1	0
2	20
3	40
4	60
5	80
6	100

Employers with a top-heavy plan can choose instead to take advantage of the 2 years' required eligibility and 100 percent immediate vesting rules. Depending upon the company's turnover characteristics, this alternative may be less expensive than a one-year-eligibility and a 3-year-cliff schedule, because contributions for an employee are not required for the extra year of delayed eligibility. When faced with this design choice, planners should take a close look at the 2-year/100 percent scenario.

Minimum Benefits and Contributions for Nonkey Employees

A top-heavy plan must provide minimum benefits or contributions for nonkey employees. For defined-benefit plans, the benefit for each nonkey employee must be at least 2 percent of compensation multiplied by the number of the employee's years of service in which the plan is top-heavy up to a maximum of 10 years. In other words, a defined-benefit plan must generally fund a 20 percent benefit for nonkey employees in the years the plan is top-heavy, which could mean additional plan costs if the minimum required benefit is more than the actual plan benefit. Extra funding is typically called for if the plan is integrated with Social Security. The reason for this is that a top-heavy plan cannot take into account benefits or contributions under Social Security to satisfy the minimum-benefit requirement. This effectively prohibits the required top-heavy minimum contribution from being eliminated or reduced by the integration of the plan with Social Security.

For a defined-contribution plan, the minimum employer contribution must be no less than 3 percent of each nonkey employee's compensation (provided the key employees receive at least 3 percent). As with defined-benefit plans, the minimum amount cannot be eliminated or reduced through Social Security integration. But unlike defined-benefit plans, defined-contribution plans are less likely to incur extra plan expense because of the required top-heavy minimum contribution. The reason for this is that defined-contribution plans generally provide a higher base amount for nonkey employees so key employees can receive adequate benefits without discrimination.

Planning Considerations

Many, if not most, plans of small businesses become top-heavy within a few years of formation. This means the top-heavy rules do have a significant impact on plan design. The top-heavy rules can cause special difficulty for the small 401(k) plan. The problem is that elective salary deferral contributions count toward determining top-heavy status, which means that even a plan that only contains salary deferral contributions can become top-heavy. This, then, would mean that the employer could be required to make the top-heavy required contributions even if the employer had intended to make no contribution. Remember, this would not happen in a traditional profit-sharing plan because a contribution of zero for the key employees means no required contribution for the nonkey employees.

The problem can even occur if the company makes matching contributions, if the contributions do not satisfy the top-heavy minimum contribution. The Economic Growth and Tax Relief Reconciliation Act of 2001 mitigated this problem somewhat by allowing matching contributions to count towards the top-heavy minimum as well as indicating that a 401(k) plan that makes a safe harbor contribution (see chapter 5) would not be considered top-heavy.

SEPs and SARSEPs (salary reduction simplified employee pensions) are also subject to the top-heavy rules. And SARSEPs have had the same type of problems as the small 401(k) plan. SIMPLE IRAs are not required to satisfy the top-heavy rules.

The following describe some other common issues that arise under the top-heavy rules:

- *Cross-tested plans*—If the employer establishes a plan that is intended to limit contributions for the rank-and-file employees, the top-heavy minimum generally creates a floor, or minimum, contribution that can be made.
- *Multiple plans*—If a sponsor maintains more than one plan, regulations provide that the top-heavy minimum contribution can be made to one, and not both, of the plans. Employers adopting

multiple plans need to address this issue in the plan design process, to make sure the plans do not both require minimum contributions.

CHAPTER REVIEW

Answers to review questions and the self-test questions start on page 673.
For additional review, see case studies in Appendix 10.

Key Terms

split-funded plan	PS 58 rule
qualified preretirement survivor annuity (QPSA)	key employee
qualified joint and survivor annuity (QJSA)	

Review Questions

10-1. Discuss the incidental-death-benefit requirements that are applicable to qualified plans.

10-2. What are the different considerations applicable to providing preretirement death benefits in the small-plan market as opposed to the medium- and large-plan market?

10-3. Your client, a small professional corporation, is unsure whether to include death benefits in its employee benefits package. What are the reasons for and against providing death benefits through a qualified retirement plan?

10-4. How are disability benefits typically provided under a qualified plan?

10-5. Describe the considerations necessary for choosing a definition of disability in a qualified plan.

10-6. a. What is the purpose of the top-heavy rules?
       b. What size organizations do these rules affect the most?

10-7. At the end of the prior year, the Trophy Shop money-purchase plan had the following participants:

Employee	Percentage of Stock Owned	Salary	Account Balance
Allen (president)	95%	$ 85,000	$100,000
McFadden (VP/treasurer)	3	140,000	60,000
McGill	2	50,000	40,000
Melone	0	45,000	12,000
Rosenbloom	0	35,000	8,000

a. Identify the employees who would be considered key employees for top-heavy testing purposes.

b. Is the Trophy Shop plan top-heavy? Explain.

10-8. What are the consequences when a plan is top-heavy?

Self-Test Questions

T   F   10-1. If universal life insurance is used to fund the plan, the aggregate premiums paid for the policy cannot exceed 50 percent of the participant's total benefit.

T   F   10-2. If the expected monthly benefit is $1,500, then the total death benefit could be $150,000 or the reserve at the date of death, if greater.

T   F   10-3. The incidental-death-benefit limitations do not apply to life insurance bought with nondeductible voluntary employee contributions.

T   F   10-4. A plan must contain a qualified preretirement survivor annuity for all of its participants.

T   F   10-5. When life insurance is purchased for an individual, the cost for current life insurance protection must be included in taxable gross income for that year.

T   F   10-6. A self-employed individual cannot deduct the part of his or her employer contribution that is allocable to the cost of pure insurance protection for himself or herself.

T   F   10-7. From an owner-employer's perspective, there is really no reason to include a death benefit in a qualified plan.

T   F   10-8. One way qualified retirement plans can provide benefits for a disabled participant is to stipulate that service for benefit purposes continues to accrue if disability occurs.

T   F   10-9. One easy way for employers to provide for determination and verification of disability is to allow the insurance policy definition and/or the insurance claims office to make the determination.

T   F   10-10. A defined-benefit plan cannot be top-heavy, because there are no participant accounts.

T   F   10-11. An individual is considered a key employee if he or she meets the requirements for a highly compensated employee as used in the nondiscrimination test area.

T   F   10-12. If a plan is top-heavy, the employees in the plan must become immediately 100 percent vested.

T   F   10-13. If a plan is top-heavy, the plan must provide minimum benefits or contributions for nonkey employees within specified limits.

Plan Funding and Investing—Part I

Learning Objectives
An understanding of the material in this chapter should enable the student to

11-1.   Describe the funding requirements that apply to a qualified plan.

11-2.   Explain a trusteed plan with respect to each of the following:

    a.   the makeup of a trust agreement
    b.   the role of the trustee
    c.   the use of a common trust fund

11-3.   Describe ERISA requirements that have an impact on plan investing.

11-4.   Identify penalties that can be imposed on fiduciaries that fail to meet their obligations.

Chapter Outline

This chapter and the next provide an overview of the issues surrounding plan funding and investing. In this chapter, three important issues are addressed. First is a review of the plan funding requirements. For defined-benefit plans, this topic is quite involved, while for other types of plans, the issue is quite straightforward. The next topic is a review of the various funding vehicles that are used in conjunction with tax-advantaged retirement plans. This discussion will also help you to become more familiar with what parties are responsible for plan investing. The third topic in this chapter addresses the legal constraints surrounding the investment of plan assets. Here we will talk about who is legally responsible for making investment decisions, what investment limitations apply, and liability for failing to meet fiduciary standards.

The following chapter focuses entirely on plan investing. There we will discuss choosing an appropriate investment policy; then, we will look at various investment options. The materials first cover typical investment classes and their role in the investment mix, and then go into specialized insurance products that have been developed to meet specific needs.

PLAN FUNDING REQUIREMENTS

The financial services professional needs to be acquainted with the plan funding requirements, much as the home buyer needs to be familiar with the plumbing and heating systems of a potential purchase. In other words, a passing knowledge of some of the buzzwords and the general implications can help you avoid an unpleasant experience. And although a detailed understanding of the complex requirements and their underlying actuarial voodoo is unnecessary, you should understand enough to be able to school your client in the basics and to deal effectively with a consulting actuary.

terminal funding approach

Once a tax-advantaged retirement plan is in place, the employer must fund it in order to meet the benefit obligations promised under the plan. At one time, it was possible for the employer to wait until the employee retired and monthly retirement obligations became due before providing for the employee's benefit. This pay-as-you-go system (also called a *terminal funding approach*) is no longer possible. Instead, retirement benefits must be prefunded according to the minimum funding standards that were set out in ERISA.

Under the minimum funding standards, employers are required to (1) set aside funds irrevocably (meaning that the pension money is beyond the reach of the employer or the employer's creditors), (2) place the funds with a trustee, custodian, or insurance company, and (3) fund their retirement obligations in advance. Advance funding basically means that the employer must pay the retirement liability according to specific rules.

Funding Defined-Benefit Plans

This section will explore the legal requirements of defined-benefit plan funding by answering three questions: (1) What is the minimum amount of funding necessary for plan qualification? (2) What role does the plan's actuary play? (3) What is the maximum amount of funding permitted in a defined-benefit plan?

Minimum Funding Standards

Under defined-benefit plans, an organization's annual liability (normal cost) is determined by an actuarial valuation. The rules regarding actuarial valuations—which are complex to start with—become even more complicated if the plan provides benefits based on past service. The intent of the minimum funding standards is to protect against situations where participants are left empty-handed because promised retirement benefits have not been delivered. To be fair, however, the rules do allow the sponsor the opportunity to spread the cost over a number of years. This means that a plan—especially a newer plan with past service liability—can satisfy the minimum funding rules but not have sufficient assets to pay promised benefits at any one time. This possibility is the reason for the Pension Benefit Guaranty Corporation (PBGC) insurance program.

There are several actuarial cost methods that can be used to determine the normal cost and, if applicable, the past-service liability. These methods are basically a pension subspecialty handled by actuaries and are beyond the scope of this text. But, we will discuss the implications that these tools of actuarial valuation, as controlled by the plan's actuary, have for your client.

The Role of the Plan Actuary

As you might imagine, the most important decision on which the plan actuary advises is what cost method to use for a defined-benefit plan (how to determine the annual employer contribution for a given set of plan benefits and a given group of employees). The right cost method should provide the plan sponsor with flexibility in funding and also meet the employer's tax objectives. It ideally allows large contributions (tax write-offs) in prosperous years and minimum liability in lean years or years when there's a cash-flow crunch.

As a rule of thumb, the actuary can generally recommend a cost method that will provide for relatively level costs from year to year (figure 11-1, chart 1, the projected-benefit cost method) or a method that will provide for lower liability at first but will increase until the plan reaches maturity (chart 2, the accrued-benefit cost method). If there is an attempt to fund for past

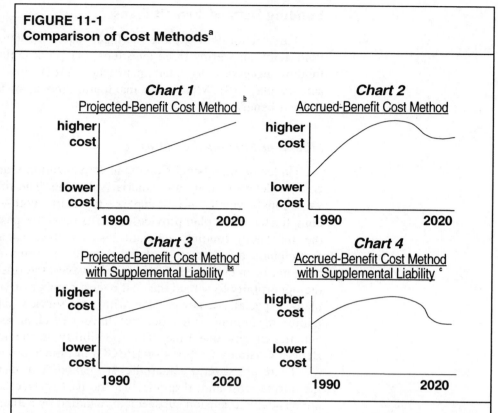

FIGURE 11-1
Comparison of Cost Methods[a]

Chart 1
Projected-Benefit Cost Method [b]

Chart 2
Accrued-Benefit Cost Method

Chart 3
Projected-Benefit Cost Method
with Supplemental Liability [bc]

Chart 4
Accrued-Benefit Cost Method
with Supplemental Liability [c]

[a] Each chart assumes an open group (one in which normal turnover occurs); if the groups are closed (just include a certain group of employees), each chart will have a sharper incline.

[b] Level funding means level as a percentage of payroll; the payroll, however, will typically increase over a given period to accommodate inflation.

[c] The drop-off for charts 3 and 4 occurs at the end of 30 years, when the past-service liability has been fully amortized. Actually, the plan sponsor can choose to amortize past service in as few as 10 years (for larger write-offs; this is generally chosen by small plans looking for tax shelter) or as many as 30 years.

service, these payments can be used either to round up the projected-benefit cost method (chart 3) or level off the accrued-benefit cost method (chart 4). If the funding for past service is not treated as enhancing the existing method, the plan is said to be with supplemental liability; if the funding for past service is treated separately, it is said to be without supplemental liability. The graphs in figure 11-1 can be compared with the projected cash-flow needs of the employer and will illustrate to the employer what system is best.

Neither the plan actuary nor the choice of an actuarial cost method bears any relationship to the ultimate cost of the plan. The ultimate cost cannot be known until the last benefit is paid and the plan is over. In other words, your client generally will never know his or her ultimate liability when adopting the plan. What the actuary does through the use of a cost method, however, is to set up a situation where there is flexibility in funding the annual liability for which your client is responsible. The actuary can help to maximize flexibility by, for example, setting up a past-service liability rather than amortizing past-service and future-service costs together.

In addition to choosing the cost method, the actuary is responsible for making certain assumptions regarding several variables; the plan's annual costs vary depending on the assumptions used. These assumptions include the following:

- the number of employees who will be eligible to receive benefits (the higher the number of employees, the higher the annual cost)
- the final-average salary that all the employees will have, if benefits are based on final-average salary (the higher the assumption, the higher the annual cost)
- the mortality rate—the rate at which active employees and already-retired workers will die (the higher the mortality assumption, the lower the annual cost)
- the disability rate—primarily for nonretired participants (the higher the disability assumption, the higher the annual cost)
- the turnover rate, including the rate of new employee replacements (the higher the turnover assumption, the lower the annual cost)
- the retirement ages, if early retirement is an option and is subsidized (the higher the early-retirement assumption, the higher the annual cost)
- the length of the benefit period for retired employees (the longer the life expectancy, the higher the annual cost)
- the investment return—the investment income earned on the accumulated assets of the plan (the higher the investment assumption, the lower the estimated annual cost)

funding standard account

No matter what cost methods or assumptions the actuary chooses, he or she must satisfy the *funding standard account,* an accounting tool (required by IRS regulations) that shows whether the plan is "adequately funded." Like an income statement, the funding standard account (which is used for accounting purposes only) is annually debited with plan costs and other amounts necessary to meet the minimum funding standard. It is also credited with the employer's contribution and such other things as decreases in plan liabilities and interest gains (interest gains occur when actual interest earnings exceed expected interest earnings). The cost methods the actuary works with are basically different approaches to funding this account, with different rules for defining the permissible limits of the actual account itself. (*Planning Note:* If there is a deficiency in the funding standard account, there is a 10 percent excise tax on the amount of the accumulated funding deficiency. If the funding deficiency is not corrected within the permitted time, an excise tax of 100 percent applies to the accumulated funding deficiency.)

What should be obvious by now is that the actuary has a certain leeway in setting the plan's annual cost. Note, however, that this leeway is not unlimited, because the actuary is restricted to reasonable assumptions and IRS-approved funding methods. But the bottom line is that the actuary is able to meet the cash-flow and tax needs of your client, within limits.

The Fully Insured Life Insurance Option

In a defined-benefit plan, the required employer contributions vary over time due to changes in the performance of plan assets. Some employers would prefer fixed costs and can sleep better knowing what their liabilities are. There is relief for these employers if the plan is fully funded with life insurance policies or annuity contracts. Under a plan that is funded by individual insurance contracts, it is the insurance company's actuary who selects the assumptions and the actuarial cost method. The premium based on that actuary's assumptions is the actual contribution due. Additionally, *fully insured* plans (plans funded in their entirety by level-premium annuities or retirement-income contracts) are exempt from the minimum funding standards (and their corresponding administrative costs, such as actuarial fees) if (1) the insurance contract provides for level premiums from participation until retirement, (2) the benefits under the plan are equal to the benefits provided under the contract, (3) the benefits are guaranteed by a licensed insurance company, (4) premiums are paid on time, (5) there are no rights under the contract subject to a security interest, and (6) there are no policy loans.

fully insured

Maximum Deductible Contributions

The minimum funding standards helped to eliminate the problem of employers who underfunded their retirement plans and eventually disappointed employees who expected to receive a retirement benefit. For some employers, however, such as small closely held corporations and professional corporations, the opposite problem exists. Small business owners generally prefer to make excessive deductible contributions to a pension fund for purposes of accelerating tax deductions and increasing the tax-shelter potential of the qualified plan. To prevent such excessive contributions, there are rules specifying the maximum deductible amount that can be made annually.

Like the minimum funding rules, the determination of the maximum deductible contribution is based upon actuarial calculations. The first rule here is that the maximum allowable contribution will never be less than the required contribution under the minimum funding rules. Then the actuary can compare this number to the contribution determined under two other calculations:

1. Determine the normal cost (the cost of the current year's liability under the plan's chosen actuarial method) plus the cost of funding one-tenth of the past-service liability (benefits based on past service).
2. Determine the unfunded cost of past and current service credits distributed at a level amount over the future service for each participant.

full-funding limit

The maximum deductible contribution is the largest of these three calculations, but is then limited by an overriding limit referred to as the *full-funding limit*. Under this limit, the maximum deduction can never exceed the lesser of (1) 165 percent (in 2002) of the plan's current liability (the present value of accrued benefits earned to date) less the value of plan assets or (2) 100 percent of the plan's actuarial accrued liability (the present value of all current and projected benefits).

Note that the 160 percent of the plan's current liability full-funding limit is troublesome. The rule was enacted to limit tax expenditures, but it can disrupt the orderly funding of the plan. The goal of any funding method is to ensure that assets are sufficient to pay promised benefits at retirement. The 160 percent limit calculation views the plan's financial status based solely upon benefits accrued currently, and it disregards the total promised benefit. The full-funding limit has been strongly criticized by actuarial groups as being inconsistent with the policy of ensuring benefit security. Because of this limit, the maximum contribution may be significant one year and zero the next—making financial and tax planning difficult. Congress has finally resolved this problem by increasing the limit to 170 percent in 2003 and repealing the limit entirely in 2004.

Funding Requirements for Other Types of Plans

Although the minimum funding requirements are most complex for the defined-benefit plan, it is important to note that the requirements do apply to other pension plans as well. This includes the two types of defined-contribution plans that are also pension plans—target-benefit and money-purchase pension plans. The minimum required contributions under this type of plan is the amount required under the plan's contribution formula each year. Failure to meet the required contribution would subject the plan to the 10 percent excise tax on funding deficiencies that applies to defined-benefit plans.

The minimum funding requirements do not apply to profit-sharing plans, stock bonus plans, ESOPs, SEPs, SIMPLEs, or 403(b) plans. Technically, this means that the 10 percent excise tax will not apply for failure to make contributions. However, if the plan document calls for a required annual contribution in one of these types of plans, the employer will have to make the contribution. Otherwise the plan will face disqualification because the employer failed to follow the terms of the plan.

When a plan has a specified contribution, this amount essentially constitutes the minimum and maximum allowable contributions. For discretionary profit-sharing plans, stock bonus plans, employee stock ownership plans, or SEPs the maximum contribution will be subject to the limitations discussed previously. That is, no individual can receive an annual allocation in excess of the lesser of 25 percent of compensation or $35,000 (as indexed for 2001) and the total employer contribution cannot exceed 15 percent of compensation of all participating employees.

FUNDING VEHICLES

funding instrument   A qualified plan must use a *funding instrument* that must be a trust, custodial account, or group insurance contract. This section will discuss these various funding instruments and how they work, as well as the typical parties involved in the investment of plan assets. The rules are different for the other tax-advantaged retirement plans.

As discussed in chapter 6, SEPs and SIMPLEs must use individual retirement accounts and annuities, while 403(b) plans must use annuity contracts or mutual fund custodial accounts.

Trusts

Trusts are the most popular funding vehicles for qualified plans. The trust approach allows for tremendous flexibility in both investments and benefit design.

A trust used for a qualified plan is based on the same principles of trust law as trusts used for other purposes. This means that the grantor of the trust is the plan's sponsor; that the grantor transfers the *res* (the plan assets) to trustees of the trust; and that the trust makes payments as specified to the beneficiaries of the trust (the plan participants and their beneficiaries).

Like all trusts, a trust used for a qualified plan contains a trust agreement, which is set up primarily to control the receipt, investment, and disbursement of funds. A typical trust agreement spells out certain particulars:

- the irrevocability of trust assets
- the investment powers of the trustee (the investment discretion of a trustee varies from plan to plan; in some cases, the employer wants to maintain full control; in others, the trustee or investment manager has almost unchecked discretion)
- the allocation of fiduciary responsibility to a named fiduciary (who is responsible for the plan and becomes the target of legal action when required)
- the payments of benefits and plan expenses
- the rights and duties in case of plan termination

If the plan is large enough, the trustees may also keep records of employer and employee contributions, each participant's salary and service, and account and benefit information. In smaller plans, this function is handled outside the trust agreement by the employer, third party plan administrator, or a consulting company.

An essential part of the trusteed plan is the plan trustees, who may be corporate (banks and trust companies) and/or individuals related to the business.

Functions of Plan Trustees

- Accept and invest employer contributions
- Pay benefits to plan participants
- Provide periodic accounting to the employer of investments, receipts, disbursements, and other transactions that involve plan assets
- Maintain administrative records, if appropriate

It is important to remember that when carrying out these duties trustees have a fiduciary relationship to plan participants. As discussed further in the next section, the fiduciaries must act in the best interest of the plan participants. Thus, a business owner who is also a plan trustee cannot act in his or her own self-interest. Also, the trustee must act prudently, as compared to other plan trustees, meaning that a business executive should think carefully before choosing to become a plan trustee.

In large plans, sometimes the trustee acts primarily as custodian of plan assets, while the fund is invested by several investment managers. Investment managers will also be plan fiduciaries, subject to essentially the same standard of care in handling plan investments. Similarly, in smaller plans, the executives will act as trustees, while one or more corporate investment managers is responsible for investing. Regardless of the arrangement, in all cases those responsible for investing plan assets are responsible to act in accordance with the plan documents and in accordance with the funding and investment policies (discussed further in the next chapter), which are established by the employer or a committee made up of executives of the employer.

In lieu of a trust agreement, the funding vehicle can also be a custodial account with a bank (or other person as authorized by IRS regulations under Code Sec. 401(f)) as custodian. With the custodial account approach, the custodian will be the record keeper, with others actually investing plan assets.

Common Trust Funds

common trust fund

Generally, the assets of a trust cannot be commingled or pooled with the assets of other trusts; a separate accounting and segregation of trust assets is usually required. However, an exception to this rule applies to common trust funds. *Common trust funds,* which are sponsored and operated by banks and trust companies, permit the pooling of funds from all participating trusts (typically many small-plan sponsors). The trust buys units of a common fund, which either increase or decrease in value depending on investment return. The common trust fund was developed because relatively small trust fund plans could not adequately diversify their investment portfolios on their own. In addition to eliminating the diversification problem, common trust funds also provide the potential for higher return (because of their size, they can attract expert investment advice), lower brokerage fees, and liquidity of funds to meet cash requirements.

Split-Funded Plans

split-funded plan

A *split-funded plan* refers to a plan that uses a trust fund arrangement, but chooses to invest a portion of plan assets in insurance and annuity contracts. Insurance products can include individual insurance and annuity contracts or any of the group funding products discussed in the next chapter. This approach can be used to take advantage of the flexibility of the trust approach while also taking advantage of the guarantees of insurance products, the ability to provide significant death benefits through the plan, or simply the yields available in a group product.

Annuity Plans

A pension plan under which retirement benefits are completely provided by annuity or insurance contracts does not have to maintain a trust fund. This applies to both individual and group products. However, to avoid the trust requirement, the terms of the plan must be incorporated in the policy. This is not practical with individual policies and, therefore, individual policies are generally issued under a trust fund agreement, with the trustee as owner of the policies. With a group policy, it is more common for the master contract to be the sole investment vehicle.

As you can see from the discussion of trusteed plans, split-funded plans, and annuity plans, the pension plan can be funded with any combination of trust fund and insurance product investments. What really will distinguish the insurance product is not the type of documentation, but the strength of the investment contracts. This subject is discussed more fully in the following chapter.

LEGISLATIVE ENVIRONMENT FOR PLAN INVESTING

The legislative scheme for making sure that plan assets are invested appropriately focuses on controlling the behavior of those individuals (and business entities) most responsible for the investment of plan assets. These individuals, referred to as fiduciaries, are required to make investment decisions in accordance with certain standards and are required to avoid certain prohibited transactions. Below is an overview of who is considered a fiduciary, affirmative obligations, prohibited transactions, and penalties these parties may face for failing to meet appropriate standards of care.

Before beginning this discussion, it is important to note that the rules discussed in this section apply to plans that are covered by title I of ERISA. This will generally include qualified plans, SEPs and SIMPLEs, and, in some cases, 403(b) plans. As discussed in chapter 6, certain 403(b) programs that allow only for employee salary deferrals (and no other employer contributions) will not be subject to the ERISA rules discussed below.

In addition to the ERISA limitations, there are several other special investment limitations. First, plans funded with IRAs (SEPs and SIMPLEs) cannot invest in life insurance or collectibles (see chapter 6). Second, 403(b) plans have even more investment limitations, as assets can be invested only in annuity contracts, mutual funds, and life insurance. On the other hand, there are no specific prohibited investment classes for qualified plans.

Individuals Considered Fiduciaries under ERISA

fiduciaries

Individuals who are considered *fiduciaries* for their role in the investment of plan assets include those persons who have discretionary authority over the disposition of plan assets and those individuals who render investment advice for a fee (or other direct or indirect compensation). Practically speaking, this will include the sponsoring company, plan trustees, investment managers (including insurance companies), and officers of the company who participate in the selection of trustees and/or investment managers.

Service providers, such as accountants, lawyers, and administrative firms, are generally not considered fiduciaries unless they have control over plan assets. Even individuals selling investments to the plan will generally not be considered fiduciaries. According to Department of Labor (DOL) regulations, rendering investment advice for a fee means

- exercising discretionary control over the purchase or sale of securities or
- providing investment advice regularly on the purchase and sale of assets, with such advice being the primary basis for the investment of plan assets

This definition is rather limited and excludes most individuals who sell insurance or other investment products. However, determining whether someone is a fiduciary is based on the facts and circumstances (regardless of whether the individual is specifically identified as a fiduciary), and even commissioned insurance agents have been determined to have been fiduciaries when the agent's advice has been determined to be the primary basis for the investment of plan assets.

Affirmative Fiduciary Obligations

Fiduciaries involved in the investment of plan assets are required to make decisions within the framework of four rules:

- the exclusive benefit requirement
- the prudent fiduciary standard
- the diversification requirement
- the requirement that investment decisions conform with plan and trust documents

Below each of these rules is described in more detail.

Exclusive Benefit Rule

exclusive benefit rule

Fiduciaries are required to discharge their duties solely in the interest of the plan's participants and beneficiaries for the exclusive purpose of providing benefits and defraying reasonable expenses. This *exclusive benefit requirement* means that the fiduciary must act in the plan participant's interest first and foremost. However, if the investment is good for the employees, it is not necessarily illegal to have a collateral benefit for the employer. Nevertheless, investment decisions that involve any consideration other than the financial interest of plan participants can be quite tricky. The DOL, in Bulletin 94-1, has indicated that a fiduciary can consider benefits to the employees (such as job security) as long as the investment return is commensurate with alternative investments with similar risks. This opinion is considered somewhat controversial and could be changed in later opinions or by legislation. If a fiduciary sees the possibility of a conflict of loyalty between the plan participants and another party (employer), according to the DOL[1] he or she should seek the advice of a competent, independent adviser and possibly elect not to participate in the decision.

Prudence

prudent fiduciary rule

According to the *prudent fiduciary standard*, fiduciaries must act with the care, skill, prudence, and diligence (under prevailing circumstances) that a prudent person acting in a like capacity and familiar with such matters would use in the conduct of an enterprise of a like character and with like aims. Note that this standard compares, for example, plan trustees with other experienced plan trustees. With regard to choosing prudent investments, DOL regulations[2] refer to six factors that should be considered:

1. the role of the investment as part of the plan's overall portfolio
2. whether the investment is reasonably designed as part of the portfolio
3. the risk of loss and opportunity for gain
4. the diversification of the portfolio
5. liquidity and current return relative to the anticipated cash flow requirements of the plan
6. the projected return of the portfolio relative to the funding objectives of the plan

One court[3] indicated that proper fiduciary procedures included

- employing proper methods to investigate, evaluate, and structure the investment, including retaining a professional adviser if the fiduciary lacks sufficient expertise
- acting in a manner consistent with others who have a similar capacity and familiarity with such matters
- exercising independent judgment when making investment decisions

Being prudent does not mean fiduciaries have to avoid risky investments. DOL Interpretive Bulletin 95-1 clarifies that an investment that has substantial risk is not in itself a problem as long as the expected return is commensurate with the risk and the risk is weighed against the anticipated return in the context of the plan's investment portfolio and of its funding, liquidity, and diversification needs.

Diversification of Investments

diversification requirement

The *diversification requirement* means that trustees have the duty to diversify the investments of the plan to minimize the risk of large losses, unless under the plan it is clearly prudent not to do so. According to legislative history of ERISA,[4] "clearly prudent" language was intended to mean that if a fiduciary were sued for failing to diversify investments, once the plaintiff demonstrated that assets were not diversified, the defendant fiduciary would have the burden of proof to demonstrate why his or her actions were appropriate. Apparently, the diversification referred to here means both diversification among asset classes and diversification within a single asset class.

Conformance with Documents

Finally, fiduciaries are required to operate the plan in accordance with the document and instruments governing the plan. Trust instruments spell out the types of investments that are allowed, whether any types of investments are prohibited, and who is responsible for making the decisions. Problems in this area do arise when trustees and others make investment decisions without carefully consulting relevant documents. If the plan has a funding policy, an investment policy, or both (discussed further below), these documents must be carefully followed as well.

Limitations: The Individual Account Plan Exception

Because qualified plans of the defined-contribution type allocate dollars to the separate accounts of participants, the sponsoring employer has the option either to direct the trustees to invest plan assets or to give participants some choice over the investment of individual accounts. Because SEPs and SIMPLEs are funded with individual IRAs, participants almost always have investment options. Similarly, 403(b) plans almost always give participants investment choices.

ERISA Sec. 404(c) (individual account plan exception)

If a defined-contribution plan, SEP, SIMPLE, or 403(b) plan gives individual participants options with regard to the investment of their own plan benefits, it makes sense that the fiduciaries should not be responsible for the participant's investment decisions. *ERISA Sec. 404(c)* grants such fiduciary relief by providing that in the case of a participant exercising independent investment direction over his or her own account, no fiduciary will be liable for losses that arise from such participant direction.

In order to qualify for this relief, the plan must conform with strict DOL requirements. The DOL's general rule is that the plan must provide an opportunity for a participant or beneficiary to exercise control over the assets in his or her account and offer the individual an opportunity to choose from a broad range of investment alternatives.

More specifically, the rules require the following:

- *Number of investment options*—Participants must have the opportunity to choose from at least three investment alternatives, each with materially different risk and return characteristics. Also, in the aggregate, the options must offer a balanced mix appropriate for a participant and, when combined with the other investments, have the effect of minimizing risks.
- *Employer stock*—Securities of the plan sponsor can also be an investment option; however, this cannot be one of the three core options.

- *Diversification*—To meet diversification requirements, the investment options generally must be "look-through investments," such as mutual funds, pooled separate accounts, or guaranteed investment contracts.
- *Election frequency*—The opportunity to change investment elections with respect to each investment alternative must be appropriate in light of market volatility. At a minimum, the three core investment alternatives must offer the opportunity to change investment choice at least quarterly.
- *Exercise of control*—The participant must be given a reasonable opportunity to give investment instructions to the fiduciary either in writing or otherwise (as long as the participant can request a written confirmation).
- *Adequate information*—The participant must also be provided with specific information regarding the investment options. The central item is a description of the investment alternatives and a general description of the risk and return characteristics of each alternative. Participants must also be informed about procedures for making elections, any expenses involved, and to whom to go for additional information. Also note that participants must be notified that the plan is seeking to qualify for the fiduciary limitations under ERISA Sec. 404(c).
- *Information upon request*—Upon request, the participant has the right to receive additional information about each investment alternative, including copies of the prospectus, description of operating expenses (as a percentage of net assets), and other detailed financial information about each option.

Note that nothing in the regulations mandates that a plan offering individual investment options meet these requirements. If the rules are not satisfied, then the fiduciary could still be liable if the participant makes an imprudent investment choice. Meeting the requirements is the best way to protect the plan fiduciaries. However, if a plan sponsor decides that meeting the requirements in the DOL regulations is impractical, yet still wants to give participants investment choices, the next best line of protection is adequate fiduciary insurance and employer indemnification. Also, in this case, employee investment education and communication can also serve to minimize risk.

If all the rules are satisfied, then ERISA Sec. 404(c) indicates that the fiduciary will not be liable for a breach of duty because of the participants' exercise of control over the investment decisions. In other words, the fiduciary is not responsible for the results of the participant's asset allocation decision.

***Example*:**   Emily, aged 60, decides to invest all of her 401(k) account in an aggressive growth stock mutual fund, shunning the four other, less risky alternatives. In the following year, the value of her account drops by 20 percent. Under 404(c), the fiduciary should not be liable for Emily's loss because it was her decision.

Still, 404(c) does not get the fiduciary completely off the hook. Fiduciaries are obligated to ensure that participant investment choices do not constitute *prohibited transactions*. Further, investment choices must conform with other fiduciary obligations—such as compliance with plan documents. Most important, fiduciaries are never granted relief from the obligation to prudently select the available options. In the example above, if the aggressive growth fund available to Emily has had inferior performance—as compared to similar aggressive growth funds—then the fiduciary may have a liability problem.

Prohibited Transactions

prohibited transactions

A large number of transactions are prohibited because they are deemed by their nature to be contrary to the interest of plan participants. Their common denominator is that they include transactions involving the plan and those parties close to the plan or employer (referred to as *parties in interest*). More specifically, these individuals are defined as any individuals in the following eight categories:

parties in interest

1. all plan fiduciaries, as well as plan counsel to and employees of the plan;
2. plan service providers;
3. sponsoring employers;
4. employee organizations (for example, unions) whose members are covered;
5. fifty percent owners of an employer or an employee organization described in paragraphs (3) or (4);
6. relatives of individuals described in paragraphs (1), (2), (3), or (5);
7. organizations (including corporations, partnerships, and trusts) that are owned by persons described in paragraphs (1), (2), (3), (4), or (5);

8. employees, officers, directors, and 10 percent owners of the sponsoring employer or others described in paragraph (2), (3), (4), (5), (7).

There are several different categories of prohibited transactions. The first category prohibits a fiduciary from causing the plan to engage in a transaction if the fiduciary knows or should know that such transaction constitutes a direct or indirect

- sale, exchange, or leasing of any property between the plan and a party in interest;
- lending of money or other extension of credit between the plan and a party in interest;
- furnishing of goods, services, or facilities between the plan and a party in interest;
- transfer to, or use by or for the benefit of, a party in interest, of any assets of the plan; or
- acquisition, on behalf of the plan, of any employer security or employer real property in violation of ERISA Sec. 407(a).

Another category of prohibited transactions involves the investment in the sponsoring employer's stock or real property. First, a plan can only hold "qualifying employer securities," (defined as stock or marketable obligations), and "qualifying employer real property" (which is property leased from the plan to the employer). Second, a plan may not acquire any qualifying employer security or qualifying employer real property if, immediately after such acquisition, the aggregate fair market value of employer securities and employer real property held by the plan exceeds 10 percent of the fair market value of the assets of the plan. However, the 10 percent limitation does not apply to profit-sharing type plans (including profit-sharing, stock bonus, 401(k), and employee stock ownership plans), as long as the plan provides that more than 10 percent of plan assets can be invested in qualifying employer real property or qualifying employer securities.

A third category of prohibited transactions involves self-dealing. Here, the fiduciary is required to avoid using plan assets for his or her own interest or account. This prohibition includes receiving compensation from any party in connection with a transaction involving assets of the plan.

Prohibited Transaction Exemptions

As you can see, the prohibited transaction rules are extremely broad. Without *prohibited transaction exemptions,* even common, everyday events—such as service providers receiving payment from the plan—would be prohibited. Because of the breadth of the prohibited transaction rules, many exceptions are provided. Exemptions come in several different forms: statutory, administrative, and individual.

Statutory Exemptions

The most commonly used statutory exemptions under ERISA include

- payment of reasonable compensation to parties in interest for services rendered necessary for the operation of the plan
- loans to parties in interest who are participants or beneficiaries of the plan if certain conditions are met. (This exception was described in chapter 9.)
- loans to employee stock ownership plans if specific conditions are met
- relief for plans for bank employees and insurance companies that want to invest in the sponsor's investment vehicles, as provided by several statutory exemptions
- certain pooled fund transactions involving banks, trust companies, and insurance companies
- distribution of assets in accordance with the terms of the plan

In addition to these exemptions, ERISA Sec. 408(c) clarifies that the prohibited transaction rules do not prohibit any fiduciary from receiving benefits as a participant from a plan, receiving reasonable compensation for services rendered to the plan (full-time employees of the plan sponsor may not be paid), receiving reimbursement for expenses incurred, or serving as fiduciary in addition to being an officer, employee, agent, or other representative of a party in interest.

Also, a plan may acquire or sell qualifying securities from any party without violating the prohibited transaction rules, as long as adequate security is paid, no commission is charged for the transaction, and the plan does not violate the 10 percent limitations.

Administrative Exemptions

ERISA Sec. 408(a) allows the Secretary of Labor to grant certain administrative exemptions from the prohibited transaction rules. These exemptions can be individual in nature, or they may be "class" exemptions, which can be relied on by the general public. Class exemptions have almost the same impact as the statutory exemptions. The DOL has granted a large number of class exemptions that can be relied upon by the employer.

Individual Exemptions

If neither a statutory nor class exemption applies, then an employer can request an individual exemption from the DOL. To grant such an individual exemption, the DOL must find that the transaction is

- administratively feasible
- in the interest of the plan and its participants and beneficiaries
- protective of the rights of the plan's participants and beneficiaries

Common Problems

Examples of common types of transactions that would be prohibited by the prohibited transaction rules include

- loans to the company, company owners, and relatives
- in most cases, contributions other than cash
- purchasing plan assets from the company or other party in interest
- property by the plan that is used by the business owner (such as art or other collectibles)
- property that is owned by the plan (like real estate) that is used by the company or other prohibited party

Especially in the small plan market, the prohibited-transaction rules pose real problems. It may not be evident to the small business owner what is wrong with the transactions described above. There are two principal reasons for this. First, the small business owner with an entrepreneurial spirit may incorrectly look at the money in the plan as capital that should be used to build the business. As the owner often sees it, what is good for the business is good for the plan participants. Second, when a significant portion of the plan assets are for the benefit of the business owner, he or she may have a hard time distinguishing plan assets from personal assets.

Fiduciary Liability

Being a plan fiduciary is a serious matter. Remember, the fiduciaries are required to both satisfy the affirmative duties and make sure that no prohibited transactions occur. Plan fiduciaries under ERISA are personally liable to the plan to make good any losses to the plan that result from the fiduciary's breach of duty. In addition, a fiduciary is required to restore to the plan any profits realized by the fiduciary through the use of plan assets. In addition, a court can subject the fiduciary to other equitable or remedial relief as the court deems appropriate. In some egregious cases, the fiduciary can even be criminally liable.

In addition to being personally liable for his or her own breaches, a fiduciary is generally liable for the acts of cofiduciaries. A fiduciary will be liable for the breach of a cofiduciary if

- the fiduciary participates knowingly in, or knowingly undertakes to conceal, an act or omission of such other fiduciary, knowing such act or omission is a breach
- by the fiduciary's failure to comply with ERISA he or she enables the other fiduciary to commit a breach
- the fiduciary has knowledge of a breach by the cofiduciary, unless the fiduciary makes reasonable efforts under the circumstances to remedy the breach

Essentially, this means that if one fiduciary knows of a breach of duty by another fiduciary, he or she must take steps to correct that situation. In many cases, this can mean suing the other fiduciary.

Segregation of Plan Assets

When a tax-advantaged retirement plan such as a 401(k) plan, SIMPLE, or 403(b) plan contains employee salary deferrals, the DOL has prescribed how quickly those salary deferrals must be contributed to the plan. Under the DOL regulations, salary deferrals have to be segregated from the employer's general assets (contributed to the plan) as soon as is administratively feasible but never later than the 15th day of the month following the month of the salary deferral. For example, deferral elections for all pay periods ending in June must be contributed by July 15. This would be true regardless of whether employees were paid weekly, biweekly, or monthly.

CHAPTER REVIEW

Answers to the review questions and the self-test questions start on page 673.

Key Terms

terminal funding approach
funding standard account
fully insured
full-funding limit
funding instrument
common trust fund
split-funded plans
fiduciaries
exclusive benefit rule

prudent fiduciary rule
diversification requirement
ERISA Sec. 404(c) (individual
    account plan exception)
prohibited transactions
parties in interest
prohibited transaction exemptions

Review Questions

11-1. Briefly describe the objective of the current minimum funding requirements that apply to qualified plans.

11-2. Discuss the role that the plan actuary plays with regard to recommending cost methods and making actuarial assumptions.

11-3. Describe a trusteed plan.

11-4. Describe the other funding vehicles available to the qualified plan.

11-5. a. What parties are generally considered fiduciaries for their involvement in the investing of plan assets?
    b. What parties close to this process are not fiduciaries?

11-6. Name the four affirmative duties that fiduciaries are required to satisfy.

11-7. What are the primary requirements for fiduciaries to be eligible for ERISA 404(c) relief?

11-8. If ERISA 404(c) relief is given, what decisions are still the responsibility of the fiduciaries?

11-9. Explain whether each of the following is a prohibited transaction:
    a. the sale of real estate owned by the ABC plan to the wife of the treasurer of the ABC Company
    b. loaning money from the plan to an officer of the corporation (the plan contains a loan provision that permits loans on a nondiscriminatory basis)

c.   the acquisition of 25 percent of employer stock by a defined-benefit plan

d.   the acquisition of real estate from the plan for less than its market value by the plan's trustee for her personal use

11-10.   Your client is a business owner who acts as the trustee of her company's pension plan. The plan owns real estate that the expanding company would like to buy at market value. What, if anything, can your client do to avoid the consequences of the prohibited-transaction rules?

Self-Test Questions

T   F   11-1.   Employers frequently use the terminal funding approach to fund their qualified plans.

T   F   11-2.   Under ERISA, the employer is required to use a trust, custodial account, or group insurance contracts as the funding instrument.

T   F   11-3.   If a defined-benefit plan meets minimum funding requirements, this means it has sufficient assets to pay currently promised benefits.

T   F   11-4.   The projected-benefit cost method provides for a lower liability at first, which steadily increases until the plan reaches maturity.

T   F   11-5.   If funding for past service is treated separately from the cost method used, the plan is said to be without supplemental liability.

T   F   11-6.   A plan sponsor can reduce the ultimate cost of a plan by choosing the proper cost method.

T   F   11-7.   The higher the final-average-salary assumption the actuary makes, the higher the annual cost.

T   F   11-8.   The higher the investment assumption the actuary makes, the higher the annual cost.

T   F   11-9.   If there is a deficiency in the funding standard account, there will be a 10 percent excise tax on the amount of the accumulated funding deficiency.

T   F   11-10.   Fully insured plans are generally exempt from ERISA's minimum funding standards.

T   F   11-11.   The minimum funding requirement does not technically apply to profit-sharing plans.

T   F   11-12.   The full-funding limitation is going to be repealed as of 2004.

T   F   11-13.   A trust for a qualified plan must be irrevocable.

T   F   11-14. Trustees generally invest plan assets, pay benefits to participants, and provide periodic accounting of investments, receipts, disbursements, and other transactions involving plan assets.

T   F   11-15. Common trust funds eliminate diversification problems inherent in small plans.

T   F   11-16. Split funding is a method by which an employer pays part of the retirement obligation while the participant is employed and part of the retirement obligation after the participant has retired.

T   F   11-17. The financial adviser who exercises discretionary control over the purchase of plan investments is not a fiduciary to the plan.

T   F   11-18. A trustee who invests plan assets in a company that is a good client of the plan's sponsor has always violated the prudence requirement.

T   F   11-19. One of the fiduciary's obligations is to operate the plan in accordance with the trust and other instruments governing the plan.

T   F   11-20. One of the requirements for obtaining relief under the ERISA 404(c) individual account plan exception is that participants must be given the option to choose from among five different investment options.

T   F   11-21. Participants must be notified that plan fiduciaries are seeking the fiduciary relief provided in ERISA 404(c).

T   F   11-22. ERISA 404(c) does not relieve plan fiduciaries from the responsibility of selecting prudent investment options from which participants may choose.

T   F   11-23. A plan that has lent money to the sponsoring company has most likely engaged in a prohibited transaction.

T   F   11-24. A fiduciary who uses plan assets for his or her own interest has engaged in a prohibited transaction.

T   F   11-25. Prohibited transactions are uncommon in the small business market.

T   F   11-26. A fiduciary is personally liable for any losses due to a breach in duty and can be liable for a breach by a cofiduciary as well.

Notes

1. DOL Adv. Op. Lty. No. 84-09A and DOL reg. 2550.408b-2(e).
2. Reg. 29 CFR 2550.404a-1(b).
3. Lanka v. O'Higgins, 810 F.Supp. 379 (N.D.N.Y. 1992).
4. Conference Committee Report to ERISA, H.R. Rep. No. 93-1280.

12

Plan Funding and Investing—Part II

Learning Objectives

An understanding of the material in this chapter should enable the student to

12-1. Discuss the importance of investment guidelines.

12-2. Describe investment characteristics that are relevant in pension investing.

12-3. Explain the role of basic investment classes, such as stocks and bonds, in the pension portfolio.

12-4. Describe the various group pension contracts and identify the circumstances under which a plan sponsor should use a separate-investment-accounts contract, a guaranteed-investment contract, and an investment-guarantee contract.

12-5. Explain how life insurance and annuities are commonly used as plan investments.

Chapter Outline

ESTABLISHING INVESTMENT GUIDELINES

Why Establish Investment Guidelines?

Now that you are familiar with ERISA's fiduciary requirements, you can see that the rules are relatively complex and that fiduciaries have a strong incentive to meet their obligations. The first, and probably most important tool for ensuring compliance, are clearly written plan investment guidelines. Essentially, *investment guidelines* are written instructions that provide guidance and structure for those involved in investing plan assets. These are crucial for the following reasons:

investment guidelines

- *Satisfying fiduciary obligations*—Investment guidelines help to establish procedures. They clarify who is responsible for what, when various tasks need to be completed, and how performance will be evaluated. They encourage a disciplined approach to fiduciary management and help to establish a paper trail.

- *First line of defense*—If the Department of Labor (DOL) or plan participants question the investment performance, courts are going to be looking for a rationale for the investments chosen. The investment guidelines should be the fiduciary's most powerful shield.

- *Investing in a vacuum*—An investment decision simply cannot be made or properly evaluated in a vacuum. A treasury bill is a great investment when the main concern is protecting principal, but a terrible investment for long-term capital growth. Appropriate investment decisions have to follow clear objectives.

For all of these reasons, it is extremely important to establish clear investment guidelines that tie the investment policy into the plan's objectives, clarify who is responsible for the various decisions surrounding the investment of plan assets, specify investment guidelines and goals, and establish procedures for reviewing both the investment performance and the plan's investment guidelines.

Funding Policy and Plan Objectives

funding policy

Every plan is required to establish a *funding policy*—procedures for establishing and carrying out a funding program consistent with the objectives of the plan and the requirements of ERISA. A funding policy addresses the level and timing of contributions necessary to fund benefit obligations throughout the life of a retirement plan.

In a defined-benefit plan, the policy should address the minimum funding requirements, provide a process for reviewing the policy periodically, and most important, require documentation of actions taken and reasons for those actions.

The funding policy and the investment guidelines are driven by the plan's objectives. In a defined-benefit plan, the primary objective is to provide sufficient funds to pay both current and future benefit obligations. In addition, there is the goal of minimizing long-term total required contributions. And, in most cases, there will be concern about the variability in annual contributions. The second and third objectives are generally at odds with one another, because minimizing costs over the long haul requires taking some risk. With risk usually comes volatility in the investment return, and, thus, a degree of variability in the required contributions. How important this is to a particular plan depends, in part, on how well-funded the plan is—the more well-funded plan has a higher tolerance for volatility. Also, the tolerance for volatility depends upon whether the sponsoring entity is cyclical in nature.

In a defined-contribution plan, the funding policy is simpler. If the plan calls for a specified contribution, the policy simply addresses the timing of contributions. With discretionary contributions in a profit-sharing plan, the employer establishes a policy for determining how and when contributions are to be made. Also, in a defined-contribution plan, there should be less conflict with the plan's objectives. Here, the employer's contribution is not tied to the plan's investment performance. The employer does not have to be concerned about the long-term cost of funding the plan or short-term variability. The only objective is to provide for the retirement needs of the participants.

However, because participants will be of different ages and have different needs and risk profiles, many defined-contribution plans pass the investment decisions on to the participants. In such plans, the objective at the trust level is somewhat different. Here the goal is to offer participants a number of sufficiently diverse investment vehicles—each with different risk and return characteristics—so each participant will be able to assemble a portfolio that will meet his or her individual investment needs. Also, to assist participants in the formation of appropriate investment objectives, the trustees will have to provide them with suitable education.

Investment Responsibilities

Investment guidelines should identify all of the parties involved in the investment of plan assets and should address each individual's specific responsibilities. Establishing this requires, first, a review of the plan and trust documents. These documents offer more detail on accountability issues than most people realize. Commonly, the document provides that either the employer or an investment committee is responsible for establishing and periodically reviewing the investment policy. The employer often retains the responsibility of choosing and monitoring the trustee and any investment managers. Trustees are responsible for investing plan assets in accordance with the stated investment goals and reporting to the employer or investment committee, unless some or all of this responsibility is passed on to one or more investment managers. The trustees will always account for and report on the status of plan assets. In some cases, there may also be consultants who help with selecting and monitoring investment managers.

Investment Policy

investment policy

The plan's *investment policy* should identify the appropriate degree of risk and yield for the trust and the importance of yield in relation to safety of principal and the plan's cash flow needs. These decisions must be made in relation to the plan's objectives and the investment objectives. When trying to determine the plan's objectives, it is helpful to ask the following questions:

- Are there other resources available to pay benefits if investment performance is bad in the short run?
- What is the appropriate investment horizon?
- What is an acceptable level of risk?
- What is the minimum level of investment return necessary to accomplish the goals?

These questions are relevant to the plan trustees, when they are responsible for investment decisions, as well as to plan participants in cases where they have investment control.

Investment Goals

The next step is to establish concrete performance objectives for monitoring investment performance. It is almost always more sensible to evaluate investments based on appropriate benchmarks as opposed to specific rates of return. If more than one investment manager is involved, a specific set of investment guidelines should be established for each manager, covering the following:

- permissible categories of investments
- asset allocation ranges among different investment classes
- appropriate investments within categories (such as specified bond quality)
- diversification concerns, such as maximum holding in specific investments, limits on small capitalization stocks, and limits on any particular sector
- policies regarding proxy voting
- limitations based on fiduciary rules, prohibited transactions, and so on

Monitoring Investment Management

Another part of the investment policy includes procedures for periodically checking performance against benchmarks. The safest course of action is to track performance on a continual basis, and to meet with investment managers on a quarterly, semi-annual, or annual basis. Investment performance should be evaluated over relatively long periods, although significant deviation in short-term performance can be a warning sign. Performance can be evaluated against peer groups as well as against benchmarks.

Reviewing Investment Guidelines

The final part of the investment procedure should be a plan for an annual review of the investment guidelines to insure that they are still appropriate. Again, it is important to keep accurate records of any meetings that discuss, reconfirm, or change the guidelines.

INVESTMENT CONSIDERATIONS

Almost every investment option available to an individual investor is available to a pension plan sponsor. In fact, pension funds can be invested in such a large number of products that it is impossible to cover them all fully in this text. Instead, in the rest of this chapter, we will concentrate on several objectives: identifying certain basic investment characteristics, clarifying the role of major asset classes in the asset mix, and finally, reviewing the makeup and merits of products that the insurance industry typically markets to pension funds.

Let's start by looking at several aspects that need to be considered before selecting investments. One factor is the investment's tax treatment. Because qualified plans and other tax-advantaged plans are tax exempt (at the trust level), investments that also have special tax advantages are generally not appropriate for the plan. This is because the investor pays a premium for the tax advantage. For example, tax-free municipal bonds have a lower investment return than comparable taxable bonds. Because the trust does not benefit from the special tax treatment, these types of investments should generally be avoided.

Another concern is investment liquidity. This refers to the ability to convert the investment to cash in a short period of time. An adequate portion of the pension assets needs to be sufficiently liquid so benefit payments can be made without the need to sell long-term investments at a bad price.

A third consideration is the investment's stability. A stable investment is one that has little fluctuation in value. Money market accounts and Treasury bills, for example, have almost no variability. As mentioned above, stability of the investments can have an impact on short-term variability of plan contributions to a defined-benefit plan. The downside of investments with little variability is that they also have low rates of return.

investment risk purchasing-power risk (inflation risk)

The variability in the value of an investment can also be called *investment risk*. Causes of investment risk are many. Here we will discuss several of the most important. First is *purchasing-power risk,* which is sometimes called *inflation risk.* With rising prices, the value of an investment asset or of the income earned thereon, or both, must increase at a rate equal to or greater than the inflation rate. Otherwise, the purchasing power of the dollars invested or earned on the asset will decline. Investment assets most susceptible to this risk are fixed-dollar investments. The next type of risk is *interest-rate risk,* in which the value of an investment changes due to changes in interest rates in the market. The third major risk factor is referred to as *market risk.* Political, economic, demographic, or social events can have an impact on the market as a whole and on the specific investment, as well. A fourth type of risk, *business risk*—consumer preference, ineffective management, law changes, or foreign competition—can affect the performance of a particular business.

interest-rate risk

market risk

business risk

INVESTMENT CLASSES

Cash Equivalents

cash equivalents

To satisfy the need to make other investment transactions and to have readily accessible money to pay benefits, plans generally invest some of a plan's assets in instruments that are known as *cash equivalents*. Typically, cash equivalents have either no specified maturity date or one that is one year or less in the future.

A number of different investments are considered cash equivalents. The investment with the least risk of default is the U.S. Treasury bill (T-bill). These obligations of the U.S. government have maturity dates when issued of 90 or 180 days, or one year, and are backed by the full taxing authority of the government. They can be readily sold and converted to cash at a modest cost. Other federal government agencies also issue short-term marketable obligations. These are available with a range of maturity dates, and generally pay a slightly higher interest rate than T-bills.

Another category, bank deposits, includes savings accounts and certificates of deposit (CDs) at banks, savings and loans, and credit unions. Savings accounts face minimal risk and are subject to few restrictions on withdrawals. CDs, which are deposits for a specified period of time such as 3, 6, or 12 months, generally impose a loss of a portion of the interest earnings as a penalty for a withdrawal before maturity, although some banks have eliminated this penalty or reduced it to a minimal amount. Also, large CDs (over $100,000) can often be sold on the secondary market.

Money market instruments, including money market deposit accounts (MMDAs) and money market mutual funds (MMMFs), are other popular cash equivalents. Both MMDAs and MMMFs hold portfolios of short-term obligations of the federal government and its agencies, of state and local governments, and of businesses. The securities are, in most cases, completely liquid without penalty. Money market instruments pay a yield slightly lower than the underlying investments (to account for management fees) but also allow greater diversification, protecting the plan from default risk.

Other investments that have the characteristics of cash equivalents include short-term obligations of state and local governments and of businesses and the long-term debt obligations of governments, businesses, and nonprofit institutions that are to mature within one year.

Bonds

Bond owners are creditors of the issuing institution, whether it is a government, business, or nonprofit organization. This status grants the investors the legal right to enforce their claims to interest income and principal repayment as contained in the agreement that specifies the terms and conditions of the debt issue. In the case of business debt instruments, debt claims have priority over any claims of its owners.

Bond issues of state and local governments (both of which are referred to as *municipals*) and of businesses, typically are quality rated by Standard and Poor's Corporation (S&P) and/or Moody's Investors Service. These ratings express the likelihood that the issuer will default on the timely payment of interest or principal. Based on a financial analysis of the issuer, a letter grade is assigned to each bond issue. Bonds rated at the top of the B grade (BBB for S&P, Baa for Moody's) or higher are considered to be "investment quality." Lower ratings are assigned for bonds assessed as "speculative." The lower the quality rating, the greater the risk of default and the higher the interest rate (return) that the investor can expect to earn.

Government Bonds

Governmental debt includes securities of the federal, state, and local governments and their agencies. Some federal bonds are backed by the full faith and credit of the U.S. government. For example, all U.S. Treasury obligations have such backing. Other U.S. government bonds issued by federal agencies or organizations, such as the Tennessee Valley Authority or the U.S. Postal Service, are not direct obligations of the U.S. Treasury. These bonds, known collectively as *agency bonds,* provide investors with a return greater than that available on U.S. Treasury bonds. A few of these agency bonds have guarantees that effectively place the full faith and credit of the U.S. Treasury behind the bonds.

Some state and local government bonds, known as *general obligations,* are backed by the taxing power of the state or local government. Others, usually issued by agencies of a state or local government, are known as *revenue bonds.* They are backed by the revenues earned from such ventures as turnpikes, airports, and sewer and water systems. Without the taxing authority behind them, these revenue bonds are viewed as riskier and pay investors a somewhat higher interest rate than do general obligation bonds.

Maturities of governmental debt instruments vary from more than one year to 30 years. Bonds with maturities of 10 years or less are often referred to as being of intermediate-term duration and have somewhat less risk than longer-term bonds. If such a risk difference does exist, intermediate-term obligations would pay a slightly lower rate than would a longer duration bond.

Corporate Bonds

Businesses are major contributors to the supply of debt securities available in the marketplace. These securities, either notes if intermediate term or bonds if long term, have various characteristics, which are detailed in the indenture. Some of the more frequently encountered characteristics include the following:

- *secured*—a promise backed by specific assets as further protection to the bondholder should the corporation default on payment of interest or principal
- *debenture*—an unsecured promise, based only on the issuer's general credit status, to pay interest and principal
- *callable*—an option exercisable at the discretion of the issuer to redeem the bond prior to its maturity date at a specified price
- *convertible*—an option exercisable by the bondholder to exchange the bond for a predetermined number of common or preferred shares

For bonds of the same quality rating, these features affect the interest rate available to the investor. If the feature provides a benefit to the bondholder, such as being secured or convertible, a lower interest rate is paid. If the feature provides a benefit to the issuer, such as the flexibility of not having specific assets pledged as collateral (debenture) or the presence of a call feature, the interest rate is higher.

Using Bonds in the Pension Environment

When plan assets are invested by the trustee, bonds are often used to ensure that the plan will have sufficient cash to pay expected benefits as they arise. For example, if a defined-benefit plan expects to pay out monthly benefits to current beneficiaries in the amount of $50,000 a month, bonds are purchased in the amount necessary to generate a stream of interest payments in such an amount. Also, bonds are used simply because they provide more stable returns than equities and higher returns than the cash equivalents mentioned above.

Equity Securities

Equity investments represent an ownership position in a business. As such, they represent a higher short-term risk for the investor than do the debt investments but they also offer higher potential long-term return. Because most retirement plans have long-term investment goals, equity investments comprise a significant role in the asset mix.

Example: The 1999 *Pension & Investments* survey of the 1,000 largest employee benefit funds showed that defined-benefit plans held 61.2 percent of their assets in equities, while defined-contribution plans held 66.1 percent of assets in equities.

By far, the most common equity investment for pension trusts is in common stock of publicly traded corporations. Investors in common stock have the ultimate ownership rights in the corporation. They elect the board of directors that oversees the management of the firm. Each common share receives an equal portion of the dividends distributed, as well as any liquidation proceeds. If the firm is unsuccessful, losses will occur that can lead to a cessation of any dividend payments and, if losses continue, to an eradication of the common equity ownership and eventual bankruptcy.

The current income distributed as dividends to the shareholder is at the sole discretion of the board of directors. The board is under no legal obligation to make dividend payments and may instead retain the profits within the business. Only by threatening to elect or actually electing a new board can the common shareholders be in the position to force a dividend payment, regardless of the profitability of the business.

The owners of common stock also vote on major issues such as mergers, name change, sale of a major part of the business, or liquidation. Finally, common stockholders usually have a *preemptive right,* which is the right to maintain their relative voting power by purchasing shares of any new issues of common stock of the corporation.

Mutual Funds

An open-end investment company, popularly called a mutual fund, continually sells and redeems its shares at net asset value, that is, the value of the fund's assets divided by the number of outstanding shares. Mutual funds acquire a portfolio of securities in which each of the fund's shares represents a proportionate interest in the total portfolio. As sales and redemptions of the fund's shares take place, the size of the fund's total portfolio changes, increasing when additional shares are sold and decreasing when shares are redeemed.

Mutual funds can be differentiated on the basis of their portfolio objectives. These major categories include:

- *money market mutual funds*—These funds own a portfolio of short-term interest-bearing securities. As mentioned earlier, they are used by investors as an alternative to cash.
- *bond funds*—These companies own a portfolio of bonds. Subcategories include some that invest only in U.S. government issues, municipal issues, corporate issues, or low-quality (junk) bonds. Further subcategories can be short-term (up to 4 or 5 years), intermediate-term (5 to 10 years), or long-term (10 or more years in duration) bond funds.

- *common stock companies*—These companies hold a portfolio of common stocks and perhaps a small number of preferred stocks. Subcategories include those that invest primarily in conservative (defensive) stocks, growth stocks, aggressive growth stocks, or foreign stocks.
- *mixed portfolio companies*—These companies own a portfolio of bonds, stocks, and other investment instruments. Subcategories include balanced companies and income companies.

Another way to distinguish funds is to look at whether they are actively managed (securities chosen individually by management) or passively managed. A common passive strategy includes those funds referred to as *index funds*. An index fund owns a portfolio that replicates a major market index such as the S&P 500. Passive strategies generally result in lower management fees.

In addition to the fees charged by the management of the fund, funds have various acquisition fees. In many cases, fees that would apply to individual investors are waived for the pension fund. If fees exist, they must be carefully evaluated.

Mutual funds are more and more commonly used in pension plans. With small plans, assets may be too small to be handled by an investment manager. Like the common trust fund (described in the previous chapter), mutual funds provide an easy way to achieve diversification. Mutual funds also provide liquidity and ease of entry and exit. As mutual fund return data is published and studied, it simplifies evaluation of investment performance.

When participants in defined-contribution plans are given investment choices, mutual funds (and other look-through investments such as common trust funds and insurance contracts) are becoming the primary form of investment. These types of investments allow participants to build individualized portfolios while still taking advantage of professional management and asset diversification. In addition, these look-through investments are required in order to take advantage of the fiduciary liability relief described in the previous chapter.

GROUP PENSION PRODUCTS

allocated

Historically, group pension departments of insurance companies offered a distinct contrast to plans invested directly in the types of assets discussed above under a trust agreement. For one thing, early group pension products were generally *allocated,* meaning that assets were committed to provide benefits for specific employees, while trust funds were unallocated. Another distinction was that the group pension products were replete with guarantees (everything from guaranteed interest rates to annuity purchase guarantees), and trust funds offered no guarantees. While the guarantees constituted something of an advantage, they also made the early group pension products less competitive, because providing long-term guarantees required conservative actuarial projections for investment return. A third difference was that group pension contracts were inflexible in the timing of contributions and restrictive regarding the types of benefit formulas for which they were suitable. As you might expect, group pension products were less than competitive in attracting pension funds.

As time wore on, new group pension products were designed to provide the employer with more flexibility in both plan design and timing of contributions. In addition, the weighty long-term guarantees that fettered companies and kept them from offering competitive investment returns were removed and replaced with guarantees on a floor rate for investment return. Also, companies began to segregate their pension assets from the insurance companies' general accounts, which permitted separate account investing that was tailored to diverse pension needs.

One final hurdle that insurance companies had to overcome was the commingling of contributions for the current and all prior years. In times of rising interest rates the insurance contracts appeared to be noncompetitive because they were selling a portfolio rate of interest that was weighed down by the lower rates of prior years. To counteract this, the new-money method (also known as investment-year method) was developed. Under the *new-money method* each deposit made by an employer is credited with the rate of interest that the funds actually earned in that year. Thus, in times of rising interest rates, the rates are not based on a company-based time-weighted portfolio but on a series of annual competitive rates (as with a trust fund plan).

The net result of all this change has placed group pension products on a par with trust funds. Distinctions between them remain, but that does not keep them from being competitive; in fact, the distinctive features of group pension products make them more advantageous under some circumstances.

Traditional Group Pension Products

Three group pension products that have been in existence for some time and still used today (although some insurance companies have discontinued underwriting them) are the group deposit-administration contract (DA), the immediate-participation-guarantee contract (IPG), and the pension-funding contract (PF).

group deposit-administration contract
unallocated group pension contract

The *group deposit-administration contract* was the first *unallocated group pension contract* (meaning that assets were not allocated to individual participants). The DA is funded by a series of employer contributions made throughout the year. Contributions are accounted for under two different systems—one that reflects investment guarantees that are given (the active-life fund) and one that reflects the actual investment experience. At retirement, the active-life fund is debited with the amount taken out, which is enough to purchase an immediate annuity for the participant in the amount provided by the plan. The annuity purchase rates are also guaranteed in the contract. Under a DA contract, the investment experience is rated annually and dividends are paid to the contract holder if the experience fund exceeds the reserve necessary for future benefits and expenses. The group deposit-administration contract is able to offer interest and annuity rate guarantees because it accumulates a contingency reserve, and because it has control (through dividend computations) over the rate at which actuarial gains pertaining to guaranteed items are created.

immediate-participation guarantee contract

Because some employers object to the reserves and other insurance company controls and, instead, seek an immediate reflection of actual investment and mortality experience, a second (and more popular) product is available—the *immediate-participation-guarantee contract*. An IPG is an unallocated funding instrument that holds benefit amounts in a commingled fund. At retirement, one of two things happens: (1) either the fund is charged directly with benefit payments or (2) the fund is charged with a single annuity premium. The IPG contract contains no interest guarantees, but, as the name indicates, it allows a plan sponsor to have an immediate reflection of the actual investment and mortality experience under the plan (which is the major selling point of a trust fund plan).

The IPG contract typically contains conservative guarantees of annuity rates for retired lives. They were, however, the first group pension contract that did not provide annuities as a matter of course. In other words, even though annuity rates are guaranteed, annuities are not automatically purchased at retirement.

pension-funding contract

A product that evolved from the IPG contract but spurned the use of any annuity guarantees was the *pension-funding contract* (PF). The only significant difference between a PF contract and an IPG contract is that, under a PF contract, there are no guarantees whatsoever for retirees, no annuity purchases are made, and no funds are earmarked for retired employees.

The Current Generation of Group Pension Products

Three newer group pension products are today's big sellers. In general, these products are giving trust fund plans stiff competition and are yielding big rewards for many insurance companies. These products include

- separate-investment accounts contracts
- guaranteed-investment contracts (GICs)
- investment-guarantee contracts (IGs)

Take note that different companies tag these products with different names and/or have special variations of the generic product, so it is important to check for the product name and any variation from the generic.

Separate-Investment Accounts Contracts

separate-investment accounts contract

The most basic of the third-generation contracts is the *separate-investment accounts contract*. Under this contract, the plan fund manager can either invest in one of the separate accounts offered by the insurance company or split investments among the various accounts offered. A separate-investment account is similar in concept to a mutual fund. Like a mutual fund, a separate-investment account is generally pooled (takes allocations from a variety of plan sponsors instead of from individual investors) and is always participating (that is, accounts are maintained at market value, and the actual investment experience is reflected directly in the value of the fund). A second similarity to mutual funds is that the separate-investment account has preestablished types of investments—for example, a bond or equity fund can be chosen. A third similarity to mutual funds is that each fund has a directed-investment philosophy and certain investment goals. (For example, an equity separate-investment account might have a directed philosophy of investing in dividend-producing equities.) And a fourth similarity to mutual funds is that the sales appeal of any separate-investment account is based on its competitive market history.

Separate-investment accounts contracts generally require a minimum deposit. The plan sponsor can allocate these funds to one or all of the different funds available and can usually transfer funds among the accounts whenever desired. This allows the plan sponsor to play the market by changing investment strategies to meet market trends.

Unlike assets held in an insurance company's general account, assets in separate accounts are not subject to the claims of the insurance company's creditors. This makes separate investment accounts especially popular in an environment of low interest rates. In such periods, institutional investors become quite concerned about the risk of loss that could result due to the failure of the insurance company. Insulation from this risk through the use of separate accounts can be an important selling point.

However, the chief selling point of a separate-investment accounts contract is the competitiveness of the investment's rate of return. Unlike that of most pension products, this competitive posture is generally well advertised in trade magazines, such as *Pensions and Investment Age;*

therefore, selling should be coordinated with the home office's advertising strategy. Another unique feature of these contracts is that there is a wealth of literature (from general philosophy reports to detailed quarterly investment reports) that can be used as a sales tool.

Guaranteed-Investment Contracts (GICs)

guaranteed-investment contract

One of the most popular types of pension-funding products issued through group pension departments of insurance companies is the *guaranteed-investment contract (GIC)*. As the name implies, a guaranteed-investment contract guarantees the pension plan's investment (both principal and interest). The insurance company receives plan assets at a specified date or dates, guarantees them at a stipulated rate of interest, and returns the principal and interest at a specified time or times. In fact, a GIC is analogous to a certificate of deposit for pension plans because, like a CD, it offers a predetermined rate of return. The GIC guaranteed rate is spot-rated—that is, it is based on the insurance company's ability to immediately purchase an underlying investment vehicle (for example, a zero coupon or deep discount bond).

A second similarity to a certificate of deposit is that a GIC guarantees the principal. Another similarity is that GICs permit withdrawals only on specified dates, sometimes only on the contract ending date. Some withdrawal flexibility is available, however, because GICs can be structured to pay out interest annually or to distribute the principal investment piecemeal (this is known as a strip feature). This flexibility is important for plan sponsors who must meet plan cash-flow needs, such as plan expenses and benefit payouts to retirees. In addition, although the length of a GIC is usually somewhere between 3 and 7 years (typically 5 years), investment flexibility can be achieved by the purchase of a short-term GIC for as little as one year.

When a GIC is offered as one of several investment options in a participant-directed defined-contribution plan, an exception is made to the withdrawal limitations that normally apply to a GIC. In this case, there is almost never a penalty for the participant who elects to move assets within the family of available investment choices.

The withdrawal limitation for the trustee-invested plan is a real consideration for the investor. However, in exchange for leaving money with the insurance company, the pension plan is assured of guaranteed interest rates that often extend for the length of the contract. These projected investment returns provide a safety net for the pension fund manager by effectively minimizing any downside risk and by allowing plan actuaries and accountants to make accurate predictions about the GIC-invested portion of the pension portfolio. On the other hand, GICs will not gain from an upside swing in the market. For this reason, they are more appropriate when interest rates are high and expected to fall or when interest rates are expected to remain stable.

Varieties of GICs. There are two basic types of GICs. The simpler of the two, the *bullet GIC*, contains a guarantee-of-interest-and-principal feature and can vary from 3 to 7 years in length. The bullet GIC is an investment vehicle structured to take a single-sum deposit for a specified period of time. Both the amount of deposit and the lock-in period are a product of the pension fund manager's investment strategy.

The bullet GIG can work well in a defined-benefit plan, but the inflexible timing of contributions led to the establishment of the *window GIC*. The window GIC helps to meet the need for periodic contributions inherent in some defined-contribution plans, which credit an employee's account balance with the plan contribution when monthly or semimonthly salaries are paid. When a window GIC is used, the interest guarantees are locked in at the contract inauguration but the timing of contributions is usually left open for up to a year. In return for this option, the guaranteed rate is lower than the rate for a corresponding bullet GIC.

A second way the window GIC is different from the bullet GIC is that the precise contribution amount is not known. And a third difference is that in a window GIC the withdrawal amounts are not known. Window GICs are marketed for defined-contribution plans because under these plans the exact yearly dollar contribution is not known when the contract is signed, but only at the end of the year, after all contributions have been made. They also are popular as a guaranteed investment option in a participant-directed defined-contribution plan.

One common twist to the window GIC is to guarantee the first-year rate but leave the years 2-through-5 rate open during that first year. Pension fund managers can then lock in a rate later that year. For example, if they gamble that rates will rise and they win, they can lock in the higher rate that comes up late in the first contract year as their 2-through-5 guarantee. If they gamble that rates will rise and they do not, the insurance company can lock in the lower rate as a guarantee for years 2 through 5. Because this involves risk for the insurance company, guarantees are generally lower.

Sales Appeal. The major selling point of a GIC is that it provides a competitive guaranteed rate of return. A second selling point is that the risk associated with GIC investments is limited. Credit risks (the inability of the carrier to pay principal and interest at maturity) are greatly minimized when one is dealing with a company that has an established investment track record. And market risk (the possibility that rates may shift during the lock-in period) can be minimized by choosing the window GIC option of floating the guarantee for a year. The third selling point of GICs is that they fit nicely in most pension portfolios by providing a conservative investment foundation on which investments that carry more risk can be placed. A fourth selling point is that assets held in GICs can be valued at book value, while assets held in bonds, for example, have to be valued at market value. In defined-benefit plans, where variability in asset valuation can cause big fluctuations in required contributions, GICs have a clear advantage over bonds. A final selling point of GICs is their pension orientation. GICs uniquely meet the investment concern of pension managers because they maximize long-term rates of return and generate cash flow to match required benefit payments while preserving safety of principal. These are the primary concerns of any pension fund manager, and GICs meet these needs effectively.

YOUR FINANCIAL SERVICES PRACTICE: GIC SALES

The bullet GIC market is extremely sensitive to interest rates. When interest rates are high, you will be able to do a lot of bullet GIC business; when interest rates are low, however, you will have problems selling. The window GIC, on the other hand, has a fairly steady market because defined-contribution plans that have a guaranteed-interest-account option under their plan have to place their money somewhere each year, regardless of interest rates.

Investment-Guarantee Contracts (IGs)

investment-guarantee contract

A third type of no-service group pension product is the *investment-guarantee contract (IG)*. The IG contract is similar to a GIC in many ways. Both GICs and IGs are often structured to receive predetermined contributions (based on the plan's contribution or benefit formula) and pay a guaranteed rate of interest; to receive contributions during a window period (like a window GIC); and to typically last 5 years. The major difference from a GIC, however, is that contributions are received for the 5-year period rather than for the one-year window or one-shot bullet payment. Also, the guarantees given to the plan sponsor for years 2 through 5 are only a floor amount. Under an IG contract, the funds may receive a higher interest rate than projected if the actual investment experience of an investment account exceeds the guarantees.

Because the insurance company is taking on more risk the farther out in time it projects guarantees, the IG interest guarantees are typically on a declining scale. The guarantee for year 3 is lower than the guarantee for year 2, and these declining guarantees are attributable to the market and investment-placement risks that insurance companies take. The plan sponsor, however, is more concerned with both the initial year's guarantee and the competitive posture of the offering company. As with any participating contract, the offering company's investment history is a key selling point because the investor is hoping that the actual results will exceed the floor guarantees.

Sales Appeal. The major selling point of an IG contract is that it allows plan funds to receive the experience account or the guarantee, whichever is better. Thus, the pension fund manager knows that downside risk is eliminated (by the guarantee) but not at the risk of locking in a static rate for an extended period. To put it another way, fund managers can sleep nights because of the guarantee, and the sky is the limit if the investment environment takes a sharp upswing turn. A second selling point is that the

TABLE 12-1
Comparison of Group Insurance Products

Type of Contract	Amount of Contribution	Timing of Contribution	Investment Guarantees	When to Sell
Separate-Investment Accounts Contract	Typically $100,000 or more	Ongoing	None; competitive history of the offering company is important	Generally, at any time; sales are easier when coordinated with home-office advertising, and/or the reporting of favorable returns
Bullet GIC	Precisely known, typically $100,000 or more	One-time, within 3 days of sale	Guaranteed at the outset for the length of the contract	When interest rates are high and expected to drop
Window GIC	Based on the plan's benefit formula, typically a percentage of annual contributions of $100,000 or more	Over a window period of up to one year	Guaranteed at the outset for the length of the contract	At all times, if the client offers a guaranteed account to employees
IG Contracts	Based on the plan's benefit formula, typically $50,000 a year or $250,000 over 5 years	Over the length of the contract	Guaranteed at the beginning of each contract year and the outset of the contract	When interest rates are low and expected to rise, or if the market is unstable and the client wants to keep options open.

risks associated with IG investments are limited. As with GICs, credit risks are minimized when the offering company has a history of good performance. But for IGs, unlike GICs, the market risk of an upturn during the investment period is eliminated because the actual experience of the fund will be credited. A final selling point for IGs is their pension orientation. Like GICs, IGs uniquely meet the investment concern of pension managers because they maximize long-term rates of return and generate cash flows to match the required benefit payments while preserving safety of principal.

LIFE INSURANCE AS A FUNDING VEHICLE

As was the case with group pension products, life insurance in qualified plans has undergone an evolution of sorts. Over the years, the use of life insurance in a qualified plan has shifted from emphasis on the fully insured plan to a split-funded, life-and-side-fund approach.

In time, fully insured plans were replaced with a split-funded approach, which combined an ordinary life contract with a side fund. The ordinary life contract generates the lowest scale of cash values, so a significant amount of funding can be provided through the side fund. This approach offers the best of both worlds—the preretirement death-benefit coverage of a fully funded plan and the investment discretion and contributions-timing discretion that is built into the side fund.

If life insurance is used in a defined-benefit plan, the trustee purchases separate contracts on the life of each participant. In defined-contribution plans, life insurance is typically offered as a participant-directed option. If the participant elects life insurance coverage, premiums are paid out of the participant's account balance. In either case, the trustee applies for the insurance, pays the premiums when due, is custodian of the individual contracts, and—even though the insured individual applies for the contract—has legal ownership of the insurance contract.

The insurability of individuals is seldom a serious problem under a life-insurance-funded plan because (1) evidence of insurability is sometimes waived, (2) substandard rates can be used, and (3) graded or graduated death benefits can be used. Also, like group term life insurance plans, some individual policy plans establish nonmedical amounts using a formula based on the amount of volume under the particular plan. The plan's disability benefit can be provided either through a waiver-of-premium clause or a rider or by fully vesting the cash value. If an employee leaves before retirement, disability, or death, his or her vested interest can be taken care of in several ways: (1) the contract can be transferred to the participant; (2) a paid-up policy in the amount that is currently funded can be transferred; (3) the trustee can borrow the unvested portion and assign the contract; or (4) the policies can be cashed in for their surrender value.

Why Life Insurance?

If you consider retirement plans in the abstract—solely as retirement vehicles—using life insurance to fund the plan does not make much sense. After all, even if investment earnings on the life insurance policy are competitive with other investments, there is still the pure life cost to consider. In addition, the use of life insurance may lead to PS 58 costs that are currently taxed to the participant. But retirement plans do not exist in a vacuum; they are a piece of the entire financial plan of the individual, whether it be the 25,000-person megacorporation or the 3-person doctor's office. And, as part of their financial plan, these people need life insurance protection.

In the large corporation, life insurance is seldom used to fund retirement plans (except for nonqualified plans). A group life plan is all that is necessary to keep these organizations competitive in the employee benefit field, and financial planning considerations for the individual come second to those of the company. But for the small professional corporation or closely held business owner, the use of life insurance to fund a qualified plan may be the best method to pay for life insurance—and, therefore, to fit in two pieces of the financial planning puzzle with one move. Using life insurance in the qualified plan satisfies the need for life insurance protection for the owner and gives a tax deduction to the business (the only nondeductible amounts being those amounts of pure insurance protection subject to PS 58 costs).

There are, of course, other reasons to use individual life insurance policies to fund a qualified plan. These include

- maximizing the preretirement death benefit
- dealing with a single individual or coordinated group in doing financial planning
- minimizing paperwork, administrative hassles, and the extra expenses that result when death benefits are provided both inside and outside the plan
- simplifying plan administration, in the case of a fully insured plan (discussed in chapter 11)

Naturally, the life insurance need must exist before funding a qualified plan with life insurance becomes a prudent maneuver. If life insurance needs have been treated adequately elsewhere in the financial plan, then the client need not carry it in the retirement plan.

ANNUITIES AS A FUNDING VEHICLE

Annuities are traditionally thought of as a common method of distributing retirement funds to retirees. However, they can play another role when it comes to funding the retirement plan. Like the use of life insurance, the use of annuities to fund retirement plans has undergone an evolution of sorts. The original retirement annuity products offered a noncompetitive investment return and lacked contribution flexibility—two drawbacks that led to their downfall. Under these contracts, the objective was to fund the retirement benefit by funding an annuity that built sufficient cash values at retirement to pay out benefits.

Annuity contracts used to fund retirement plans are typically deferred annuities, with the plan sponsor agreeing to fund (over the employee's career) an annuity that will begin spinning out payments at retirement. These annuities can be either fixed (where the monthly return is predetermined and guaranteed) or variable (where the underlying annuity investments, such as stocks, bonds, and money markets, let the annuities' return float with market conditions). The variable annuity tends to be the more popular of the two because it gives the plan sponsor more investment discretion—within limits. This is particularly important when the plan sponsor is a small business owner who wants some investment control over his or her own retirement. It is in this small closely held business/professional-corporation market that most plan-funding annuities are sold.

Annuities are sometimes used to fund plans in situations where life insurance is not available because of underwriting considerations. Although life insurance underwriting requirements are not typically stringent in the retirement arena, there are times when a prospect is uninsurable and the "guaranteed issue" or graded death benefit amount is not sufficient. In these cases, annuities are suitable substitutes for life insurance in filling the funding need. A second reason annuities are used to fund plans is the guaranteed payout rates they sometimes offer. If this is the case, the same annuity that is used for funding purposes is also used for payout purposes.

CHAPTER REVIEW

Answers to the review questions and the self-test questions start on page 673.

Key Terms

investment guidelines   investment risk
funding policy   purchasing power risk
investment policy   (inflation risk)

interest-rate risk

market risk

business risk

cash equivalents

allocated

group-deposit administration
    contract

unallocated group pension
    contract

immediate-participation-
    guarantee contract

pension-funding contract

separate investment accounts
    contracts

guaranteed-investment
    contract (GIC)

investment-guarantee
    contract (IG)

Review Questions

12-1.   Why is it so important to establish investment guidelines?

12-2.   Name the common objectives of a defined-benefit plan.

12-3.   Name the common objective of a defined-contribution plan.

12-4.   What is the primary objective that the trustees must satisfy when plan participants have investment options?

12-5.   What questions are helpful to ask when determining the plan's investment policy?

12-6.   Name the specific areas that should be addressed when identifying investment goals.

12-7.   Identify four types of investment risk relevant to the selection of the pension portfolio.

12-8.   Explain the role that cash equivalencies, bonds, and stocks have in the pension portfolio.

12-9.   Describe the major characteristics of the immediate-participation guarantee contract.

12-10. A separate-investment-accounts contract can be compared to a mutual fund. Explain some of the similarities.

12-11. Why does the separate-account contract reduce the risk to the investor?

12-12. A guaranteed-investment contract (GIC) is similar to a certificate of deposit. Explain some of the similarities and differences.

12-13. Plan sponsor Gillman owns a lacrosse equipment manufacturing company. Gillman's investment objectives for his defined-benefit plan include (1) receiving a guaranteed rate of return, (2) maintaining principal, and (3) protecting against downside risk.

    a. Why is a GIC desirable for Gillman?

    b. What investment strategy should the Gillman Company take if it wants to avoid placing interest-rate bets?

    c. Which GIC variety should Gillman choose if he suspects interest rates are high and are expected to drop?

12-14. What are the major advantages of an investment-guarantee contract, and when should it be used?

12-15. Explain what type of pension contract is most appropriate under each of the following circumstances:

    a. The plan sponsor is small ($50,000 in annual contributions) and expects the current low interest rates are going to increase.

    b. The plan sponsor has a defined-contribution plan (annual contributions of $200,000) and expects interest rates to drop.

    c. The plan sponsor intends to maintain certain investment discretion, wants to make ongoing contributions, and does not require guarantees to be made.

    d. The plan sponsor has a defined-benefit plan, has annual contributions of $200,000, and expects interest rates to drop.

12-16. Why are annuities typically used as investments in retirement plans?

Self-Test Questions

T F   12-1. Investment guidelines offer direction for the responsible parties, but they are not of much use to the fiduciary whose actions have been questioned.

T F   12-2. Investment guidelines should tie the investment policy into the plan's objectives, clarify who is responsible for various decisions, specify investment goals, and establish procedures for reviewing investment performance.

T F   12-3. Qualified plans should take advantage of tax-free investments such as municipal bonds.

T F   12-4. Variability or investment risk can be an important consideration in a defined-benefit plan, because this factor can affect annual plan contributions.

T F   12-5. Purchasing power, or inflation risk, can be the most important risk factor facing a plan participant in a defined-contribution plan.

T F   12-6. Today, less than 25 percent of plan assets are held in equity securities.

T F   12-7. The immediate-participation-guarantee contract contains a guarantee of both principal and interest.

T   F   12-8.   Separate-investment accounts contracts include separate accounts in equities, bonds, and securities.

T   F   12-9.   Separate-investment accounts contracts are always pooled.

T   F   12-10.   The guaranteed-investment contract guarantees both principal and interest.

T   F   12-11.   GICs can effectively minimize downside risk for a pension fund.

T   F   12-12.   Window GICs specify a precise dollar contribution.

T   F   12-13.   The major selling point of a GIC is that it provides a competitive guaranteed rate of return.

T   F   12-14.   In a partially insured plan, the individual life insurance policies are held by a trustee.

T   F   12-15.   Using life insurance in a qualified plan satisfies the need for life insurance protection for the owner and gives a tax deduction to the business.

13

Plan Installation and Administration

Learning Objectives

An understanding of the material in this chapter should enable the student to

13-1. Explain the financial services professional's role in the plan-installation and plan-administration processes.

13-2. Describe the steps that must be taken to install a corporate plan.

13-3. Identify the various responsibilities of plan administration.

13-4. Describe the makeup and use of a summary plan description.

13-5. List the tax forms used to report to the Internal Revenue Service.

13-6. Describe how the installation and administration of a Keogh plan differs from that of a corporate plan.

Chapter Outline

Once the plan has been selected and designed according to employer specifications and the funding approach has been decided upon, the tasks of plan installation and plan administration begin. The role of the financial services professional in these processes varies from case to case. Some clients desire that you provide ongoing consulting, while others allow you to take a more passive posture. Most financial services professionals will want to choose the latter role and delegate the responsibilities associated with plan installation and administration to a third-party administrator. This will enable you to use your time more efficiently, freeing you up for sales and design consulting. There are, however, occasions that call for client hand-holding and troubleshooting on your part. For these times, you need a general understanding of the installation and administration processes and the documents that are an integral part of these processes. The objective of this chapter is to provide you with this understanding through an overview of plan installation and plan administration. If a more detailed review of the plan installation and administration process is needed, the loose-leaf services described in chapter 2 should be consulted. These services provide a wealth of information about filing requirements, as well as supplying copies of current forms and instructions.

SETTING UP A CORPORATE PLAN

The first step in the plan installation process is for the employer to legally adopt the plan. This can be done through a resolution of the corporate board of directors, which can either adopt a particular plan document or simply adopt the major provisions of the plan. The corporate resolution should be adopted before the end of the tax year, if the employer wants the plan to be effective in that year. If the company's securities are offered in the open market, the plan is also generally submitted for stockholder approval (although it is not legally necessary). Notice of the establishment of the plan and details about the plan should be presented to stockholders in a proxy statement.

At the same time that the plan is approved, the corporate board of directors should also approve the trust instrument (if any) that will be used. Recall that a trust provides for the irrevocable deposit of plan assets. In other words, once assets such as individual life insurance policies or cash are transferred to the trust, the employer or the employer's creditors cannot recapture these assets. (The employer may, however, recapture assets that exceed promised benefits at the termination of the plan.) Under some state laws, a nominal contribution to the trust may be necessary in order to establish its existence.

If a group pension contract is used instead of a trust, the board will review a specimen contract. If the board wishes to adopt the contract, it will authorize the submission of a letter of application with premium. Note that the group pension contract must be submitted for approval to the state insurance department in the state where the corporation is domiciled. The state insurance department reviews the contract to see if the insurer has sufficient reserves to pay benefits and if the contract meets other state specifications.

Another step that must be completed before the end of the first tax year is notifying the participants of the new plan. This can be an oral explanation at an employee meeting or a written letter that is either mailed or posted at work—for example: "It is our pleasure to announce the ABC Company is adopting a qualified 401(k) plan. The details of the plan are as follows. . . ." Alternatively, the summary plan description (see below) can be used to satisfy this requirement.

For a plan funded with employer contributions, the employer typically adopts the plan at the end of the tax year in which it wants to receive a tax-deductible contribution. The reason is that the employer may not know until the end of the year whether it has funds available to contribute to a plan. In this case, the plan is made effective retroactive to the first day of the year, and a tax-deductible contribution can be made for the whole year. For example, if the employer is on a calendar tax year, the plan may be adopted on December 31, effective as of the previous January 1. However, if the plan is a contributory plan (a 401(k) plan or 403(b) plan), it should be adopted prior to the beginning of the first year of the plan's operation. This is necessary to allow time to enroll participants in the program. For such a plan, application is best accomplished through one or more enrollment meetings.

enrollment meeting

If the plan is contributory or if salary reductions are required under a 403(b) plan or a 401(k) plan, an additional step must be taken. When this is the case, the employees are asked to attend an *enrollment meeting*. The enrollment of an adequate number of employees in the plan is crucial for purposes of meeting the nondiscrimination rules and passing the actual deferral percentage test (401(k) plans only). Employers usually request the financial services professional to attend the enrollment meeting and use his or her selling skills to persuade the rank-and-file employees to make the necessary contributions or salary reductions.

YOUR FINANCIAL SERVICES PRACTICE:
401(k) PLANS AND THE NEGATIVE ELECTION

The IRS has approved a strategy that can increase enrollment in 401(k) plans. A plan can require that all participants start off with a default contribution of a specified amount (typically 3 percent) into a default investment account. Participants have to make an affirmative election to choose not to participate. This "negative election" approach can help to include those individuals who fail to participate because they never get around to filling in the form.

The enrollment meeting begins with the financial services professional describing the plan and spelling out the benefits and trade-offs of plan participation for the employees. The meeting typically contains a question-and-answer period during which the employees get to voice their concerns and receive clarification on important issues. (*Planning Note:* Many financial services professionals present a slide show or movie that addresses the most typical questions. This often heads off the common problem of having one or two employees cause trouble by harping on the negative aspects of the plan.) The meeting typically concludes with the completion and signing of enrollment forms and salary reduction agreements or authorization to withhold mandatory contributions from an employee's pay.

The enrollment meeting (or if an enrollment meeting is not required, a separate meeting) can be used to secure the information to apply for individual life insurance contracts if they are being used wholly or in part to fund the plan. In addition, medical examinations can also be conducted at this time, if required by underwriting.

Regardless of whether a trust or group pension contract is used, the entire first year's contribution should be made by the time for filing the employer's tax return for the year in which the plan is adopted. (For a corporate employer using a calendar year, the date for filing the tax return for a given year is generally March 15 of the following year, but this can be extended to September 15.) As long as this requirement is met and the plan is in final form, the employer will be able to deduct contributions if the plan qualifies. (*Planning Note:* The plan should be adopted subject to the right to be rescinded if it does not qualify, and the trust or group pension contract should allow contributions to be returned if the plan does not qualify.)

advance-determination letter

In order to determine whether the plan qualifies, the employer should file an application for an *advance-determination letter* with the IRS. The employer is not required to receive IRS approval, but instead can wait for an IRS audit to determine whether the plan is qualified. However, this is not recommended because of the risk of disqualification (which means a retroactive loss of the tax deduction). The forms and documents used to file for an advance-determination letter include the following:

- IRS Form 5300 (Application for Determination for Employee Benefit Plan) or IRS Form 5307 (Short Form Application for Determination for Employee Benefit Plan—this form is used for master or prototype plans and volume submitter plans)
- IRS Form 8717 (User Fee for Employee Plan Determination Request)
- Schedule Q (Nondiscrimination requirements)

- IRS Form 2848 (Power of Attorney and Declaration of Representative)
- copies of the plan and the trust or group pension contract

Make sure the determination letter is applied for before the tax return filing date (plus extensions). If the request for an advance-determination letter is submitted before the tax return is due, the IRS will extend the time limit for amending the plan. A retroactive amendment will then be possible, enabling the employer to receive a deduction for the current year. If the filing deadline is missed, it is highly unlikely that the IRS will allow the plan to be amended retroactively or that a deduction will be allowed for the initial contribution. Retroactive amendment is common if the IRS objects to some provisions of the proposed plan. (*Planning Note:* A determination letter is typically issued within 6 months after the application is filed. Although the IRS has a maximum of 270 days to make a ruling, no determination letter will be received before 60 days to give interested parties a chance to comment.)

YOUR FINANCIAL SERVICES PRACTICE: SMALL EMPLOYER TAX INCENTIVES

The Economic Growth and Tax Relief Reconciliation Act of 2001 provides for several new incentives to encourage small employers (100 or fewer employees) to establish a plan. The new law provides up to a $500 income tax credit for administrative and retirement-education expenses for any small business that adopts a new qualified defined-benefit or defined-contribution plan (including a section 401(k) plan), SIMPLE plan, or simplified employee pension (SEP). The credit is available for each of the first 3 years of the plan.

In addition, a small employer that sponsors a plan covering at least one non-highly compensated employee is not required to pay a user fee for a determination letter request in the first 5 years of the plan.

---

notice to interested parties

Immediately preceding the filing of the request for an advance-determination letter, the employer should issue the *notice to interested parties* of the intent to install a qualified plan. The IRS will not issue an advance-determination letter unless interested parties have been notified that an application for one has been filed. The notice to interested parties goes to all employees eligible to be in the plan and to ineligible employees if they work at the same location as the eligible employees. The notice should indicate that qualification is being sought and that the employees have the right to submit comments on the plan to the IRS and the Department of Labor.

**summary plan
description (SPD)**

The final and most important step in the employee communications process is the issuing of the *summary plan description (SPD)*. A summary plan description is an easy-to-read booklet that explains the plan to the participants. The SPD may be prepared by the financial services professional, the insurer, or the employer. In any case, employers are required to give summary plan descriptions to participants within 120 days after the plan is adopted by the board of directors. (*Planning Note:* In addition to being used with retirement plans, summary plan descriptions are also required for most welfare benefit plans. For this reason, it may be wise to suggest that your client combine all the summary plan descriptions [and other information] in an employee handbook.)

A summary plan description bridges the gap between the legalese of the pension plan and the understanding of the average participant by effectively communicating how a plan works, what benefits are available, and how to get these benefits. The SPD must strike a balance between clarity and depth. To this end, the Department of Labor suggests the frequent use of examples, the elimination of technical jargon and long complex sentences, the inclusion of a table of contents, and the use of clear cross-references. Other good ideas include the following:

- cross-referencing only to materials already discussed, not to materials that have yet to be discussed
- using short paragraphs (three or four sentences)
- using short sentences (20 words or less) and short, familiar words with few syllables

A summary plan description must be fair and evenhanded. It cannot be used to persuade employees to join the plan, but must merely explain the plan. The regulations specifically state that a summary plan description cannot downplay the negative consequences of involvement—for example, it cannot gloss over plan terms that may cause a participant to lose benefits or fail to qualify for them.

At the same time the SPD must be accurate. Employees have sued and won cases where the SPD promised something that was not contained in the document. The best way for the employer to protect itself is to include a disclaimer stating that if there is a conflict between the plan and the summary plan description, the plan provisions will be determinative.

The summary plan description regulations dictate what kind of language to use, what kind of information to have, and what group of people must get the information. The regulations also require that every 5 years participants whose plans have been modified must receive an updated summary plan description, and every 10 years—regardless of whether the plan has been modified—a new summary plan description must be issued. The following is a list of items that the SPD must contain:

- a provision identifying the plan—for example: "This is the ABC Company profit-sharing plan"
- the names and addresses of people responsible for the plan
- the employer identification number
- the plan administrator's name, address, and telephone number
- the name and address of the person designated for service of legal process
- the name, title, and business address of each trustee
- a statement to the effect if the plan is collectively bargained
- an explanation of the plan's eligibility requirements for participation and benefits and normal retirement age
- an explanation of any joint and survivor benefits
- an explanation of any terms that could result in a participant's losing benefits
- a PBGC insurance provision, if applicable
- a description and explanation of the plan provisions for determining years of service for eligibility to participate, vesting, breaks of service, and benefit accrual
- a list of the sources of plan contributions
- the name of the funding agency
- the plan year's ending date
- the procedures for presenting claims for benefits under the plan and remedies for benefits denied under the plan
- a statement of ERISA rights (this statement is standard text promulgated by the Department of Labor)

Table 13-1 summarizes all of the steps required to establish a qualified retirement plan.

TABLE 13-1
Summary of Steps in Setting Up a Corporate Plan

Steps	Timetable
1. Secure a corporate resolution adopting the plan.	Before the end of the tax year
2. Secure a corporate resolution approving the trust document or group pension contract.	Before the end of the tax year
3. Notify participants of the plan's adoption and its major terms.	Before the end of the tax year
4. Conduct an enrollment meeting if necessary.	For 401(k) and 403(b) plans, shortly after plan adoption
5. Give notice of the filing for advance determination to interested parties.	Before the date for filing the employer's tax return
6. File for an advance-determination letter.	Before the date for filing the employer's tax return
7. Make the first year's contribution.	Before the date for filing the employer's tax return
8. Supply a summary plan description to employees.	Within 120 days after the plan is adopted

ADMINISTRATION OF A CORPORATE PLAN

Every qualified plan has a plan administrator who is responsible for the administration of the plan. Typically, the plan administrator is the employer (in larger plans, the employer's director of human resources) or an individual or committee designated by the employer. The plan administrator receives help from a variety of sources. If the plan has a trust, the trustee may assist the plan administrator with administrative matters, but more frequently the trustee restricts his or her activities to investing the plan's assets. With insured plans, the insurer will generally provide a great number of administrative services, from computer support to producing manuals, which guide the plan administrator through the administrative process. In addition to the trustee or insurance company, the plan administrator can also look to a variety of third-party administrators (TPAs) who perform everything from turnkey services to only one specific service, such as administering the actual deferral percentage test. As a financial services professional, you will sometimes be asked to suggest or secure a TPA. (A list of third-party administrators can be found in chapter 2.)

One of the principal duties of the plan administrator is to comply with the reporting and disclosure requirements of ERISA. All qualified plans are subject to these reporting and disclosure requirements (except some church and state plans). The most important reporting and disclosure requirement is filing the annual return/report with the IRS. (*Planning Note:* Financial services professionals are sometimes asked to advise plan administrators on how to comply with the reporting and disclosure requirements and may be called on to help in the filing of forms.)

Beginning for the year 1999, the filing requirements were changed substantially. Now almost all filers are required to file Form 5500, which is now a short main form with basic identifying information. Under the new scheme, there are 13 schedule attachments focused on particular subjects and/or filing requirements—five pension schedules, seven financial schedules, and one fringe benefit schedule. Filers will have to complete only those schedules applicable to the filer's specific type of plan. The schedules most commonly filed by pension plans include:

- Schedule A of Form 5500 (Insurance Information). This form is filed if any benefits are provided by an insurance company.
- Schedule B of Form 5500 (Actuarial Information). This form is used for most defined-benefit plans.
- Schedule P of Form 5500 (Annual Return of Fiduciary of Employee Benefit Trust). This form starts the statute of limitations running on fiduciary responsibilities.
- Schedules H and I (Financial Information). These forms (H for large plans and I for small plans) report financial information about the plan.
- Schedule R (Retirement Plan Information). This form includes information on pension plans distributions and funding requirements.
- Schedule T (Qualified Pension Plan Coverage Information). This form reports information on the coverage requirements for tax-qualified plans.
- Schedule SSA of Form 5500 (Annual Registration—Statement Identifying Separated Participants with Deferred Vested Benefits). This form is filed if a covered participant separates from service and the participant is entitled to a deferred vested benefit.

Qualified plans referred to as "one-participant plans" are allowed to file Form 5500-EZ instead of Form 5500. A plan is considered to be a one-participant plan if it only covers (a) the business owner and his or her spouse (if the business is wholly owned by the owner and spouse) or (b) partners in a business partnership, or the partners and their spouses. In addition, to qualify as a one-participant plan, the plan must meet the minimum-coverage requirements on its own, and the plan cannot cover a business that is a member of an affiliated service group, a controlled group of corporations, or a group of businesses under common control.

A plan that satisfies the above one-participant requirements does not have to file Form 5500-EZ if the plan satisfies all of the conditions above and the plan has total plan assets of $100,000 or less at the end of every plan year. The same exception applies for an employer that has two or more one-participant plans that together had total plan assets of $100,000 or less at the end of every plan year. However, note that all one-participant plans *must* file a Form 5500-EZ for their final plan year even if the total plan assets have *always* been less than $100,000. The final plan year is the year in which distribution of all plan assets is completed.

When Form 5500 or Form 5500-EZ is required, it must be filed annually by the last day of the seventh month after the plan year ends. An extension of time up to 2 1/2 months may be granted if Form 5558 is filed.

In addition to filing the 5500 family of forms with the IRS, administrators of defined-benefit plans must also supply the Pension Benefit Guaranty Corporation with annual premiums and filings (Form PBGC-1). Form PBGC-1 is due no later than 7 months after the close of the plan year (July 31 for a calendar-year plan).

Plan administrators are required not only to file forms with appropriate federal agencies, but also to keep plan participants informed. Two of the most important ways of doing this are through the summary plan description (for an existing plan, the SPD must be furnished to an employee within 90 days of becoming a participant) and employee meetings. Other paperwork is also required, however; this includes supplying plan participants with a *summary annual report (SAR)* each year. This document is a summary of the information on the annual report—5500 form(s)—and is provided to each participant in the plan every year.

summary annual report (SAR)

In addition to a summary annual report, plan participants must also be supplied with a *summary of material modification (SMM)*. A summary of material modification informs the employees about changes in the plan. For example, if the vesting schedule was changed from 10-year-cliff vesting to 5-year-cliff vesting, the participants should be supplied with notification of the change within 210 days after the close of the plan year in which the material modification occurred. A material modification does not include every plan change but only the major changes shown in table 13-2.

summary of material modification (SMM)

Furnishing plan participants with a personal benefit statement is another important aspect of plan administration. Upon written request, each plan participant or beneficiary is entitled to receive a statement of the individual's own accrued benefit or account balance under the qualified plan. This statement need not be furnished more than once in any 12-month period but must be furnished upon a participant's termination of employment. Many plan administrators, however, feel it appropriate to provide a personal benefit statement every year to each participant and beneficiary even if there is no formal request for one. This is good practice because it makes employees more aware of their benefits and enables the employer to meet the organizational objectives of retaining and motivating employees.

TABLE 13-2
List of Material Modifications

- name and address of sponsor/employer
- name and address of plan administrator
- structure of plan
- name of plan
- type of plan
- agent for service of process
- persons performing functions for the plan
- sources and method of determining contributions
- method of asset accumulation
- procedure for presenting claims
- eligibility requirements
- vesting provisions
- features of portability or reciprocity
- length of service to determine participation, vesting, benefit accrual
- break-in-service rules
- requirements for pension benefits
- basis for computing retirement benefits
- circumstances causing loss of pension benefits
- joint and survivor annuity rules
- disposition of employee's contributions
- requirements for welfare benefits
- circumstances causing loss of welfare benefits
- fiduciaries' names and addresses

Another aspect of plan administration is counseling participants about plan choices—especially about participant contributions and investment alternatives (assuming that the participants have them). Periodic notices of the plans terms, enrollment meetings, investment alternative education, and even more general retirement planning education has become common place in the American work force today.

The distribution of benefits from qualified plans has become an extremely complicated and time-consuming process. The distribution process typically looks like the following:

- distribution information—the process typically begins when the participant requests a distribution from the plan
- election forms—participants will be given forms identifying the optional forms of distribution. These forms will be supported with written materials (and sometimes personal meetings) explaining the value of each option and the impact of electing one option over another.
- qualified joint and survivor annuity—if the distribution is to a married participant and the qualified joint and survivor annuity rules apply, the participant and spouse will have to sign off on any optional form of distribution
- direct rollover—virtually all participants receiving a distribution from a qualified plan must be given an election form that allows them to elect to roll the benefit directly to an IRA
- income tax treatment—in most cases, participants must be given general information about tax implications of a pension distribution
- 1099R forms—tax forms distributed to participants (and filed with the IRS) identifying the amount of the distribution and whether any portion is considered basis (not subject to income tax)

Another facet of plan administration involves amending plan documents. This may be required because the sponsor wants to make a design change or plan enhancement, or because the law has changed requiring plan amendments for the plan to remain "qualified." When a plan is amended, in

---

Summary of Plan-Administration Responsibilities

- Filing annual return or report (5500 or 5500-EZ)
- Filing annual premiums with PBGC (Form PBGC-1)
- Holding employee meetings
- Distributing SPDs to new participants
- Distributing summary annual report (SAR)
- Distributing SMM (if plan is amended)
- Furnishing personal benefit statements
- Counseling participants on participant options
- Handling benefit distributions
- Amending the plan when necessary

general, the sponsor needs to consider whether or not to resubmit the plan for an IRS determination letter. As with the initial qualification letter, submitting the plan is generally the safer approach. In some cases, the submission process is simpler because the IRS only reviews the amendment, not the entire plan.

SETTING UP AND ADMINISTERING A KEOGH PLAN

The rules for setting up and administering a qualified plan for a sole proprietor or partnership (still referred to as Keogh plans) are essentially the same as for a corporation. There are a few differences, however.

- A Keogh plan that satisfies the one-participant rules either files form 5500-EZ or has no filing requirements if assets are $100,000 or less (see former discussion).
- A plan that only covers owners (and their spouses) may not be subject to ERISA, meaning that no summary plan description is required.
- The deductible contribution is calculated differently due to the "net income" calculation discussed in chapter 3.
- Such plans can not make loans to owners who are plan participants.
- A letter or some other document should be used by a sole proprietorship or partnership to formally adopt the plan. This is the corollary to the corporate resolution that adopts the plan.

The following are some other considerations that are important when installing a Keogh plan:

- The role of the financial services professional takes on greater significance when the client establishes a Keogh plan, because such clients typically do not have an administrative arm to carry out the multiple functions associated with plan installation and administration.
- Like corporate plans, a qualified plan must be established by December 31 (with a calendar year tax year) in order for a deduction to be taken for the year. Plan contributions, however, can be made up until the tax return deadline plus extensions. If the year has ended, it may still be possible to adopt a SEP (simplified employee pension), which can be established up to April 15.
- A business owner can shift documents—for example from one master plan to a different one—without incurring any penalties. (*Planning*

Note: If your client is currently under another organization's master Keogh plan, the possibility for a "painless" switch exists.)

SOFTWARE PACKAGES USED FOR PLAN INSTALLATION AND ADMINISTRATION

A variety of software packages are available from insurance company home offices and pension vendors that aid in the process of plan installation and administration. Software packages are widely available in the following areas:

- actual deferral percentage test calculation (monitors whether 401(k) plans meet the ADP test)
- actuarial valuations (a must for firms with defined-benefit plans)
- claims processing (typically used in conjunction with welfare benefit plans)
- document preparation (both plan and summary plan description)
- employee benefit statement preparation (typically used in conjunction with welfare benefit plans)
- nondiscrimination testing (monitors whether plans meet 410(b) and 401(a) 26 tests)
- top-heavy analysis (monitors top-heavy status of plan)
- 5500 forms preparation (very popular method for simplifying government filings)
- pension check processing (processes benefit payments)
- loan processing (useful for processing loans and tracking plan loan repayments)

CHAPTER REVIEW

Answers to the review questions and the self-test questions start on page 673.

Key Terms

enrollment meeting
advance-determination letter
notice to interested parties
summary plan description (SPD)

summary annual report (SAR)
summary of material modification
    (SMM)

Review Questions

13-1.   What role does the financial services professional play in the plan-installation and plan-administration processes?

13-2.   What are the steps involved in adopting a corporate plan?

13-3.   a.   Who is typically appointed to be the plan administrator?
        b.   What individuals and organizations help the plan administrator administer the plan?

13-4.   Why is the summary plan description (SPD) frequently used as a means of fulfilling the employer's obligation to explain the plan to participants?

13-5.   Discuss the makeup of a summary plan description with regard to
        a.   the limitations on using the SPD as a marketing piece
        b.   the plan provisions that it must explain

13-6.   Identify each of the following:
        a.   Form 5500
        b.   Schedule A of Form 5500
        c.   Schedule SSA of Form 5500
        d.   Form 5500-EZ
        e.   Form PBGC-1

13-7.   Describe the responsibility of the plan administrator with regard to
        a.   distributing the summary annual report
        b.   issuing personal benefit statements
        c.   counseling participants concerning plan options
        d.   amending the plan document

13-8. How do the installation and administration of a Keogh plan differ from the installation and administration of a corporate plan?

Self-Test Questions

T   F   13-1.   To receive a deduction for the tax year, a corporation the board of directors must adopt a qualified plan before the end of the tax year.

T   F   13-2.   At the same time the corporate board of directors approves the plan, it should also approve the trust instrument or the specimen group pension contract that is provided.

T   F   13-3.   The entire first-year plan contribution must be made in time for filing the employer's tax return (plus extensions) for the year in which the plan is adopted in order for the employer to take a deduction.

T   F   13-4.   401(k) and 403(b) plans are typically set up at the end of the first year for which a deduction is going to be taken.

T   F   13-5.   The employer must file an application for an advance-determination letter with the IRS in order for the plan to be considered qualified.

T   F   13-6.   If the filing for an advance determination letter is not made on a timely basis, the IRS could prohibit the sponsor from making corrective retroactive amendments.

T   F   13-7.   A summary plan description can be used as a marketing tool that emphasizes only the attractive features of the plan in order to persuade employees to join the plan.

T   F   13-8.   The summary plan description must spell out any terms that could result in a participant losing benefits.

T   F   13-9.   A summary plan description must contain a description and explanation of the plan's vesting schedule.

T   F   13-10.   The summary plan description must contain a statement of ERISA rights.

T   F   13-11.   The plan administrator is prohibited by ERISA from delegating any of his or her plan administration duties.

T   F   13-12.   One of the principal duties of the plan administrator is to comply with the reporting and disclosure requirements of ERISA.

T   F   13-13.   The plan administrator of a small corporation (50 employees) must file a detailed annual report (Form 5500) each year.

T   F   13-14.   The plan administrator of a profit-sharing plan covering only a self-employed person (with no employees) with $60,000 of assets at the end of the year generally must file Form 5500-EZ each year.

T   F   13-15.   Participants in a qualified plan must receive a summary annual report each year.

T   F   13-16.   A summary of material modification must be supplied if the plan changes its vesting schedule.

T   F   13-17.   The plan administrator is required to issue a personal benefit statement only when a person retires.

T   F   13-18.   A 1099-R form is used to notify participants of the amount of their plan's lump-sum or periodic distribution for tax purposes.

T   F   13-19. A Keogh plan (with a sponsor that has a calendar tax year) must be established by December 31 in order for a deduction to be taken for the year.

14

Plan Termination

Learning Objectives

An understanding of the material in this chapter should enable the student to

14-1. State the reasons for terminating plans and identify typical problems.

14-2. Describe the steps for terminating a defined-contribution plan.

14-3. Describe the steps for terminating a defined-benefit plan.

14-4. Identify the process for distributing plan assets from a terminating plan.

14-5. Review the circumstances in which a plan may be terminated by operation of law

---

Chapter Outline

Business owners contemplating the establishment of a retirement plan need to know that qualified plans must be permanent, rather than temporary, programs. The IRS seeks assurance that the plan is intended to meet the retirement needs of present and future employees rather than as a tax shelter for key employees. This does not mean, however, that the business owner must be saddled with a plan indefinitely. If business conditions change substantially, the plan can still be terminated, as long as the plan has been drafted to reserve the employer's right to terminate it.

The term *plan termination* used herein means the complete dissolution of the plan: participants receive no additional plan benefits, contributions cease (after meeting remaining obligations), plan assets are liquidated, and benefits are distributed. The employer considering termination of a plan may not be fully aware of the consequences and administrative burdens of such a decision. This chapter explores the procedures and ramifications of plan termination and reviews less drastic alternatives.

TO TERMINATE OR NOT TO TERMINATE

Why Plan Termination?

The employer may wish to terminate a plan for any number of business reasons, such as the following common ones:

- The employer is no longer in a financial position to make further plan contributions.
- The plan benefits are not meaningful amounts, and participants are limited in their ability to make deductible IRA contributions.
- To lower plan costs and ease administrative complexity, the employer may want to switch plan designs (for example, switching from a defined-benefit to a defined-contribution approach).
- The company may want to switch to an employee stock ownership plan (ESOP) to purchase the stock of a retiring owner.
- The employer may want to accommodate a substantial change in business operations, such as the sale or merger of the business.

Alternatives to Plan Termination

Plan termination is much more than simply ceasing additional employer contributions. It also means notifying proper governmental agencies, liquidating assets, and distributing funds to participants—all of which generate a great deal of paperwork and administrative expense. Before deciding to terminate a plan, the employer should consider other alternatives.

Ceasing Further Benefit Accruals

A defined-benefit or defined-contribution plan can be amended to cease further benefit accruals—as long as benefits already earned are not reduced. With defined-contribution plans, this strategy can be used to cease employer contributions. This approach may make sense to the employer who expects to resume making contributions later or who is concerned about participants squandering retirement benefits if they receive them now. Ceasing accruals in a defined-benefit plan does not always result in a complete cessation of contributions, depending upon the funding status of the plan. Ceasing accruals will, however, limit the plan sponsor's future funding obligations.

Regardless of the type of plan involved, one issue that must always be considered is whether additional benefit accruals must be awarded for the current year. Under ERISA, benefit accruals cannot cease until 15 days after plan participants have been notified of the amendment. Therefore, the effective date of the amendment ceasing accruals must be a minimum of 15 days after notice is given. Once the effective date is established, a determination is made whether participants are entitled to another year of benefit accrual. The rule is that participants are entitled to an accrual if they meet all service eligibility requirements *prior to* the effective date of the amendment.

***Example*:**	Alpha Corporation maintains a money-purchase pension plan with a calendar plan year. The plan is amended to cease accruals effective September 1 (and participants are given notice of the amendment by the preceding August 15). If the plan awards a benefit accrual to participants completing 1,000 hours of service, full-time employees will have met the 1,000-hour requirement by September 1 and will be entitled to an accrual for the current plan year.

An amendment ceasing accruals for current participants usually should include a provision prohibiting other employees from becoming new plan participants. Because new participants will not be eligible for any benefits, adding them simply compounds the administrative burden. Under the law, a plan that is not currently providing benefit accruals does not have to satisfy any minimum coverage requirements, so prohibiting new members does not cause any coverage problems.

Effect on Defined-Benefit Plans. Ceasing further benefit accruals in a defined-benefit plan does not change the plan's essential nature—the plan is still required to pay promised benefits as they become due, employees continue to vest under the same vesting schedule,[1] and the employer is still required to meet the minimum funding obligations. If assets are not sufficient to meet the projected payouts, the actuary may determine that additional contributions are still necessary. Plans subject to the PBGC insurance program must continue paying insurance premiums. The rising costs of these premiums over the last few years could weigh in favor of terminating the plan versus discontinuing further benefit accruals.

Effect on Defined-Contribution Plans. In a money-purchase plan, or any other plan with required contributions, the only additional contributions necessary when accruals cease are those to fund the prior or current year's obligation.

Whether the same vesting provisions can continue to apply or whether full vesting occurs depends upon the type of plan involved. Any defined-contribution plan that is a pension plan (money-purchase and target-benefit plans) should be able to continue using the same vesting schedule. On the other hand, in profit-sharing plans, participants become fully vested when employer contributions are completely discontinued. (See below for a more complete discussion.)

Amending the Plan into Another Type

In some circumstances, the employer has the choice to amend the plan into another type of plan, rather than terminating the plan and starting up a new one. This is a tricky area and legal consultation should be sought. However, some general guidelines can be provided. A defined-contribution plan of one type usually can be amended into another type of defined-contribution plan; for example, a money-purchase plan can be amended into a profit-sharing plan. The amendment must be carefully drafted to ensure that subtle differences between the types of plans are addressed.

Likewise, a defined-benefit plan of one type can be amended into another type of defined-benefit plan. In the large plan market, this sometimes happens when a traditional defined-benefit plan is amended into a cash-balance-type plan. One type of amendment is clearly prohibited: defined-benefit plans cannot be amended into defined-contribution plans, and defined-contribution plans cannot be amended into defined-benefit plans.

Limitations on Plan Termination

Several issues may discourage or prohibit the plan sponsor from terminating the plan. These issues are addressed below.

Temporary Tax Shelters

As a general rule, retirement plans may not be set up as a subterfuge to tax-shelter funds for the benefit of key employees. If they have been, plan termination can result in retroactive disqualification. For plans terminated within a few years after establishment, the IRS presumes that the employer did not intend for the plan to be permanent. To rebut this assumption, the employer must provide a reason of "business necessity beyond the employer's control." Acceptable reasons for an early termination appear to be change in ownership by merger, the liquidation or dissolution of the business, a change in ownership by sale or transfer, adverse business conditions, a significant change in the pension law, or a change in the company's retirement plan strategy, resulting in the adoption of a replacement plan. Practically speaking, the permanency issue is not a concern when the plan has been maintained for at least 10 years.

Insufficient Plan Assets

In defined-contribution plans, plan benefits are based upon the individual accounts, which represent all the assets held by the plan. This means that additional employer contributions are generally not required when a plan is terminated. However, for any plan that requires specified employer contributions, promised contributions that have not been made at the time of termination must still be made.

Defined-benefit plans, on the other hand, are a totally different story. In defined-benefit plans, assets never equal the present value of promised benefits. The plan will either have more than enough or not enough assets to pay promised benefits. When assets are insufficient to pay benefits, plans subject to the Pension Benefit Guaranty Corporation (PBGC) insurance program may not be able to be terminated at all. The PBGC has a financial interest at this point, and strict rules (described below) apply. If the plan cannot be terminated, the employer generally will want to amend the plan to cease all further benefit accruals in order to limit its future liability. If a plan with insufficient assets is not subject to the PBGC program, the plan may be terminated, and strict rules regarding how plan assets are allocated to the participants apply. The rules that apply to plans with excess assets are discussed more fully below.

Plan Problems

Plan termination is a time when the IRS scrutinizes the operation of the plan. The sponsor of a plan should correct any compliance problems prior to considering plan termination. The IRS currently maintains a voluntary compliance program, which allows sponsors willing to correct compliance problems to do so with a minimum of penalties.

TERMINATING A DEFINED-CONTRIBUTION PLAN

Compared with the termination of a defined-benefit plan covered by the PBGC insurance program, termination of a defined-contribution plan is relatively easy. However, each of the following steps needs to be taken:

- A corporate resolution terminating the plan must be adopted, and the plan and trust must be amended to terminate further accruals. As discussed above, the issue of whether participants have accrued a benefit for the current year has to be carefully considered.
- The plan termination date must be scheduled at least 15 days after participants are notified. Because the termination effectively ceases benefit accruals, the ERISA rule requiring that participants be notified 15 days before the amendment becomes effective applies.
- The employer must make any remaining required contributions for the previous year or for this year's benefit accruals.
- Sometimes when the laws regarding qualified plans change, plan sponsors are allowed an extended period in which to incorporate amendments reflecting the new law. If this is the case at the time of a plan termination, conforming amendments should be added to the plan.
- Plan assets must be liquidated in preparation for distribution. Note that assets can be distributed in kind as long as the highly compensated employees are not given special treatment.
- Benefit distribution paperwork (described below) must be prepared.
- In the year that benefits are distributed, when the annual IRS Form 5500 is filed, it is marked as the "final form."

Submitting the Plan to the IRS

At the time of plan termination, the sponsor of a qualified plan can voluntarily request an IRS approval letter. If granted, the IRS letter states that the plan termination does not adversely affect the qualified status of the plan. Although the submission is voluntary, in recent history, the IRS has audited a large number of plans that terminate without requesting such a determination letter.

The determination letter gives the sponsor and plan participants the assurance that distributed benefits will be eligible for the special tax treatment afforded to qualified plans. Unfortunately, the IRS determination letter is not a guarantee that the plan will not be audited later. However, the auditing process should go more smoothly if the determination letter had been requested. For these reasons, it is generally a good idea for the plan sponsor to request the IRS determination letter.

To request a determination letter, the plan sponsor must complete and submit Form 5310. Also, all plan participants and beneficiaries must be given notice of the submission. Besides announcing the submission, the notice should inform participants that they are allowed to send comments to the IRS or Department of Labor (DOL). Strict rules apply to who must receive the notice as well as how and when it is to be distributed.

TERMINATING A DEFINED-BENEFIT PLAN

An extremely complex termination procedure applies for defined-benefit plans covered under the PBGC insurance program. For plans that are not covered, the procedures are similar to those described above.

Plans Covered under the PBGC Insurance Program

Overview

The Pension Benefit Guaranty Corporation (PBGC) is a federal agency that insures participants against the loss of benefits arising from complete or partial termination of a defined-benefit plan. When this agency was discussed in chapter 2, we mentioned that the PBGC

- covers all qualified defined-benefit plans (except for plans of professional-service employers with 25 or fewer active participants)
- collects compulsory premiums
- guarantees benefits (up to a maximum of approximately $3,200) in case of employer default
- oversees plan terminations initiated by the employer
- initiates terminations if a plan is financially strained
- taps up to 30 percent of the net worth of employers whose plans have terminated and left the PBGC liable for payments

Here, we will explore the PBGC's practices and requirements for plan terminations initiated voluntarily by the employer. But note that the PBGC also has the right to terminate a plan in financial difficulty (as discussed further at the end of the chapter).

Voluntary Plan Termination

When an employer wishes to terminate a defined-benefit plan covered under the PBGC program, the employer faces three issues:

- Can the plan be voluntarily terminated?
- When can the plan be terminated?
- How can the plan be terminated?

The Single Employer Pension Plan Amendments Act (SEPPAA) addresses and provides answers to each of these questions. SEPPAA introduced a major change to the plan termination process. Now a plan can be terminated only if it meets specific conditions; if not, the plan must continue until the conditions are satisfied. Technically speaking, a termination is allowed only if the plan satisfies conditions for a standard or a distress termination.

standard termination

Standard Termination. The employer can initiate a *standard termination* only if the plan has sufficient assets to pay all plan benefits. If the plan does not currently have sufficient assets, the plan may still qualify for a standard termination if the employer agrees to make up the difference with a single payment, or if a 50 percent owner of the company agrees to waive benefits due under the plan.

distress termination

Distress Termination. If the plan does not have sufficient assets to pay promised benefits, the plan may qualify—in extreme circumstances—for a *distress termination.* To qualify, the employer must fall within one of the following categories:

- It faces liquidation in bankruptcy or insolvency proceedings.
- It faces reorganization in bankruptcy or insolvency proceedings.
- It can demonstrate to the PBGC that it will be unable to pay its debts when due and will be unable to continue the business.
- It can prove that the cost of providing coverage has become unreasonably burdensome as a result of a decline in the workforce.

Setting the Termination Date. Assuming an employer is able to terminate the plan under SEPPAA, the next consideration is the termination date. This date has great importance because it establishes the limits on the employer's liability. The date is contingent upon notification of participants of the upcoming termination. The actual termination date must be from 60 to 90 days after the notification.

Steps in a Plan Termination. Once the date is established, in order to keep the termination date, all of the following PBGC-required procedures must be completed in a timely manner:

- issuing a notice of intent to terminate to participants and beneficiaries at least 60 days and no more than 90 days before the proposed termination date
- filing a notice of the termination on Form 500 (including an actuaries certificate that assets are sufficient to pay promised benefits) with the PBGC on or before the 180th day after the proposed termination date
- distributing assets to satisfy plan obligations within 180 days after the PBGC 60-day review period

In addition to the requirements established by the PBGC, the plan also must take each of the steps required for terminating a defined-contribution plan. To summarize, these include:

- adopting a corporate resolution to terminate the plan and amending the plan and trust to terminate further accruals
- making any remaining required contributions
- adopting plan amendments to conform with law changes
- deciding whether to voluntarily request IRS approval on Form 5310 and notifying participants
- liquidating plan assets in preparation for distribution
- preparing benefit distribution paperwork (described below)
- filing the final 5500 annual return/report

Plans Not Covered under the PBGC Insurance Program

When a plan is not subject to PBGC regulation, it need not conform to the PBGC's rigid termination procedures. Because of this, a non-PBGC plan can be terminated even if it does not have sufficient assets to pay all plan benefits. When this is the case, the law prescribes a specific method for dividing the plan assets among the participants. In many cases, to avoid bad feelings (and potential lawsuits), the owners will decide to have all of the deficiency taken from their own benefits.

The administrative burden is not as great with the non-PBGC plan, because the PBGC filing requirements do not have to be satisfied. However, the sponsor does have to take all of the steps required for terminating a defined-contribution plan, as described above.

Reversion of Excess Plan Assets

As stated earlier, a defined-benefit plan may, at any point in time, have more assets than necessary to pay benefits promised under the plan. This generally occurs when plan assets outperform the actuaries' assumptions. Before the mid-1980s, an employer could terminate a plan and receive an asset reversion from an overfunded terminated defined-benefit plan without penalty (although the amount was and still is treated as taxable income to the employer).

However, beginning in the mid-1980s, the law began to make the practice of terminating plans to recover surplus assets less desirable by adding penalty taxes to the amount of excess assets returned to the employer. Congress took its strongest action to date in promoting these goals when it passed the Revenue Reconciliation Act of 1990. The Act (Code Subsection 4980) created a 50 percent excise tax on all reversions except when the employer shares the reversion with employees, in which case the excise tax is only 20 percent.

To qualify for the 20 percent tax rate, the employer must either (1) establish a qualified replacement plan to which it transfers assets equal to 25 percent of the reversion or (2) provide pro rata increases in benefits of qualified participants in connection with the plan termination equal to at least 20 percent of the reversion.

Note that in order to revert plan assets to the employer, the plan must specifically state that excess assets will revert at the time of plan termination. Under a recent law change, a plan that does not have such a provision may not be amended to do so at the time of the termination.

When a plan has excess assets, the employer is not under any obligation to revert the excess. The assets may be, and often are, allocated among plan participants. The law provides some discretion in the allocation method, and the actuary should provide several alternatives. In the small-plan setting, the actuary generally looks for a method that allocates the lion's share of the excess to the business owner. This can work quite well, unless the owner's benefit is already approaching the maximum benefit limitations. If the owner can get a significant piece of the excess, the reallocation method has clear tax advantages—benefits can be rolled into an IRA and tax deferral can continue. On the other hand, if the owner's share of the excess is limited, he or she may prefer the reversion approach.

DISTRIBUTIONS FROM A TERMINATING PLAN

In one significant way, the process of distributing plan benefits at the time of plan termination is different than in other situations. If the plan is to pay single-sum benefits, then the paperwork involved is the same as for normal benefit payouts. On the other hand, if participants are to receive deferred annuity payments at retirement, the plan purchases deferred annuities and much of the normal distribution paperwork will be completed at the time the annuity begins.

The form of benefit payout at plan termination depends solely upon the terms of the plan. If the plan does not offer a lump-sum option, the employer purchases a single-premium annuity contract (SPAC) from an insurance company, and all benefit payouts are made through that contract. If the plan does offer a lump-sum option, participants must be given a choice to receive a single sum or the deferred annuity. At the employer's election, a single-sum option can be added at the time of termination; however, such an option may not be removed. When a plan has a lump-sum option, in most cases, participants elect this option.

The employer considering the addition of a lump-sum option in a defined-benefit plan should do so carefully. Under the law, single-sum benefits are calculated using the lower of the plan's specified interest rate or a rate specified by the PBGC. When interest rates in the market are low, the PBGC rate can also be quite low. Therefore, in many cases, providing benefits in the form of a lump sum can prove to be more expensive than purchasing a deferred annuity.

Single-Premium Annuity Contracts

single-premium annuity contract

Employers wishing to purchase paid-up annuities to satisfy the distribution obligation from a terminating plan purchase a *single-premium annuity contract*. SPACs are issued through group pension departments of insurance companies and sold to plans that are terminating. In return for the single premium, the insurance company assumes the transferred plan liabilities and issues annuity certificates that ensure participants receive their benefits.

At the time that participants retire, they choose a distribution option from among the various ones available. The law requires that the SPAC distribution options match the original plan distribution options. At the time of payout, the insurer provides election forms, qualified joint and survivor notices, and so on.

SPACs are typically difficult for an insurer to price (that is, to determine how much money is required from the employer to pay the benefit obligations under the plan). The insurer must first assess the liabilities under the plan, a process complicated by discrepancies in terminology from plan to plan and the presence of any atypical design features. The second step, finding the present value of future obligations, can be even trickier. At this stage, the insurer must apply assumptions regarding interest return, mortality, early retirement (which is particularly important if the early-retirement benefit is subsidized), and other variables. A third difficult aspect of pricing a SPAC lies with the one-time expense charge. Theoretically, the employer could be making benefit payments 50 years or more in the future. Determining expenses for that length of time can be almost impossible. All of these pricing difficulties affect the insurance company because (1) the single premium required can vary significantly from company to company and (2) a SPAC that is priced too high will not be competitive and a SPAC that is priced too low will lose money.

With the failure of several insurance companies, note that the DOL is quite concerned about the choice of carriers when a SPAC is purchased. The employer and other plan fiduciaries may be held personally liable if the insurer cannot pay up—if it is determined that the fiduciaries did not use reasonable care when choosing the carrier. On a practical level, this means the fiduciaries should

- obtain several SPAC quotes
- document how and why the particular choice was made
- review the company's insurance ratings using a number of rating services
- be especially careful when they choose a lower quote, if that insurer is also rated lower than the competition
- consider hiring independent consultants to further analyze the financial condition of the company

Remember that fiduciaries are not liable simply if the insurer fails—only if they behaved in an imprudent manner.

**YOUR FINANCIAL SERVICES PRACTICE:
SELLING SPACs**

The SPAC is a relatively convenient product for the financial services professional to sell. The market is easily identifiable (terminating plans), the sale depends solely on the single premium being requested, and commissions are received promptly. The sale of a SPAC is a one-step process that does not call for an ongoing commitment to the client. The most difficult part of the sale is making sure the home office receives the proper documents for underwriting purposes and that the single-premium quote is competitive with other quotes. Also, the agent needs to carefully consider the fiduciary issues mentioned above.

Distribution Paperwork

If the plan does not allow lump-sum payments and a SPAC is being purchased, participants do not make a distribution election at the time of the termination. The actual benefit election is made later at retirement. However, if participants have the option to receive a lump sum, then the paperwork is similar to any other plan distribution (discussed in detail in the previous chapter). The following summarizes the various items that must be given to and completed by participants:

- benefit election form
- notice and election forms for applicable qualified joint and survivor annuity rules
- notice and election forms for the right to have benefits transferred directly to an IRA or other qualified plan
- IRS Form 1099R for lump-sum distributions

TERMINATIONS BY OPERATION OF LAW

In the preceding part of this chapter, we discussed plan terminations initiated by the employer. Here we discuss a quite different topic, plan terminations that occur due to the operation of law. This may occur in three separate situations:

- a partial termination of any qualified plan, resulting from a sudden reduction in the number of plan participants or a reduction in plan benefits
- the termination of a profit-sharing plan as a result of a complete discontinuance of contributions
- the involuntary termination of a defined-benefit plan by the PBGC

Partial Terminations

partial plan termination

As mentioned previously, when a plan is terminated, the Tax Code requires that plan benefits become fully vested. This rule also applies to those participants affected by a *partial plan termination*. Unfortunately, this term is not defined in the Code. Under the regulations, the decision whether a partial termination exists is based on a review of all the facts and circumstances. The factors in this determination are

- whether the number of plan participants has been substantially reduced, *and*

- whether plan amendments have adversely affected the rights of employees to vest in benefits under the plan

When there is a reduction in the number of participants, there is no specified number or percentage drop that triggers a partial termination. Each case is decided by the facts and circumstances. However, any time plan participation drops by more than 20 percent, corporate counsel should look into the issue. Drop-offs in participation may occur due to layoff, an amendment excluding previously eligible participants, or (in rare occurrences) voluntary termination of employment. Under the various cases and rulings, a partial termination is certainly more likely if the reduction is within the control of the employer; however, the IRS has indicated that a partial termination may exist even when participants terminated employment voluntarily. The result of a determination that a partial termination exits is that all participants eliminated from the plan become fully vested.

Reduction in the number of participants is the most likely scenario in which the partial termination issue will arise; still, whenever the plan's vesting provisions are amended, the second rule must be considered. Amendments adversely affecting participants' rights to vest can result in a partial termination. This provision seems unnecessary, because other provisions in the Code prohibit the reduction of vested benefits already accrued and allow participants with 3 years of service to select an old vesting provision over a new, less favorable one.

The regulations identify a third type of partial termination. Under this special rule, a defined-benefit plan is deemed to be partially terminated if the reduction (or cessation) of benefit accruals results in—or increases the possibility of—a reversion to the employer. This means that the determination depends entirely on the plan's funding status at the time of the amendment. In other words, an amended plan that is not fully funded does not result in a partial termination, whereas a plan with excess assets at the time of the amendment would create a partially terminated plan. When a partial termination exists under this special rule, all participants become fully vested in their benefits as of the time of the amendment.

Profit-Sharing Plans

The same Code section governing partial terminations states that in profit-sharing type plans (which include 401(k) plans and ESOPs), participants become fully vested at the time of a complete "discontinuance of contributions." Again, the determination is based on a facts-and-circumstances test. In making the determination, the IRS considers whether contributions have been recurring and substantial, and whether there is any reasonable probability that the lack of contributions will continue indefinitely. This vague standard makes it difficult for the sponsor to determine whether the rule applies in a particular case. As a practical matter, the issue should be reviewed if no substantial contributions are made to a plan for 2 years or more.

The IRS—especially at the time a plan terminates—will definitely review the complete discontinuance issue. In many situations, plans are terminated well after the date that contributions have ceased. In this scenario, the IRS is likely to determine that benefits became fully vested at the time contributions stopped, not when the plan was actually terminated. Such a determination can cause major headaches when forfeited benefits have already been reallocated to other participants.

Involuntary Terminations of Defined-Benefit Plans

involuntary
terminations

In the case of a defined-benefit plan covered by the PBGC insurance program, the PBGC has the right to involuntarily terminate a plan in very limited circumstances. The reason that it does so is to protect itself from mounting liabilities under a plan that shows no promise of meeting its obligations. The PBGC can institute termination proceedings if it determines that the interests of the plan participants would be better served by the termination, and if any one of the following occurs:

- Minimum funding standards have not been satisfied.
- Benefits cannot be paid when they are due.
- A substantial lump-sum payment has been made to a substantial owner who is a plan participant.
- The long-run liability of the company to the PBGC is expected to increase unreasonably.

CHAPTER REVIEW

Answers to review questions and the self-test questions start on page 673.

Key Terms

standard termination   partial plan termination
distress termination   involuntary terminations
single-premium annuity contract

Review Questions

14-1.   Explain the reasons employers typically terminate a qualified plan.

14-2.   Identify alternatives to plan termination.

14-3.   What problems can get in the way of a plan termination?

14-4.   Describe the steps required for terminating a defined-contribution plan.

14-5.   Explain why the employer should consider submitting the plan for IRS approval upon plan termination.

14-6.   What is the major difference between terminating defined-benefit plans covered by the PBGC and terminating those that are not covered?

14-7.   What does the employer have to do to qualify for the lower 20 percent reversion excise tax?

14-8.   Describe a single-premium annuity contract (SPAC).

14-9.   Identify the three situations in which a termination by operation of law can occur.

Self-Test Questions

T   F   14-1.   A qualified plan may not be terminated within 10 years of the date it is adopted.

T   F   14-2.   The Pension Benefit Guaranty Corporation (PBGC) collects compulsory premiums from defined-benefit and defined-contribution plans.

T   F   14-3.   Employers with a defined-benefit plan covered by the PBGC who do not meet the requirements for either a standard or distress termination cannot terminate their plans.

T   F   14-4.   A distress termination is available if the employer can demonstrate to the PBGC that it is facing liquidation in bankruptcy.

T   F   14-5.   A penalty tax applies to assets that revert to the employer because of a defined-benefit plan termination.

T   F   14-6.   In order for an employer to qualify for the lower 20 percent penalty tax, the employer must allocate at least 50 percent of the excess assets to the participants.

T   F   14-7.   When single-premium annuity contracts are issued, the insurance company takes over the employer's responsibility to make benefit payments.

T   F   14-8.   Single-premium annuity contracts are risk-free contracts from the insurer's point of view.

T   F   14-9.   If 5 percent of the workforce is laid off, a partial termination has occurred and affected participants must become fully vested in their benefits.

T   F   14-10. The PBGC has the power to involuntarily terminate a plan.

Note

1. Participants may have to become fully vested in accordance with the rule discussed in the section on partial plan terminations. Under this rule, full and immediate vesting is only an issue if the plan has excess assets at the time the amendment is adopted.

Nonqualified Retirement Plans: An Overview

Learning Objectives

An understanding of the material in this chapter should enable the student to

---

15-1. Identify the planning situations in which a nonqualified deferred-compensation plan should be used.

15-2. Compare and contrast the various types of nonqualified deferred-compensation plans.

15-3. Identify the various design provisions that can be inserted in a nonqualified deferred-compensation plan.

15-4. Discuss stock option programs.

Chapter Outline

Up to this point, the emphasis has been on the use of a tax-sheltered retirement plan to meet the needs of the small business and the small-business owner. However, a second lucrative market is open to financial services professionals who are servicing the retirement needs of the business and the business owner. This market is the nonqualified plan market, which includes nonqualified deferred-compensation plans and executive-bonus plans. These plans help the business owner and selected employees save for retirement without being subject to the requirements that apply to qualified plans. As a trade-off for allowing the employer complete discretion in plan design and in choosing the employees that will be covered by the plan, the employer loses the central advantage of a qualified plan—that is, the ability to make a before-tax contribution on the employee's behalf that is simultaneously deductible to the business. Instead, the employer is entitled to an immediate deduction only if the employee is currently taxed, or conversely, the employee may defer tax only if the employer's deduction is deferred.

One housekeeping detail needs to be discussed before we start to explore the nonqualified market. Nonqualified deferred-compensation plans are sometimes referred to as salary continuation plans, deferred-compensation plans, and nonqualified plans. These aliases, however, can be misleading because they all have other meanings. For example, the term *salary continuation plan* is sometimes used to refer to sick days and disability benefits. Likewise, *deferred compensation* sometimes refers to qualified pension and profit-sharing plans. The term *nonqualified plans* can refer to a myriad of plans that fail to meet various qualification standards. Because we are going to discuss only nonqualified deferred-compensation plans in chapters 15 and 16, we will call them nonqualified plans for short. In the marketplace, however, it is wise to make sure everybody is on the same wavelength and is not tripped up by the confusing nomenclature.

YOUR FINANCIAL SERVICES PRACTICE: THE ALLURE OF THE NONQUALIFIED MARKET

Several factors prompt financial services professionals to become involved in the nonqualified market. Some get involved because nonqualified deferred-compensation and executive-bonus plans help them to provide comprehensive services to their clients. A combination of life insurance, individual annuities, qualified plans, and nonqualified plans allows the financial service professional to provide a comprehensive umbrella of retirement coverage. Others prefer the nonqualified market because it means contact with an upscale clientele, and this, in turn, provides networking opportunities. A third reason to be involved is that life insurance is often the most appropriate funding vehicle.

PROBLEM SOLVING WITH NONQUALIFIED PLANS

The nonqualified market is a very important part of a financial services practice in the retirement field because it allows financial services professionals to successfully deal with client situations that are otherwise unsolvable, such as these:

- The client wants to provide a second tier of executive retirement benefits in addition to the qualified plan in order to attract and retain strong executives.
- The client wants to limit coverage to certain executives.
- The client wants a plan that is less administrative burden than a qualified plan.
- The client wants to give executives the opportunity to save more of their current income. Sometimes the program dovetails with a 401(k) plan, and only salary deferrals above the 401(k) plan go into the nonqualified program.
- The client is an owner of a closely held business who is looking to temporarily save taxes may want to have income retained in the company. This makes sense when the corporate tax rate is lower than the individual tax rate. Note, however, that the IRS may challenge a plan that allows a controlling (50 percent) shareholder to defer compensation.[1]
- The client is the owner of a closely held business that is just starting up and the company lacks the cash to pay owner-employees their full salaries. Making the promise to pay the executive compensation later establishes the obligation to pay additional income and helps avoid problems with the IRS about "reasonable compensation" in later years when the owners are receiving large payouts.
- The client wants to meet the organization's objectives of attracting executives, retaining executives, and providing for a graceful transition in company leadership. Although qualified plans can achieve similar objectives, nonqualified plans can be more effective because they are subject to fewer design restrictions.

DETERMINING THE COMPANY'S NEEDS

Once your client has indicated that one or more of the above situations is applicable, your next step is to focus the client on the important issues involved in selecting and designing a nonqualified plan. In addition, you need to discern the organization's needs and objectives. The device used to accomplish these steps is a nonqualified plan fact finder.

NONQUALIFIED PLAN FACT FINDER

Client Name: _____

Step 1: Identify concerns

Listed below are some typical concerns that organizations have when instituting a nonqualified plan. Grade each of these concerns by scoring 1 for very valuable, 2 for valuable, 3 for moderately valuable, and 4 for least valuable.

1.	Avoid the nondiscrimination requirements of a qualified plan.	[1][2][3][4]
2.	Allow executives to defer current income for their own tax-shelter purposes.	[1][2][3][4]
3.	Exceed the 415 maximum benefit and contribution limits of a qualified plan.	[1][2][3][4]
4.	Supplement qualified-plan benefits that are not stretched to the maximum limits.	[1][2][3][4]
5.	Recruit talented executives from outside the company.	[1][2][3][4]
6.	Retain executives by inducing them to stay with the company.	[1][2][3][4]
7.	Induce executives to take early retirement.	[1][2][3][4]
8.	Induce executives to provide consulting services after retirement.	[1][2][3][4]
9.	Keep executives from competing with the company.	[1][2][3][4]
10.	Adjust executive retirement benefits to include not only the compensation considered under the qualified plan but all compensation.	[1][2][3][4]

Step 2: List in order the primary reasons for establishing a nonqualified plan
1.
2.
3.

The fact finder (above) will

- provide a working framework for soliciting the client's goals
- serve as a due-diligence checklist, which will ensure that important discussions have not been omitted
- operate as a training tool for those who have little or no experience with nonqualified plans
- educate the client about the various needs, objectives, and considerations that are relevant to plan selection and design

CHOOSING THE BEST NONQUALIFIED RETIREMENT PLAN

When you have a full understanding of the client's objectives, you can choose the proper nonqualified plan. There are many varieties of nonqualified plans, but our focus will be primarily on deferred-compensation plans. However, due to their growing popularity, stock option programs are discussed at the end of this chapter. Several other terms commonly used in this field that there are helpful to understand include

golden handshakes

- *golden handshakes*—are additional benefits that are intended to induce early retirement

golden parachutes

- *golden parachutes*—substantial payments made to executives who are terminated upon change of ownership or corporate control
- *incentive pay*—refers to bonuses given for accomplishing short-term goals that can be used by the executive for retirement purposes

There are two major types of nonqualified deferred-compensation plan designs: the salary reduction plan and the supplemental executive-retirement plan. Nonqualified plans sponsored by nonprofit organizations or government entities are subject to a special set of rules set forth in Code Sec. 457. Nonqualified plans of these entities are referred to as Sec. 457 plans. Each approach is discussed below.

Salary Reduction Plans

If the employer's objective is to provide a method for executives to defer current income (in essence, to allow a nonqualified 401(k) look-alike arrangement), a so-called salary reduction plan can be used. *Salary reduction plans* typically give participants the option to defer regular compensation, bonuses, or commissions. This type of plan is appropriate when executives, currently in the highest marginal income tax bracket anticipate being in a lower tax bracket after retirement. It can also be appropriate simply as a means of income leveling for highly compensated employees whose income would otherwise drop sharply after retirement. What makes the nonqualified salary reduction plan more flexible than the 401(k) plan is that it has no maximum deferral limits and can be designed to exclude rank-and-file employees.

salary reduction plans

A salary reduction plan can be either initiated at the individual option of an executive during contract negotiations or offered as a package of perks to selected managers or highly compensated employees. In either circumstance, however, the agreement of deferral should be entered into prior to the date that the services are actually performed to avoid unwanted tax consequences.

Candidates for a salary reduction plan include

- employers who are looking to provide a low-cost benefit for highly compensated and management employees (the only employer cost is the cost of the deferral of the tax deduction)
- small closely held businesses whose owners' individual tax rate is higher than the corporate tax rate
- organizations that wish to set conditions on a certain amount of executives' salaries to induce desired results

---

***Example*:**   At the beginning of each year, The Baltimore Company offers its top executives the opportunity to defer up to $50,000 of their following year's compensation. Deferred amounts grow at some specified interest rate and the accumulated amount will be paid out over a 15-year period, beginning at the later occurrence of either age 55 or termination of employment.

Supplemental Executive Retirement Plans

supplemental executive retirement plan (SERP)

A *supplemental executive retirement plan (SERP)* satisfies the employer objective of complementing an existing qualified plan that is not already stretched to the maximum limits, by bringing executive retirement benefits (or contributions) up to desired levels. Unlike salary reduction plans, SERPs are additional, employer-provided benefits.

Regular and Offset SERPs

SERPs can complement the underlying qualified plan in one of two ways. They can be designed to provide the "missing piece" of retirement benefit (or contribution) that the employer wants the executive to have. For example, if the employer is looking to provide a replacement of 60 percent of an executive's final-average salary and the underlying qualified plan only provides for a 40 percent replacement, the SERP can be designed to provide a benefit equal to 20 percent of the final-average salary. In cases where the exact benefit (or contribution) is unknown, however, such as when an integrated unit-benefit formula is used, SERPs can be designed a second way: to provide for the total benefit or contribution desired (for example, all 60 percent), taking into account, or offsetting, the benefits provided by the qualified plan. This type of SERP is called an offset SERP.

Candidates for SERPs

Candidates for SERPs include employers who want to

- cut back benefits under their qualified plan due to increased costs
- provide a higher income replacement ratio for executives than they can afford (or want) to provide for all employees
- defeat the $200,000 cap (as indexed for 2002) on compensation that can be considered in determining benefits

---

Nonqualified Plan Objectives

- Alternative to qualified plan
- Second tier of benefits
- Cover limited group of employees
- Salary deferral for executives
- Instant benefit program for new company
- Meet a wide range of compensation goals
- Satisfy special needs of specific employees

---

457 Plans

457 plan

Sec. 457 of the Internal Revenue Code provides rules governing nonqualified plans of government organizations and non-church-controlled tax-exempt organizations. A nonqualified plan sponsored by one of these organizations is referred to as a *457 plan*. A 457 plan is similar to a salary reduction 401(k) plan. The maximum amount that can be deferred in any year cannot exceed the same salary deferral limit that applies to 401(k) and 403(b) plans ($11,000 for 2002). The catchup election for those over age 50 also applies, except for during the last three years prior to retirement, when a special catchup rule that only applies 457 plans allows the limit to double. - In addition, the following rules apply:

- Elections to defer compensation must be made before the compensation is earned.
- Special distribution restrictions apply.
- The employer may discriminately choose any or all employees for coverage.

Because the employer in a Sec. 457 plan does not pay federal income taxes, deductibility is not an issue.

DESIGN CONSIDERATIONS

To the extent that they are designed to avoid the rules of ERISA (which, as discussed later, most plans are), salary reduction plans and SERPs have tremendous design freedom. Without legislative and regulatory constraints, plan design is an interesting and challenging assignment. Let's look at the most common design features used in these plans.

Forfeiture Provisions

A forfeiture provision in a nonqualified plan sets forth certain conditions under which an employee forfeits the benefits he or she would normally get under the plan. Salary reduction plans do not typically contain forfeiture provisions because they represent an employee election to reduce salary. But forfeiture provisions are very common in SERPs because they help to achieve a multitude of employer objectives. Let's look at some client problems and see how forfeiture provisions can help solve them.

Client Problem: *Successful Transition of Company Leadership.* Some businesses are dependent on the special contributions of a few key executives. The retirement of these executives may prove devastating to the profit-making ability of the organization. To prevent a drop in revenue and to ensure a smooth transition, a nonqualified deferred-compensation plan can contain a provision that requires the executive to provide consulting services after retirement or else forfeit any benefit under the plan.

Client Problem: *Retention of Executives.* If your client is concerned about inducing an executive to stay on board instead of leaving prematurely, a so-called golden-handcuffs provision should be incorporated into the plan. There are any number of ways to design this provision. The employer who is not concerned about recruiting executives will probably prefer a provision requiring the executive to forfeit *all* rights under the plan if he or she terminates employment prior to normal retirement age. If executive recruiting is a strong concern, the forfeiture of benefits can be designed to include liberal vesting requirements. For example, the plan may provide *no* vesting to an employee who works less than 5 years, 50 percent vesting to an employee who terminates between 5 and 10 years, and 100 percent vesting to an employee who terminates after 10 or more years. If recruiting is a concern but not a priority, a more conservative vesting schedule can be used.

Client Problem: *Competition from Former Employees.* A major problem for employers in service industries is an employee who leaves and goes to work for a competitor or sets up a competing business. A covenant-not-to-compete provision can deter this behavior. A covenant-not-to-compete provision calls for the forfeiture of nonqualified benefits if the employee enters into competition with the employer by opening a competing business. To avoid legal problems the covenant-not-to-compete provision must be carefully drafted. The provision should be reasonable in terms of the geographical area and the time period it covers. For example, a covenant that says a former employee cannot compete in the Northeast for 10 years after the employee leaves employment is probably a violation of public policy and not valid. If the employee is restricted from working for 2 years in the same county, however, the provision is probably valid. The facts and circumstances will be determinative. Because the rules for noncompetition clauses vary from state to state, your client should consult an attorney before designing such a provision.

Designing a Nonqualified Plan for Executives

Up to this point, the assumption has been that your client is a business entity. However, your financial services practice may also include solving problems for executives who are negotiating a nonqualified arrangement with their employer. If this is the case, keep the following points in mind:

- A supplemental executive retirement plan can be set up to protect selected executives against involuntary termination if the company changes hands, by structuring the SERP to pay out or increase benefits under this contingency (a so-called takeover trigger—the executive's alternative if a golden parachute does not exist).
- Nonqualified plans can be designed to protect your client against involuntary termination because of declining earnings or change in control of the business by providing immediate vesting in nonqualified benefits if either of these contingencies occurs. This provision is called an *insolvency trigger*. The challenge, however, is to design the nonqualified plan so that the existence of an insolvency trigger does not trigger immediate taxation. If a rabbi trust is used (discussed in chapter 16), this probably cannot be done. If the plan is completely unfunded, however, the insolvency trigger can be incorporated into the plan.
- Nonqualified plans can be designed to allow withdrawals prior to termination in cases of financial hardship. If desired, the plan should spell out the circumstances that constitute a hardship, or it should provide for an independent third party to make the determination. This way your client can avoid adverse tax consequences.

- Your client should ask for a binding-arbitration clause in case of a dispute. This will help to save litigation costs.

Other Features in Plan Design

In addition to forfeiture provisions, there are several other important design features to be considered in nonqualified plans. In fact, if a plan is not required to meet ERISA standards, the only real constraints on plan design are the market forces at work and the designer's imagination. In general, however, the design features of a nonqualified plan are similar to those of a qualified plan except that they are not inhibited by IRS restrictions. Here is an overview of some standard design features.

Benefit or Contribution Structure

Nonqualified plans can be designed as either defined-benefit or defined-contribution plans. Salary reduction plans are usually designed as defined-contribution plans because they allow executives to *contribute* a deferred amount of salary each year. Salary continuation nonqualified plans (SERPs) can also be set up as defined-contribution plans but are more frequently set up as defined-benefit plans. When SERPs are set up as defined-benefit plans, the benefit formula should jibe with the employer's objectives. This may mean supplementing the employer's qualified plan or avoiding duplication in benefits by the coordination of all benefits received under the employer's qualified and other benefit plans, retirement benefits earned with other employers, and Social Security benefits. Meeting employer objectives may also mean indexing benefits, weighing benefits for length of service (such as in a unit-benefit formula), or both.

Eligibility

Participation in nonqualified plans is typically restricted to company executives. In fact, to a certain extent, it is necessary to restrict participation for the plan to be exempt from the requirements of ERISA. Under what is referred to as the "top-hat exemption" of ERISA, the plan *must* by definition be maintained "primarily" for a select group of management or highly compensated employees.

In a salary reduction plan or a SERP, the executive's title or position typically dictates inclusion in or exclusion from the plan (for example, all executives above the level of first vice president might be included). A second way to determine eligibility is by salary. When salary determines eligibility, the chosen dollar amount should be indexed; by taking this precaution, the employer does not risk substantial cost increases caused by the inclusion of executives who are not at the top level but whose salaries have inflated over time. A third common way to determine eligibility is to appoint a compensation committee. When this is done, the employer, who heads the committee, retains absolute control over plan membership.

Disability Provisions

Nonqualified plans frequently contain disability provisions. The employer can stipulate whether disability will be treated like any other termination of employment or whether special disability provisions will apply. In addition, the employer must choose whether service will continue to accrue if a disability occurs—in which case the plan should contain a definition of disability.

Retirement Age

Another key plan design issue is retirement age. In general, the normal retirement age of the nonqualified plan is the age at which benefits become payable without any forfeiture. The employer's personnel objectives determine whether a "young" retirement age (50–62) or an "old" retirement age (65–70) is chosen. If the employer wants to control salary costs by keeping a young work force, then a young retirement age should be chosen (typically, this is coordinated with a young normal retirement age in the qualified plan). If the executives involved have knowledge or experience that is crucial to the company, however, a later retirement age should be selected.

Death Benefits

Nonqualified plans can provide death benefits, which can cover the preretirement period, the postretirement period, or both. The death benefit chosen depends in part on what type of life insurance is used to fund the plan (if any) and what type of annuity is used for distribution from the plan. The choice of a death benefit should, therefore, be closely coordinated with the life insurance product used in the plan.

Key Design Considerations

- Salary deferral or supplemental benefit
- Benefit structure
- Eligibility
- Disability and death benefits
- Forfeiture provisions
- Hardship withdrawals
- Change in control and insolvency triggers

STOCK OPTION PLANS

Stock option programs have become a very popular benefit both from the employer's perspective as well as from the participant's perspective. In this section, we will review the two types of stock option plans, design considerations, and planning for the participant. Even if a financial services professional does not work with employers to design programs, he or she must be familiar with the tax considerations when working with employees.

Nonqualified Stock Options (NQSOs)

nonqualified stock options

Nonqualified stock options are options to purchase shares of company stock at a stated price over a given period of time (frequently 10 years). The option price normally equals 100 percent of the stock's fair market value on the date the option is granted, but it may be set below this level. Typically, the employee may exercise the options by paying cash equal to the exercise price or by tendering previously owned shares of stock.

At the time the option is exercised, the excess of the fair market value of the stock over the option price is taxed as ordinary income and is subject to income tax withholding. The company receives a tax deduction in the amount of the executive's income from the exercise of the option in the year the employee is taxed, as long as the withholding requirements are met.

Example: The employer grants to Ellie Executive the right to purchase 500 shares of common stock at the market price ($20/share at the time of issuance) at any time over the next 10 years. After 3 years, the market price has risen to $60/share. Ellie purchases all 500 shares at $20/share ($10,000). She now has $20,000 ($40 x 500) of ordinary income, which is the difference between the purchase price ($10,000) and the current market value ($30,000).

Clearly these options will be valuable to the employee only if the price of stock has risen since the date the option was issued. However, there is a possibility of large gains if the price is increased substantially. The employee generally may choose to exercise the options over a specified period (typically 10 years) without limitation. But, there *is* a limitation for employees who are considered "insiders" under SEC rules. Essentially, an *insider* is any employee who would have access to information that is not available to the general public. Insiders are subject to an insider-trading rule that limits the sale of stocks by the employee to within 6 months of the time he or she has been issued the option. Therefore, the 6-month period begins when the option is issued and ends when the stock is sold.

Many options are not exercisible for a period of time after the options are granted. Sometimes all options granted at a specific time become vested at once (referred to as *cliff-vesting*) after a specified number of years. For example, the company grants 500 options that become exercisable 3 years from the date of the grant as long as the participant is still employed on that date. Another option is to vest a portion of the options each year (referred to as *graded vesting*). For example, one third of the options is vested after one year, two thirds after 2 years, with full vesting after 3 years. It is also possible to have accelerated vesting upon the occurrence of a change in control of the company or the participant's death or disability. Also, be aware that the vesting provisions within a single company can be different for options granted at different times.

Several newer vesting approaches are being used today. In some cases, vesting is subject to the company (or employee) satisfying certain performance goals. Another approach offered in some pre-IPO (prior to the initial public offering) companies is referred to as *early exercise*. Under this arrangement, the participant is allowed to immediately exercise options when they are granted, but the stock remains restricted (forfeitible if the participant does not complete a specified period of service). Because the participant could forfeit the stock, there is generally no income tax treatment until the vesting restrictions lapse. As an alternative, the participant can elect a Section 83(b) election and pay tax at the time of exercise. Once exercised, the program is really a restricted stock plan (discussed below).

The duration of the exercise period is most often 10 years, but termination of employment prior to that can shorten the duration. It is common for a terminating employee to have the options lapse between 60 and 180 days after termination of employment, and even possible for the options to lapse at termination of employment if the participant is terminated for cause or violates a *do not compete clause.*

In order to exercise the options, the employee needs cash to pay the option price for the stock. Although this often requires borrowing, once the options are exercised, the employee may sell a sufficient number of the shares to repay the loan. Many stock option programs today offer cashless transactions where a designated broker exercises the options and sells some or all of the stock to cover the cost of the options at the same time.

If the employee prefers to hold the shares for their potential future appreciation, devising a method to raise the cash necessary to purchase shares becomes an important part of retirement planning. In addition, if employer stock constitutes a disproportionate share of a retiring employee's investment portfolio, planning for the systematic repositioning of the portfolio is another consideration for the practitioner.

Incentive Stock Options (ISOs)

An *incentive stock option (ISO)* is an option to purchase shares of the company stock at 100 percent or more of the stock's fair market value on the date that the option is granted, for a period of up to 10 years. ISOs are taxed more favorably to the participant than nonqualified stock options but are less flexible. There are certain limits on the value of options that can become exercisable annually, and there are certain holding period requirements before sale. In addition, any option granted to a shareholder of 10 percent or more of a company's voting stock must be priced at 110 percent or more of the stock's fair market value, with an option term of no more than 5 years. As in the case of nonqualified stock options, the options may be exercised by paying cash or by tendering previously owned shares of stock.

When the employee exercises the ISO, there is no regular income tax owed. However, the excess of the stock's fair market value at the time of exercise over the option exercise price—that is, the *spread*—is a tax preference item that may trigger an alternative minimum tax obligation. If the shares are held for at least 2 years from the date the option was granted and at least one year from exercise, the tax on sale is payable at a long-term capital-gains rate on the increase in the stock's value from the date of the grant of the option to the date of sale of the stock. If the holding period requirements are not met, the gain to the extent realized from the time the option is granted to the time of exercise of the option is taxed as ordinary income; the remainder is taxed as capital gain.

Because the capital gains rate can be significantly lower than ordinary income tax rates, satisfying the holding requirements is quite important. In addition to the lower rate, capital gains on the sale of stocks acquired through incentive stock options can be used to offset capital losses from the sale of other securities. Still, the participant needs to consider the alternative minimum tax implications of holding stock after exercise.

As with NQSOs, ISOs provide the employee with the possibility of large gains. Within limits, the employee can choose the timing of exercise of the options to maximize gains; however, options granted prior to December 31, 1986 must be exercised in the order in which they were granted. Also, as with NQSOs, the participant needs to have a full appreciation of the terms of the program, including the vesting and duration provisions, before any liquidation strategy can be conceived.

Choosing and Designing a Plan

Similar to plans of deferred compensation, stock option programs can be used as a tool to attract, motivate and retain the services of an employee. Unlike compensation programs, stock programs can transform the executive's interest in the company from that of an employee to a part-owner. A stock option program also does not involve the outlay of any cash by the employer, either at the time of issuance or at the time the participant exercises the option.

This does not mean there is not a cost associated with the establishment of a stock option program. If the value of the company's stock increases a great deal, there is the lost opportunity of selling the stock to a third party at the market price. A company should not consider a stock option program unless it has first carefully evaluated the potential costs and has a clear understanding of the objectives it is trying to accomplish.

When choosing between the two types of stock option programs, remember that the tax impact on the employer is quite different. With an ISO, the employer gets no tax deduction, while with the nonqualified program, the employer receives a deduction in the amount that the participant declares as income at the time of exercise. This makes the cost of providing benefits with an ISO more expensive than with a nonqualified program. In addition, the nonqualified program is more flexible.

In the review of nonqualified stock options and ISOs, we discussed the major plan design options that the employer has with each type of plan. As you can see, as with nonqualified deferred compensation, there is a great deal of flexibility in choosing the proper plan design. The issues are similar to the design considerations discussed earlier in the chapter.

Exercising Stock Options and ISOs

Employees that participate in a nonqualified stock option program or ISO have a difficult time choosing the optimal timing strategy for stock options. There are no rules of thumb that apply to every situation. Because there is a risk to every alternative, in some ways choosing the right option is more of an art than a science. Also, remember that the most serious problems mistakes that participants mare are often the simplest ones—for example, letting valuable options lapse because of a misunderstanding or failing to monitor the options.

A participant's decision making can be facilitated by having a clear structure to the process. The following provides a logical process to follow. The first step is to identify clear financial goals. Knowing what the proceeds will be used for, such as buying a home in 2 years or retiring in 10 years, will go a long way to bringing the right decision into focus.

The next step is to get a complete understanding of the option program. Here is a list of the types of questions to ask.

- Are the options nonqualified or ISOs?
- When do options become vested and doe vesting occur at once (cliff vesting) or over time (graded vesting)?
- Will the options become vested earlier if the participant dies, becomes disabled, or if there is a change in ownership?
- Are the options exercisable before they become vested?
- What is the duration of the option period?
- How long are options exercisable after termination of employment due to (a) death, (b) disability, (c) retirement, (d) voluntary termination, or (e) involuntary termination of employment?
- Do options lapse if the participant goes to work for a competitor?
- Does the company intend to grant additional options in the future?

Knowing the rules also means understanding the tax implications. Once the type (nonqualified or ISO) is determined, the client needs to have a full appreciation of the tax timing issues. A participant does not really know the value of the options until he or she knows the value after the exercise price and after all taxes have been paid. With ISOs, the alternative minimum tax is a real issue for those participants who choose to hold the stock to take advantage of the lower capital gains rate.

Once the participant understands the plan and has a general idea of what the funds will be used for, the next step is to develop a long-term liquidation plan. This can be facilitated by asking questions, such as

- How many additional options are likely to be granted?
- How much wealth should be tied into the employer's stock?
- How long will employment with the company continue?

Because many employees acquire sizable blocks of stock in their company through various incentive plans, one important planning consideration is often the systematic liquidation of this stock and the purchase of other securities to better diversify the employee's investment portfolio at his or her retirement. The plan should also include a strategy for which stock to liquidate first.

The plan should also have an action strategy. For example, who is going to notify heirs if the participant dies and still has stock options? What steps are in place to ensure that valuable options do not lapse? How often will the plan be reevaluated and adjusted for changing conditions?

The financial advisor can be a very important part of the process, because the professional is typically better suited than the participant to help model asset allocation, long-term projections, and tax analysis.

When devising a long-term plan, in addition to taking the above steps, the participant may want to consider some of the following strategies.

- Because stock prices historically rise over time, the strategy of holding the options until the end of the exercise period is a good place to start when formulating a strategy.
- Countervailing considerations such as diversifying the portfolio, exercising the options to meet a specific financial goal, or a realistic assessment that the stock price is unlikely to continue to increase can be good reasons to sell sooner.
- Arguably, because options are a bonus, liquidating the position (selling the stock) at the time the options are exercised ensures a positive cash position—and does not tie up the participant's assets.
- Alternatively, if stock appreciation is relatively certain, a participant in a high tax bracket (who can afford to take some risk) should exercise early and hold the stock to change the tax treatment from ordinary income (up to 39.9 percent tax rate) to long-term capital gains (20 percent tax rate). However, this strategy requires cash to purchase the stock and the possibility that the gain will be lost.
- When choosing which options to sell, first consider selling the oldest options even if they are not the lowest priced.
- Pay attention to the price behavior of the company's stock.
- Consider exercising the options and selling the stock (cashless transactions) over a period of time instead of all at once. This allows the price to be averaged and reduces the risk of receiving a low price for all the options, and it allows the participant to invest the proceeds into new investments over time, also reducing risk.

CHAPTER REVIEW

Answers to the review questions and the self-test questions start on page 673.

Key Terms

golden handshakes
golden parachutes
salary reduction plans
supplemental executive retirement
  plan (SERP)

457 plan
nonqualified stock options
incentive stock options (ISOs)

Review Questions

15-1.   What are the advantages for a financial services professional of becoming involved in the nonqualified deferred-compensation market?

15-2.   Identify the planning situations in which a nonqualified deferred-compensation plan should be used.

15-3.   Rhonda Rolodex is the owner of The Mainline Office Supply Company. In order to "keep her top people happy," Rhonda would like to set up a nonqualified plan for the top 20 executives in her 200-employee company. Rhonda has asked her financial services professional how she can best accomplish this objective. How should the planner advise Rhonda?

15-4.   Briefly describe the following:
   a.   golden handshakes
   b.   golden parachutes
   c.   incentive pay

15-5.   Describe a salary reduction plan.

15-6.   Describe a supplemental executive retirement plan (SERP).

15-7.   Describe a 457 plan.

15-8.   Jersey Technical Electronics (JTE) has been a very successful business, thanks to the personal contacts Sue Edison has throughout the industry. The owners of JTE fear that Sue, now 60, will retire shortly and the business will suffer. How can a nonqualified plan with a consulting clause help?

15-9.   Explain how a nonqualified plan can be designed to help in the following situations:
   a.   Rayco, Inc. is concerned about its key executives leaving prior to retirement age.
   b.   Lawyer Prudence Juris is concerned that one of her junior partners will leave, taking with her some of the firm's clients.

15-10. Howard Hayes, an executive at a local manufacturing firm, has asked his insurance agent what provisions he should ask the firm's owners to put into his nonqualified plan. What provisions should the agent suggest?

15-11. Briefly describe how nonqualified plans can be designed with regard to their
   a.   benefit structure
   b.   eligibility provisions
   c.   disability provisions
   d.   retirement age provisions
   e.   death benefit provisions

15-12. What are the tax consequences of nonqualified stock option?

15-13   What are the tax consequences of incentive stock options?

Self-Test Questions

T   F   15-1.   Nonqualified deferred-compensation plans are sometimes referred to as salary continuation plans, deferred-compensation plans, and nonqualified plans.

T   F   15-2.   Nonqualified plans can bring an executive's retirement benefits up to desired levels when they are used as a second tier of benefits on top of a qualified plan.

T   F   15-3.   Nonqualified plans are subject to nondiscrimination requirements similar to those used in qualified plans.

T   F   15-4.   Fewer formalities are required to establish a nonqualified plan than to establish a qualified plan.

T   F   15-5.   Nonqualified plans are generally considered to be more effective than qualified plans for recruiting, retaining, and retiring executives.

T   F   15-6.   A golden handshake is a substantial payment made to corporate executives who are terminated upon change of ownership or corporate control.

T   F   15-7.   A salary reduction plan is similar to a 401(k) plan because it restricts salary deferrals to a stated dollar amount.

T   F   15-8.   A SERP is used to meet the objective of bringing executive pension benefits up to an acceptable level.

T   F   15-9.   If an offset SERP is used, benefits provided by the SERP are reduced by the benefits payable under the employer's qualified plan.

T   F   15-10.   Under the rules governing 457 plans, the maximum amount that may be deferred under the plan in any year can not exceed the lesser of $11,000 (as indexed for 2002) or 100 percent of the participant's compensation.

T   F   15-11.   When a business is dependent on the special contributions of a few key executives, and the retirement of these executives may prove devastating to the profit-making ability of the organization, a consulting services provision should be part of the nonqualified plan design.

T   F   15-12.   If the client is concerned about persuading an executive to stay with the corporation until retirement, a so-called golden-handcuffs provision should be incorporated into the plan.

T   F   15-13.   If executive recruiting is a strong concern, the golden-handcuffs provision should contain liberal vesting requirements.

T   F   15-14. A covenant-not-to-compete provision can bar a former employee from working in the same geographic region for the rest of his or her life.

T   F   15-15. Nonqualified plans can be designed to allow withdrawals prior to termination in the event of a financial hardship.

T   F   15-16. A nonqualified plan is restricted by ERISA from containing a death or disability benefit.

T   F   15-17. Incentive stock options are more flexible than nonqualified stock options.

Note

1. The IRS will not issue a private letter ruling on a plan for a 50 percent controlling shareholder. They have challenged such plans, arguing that the shareholder has the legal right to receive the payments and, therefore, hasn't successfully elected to defer income. When working with such a plan, legal advice should be sought to identify risks and determine strategies for reducing the sponsor's exposure.

16

Nonqualified Retirement Plans: Issues and Answers

Learning Objectives

An understanding of the material in this chapter should enable the student to

16-1. Compare nonqualified plans with qualified plans.

16-2. Discuss the tax and funding implications of a nonqualified plan.

16-3. Discuss the application of ERISA to nonqualified plans.

16-4. List the reasons why life insurance is used to fund a nonqualified plan.

16-5. Discuss the installation and administration concerns for qualified plans.

Chapter Outline

Chapter 15 served as an introduction to the nonqualified market by surveying nonqualified plan use, choice, and design. In order to fully understand the nonqualified market, however, we also need to review many of the issues involved in the implementation of nonqualified plans. The questions that must be addressed include the following:

- Is it more advantageous for a cost-conscious client to use a qualified or a nonqualified plan?
- What tax considerations underlie the use, design, and funding of a nonqualified plan?
- Should a plan be funded, unfunded, or informally funded?
- Should a rabbi trust be used, and if so, how can it be designed in a state-of-the-art manner?
- Should a secular trust or a surety bond be used to secure payments under a nonqualified plan?
- What are the ERISA implications of using nonqualified plans?
- How are nonqualified plans installed and administered?
- Should life insurance products be used to pay for nonqualified plan benefits?

It is only after understanding these issues that we can accurately serve our clients' needs.

NONQUALIFIED VERSUS QUALIFIED

As we have seen, qualified pension and profit-sharing plans are retirement plans that meet standards set out in the Employee Retirement Income Security Act (ERISA) and Internal Revenue Code. The major requirements for qualification have been identified and discussed in earlier chapters. As a payback for adhering to these burdensome rules, plan contributions are immediately deductible by the employer, earnings on plan funds are tax deferred and, when qualified plan funds are distributed to employees, several tax-saving strategies such as forward averaging and rollovers may be available. The case study in chapter 2 illustrates the vast economic gain available through this tax-saving "interest-free loan."

In contrast, a nonqualified plan cannot simultaneously give the employer the benefit of an immediate tax deduction and give the employee the benefit of a tax deferral. Most nonqualified plans are structured to defer the taxation of retirement benefits for executives. Unlike qualified plans, however, nonqualified deferred-compensation plans postpone the employer's deduction until the benefit has been paid to the executive and has been included in his or her income. In addition, earnings on money put aside to fund the plan will be taxed in the year it is earned unless a tax shelter, such as life insurance, is used. Finally, distributions from nonqualified plans cannot be forward averaged to reduce the effective tax rate or rolled over to delay taxation (see table 16–1).

TABLE 16-1
Qualified and Nonqualified Plans Compared

Characteristic	Qualified Plan	Nonqualified Plan
Tax deferred to employee	Yes—always	Yes (unless considered funded)
Tax consequences to employer	Immediate deduction	Deduction deferred (unless considered funded)
Earnings accumulate tax free	Yes—always	No (unless tax shelter used)
Special tax treatment at retirement for employee	Yes (rollovers and forward averaging)	No
Ability to lower costs by only covering selected employees	No (must meet nondiscrimination rules)	Yes—always
Plan administration requirements	Burdensome and expensive	Minimal and inexpensive
Reporting and disclosure requirements	Burdensome and expensive	Minimal and inexpensive
Ability to attract, retain, and motivate employees	Effective	More effective

Despite the dismal tax comparison, nonqualified plans are favored over qualified plans in many cases for a variety of reasons, including

- design flexibility (chapter 15)
- lower administrative costs
- cost-saving discriminatory coverage

This last reason is perhaps the chief motivation for an employer to install a nonqualified plan. Business owners claim they can save significant sums of money by excluding rank-and-file employees from the plan. In the minds of many employers, the tax savings garnered under a qualified plan are overshadowed by the ability to avoid paying benefit costs for the majority of their employees. A short case study helps to illustrate this point (see also table 16-1).

CASE STUDY: THE SMALLCO COMPANY

Smallco is a company of 10 people and is owned by two sisters. The sisters earn a salary of $100,000 each; the payroll for the additional employees is $240,000 (average salary, $30,000). If Smallco were to install a profit-sharing plan that provides a benefit of 15 percent of salary to all employees, the qualified plan would cost $66,000 plus administrative expenses ($66,000 equals 15 percent of the total payroll of $440,000). If Smallco were to provide a 15 percent nonqualified plan for the two owners and no benefits for the other employees, however, then the cost to the plan would be reduced to $30,000 plus the cost of deferring the deduction.

Determining the Cost of Deferring the Deduction

Smallco is in the 34 percent marginal tax bracket. The deferral of the deduction would, thus, immediately cost Smallco 34 cents on every dollar put into the plan. Because $30,000 is being contributed, Smallco would, thus, "lose" $10,200 in tax savings (34 percent tax rate multiplied by the $30,000 contribution). In addition, Smallco loses the amount it could have gained by investing the $10,200. This, of course, will be offset by the amount that will be deducted when the benefits are paid. There is no way to accurately predict the employer's cost for deferring the deduction because of the interest and time assumptions that must be used (not to mention potential shifts in tax rates). But even assuming that it costs Smallco $1.40 (a conservatively high figure) to provide $1 in benefits, the total plan cost in real dollars will only be $42,000. This amount is $24,000 less than what the qualified plan would cost. In addition, Smallco's administrative costs will be significantly lower. To put it another way, even though it will cost Smallco more than a dollar to provide a dollar's worth of benefits, the additional cost is more than offset by increased benefit costs brought about by providing benefits for rank-and-file employees.

YOUR FINANCIAL SERVICES PRACTICE:
EFFECTIVE COMPENSATION PLANNING

Clients often mistakenly believe that implementing a qualified plan will increase costs because the benefits are an additional compensation—sort of a windfall—for rank-and-file employees. This commonly held opinion is correct only if benefits are an increase to the overall compensation package. If benefits are a piece of what is already being paid to an employee, however, employer costs are not increased. In other words, the employer should focus on how employees are paid, not how much he or she pays them. Effective compensation planning dictates that employers give employees (and themselves) the opportunity to save for retirement with the tax advantages that are only available through a qualified plan. Unfortunately, for many employers it is the perception that counts, not the reality.

One way to satisfy stubborn prospects is to *gradually* shift current compensation to deferred compensation. This can be accomplished by lowering future salary increases by a small percentage, which will be used to fund a deferred-compensation plan.

TAX CONSIDERATIONS

A client who desires a nonqualified plan must be made aware of the tax implications of having such a plan. Unlike qualified plans, nonqualified plans are subject to the matching rule that generally applies to compensation paid to employees. The employer is eligible for a deduction in the year that the employee is taxed on the income. Because most plans are designed to defer employee taxation until the benefits are distributed, the employer's deduction is deferred until benefits are paid out.

Although income tax deferral is usually the objective, several tax law concepts can defeat the goal. These concepts must be fully understood when working with nonqualified plans.

Constructive Receipt

constructive receipt

Under IRS regulations, an amount becomes currently taxable to an executive even before it is actually received if it has been "constructively received." *Constructive receipt* is deemed to have occurred in a nonqualified plan if the deferred compensation is credited to an executive's account, set apart for the executive, or made available to the executive so that he or she can draw upon it anytime or could draw on it if notice of intention to draw had been given. In other words, if the executive had the choice of taking compensation but refused to take possession, the IRS treats that person as having taxable income. There is, however, no constructive receipt if either of the following conditions is met:

- The deferred compensation is subject to substantial limitations or restrictions.
- The election to defer compensation is a mere promise to pay, not represented by notes or secured in any way (that is, if it is an unsecured promise to pay).

Consequently, an executive in a salary reduction plan, for example, is deemed to be in constructive receipt of income because he or she has, in effect, postponed income in order to avoid current taxation—*unless* the nonqualified plan meets either one of the two criteria outlined above. Because the major advantage to an executive of a nonqualified plan is the deferral of taxes, it is essential that the plan be designed to meet one of the two specified criteria.

Substantial Limitation or Restriction

Whether or not constructive receipt applies is a facts-and-circumstances decision. Substantial limitations have been held to exist if the executive must wait until the passage of a given period of time to receive the money (under a golden-handcuffs provision, for example). In addition, the employer can avoid constructive receipt by setting up the plan to require the occurrence of an event that is beyond the executive's control. (Recall the forfeiture provisions discussed in chapter 15.)

Unsecured Promise to Pay

What constitutes an unsecured promise to pay will be covered in detail later when unfunded plans, informally funded plans, and rabbi trusts are discussed. The question of *when* the unsecured promise to pay should be made is another matter, however. The executive is better off entering into the agreement to defer compensation before services are rendered. If the executive waits to make an election later, the plan can only avoid constructive receipt if there is a "substantial risk of forfeiture." A substantial risk of forfeiture is a significant limitation or duty that requires a meaningful effort on the part of the executive to fulfill, and there must be a definite possibility that the event that will cause the forfeiture could occur. In other words, the executive will have a much higher hurdle to jump to avoid IRS claims of constructive receipt if he or she procrastinates in making the election.

When Does It End?

One final point concerning constructive receipt needs to be made. The problem of constructive receipt can last beyond the asset buildup period. In other words, plan provisions also have to ensure that the executive is not taxed on more than he or she receives in the distribution period. For example, an executive cannot elect to accelerate the balance of payments due under the plan after retirement. An executive can, however, elect the time and manner of payment under the nonqualified plan without triggering constructive receipt if the election is made before the deferred amount has been earned.

Economic Benefit

economic benefit

Under the economic-benefit doctrine an *economic* (or financial) *benefit* conferred on an executive as compensation should be included in the person's income to the extent that the benefit has an ascertainable fair market value. In other words, if a compensation arrangement provides a current economic benefit to an executive, that person must report the value of the benefit even if he or she has no current right to receive the benefit. The economic-benefit doctrine is different from the constructive-receipt doctrine because the tax issue is *not* whether the taxpayer can control the timing of the actual receipt of the income (as it is in constructive receipt); the issue is whether or not there has been an irrevocable transfer of funds made on the executive's behalf that provides an economic benefit to the executive. The economic-benefit doctrine is a higher hurdle for taxpayers to jump than the constructive-receipt doctrine because it requires the executive to be taxed when funds are irrevocably paid out on the executive's behalf to a fund in which the executive has vested rights—regardless of whether there are substantial limitations or restrictions on the deferred income. For purposes of the economic-benefit doctrine, a fund is created when property is irrevocably placed with a third party. The economic-benefit doctrine *does not* apply, however, when the property involved is subject to the rights of the employer's creditors, because theoretically no property has been transferred and the obligation remains an unsecured promise to pay.

Section 83

Under Sec. 83 of the Internal Revenue Code, the executive is not taxed until his or her rights in the property become transferable or are no longer subject to a substantial risk of forfeiture (discussed above). A substantial risk of forfeiture is deemed to occur if the plan contains forfeiture provisions, that is, if the rights to deferred compensation are conditional on the performance—or nonperformance—of substantial services. Whether or not the forfeiture provisions accomplish this is a facts-and-circumstances determination. One final note: "Property" that is transferred and is subject to the creditors of the corporation is *not* really property for tax purposes, because the transferred interest cannot be valued and the obligation remains an unsecured promise to pay.

Let's look at some examples.

Example 1: Employer Able sets up a separate account that will be used to pay off nonqualified benefits. Able retains ownership over the assets in the fund and can direct the fund's assets to business use if necessary. Under this scenario, the executives avoid taxation because they cannot control the timing of the actual receipt of the income, and the employer has not made an irrevocable transfer of funds on the executives' behalf. The executives in this example, however, may not feel secure that they will receive their benefit because they have only an unsecured promise to receive benefits.

Example 2: To provide the executives with more security, employer Able transfers the funds to a trust. The assets placed in the trust cannot revert back to the employer and are not subject to attack by the employer's creditors if the company files for bankruptcy. Under this scenario, the executives are certain that they will receive their nonqualified benefit—but they are also subject to immediate tax on the transferred assets. The reason for this is that the transferred assets are no longer an unsecured promise to pay and are not subject to a substantial risk of forfeiture; therefore, the executives have constructively received and derived an economic benefit from the assets—even though they have not actually received the assets.

PLAN FUNDING

Nonqualified plans can be funded, unfunded, or informally funded. As you have probably concluded by now, plan funding for tax purposes and "storing" assets to pay future nonqualified promises are two different things from a tax standpoint. Let's take a closer look.

Funded Plans

A nonqualified deferred-compensation plan is considered funded for tax purposes when, in order to meet its promise of providing benefits under the plan, the company contributes specific assets to an escrow or trustee account in which the executive has a current beneficial interest. In other words, to pay benefits, the company sets aside funds that are beyond the reach of the general creditors of the corporation. In addition, a nonqualified plan is funded if the executive's obligation is backed by a letter of credit from the employer or by a surety bond obtained by the employer. If a nonqualified deferred-compensation plan is considered funded, the executive is subject to taxation upon the later occurrence of either when contributions are made to the plan or when the employee becomes vested in the benefit (under the economic benefit doctrine codified in Sec. 83). As discussed later, ERISA rules concerning participation, funding, vesting, fiduciary enforcement, and reporting and disclosure also apply to a funded plan. Because this generally defeats the purpose of the plan, most plans are designed to be unfunded for both tax and ERISA purposes. One exception, discussed later, is the secular trust, in which benefit security is determined to outweigh the need for income tax deferral.

Unfunded Plans

A nonqualified deferred-compensation plan is considered unfunded for tax purposes if there is no reserve set aside to pay the promised benefit under the plan. Rev. Rul. 60-31 states that a mere promise to pay that is not represented by notes or secured in any way is not regarded as a receipt of income. Therefore, an unfunded, unsecured promise by an employer to pay compensation at some future date does not constitute current taxable income to an executive.

Informally Funded Plans

Unfunded plans that do not make contingencies for storing funds to pay nonqualified promises pose a major problem for the executive because benefit payments hinge on the fiscal health of the employer at the time benefits become payable. In addition, many executives wonder if their own status will be different by the time they collect. Management change, business buyouts (through hostile takeover or otherwise), or a demotion due to performance problems or "office politics" may put the employee in an untenable position when he or she approaches the time to collect benefits. The executive is relying mainly on the corporation's unsecured (albeit contractual) promise to pay. Thus, executives are caught between the horns of a dilemma. On one hand, if the plan is funded, executives will be taxed immediately. On the other hand, executives do not want to risk their retirement on an unsecured promise to pay. Because executives want the best of both worlds—as much security as possible without triggering immediate taxation—many plans are informally funded. A plan is informally funded when a reserve is set up to pay the nonqualified benefit, but the assets of the reserve are retained as assets of the corporation, subject to attack by creditors of the corporation. In other words, as long as the executive does not have a current beneficial interest, the plan is considered unfunded for tax purposes. When a plan is informally funded, it is important to consider the other side of the equation—the employer's deduction.

Income Tax Effects on the Employer

Under the cash method of accounting, a taxpayer is not entitled to a deduction until benefits have been paid to executives, some employers are subject to the accrual method of accounting. However, under the accrual method of accounting, a taxpayer is entitled to a deduction in the year during which all events have occurred that gave rise to the liability and the amount of such liability can be determined with reasonable accuracy. However, the timing of deductions for the payment of nonqualified deferred compensation comes under special IRS regulations. Unlike the usual tax accounting rules applicable to other deductions, Reg. 1.404(b)-1T allows a deduction for nonqualified deferred compensation only in the year in which the payment is includible in the employee's gross income. Although unfunded deferred-compensation arrangements often qualify as deductible expenses under the usual accrual requirements, Reg. 1.404(b)-1T takes precedence and delays the deduction for the employer until the income is taxable to the employee.

BENEFIT SECURITY

Because of the income tax and ERISA issues involved in nonqualified plans, it is quite difficult to make benefits as secure for the participants as they are with qualified plans. To solve the security issue, there are three possible solutions (unfortunately none is totally satisfactory): the rabbi trust, the secular trust, and the surety bond.

Rabbi Trust

rabbi trust

With the *rabbi trust* (first conceived in 1981 to provide benefit security for a rabbi), contributions are made to a separate trust. Under the terms of the trust, assets generally can not revert to the company—meaning that plan assets will be available to pay plan benefits, even if new hostile management takes over the company. However, to avoid current taxation to the participants, the trust's assets remain subject to the claims of the employer's creditors.

For many years, a sponsor wanting the IRS to rule on the validity of the rabbi trust agreement had to request a private letter ruling. In Rev. Proc. 92-64, the IRS made the use of the rabbi trust more secure by providing a model trust agreement. In order to have IRS approval of a deferred compensation agreement today, the sponsor in almost all cases must use the IRS's model rabbi trust form.

The model trust generally conforms with IRS guidelines already well known from prior IRS private letter rulings. Optional paragraphs are provided to allow some degree of customization. The model contains some relatively favorable provisions. For example, it allows the use of "springing" irrevocability. That is a provision under which, if there is a change of ownership of the employer, the trust becomes irrevocable. Similarly, at the change in control, the employer can be required to make an irrevocable contribution of all remaining deferred compensation. Also, the model permits the rabbi trust to own employer stock. However, the model does not allow "insolvency triggers" that hasten payments to executives when the employer's net worth falls below a certain point. (The IRS fears that accelerating benefit payments when the employer's financial position deteriorates may result in all benefits being paid before any creditors have a chance to attach the assets of the trust.) Other requirements, either contained in the model trust or in prior rulings, include the following:

- The assets in a rabbi trust must be available to all general creditors of the company if the company files for bankruptcy or becomes insolvent.
- The participants must not have greater rights than unsecured creditors.
- The plan must provide clear rules describing when benefits will be paid.

- The company must notify the trustee of any bankruptcy or financial hardship that the company is undergoing. When a bankruptcy or financial hardship occurs, the trustee should suspend payment to the trust beneficiary and hold assets for the employer's general creditors.

Over the years, other planning devices have become commonly accepted as ways to protect the executive.

Example: Another way to protect the participants in the event of a hostile takeover is to give the trustee control over the investment of plan assets upon the change in control. This prevents the "bad guys" from making investments in illiquid employer-leased real estate or an employer-related venture.

Participants can elect the form of distribution from the rabbi trust when contributions to the trust are made without triggering constructive receipt. In addition, a change in the form of business organization by the employee's company (from a partnership to an S corporation, for example) will not adversely affect the rabbi trust.

Finally, executives can take a hardship withdrawal from a rabbi trust without triggering constructive receipt. The withdrawal is limited to an amount reasonably needed to meet the emergency. In addition, the emergency must be unforeseeable, that is, pose a severe financial hardship to the participant or result from a loss of property due to casualty or other similar extraordinary and unforeseeable circumstances beyond the control of the participant.

Although rabbi trusts accomplish the dual objective of deferring taxation and providing a measure of retirement security to executives, they have one important disadvantage: rabbi trusts provide no benefit security for executives should the employer go bankrupt. In other words, the executive must stand in line with other creditors if the employer files for bankruptcy. Rabbi trusts, therefore, are very effective in providing retirement security if the employer is unwilling to pay promised benefits, but they do not provide security if the employer is unable to pay benefits.

Secular Trusts

In situations where the employer's ability to pay promised benefits comes into question, some professionals have been recommending a secular

secular trust

trust in lieu of a rabbi trust. Like a rabbi trust, a *secular trust* calls for an irrevocable contribution on the employer's part to finance promises under a nonqualified plan. Unlike a rabbi trust, however, funds held in a secular trust cannot be reached by the employer's creditors. This means that executives can expect to receive promised benefits even if the employer goes bankrupt (giving the participant's a similar level of security that qualified plans have). However, there is a significant price for this security. Contributions to the trust are taxable at the later of the date that contributions are made or benefits become nonforfeitable (see discussion of Sec. 83).

Unfortunately, several IRS private-letter rulings have also indicated that in some circumstances trust earnings would be subject to double taxation, once when earned at the trust level and again when actually paid out to the employee. Because of the tax issues and because individual tax rates (for executives) are generally higher than the corporate rate, secular trusts are not commonly used today.

TABLE 16-2
Comparison of Funding Approaches

Type of Plan	Funds Set Aside Prior to Retirement	Secured against Unwillingness to Pay	Secured against Employer Insolvency	Delayed Taxation for Executives
Unfunded pay-as-you-go plan	No	No	No	Yes
Rabbi trust	Yes	Yes	No	Yes
Secular trust	Yes	Yes	Yes	No

Surety Bonds

For the executive who feels uncomfortable with the possibility of benefits going unpaid from a rabbi trust because of an employer bankruptcy but who wants to avoid the use of a secular trust because of the tax consequences, an alternative may be available. For these executives you should look into the use of a surety bond. A *surety bond* provides for a bonding company to pay promised benefits if the employer defaults on the promise to pay nonqualified benefits—thus providing the executive with an indirect means of securing the employer's unsecured promise.

surety bond

In order to prevent the purchase of a surety bond from triggering a constructive-receipt, economic-benefit, or Sec. 83 problem, certain precautions must be taken. The executive must bear the cost of the surety bond, and the employer should not have an involvement with the bonding company. If these precautions are taken, the executive can have the security of continued protection for nonqualified retirement payments.

The downside is that surety bonds for nonqualified plans can be expensive and difficult to obtain. Premiums are typically one to 3 percent of the annual amount deferred, plus earnings. In addition, very few companies provide this coverage. Finally, renewal of the bond can be difficult if the employer experiences an economic downturn. Surety bonds are issued for from 3 to 5 years and may not be renewed if bankruptcy is on the horizon. Ironically, this is when they are most needed!

ERISA CONCONSIDERATIONS

top-hat exemption

When designing a nonqualified deferred-compensation plan, in almost all cases, the employer will want to avoid coverage under ERISA by satisfying the *top-hat exemption* of ERISA. This requires that the plan be unfunded and maintained by an employer, primarily for the purpose of providing deferred compensation for a select group of management and/or highly compensated employees. The "unfunded" requirement is generally not problematic, as the employer can still utilize one of the informal funding approaches discussed above. The more difficult task is determining which employees can be covered as "highly compensated" employees. Unfortunately, the DOL has not provided any clear guidance on this issue. It is clear, however, that the Tax Code's definition of highly compensated (5 percent owners and those earning more than $80,000) is not determinative here. From a practical perspective, a plan that covers only a few highly paid executives will probably comply. As the group gets bigger, however, there is less certainty. To safeguard the plan, the plan documents should specify that the employer has the right to amend the plan to limit the group of covered employees, conforming to any future DOL guidance on this issue.

An unfunded top-hat plan is exempt from ERISA's participation, vesting, benefit, accrual, funding, and fiduciary provisions. It is still subject to ERISA's reporting, disclosure, administration, and enforcement provisions. However, the reporting provisions can be satisfied simply by filing with the DOL (at the time the plan is established) a statement including the following information: the name and address of the employer, the employer's identification number, a declaration that the employer maintains the plan primarily to provide deferred compensation to a select group of management or highly paid employees, the number of such plans maintained by the employer, and the number of employees in each plan.

"FUNDING" NONQUALIFIED PLANS WITH LIFE INSURANCE

Corporate-owned life insurance (COLI) is a popular way for most publicly held and almost all closely held businesses to set up a reserve against future obligations under a nonqualified plan. No single type of contract is best. Most employers, however, prefer policies with premium and investment flexibility and low mortality and expense costs. In addition, because the policy values are generally used to finance retirement benefits, permanent rather than term coverage is indicated.

Advantages of COLI

The use of COLI is attractive for many reasons:

- The tax-free inside buildup that occurs in a life insurance policy is important to a nonqualified plan because, unlike those of a qualified plan, earnings on nonqualified-plan assets are not tax deferred.
- Life insurance proceeds received by the company can protect the company against the premature death of an executive. This works two ways. If the executive is not fully vested in his or her promised benefit at death, or if no death benefit is provided at all, the excess death benefit received by the company can be used to cushion the company against anticipated losses owing to the executive's death. If the executive is fully vested in a substantial death benefit and dies shortly after entering the plan, the life insurance policy will be able to pay the promised benefit in full, whereas the other reserves would have been inadequate.
- Life insurance proceeds received by the company upon the death of the executive are tax free.
- Policies can be borrowed against to help pay the cost of future premiums. Knowing that if cash flow is a problem the funding of his or her benefit will not suffer should give the executive an added sense of security. An added benefit of a leveraged insurance contract is that the employer is allowed to deduct any interest paid on policy loans that total $50,000 or less. (*Planning Note:* The $50,000 ceiling on policy loans was added by TRA '86. Prior to that time, leveraged life insurance products had been a highly desirable way to fund nonqualified plans, but the trend now seems to be away from leveraged policies and toward variable life insurance.)
- Life insurance funding provides the employer with flexibility. The employer can either use the cash values of the policy to pay nonqualified benefits or use other assets and keep the policy in force

until death. If the latter course is taken, the employer can often receive more from the insurance company as death proceeds than it pays out under the plan.

- Life insurance policies can be used to provide a supplemental disability benefit. The waiver-of-premium clause in a life policy will enable the executive to get the full nonqualified benefit even if he or she becomes disabled.

- If life insurance purchased on the life of the executive is owned by the company, premiums are paid by the company, and the company is the sole beneficiary, then constructive-receipt, economic-benefit, and Sec. 83 problems are avoided.

- If the nonqualified plan requires the plan to pay a life income to the executive, by electing a life-income option, the employer can pass on to the insurance company the risk that the executive will live beyond his or her normal life expectancy.

Disadvantages of COLI

Two major disadvantages of using life insurance to fund a nonqualified plan concern the limitation on a corporate deduction for interest paid on policy loans (previously discussed) and the alternative minimum tax on corporate assets. The alternative minimum tax (AMT) offers some impediment to the use of life insurance to fund a nonqualified plan because the life insurance that is payable to the corporation, although not subject to regular taxes, may be subject to the AMT. If so, employer costs are increased. Employers should be advised that they may need to purchase additional insurance so they can pay any AMT as well as their obligations under the plan. Although the AMT is usually about 15 percent of the death benefit (and in many cases far less), some experts suggest that the employer obtain slightly over 15 percent more life insurance than the amount needed to fund the plan. In any case, the employer's tax adviser should be consulted to determine whether the alternative minimum tax will apply.

THE INSTALLATION AND ADMINISTRATION OF NONQUALIFIED PLANS

The final issue we will consider in this chapter is the installation and administration of your client's nonqualified plan. In order to install a nonqualified plan, the employer should adopt a corporate resolution authorizing the purchase of life insurance to indemnify the business for the expenses it is likely to incur. A second restriction should authorize the production of either a contract or plan document that will spell out both the corporation's and the executives' benefits and obligations. In addition, a rabbi trust document or a secular trust document should be created. Finally, a one-page ERISA notice should be completed and sent to the Department of Labor. This notice is a letter informing the DOL that a nonqualified plan exists and that certain named employees are covered by the plan.

CHAPTER REVIEW

Answers to the review questions and the self-test questions start on page 673.

Key Terms

constructive receipt

economic benefit

rabbi trust

secular trust

surety bond

top-hat exemption

Review Questions

16-1.   Discuss the differences between a qualified and a nonqualified plan.

16-2.   What is the doctrine of constructive receipt?

16-3.   How does the economic benefit rule work?

16-4.   Discuss the implications of the Code Sec. 83 rule as it applies to nonqualified plans.

16-5.   Which of the following transactions are subject to taxation under the economic benefit, constructive receipt, or Sec. 83 rules? Explain.

   a.   ABC Corporation buys life insurance on the lives of its key executives in order to pay their nonqualified plan, which contains a golden-handcuffs provision. ABC owns the policies, pays the premiums, and is the beneficiary under the policies. ABC has direct control over the cash values in the policies and can divert these funds to business use.

   b.   DEF Corporation makes a bonus available to its officers that can be taken as current income or deferred by leaving the funds in an irrevocable trust in which the officers are the beneficiaries.

   c.   GHI Corporation transfers assets to an irrevocable trust in which a key executive is the beneficiary. The trust is subject to the claims of the employer's creditors.

16-6.   How does a rabbi trust work?

16-7.   How does a secular trust work?

16-8.   What is the top-hat exemption from ERISA?

16-9.   List the reasons why life insurance is frequently used to fund nonqualified deferred-compensation plans.

16-10. Discuss the procedures for installing and administering a nonqualified plan.

Self-Test Questions

T   F   16-1.   A nonqualified plan simultaneously gives an employer the benefit of an immediate tax deduction and an employee a deferral of tax.

T   F   16-2.   Nonqualified plans have lower administrative costs than qualified plans.

T   F   16-3.   It generally costs more than a dollar to provide a dollar's worth of nonqualified plan benefit.

T   F   16-4.   The doctrine of constructive receipt is triggered if there is an irrevocable transfer of funds made on the executive's behalf that provides a benefit to the executive.

T   F   16-5.   Sec. 83 is essentially a codification of the constructive-receipt and economic-benefit doctrines.

T   F   16-6.   A plan is considered funded if a reserve is set up to pay a nonqualified benefit, but the assets of the reserve are retained as assets of the corporation and are subject to attack by creditors of the corporation.

T   F   16-7.   Key executives always prefer that their nonqualified plan be an unfunded, unsecured promise made by the employer.

T   F   16-8.   Funds placed in a rabbi trust are not subject to the claims of an employer's creditors.

T   F   16-9.   A rabbi trust can contain an insolvency trigger that requires accelerated payments to executives if the company's net worth falls below a certain point.

T   F   16-10. Rabbi trusts provide no benefit security for executives if an employer goes bankrupt.

T   F   16-11. Like a rabbi trust, a secular trust can be used to defer the taxation of an employee on a contribution made in his or her behalf.

T   F   16-12. The employer should buy an executive's surety bond in order to avoid unwanted tax consequences.

T   F   16-13. A top-hat plan must be maintained primarily for the purpose of providing deferred compensation for a select group of management or highly compensated employees.

T   F   16-14.   If a nonqualified plan is used, a one-page ERISA notice should be completed and sent to the Department of Labor.

T   F   16-15.   The tax-free inside buildup that occurs in a life insurance policy is important to a nonqualified plan because earnings on nonqualified plan assets are not tax deferred.

T   F   16-16.   Life insurance proceeds received by a company upon the death of an executive are received tax free.

T   F   16-17.   By electing a life-income option, the employer can transfer to the insurance company the risk of an employee living beyond his or her normal life expectancy.

17

Individual Retirement Plans—Part I

Learning Objectives

An understanding of the material in this chapter should enable the student to

---

17-1. Describe the different types of individual retirement arrangements.

17-2. Identify the IRA contribution rules with regard to

    a. regular IRA contribution limits
    b. spousal IRA contribution limits
    c. the timing of contributions
    d. the consequences of excess contributions

17-3. Discuss the eligibility requirements for a deductible IRA.

17-4. Discuss the eligibility requirements for a Roth IRA.

17-5. Identify the different types of rollover contributions and explain how they can be applied when conducting financial planning for a client.

Chapter Outline

OVERVIEW

Individual retirement plans are a vital part of the financial planning business. They are important both to the financial security of clients and to the business efforts of financial services professionals. Even though the best opportunities are for lower- and middle-class workers, wealthy individuals often have plans with large sums that have been rolled over from employer-sponsored tax-advantaged retirement plans.

Over the years, Congress has changed the IRA rules numerous times. The changes in the last few years have all been favorable. The Taxpayer Relief Act of 1997 added the Roth IRA and made the deductible IRA available to more taxpayers. The Economic Growth and Tax Relief Reconciliation Act of 2001 increased the maximum allowable contribution limits and added a catch-up contribution for older participants. As a result, proper use of traditional IRAs, the new Roth IRAs, and rollover IRAs can go a long way toward providing retirement security, and the financial services professional can help clients achieve their goals by explaining the IRA rules, encouraging saving for retirement, and marketing IRA investments.

IRA

Roth IRA

With the introduction of the Roth IRA, there are now two types of savings vehicles that are called IRAs (individual retirement accounts). The traditional plan is still referred to as an *IRA*; the new plan is referred to as the Roth IRA. Traditional IRAs are similar to employer-sponsored tax-sheltered retirement plans in many ways. Both are tax-favored savings plans that encourage the accumulation of savings for retirement because they allow contributions to be made with pretax dollars (if the taxpayer is eligible) and earnings to be tax deferred until retirement. With *Roth IRAs*, contributions are made on an after-tax basis, but earnings are not taxed and qualifying distributions are tax free. These tax benefits of both types of plans result in a significant loss of revenue to the federal government and stringent rules are in place to ensure that the goal of encouraging retirement savings is achieved and revenue loss is minimized.

The funding vehicles and types of allowable investments are the same for both traditional IRAs and the Roth IRA. As will be discussed in chapter 18, both types of IRAs can have as funding instruments a trust or custodial account (individual retirement account) or an annuity contract (individual retirement annuity). With either type of funding vehicle, a wide array of traditional investment strategies can be used.

CONTRIBUTION LIMITS

The maximum allowable contribution to an IRA or Roth IRA for 2002 is the lesser of $3,000 or 100 percent of compensation. The $3,000 limit applies to all traditional IRAs and Roth IRAs to which a taxpayer contributes for the year. For example, if the taxpayer makes a $3,000 contribution to a traditional IRA, no contributions can be made to a Roth IRA for the year. The maximum allowable contribution limit is scheduled to increase in future years to $4,000 in 2005 and to $5,000 in 2008. (See Appendix 8.)

It is important to remember that a contribution cannot exceed a person's compensation. *Compensation* is earnings from wages, salaries, tips, professional fees, bonuses, and any other amount a taxpayer receives for providing personal services. In addition, alimony and separate-maintenance payments are also considered compensation for IRA purposes. Compensation does not include earnings and profits from property, such as rental and dividend income, or amounts received as a pension or annuity. As a general rule, if it is income the taxpayer worked for in a given year, the contribution can be made; if it is derived from investments or retirement income, it is not eligible.

For self-employeds, compensation includes earned income from personal services, reduced by any contributions to a qualified plan on behalf of the individual. Self-employeds with a net loss from self-employment cannot make IRA contributions unless they also have salary or wage income. In this case, they do not have to reduce the amount of salary income by the net loss from self-employment. If there are both salary or wage income and net income from self-employment, the two amounts are combined to determine the amount that can be contributed.

***Example*:**   In his first year in business, Don, a self-employed creator of computer software, has a net loss of $17,000, largely because of start-up costs. However, he received $4,000 from part-time teaching. Don may contribute up to $3,000 to an IRA because his salary will not be reduced by his self-employment loss.

margin note: spousal IRA

Spousal IRAs

If a married person does not work or has limited compensation, his or her spouse can contribute up to $3,000 to a *spousal IRA*—which can be either a traditional IRA or a Roth IRA—as long as the following conditions are satisfied:

- The taxpayer is married at the end of the year and files a joint tax return.
- The spouse earns less than the taxpayer.
- The couple has compensation that equals or exceeds contributions to the IRAs of both persons ($6,000 if $3,000 is contributed for each).

Spousal IRAs can be set up even if the taxpayer does not contribute to his or her own account, or contributions can be made for both spouses, or the taxpayer can make contributions just to the taxpayer's IRA even though a spousal IRA already exists. However, no more than $3,000 can be placed in either IRA for any year.

Catch-up Election

Beginning in 2002, an individual who has attained age 50 before the end of the taxable year can contribute an additional $500. For example, in 2002 a 55 year-old individual could contribution up to $3,500 to an IRA or Roth IRA (assuming that they were otherwise eligible under the phaseout limits discussed below). The catch-up amount is also scheduled to increase in future years. It remains at an additional $500 through 2005 and then becomes $1,000 in 2006. (See Appendix 8).

Example: In 2002, John and Sarah are married, file jointly, and have an AGI of $120,000. They are each eligible to make Roth IRA contributions. Because they are both over 50 years old, the maximum contribution for each is $3,500, or in total $7,000.

Timing of Contributions

Contributions to an IRA or Roth IRA can be made at any time during the tax year for which the contribution relates or up to April 15 of the following year. Contributions for the year can be made at once or over time.

Excess Contributions

excess contribution

An *excess contribution* is any amount contributed to an IRA or Roth IRA that exceeds the maximum contribution limit. Excess contributions will result in an excise tax of 6 percent on the excess. If the excess amount (plus interest) is withdrawn by the tax deadline in the year the excess contribution is made, however, the taxpayer does not have to pay the penalty. The taxpayer does have to include the excess amount in his or her gross income for that year and may have to pay a 10 percent premature distribution penalty on the interest. With traditional IRAs, excess contributions are relatively rare because most taxpayers can contribute $3,000—even though only a portion of that may be deductible. However, excess contributions may be more common in the Roth IRA because the maximum allowable contribution is reduced when the taxpayer's adjusted gross income (AGI) exceeds a specified amount

TRADITIONAL IRAs

Individual retirement plans have certain ground rules regarding eligibility, contribution and deduction limits, and distributions. Generally, these rules ensure that the federal government is promoting retirement savings, not merely providing a tax shelter. These rules also protect against the loss of excess federal revenue by limiting the amount of contributions, prescribing the dates by which distributions must occur, and limiting participation to those who are considered middle class or below or who are not considered active participants in a pension program.

Who Is Eligible

Any person under age 70 1/2 who gets compensation (either salary or self-employment earned income) can make a contribution to an IRA. For some, the contribution will not be deductible, but the interest earnings will be tax deferred. For others, the contribution (as well as any interest earnings) will be tax deferred through an income tax deduction. The contribution will be deductible if neither the taxpayer nor the taxpayer's spouse is an active participant in an employer-maintained retirement plan. If the taxpayer is an active participant, then the contribution is deductible only if his or her adjusted gross income falls below prescribed limits (designed to approximate a middle-class income). If an individual is not an active participant, but his or her spouse is, then the contribution is deductible (for the nonparticipant) if the couple's income is less than a different higher income threshold.

Active Participant

active participant

The first issue that arises under the eligibility question is specifying who an *active participant* is in an employer-maintained plan. The employer-maintained plan basically takes into account every type of qualified plan: defined-benefit pension plans, money-purchase plans, target-benefit plans, profit-sharing plans, and stock plans. It also includes 403(b) tax-sheltered annuity plans, SEPs, and SIMPLEs. Federal, state, or local government plans are also taken into account. However, nonqualified retirement arrangements are not included. An employee who is covered only by a nonqualified plan will not be considered an active participant and can, therefore, make deductible IRA contributions.

Active participant has a special meaning that depends on the type of plan involved.

Defined-Benefit Plans

Generally, a person is an active participant in a defined-benefit plan unless excluded under the eligibility provision of the plan for the entire year. This is true even if he or she elects not to participate in the plan. For example, ABC Company has a plan that requires employees to contribute in order to participate. Because Kim does not feel she can afford to make contributions, she does not participate. But, she is still considered an active participant for IRA purposes, even though she is not active in the plan.

Nevertheless, there are situations in a defined-benefit plan when a client will not be considered an active participant, such as:

- if your client is not covered under the plan's eligibility provisions (for example, employees who are not currently eligible or who will never be eligible for plan participation)
- if the defined-benefit plan is frozen—meaning that no additional benefits are accruing currently for any participant

Defined-Contribution Plans

In general, a person is an active participant in any type of defined-contribution plan if the plan specifies that employer contributions must be allocated to the individual's account. This category also includes SEPs, 403(b) plans, and SIMPLEs. In a profit-sharing or stock plan where employer contributions are discretionary, the participant must actually receive some contribution (even if the contribution amounts to a reallocated forfeiture) for active-participant status to be triggered. Furthermore, mandatory contributions, voluntary contributions, and contributions made pursuant to a salary reduction SEP, 403(b) plan, SIMPLE, or 401(k) arrangement will also trigger active-participant status.

A special rule applies when contributions are completely discretionary under the plan (like a profit-sharing plan) and contributions are not made until after the end of the plan year (ending with or within the employee's tax year in question). In this case, to recognize that a plan participant may not know whether he or she is an active participant by the time the IRA contribution deadline arrives, the employer's contribution is attributable to the following year.

Example: Sally first becomes eligible for XYZ Corporation's profit-sharing plan for the plan year ending December 31, 2001. The company is on a calendar fiscal year and does not decide to make a contribution for the 2001 plan year until June 1, 2002. Sally is not considered an active participant in the plan for the 2001 plan year. However, due to the 2002 contribution, she is an active participant for the 2002 plan year.

When the plan year of the employer's plan (regardless of whether the plan is a defined-benefit or defined-contribution plan) is not the calendar year, an individual's active-participant status is dependent upon whether he or she is an active participant for the plan year ending with or within the particular calendar year in question.

Example: Susan first becomes eligible for the ABC money-purchase pension plan for the plan year June 1, 2001 to May 30, 2002. Susan is an active participant for 2002 (but not 2001) because the plan year ended "with or within" calendar year 2002.

Finally, note that in determining active-participant status, participation for any part of the plan year counts as participation for the whole plan year, and that whether or not the participant is vested in his or her benefit has no bearing on the determination.

Income Level

The second issue that arises under the eligibility question is whether the taxpayer can make deductible contributions under the income-level rules. In general, people who are not active participants can deduct contributions to an IRA no matter what they earn. For an active participant, however, fully deductible contributions are allowed only if the taxpayer has AGI below a specified level. If the AGI exceeds the specified limit but falls below a maximum level, the $3,000 IRA limit (or $3,500 for an individual over age 50) is proportionately reduced by a formula (table 17-1 shows the phaseout limits for 2002). Note that the phase-out limits continue to increase until they level off in the year 2007. (Appendix 8 shows the phase-out limits for future years.)

The level for unreduced contributions depends upon the taxpayer's filing status. In 2002, married couples filing a joint return will get a full IRA deduction if their AGI is $54,000 or less (special rules apply to marrieds filing separately—see Appendix 8). In 2002, individual taxpayers will get a full IRA deduction if their AGI is $34,000 or less. The maximum level for deductible contributions is $63,999.99 for marrieds filing jointly and $43,999.99 for individuals. In other words, if an active participant's AGI exceeds these levels, no part of an IRA contribution can be deducted.

When applying the phase-out limits, calculation of the AGI is somewhat modified. AGI is determined without regard to the exclusion for foreign earned income, but Social Security benefits includible in gross income and losses or gains on passive investments are taken into account. Also, contributions to an IRA or Roth IRA are not deducted.

TABLE 17-1
2002 Limits for Deductible IRA Contributions

Filing Status	Full IRA Deduction	Reduced IRA Deduction	No IRA Deduction
Individual	34,000 or less	$34,000.01- $43,999.99	$44,000 or more
Married filing jointly	54,000 or less	$54,000.01- $63,999.99	$64,000 or more

For taxpayers whose AGI falls between the no-deduction level and the full-deduction level, their deduction is reduced prorata. To compute the reduction use the following formula:

$$\text{Deductible amount} = \text{max. contribution} - \left(\text{max. contribution} \times \frac{\text{AGI} - \text{filing status floor}}{\text{phase out range}}\right)$$

Two operational rules apply to taxpayers who fall into the reduced IRA category. First, the IRS allows the adjusted limitation to be rounded up to the next $10 increment. For example, if the formula for Kay shows her eligible to make a deductible contribution of $758.43, her deductible contribution is rounded up to $760. The second rule that applies to the reduction formula is that there is a $200 floor. In other words, even if Ed's deductible IRA

***Example*:**   Bob and Rita Dufus (a married couple under age 50 filing jointly) are both working, are both active participants, and have a combined adjusted gross income of $59,000 for 2002. Bob and Rita can each make the full IRA contribution of $3,000 (total $6,000). However, only a portion of each contribution is deductible. Because their AGI is $5,000 more than the lower limit for married couples ($54,000) they each lose one half (totally phased out over $10,000) of the deductible contribution. Each can deduct $1,500 (total $3,000). Using the formula

$$\$3,000 - \left(\$3,000 \times \frac{\$59,000 - \$54,000}{\$10,000} \right)$$

---

contribution works out to $57, Ed is still entitled to make a $200 deductible contribution. This means that a one-cent difference can mean the loss of a $200 deduction.

Married Taxpayers with Spouses Who Are Active Participants

If a married taxpayer and his or her spouse are both active participants, then the deduction rules just described apply to both IRAs. However, the rules are different when only one spouse is an active participant. In this case, a $3,000 deductible IRA contribution is allowed for the nonactive participant spouse as long as the couple's AGI does not exceed $150,000. The deduction is phased out if the couple's joint AGI exceeds $150,000 and will be gone entirely if their AGI is $160,000 or more. These phase-out rules apply in the same way as the other deductible IRA phase-out rules. A deductible contribution is not available for the nonactive participant spouse if the couple files separate tax returns.

Example: Joe and Jane Morgan, each aged 32, are considering establishing IRAs for themselves and ask you whether contributions are deductible. Joe earns $80,000 and Jane does not have any income because she stays at home with the children. Joe is an active participant in a retirement plan and Jane, of course, is not. Joe cannot make a deductible IRA contribution on his own behalf because their income exceeds $64,000. However, he can make a $3,000 deductible IRA contribution for Jane because their joint income is less than $150,000.

ROTH IRAs

Today, most individuals have a choice between contributing to the traditional IRA or to a Roth IRA each year. The newer Roth IRA is tied to the old rules in that total contributions for the year (to either type of IRA) cannot exceed the maximum limit for the year (for 2002, $3,000 or $3,500 for a taxpayer aged 50 or older). As with traditional IRAs, spousal Roth IRAs are allowed. Contributions to a Roth IRA are not deductible, but distributions are tax free as long as certain eligibility requirements are satisfied. The maximum contribution to a Roth IRA is phased out for single taxpayers with an AGI between $95,000 and $110,000 (pro rata reduction over $15,000 income spread) and for married joint filers with an AGI between $150,000 and $160,000 (pro rata reduction over $10,000 income spread). For purposes of this calculation, the AGI is modified in the same way as for traditional IRAs.

Unlike traditional IRAs, contributions can even be made after attainment of age 70 1/2, and the minimum-distribution rules that require distributions from IRAs beginning at age 70 1/2 do not apply. However, the IRA minimum-distribution requirement that applies to payments after the death of the participant does apply to Roth IRAs.

For distributions to be "qualified distributions" that are entirely tax free, they have to meet two requirements. First, the distribution must be made after the 5-tax-year period beginning with the first tax year for which a contribution was made to an individual's Roth IRA. Second, the distribution must be made after one of the four following events has occurred:

- The participant has attained age 59 1/2.
- The distribution is paid to a beneficiary due to the participant's death.

- The participant has become disabled.
- The withdrawal is made to pay qualified first-time homebuyer expenses.

Qualified first-time homebuyer expenses include acquisition costs of a first home (paid within 120 days of the distribution) for the participant, spouse, or any child, grandchild, or ancestor of the participant or spouse. This exception, however, has a $10,000 lifetime limit per IRA (or Roth IRA) participant. If a distribution does not meet these requirements, it is referred to as a nonqualifying distribution. (The tax rules that apply to nonqualifying distributions are discussed later.)

ROLLOVER CONTRIBUTIONS

The ability to roll benefits from an employer-sponsored tax-sheltered retirement plan to an IRA is a powerful concept. It gives participants the opportunity to defer income taxes and to continue to accrue tax-deferred interest until distributions are needed for retirement. It also gives the participant complete control over the investment direction of retirement funds as well as the timing of distributions.

The IRA rollover also permits the financial services professional to manage and service large asset accumulations. This opportunity continues to grow as more company pension plans today give participants a lump-sum option and workers continue to accumulate large sums in their company's 401(k) plan.

Traditional IRAs

To facilitate portability of pensions and transferability when a taxpayer changes jobs, distributions from a qualified plan (except life insurance distributions), 403(b) plan, 457 plan, or from an individual retirement arrangement can be made on a tax-free basis if the distribution is reinvested within 60 days in an individual retirement arrangement. This transaction is known as a *rollover*—the tax-free transfer from one retirement program to another.

There are several types of rollovers involving individual retirement arrangements:

- *Rollover from one individual retirement arrangement to another individual retirement arrangement.* Taxpayers can withdraw all or part of the balance in an IRA and reinvest it within 60 days in another IRA. The reasons for doing this include changing trusts or custodial accounts (because of dissatisfaction with investment performance or service) or temporarily boosting cash flow.

- *Rollover from a qualified plan or 403(b) plan to an IRA.* Under the rules applicable today, most distributions made from a qualified plan, 403(b) plan, or 457 plan can be rolled over (in full or in part) into a new or existing IRA. The rollover is not allowed when the distribution is part of a series of periodic payments over the life expectancy of the participant or over a period of 10 years or more or if the distribution is a hardship withdrawal from 401(k) plan. A participant wanting to make such a rollover should generally choose what is referred to as a *direct rollover* from the plan to the IRA. This allows the participant to avoid the 20 percent income tax withholding requirements on the distribution paid directly to the participant. Electing the direct rollover is relatively easy to accomplish because the law now requires that qualified plans, 403(b) plans, and 457 plans give participants the option to make the direct transfer to an IRA.

One final word on traditional IRA rollovers: Because rollovers are permitted only once a year, one way around this one-year rule is to make a *trustee-to-trustee transfer*—a transfer of IRA funds from one trustee directly to another trustee. However, a trustee-to-trustee transfer does not constitute a rollover because the money is never distributed.

Roth IRAs

Distributions from one Roth IRA can be rolled over tax free to another Roth IRA. Also, amounts in a traditional IRA can be rolled over to a Roth IRA if the individual's AGI for the tax year does not exceed $100,000. The dollar limit is the same for both single and married couples filing jointly—marrieds filing separately are not eligible for the rollover. Rollovers from Roth IRAs and conversions from traditional IRAs are subject to the 60-day rollover rules. The once-a-year rollover rule also applies to Roth IRAs but not to conversions from traditional to Roth IRAs. The 60-day rollover means that an individual can convert to a Roth IRA in 2002 by withdrawing the funds from the traditional IRA up to December 31, 2002 and then rolling the amount into the Roth IRA as late as the end of February in the year 2003. Under the rules, this is treated as a Roth IRA conversion for 2002.

Because a conversion has to occur before the end of the year, it is quite possible that the individual's AGI is not yet known at the time of the conversion. For example, Sally, who is single, expects to have AGI of $95,000. On December 1, 2002 she converts a $10,000 IRA. After the year ends and she calculates her taxes, it turns out that she had AGI of $102,000 for 2002. The law allows an undoing of the Roth IRA conversion without penalty as long as the amount is transferred back to a traditional IRA by the due date of the tax return (plus extensions) for the year, and that any earnings on the account are also returned.

When an amount is rolled over from a traditional IRA, the distribution is subject to income tax (taxed as ordinary income), but is not subject to the 10 percent early distribution excise tax. However, because this could result in the avoidance of the 10 percent early distribution tax, individuals who withdraw converted amounts from a Roth IRA within 5 tax years of the conversion will be subject to the 10 percent penalty on early withdrawals.

Once in the Roth IRA, future growth is not taxed as long as distributions qualify for the income exclusion, using the same rules that apply to new Roth IRAs. With a converted Roth IRA, the 5-year measuring period begins for the first year that contributions to any Roth IRA were made. This means that if an individual made a $2,000 contribution to a Roth IRA for 1998 and then in the year 2002 converted a $50,000 IRA to another Roth IRA, the 5-year measuring period for the Roth IRA would start in 1998.

DISTRIBUTIONS

Chapters 25 and 26 cover the taxation of qualified plan and IRA distributions in-depth. Here we will summarize the rules that apply to both traditional and Roth IRAs.

Traditional IRAs

Taxpayers can withdraw all or part of their IRAs any time they wish. Unless the participant has made nondeductible contributions, distributions from IRAs are treated as ordinary income and are subject to federal income tax. Nondeductible contributions are withdrawn tax free on a pro rata basis. If the participant dies, payments to beneficiaries are still subject to income tax. However, the income is treated as "income in respect to a decedent," which means that income taxes are reduced by the amount of estate taxes paid as a result of the IRA.

If distributions are made prior to age 59 1/2, the Sec 72(t) excise tax imposes an additional 10 percent tax unless an exception applies. Exceptions are made for payments on account of death, disability, or for the payment of certain medical expenses. Another exception allows substantially equal periodic payments over the remaining life of the participant and a chosen beneficiary. Another allows payments for qualified higher education expenses for education furnished to the taxpayer, the taxpayer's spouse, or any child or grandchild of the taxpayer or taxpayer's spouse at an eligible educational institution. A final exception is for distributions to pay for acquisition costs of a first home for the participant, spouse, or any child, grandchild, or ancestor of the participant or spouse. This exception, however, has a $10,000 lifetime exception per IRA participant.

IRAs are also subject to rules that control the maximum length of the tax-deferral period. These are the minimum-distribution rules that generally require that distributions begin when the participant attains age 70 1/2 and also require specified payments at the death of the participant.

Roth IRAs

What makes Roth IRAs unique is that qualifying distributions are tax free. As described above, to qualify, distributions must be made more than 5 years after the Roth IRA was established, and be distributed after the participant attains age 59 1/2, or dies, or becomes disabled. Also, up to $10,000 of homebuying expenses can be distributed tax free as well, as long as the 5-year rule is satisfied.

If a nonqualifying distribution is made, the situation is somewhat more complicated. Generally, an individual can withdraw his or her Roth IRA contributions (or converted contributions) without income tax consequences. Once all contributions have been withdrawn, amounts representing earnings are subject to both income tax and the 10 percent Sec. 72(t) excise tax.

A special rule applies to converted Roth IRAs. The 10 percent excise tax continues to apply for 5 years after the conversion—even if no income tax is due. Remember, however, that all of the exceptions to the premature distributions penalty that apply to traditional IRAs will apply to distributions from the Roth IRA as well.

CONCLUSION

With the new Roth IRA, the increases in the deductible IRA phase-out limits, the special deduction rules where one spouse is not an active participant, and the income limits for Roth IRA rollovers, the expertise required to advise clients regarding their IRA options has become much more extensive. Table 17-2 should help by summarizing these rules.

TABLE 17-2 2002 IRA Phase-Out Limits			
Tax Benefit	**Phase-Out Income Levels**		
	Single	Married filing jointly	Married filing separately
Deductible IRA contributions for active participants	$ 34,000 $ 44,000	$ 54,000 $ 64,000	$0 – $10,000
Deductible IRA contributions for spouse of an active participant	Not applicable	$150,000 $160,000	Not available
Roth IRA contributions	$ 95,000 $ 110,000	$150,000 $160,000	$0 – $10,000
Roth IRA conversions	$ 100,000	$100,000	Not allowed

CHAPTER REVIEW

Answers to the review questions and the self-test questions start on page 673.

Key Terms

IRA   excess contribution
Roth IRA   active participant
spousal IRA

Review Questions

17-1.   How are traditional IRAs similar to qualified plans?

17-2.   How is the Roth IRA different from the traditional IRA?

17-3.   a.   Explain the annual limit for contributions to either type of IRA.
      b.   When can a catchup election be made?
      c.   When can a spousal IRA be established?
      d.   Discuss the timing of IRA contributions.
      e.   What happens if too much is contributed to the plan?

17-4.   Who is eligible to make deductible IRA contributions?

17-5.   Which of the following employees is considered an active participant?
      a.   John has a target-benefit Keogh plan to which he contributes annually.

    b.   Barb works for an employer who maintains a defined-benefit plan, but Barb is not eligible to participate in the plan.

    c.   Patty is a member of a 401(k) plan and makes a 5 percent salary reduction that is not matched.

    d.   Bob is a member of his employer's profit-sharing plan; the employer has announced that no contribution will be made for the year.

    e.   Tim's employer does not have any form of retirement plan. Tim's wife works for an employer who contributes an amount equal to 10 percent of her salary each year to a money-purchase plan.

17-6.   List the income limits for deductible IRA contributions in 2002 for
    a.   a single taxpayer
    b.   a married taxpayer who is filing jointly

17-7.   George and Mary Barke (marrieds filing jointly) have a combined adjusted gross income of $57,317 in 2002. Each are aged 45. George is an active participant in an employer-maintained plan but Mary is not. What is the amount of the deductible IRA contribution that George and Mary can make for 2002 assuming that both earn more than $3,000?

17-8.   Explain Roth IRAs with regard to
    a.   eligibility for contributions
    b.   whether contributions can be made after attainment of age 70 1/2
    c.   tax-free withdrawals

17-9.   What are the various types of rollover contributions from a traditional IRA?

17-10. Under what circumstances can a traditional IRA be converted to a Roth IRA?

17-11. What are the tax implications of converting a traditional IRA to a Roth IRA?

17-12. a.   Explain the tax treatment of distributions from traditional IRAs.
        b.   Explain the tax treatment of distributions from Roth IRAs.

Self-Test Questions

T F   17-1. A taxpayer can make nondeductible contributions to an IRA even if he or she only has passive income (such as investment earnings).

T F   17-2. Self-employeds who have a salary income from another job cannot make an IRA contribution if they have a net loss from self-employment.

T F   17-3. The maximum contribution to a spousal IRA for 2002 is $3,000 if the spouse is under age 50.

T F   17-4. A spousal IRA can be set up only if the taxpayer contributes to his or her own account.

T   F   17-5.   An excess contribution is subject to a 50 percent excise tax.

T   F   17-6.   A single individual, aged 40, with an AGI of $100,000 in 2002 who is not an active participant can make a $3,000 deductible IRA contribution for 2002.

T   F   17-7.   Generally, a person is an active participant if he or she is covered by a simplified employee pension plan.

T   F   17-8.   An employee who is covered by only a nonqualified plan will be considered an active participant.

T   F   17-9.   A person is an active participant for IRA purposes even in years when the profit-sharing plan does not make contributions and no other allocations are made to the participant's account.

T   F   17-10. An IRA deduction that is partially reduced under the limits for deductible contribution rules is always rounded up to the nearest $100 increment.

T   F   17-11. If a married couple filing jointly earns less than $150,000 in 2002, a $3,000 deductible contribution to a spousal IRA is generally allowed for a nonworking spouse.

T   F   17-12. Contributions to a Roth IRA are sometimes eligible for a tax deduction.

T   F   17-13. A single person who is an active participant and has an AGI of $60,000 in 2002 cannot make a Roth IRA contribution.

T   F   17-14. A Roth IRA distribution is always tax-free withdrawal if the participant is aged 63 at the time of the distribution and has maintained the Roth IRA for at least 3 years.

T   F   17-15. An IRA to an IRA rollover must be made within 6 months of the distribution.

T   F   17-16. Rollovers from one IRA to another IRA may only be made once a year.

T   F   17-17. An IRA can be converted to a Roth IRA if the taxpayer has an AGI of less than $100,000 for the year and the individual is not married or is married and files a joint return.

T   F   17-18. A conversion from an IRA to Roth IRA can be accomplished tax free.

T   F   17-19. Distributions from an IRA to pay for qualifying education expenses will not be subject to the 10 percent premature distributions excise tax.

Individual Retirement Plans—Part II

Learning Objectives

An understanding of the material in this chapter should enable the student to

18-1. Explain the tax treatment of IRAs and Roth IRAs.

18-2. Describe the investment considerations and restrictions that apply to IRAs.

18-3. Discuss appropriate uses of IRAs and Roth IRAs.

Chapter Outline

In addition to the legal and tax implications concerning IRAs, there are also several financial implications. Note that both traditional IRAs and Roth IRAs are subject to the same investment rules. Let's take a closer look.

FUNDING VEHICLES

Individual retirement plans can be established with one of two different funding vehicles:

- individual retirement accounts
- individual retirement annuities

Individual Retirement Accounts (IRAs)

Individual retirement accounts (IRAs) are the most popular type of individual retirement arrangement. The IRA document itself is a written trust or a custodial account whose trustee or custodian must be a bank, a federally insured credit union, a savings and loan association, or a person or organization that receives IRS permission to act as the trustee or custodian (for example, an insurance company). No one receives IRS permission to be the trustee of his or her own IRA because the IRS mandates arm's-length dealing between the beneficiary of the IRA trust and those in charge of enforcing IRA rules. IRA funds may not be commingled with other assets.

Individual Retirement Annuities (IRA Annuities)

An *individual retirement annuity (IRA annuity)* is an annuity contract typically issued by insurance companies. IRA annuities are similar to IRAs except that the following additional rules apply because of their annuity investment feature:

- The IRA annuity is nontransferable. In other words, unlike the proceeds from other annuities, the IRA annuity proceeds must be received by either the taxpayer or a beneficiary. Individuals cannot set up an IRA annuity and then pledge the annuity to another party or put the annuity up as a security for a loan. For example, if loans were made under an automatic premium-loan provision, the plan would be disqualified.
- IRA annuities may not have fixed annual premiums. It is allowable, however, to charge an annual fee for each premium or to have a level annual premium for a supplementary benefit, such as a waiver of premium in case of disability.

TYPES OF INVESTMENTS

self-directed IRAs

IRAs can be invested in a multitude of vehicles running the gamut from mutual funds to limited partnerships, from investments with minimal risk and modest returns to speculative investments with promises of greater return. IRAs are typically invested in certificates of deposit, money market funds, mutual funds, limited partnerships, income bond funds, corporate bond funds, and common stocks and other equities. *Self-directed IRAs* (IRAs in which the taxpayer is able to shift investments between general investment vehicles offered by the trustee) are also popular because they give the investor investment flexibility and the ability to anticipate or react to interest-rate directions and market trends.

Choosing the best investment for an individual retirement arrangement is similar to choosing any other investment: lifestyle. Other financial resources, as well as the client's degree of risk aversion, must be considered. There is, however, one hitch with an IRA or IRA annuity investment: The *R* stands for *retirement*. The client's retirement goals must be considered to make the proper IRA or IRA annuity investment. In rendering IRA or IRA annuity advice, the job of a financial services professional is to induce the client to generate a retirement strategy first and an investment strategy second.

However, investing in tax-sheltered vehicles, such as municipal bonds, is generally not a good idea because the tax shelter is not necessary. Because an IRA provides for tax deferral already, the overkill of investing in a tax-free bond will not make it worthwhile for an investor to take the lower yield that municipal bonds offer.

Investment Restrictions

Investment of IRAs is generally open to all of the investment vehicles available outside IRAs. There are, however, a few exceptions:

- investment in life insurance
- investment in collectibles
- prohibited transactions

Life Insurance

Investment in life insurance is not allowed for an IRA even though defined-benefit and defined-contribution retirement plans allow an "incidental" amount of life insurance. IRAs, however, are not subject to the same rules (or underlying logic) and are considered to be strictly for retirement purposes. Therefore, no incidental insurance is available. But there is an interesting method for linking the sale of life insurance with an IRA.

**YOUR FINANCIAL SERVICES PRACTICE:
LIFE INSURANCE AND IRAs**

Dividend-paying cash value life insurance (for example, whole life) can be used to fund an IRA indirectly. The client should use an existing policy or purchase a life policy capable of generating $3,000 worth of dividends after a sufficient time has passed to allow cash buildup. The $3,000 can then be distributed as a "tax-free" dividend if it is used to fund an IRA or IRA annuity. The taxpayer gives up contributions to a life policy for several years but gains the face value (plus any reinvested dividends) as insurance coverage, a perpetually tax-free-funded IRA or IRA annuity, and a possible IRA or IRA annuity tax deduction.

Collectibles

If an IRA is invested in collectibles, the amount invested in collectibles is considered a distribution in the year invested. This means that the tax advantages of IRAs have been eliminated, and if the investment is made prior to age 59 1/2, a 10 percent excise tax will be applicable unless the payment is made in the form of a life annuity or its equivalent. Collectibles include works of art, Oriental rugs, antiques, rare coins, stamps, rare wines, and certain other tangible property.

There are two exceptions to the prohibition on investments in collectibles. First, specified gold, silver, and platinum coins issued by the United States and coins issued under state law can be bought with IRA funds. However, gold and silver coins of other countries are still prohibited. In addition, investments in gold, silver, platinum, or palladium bullion of a quality eligible for a regulated futures contract (as described in section 7 of the Commodity Exchange Act, 7 U.S.C. 7) are also allowed. This provision allows individuals to invest in precious metals within their IRA accounts. However, these types of investments are allowed only when the IRA trustee has physical possession of the bullion.

Prohibited Transactions

Prohibited transactions for an IRA include borrowing money from the account or annuity, selling property to the account, or using the account or annuity as security for a loan. If a nonexempt prohibited transaction occurs, the IRA will be "disqualified" and the taxpayer must include the fair market value of part or all of the IRA assets in his or her gross income for tax purposes in the year in which the prohibited transaction occurs. There also will be a 10 percent premature distribution penalty (if prior to age 59 1/2). In effect, prohibited transactions are treated as distributions from the plan.

Choosing an Individual Retirement Annuity

The primary reason for choosing one IRA funding vehicle over another is the investor's desired return balanced against the amount of risk he or she is willing to accept. There are, however, secondary reasons that make IRA annuities worth considering when the return/risk factors are comparable with other investments: the waiver-of-premium coverage in case of disability and the lifelong payments that are afforded by a life annuity. The waiver-of-premium coverage provides an investor with valuable protection should disability occur. This is especially important for those relying on individual-retirement-arrangement funds as a major source of retirement income. In fact, for some people the waiver of premium in case of disability may be the only assurance of retirement income (aside from Social Security). The lifetime payments offered by an IRA annuity are a second reason for choosing it. As with any annuity, the investor is betting he or she will outlive the mortality table. If the investor does, the excess payments represent mortality gain, which can be thought of as an additional return on investment. The IRA annuity also quells a common fear of retired persons—running out of funds and becoming dependent on others. Ideally, investors would like to live off the interest provided by their personal savings and IRA, but this is not possible for many. Life annuities provide a structured way to use up both principal and interest without the danger of funds running out.

IRAs USED WITH SEPs AND SIMPLEs

IRAs are also used as the funding vehicle for two types of employer-sponsored retirement plans, SEPs and SIMPLEs. Obviously, the contribution limits are different, but in most other ways the IRAs operate under the same rules that apply to IRAs established by individuals. This means that the investment restrictions are same, benefits must be fully vested at all times, distributions are taxed the same, and in most instances benefits can be rolled from one IRA to another. (Note that the IRA rules prohibit loans to participants. This prohibition means that SEPs and SIMPLEs cannot include participant loan programs.)

When an employer establishes a SEP, regular IRA accounts are established for each participant. Unfortunately, this is not true when an employer establishes a SIMPLE. Here a vehicle called the SIMPLE IRA is adopted for each participant. Even though these accounts are essentially IRAs, the new name is required because they differ from regular IRAs in one regard: Distributions from SIMPLE IRAs in the first 2 years of participation are subject to a 25 percent early withdrawal penalty tax. Because of this tax, there is a prohibition on the transfer out of a SIMPLE IRA and into a regular IRA in the first 2 years of participation. Otherwise, participants could circumvent the 25 percent tax. In all other regards, SIMPLE IRAs are the same as other IRAs.

IRAs AND THE FINANCIAL SERVICES PROFESSIONAL

For the financial services professional, understanding IRAs requires more than just knowing the various rules, restraints, and tax implications associated with them. The financial services professional must also analyze whether a current client's interests are best served by making IRA contributions and must identify potential clients who need IRA assistance. Many financial services professionals must even ask themselves whether selling IRAs is appropriate for them.

Should Your Client Make an IRA or Roth IRA Contribution?

The first step in determining whether a client should use IRAs is to determine their eligibility for the various options. Tables 18-1 and 18-2 summarize the available options for both single and married (filing jointly) taxpayers in 2002.

The last several years have seen important favorable changes for IRAs. Even though IRA planning has become considerably more complicated, it has also opened up new opportunities for your clients. Looking at IRAs under the new playing field, here are some general observations for your clients:

- The maximum contribution to IRAs is rising. For 2002, the limit is $3,000 and will continue to increase until 2006, when it becomes $5,000. Those aged 50 or older can make an additional contribution each year through 2005 and then can make a $1,000 additional contribution after that.
- The special spousal rule provides that for married couple filing jointly with AGI less than $150,000 and only one spouse covered in an employer sponsored retirement plan, the other spouse can contribute the maximum amount on a deductible basis to a traditional IRA.

TABLE 18-1
IRA Options for Singles in 2002

Type of contribution	Tax benefit	Availability
Nondeductible	–After-tax contributions with tax deferral on earnings –Distributions of earnings taxed as ordinary income	Individuals who have not yet attained age 70 1/2 with compensation from personal services (does not include investment income)
Deductible	–Tax deduction on contributions with tax deferral on earnings –All distributions taxed as ordinary income	–Individuals who have not yet attained age 70 1/2 with compensation who are not active participants in an employer sponsored retirement plan –Deduction phased out for individuals who are active participants with AGI between $34,000 and $44,000
Roth	–After-tax contributions –No tax on qualifying distributions	–Individuals of any age with compensation –Ability to make contribution phased out with AGI between $95,000 and $110,000
Converting an IRA to a Roth IRA	Income tax paid at the time the IRA is converted to the Roth IRA	Cannot make conversion if AGI exceeds $100,000 for the year

- The ability to make withdrawals from IRAs without penalty for family educational expenses and first homebuying expenses takes away one of the major reasons not to use an IRA.
- The Roth IRA offers a significant tax benefit that is available to a lot of taxpayers who cannot make deductible IRA contributions. For example, an individual earning $50,000 and who is a 401(k) plan participant cannot make a deductible IRA contribution, but can make a $3,000 contribution to a Roth IRA.
- Choosing between the Roth IRA and a deductible IRA (or other pre-tax savings vehicle like a 401(k) plan) can be a difficult choice (see below). However, do not forget that both are great ways to save for retirement.

- Many taxpayers will resist converting traditional IRAs to Roth IRAs. Doing so creates a current tax liability. However, conversions can accomplish a number of objectives and can be the appropriate economic choice for many individuals, that is, as long as the law does not change again.

TABLE 18-2
IRA Options for Marrieds Filing Jointly in 2002

Type of contribution	Tax benefit	Availability
Nondeductible	–After-tax contributions with tax deferral on earnings –Distributions of earnings taxed as ordinary income	Individuals* who have not yet attained age 70 1/2, with compensation from personal services (does not include investment income)
Deductible	–Tax deduction on contributions with tax deferral on earnings –All distributions taxed as ordinary income	–Individuals* who have not yet attained age 70 1/2 with compensation who are not active participants in an employer-sponsored retirement plan –If one spouse is an active participant, then the deduction is phased out (for the spouse who is not an active participant) for AGI between $150,000 and $160,000 –Deduction phased out for individuals who are active participants with AGI between $53,000 and $63,000
Roth IRA	–After-tax contributions –No tax on qualifying distributions	–Individual's* of any age with compensation –Ability to make contribution phased out with AGI between $150,000 and $160,000
Converting an IRA to a Roth IRA	–Income tax paid at the time the IRA is converted to the Roth IRA	Cannot make conversion if AGI exceeds $100,000 for the year

*For a married couple, a spousal IRA can be established if one spouse does not have compensation from employment.

- The IRA rules offer little for taxpayers with high-end income. However, older, more affluent individuals can provide encouragement—and funds—to their children and grandchildren to take advantage of these new opportunities. Also, some advisors are so enthusiastic about the advantages of the Roth IRA conversion that they may be encouraging clients to manipulate their income to get below the $100,000 AGI threshold.

- The IRA rules offer little to those at the lower end of the earnings scale. These individuals are least likely to be able to have sufficient income to afford a contribution, and will be most likely to need emergency withdrawals that will not qualify for special tax treatment.

Let's look at several of these points in greater depth.

Easier Access to IRA funds

Sometimes it is difficult to convince your clients of the importance of saving for retirement. With younger clients, it can be helpful to point out that by making just nine $2,000 contributions from age 18 to age 26—and no contributions thereafter—an IRA at age 65 will be larger than an IRA funded with a $2,000 contribution each year from age 27 to age 65 (see table 18-3). For clients who think their company-sponsored retirement plan is sufficient, point out to them that if postretirement inflation is 4 percent per year, a $1 loaf of bread at age 65 will cost $2.19 at age 85.

Another concern of clients is the effect of the 10 percent premature excise tax. If money is withdrawn too soon, the tax will reduce the client's savings. For some, this is good news because it acts as an incentive to keep the money in the plan. However, it would also be irresponsible to advise a client to make IRA contributions if he or she could not leave the money in the plan for a significant period of time. Still, there is a point at which it pays a taxpayer to make IRA contributions even when a premature withdrawal is the taxpayer's intention. The break-even or get-ahead date depends on the tax bracket of the employee when contributions are made, the interest earned under the IRA, the tax bracket of the person when distributions are withdrawn, and the ratio of nondeductible contributions to the total IRA balance at the time of withdrawal. If the taxpayer's tax bracket is lower at the time of withdrawal, the break-even point will be shorter. (The converse is also true: a higher tax bracket at distribution time will mean a longer break-even point.)

Another answer to a client's concerns about the premature excise tax is that withdrawals can be made to pay for educational expenses and up to $10,000 of first homebuying expenses. These exceptions mean that young persons who are also concerned about saving for homeownership and for their children's college education can withdraw funds for these purposes without penalty.

Choosing the Roth IRA over the Nondeductible IRA

Many taxpayers who do not have the option to make deductible IRA contributions will, however, have the opportunity to make Roth IRA contributions. The ability to contribute to Roth IRAs is phased out for single taxpayers with AGI between $95,000 and $110,000 and married couples filing jointly with AGI between $150,000 and $160,000. Individuals who have the choice between nondeductible IRA contributions and Roth IRA

TABLE 18-3 IRA Funding Plans[1]					
Plan One			**Plan Two**		
Age start		18	Age start		27
Age end		26	Age end		65
Amount per year		$2,000	Amount per year		$2,000
Rate of return		10%	Rate of return		10%
Value at age 65		$1,229,194	Value at age 65		$883,145
Total amount contributed		$18,000	Total amount contributed		$78,000
Age	**Amount**	**Value**	**Age**	**Amount**	**Value**
18	$2,000	$ 2,200	18	0	0
19	2,000	4,620	19	0	0
20	2,000	7,282	20	0	0
21	2,000	10,210	21	0	0
22	2,000	13,431	22	0	0
23	2,000	16,974	23	0	0
24	2,000	20,871	24	0	0
25	2,000	25,158	25	0	0
26	2,000	29,874	26	0	0
27	0	32,861	27	$2,000	$ 2,200
28	0	36,147	28	2,000	4,620
29	0	39,762	29	2,000	7,282
30	0	43,738	30	2,000	10,210
.	.	.	.	.	.
60	0	763,233	60	2,000	540,049
61	0	839,556	61	2,000	596,254
62	0	923,512	62	2,000	658,079
63	0	1,015,863	63	2,000	726,087
64	0	1,117,449	64	2,000	800,896
65	0	1,229,194	65	2,000	883,145

[1]This comparison is hypothetical; no guarantees are implied for specific investments. The interest rate is assumed to remain unchanged for the entire period.

contributions should almost always choose the Roth IRA. Tax-free distributions are clearly better than tax deferral. In fact, beginning in 1998 nondeductible contributions really lost their tax luster. Today, investing in securities (outside of the IRA context) may be more attractive, because capital gains can be deferred until the sale and qualifying sales will be taxed at a maximum 20 percent tax rate. Also, securities left to heirs avoid income taxes on the growth over the participant's life.

In contrast, the tax advantages of the Roth IRA are clear. As long as distributions satisfy the eligibility requirements, the entire distribution avoids income tax—even distributions to death beneficiaries. The Roth IRA can even be used to save (up to $10,000) as a down payment for a first home. Like other IRAs, Roth IRA funds can be invested in stocks, bonds, or other investment vehicles.

Still, if an individual has to withdraw funds for other purposes, withdrawals of earnings will be subject to income tax and the 10 percent penalty. Under the new statute, Roth IRA contributions can be withdrawn first without tax consequences. This gives the Roth IRA participant a safety net (up to the amount of accumulated contributions) in case of emergency. Also, because the penalty tax applies in the same manner as to traditional IRAs, withdrawals from a Roth IRA for educational expenses would be subject to income tax (to the extent that withdrawals exceed the participant's accumulated contributions) but not the 10 percent penalty tax.

A good candidate for the Roth IRA is, for example, the 401(k) participant who has maximized his or her contribution to the 401(k) plan, is not eligible for a deductible IRA contribution, and still wants to save more for retirement. In this case, the next place to save is definitely the Roth IRA. The harder question to answer would be, "Should the 401(k) participant who has been putting away 6 percent of compensation each year and who wants to save more, contribute more to the 401(k) plan or contribute to a Roth IRA?" This individual is now choosing between the deductible savings and the tax-free saving alternatives. The issues involved in this decision making are discussed below.

Choosing the Roth IRA over the Deductible IRA

Some taxpayers will be in the position to choose between a deductible IRA contribution or the Roth IRA. Similarly, many employees may be choosing between making additional contributions to a 401(k) plan or the Roth IRA. In the 401(k) setting, if the employer is going to match the contribution, the advantage usually goes to the 401(k) plan, because the employer match is like an instant return on the participant's contribution. However, if the contribution is not matched, then the 401(k) to Roth IRA comparison is essentially the same as the deductible IRA to Roth IRA comparison.

Comparing the financial effect of the two options is difficult, partially because it involves assumptions about rates of return in the future, tax rates in the future, and the timing of withdrawals. Numerous computer software programs are available to help with this comparison, and they can be quite valuable in helping to make choices.

Even though individual analysis is best, here are some general considerations. It is clearest that when the individual expects to be in a higher tax bracket in retirement than at the time of the contribution, the Roth IRA is the more appropriate vehicle. For example, take the young person in the 17 percent (15 percent federal and 2 percent state) bracket today who expects to be in the 42 percent bracket at the time of distribution. Table 18-4 gives an example of such an individual, who has $2,000 to contribute at age 25 and withdraws this amount at age 70. If $2,000 is contributed to the traditional IRA, after taxes are paid at age 70 she will have $37,042. However, if $1,660 is contributed to a Roth IRA ($2,000 less taxes), at age 70 she will have $53,006. This is a significant difference. As seen in table 18-5, this trend is consistent when contributions are made at age 45.

TABLE 18-4
Comparing Deductible IRAs to Roth IRA Accumulations

Age	30%/30%*		17%/42%*		30%/42%*	
	Roth	Deductible	Roth	Deductible	Roth	Deductible
25	$ 1,400	$2,000	$ 1,660	$ 2,000	$ 1,400	$ 2,000
70	$44,691	$44,706**	$53,006	$37,042**	$44,691	$37,042**

* The first number represents the combined federal and state income tax rate at the time of contribution and the second number represents the tax rate at the time of distribution.

** Assumes that the entire accumulation is distributed and taxed at age 70. Assumes growth at 8%.

Looking at the columns in tables 18-4 and 18-5 showing the individual's tax rates to be the same (30 percent) at the time of contribution and distribution, it may appear at first glance that the Roth IRA is *not* more effective for taxpayers who will have the same or lower tax rates at the time of withdrawal. However, this will not always be the case. In our example, the participant withdraws all of the Roth IRA at age 70, but one of the Roth

IRA's powerful features is that distributions are not required during the participant's lifetime. If the beneficiary is the spouse, distributions can be delayed even further to the death of the spouse. After that, distributions can be made over the expected lifetime of the beneficiary or beneficiaries. This tax deferral can be quite powerful, and makes the Roth IRA a good way to pass on wealth to the next generation.

Also, there is another strength to the Roth IRA. The tax-free source of income gives the participant more flexibility in how and when to liquidate other taxable assets in retirement. The tax-free funds in a Roth IRA can be used in retirement to

- minimize taxable withdrawals from traditional IRAs or qualified plans
- minimize taxable income to stay in a lower tax bracket
- provide for a source of income that will not increase the portion of Social Security benefits that are taxed
- fund life insurance premiums for estate planning purposes
- provide liquidity for estate taxes
- minimize liquidation of other taxable investments such as stocks and mutual funds—which receive a step-up if left intact to heirs

TABLE 18-5
Comparing Deductible IRA to Roth IRA Accumulations

Age	30%/30%*		17%/42%*		30%/42%*	
	Roth	Deductible	Roth	Deductible	Roth	Deductible
45	$1,400	$2,000	$1,660	$2,000	$1,400	$2,000
70	$9,589	$9,591**	$11,372	$7,947**	$9,589	$7,947**

*   The first number represents the combined federal and state income tax rate at the time of contribution and the second number represents the tax rate at the time of distribution.

** Assumes that the entire accumulation is distributed and taxed at age 70. Assumes growth at 8%.

Because of the many strengths of the Roth IRA, the following types of clients should consider the Roth IRA over the deductible IRA:

- individuals in the 15 percent federal income tax bracket
- individuals in the 28 percent federal income tax bracket who expect to be in a higher bracket at retirement

- individuals who have already accumulated significant assets for retirement on a tax-deferred basis and who may want to use the Roth IRA as a way to create a more balanced portfolio
- individuals who are more concerned about estate planning than retirement planning

IRA-to-Roth IRA Conversions

In the coming years, everyone will be intrigued by the idea of paying tax now to avoid taxes later. Before getting too excited about it, remember that the individuals who would be most interested—singles and couples earning more than $100,000—will not be eligible to do it. Others simply will not be willing to pay the taxes before they have to. However, in a significant number of cases, it appears that the Roth IRA conversion can really result in greater after-tax accumulations. It is a good idea to run computer simulations for real clients to see for yourself the effect of a conversion. Consider the following when considering the conversion decision:

- Conversions work for young persons because there will be a long accumulation period over which the Roth IRA is growing tax free.
- Individuals who have most of their retirement savings in IRAs and Roth IRAs should consider converting at least some of those amounts to Roth IRAs. As discussed above, a nontaxable source of income in retirement can be used for a number of retirement or estate planning purposes.
- If taxes are paid out of the IRA when it is converted to a Roth IRA, the 10 percent premature excise tax may apply. This detracts from the value of the conversion. If possible, other sources should be used for paying the taxes.

Even though it may appear at first glance that older persons should not convert, conversion can have significant estate-planning implications. Remember that if the taxpayer does not need to make withdrawals for living expenses, the law does not require any withdrawals until after the participant's death. If the spouse is the beneficiary, no withdrawals are required over his or her life either. This means that the tax-free accumulation period for even an older person can be quite long. In addition, after death, the Roth IRA can be distributed over the entire lifetime of the beneficiary. Even if the older participant were to die shortly after the conversion, the income taxes paid at the conversion reduce the value of the estate, offsetting the Roth IRA accumulation period.

THE IRA MARKET—POTENTIAL CLIENTS

As you have just seen, just about every taxpayer is a candidate for an IRA. In fact, because of their broad-based appeal and general attractiveness to the public, IRAs make a great door opener. Also, mass marketing of IRAs is possible—and this opens the way to an increased client base. Once the door is open, you can easily explain IRAs, which will lead naturally into a discussion of the overall retirement and financial plan.

For financial services professionals who work primarily with employers, employer-sponsored IRAs are possible. The usual IRA rules apply, and there are none of the qualified retirement plan hassles, such as reporting requirements and nondiscrimination rules. In fact, there is no requirement that employer-sponsored IRAs be available to all employees, so it is possible to provide them just for key employees and owner-employees. Contributions to an employer-sponsored IRA may be made as additional compensation or as a salary reduction and, in the latter case, payroll deduction is a good way to simplify administration.

If you decide to advise your employer-client to institute employer-sponsored IRAs, your client must consider the following factors:

- Amounts contributed are taxable to the employee; if an employee earns less than the compensation limits for his or her particular tax bracket, the employee may deduct the contribution.
- Social Security and unemployment taxes are applicable because the contribution represents extra compensation. If the employer believes that the employee will be entitled to an IRA deduction, however, no federal income tax withholding is required.

Whether you are involved with IRAs in the individual market or through the employee benefit market, it is important to be aware that selling IRAs has its drawbacks. First, IRA commissions are generally not generous. (They are typically lower than on most insurance products.) Second, because of the wide variety of investments and the fluctuating returns offered, clients tend to shift investment vehicles, which translates into administrative and financial headaches. However, many planners believe that IRAs represent an ideal supplemental sale despite these drawbacks and that involvement with the IRA products leads to financial success for themselves and their clients.

CHAPTER REVIEW

Answers to the review questions and the self-test questions start on page 673.

Key Term

self-directed IRAs

Review Questions

18-1.   a.   What is an individual retirement account (IRA)?
      b.   What is an individual retirement annuity, and what special rules apply to the annuity contract?

18-2.   Which of the following items is/are permissible IRA investments?
      a.   investment in life insurance
      b.   investment in antiques
      c.   investment in gold bullion
      d.   investment in real estate that is owned by the client

18-3.   What are some of the advantages of investing in an individual retirement annuity?

18-4.   Why are IRAs associated with SIMPLE plans referred to as SIMPLE IRAs?

18-5.   Explain the IRA and Roth IRA options for the following individuals in 2002:
      a.   Carlos, a single 35-year-old taxpayer, has an adjusted gross income (AGI) of $80,000 and is not an active participant in an employer-sponsored retirement plan in 2002.
      b.   Anthony, a single 45-year-old taxpayer, has an AGI of $120,000 and is an active participant in a qualified retirement plan.
      c.   Sam and Sally, each under age 50, are married and file a joint tax return. Sam has an AGI of $120,000 and is an active participant in an employer-sponsored retirement plan. Sally does not work outside of the home.
      d.   Della and George, aged 40, are married and file a joint tax return. Della earns $90,000 and George earns $75,000 (joint AGI is $165,000). They are both active participants in employer-sponsored retirement plans.

18-6.   Why may the nondeductible IRA be an inappropriate retirement investment vehicle in 2002?

18-7.   When is the Roth IRA potentially more advantageous than the deductible IRA contribution?

18-8.   Describe employer-sponsored IRAs.

Self-Test Questions

T   F   18-1.   Individual retirement annuities may not be transferable.

T   F   18-2.   IRAs are typically invested in life insurance.

T   F   18-3.   IRAs cannot be invested in any type of collectible.

T   F   18-4.   One reason for the popularity of individual retirement annuities is that the annuity quells the retiree's fear that he or she may run out of funds.

T   F   18-5.   Taxpayers should generally choose Roth IRA contributions over nondeductible IRA contributions.

T   F   18-6.   A traditional IRA contribution is generally a better choice than a Roth IRA contribution for the taxpayer who expects to be in a much lower tax bracket upon retirement.

T   F   18-7.   A taxpayer in the 15 percent tax bracket who expects to be in a higher bracket in retirement should consider the Roth IRA over the deductible IRA contribution.

T   F   18-8.   An individual who has all of his or her retirement savings in tax-deferred vehicles should consider a Roth IRA in order to develop a source of non-taxable income in retirement.

T   F   18-9.   Individuals who have estate planning problems with large pension accumulations should never consider converting some or all of the their IRA funds into a Roth IRA.

T   F   18-10.   Employer-sponsored IRAs must be made available to all employees on a nondiscriminatory basis.

Introduction to Individual Retirement Planning

Learning Objectives
An understanding of the material in this chapter should enable the student to

19-1. Identify the reasons that clients should be encouraged to plan for retirement.

19-2. Describe the roadblocks to retirement saving and explain some planning strategies that might be recommended to help clients overcome these roadblocks.

19-3. Explain the typical retirement objectives that clients have.

19-4. Describe several elements of a retirement planning practice.

Chapter Outline

All too often clients are only vaguely aware of problems associated with the retirement years. Other clients recognize that retirement problems exist but feel there is no way to cope with the magnitude of the financial requirements. Instead, they choose to concentrate on today and let tomorrow take care of itself. Many clients used to feel the same about life insurance until efforts by the insurance industry and its agents brought about the general acceptance that life insurance is a basic piece of a client's financial plan. This change has been fostered by agents educating their clients about the problems that exist when a major source of income is lost because of death and about how life insurance products can help. A similar effort by agents is now required to educate an aging population about the need to plan for retirement and to provide the financial planning tools that can be used to replace lost income in the retirement years. If the track record of the insurance industry is any indication, retirement planning will soon be included in every individual's financial plan.[1]

WHY PLAN FOR RETIREMENT?

Because a larger percentage of the population will live until retirement and will live longer during retirement than previous generations, it is more essential than ever that today's population plan for retirement. Retirement planners need to help their clients understand the following:

- the magnitude of the financial requirements facing them during retirement
- the impact of inflation on retirement
- the effect that financial well-being has on the quality of life
- the importance of planning to achieve financial self-sufficiency

In addition, clients who are complacent about saving for retirement should be made aware of the financial problems that force retirees to worry about the adequacy of their retirement income or that make them financially dependent on others. Have your clients consider the following:

- Retirees are sometimes forced to reduce or eliminate their consumption of some nonessential items so that they can afford the increasing costs of items necessary for the maintenance of life. These nonessential items (such as home maintenance), however, are themselves critical to a person's self-dignity and future financial welfare.

- Studies indicate that 75 percent of elderly families cannot afford luxury items because the routine costs of living absorb all of their income.
- According to one study, 65-year-olds without a written financial plan are twice as likely to find retirement a time of financial worry as their counterparts that have a plan.
- Even in the most generous employer-sponsored retirement plans the employer typically only replaces about one-half of a person's salary.
- The combination of an employer-sponsored plan and Social Security will not provide adequate funds for maintaining the preretirement standard of living during retirement.
- Clients should be sensitive to the long-term viability of Social Security as it exists today. They should consider the economic trouble the Medicare system is currently experiencing and the bailouts of the Social Security system in the early 1980s. If these problems can occur when only one out of eight Americans is retired, what will happen in the year 2027 when one out of five Americans will be retired?
- Many clients will have to deal with deteriorating health during retirement. Poor health not only creates the problem of increased medical bills, but also means increases in the purchase of services that clients were once able to do for themselves (for example, home maintenance).
- Rising inflation during retirement forces many retirees to either work part-time at low wages to replace lost purchasing power or liquidate the family home or other financial or personal assets to pay bills.
- If inflation goes up 4 percent per year, an item that costs $1 at age 65 will cost $2.19 at age 85.

BABY BOOMERS AND RETIREMENT—DEMOGRAPHICS WORTH THINKING ABOUT

baby-boom generation

Make no mistake that retirement planning is important for every generation—you are never too old or too young to plan for retirement. Special attention must be paid, however, to the needs of those born from 1946 to 1964, the so-called *baby-boom generation*. This generation represents roughly one-third of the population and, as it has progressed through the life cycles, it has greatly impacted everything from crowding in grammar schools to the housing market. The question remains: What will the implications of this demographic tidal wave have on retirement? The following should be considered:

- According to one survey, 86 percent of baby boomers feel this generation is not saving enough for retirement.
- Sixty-six percent of baby boomers say they should have started saving sooner.
- The baby-boom generation spends freely and has low personal savings rates.
- Sixty-eight percent of baby boomers admit to not having spent enough time planning for retirement.

Baby boomers who work for medium- and large-sized employers typically have a leg up toward retirement over their counterparts in small firms. Eighty-five percent of workers at employers with 100 or more employees have an employment-based plan available to them. Fifty percent of workers at employers with 25–99 employees have an employment-based plan available to them. However, only 20 percent of workers at employers with less than 25 employees have an employment-based plan available to them. The Employee Benefit Research Institute estimates that over 25 million employees working for small businesses are not covered by company pension plans.

Baby boomers may be helped to a more successful retirement by inheritances—over $10 trillion will be inherited between now and 2040. The numbers can be misleading, however, because one percent will inherit one-third, 9 percent will inherit one-third, and 90 percent will inherit one-third.

Baby boomers will also face a different retirement than their parents. For one thing, they are less likely to be offered retirement incentives, because there will possibly be a labor shortage and also because incentive packages are on the decline. For another thing, some surveys also show that baby boomers expect to work during retirement. Finally, current retirees are most likely to identify Social Security as their most important source of income but current workers are most likely to say that personal savings will be their most important source of income in retirement (see table 19-1).

TABLE 19-1 Median Amounts Accumulated By Generation	
Pre-retirees	$55,556
Older boomers	$53,125
Younger boomers	$34,091
Generation X	$11,034

ROADBLOCKS TO RETIREMENT SAVING

No matter what the generation, the question remains: Why don't more Americans plan for retirement? After all, the so-called golden years are part of the American dream. The answer lies in the many distractions that hinder retirement savings.

Perhaps the biggest roadblock to retirement planning is the tendency of many working people to use their full after-tax income to support their current standard of living. These people will not have any private savings to supplement Social Security and pension funds. Many of them also may have experienced adversities like unemployment that pushed them into debt. In other cases, a lifestyle that incurs debt can stem from a spendthrift attitude or from the desire to emulate or improve upon their parents' standard of living. Whatever the reason for their lack of retirement savings, clients must follow a budget that allows them to live within their means and that also provides for retirement savings. (*Planning Note:* Make your clients aware that a 90/10 spending ratio is generally desired. Under a 90/10 spending ratio, 90 percent of your clients' earnings is directed toward their current standard of living, and at least 10 percent is directed toward other long-term financial objectives, such as their children's education and their own retirement. For example, a family with a gross annual income of $60,000 should allocate no more than $54,000 [including taxes] of its total income to standard-of-living and lifestyle items, leaving at least $6,000 for long-term objectives. Furthermore, as income rises, the percentage spent on the current standard of living should decline, eventually approaching an 80/20 split.)

A second impediment to retirement saving is unexpected expenses, including uninsured medical bills; repairs to a home, auto, or major appliance; and periods of unemployment. (*Planning Note:* The client should set up an emergency fund to handle these inevitable problems. Approximately 3 to 6 months' income is usually set aside for this objective. If a client's salary is stable and other income such as dividends is part of the individual's income flow, then a 3 to 4 months' income level in the emergency fund can be sufficient. However, if the main source of income is commissions that fluctuate between pay periods, 6 months' income held for emergencies is more appropriate.)

Inadequate insurance coverage is a third impediment to retirement saving. Regardless of whether it is life, disability, health, home, or auto, many individuals continue to remain uninsured or underinsured. Because the client cannot always recover economically from such losses, one important element of retirement planning is protection against catastrophic financial loss that would make future saving impossible. (*Planning Note:* Agents should conduct a thorough review of their clients' insurance needs to make sure they are adequately covered. Two often overlooked areas are disability insurance and liability insurance for the professional. Make sure your client is adequately protected in both areas.)

A fourth roadblock to saving for retirement occurs in the case of a divorced client. Divorce often leaves one or both parties with little or no accumulation of pension benefits or other private sources of retirement income. They only have a short time to accumulate any retirement income and are not able to earn significant pension or Social Security benefits. If the marriage lasted 10 years or longer, divorced persons are eligible for Social Security based on their former spouse's earnings record. In addition, a spouse may be entitled to a portion of the former spouse's retirement benefits if the divorce decree includes a *qualified domestic relations order (QDRO)*. QDROs are judgments, decrees, or orders issued by state courts that allow a participant's plan assets to be used for marital property rights, child support, or alimony payments to a former spouse or dependent.

qualified domestic relations order (QDRO)

Another common retirement planning problem is the lack of a retirement plan at the place of employment. Some workers have never had the opportunity to participate in a qualified pension plan because their employer(s) did not provide such benefits.[2]

Workers who have frequently changed employers also face the problem of arriving at retirement with little or no pension. Statistics show that employees today are unlikely to remain with one employer for their working life and will typically hold seven full-time jobs during their career. Generally, these people will not accumulate vested pension benefits because they never stayed with an employer long enough to become vested. Even if they did become vested, they may have received a distribution of their accumulated pension fund upon leaving the job and probably spent this money rather than investing it or rolling it over for retirement. According to the most recent statistics available, 6 in 10 people who change jobs cashed out their retirement savings instead of rolling them over into another type of plan.[3] (*Planning Note:* Advise clients who change jobs to roll over vested benefits into an IRA or into their new qualified plan to preserve the tax-deferred growth on their retirement funds. Advise clients who have recently changed jobs that if they have not met the participation requirements of their new employer's plan, then annual tax-deductible contributions can be made to an IRA in those years, regardless of salary.)

Another problem that inhibits people from saving for retirement is a lack of financial literacy. Employees have never been properly schooled about investments and finance. For this reason, investment education has replaced health care as the top concern for employee benefit professionals and employees.[4] (*Planning Note:* There is a window of opportunity opening to do seminar selling by conducting educational workshops for employee groups.)

YOUR FINANCIAL SERVICES PRACTICE: UNDERSTANDING QDROs

There are two ways in which a settlement of pension rights can be made under a Qualified Domestic Relations Order (QDRO):

- an immediate cash settlement (which is often made from nonpension sources)
- a settlement under which payments to the nonparticipant spouse are deferred until payments are due to the participant spouse

In both cases, valuation is fundamental. Before the parties can agree on how to divide the pension, its value must be determined. If the plan is a defined-contribution plan, valuation is relatively easy—the participant has an individual account and the plan sponsor must provide its value to the participant at least annually. However, if participation in the plan has extended over a period longer than the marriage, this amount must be reduced by a "coverture fraction" that is based on the relation between the length of the marriage and the duration of the plan coverage. This can be a simple mathematical ratio, or it can reflect rates of contribution and interest over time.

If the plan is a defined-benefit plan, the parties will probably need an actuary's assistance in determining the present dollar value of pension benefits. For a participant in a defined-benefit plan, the benefit at any time before retirement is expressed as an amount of expected pension at retirement age that the participant has accrued up to that point. For example, if the participant is aged 45, the plan might express his accrued benefit as "$10,000 per month beginning at age 65." In order to determine current worth, at age 45, an actuarial calculation must be made. In this calculation, the interest rate and mortality assumptions are critical. The assumptions do not necessarily have to be the same as those used by the plan for funding purposes. There is no federal standard for actuarial assumptions in this area, although PBGC interest rates for valuing plans on termination are sometimes used as guidelines. The total amount determined must also be multiplied by a coverture fraction, as for the defined-contribution plan where the participant was not married to the current (imminently departing) spouse during the entire time of his or her plan coverage.

Many open and controversial issues exist in these determinations. For example, should the valuation take taxes into account? What about inflation? Or possible future increases in the participant's salary? These are issues of state law that may vary and may not have been considered or decided by the state's courts. The use of an expert actuary is advisable, particularly in disputed cases, so that the actuarial assumptions and other valuation assumptions can be supported in court proceedings if necessary.

A final impediment to acquiring adequate retirement savings is the tendency to direct retirement funds for other purposes. The down payment on a primary residence and/or vacation home and the education of children can consume any long-term savings that people have managed to accumulate. Because these objectives have a greater urgency for completion than retirement, they supplant retirement as a saving priority. Although these objectives are worthy, it is important to remind clients that savings must be carved out for retirement purposes in addition to other long-term objectives.

Whatever distractions face your clients, it is important to educate them about the need to plan and save for retirement. Clients must realize that saving is possible only for a limited time period during their life, but consumption occurs throughout their lives and can drastically increase at any time because of illness or inflation. This imbalance makes it essential for clients to save sufficient assets during the working years in order to ensure attainment of retirement goals. You cannot force clients to make lifestyle choices that will provide an adequate source of retirement funds. You can, however, make clients aware of the large sums needed for retirement and point out that a spendthrift lifestyle (one that uses the full aftertax income to support the current standard of living) hurts retirees in two ways. First, it minimizes their ability to accumulate savings that will produce an adequate income stream to complement their employer pension and Social Security. Second, retirees become accustomed to an unnaturally high standard of living. By living below their means before retirement, clients will establish a lifestyle that is more easily maintained in the retirement years. You can motivate clients to undertake a savings plan by first helping them to identify the retirement objectives for which they should be striving.

RETIREMENT OBJECTIVES

Clients' objectives will vary significantly depending on many factors, including health, age, marital status, number and ages of children, differences in the ages of the husband and wife, and personal preferences. Also, a client's objectives will vary depending upon his or her personal definition of retirement. For some, retirement is the last day they *have* to work, for others it is the last day they *want* to work, and for still others it is the last day they *can* work.[5] Table 19-2 contains a ranking of some typical retirement objectives. (The ranking identifies how a surveyed group of CLUs, ChFCs, and members of the Registry of Financial Planning Practitioners feel their clients would generally rate their retirement objectives.)

Maintaining a Preretirement Standard of Living

Maintaining their preretirement standard of living despite the loss of income from employment can mean a variety of things to clients. For some clients it may mean being able to stay where they are (in the same home or the same area) without a dramatic loss of purchasing power. Other clients

TABLE 19-2
Ranking of Retirement Objectives in Order of Priority
Retirement Objectives
1. Maintaining preretirement standard of living 2. Maintaining economic self-sufficiency 3. Minimizing taxes 4. Retiring early 5. Adapting to noneconomic aspects of retirement 6. Passing on wealth to others 7. Improving lifestyle in retirement 8. Caring for dependents

may be willing to move to a less costly area in order to maintain their purchasing power. Clients who are active in leisure activities such as golf or clients who hold memberships in such groups as the local Rotary club will want to continue (if not expand) these activities. It is important to remind clients that a continued subscription to the local orchestra's performances or continued winter trips to Florida can be as important a planning objective as providing food and shelter. (*Planning Note:* The client's priorities often differ from the planner's. Thus, planners should be careful not to impose their own values on the client.)

Maintaining Economic Self-Sufficiency

An objective that goes hand in hand with maintaining one's preretirement standard of living is the desire to remain self-sufficient throughout retirement. Many clients fear becoming dependent on children, charity, or the government. This may be a significant reason that clients actually cut back on spending in retirement. Financial independence takes on even more importance when one considers that many other constraints may be imposed on their independence such as their ability to work, drive, or be physically mobile.

Minimizing Taxes

An important objective common to all clients is their desire to be taxwise regarding their retirement funds. Paying the least amount of taxes on their retirement distribution(s) (chapter 26), investing for the best aftertax yield (chapter 24), and maximizing tax-shelter opportunities with their retirement capital (chapter 24) are special priorities that your clients will have. One reason clients strive for tax savings is a propensity to play the tax game by concentrating on tax consequences as opposed to economic consequences. While this motivation *may* serve your clients in the proper manner, their primary concern should be aftertax income, not paying less taxes, and a risky venture that promises tax deductions may not be as profitable as some taxed investments.

Retiring Early

A characteristic of modern times is that many people want to "get out of the rat race" as soon as possible. According to a study done by Charles D. Spencer & Associates, most workers working for employers with retirement plans choose to retire prior to age 65 (see table 19-3). This data shows that early retirement is a common client priority. The Spencer Survey, which polled 147 companies, showed that 75 percent of employees retire before age 65. Early retirement is popular for several reasons:

- health problems that the client is currently facing
- fear of future health problems (the "get out now while I can still enjoy it" philosophy)
- caregiving concerns due to the health problems of a loved one
- corporate downsizing
- retirement of a spouse
- death of a spouse

TABLE 19-3 Retirement Experience*		
Timing of Retirement	Number	Percent of Total
Retirement prior to age 65	14,001	75.04%
Retirement at age 65	2,004	9.55
Retirement after age 65	2,229	9.20
Disability retirement, all ages	488	6.20
Total	11,063	100.00
*Based on a survey by Charles D. Spencer & Associates		

If a client seeks an early retirement, it is even more important to start retirement planning at a young age and to accurately estimate the retirement need. These extra precautions are necessary because the lengthened retirement period is subject to compounded increases in inflation.

Furthermore, the shortened preretirement period is subject to increased drain on current cash in order to fund the extended retirement period and pre-age 65 costs for medical protection. In addition, pension benefits will be lower because of the loss of peak earning years from the benefit or contribution formula. Finally, the Social Security calculation will also be adversely affected.

Adapting to Noneconomic Aspects of Retirement

In addition to the relevant economic objectives your clients will have to meet, they will also have noneconomic objectives, such as

- using leisure time more effectively
- adapting to a nonworking environment
- coping with deteriorating health
- coping with caregiving responsibilities (a Norman Rockwell-type picture of American retirement in the next century might have the 73-year-old son taking the 95-year-old mother to the doctor)
- adapting to a fixed income
- relocating after retirement
- finding the best residence for the retirement years

These and other noneconomic factors also have important economic implications. For example, relocating after retirement can affect the overall pool of retirement assets because the sale of the home may provide surplus assets.

Passing on Wealth to Others

For some clients, the wherewithal for an adequate retirement income is not the problem. Instead, the problem is how to plan their estate without subjecting the "family money" to inheritance or gift taxes. These clients present the financial services professional with an entirely different set of planning problems. In essence, the need is not to secure enough money to finance retirement but rather to shelter as much as possible from taxes as money passes from generation to generation.

Improving Lifestyle in Retirement

Clients with the objective of improving their lifestyle in the retirement years are willing to make extra sacrifices prior to retirement in order to enjoy some luxuries, such as travel, during retirement. Another set of planning problems is created if the person's objective is to plan for a more costly lifestyle during retirement. These individuals will need extra resources in order to fulfill their dreams.

Caring for Dependents

Another retirement objective for some people is to have the ability to support a dependent. This typically occurs when a dependent needs frequent physical or medical care. Special and distinct planning considerations are required depending on whether the dependent is a child, sibling, or parent. In addition to the normal living expenses during the dependent's life expectancy, the planner must also consider whether there will be medical bills, additional living expenses, and any other financial drains on the client's retirement income.

Other Objectives

In addition to the general retirement objectives, your client may have one or more of the following specific retirement objectives:

- *providing for secure investments*—investing assets to minimize potential losses and make the client feel secure about his or her investments
- *coping with health care costs*—purchasing a Medicare supplement may be required to cover health care costs not covered under the Medicare program
- *continuing the family business*—special planning is needed for clients who would like to see their business successfully continue after their retirement
- *obtaining reasonable value for the sale of a closely held business*—maximizing the amount received upon the sale of a business if clients wish to discontinue operations after retirement
- *staying as healthy as possible*—ensuring adequate funding for health clubs and other leisure activities

THE RETIREMENT PLANNER

Holistic Retirement Planning

Retirement planning is a multidimensional field that requires the planner to be schooled in the nuances of many financial planning specialties as well as other areas. Unfortunately, many so-called planners approach retirement planning from only one point of view (for example, investments). The perspective offered by specializing, however, is inadequate for dealing with the diversified needs of the would-be retiree. A client is better served by a team of planners who have specialized backgrounds that are complementary or by a single planner who is experienced in a variety of important retirement topics.

Whether the retirement team or the multitalented individual is the vehicle, the holistic approach to retirement planning is the only means by which a client's needs can be fully and adequately met. Under the *holistic* approach to *retirement planning,* the planner is required to communicate with clients concerning the following topics:

holistic retirement planning

- employer-provided retirement plans
- Social Security
- personal savings and investments
- IRAs and Roth IRAs
- income tax issues
- distribution issues
- insurance coverage
- asset allocation and risk
- long-term care options
- retirement communities
- relocation possibilities
- wellness
- nutrition
- lifestyle choices

Your Retirement Planning Practice

Retirement planning requires planners to undertake several responsibilities that may not have been a part of their traditional financial practice. These aspects of a retirement planning practice include the following:

- *incorporating retirement planning as a segment of comprehensive financial planning.* This means using financial planning techniques such as fact finding, budgeting, income-flow regulating, and rendering investment advice.
- *dealing with other professionals who advise the client.* These professionals include the client's lawyer, accountant, banker, investment adviser, and—if the planner is not the client's sole insurance agent—other insurance agents. By communicating with

this group, planners gain many advantages, including a better understanding of the client's needs, a team approach for motivating the client to save for retirement, and referral sources for future business.

- *dealing with relatively young clients.* One common mistake is to start retirement planning only after a client has satisfied his or her other long-term responsibilities such as buying a home or educating a child. Retirement planning is best, however, if clients start saving for retirement at a relatively young age. (*Planning Note:* When approaching a younger client about retirement, planners often refer to retirement planning as "financial independence planning.")

- *monitoring and updating the client's plan.* The client's plan needs continued service because of changes in family circumstances (such as job changes, births, deaths, divorces, and the acquisition of inheritances) and because of changes in the tax and economic environment.

- *conducting seminars for employers.* Many planners are asking employers for time to speak to employees during working hours. The employer sees this as an opportunity to provide a low-cost employee benefit, and the employees appreciate a retirement planning seminar offered by the employer. Planners who are also designing the employer's qualified or nonqualified plan can point out to the employer that work-sponsored retirement planning seminars help the plan accomplish its main objective—a successful retirement for employees.

In addition to undertaking these obligations, retirement planners must also familiarize themselves with the various resources available in the retirement planning field. Organizations such as the American Society of Financial Service Professionals, the Financial Planning Association, the National Council on Aging, and the American Society on Aging offer a forum that provides newsletters, conferences, and a chance for interaction with other planners. In addition, planners should make their clients aware of the American Association of Retired Persons (AARP), an organization that provides information on services for the elderly and is a valuable resource for retirement information. Planners may also want to check retirement planning websites. There are hundreds of them! Here are a few samples:

- T. Rowe Price "Retirement"
  http://www.troweprice.com
  (covers new tax laws, Social Security and Medicare issues, medigap insurance; has a retirement calculator; offers free kits for lump-sum distributions, annuity distributions and minimum distributions)

- New England Financial "Retirement Planning Center"
  http://www.tne.com/needs/retirement/retirement.cfm
  (contains a special kids' section for dealing with mentally, physically or emotionally challenged children after the client passes on)
- New York Life Education Center "Planning for Retirement"
  http://www.newyorklife.com
  (talks about the importance of retirement planning; contains a retirement planning calculator)
- Columbia Funds
  http://www.columbiafunds.com
  (contains a traditional IRA to Roth IRA calculator)
- Putnam Investments "Retirement Planning"
  http://www.putnaminv.com/frames/cond.htm
  (covers 401(k) plans in depth; contains a 401(k) calculator)
- The Vanguard Group "Retirement Planning"
  http://www.vanguard.com
  (contains an excellent glossary; contains a calculator for retirement needs)
- Quicken Retirement
  http://www.quicken.com/retirement/planner/
  (contains retirement planning calculations and articles on retirement planning)

CHAPTER REVIEW

Answers to the review questions and the self-test questions start on page 673.

Key Terms

baby-boom generation   holistic retirement planning
qualified domestic relations order
    (QDRO)

Review Questions

19-1. Kathy Williams is an insurance agent who would like to conduct individual retirement planning for her clients.
   a. What are four of Kathy's primary goals as a retirement planner?
   b. What factors should Kathy bring to her clients' attention in order to motivate them to save for retirement?

19-2. Discuss the retirement planning implications for baby boomers.

19-3. a. List seven factors that hinder a client's ability to save for retirement.
     b. Discuss some strategies that a retirement planner might recommend to the client in order to overcome the roadblocks to retirement saving listed in your answer to part (a).

19-4. What factors tend to influence a client's retirement objectives?

19-5. Explain the typical retirement objectives that a client may have.

19-6. a. List the variety of topics that are covered in a holistic retirement planning practice.
     b. What are five elements of a retirement planning practice?

19-7. What resources are available to aid a retirement planner?

Self-Test Questions

T   F   19-1. Poor health during retirement can cause an economic hardship because it forces retirees to purchase services they were once able to perform for themselves.

T   F   19-2. In order to save properly for retirement and other long-term objectives, clients should establish a 50/50 spending ratio in which half of their money is used for current consumption and the other half is saved.

T   F   19-3. An emergency fund should contain 3 months' income if a client's major source of income is commissions.

T   F   19-4. Divorced persons are eligible for Social Security based on their former spouse's earnings record if the marriage lasted 10 years or longer.

T   F   19-5. When a pension plan is split under a qualified domestic relations order (QDRO), the pension assets are divided according to a court order.

T   F   19-6. Job changes often hurt a person's chance to save for retirement because leakage from qualified plans occurs at that time.

T   F   19-7. Most clients are considered to have a thorough understanding of financial products and services.

T   F   19-8. In order to maximize wealth, clients should always seek to minimize taxes.

T   F   19-9. The current retirement trend is for employees to take early retirement.

T   F   19-10. An important retirement goal is adapting to a nonworking environment.

T   F   19-11. There is a trend among financial services professionals to include or expand retirement planning as part of their financial services practice.

T   F   19-12. Retirement planning should be started only after a client has satisfied his or her other long-term responsibilities, such as buying a house or educating a child.

Notes

1. According to one study, nearly 60 percent of American adults have not calculated how much they need for retirement. Strides are being made, however, because the number of those who have done a "needs analysis" has increased in recent years.
2. Only 57 percent of American workers have a retirement plan where they work. Lack of coverage is the worst in companies with under 100 employees. These smaller firms, therefore, are the most significant market of the next century for pension and retirement planners.
3. According to a January 1998 article "Take the Money and Run," by Shannon Dortch in American Demographics.
4. According to a 1997 survey conducted by the International Society of Certified Employee Benefit Specialists and the Employee Benefits Group of Deloitte and Touche LLP.
5. From "Planning Ahead for a Secure Retirement," an employee seminar software package by David Littell and Kenn Tacchino.

20

Planning for the Client's Needs

Learning Objectives

An understanding of the material in this chapter should enable the student to

---

20-1. Discuss retirement planning for clients with respect to the client's

    a. attitudes about retirement
    b. health
    c. life expectancy
    d. attitudes toward saving
    e. investment savvy
    f. marriage stability

20-2. Explain the retirement strategies that can be used when planning for each of the following:

    a. the business owner
    b. the baby boomer client
    c. the client whose plan is terminated
    d. the client's estate
    e. the homeowner
    f. the client who is considering relocation
    g. the client who is considering postretirement employment

---

Chapter Outline

There are many factors that affect a client's ability to achieve his or her retirement goals. Despite careful planning, events occur that are beyond the client's control (for example, a merger or plant closing that forces the client into early retirement). Furthermore, as people mature their goals and situations also change. In addition, the fact that each client is unique and requires planning that accommodates his or her individual needs provides a challenge that will test the best of planners. This chapter explores this challenge and provides strategies that deal with the many obstacles to effective retirement planning.

THE NATURE OF CLIENTS AND THE ROLE OF THE PLANNER

It is often said by financial services professionals that the only thing clients have in common is that they are different. As a planner, you must become familiar with each client's attitude and conduct retirement planning consistent with the unique situations that make up the client's profile. Understanding these factors starts with an overview of the following:

- attitudes toward retirement
- health issues
- perception of life expectancy
- attitudes toward saving for retirement
- client investment savvy
- stability of the marriage

(*Planning Note:* For retirement-planning purposes the "client" constitutes *both* the husband and the wife. Many planners mistakenly meet with only one spouse and later find out that the retirement plan must be revamped to accommodate the other spouse's input. For this reason, when dealing with married individuals, planners should make every effort to understand the feelings of both the husband and the wife and the influence each exerts over important planning decisions.)

Attitudes toward Retirement

Planners should take into account their clients' attitudes toward retirement when developing a retirement plan. In general, clients who have many activities that they have been unable to pursue because of the demands of the workplace usually look forward to retiring as soon as it is economically feasible. Retirement is not a panacea for all workers, however. Persons who have no outside interests or hobbies to pursue after they leave the workforce often find retirement boring and unfulfilling. For these individuals, retirement takes the regimen out of life by eliminating the scheduled workday.

Clients may defer retirement as long as desired because recent amendments to the Age Discrimination in Employment Act (ADEA) prohibit involuntary retirement at any age (subject to a few exceptions, such as the exception for certain highly paid executives). On the other hand, there has been a recent trend among employers to offer employees incentives to take early retirement. These so-called golden handshakes may include an increase in the age and/or service factor in the client's defined-benefit plan, an offer of a lump sum cash bonus, or the payment of health insurance benefits for a stipulated period of time.

From a financial standpoint, the longer retirement is deferred, the better it is for the client. Continued employment generally means an opportunity to continue the accumulation of assets for retirement and the continuation of full medical benefits. In addition, some less obvious benefits of continued employment exist. These benefits include

- inflation protection, assuming your client's salary keeps pace with inflation
- continuation of employment-related activities, such as memberships in athletic clubs and other organizations
- travel on behalf of the employer, which makes it less costly to travel with the spouse because the client need only pay the spouse's costs
- continued interaction with colleagues in the workplace
- a bolstered sense of self-esteem for clients who base their sense of self-worth on employment production

Health Issues

In addition to your client's attitude toward retirement, you must also account for your client's health when planning for retirement. Persons in extremely poor health may not be able to continue employment after early retirement regardless of their desire to do so. In contrast, persons in good health may decide to remain in the workforce until normal retirement age or to defer retirement beyond normal retirement age. Be wary, however, because health issues are not restricted to the client alone but may also encompass family members. For example, a spouse in extremely poor health may need extra care and attention that could be provided by the employed spouse. This can serve as an impetus to retire early. In addition, a permanently disabled child who requires expensive care may make the worker feel that employment must be continued as long as possible regardless of his or her own health. Finally, it is important to note that perceived health issues may also affect retirement. Clients may retire early based on the fear of poor health in later retirement years.

When developing a client's retirement plan, it may be impossible to say with certainty whether a given health condition will prompt the client to retire early or to remain longer in the workforce. It is important, however, to recognize that the client's retirement plan may have to be adapted to changes in the health of the client or of his or her family.

Perception of Life Expectancy

As we shall see later, one of the most important assumptions a planner will make when liquidating retirement assets is the life expectancy of the client. Ideally, clients would accumulate enough assets so they could live on interest alone and never have to liquidate the principal. However, for many this is not possible and they must liquidate financial resources over the retirement period. All things being equal, changing the liquidation period in an accumulation model from 20 to 25 years meant an increase of 19 percent in the funds the client needed to save. Therefore, the planner must be familiar with the client's perception of his or her life expectancy and, if married, his or her spouse's life expectancy. This perception is often generated by the ages at which parents and grandparents have died. If family life expectancy reaches into the 80s and beyond, the client is often concerned about the adequacy of accumulated funds for the enjoyment of a relatively long retirement. Conversely, in families where most relatives die before the end of their 60s, working family members frequently seek early retirement in order to enjoy some of their accumulated retirement benefits. Persons whose ancestors have widely varied life expectancies may not have any strong personal perception about their own life expectancy. In any case, the planner should also keep in mind the projected life expectancies used by insurance companies for annuity purposes (appendix 3). These life expectancies provide guidelines for choosing life-expectancy assumptions. Note that many planners typically add 5 to 10 years to a life expectancy because the effect of using a projected life expectancy and, consequently, underestimating the actual life span can be disastrous.

Attitudes toward Saving for Retirement

Most retirement planning comes down to a question of now or later. Is the individual willing to allocate funds toward retirement now and reduce the current standard of living so an adequate standard of living will be possible during retirement? Conversely, is there an unwillingness to reduce the current living standard and allocate funds toward retirement that will result in a forced reduction in the standard of living at the onset of retirement? Most clients easily consume their disposable income during years of employment. Human wants seem to be insatiable as spending up to and beyond an individual's means is typical. Furthermore, people would like to increase whatever standard-of-living level they currently enjoy. However, by cutting back on the standard of living (or forsaking increases) during the employment years, individuals can accumulate assets and sources of income that will help fund retirement needs. Compound interest and the ability to secure higher yields on long-term investments allow clients to accumulate sizable funds over long periods of time with relatively small periodic contributions.

Example: Jane Jones (aged 30, 28 percent tax bracket) can accumulate $400,000 by the time she reaches age 65 by investing $251 a month between the ages of 30 and 65 (assuming a 9 percent taxable yield). If, however, Jane waited until age 55, she would be required to invest $2,378 a month (at 9 percent taxable yield) to acquire the same $400,000.

Investment Savvy of the Client

Survey after survey of American households conclude that Americans are remarkably ill-informed about the nuts and bolts of personal finance. In one survey, only 50 percent of those surveyed understood bank certificates of deposit or IRAs. If these are accurate percentages for such relatively simple products, consider for a moment what the percentages might be for more complex investments such as common stocks, options, real estate syndications, or futures.

It is essential for the planner to ascertain the degree of the client's investment expertise for two reasons. First, to recommend investment vehicles that go beyond the understanding of the client would be unproductive. If the client lacks understanding, the planner should explain the investment characteristics of the vehicles being suggested. Second, for

---

YOUR FINANCIAL SERVICES PRACTICE:
CASH VALUE LIFE INSURANCE AND ANNUITIES

Two products that can be used to accomplish the goal of periodic saving over a long accumulation period are cash value life insurance and deferred annuities.

Cash value life insurance holds the following retirement planning advantages:

- Forced savings occur in a painless way. If the premiums are paid in a direct-deposit manner, the client never has a chance to spend the money.
- Cash-value buildup is tax deferred until withdrawn at retirement.
- Interest rates used with some products are market sensitive and yield earnings that may outdistance inflation.
- Death benefits are offered that can be used for a surviving spouse's retirement.

If there is no need for additional life insurance protection, deferred-annuity contracts are well suited for accumulation and provide many of the advantages offered by cash value life insurance, including forced savings, tax deferral, and market-sensitive yields, without the expenses associated with the life insurance element. Flexible premium annuities are also available for those who are unable to make level premium payments.

---

every investment alternative that is suggested, investment risks must be thoroughly explained to prevent unpleasant surprises for the client and potential legal liability for the planner. In addition to educating clients about the risk characteristics of various investment media, the planner must assess the propensity of both the client and spouse to accept risk. In general, many Americans want to avoid undue risk when it affects their financial affairs. Consequently, most clients will tend to opt for investment media that produce relatively low returns. A second consequence of your client's risk propensity is that any recommended investments must be consistent with the client's risk profile; otherwise, the recommendation will either not be accepted or, if acquired, will not be retained.

Stability of the Marriage

When assembling a retirement plan, it is essential that you become aware of the status of the client's marriage. If a divorce or separation is a possibility, separate retirement planning for each spouse (although funded out of the family income) may be prudent. Even if the marriage seems sound, the high divorce rate and the increasing frequency of both spouses being employed dictate that the planner raise the issue of separate planning with both parties. Regardless of the status of the marriage, however, the client must make the decision and the planner should not force a client into an awkward situation.

Not only are the consequences of divorce important for the planner to consider, but it is also important to consider the consequences of remarriage on the retirement plan. This is particularly important when there are children from the prior marriage(s). Until the children are self-supporting, child support and education payments may constrain the noncustodial parent's ability to adequately plan for retirement. In addition, a client might want to provide for offspring from several marriages after his or her death. When this is the case, target amounts for retirement income purposes are established that do not include liquidation of principal during retirement.

STRATEGIES FOR THE CLIENT'S SITUATION

One of the most challenging aspects to retirement planning is dealing with the many issues confronting clients. These issues include a variety of personal decisions that are made by your client (such as the desire to relocate after retirement) or that are a result of the client's specific circumstances (such as the ownership of a business). In either case, any retirement plan must effectively accommodate the client's personal decisions or account for the client's special circumstances.

Planning for a Business Owner

Retirement planning for clients who have an ownership interest in a business is strongly influenced by the nature of the business, the decision-making power of the client, and the long-term stability of the business. These factors determine whether the client has the influence to maximize contributions or benefits under the qualified plan, whether (or to what extent) saving outside the business is necessary, and whether the client will be able to use his or her ownership-interest as a retirement asset. For example, if the client has the ability to maximize benefits under a business's qualified plan, then little, if any, additional retirement saving will be necessary. Furthermore, funds saved in a qualified plan are not subject to the reach of the business's general creditors in case of bankruptcy. On the other hand, a business owner may be forced to forgo making contributions to a qualified plan or to tap personal retirement funds to keep the business from failing, and the business may go bankrupt in spite of these efforts.

When planning for the business owner, the planner's primary obligation is to set up a qualified plan for the business and to monitor the plan to make sure it meets the retirement planning needs of the business owner. Provided saving for retirement is economically feasible, the tax advantages available under a qualified plan make this plan the most effective method of saving for retirement. In the event that the business owner has maximized contributions or benefits under a qualified plan or it is prohibitively expensive to maximize benefits because of the nondiscrimination requirements for qualified plans, an alternate plan can be set up to save funds for the owners on a nonqualified basis, or the client can use personal income from the business for retirement savings.

In addition to becoming involved with the client's qualified plan, nonqualified plan, and individual retirement savings from company compensation, the planner must also

- *monitor the performance of the business*—retirement planning must account for the fact that a failing business will put constraints on savings and a successful business will require special tax planning
- *account for the business owner's ability to receive payment for business interests sold at retirement*—this can involve setting up a buy-sell agreement that includes methods for valuing the business whenever needed
- *plan for the continued employment of the former business owner as a consultant to the business*—especially if the business remains in the family

Planning for Baby Boomers

Baby boomers are defined as the demographic cohort born during the years 1946 to 1964. The first baby boomer turned 53 on January 1, 1999. Since the average age of retirement in this country is 62, they are less than 10 years from retirement! What makes this significant is that baby boomers represent one-third of the country's population. A national debate rages over baby boomers' preparedness for retirement, and there are a variety of surveys and studies that indicate problems. The most damning of these is a Merrill Lynch study that concludes baby boomers need to triple their current savings rates to maintain their standard of living during retirement. Conversely, the Employee Benefit Research Institute predicts that baby boomers are on the track to exceeding their parents when it comes to retirement. Conflicting statistical studies and news reports make it difficult to understand the boomers' prospects for a successful retirement. Here is what we do know:

- *Baby boomers must plug the leak.* Nearly one-half of all workers with 401(k) plans report having money withdrawn before retirement.

Planners must persuade their clients to hold onto their funds and stop raiding their accounts.

- *Baby boomers need financial counseling.* According to Scudder Kemper Investments, 25 percent of those 55 and older admit they do not know the form in which they will receive the money from their retirement savings plans. Planners need to educate their boomer clients concerning the myriad issues facing them.

- *Women need extra planning when it comes to retirement.* Statistically, boomer women have lower earnings and experience higher turnover than boomer men. What is worse, women tend to be employed in industries with low or no pension coverage. Combine this with the facts that women statistically outlive their spouses and are more likely to be caregivers, and you have a recipe for disaster. Planners must pursue special strategies for their female boomer clients.

- *Clients in medium and large plans typically have a leg up toward retirement over their counterparts in small firms.* According to the Bureau of Labor Statistics, 80 percent of full-time employees in medium and large private establishments participated in one or more retirement plans. However, only 26 percent of the 130,000 companies with fewer than 100 employees have a 401(k) plan. Planners need to use SEPs, SIMPLEs and other plans to bolster the numbers.

- *Diversification is a problem for some boomers.* According to some studies, Americans have as much as one-third of the 401(k) and other retirement plan savings invested in their own employer's stock. Planners need to account for this and help participants have a balanced portfolio.

Planning for the Client Whose Plan Is Terminated

When your client is not the business owner, he or she may still be a participant in a company pension plan. Your client may be counting on this plan to provide a significant portion of his or her retirement benefit and will be quite upset if the plan is terminated. You should be aware of the protection that the law provides your client in such a case. The law provides that if a plan is terminated (or partially terminated), participants under the plan are endowed with certain rights. One of the most important rights is that the participant becomes 100 percent vested in the account balance (defined-contribution plans) or accrued benefit (defined-benefit plans). One hundred percent vesting occurs whether the participant was zero percent vested or 80 percent vested on the day before the termination. A second right that your clients have is to be informed by the employer about the termination. Employer communications include

- a notice of the termination
- a notice that the IRS's approval of the termination is being sought
- modifications of the summary plan description, describing coincident changes to the terms of the plan
- the issuance of election forms that explain distribution options, describe the tax consequences of each option, and request participant elections

For participants in a defined-benefit plan, the consequences of plan termination trigger Pension Benefit Guaranty Corporation (PBGC) protection. If the employer is unable to make benefit payments, the PBGC will guarantee the payment of certain benefits known as basic benefits (special benefits and benefits that become vested due to the plan termination are generally not covered). The PBGC insurance only covers up to a maximum benefit level. The maximum insured benefit equals the lesser of

- approximately $3,200 (as indexed for inflation) a month, adjusted upward each year to reflect changes in the Social Security wage base, or
- 100 percent of average monthly wages during the participant's 5 highest-paid consecutive years

Because not all benefits are guaranteed by the PBGC, participants may not get all of their benefits. Also, some defined-benefit plans are not covered under the PBGC insurance program, and these plans may terminate with insufficient assets to pay benefits. In either case, the insufficient assets are distributed to participants in a required priority. From high to low priority, the order is

- employee voluntary contributions
- employee mandatory contributions
- annuity payments begun at least 6 years before the plan termination
- all other guaranteed benefits
- all other vested benefits
- all other benefits under the plan

If the plan owns life insurance policies, it may, and generally will, allow participants the right to purchase the policies. If the participant elects to receive the policy, he or she will be taxed on the cash value of the policy less any basis (PS 58 costs) and will assume premium payments thereafter. To minimize taxation, the trustee can take out the full loan value of the policy and have the stripped policy distributed out of the plan. If the trustee takes out the loan, the loan proceeds will then be distributed to the participant as part of the cash portion of his or her distribution.

Coordinating Retirement Planning with Estate Planning

For some clients, retirement planning plays a secondary role to estate planning. In many respects, the goals of retirement and estate planning seem incongruous. Retirement planning involves the accumulation of funds primarily for consumption during the client's (and/or spouse's) retirement. The primary goal of retirement planning is to maintain the preretirement lifestyle. This generally requires the expenditure of a significant percentage of the client's accumulated wealth, particularly if the client lives well past the chosen retirement age.

The primary goal of estate planning, on the other hand, is to accumulate assets during the client's lifetime for the appropriate distribution to selected heirs at a client's death. Generally speaking, clients wish to pass as much wealth to their heirs as circumstances permit. Methods employed to reach this goal include the conservation of wealth during retirement and minimization of the federal and state tax costs of transferring wealth.

The first of these methods requires little explanation. The less wealth consumed by a client during retirement, the greater the distributable estate will be at his or her death. The ability to conserve wealth during retirement is a client-specific question. That is, the amount of wealth consumed necessarily depends upon the client's target retirement lifestyle, continued health, and actual lifespan.

The minimization of estate taxes depends on the answer to the "who," "what," and "how" questions. The "who" question determines the level of transfer tax based on the target of the client's distribution. The net amount of assets passing to heirs depends upon their relationship to your client. Assets passed to the surviving spouse will be free of transfer taxes under typical circumstances due to a federally permitted 100 percent marital deduction. A generation-skipping transfer tax, however, may cause a double federal tax burden for gifts or bequests to grandchildren. Furthermore, state transfer taxes are often higher if assets are distributed outside of the client's lineal heirs.

The "what" question refers to the difference in taxes resulting from various types of transferred wealth. Under some circumstances, property is transferred to the surviving spouse free of federal estate tax. In other circumstances, however, transfers to a spouse will not qualify for the estate tax marital deduction. For this reason, a large part of the estate-retirement planning dichotomy is the determination by the client of what assets to consume during retirement and what to leave to his or her heirs. (*Planning Note:* Because there are estate tax implications concerning consumption of certain assets during retirement, planners should consult with their clients' estate planner to determine what assets should be used during retirement and what assets should be left intact.)

Finally, the "how" decision determines the manner in which property passes to the heirs. Some transfer mechanisms create greater tax liability than others. For example, direct probate transfers cause full imposition of estate and/or inheritance tax (ignoring marital deduction and unified credit). On the other hand, properly designed irrevocable life-insurance-trust transfers will result in substantial wealth passing to the beneficiaries at zero tax costs. Of course, the client may have to reduce current consumption and lose some degree of control to gain these transfer planning advantages.

Planning for a Homeowner

Retirement planning for a homeowner requires special consideration regardless of whether the homeowner intends to continue ownership after retirement or relocate to a new residence.

Continuing to Live in the Preretirement Residence

If your client decides to stay in the preretirement residence, you must account for the stream of mortgage payments, if any, and the cost of home maintenance and repair when determining the postretirement standard of living. From an emotional standpoint, continued ownership may be desirable considering that the very act of retirement is sufficiently stressful without experiencing other important lifestyle changes at the same time. From an economic standpoint, however, it may be desirable for the client to take some equity out of the home to be used for retirement purposes. Even a mortgage-free house can be costing your client income, because the equity that can be pulled from a home can be annuitized or used as capital to produce an income stream for retirement.

reverse annuity mortgage (RAM)

If your client would like to take some equity out of his or her house but is reluctant to leave the home, alternatives are available that can achieve the desired results without bringing the negative consequences. One option is to engage in a transaction known as a *reverse annuity mortgage* (RAM). Under one type of reverse annuity mortgage, the client sells a remainder interest in the home but retains the right to occupy the house until death. The purchaser of the remainder interest acquires the right to take possession of the property after the homeowner's death (or the death of the homeowner and the spouse). The consideration for acquiring the remainder interest in the house is that the purchaser agrees to make periodic payments to the seller during the seller's life.

Under another type of reverse annuity mortgage, the annuity payments plus interest are held as a series of loans against the value of the home. In this case, the amount paid out in an income stream plus interest will be recovered by the lender from eventual sale proceeds after the death of the retiree or by other payment.

The reverse annuity mortgage is a relatively new concept, and only a few financial institutions are currently active in this market. Therefore, this option may not be available in all parts of the country or to all those homeowners in areas where the service is available unless the federal, HECM (Home Equity Conversion Mortgage) is used. Beware, however, of these programs. Many scholars have warned that the underwriting restrictions are so tight they may prove to be a bad deal for the client. Another potential impediment to the use of a reverse annuity mortgage is that the homeowner may not have enough home-equity to make a reverse annuity mortgage feasible. This is especially true for clients who have just recently taken out a second mortgage on their home. A third problem with a reverse annuity mortgage is that the financial institution making the purchase has a vested interest in preserving the value of the property. This typically means that the client must go through the unpleasant tasks of (1) acquiring permission to make renovations, (2) maintaining the property according to contractual specifications, and (3) allowing periodic inspections of the property by the purchaser. (*Planning Note:* Reverse annuity mortgages have not yet become popular because of the feeling clients have about giving up their home. Furthermore the feelings of clients' children may preclude this course of action. Make sure the family has settled the matter before proceeding with the transaction.)

A second option available to the client who wants to remain in his or her home but needs to capitalize on its value is to rent space to occupants. A tenant may prove to be not only a valuable financial resource but also a companion for the retiree. Conversely, minor alterations of the property could be made so that the retiree and the tenant have full privacy. (*Planning Note:* Have your clients check with their local zoning boards before renting out space. In some communities, taking in tenants may not be permitted, or the town may impose restrictions on the property. In addition, have the client check his or her homeowner's policy to see if additional coverage is necessary.)

sale-leaseback agreement

Another means of unlocking the equity tied up in your client's home while allowing the client to remain in the residence is a *sale-leaseback agreement.* Under a sale-leaseback, your client sells the house to an investor and rents the property from the investor for the rest of his or her life (or if married, both lives). The sale-leaseback agreement can specify future rents or can provide for an agreement about how changes in the rental rate will be determined (for example, a periodic market value appraisal by a neutral third party).

The most desirable type of a sale-leaseback involves younger family members buying the home for investment purposes. The family relationship between the buyer and seller often makes the arrangement run more smoothly, but is sure to produce an IRS audit. Make sure that the transaction was conducted in an arm's-length businesslike manner. Regardless of who the buyer is, however, the new owner will be able to deduct mortgage interest, depreciation, and other expenses, and must include the rents as income.

Relocation to a Retirement Residence

If your client decides to sell his or her home and relocate to a smaller, less expensive residence, the money made available from the transactions should be counted as a retirement asset. For example, if your client can sell the house for $200,000 after taxes and relocate to a new residence costing $100,000, the extra $100,000 can be used to produce an extra $10,000 a year in income (assuming a 10 percent interest rate). As discussed, this can be very desirable from a financial perspective because retirees can capitalize on what, for many, is their single most important financial asset—their home. In addition, this can be very desirable from a tax standpoint because the IRS allows an exclusion of up to $500,000 ($250,000 for a single taxpayer or married taxpayer filing separately) on the taxation of gain from the sale of a home for a person who has lived in their home for two or more years.

In addition to advising a client who is relocating about the exclusion of gain from the sale of a home, you must also give advice on several alternative decisions. One such decision is about the relocation itself. Typical relocation patterns today include moves to less expensive housing in the same town as well as moves to the preferable climates of southeastern or southwestern United States.

Many planners advise caution when relocating to an unfamiliar geographic area. It might be advantageous for retirees to retain ownership of their previous home by renting it out while they temporarily rent in the new geographic area. By retaining their family home retirees have a house to return to if the relocation proves to be unsatisfactory. Problems with relocations occur because retirees miss the close proximity to friends and family or because retirees move to a location where they frequently vacationed prior to retirement and find postretirement year-round living undesirable.

Whether relocating across town or across country, the client will have to decide on the type of housing facility that best suits his or her needs. In general, smaller one floor units in a home or an apartment are preferred. A smaller unit minimizes the cleaning drudgery, maintenance burdens, and heating and cooling expenses.

life-care retirement communities

Some retirees choose not to move into either single family homes or apartments, but instead move into *life-care retirement communities.* Life-care retirement communities, sometimes called continuing-care retirement communities, are villages that provide housing and services to retired parties in exchange for up-front and/or monthly fees. These communities often provide some level of housekeeping and meal preparation in addition to facilities for activities, including crafts, tennis, golf, and swimming. Some of these retirement communities can be quite expensive, however, and frequently require a substantial nonrefundable fee for admission as well as an ongoing monthly fee. Paying a nonrefundable fee makes the decision almost irreversible for your client. For this reason, you should recommend that the client spend time conversing with current residents of the community and try to experience living in the community before making a financial commitment. Communities that promise lifetime care, especially those without ongoing fees, should be scrutinized by the planner. The communities' funding calculations should be based on sophisticated actuarial evaluations. An absence of proper management and financing could lead to inadequate funding and subsequent financial failure of the community. Some retirement communities fail financially from inadequate pricing and inadequate subscriptions.

Planning for Postretirement Employment

Some retirees continue working beyond retirement on a part-time basis as either a consultant to their former employer or in another capacity. Retirees who work as consultants to their former employer benefit by continuing to interact with coworkers and friends and maintaining the sense of purpose and self-worth they received from employment. Employers who hire former employees as consultants gain the advantage of being able to capitalize on the former employees' expertise, skills, and business connections.

A potential problem with providing consulting services to a former employer (or working after retirement in any capacity) is that retirees can lose Social Security benefits if earnings exceed specified limits. Under the so-called *wage test* for the 62- to 65-year-old retiree, Social Security benefits are reduced $1 for every $2 in earnings in excess of prescribed limits. For clients under age 65, the earnings limit is $10,680 (this 2001 figure is increased annually to reflect inflation). So, if your 63-year-old client earns $12,680, his or her Social Security benefits will be reduced $1,000 annually. (To calculate the reduction, subtract the earnings limit [$10,680] from the actual amount earned [$12,680] and divide by 2.) For clients aged 65 and older, there is no reduction to Social Security regardless of the amount earned.

CHAPTER REVIEW

Answers to review questions and the self-test questions start on page 673.

Key Terms

reverse annuity mortgage   life-care retirement communities
sale-leaseback agreement

Review Questions

20-1. What are some of the advantages of deferring retirement as long as possible?

20-2. Why must a client's health be accounted for in the retirement planning process?

20-3. What effect do a client's feelings about his or her life expectancy have on retirement planning?

20-4. Why might cash value life insurance and annuities be used as funding vehicles for retirement savings?

20-5. Why is it important for a retirement planner to understand the investment savvy of his or her client?

20-6. What special considerations and strategies are used when conducting retirement planning for a business owner?

20-7. List five reasons why female baby boomers need extra special strategies for retirement.

20-8. Describe how planning should occur for a client whose plan is terminated.

20-9. Discuss the relationship between retirement planning and estate planning.

20-10. a. What is a reverse annuity mortgage, and how can it be used to produce retirement income?

        b.   What are some of the major problems in relying on a reverse annuity mortgage as part of the retirement plan?

20-11. a.   Explain the advantages of relocating to a smaller home.

        b.   Why should clients be cautious when relocating?

20-12. Your client, Jane Able, retired at age 62 and started collecting Social Security. Jane is now age 63 and has been offered a part-time consulting job that pays $15,080 a year. What effect will this job have on Jane's $10,000-per-year Social Security benefit in this year (2001)?

Self-Test Questions

T   F   20-1. When dealing with married individuals, planners should make every effort to understand the feelings of both the husband and the wife.

T   F   20-2. In most cases, an employer may require an employee to retire at age 70.

T   F   20-3. One of the advantages of deferring retirement is that it provides inflation protection for a client whose salary keeps pace with inflation.

T   F   20-4. Health issues in retirement planning are not restricted to the client alone but may encompass all family members.

T   F   20-5. Retirement planners should only use life insurance company projected life expectancy tables when estimating a client's life expectancy.

T   F   20-6. Clients can accumulate sizable funds with relatively small periodic contributions over long periods of time.

T   F   20-7. If there is no need for additional life insurance protection, a cash value life insurance policy should be used instead of a deferred-annuity contract.

T   F   20-8. Any recommended retirement investments must be consistent with a client's risk profile; otherwise, the recommendation will either not be accepted, or, if acquired, will not be retained.

T   F   20-9. If a divorce or separation is a possibility, separate retirement planning should be done for each spouse.

T   F   20-10. Funds saved in a qualified plan are subject to the reach of the business's general creditors in cases such as bankruptcy or corporate liability.

T   F   20-11. When planning a business owner's retirement, retirement planners usually feel that the value of the business is too tentative to be considered a retirement asset.

T   F   20-12. For some clients, retirement planning plays a secondary role to estate planning.

T   F   20-13.   When planning the retirement of a surviving spouse, retirement planners must ensure that the amount of all assets available is discounted to account for federal estate taxes.

T   F   20-14.   Even a mortgage-free house can cost your client income.

T   F   20-15.   Under one type of reverse annuity mortgage, the client receives an annuity in consideration for selling the remainder interest on his or her home.

T   F   20-16.   Clients who want to remain in their home but need to capitalize on its value can use the strategy of renting space to tenants.

T   F   20-17.   Under a sale-leaseback arrangement, the client leases the home to a potential seller until the client's death, at which point the lessee acquires ownership.

T   F   20-18.   A married couple who have lived in their home for 2 or more years do not have to recognize up to $500,000 of gain on the sale of their home.

T   F   20-19.   Planners should recommend full and immediate commitment when advising a client to relocate to a new area.

T   F   20-20.   Retirement communities frequently require a substantial nonrefundable fee for admission as well as an ongoing monthly fee.

T   F   20-21.   Becoming reemployed after starting to receive Social Security benefits will have no effect on a 63-year-old client's earnings.

Determining Postretirement Monetary Needs: Preliminary Concerns

---

Learning Objectives

An understanding of the material in this chapter should enable the student to

---

21-1. Describe the standard of living that clients should plan for retirement.

21-2. Describe the replacement-ratio approach for determining the income needed in the first year of retirement, considering the

  a. estimated replacement ratio
  b. decrease in taxation for retirees
  c. factors that reduce living expenses for retirees
  d. factors that increase living expenses for retirees

21-3. Describe the expense-method approach for determining the income needed in the first year of retirement.

21-4. Explain the factors that should be considered when estimating a retirement date for a client.

21-5. Describe the impact inflation has on funds needed for retirement.

Chapter Outline

One major question that almost every individual encounters when planning for retirement is whether sufficient income and assets exist to provide for the retirement years: There is no exact method that calculates how much is enough. However, the planner can take several steps to create a workable retirement plan. This chapter and chapters 22 and 23 will explore these steps by

- addressing four crucial elements of postretirement monetary need (chapter 21)
- exploring the various sources of retirement income (chapter 22)
- providing a method for computing and for funding the client's retirement need (chapter 23)

In this chapter, we will look at four of the five major components of the postretirement monetary need: the expected standard of living during retirement, the estimate of the first year's retirement needs, the expected starting date for retirement, and the expected inflation rate before and after retirement. Chapter 22 will address the fifth major factor in determining the postretirement monetary need—the client's sources of retirement income.

EXPECTED STANDARD OF LIVING DURING RETIREMENT

The standard of living enjoyed during the years just prior to retirement largely influences the client's expectations for his or her postretirement standard of living. For this reason, the planner encounters different situations depending on how close the client is to his or her retirement date. With this in mind, let's examine the differences that exist between clients of various age groups.

Late-Career Clients

For almost all clients, the years immediately prior to retirement represent their peak earning years and their highest standard of living. Clients who are near the end of their careers are concerned about maintaining their current standard of living. As a group, these clients are the most interested in retirement planning and are the most willing to make some adjustments to their preretirement lifestyle to compensate for inadequate retirement savings. The reason for such interest is that their close proximity to retirement makes planning for retirement one of their highest priorities.

Mid-Career Clients

The client who is in the middle of his or her career has a different perspective on his or her postretirement standard of living. Employment has permitted this client to establish a comfortable standard of living, but the client envisions still further increases in income and in lifestyle. For these clients, the desired standard of living during retirement will be based on their expectations of success in their career and the attendant increases in their standard of living. In other words, these clients will prefer to enjoy an unknown and yet to be realized standard of living during their retirement years. This expectation provides planners with a special challenge. Although sufficient time remains to develop and implement accumulation plans to provide for the client's retirement years, the actual retirement standard of living is speculative at best. For this reason, planners must first make the best estimate possible based on the client's educational background, job experiences, personal ambitions, and career plan. The estimated retirement standard of living can be computed by applying a growth factor to the client's current salary (for example, 1 1/2 times an expected inflation rate of 4 percent) and approximating the client's final-average salary. A second method would be to estimate the current annual expenses that are owed by a person in the position the client aspires to by the end of his or her career and inflate this amount. Regardless of the method used, it is important for planners to monitor the careers of their younger clients and make corresponding adjustments to the retirement plan to reflect the difference between their actual growth rate and their estimated growth rate. If this is done as the client gets closer to retirement, the estimated standard of living becomes more accurate.

Early-Career Clients

These clients typically have too little experience to estimate what their retirement needs will be and probably have not thought too much about the standard of living they will expect at that time. Most likely, if any such thought has been entertained, these clients anticipate a standard of living approximately equal to or slightly greater than their parents' current standard. For this reason, estimating a retirement standard of living at this stage is too tentative. The planner should instead concentrate efforts on encouraging their clients to use regular IRAs or Roth IRAs, to make contributions to the employer 401(k) plan, or to acquire long-term savings vehicles such as deferred annuities.

Note also that early-career clients as well as mid-career clients are less likely than a late-career client to adjust their current lifestyle for retirement planning purposes. Younger clients are more likely to be distracted by other priorities and will tend to ignore the future because current problems take precedence. In this situation, the retirement planner must try to make saving for retirement a priority in spite of these distractions. One way to accomplish this is to talk about retirement planning in terms of financial independence planning. The change in terminology focuses clients on the goal of being able to control their own financial future. This is something that is desirable even to younger clients.

ESTIMATING THE FIRST YEAR'S INCOME

In addition to understanding the standard of living the client expects during retirement, planners must also be prepared to estimate the income stream that a client will need during retirement. One of the essential parts of this process is estimating the income that a client will need in the first year of retirement. Let's examine the two generally accepted methods for determining this, the replacement-ratio method and the expense method.

The Replacement-Ratio Method

replacement-ratio method

One way to estimate how much a client will need in the first year of retirement is to apply the replacement-ratio method. The *replacement-ratio method* assumes that the standard of living enjoyed during the years just prior to retirement will be the determinant of the standard of living needed in the first year of retirement. Under the replacement-ratio method, the planner can estimate the amount needed in the first year of retirement regardless of the client's age by using a replacement ratio that is geared to continue the same standard of living (for late-career clients) or the estimated standard of living (for mid-career clients). In general, a 60 to 80 percent replacement ratio is used. In other words, the amount of income needed to be financially independent in the first year of retirement without drastically altering the client's standard of living varies between 60 and 80 percent of the average gross annual income of the average of the last 3 years of employment. For example, if a client with an income in the years prior to retirement of $95,000, $100,000, and $105,000 respectively has an 80 percent target rate, then the client should target a replacement ratio of about $80,000 (80 percent of the $100,000 average). Support for this range rests upon the elimination of some employment-related taxes and some expected changes in spending patterns that reduce the retiree's need for income (such as expenditures that will either decrease or disappear in the retirement years).

Factors that Influence the Amount of Income Needed during Retirement

Reductions in Taxation

In many circumstances, retirees can count on a lower percentage of their income going to pay taxes in the retirement years. Some taxes are reduced or eliminated, and in other cases retirees may enjoy special favorable tax treatment. Let's take a closer look at the potential reductions in taxation that are granted to retirees.

Social Security Taxes. FICA contributions (old-age, survivors, disability, and hospital insurance) are levied solely on income from employment. Distributions from pensions, IRAs, retirement annuities, and other similar devices are not considered income subject to FICA or SECA (self-employment FICA) taxes. Hence, for the retiree who stops working entirely, Social Security taxes are no longer an expenditure. Note also that FICA and SECA amounts will increase each year to reflect increases in the wage base for the old age, survivors, and disability portion of Social Security (in 2001, 6.2 percent of $80,400). The hospital insurance portion of Social Security is not subject to a wage cap, and the tax in 2001 is 1.45 percent of all covered wages.

Increased Standard Deduction. For a married taxpayer aged 65 or over, an additional $900 (in 2001) is added to the standard deduction. If the taxpayer's spouse is also 65 or older, an additional $900 increase in the standard deduction can be taken ($900 for each spouse, or $1,800 total). For any taxpayer over age 65 who is not married and does not file as a surviving spouse, $1,100 is added to the standard deduction.

Social Security Benefits Exclusion. Until 1984, all Social Security benefits were received free of federal income taxation. Since then, however, the rules have changed several times, so that now many individuals are required to pay tax on a large portion of their benefits. Until 1994, the maximum amount of Social Security benefits subject to tax was 50 percent. However, beginning in 1994, the maximum percentage increased to 85 percent for certain taxpayers.

provisional income   The portion of the OASDI benefit that is subject to tax is based on what is referred to as the individual's *provisional income*. Provisional income is the sum of the following:

- the taxpayer's adjusted gross income
- the taxpayer's tax-exempt interest for the year
- half of the Social Security benefits for the year

If the provisional income is less than what is referred to as the *base amount*—$25,000 for a single taxpayer and $32,000 or less for a married taxpayer filing jointly—Social Security benefits are not taxable. If the provisional income is between the base amount and $34,000 ($44,000 for a married taxpayer filing jointly), up to 50 percent of the Social Security benefit will be includible in taxable income. If the provisional amount exceeds $34,000 ($44,000 for a married taxpayer filing jointly), up to 85 percent of the Social Security benefit will be includible in taxable income. To summarize, the table below identifies the various cutoff points.

TABLE 21-1
Portion of OASDI Benefits Subject to Federal Income Tax

Taxpayer Filing Status	Provisional Income Threshold	Amount of Benefits Subject to Federal Income Tax
Single	under $25,000	0 percent
Single	$25,000–$33,999	up to 50 percent
Single	$34,000 or more	up to 85 percent
Married filing jointly	under $32,000	0 percent
Married filing jointly	$32,000–$43,999	up to 50 percent
Married filing jointly	$44,000 or more	up to 85 percent
Married filing separately (and living in the same household)	$0	up to 85 percent

The general description of how much is included and the various cutoffs is often sufficient for planning purposes. However, the planner may have occasion to actually calculate the specific amount of benefits includible as taxable income. The following explanation and example can be used to make this determination:

Step 1: Calculate provisional income.
Step 2: Determine appropriate thresholds, based on the individual's tax filing status.
Step 3: The amount of Social Security benefits included as taxable income is the smallest number obtained from performing the following three calculations:

   (a) 50 percent of any provisional income that exceeds the base threshold plus 35 percent of any amount in excess of the second threshold

   (b) 85 percent of the benefits

   (c) 50 percent of the benefits, plus 85 percent of any amount in excess of the second threshold

---

Example: Peggy and Larry Novernstern are married and file jointly. They have an adjusted gross income of $40,000 (not considering Social Security benefits) plus $5,000 of tax-free bond interest, and are entitled to a $15,000 Social Security benefit.

Step 1:   <u>Calculate provisional income</u>

preliminary adjusted gross income	$40,000
tax-free bond interest	5,000
50 percent of Social Security benefits	7,500
provisional income equals	$52,500

Step 2:   <u>Determine income in excess of the applicable thresholds</u>

- Excess over base threshold equals ($52,500 – $32,000) $20,500
- Excess over second threshold equals ($52,500 – $44,000) $8,500

Step 3:   <u>Amount includible in taxable income is the lowest of the following three amounts</u>

   (a) 50 percent of excess over base threshold plus 35 percent of excess over second threshold

       ($.5 \times \$20,500 + .35 \times 8,500$)   = $13,225

   (b) 85 percent of $15,000   = $12,750

   (c) 50 percent of $15,000 + 85 percent of $8,500   = $14,725

In this case, the $12,750 (85 percent of the benefit) is included as adjusted gross income.

State and Local Income Taxation. In some states, Social Security benefits are fully exempt from state income taxation; in others, some taxation of these benefits might occur if the state's income tax is assessed on the taxpayer's taxable income as reported for federal income tax purposes. In addition, some states grant extra income tax relief for the elderly by providing increased personal exemptions, credits, sliding scale rebates of property or other taxes (the amount or percent of which might be dependent on income), or additional tax breaks.

Deductible Medical Expenses. For taxpayers that itemize deductions, it might be easier to exceed the 7.5 percent threshold for deductibility of qualifying medical expenses (including costs for long-term care insurance) owing to the reduced retirement income level and often increased medical expenses.

Reduced Living Expenses

In addition to the possible reductions in taxation, retired individuals can experience reduced living expenses that permit them to maintain their same standard of living on a lower income. Let's take a closer look at some of the reduced living expenses.

Work-Related Expenses. The costs of proper clothing for work, commuting, and meals purchased during work hours are eliminated when a person retires. In addition, other expenses, such as membership dues in some professional or social clubs, may be reduced because of retired status or may be eliminated if no longer necessary.

Home Ownership Expenses. By the time of retirement, many homeowners have "burned the mortgage" and no longer have this debt reduction expenditure. (*Planning Note:* It may be worthwhile for a client to pay off the mortgage at or near the date of retirement. This mortgage redemption not only eliminates the debt repayment expenditure but also reduces income from interest or dividends on assets used to pay the mortgage, thereby reducing income for federal and state tax purposes. For taxpayers of modest means, the income reduction might place them just below the threshold for taxation of Social Security benefits. Also, most of the monthly mortgage payments typically are applied to principal reduction, thus interest deductibility would be a minor tax benefit. Furthermore, the interest being paid could exceed the rate of earnings on invested funds, thereby producing a real saving for the retiree.)

Absence of Dependent Children. The expense of supporting dependent children is usually completed by the time a client enters retirement. Be cautious, however, because retirees, especially those who married later in life, occasionally have children who are not self-supporting and will require continued financial support during some of the clients' retirement years.

Senior Citizen Discounts. Special reductions in price are given to senior citizens. Some reductions, such as certain AARP discounts, are available at age 50. Many businesses, however, require proof of age 65 (usually by having a Medicare card) to qualify for discounts on prescriptions, clothing, and restaurant meals. Discounts typically range from 5 to 15 percent of an item's cost.

No Longer Saving for Retirement. For many retirees, retirement is not a time to continue to save for retirement. Payments to contributory pension plans, lack of eligibility for IRA or Keogh plan contributions, or just the psychological fact of being retired help to weaken retirees' motivation to save for the future. Note that a retired worker's income can fall by the amount being saved with no concurrent reduction in standard of living. Therefore, a retired worker who has been saving 20 percent of income needs only to maintain an "inflation protected" 80 percent (before tax) of income to enjoy the same purchasing power.

Fewer Automobiles. Retirees often consciously decide to reduce their automobile expenditures either by owning fewer automobiles or by purchasing a replacement less frequently. In either case, the dollar cost for automobile insurance and the cash flow for financing automobiles tend to decline during the retirement years.

Age-Related Reductions. As a client grows older in retirement, he or she often cuts back on expenses and adopts a more sedentary lifestyle. For example, at some age driving becomes impossible or restricted and, at that point, car and other expenses decline. Some practitioners argue that these declines are mitigated by increased costs for medical care. Data from the Bureau of Labor Statistics, however, indicates that even though health care expenses increase over retirement, the increase does not significantly mitigate the decrease in other expenses.

Living Expenses in the Early Years of Retirement

Some retirement planners are rather uncomfortable with recommending a planned reduction in income in the first year of retirement. These planners believe that certain factors suggest that during the first year of retirement at least as much, if not more, income will be required to maintain the preretirement standard of living. Let's take a closer look at these factors.

Medical Expenses. Without question, medical expenses will increase over time for virtually all clients. The mere act of aging and the associated health problems generate additional demands for medical services. Even if

---

ILLUSTRATION 21-1
Justification of a 60 to 80 Percent Replacement Ratio

Joe Jones, aged 64, has a fixed salary of $100,000 and would like to maintain his current purchasing power when he retires next year. If Joe has no increased retirement-related expenses, he can do this by having a retirement income of 70 percent of his final salary (as illustrated below). If Joe has increased retirement-related expenses, a somewhat higher figure should be used. (Note that postretirement inflation will be accounted for later.)

Working salary			$100,000
less retirement savings		18,000.00	
less FICA taxes		5,504.80	
less reduction in federal taxes	(extra $1,000 deduction for being 65)	280.00	
	(no tax on portion of Social Security received)	1,138.40	
less annual commuting expenses to work		450.00	
less mortgage expenses	(mortgage expires on retirement date)	4,626.80	
Reductions subtotal			30,000
Total purchasing power needed at 65			$ 70,000
Percentage of final salary needed			70%

---

advancing age does not create an increase in an individual's demands for medical services, inflation in these costs will. Furthermore, increases in inflation are not evenly distributed in the various medical care disciplines, and those services that will potentially affect retirees have been hit hardest. For example, the cost of hospital rooms rose 719 percent; professional medical services rose 406 percent; and prescription drugs rose 196 percent over the past 20 years. This does not consider the prices for some of the newer, more costly wonder drugs. Although retirees are often covered by Medicare and other health insurance, the trend in these coverages has been toward cost containment—defined by the government and the insurance companies as that of shifting more of the medical cost to the insured by means of larger deductibles and coinsurance payments. These higher medical expenses would be in addition to the increased premiums for the insurance.

**YOUR FINANCIAL SERVICES PRACTICE:
WARNING YOUR CLIENTS ABOUT THE RISKS**

Whether or not your clients accept a 60 to 80 percent replacement ratio or feel something more is necessary, it should be stressed that there is no definitive answer to absolutely determine if the postretirement income should be less than, equal to, or greater than that of the preretirement years.

Estimating financial needs during the first year of retirement is like trying to hit a moving target when you are blindfolded: Your aim is obscured by many unknown variables and it is hard to draw a bead on the target. For example, the planner and client must establish what standard of living is desired during retirement, when retirement will begin, what inflation assumptions should be made before and after retirement, and what interest can be earned on invested funds. In addition, for clients who are forced by economic necessity to liquidate their retirement nest egg, the client and planner must estimate the life expectancy over which liquidations will occur. Many of these variables can dramatically change overnight and without warning, for example:

- The client may be planning to retire at age 65 when health considerations, or perhaps a plant shutdown, force retirement at age 62.
- A younger client may be planning on a relatively moderate retirement lifestyle, but business success mandates that a more lucrative retirement lifestyle be planned.

Travel, Vacations, and Other Lifestyle Changes. Many clients expect to devote considerably more time to travel and vacations upon retirement than they did during their working years. Increased leisure time, once a scarce commodity, now provides the opportunity to travel. Unfortunately, vacationing can be an expensive activity. Indeed, an increase in vacation activities represents a rise in the standard of living and will require additional income.

Dependents. As previously stated, parents usually need less income during the first year of retirement because they no longer financially support their children, who typically become self-supporting prior to parental retirement. However, many retirees still have dependents to support. Many parents have children with mental or physical problems who will require long-term custodial and financial care throughout the retirement years. Other retirees, because medical care, surgical techniques, and drugs are helping to prolong life, may have to provide for their aged parents who no longer possess the wherewithal to do so themselves.

The Expense Method

A second way planners can estimate their client's retirement needs is by using the expense-method approach. The expense method of retirement planning focuses on the projected expenses that the retiree will have in the first year of retirement. As with the replacement-ratio method, it is much easier to define the potential expenses for those clients who are at or near retirement. For example, if the 64-year-old near-retiree expects to have $3,000 in monthly bills ($36,000 annually), then the retirement income for that retiree should maintain $36,000 worth of purchasing power in today's dollars. If, however, a younger client is involved, more speculative estimates of retirement expenses must be made (and periodically revised).

A list of expenses that should be considered includes expenses that may be unique to the particular client as well as other more general expenses.

Some expenses that tend to increase for retirees include the following:

- utilities and telephone
- medical/dental/drugs/health insurance
- house upkeep/repairs/maintenance/property insurance (until a move occurs)
- recreation/entertainment/travel/dining (during the early years of retirement)

Conversely, some expenses tend to decrease for the retiree. These include the following:

- mortgage payments
- food
- clothing
- income taxes
- property taxes
- transportation costs (car maintenance/insurance/other)
- debt repayment (charge accounts, personal loans)
- child support/alimony
- household furnishings

EXPECTED STARTING DATE FOR RETIREMENT

Estimating the target date for the start of retirement is another crucial element in determining postretirement monetary needs. The advent of Social Security in the 1930s created an image that Americans would retire when Social Security benefits began. Until recently, most pension planning tended to support this perception by specifying retirement to occur at age 65. Thus, workers and planners almost invariably planned, economically and psychologically, for retirement to begin at age 65.

This assumption may not be wise, however, when you consider the following factors:

- Only 67 percent of men 55 to 65 years old were still in the workforce in 1987 compared to 90 percent in 1947.
- The retirement date for full Social Security benefits will be gradually increased to age 67 between 2003 and 2027. (In addition, many are predicting an increase in the age for full benefits.)
- According to one study, nearly five out of six individuals retire early.
- According to another study, 80 percent of people in large companies with pension plans retired before age 65.
- Health issues will affect the choice of a retirement date.
- An increasing number of individuals are forced to retire early in cases where jobs are being eliminated.
- The average retirement age of American workers is 62.

Planners must, therefore, rely on their best judgment and account for the client's specific circumstances when estimating a retirement date. (*Planning Note:* If you err on the conservative side and plan for a retirement date that occurs prior to your client's actual retirement date, you will overestimate the retirement need and, consequently, the client will have more funds than necessary. Conversely, a planned retirement date that occurs after the actual retirement starting date will tend to underestimate the retirement income need and leave the client with less funds than necessary.)

Planners who feel that retirement prior to age 65 is likely to occur should keep in mind its impact on their clients' pension benefits. In a defined-contribution plan, the account balance will be lower than if the client continued working until normal retirement. In a defined-benefit plan, early retirement benefits are usually actuarially reduced to account for the longer payout period. Therefore, it is not unusual for a plan that provides a 50 percent replacement ratio of final-average salary at normal retirement age to provide a 40 percent replacement ratio at the plan's early retirement age (less, if the early retirement benefit is not subsidized by the employer). Note also that the final-average salary at an early retirement age will be less than if the client remained employed until normal retirement age. This, plus the actuarial reduction, tends to severely restrict the amount of pension income you can count on for a client who retires early compared to a client who retires at normal retirement age.

The planner must also account for the retirement dates for the two-wage-earner family. In two-wage-earner families, the spouses will often choose to coordinate their retirement dates. If the spouses are close in age, they typically desire to retire in the same year. If a wide age disparity exists, clients typically stagger retirement dates. Keep these trends in mind when planning for the two-wage-earner family.

ILLUSTRATION 21-2
Understanding the Expense Method

Your clients, Bob and Betty Smith, both aged 64, would like to maintain their current purchasing power when they retire next year. They can do this by having an annual income of $40,860 as illustrated below. Note that the figures are estimates of their expenses during retirement (some are higher than their current expenses and some are lower than their current expenses). Also note that postretirement inflation will be accounted for later.

Estimated retirement living expenses and required capital (in current dollars)

	Per Month x 12 =	Per Year
1. Food	$ 500	$ 6,000
2. Housing		
a. Rent/mortgage payment	400	4,800
b. Insurance (if separate payment)	25	300
c. Property taxes (if separate payment)	150	1,800
d. Utilities	180	2,160
e. Maintenance (if owned)	100	1,200
3. Clothing and Personal Care		
a. Wife	75	900
b. Husband	75	900
4. Medical Expenses		
a. Doctor (HMO)	75	900
b. Dentist	20	240
c. Medicines	75	900
5. Transportation		
a. Car payments	130	1,560
b. Gas	50	600
c. Insurance	50	600
d. Car maintenance (tires and repairs)	30	360
6. Miscellaneous Expenses		
a. Entertainment	150	1,800
b. Travel	200	2,400
c. Hobbies	50	600
d. Other	100	1,200
e. Club fees and dues	20	240
7. Insurance	100	1,200
8. Gifts and contributions	50	600
9. State, local, and federal taxes (if any)	800	9,600
10. Total expenses (current dollars)	$3,405	$40,860*

*Note an adjustment should be made for future years to reflect a more sedentary lifestyle and reduced spending on the part of the client.

A final consideration when determining a target retirement date is the burdensome fixed long-term liabilities of the client. In some cases, the client has very little discretion over the retirement date until these liabilities have been paid. For example, the client may have large debts from medical expenses and/or educational expenses.

EXPECTED INFLATION BEFORE AND DURING RETIREMENT

A final element that greatly affects the postretirement monetary need is the amount of expected inflation before and after retirement. Forecasting inflation is not an easy task. Lacking a crystal ball, a proxy for the expected inflation rate is needed. Because retirement income planning can encompass a long time span, one school of thought is to recommend taking a long-term view of inflation. For example, for the period from 1962 to 1996 inclusive, the average compound increase in prices was 4.9 percent, and proponents of the long-term view would perhaps use 4.5 percent as a reasonable measure for expected inflation.

A second school of thought suggests that the structure of the economy and prices have changed too drastically to use long-term figures. This group would argue that the figures from the last 15 years are a more appropriate measure of inflation. For this period, the compound inflation rate was 3.5 percent.

Rather than accept any one of these inflation rates, or any other historical rate, the planner must be aware of the forces that were operating during those periods and the forces that are likely to operate in the future. Because there is no method of determining the inflation rate based on historical data, you must use your best judgment as to future economic prospects and your clients' risk-aversion tendencies. A risk-averse client will probably want a more conservative figure projected, whereas a risk taker may feel comfortable with an optimistically low-inflation assumption. For someone in the middle, a 4 percent assumption could prove to be a viable rate to use during both the accumulation period and the retirement period. However, both you and your client must recognize that if actual inflation begins to exceed the expected rate, revisions in the planning must be made. (*Planning Note:* If you err on the conservative side and assume a higher inflation rate than the actual inflation rate, you will overestimate the retirement need and consequently the client will have more funds than necessary. Conversely, an estimate that assumes a lower inflation rate than the actual inflation rate will underestimate the retirement need and leave the client with less funds than necessary.)

ILLUSTRATING THE EFFECT OF INCREASES IN INFLATION AND STANDARD OF LIVING

In general, the higher the inflation rate and standard-of-living increases that a client experiences, the greater the amount of retirement income that will be needed. The compound interest formula can be used to make the necessary projection for the purpose of illustrating this. This formula is

$$FV = PV \, (1 + r)^n$$

where   FV = the target dollar expenditure at retirement
        PV = the dollar expenditures for the current standard of living
        r   = a rate of growth in the dollar expenditures for the standard of living
        n   = the number of years from time of planning until target retirement date

The rate of growth, or r, can stand for either (1) the rate of increase in the level of the standard of living, (2) the rate of inflation that requires more dollars being spent to maintain the current standard of living, or (3) a combination of both. For example, if no inflation is expected, but the client anticipates a 20 percent increase in his or her standard of living between now and retirement 10 years hence, the result is an average annual 1.84 percent compound increase in the standard of living and r equals .0184 in the formula. If no growth in the standard of living is anticipated before retirement, but inflation is expected to average 4 percent annually over the 10 years to retirement, then r equals .04 in the above formula.

When the standard of living is expected to rise during the planning period and inflation is expected to continue, then r, the growth rate, can be *approximated* by adding the rates of growth in both the standard of living and inflation to estimate the needed income at or during retirement. For example, if the standard of living is expected to rise at 1.84 percent annually and inflation at 4 percent annually, then the combined result is a needed 5.84 percent increase in income. In this case, r equals 5.84. (For technical accuracy, these rates should be multiplied together [1.0184 x 1.04 = 1.059] rather than added, but because of the many necessary assumptions about the future the inaccuracy from approximating is acceptable.)

Applying the Formula

Earlier in this chapter, we introduced three disparate clients: the late-career client, the mid-career client, and the early-career client. At this point, the concepts developed in this chapter can be applied to illustrate the effect that inflation and standard-of-living assumptions have on his or her needed retirement income.

For the purpose of simplicity, the following assumptions will apply to each client:

- target retirement at age 65
- inflation of 4 percent each year until retirement
- a retirement standard of living equal to 90 percent of the preretirement standard of living

The Late-Career Client

This client, Ed Ferguson, aged 60, currently is spending $50,000 per year to maintain his standard of living. Ed does not anticipate any increase in his standard of living between now and retirement. To begin planning for Ed's retirement, the starting point requires an estimation of his needed retirement income at and during retirement. Using the compound interest formula, Ed's estimated retirement income need at age 65 would be

$$FV = \$50,000 \ (1.04)^5$$
$$FV = \$60,832$$

This is the amount Ed would be spending on standard of living before retirement. Because it is assumed that the retirement standard of living will be 10 percent less than the preretirement standard, the following adjustment determines the amount Ed needs for his first year's retirement income:

1st year's Retirement Income = 90% of preretirement standard of living expenditures
1st year's Retirement Income = .90 ($60,832)
1st year's Retirement Income = $54,749

Because inflation will continue after retirement, Ed will need income in his second year of retirement.

$$FV = 54,749 \ (1.04)^1$$
$$FV = \$56,939$$

By the same process, Ed's retirement income could be calculated for each and every year. Table 2 shows the retirement income needed in 5-year increments until age 80 and in 10-year increments until age 100.

Note that there will be a change in retirement needs for Ed if the inflation or standard-of-living assumptions are altered. In general, the higher the inflation and standard-of-living assumptions the greater the amount of income that is needed and vice versa. For example, if a 2 percent inflation rate is assumed and an 80 percent of final salary replacement ratio is used, Ed will need only $44,163 at age 65 (that is $10,586 less income needed at age 65 than is shown in table 21-2). If, however, a 6 percent inflation rate is assumed and a 100 percent of final salary replacement ratio is desired, Ed will need $12,162 more than shown in table 21-2 at age 65, or $66,911.

TABLE 21-2 Retirement Income for Ed Ferguson	
Ed's Age	Income
65	$54,749
70	66,610
75	81,042
80	98,600
90	145,951
100	216,044

The Mid-Career Client

Susan Hughes, aged 43, currently is spending $40,000 to maintain her standard of living. But Susan feels that her future is bright and she expects expenditures for standard of living will grow by 2 percent over inflation each year from now until retirement. She, like Ed in the preceding example, will want to use a 90 percent replacement ratio to maintain her preretirement standard of living. Based on this information, Susan's preretirement standard-of-living expenditures will be

$$FV = \$40,000 \, (1.06)^{22}$$
$$FV = \$144,141$$

Her first year's retirement income will be

1st year's Retirement Income = .90 ($144,141)
1st year's Retirement Income = $129,727

Table 21-3 shows the estimated retirement income for Susan until age 100 using the formula $FV = \$129,727 \, (1.04)^n$.

TABLE 21-3
Retirement Income for Susan Hughes

Susan's Age	Income
65	$129,727
70	157,833
75	192,028
80	233,632
90	345,832
100	511,916

As with Ed, Susan's retirement income needs will vary with the inflation and replacement-ratio assumptions used. In addition, if Susan expects more than a 2 percent per year growth to occur in her living standard, her retirement income need will increase. For example, if Susan expects a 4 percent per year growth to occur, she will need $195,715 at age 65 (that is $65,988 more than the amount needed at 2 percent). Note also that if Susan has a 4 percent growth per year but inflation drops to an average of 2 percent a year, then the numbers in table 21-3 will still be correct.

The Early-Career Client

John Jones, aged 25, currently spends $15,000 to maintain his standard of living. He is less optimistic about the future than Susan is and expects his standard-of-living expenditures to increase about 1.25 percent annually until retirement. He expects the standard of living during retirement to be equal to 90 percent of his last year of employment. Thus, John would have anticipated standard-of-living expenditures during his last year of employment as follows:

$$FV = \$15,000\,(1.0525)^{40}$$
$$FV = \$116,138$$

His first year's retirement income will be

1st year's Retirement Income = .90 ($116,138)
1st year's Retirement Income = $104,524

Table 21-4 shows John's retirement income needs to age 100 using a 4 percent rate of inflation.

TABLE 21-4 Retirement Income for John Jones	
John's Age	Income
65	$104.524
70	127,170
75	154,722
80	188,241
90	278,644
100	412,462

Summing Up

As can be observed from the three examples, if the assumptions used to develop the estimated retirement income needed to maintain a particular standard of living are valid, each client will require, if he or she lives to age 100, an amount of income beyond expectations.

Suppose, however, inflation was ignored. If the inflation assumptions during employment and retirement could be zero, then table 21-5 shows the resulting retirement income needs.

TABLE 21-5 Retirement Projections without Inflation	
	Income
Ed	$45,000 (.90 x $50,000)
Susan	$55,655 [.90 x $40,000 $(1.02)^{22}$]
John	$22,188 [.90 x $15,000 $(1.0125)^{40}$]

There is quite a difference. Think how much easier the potential for meaningful retirement income planning could be for both the client and the planner if the rate of inflation were zero. Unfortunately, like death and taxes, long-term inflation is a fact of life and the prudent planner must assume it will continue and plan accordingly.

CHAPTER REVIEW

Answers to the review questions and self-test questions start on page 673.

Key Terms

replacement-ratio method   provisional income

Review Questions

21-1. Describe the planning differences between late-career, mid-career, and early-career clients when estimating postretirement standards of living.

21-2. What ranges of replacement ratios are generally chosen by retirement planners in order to maintain a client's preretirement standard of living during the first year of retirement?

21-3. Why can retirees in some cases count on less of their income going to pay taxes during their retirement years? Explain.

21-4. James Stone, aged 65, is retired and receives $29,000 in pension income and $9,000 in Social Security income. James has no other sources of income and would like to know how his Social Security income will be taxed for federal tax purposes. James is married and files jointly.

21-5. a.   What factors tend to reduce a client's living expenses after retirement?
       b.   What factors tend to increase a client's living expenses after retirement?

21-6. Why is it so hard to accurately estimate the amount of income needed in the first year of retirement?

21-7. Explain the expense-method approach to retirement planning.

21-8. What factors should be considered when estimating a client's expected starting date for retirement?

21-9. Why is a 4 percent inflation assumption considered appropriate for a client who is willing to accept a moderate risk?

21-10. Discuss the impact that rate-of-inflation and standard-of-living increases have on the amount of income needed for retirement.

Self-Test Questions

T   F   21-1. The standard of living enjoyed during the years just prior to retirement largely influences the client's expectations for his or her postretirement standard of living.

T   F   21-2.   Clients in the middle of their careers typically wish to account for a higher standard of living than they are currently enjoying.

T   F   21-3.   A replacement ratio of 50 percent of final-average salary should be used when planning an individual's retirement.

T   F   21-4.   A retiree's Social Security taxes are reduced one dollar for every two dollars of Social Security income.

T   F   21-5.   For taxpayers over age 65 who are not married, $600 is added to the standard deduction.

T   F   21-6.   A married taxpayer who files jointly can exclude all Social Security benefits from income for tax purposes if the taxpayer's modified adjusted gross income is $15,000 and his or her Social Security benefit is $12,000.

T   F   21-7.   Some states grant income tax relief for the elderly by providing sliding scale rebates of property taxes.

T   F   21-8.   A retired worker's income can fall by the amount being saved for retirement with no concurrent reduction in standard of living.

T   F   21-9.   Some expenses that tend to increase for retirees include medical bills, recreation expenditures, and house repair costs.

T   F   21-10.   The retirement date for full Social Security benefits will be gradually increased to age 67 between 2003 and 2027.

T   F   21-11.   If a planned retirement date occurs after an actual retirement date, the retirement need will be overestimated.

T   F   21-12.   It is not unusual for a plan that provides a 50 percent replacement ratio of final-average salary at normal retirement age to provide a 40 percent or lower replacement ratio at early retirement age.

T   F   21-13.   A 4 percent inflation assumption can be used for retirement planning purposes, but this rate must be monitored to recognize disparity with the actual inflation rate.

Determining Postretirement Monetary Needs: Sources of Postretirement Income

---

Learning Objectives

An understanding of the material in this chapter should enable the student to

---

22-1. Discuss the retirement and medical benefits available to a retiree under Social Security.

22-2. Identify the documents a retirement planner uses to understand his or her client's pension benefit.

22-3. Explain why Social Security and pensions do not provide an adequate level of benefits for retirement.

22-4. Identify the various sources of private savings that clients use for retirement purposes.

Chapter Outline

In addition to analyzing the expected standard of living during retirement, the expected starting date for retirement, and the expected inflation rate before and after retirement, planners must also account for the resources that the client has available for retirement. These resources are compared to the client's expected retirement needs to determine the short fall—the amount of additional savings needed. These resources typically include benefits payable under Social Security, pension benefits from employer-provided plans, and private savings that the employee has accumulated for retirement purposes. These three sources have come to be known as the three-legged stool of retirement security. This chapter analyzes these resources with an emphasis on the facets that are important for the retirement planner to know.

SOCIAL SECURITY

When people use the term *Social Security*, they are actually referring to the old-age, survivors, disability, and health insurance (OASDHI) program of the federal government. For retirement planning purposes, planners should be familiar with the entire Social Security system, particularly the old-age insurance programs and health insurance programs. Let's take a closer look at these two programs.

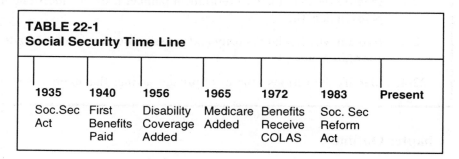

TABLE 22-1
Social Security Time Line

1935	1940	1956	1965	1972	1983	Present
Soc.Sec Act	First Benefits Paid	Disability Coverage Added	Medicare Added	Benefits Receive COLAS	Soc. Sec Reform Act	

Old-Age Insurance under Social Security

Eligibility

Your client is eligible for retirement benefits under the old-age provisions of Social Security if he or she is covered by Social Security (groups that are not covered are discussed later) and has "credit" for a stipulated amount of work. Credit for Social Security purposes is based on *quarters of coverage*. For 2001, a worker receives credit for one quarter of coverage for each $830 in annual earnings on which Social Security taxes are paid. However, credit for no more than four quarters of coverage may be earned in any one calendar year. Consequently, a worker paying Social Security taxes on as little as $3,320 (that is, $830 x 4) during the year will receive credit for the maximum four quarters. Furthermore, the amount of earnings necessary for a quarter of coverage is adjusted annually according to changes in the national level of wages. Also note that prior to 1978 a worker could receive credit for only one quarter of coverage in any given calendar quarter. In the past, it was necessary to earn wages throughout the year to receive the maximum number of credits. Now a worker with the appropriate level of wages can receive credit for the maximum number of quarters even if all wages are earned within one calendar quarter.

Fully Insured Status

A person is fully insured for purposes of receiving Social Security retirement benefits if he or she has 40 quarters of coverage. Once a person acquires this much credit, he or she is fully insured for life even if covered employment under Social Security ceases.

Retirement Benefits

A worker who is fully insured is eligible to receive monthly retirement benefits as early as age 62. Electing to receive benefits prior to age 65, however, results in a permanently reduced benefit. In addition, the following dependents of persons receiving retirement benefits are also eligible for monthly benefits based on the retiree's own account:

- *a spouse aged 62 or older*—A nonworking spouse will receive 50 percent of the working spouse's primary insurance amount. Benefits are permanently reduced if this benefit is elected prior to the spouse's reaching age 65. This benefit is also available to a divorced spouse under certain circumstances if the marriage lasted at least 10 years.
- *a spouse of any age if the spouse is caring for at least one child of the retired worker*—The children must be (1) under age 16 or (2) disabled and entitled to a child's benefit as described below. This benefit is commonly referred to as a mother's or father's benefit.
- *dependent, unmarried children under 18*—This child's benefit will continue until age 19 as long as a child is a full-time student in elementary or secondary school. In addition, disabled children of any age are eligible for benefits as long as they were disabled before reaching age 22.

It is important to note that retirement benefits are not automatically paid upon eligibility. Instead, workers must apply for retirement benefits, as well as all other Social Security benefits. (*Planning Note:* Clients should apply for benefits three months in advance. Application can be made at the local Social Security office. For clients who did not file timely, note that benefit claims can be filed up to six months after benefits are due to commence because benefits can be paid retroactively for six months.

Benefit Amounts

Old-age insurance benefits are based on a worker's primary insurance amount (PIA). The PIA, in turn, is a function of the worker's average indexed monthly earnings (AIME) on which Social Security taxes have been paid. For retirement planning purposes, the planner need not know how to calculate the AIME and PIA. Instead, the best method to estimate a client's expected Social Security benefits would be to examine the employee's data from the Social Security administration. This data is mailed annually to all clients who are 25 and older and who are not already receiving Social Security benefits. The new Social Security statements were first mailed in October of 1999. If your client has not received one (they are typically received 3 months prior to your client's birthday), he or she can file Form SSA-7050-F3 or Form SSA-7004-PC-0P1 (appendix 4). The Social Security office will then provide data relating to your client's earnings history and estimated primary insurance amount. Also note that much information can be garnered on line at http:\\www.ssa.gov.

Cost-of-living Adjustments. Old-age insurance benefits are increased automatically each January as long as there has been an increase in the Consumer Price Index (CPI) for the one-year period ending in the third quarter of the prior year. The increase is the same as the increase in the CPI since the last cost-of-living adjustment, rounded to the nearest 0.1 percent.

There is one exception to this adjustment. In any year that the combined reserves of the Social Security trust funds drop below certain levels, the cost-of-living adjustment will be limited to the lesser of the increase in the CPI or the increase in national wages used to adjust the wage base for Social Security taxes. When benefit increases have been based on wage levels, future cost-of-living increases can be larger than changes in the CPI to compensate for the lower benefit increases in those years when the CPI was not used. However, this extra cost-of-living increase can be made only in years when the reserve is equal to at least 32 percent of expected benefits.

Benefits Taken Early. If a worker elects to receive retirement benefits prior to age 65 (full retirement age for those born in 1937 or earlier), benefits are permanently reduced by 5/9 of one percent for every month that the early retirement precedes age 65. For example, for a worker who retires at age 62, the monthly benefit will be only 80 percent of that worker's PIA. (Note that table 22-2 shows the full retirement age for other years of birth.) A spouse who elects retirement benefits prior to age 65 will have benefits reduced by

25/36 of one percent per month; a widow or widower will have benefits reduced by 19/40 of one percent per month. In the latter case, benefits at age 60 will be 71 1/2 percent of the worker's PIA. If the widow or widower elects benefits between the ages of 50 and 60 because of disability, there is no further reduction.

TABLE 22-2	
Year of Birth	Social Security Normal Retirement Age
1937 and earlier	65 years
1938	65 and 2 months
1939	65 and 4 months
1940	65 and 6 months
1941	65 and 8 months
1942	65 and 10 months
1943–54	66 years
1955	66 and 2 months
1956	66 and 4 months
1957	66 and 6 months
1958	66 and 8 months
1959	66 and 10 months
1960 and after	67 years

Your Financial Services Practice: Helping clients with the decision of when to start Social Security benefits. Many clients wonder what is the best time to take Social Security benefits. Nearly half of males and 60 percent of females get benefits at age 62, but it is questionable whether this is a prudent idea. From an economic standpoint, the answer depends on certain factors. A break-even analysis needs to be conducted to decide what is best for your client. On one hand, if he or she takes benefits early (for example, age 62), he or she will receive only 80 percent of what they would have been entitled to at age 65 (if age 65 was their full retirement age). On the other hand, they will receive 36 additional checks by starting benefits at age 62. The Social Security administration is often quoted as saying the break-even age is 76. That is, people who die earlier than this age would have been better off economically taking a reduced benefit at 62. On the other hand, people who live longer than the break-even age would be better off taking full benefits at 65. The age of 76, however, is not etched in stone. Several factors can affect the calculation, such as whether funds taken early are invested and the discount rate used. (More detailed information can be obtained in *Financial Decision Making at Retirement*, Littell et al, The American College.)

One final note: economics alone will not always be determinative. Consider the following questions:

- Does the client need the money early from a cash flow perspective or can other investments be used to bridge the gap to normal retirement age?
- At what age will the client retire?
- What are the client's desires?

Delayed Retirement. Workers who delay applying for retirement benefits until after age 65 are eligible for an increased benefit. For persons born from 1917–1924, the increase is 3 percent for each year of delay up to age 70. For persons born from 1925–1926, the increase is 3 1/2 percent per year. To encourage delayed retirement, the percentage will gradually increase to 8 percent by 2009.

Earnings Test. Benefits are reduced for Social Security beneficiaries under the age of 65 if they have work wages that exceed a specified level. The rationale behind having such a reduction tied to wages, referred to as an earnings test, is that Social Security benefits are intended to replace lost wages but not other income such as dividends or interest. In 2001, Social Security beneficiaries under age 65 are allowed earnings of $10,680. This figure also is adjusted annually on the basis of national wage levels. If a beneficiary earns in excess of the allowable amount, his or her Social Security benefit is reduced. For persons under age 65, the reduction is $1 for every $2 of excess earnings. Social Security beneficiaries aged 65 or older can earn any amount of wages without a reduction of benefits.

The reduction in a retired worker's benefits resulting from excess earnings is applied to all benefits paid to the family. If large enough, this reduction may totally eliminate all benefits otherwise payable to the worker and family members. In contrast, excess earnings of family members are charged against their individual benefits only. For example, a widowed mother who holds a job outside the home may lose her mother's benefit, but any benefits received by her children will be unaffected.

Social Security Coverage

Although most workers in the United States are covered under the Social Security program, some clients may belong to a group that is not covered. Let's examine these groups and what, if any, alternatives they offer to Social Security coverage.

One of the largest groups of employees not covered by Social Security are most civilian employees of the federal government who were employed by the government *prior to* 1984 (those hired after 1984 and others who elected Social Security coverage are covered by Social Security). Most of those hired before 1984 are typically covered under the Civil Service Retirement System, which is similar to the Social Security system.

A second group generally not covered by Social Security is the railroad workers. Railroad workers are covered under a benefit system similar to Social Security known as the Railroad Retirement Act.

Employees of some state and local governments and subdivisions of state and local governments make up a third group that is not covered by Social Security. These employees are covered under a state or local pension system. Information about a particular state or local system can be obtained from the human resources department of the applicable governmental agency. Note, however, that most state and local governments and their subdivisions have entered into voluntary agreements with the Social Security Administration resulting in Social Security coverage for employees.

Other groups not covered by Social Security include ministers who elect out of coverage because of religious principles or conscience and some American citizens who work abroad for foreign affiliates of U.S. employers.

Medicare

In addition to understanding the amount of retirement benefits provided by Social Security and the people who are covered by Social Security, retirement planners need to understand the Medicare system.

Eligibility for Medicare

Part A, the hospital portion of Medicare, is available at no monthly cost to any person aged 65 or older as long as the person is entitled to monthly retirement benefits under Social Security or the railroad retirement program. In addition, civilian employees of the federal government aged 65 or older are also eligible. Workers do not have to be actually receiving retirement benefits, but they must be fully insured for purposes of retirement benefits. In addition, dependents aged 65 or older of fully insured workers aged 62 or older are also eligible for Medicare.

Most persons who are 65 or over and do not meet the previously discussed eligibility requirements may voluntarily enroll in Medicare. However, they must pay a monthly premium. In addition, these persons must also enroll in part B.

Any person eligible for part A of Medicare is also eligible for part B. However, a monthly premium must be paid for part B. This monthly premium—$50.00 in 2001—is adjusted annually and represents only about 25 percent of the cost of the benefits provided. The remaining cost of the program is financed from the federal government's general revenues.

Persons receiving Social Security or railroad retirement benefits are automatically enrolled in Medicare if they are eligible. If they do not want part B, they must elect out in writing. Other persons eligible for Medicare must apply for part B benefits. Anyone who elects out of part B or who does not enroll when initially eligible, may later apply for benefits during the general enrollment period between January 1 and March 31 of each year. However, the monthly premium will be increased by 10 percent for each 12-month period during which the person was eligible but failed to enroll.

Medicare: Part A Benefits

Part A of Medicare provides benefits for expenses incurred in hospitals (for stays up to 90 days in each benefit period), skilled nursing facilities (if a physician certifies that skilled nursing or therapeutic care is needed for a condition that was treated in a hospital within the last 30 days), and hospices (for terminally ill persons who have a life expectancy of 6 months or less). In addition, the first 100 home health service visits following a hospital or skilled nursing facility stay are covered. Benefit periods are renewable, that is, a new benefit period starts 60 days after your client is out of the hospital. Also, benefit periods can be supplemented by 60 lifetime reserve days. These are not renewable but do represent a bank of days that can be factored out of the 90-day benefit period. In order for benefits to be paid, the facility or agency providing benefits must participate in the Medicare program. Virtually all hospitals are participants, as are most other facilities or agencies that meet the requirements of Medicare.

Medicare: Part B Benefits

Part B, the supplementary medical insurance portion of Medicare, provides benefits for the following medical expenses not covered under part A:

- physicians' and surgeons' fees that result from house calls, office visits, or services provided in a hospital or other institution (under certain circumstances benefits are also provided for the services of chiropractors, podiatrists, and optometrists)
- diagnostic tests in a hospital or in a physician's office
- physical therapy in a physician's office, or as an outpatient of a hospital, skilled nursing facility, or an approved clinic, agency, or public-health agency
- home health care not covered under part A
- drugs and biologicals that cannot be self-administered
- radiation therapy

- medical supplies, such as surgical dressings, splints, and casts
- rental of medical equipment, such as oxygen tents, hospital beds, and wheelchairs
- prosthetic devices, such as artificial heart valves or lenses after a cataract operation
- ambulance service if a patient's condition does not permit the use of other methods of transportation
- pneumococcal vaccine and its administration
- mammograms

With some exceptions, part B pays 80 percent of the approved charges for covered medical expenses after the satisfaction of a $100 annual deductible.

Exclusions. Although the preceding list may appear to be comprehensive, numerous medical products and services are not covered by part B. Some of these products and services that represent significant expenses for the elderly include the following:

- drugs and biologicals that can be self-administered
- routine physical, eye, and hearing examinations
- routine foot care
- immunizations, except pneumococcal vaccinations or immunization required because of an injury or immediate risk of infection
- cosmetic surgery unless it is needed because of an accidental injury or to improve the function of a malformed part of the body
- dental care unless it involves jaw or facial bone surgery or the setting of fractures
- custodial care
- eyeglasses, hearing aids, and orthopedic shoes

In addition, benefits are not provided to persons who are eligible for workers' compensation or treated in government hospitals. Benefits are provided only for services received in the United States, except for physicians' services and ambulance services rendered for a hospitalization that are covered in Mexico or Canada under part A.

FINDING OUT ABOUT PENSION BENEFITS

Information concerning the benefits available from the employer's pension plan is typically provided to plan participants on an annual basis. A client participating in an employer-sponsored plan usually receives a statement containing the following information:

- vesting percentage (all participants are 100 percent vested at retirement)
- dollar amount of pension benefit from plan at normal retirement age in current (uninflated) dollars (defined-benefit plans)
- current account balance (defined-contribution plans)
- estimated Social Security benefit
- benefit to spouse from pension plan should the employee die prior to normal retirement age
- value of contributions made by the plan participant and other payments that are considered part of the participant's basis

If your client's employer does not provide an annual benefit statement, the planner should have the client request one. Under the Employee Retirement Income Security Act (ERISA), most employers (the federal government and some other employers are exempted) are required to provide benefit statements on request (no more than one per year, however).

Another way to analyze your client's pension benefits is to examine your client's summary plan description (SPD). ERISA requires that most employers (the federal government and some other employers are exempted) provide a description of the plan to employees. The SPD will contain a wealth of information about your client's options under the plan, including information about

- early retirement
- normal retirement age
- benefit accruals after normal retirement (defined-benefit plans)
- contributions after normal retirement (defined-contribution plans)
- annuity options available at retirement
- lump-sum payouts (if allowed)
- claims procedures for denial of benefits

1099R forms

In addition to the summary plan description and the annual benefit statements, the employer will supply *1099R forms*. These forms are filed with the IRS and sent to any participant or participant's beneficiary who receives a lump-sum or periodic distribution. They will indicate the amount of the distribution and whether any portion of the distribution will not be subject to tax.

The following worksheet should be used to help you in your fact-finding process.

```
┌─────────────────────────────────────────────────────────────────────┐
│ WORKSHEET 22-1                                                         │
│ Employer-Provided Documents Used for Retirement Planning              │
├─────────────────────────────────────────────────────────────────────┤
│ Name of Plan Administrator_____            │
│ Phone Number (____)_____             │
│                                                                       │
│ 1.  Summary Plan Description                            [  ]          │
│ 2.  Annual Benefit Statements                           [  ]          │
│ 3.  1099R Form                                          [  ]          │
└─────────────────────────────────────────────────────────────────────┘
```

WILL EMPLOYER PENSIONS AND SOCIAL SECURITY PROVIDE ENOUGH RETIREMENT INCOME?

Clients having retirement expectations need to plan so their expectations can be fulfilled. In many ways, it is similar to taking a trip. Just knowing that you want to go somewhere is not enough to get you there. You have to make plans depending on the availability of funds at the time the trip will be made. The situation is the same in retirement—what can be done in retirement depends on the funds the retiree has accumulated. Unfortunately, some clients do not approach you about planning for retirement until it is too late to accumulate sufficient retirement assets. These clients probably assumed that the combination of pension benefits and Social Security would be adequate for retirement needs. In most cases, however, Social Security and pension benefits will not provide enough retirement income to enable a retiree to continue his or her preretirement standard of living. Consider the following:

- Most defined-benefit plans are geared toward providing a replacement ratio between only 40 and 60 percent of final-average salary. This amount generally will only be paid if the employee has 25 or more years of service with the employer (for employees whose service is less, the replacement ratio is reduced accordingly). Furthermore, the defined-benefit pension is often reduced for payments to Social Security, and under typical circumstances the actual replacement ratio can drop to between 20 and 30 percent of final-average salary for a rank-and-file employee.

- Defined-contribution plans are not protected against preretirement inflation. Defined-contribution plans can only provide benefits based on the average earnings of your client, which are less than the earnings in your client's final years. This means that half the contributions to your client's account were made based on salaries that were lower than the average salary your client earned during his or her participation in the plan. These contributions based on lower "uninflated salaries" tend to limit the replacement ratio in a defined-contribution plan. What's more, poor investment performance of the defined-contribution account or lack of contributions for employees who joined a defined-contribution plan later in their careers also tends to limit the amounts that are available under these plans.

- Most profit-sharing plans allow employers to skip annual contributions and allow employees to make in-service withdrawals.

- Assuming the employer's plan has a loan provision, any loaned amount may reduce the pool of plan assets available at retirement if the loan was taken out within 5 years of retirement, since the outstanding balance will not be distributed to the participant.

- Employers may terminate their qualified plans leaving employees to continue working without any future benefits or contributions.

- Social Security is geared toward providing benefits for the lower paid. For example, a person with a $10,000 salary prior to retirement will receive approximately a 50 percent income replacement ratio from Social Security whereas a person with a $100,000 salary will only receive a 10 percent income-replacement ratio.

- Most nonqualified plans provide for abundant retirement savings for an employee. Retirement planners must be wary of certain traps awaiting their clients. First, lump-sum distributions from a nonqualified plan will be subject to significantly more taxes than similar distributions from a qualified plan, because qualified plan distributions are eligible for favorable 10-year averaging and nonqualified distributions are not. Second, retirement funds are more secure in a qualified plan than in a nonqualified plan. Promised benefits from a nonqualified plan are subject to loss for a variety of reasons such as

  - *The nonqualified plan may contain a forfeiture provision.* For example, the plan may provide that benefits are forfeited if the employee terminates employment prior to age 65.

  - *The nonqualified plan will typically not pay benefits if the employer goes bankrupt.* Nonqualified plan funds are typically held as corporate assets, which are subject to the claims of corporate creditors.

  - *Benefits payable under a nonqualified plan may be defaulted by an employer who has not prefunded the plan and who lacks current resources to pay.*

Case Study

The following case study illustrates the fact that the combination of just pensions and Social Security will not provide an adequate retirement benefit.

Gene Splicer went to work as a biologist for DNA Corporation in 1969 for a $10,000 salary. Gene's salary has increased at an annual rate of 7 percent over his 32 years with DNA and in 2001, Gene, aged 65, earned $81,443. During his tenure with DNA, a 7-percent-of-salary contribution was made annually on Gene's behalf into a money-purchase plan that earned 7 percent interest. The amount of money in Gene's plan in 2001 was $182,450. Gene has approached you about retirement and has disclosed that he has always believed that his pension and Social Security would be enough to sustain him through retirement. Thus, he has virtually no personal savings (the personal savings he had managed to accumulate were recently spent on his children's education). Gene would like answers to the following questions:

- How much per month will the $182,450 money-purchase plan provide if an annuity is purchased that provides for equal payments to Gene's spouse should he die first?
- How much Social Security will Gene and his (nonworking) spouse receive?
- Will these amounts be enough to sustain Gene's current standard of living through retirement?

For Gene and his wife (both aged 65) the $182,450 account balance in his money-purchase plan will provide a $1,976 a month benefit in the form of a 100 percent joint and survivor benefit. Gene and his wife can also expect to receive an additional $1,752 a month ($21,024 combined annual benefit) from Social Security (based on his most recent Social Security benefit statement). The combination of the $1,976 pension benefit and $1,752 Social Security benefit will give Gene a gross monthly salary of $3,728. Gene's current gross monthly salary is $6,787, which is about twice the amount he will receive in retirement! Gene's replacement ratio will be an inadequate percentage of his final-average salary. Gene will have to suffer drastic cutbacks in his standard of living during the retirement years.

**YOUR FINANCIAL SERVICES PRACTICE:
PLANNING FOR CLIENTS WHO HAVE PROCRASTINATED**

The client who starts planning for retirement within a few years of the retirement date is precluded from pursuing options that could have been available with a minimal amount of planning and preparation. These clients have lost the ability to set aside savings on a systematic basis and to let compound interest work for them. This does not mean, however, that planning cannot be conducted for them. Important decisions must be made about distributions from qualified plans, liquidation of personal assets, and investment of any private savings. In addition, developing a retirement plan for the client who has procrastinated includes determining what funds are available for retirement and creating strategies even if the funds are inadequate.

One such strategy calls for the planner to suggest that the client postpone retirement. The combined effect of both lengthening the accumulation period and shortening the retirement period is financially desirable. If delaying retirement from his or her current job is not feasible, the client can achieve similar results by working for another employer after forced retirement. A second strategy is to recommend that the client move to an area with a lower cost of living. This move will enable the client to stretch his or her retirement dollars. By freeing up some of the equity in the home, the client can make available assets for investment purposes. In addition to recommending these strategies, it is an essential part of the planner's job to help the client change his or her expectations about retirement. By forcing the client to look realistically at the lifestyle he or she will be able to afford, you can save your client from overspending during the early retirement years and, thus, from becoming financially destitute in the later retirement years.

PRIVATE SAVINGS

Clients commonly have savings for retirement even before they seek help in retirement planning. These savings must be considered for planning purposes. Typically, these savings will be inadequate to fully fund the retirement need and additional saving will be required. Finally, the pattern of saving used by the client provides the planner with good ideas about potential investments that the client may be comfortable with for retirement-accumulation purposes. (*Planning Note:* One saving technique that should be suggested to clients is to have any income earned on investments immediately reinvested in the accumulation vehicle, such as dividend reinvestments. These convenient reinvestments promote long-term saving because the client never has the chance to spend the money.)

Clients will typically have retirement savings in one or more of the following vehicles:

- *IRAs*—IRAs can contain both private savings and amounts rolled over from a former employer's qualified plan. In addition, IRAs can contain funds that will be subject to taxation at distribution and funds that will not be taxed because they were originally contributed on an after-tax basis. (*Planning Note:* If the client intends to make both deductible and nondeductible contributions, separate IRAs should be established for each type of contribution to simplify record keeping.)

- *Roth IRAs*—The unique thing about Roth IRAs is that funds received from these accounts are generally not subject to tax.

- *Retirement Annuity Plans*—Your client is likely to have a personally owned deferred-annuity contract issued by a life insurance company and designed to accept contributions over a period of years. Upon the individual's retirement, the accumulated sum can be either converted to an annuity or withdrawn in a lump sum.

- *Personally Owned Life Insurance*—Upon reaching retirement, an individual often finds that the amount of cash value life insurance carried on his or her life is more than adequate for the future needs of providing protection for survivors or for estate liquidity purposes. Thus, the policy surrender value for one or more policies can be taken either in the form of an annuity or as a lump sum used for investment in alternative income-producing investment vehicles.

- *Financial Assets*—Many clients have accumulated a portfolio of stocks, bonds, mutual funds, master limited partnership units, unit trust shares, real estate investment trust shares, ownership interests in nontraded limited partnerships, CDs, or other investment assets.

- *Tangible Assets*—Some individuals have acquired considerable tangible investment assets. These can take the form of investment real estate, precious metals or gemstones, art, or other collectibles. (*Planning Note:* Most tangible assets require an annual cash outlay for their protection. This outlay could be for insurance, storage costs, or other expenses associated with their ownership. Unless the client's income level exceeds the amount needed for maintaining the retirement standard of living, these negative cash-flow investments become candidates for resale when the client nears retirement. This transaction will not only eliminate the cash drain but more importantly convert the investment into an income-producing form.)

CHAPTER REVIEW

Answers to the review questions and the self-test questions start on page 673.

Key Terms

1099R forms

Review Questions

22-1.   What are the eligibility requirements for retirement benefits under Social Security?

22-2.   Identify the dependents of a worker that are eligible for Social Security retirement benefits.

22-3.   How is Social Security adjusted for changes in the cost of living?

22-4.   Robert Rose, whose Social Security full retirement age is 65, has decided to take early retirement when he reaches age 63. By what percentage will Robert's benefit be reduced if he elects to receive Social Security at age 63?

22-5.   Jane Maple (born in 1923) plans on taking deferred retirement from her employer and starting her benefit at age 68. What percentage will Jane's benefit be increased?

22-6.   Describe the eligibility requirements for part A and part B of Medicare.

22-7.   What benefits are available under part A of Medicare?

22-8.   a.   What benefits are available under part B of Medicare?
        b.   What benefits are not provided under part B of Medicare?

22-9.   What resources are available to help a planner understand a client's pension benefit?

22-10. Why will the combination of Social Security and employer-sponsored pension benefits alone be inadequate for a retiree?

22-11. What strategies can be suggested to help a client who has inadequate retirement savings at retirement time?

22-12. What investment vehicles are typically used to invest a client's retirement savings?

Self-Test Questions

T   F   22-1.   When people use the term *Social Security,* they are actually referring to the old-age, survivors, disability, and health insurance programs of the federal government.

T   F   22-2.   Credit for Social Security eligibility purposes is based on years of coverage.

T   F   22-3.   A worker with the appropriate level of wages can receive credit for four quarters in a year, even if the worker had earnings in only one month during the year.

T   F   22-4.   A person is fully insured for purposes of receiving Social Security retirement benefits if that person has credit for 40 quarters of coverage.

T   F   22-5.   A worker who is fully insured is eligible for reduced monthly Social Security retirement benefits as early as age 55.

T   F   22-6.   A spouse aged 62 or older is entitled to full Social Security benefits based on the other spouse's eligibility for Social Security retirement benefits.

T   F   22-7.   Social Security retirement benefits are generally increased each year to reflect increases in the consumer price index.

T   F   22-8.   A worker who retires at age 62 and elects Social Security coverage will receive 50 percent of the benefit that he or she would have received at age 65.

T   F   22-9.   Workers who delay applying for benefits until after age 65 receive the same Social Security retirement benefit they would have received if they had started benefit payments at age 65.

T   F   22-10. All civilian federal employees are now covered by the Social Security system.

T   F   22-11. Part A of Medicare is available at no monthly cost if a person is entitled to monthly benefits under Social Security.

T   F   22-12. Any person eligible for part A of Medicare is eligible for part B of Medicare at no cost.

T   F   22-13. If requested, an annual statement of pension benefits must be provided by an employer.

T   F   22-14. A retirement planner can learn a great deal about his or her client's retirement benefit by examining the client's summary plan description.

T   F   22-15. Participants of a qualified plan receiving a distribution receive form 1099R, which indicates the amount of the distribution and whether any portion of it is excluded from tax.

T   F   22-16.   An integrated defined-benefit plan typically provides a replacement ratio of 60 percent of final-average salary for a rank-and-file employee.

T   F   22-17.   Defined-contribution plans are protected against preretirement inflation because they provide benefits based on a client's final salary.

T   F   22-18.   Profit-sharing plans may allow employers to skip annual contributions.

T   F   22-19.   The combination of a pension benefit and a Social Security benefit will generally be adequate to provide the proper amount of retirement income.

T   F   22-20.   One important facet of developing a retirement plan for a client who has not saved for retirement is to force the client to look realistically at the lifestyle he or she will be able to afford.

T   F   22-21.   If your client makes both deductible and nondeductible IRA contributions, the funds should be commingled for simplification purposes.

Determining Postretirement Monetary Needs: Case Study

Learning Objectives
An understanding of the material in this chapter should enable the student to

23-1. Explain the steps used when determining the amount of the postretirement monetary need.

23-2. Discuss the methods that can be used for establishing a savings schedule.

Chapter Outline

In this chapter, we turn our attention from the various pieces of the retirement-planning puzzle (the expected standard of living, the expected retirement date, the expected inflation rate, and the sources of retirement income) to a method for actually solving the puzzle of putting together a retirement plan. Putting together a retirement plan for a client is basically a three-step process. In the first step, the planner conducts fact finding to become familiar with the client's feelings, goals, and factual circumstances. In the second step, the planner must calculate the amount of the client's retirement need. This process is complicated by the mathematical equations that are involved, because planners must account for the time value of money and inflation (in other words, a dollar today is not the same as a dollar tomorrow). The third and final step in putting together a retirement plan is to establish a savings schedule and investment portfolio for the client so he or she can fund the amount of the needed savings.

Because the best way to understand these steps is to examine how they apply in a particular situation, this chapter presents a case study that examines the retirement needs of Joe and Betty Brown.

FACT FINDING

Your clients, Joe and Betty Brown, have provided the following information:

- Joe is married and his wife, Betty, is a homemaker.
- Both Joe and Betty are currently 55 years old.
- Joe expects to retire at age 65.
- Joe earns $54,000 a year.
- Joe is in the 28 percent tax bracket.
- Joe's company has a defined-benefit pension plan. If Joe continues employment until age 65, he can expect to receive a $20,000-a-year pension. (That figure is in today's dollars; his actual pension at retirement will be larger.) Joe's pension will be payable in the form of a 50 percent joint and survivor annuity (see chapter 25). Joe's pension will not be offset by Social Security payments.

- Joe owns $150,000 in common stock, which pays $6,000 per year in dividends. Joe has reinvested all aftertax income from the portfolio every year except one, when he and Betty spent the money on a trip to Europe.
- Joe owns some non-income-producing assets, such as a home (current market value $250,000) and personal effects (worth about $100,000). The mortgage on the home will be paid off in 2 years.
- Both Joe and Betty have a fairly sophisticated understanding of investments.
- Joe and Betty have been married for 30 years, and the marriage is very stable.
- Both Joe and Betty are in good health.
- Both Joe and Betty feel they have average, or better than average, life expectancies.

FINANCING THE DESIRED RETIREMENT LIFESTYLE

Several steps must be taken to determine the finances necessary for providing Joe and Betty with a continuation of their current lifestyle throughout retirement. These steps include

(1) adding up the existing sources of retirement income
(2) finding the amount of income needed to achieve the desired retirement lifestyle
(3) estimating the retirement-income status (RIS)
(4) determining what resources need inflation protection
(5) calculating the target amount

Step 1: Adding Up the Existing Sources of Retirement Income

Joe indicates that he will have the following sources of income:

- *Social Security*—The Social Security Administration has informed Joe that he will receive $1,407 monthly ($938 for Joe and $469 for Betty) in Social Security benefits (current dollars) at age 65. This translates into a $16,884 annual income in current dollars.
- *Pension*—Joe's pension is $20,000 a year in current dollars.
- *Private Savings*—Joe does not intend to liquidate his $150,000 equity portfolio. Joe will, however, use the $6,000 in dividends for living expenses during retirement. Because he has no desire to either take the equity out of his home or sell any personal effects, these assets will not be used to produce a stream of income for retirement.

Step 2: Finding the Amount of Income Needed to Achieve the Desired Retirement Lifestyle

To find the amount of income needed to achieve the desired retirement lifestyle, you can either apply the desired replacement ratio to your client's salary or use the expense-method approach.

Replacement-Ratio Method

If the client expects an increase in his or her standard of living, a growth factor must be incorporated to determine Joe's final salary. Joe, however, would like his retirement income to provide a standard of living comparable to his existing standard of living and does not need to apply a growth factor to his current lifestyle. Because he will no longer be saving for retirement, paying Social Security taxes, or incurring work-related expenses, Joe estimates that 80 percent of his preretirement income from employment will be sufficient. In other words, in today's dollars Joe wants to have $43,200 (80 percent of his current salary of $54,000) when he retires. In tomorrow's dollars, Joe is looking to have this amount keep pace with inflation. (For example, if inflation rose 4 percent per year for 10 years, Joe would need $63,947 to have his current purchasing power during the first year of his retirement.)

Example: Suppose instead that Joe had anticipated that his standard of living would increase 2 percent per year until retirement. (In other words, his salary would increase 2 percent more than inflation, and Joe would use the commensurate increase in real income to improve his lifestyle.) If this is the case, a growth factor of 2 percent should be applied to Joe's current $54,000 salary using the future value formula discussed in chapter 21:

$$PV = PV(1 + r)^n$$

where n = number of years before target retirement date

r = inflation rate

(Example cont'd):

In this case, however, instead of inflation the r would stand for the desired growth rate that the client expects (2 percent). Under these circumstances, the salary considered would be

$$V = \$54,000(1+r)^n$$
$$= \$54,000(1+.02)^{10}$$
$$= \$65,826$$

Because Joe only needs 80 percent of this salary in current dollars, Joe would want $52,660 in today's dollars when he retires in order to maintain his anticipated purchasing power. In tomorrow's dollars, Joe would want this amount to keep pace with inflation.

Since Joe had not anticipated any real growth or inflation factor, we can use the $43,200 target achieved by applying an 80 percent replacement ratio to his current salary when estimating Joe's retirement income status.

Expense-Method-Approach

If Joe were to use the expense-method approach to determine the amount of income he would need during retirement, he and Betty would sit down with the planner to estimate their expenses in their first year of retirement. Let's assume that Joe will have annual expenses of $43,200 (the same as the replacement-ratio method). Note, however, that the expense-method approach and the replacement-ratio method will seldom provide the same number.

Step 3: Estimating the Retirement-Income Status (RIS)

To determine the amount of additional savings he will need to accumulate, Joe must subtract his annual target for retirement income from his estimated amount of annual retirement income (table 23-1).

The retirement-income status (RIS) can be either a positive or negative number. A positive RIS indicates a surplus because current sources exceed the target amount. A negative RIS indicates a deficit and suggests the need for additional savings. When the RIS is negative, it will be labeled RID (retirement-income deficit) and used with a positive sign to avoid dealing with negative numbers.

TABLE 23-1 **Calculation of Annual Retirement-Income Status** **(in today's dollars)**		
Estimated annual retirement income		
Social Security	$16,884	
Pension	20,000	
Private savings (dividends)	6,000	$42,884
Annual target retirement income		$43,200
Annual retirement-income status (RIS)		$ – 316

In current dollars, Joe appears to be in the enviable position of having nearly adequate retirement income to meet his desired retirement standard of living (a RID of only $316). However, this may be misleading because these values ignore the effects of inflation before and after retirement.

Step 4: Determining What Resources Need Inflation Protection

Up to this point, we have determined that Joe will have a $316 gap between what his Social Security, pension, and private savings will provide and what his desired annual income during retirement will be. At this point, we have a partial picture of the retirement need for Joe and Betty. To calculate the true retirement need, however, we must provide inflation protection, both before and after retirement, for all Joe's retirement resources. In chapter 21, when the effect of inflation was explored, it was determined that a 4 percent rate of inflation could be used as an estimate. Using that estimate, let's take a closer look at each of the retirement resources.

Social Security

To a certain extent, Social Security is inflation protected because it is geared toward increases in the consumer price index (CPI). This assumes, however, that the law will remain unchanged and that the CPI accurately reflects inflation as it affects Joe. For Joe's purposes, we can assume that the law will not change and that the indexation of Social Security is a reasonable reflection of inflation increases.

Pension

We can assume that Joe's pension is inflation protected until retirement because it is a defined-benefit plan based on final-average salary. We cannot, however, assume any inflation protection after retirement. For this reason, in addition to funding the retirement-income deficit (RID), Joe will need to fund an amount that can be used to bolster his non-inflation-proof pension benefits (that is, to keep pension purchasing power constant). This amount is called the decline in purchasing power (DIPP).

Dividends

Dividend income from a stock portfolio is generally considered to be inflation protected if the principal is left intact. For Joe's purposes, we can assume his dividend income will be inflation protected both in the preretirement and postretirement periods. The fact that Joe is not liquidating his principal provides a hedge against inflation, because he can annuitize the principal if he needs additional retirement income.

Retirement-Income Deficit (RID)

Joe must account for the effect of preretirement and postretirement inflation on the purchasing power of the income from the monies that he will accumulate to fund the RID. For example, when a 4 percent rate of inflation is added to the RID ($316 in today's dollars), the RID grows to $468 by the time Joe reaches age 65.

Table 23-2 summarizes the impact of inflation on Joe's resources.

Step 5: Calculating the Target Amount

The next step is to examine how much Joe will need to accumulate to fund the RID and the pension DIPP. This sum is the target amount of funds that Joe needs in addition to his current stock portfolio to achieve his desired standard of living during retirement. To accomplish this, the planner must make many assumptions about the future. In addition to estimating inflation at, for example, 4 percent, assumptions must be made about the amount of investment return that Joe will earn on accumulated funds and about the method Joe will use to liquidate his saved funds.

Investment Return

Generally, a higher rate of return means a greater variability of the return and hence a greater risk. Thus, if your client seeks a higher return on invested

TABLE 23-2
Inflation's Impact on Joe's Resources

Source of Income	Inflation Protected
Social Security benefits	Yes
Pension	Not after retirement
Dividends	Yes
Retirement-income deficit	No

invested monies, there will be a commensurate increase in the likelihood that the targeted amount of retirement funds will not be accumulated. A general guideline for this risk-return tradeoff is that the more important the financial objective is to the client, the less the risk that should be assumed. Some planners believe that accumulating funds for retirement is the most important reason for investing and would recommend investment vehicles that have relatively low risk. They argue that because Joe's retirement date is only 10 years away, he will have little opportunity to make up any investment losses that might occur during this relatively short period. For this reason, a conservative investment strategy might be best. Others argue that because Joe and Betty are likely to live many years in retirement, it is not the time to change strategies because the holding period will still be significant. In the end, it is the clients' decision to make after both schools of thought have been explained to them.

An additional consideration is whether Joe can use a tax-deferred investment vehicle, such as a traditional IRA, or can make a nondeductible voluntary contribution to his pension plan during the accumulation period. If so, earnings on monies set aside would accumulate free of current income taxation. With such a vehicle, 8 percent could be earned on relatively low-risk investments. If currently taxable investments of the same risk characteristic were employed, then the return (r) times one minus the client's marginal tax rate (t), or $r(1-t)$, would be earned after tax. In other words, because Joe is in the 28 percent marginal tax bracket, he would have an aftertax yield of 5.76 percent on an investment that yields 8 percent interest before tax [$.08(1-.28)$].

Liquidation of Funds

Several paths can be followed when using the funds accumulated to meet Joe's retirement-income deficit and to meet the decline in purchasing power of Joe's pension. One such option is to not liquidate the assets at all. Under this option, Joe will need to accumulate a fund that would earn sufficient income each year without reducing the accumulated capital. A second alternative would involve accumulating a fund that could be systematically liquidated over a specified number of years. At the end of the specified time, the capital would be depleted. (*Planning Note:* The longer the liquidation period that is assumed for depleting assets, the greater the amount of funds that will be needed for the retirement target.)

YOUR FINANCIAL SERVICES PRACTICE:
PROTECTING CLIENTS FROM OUTLIVING INCOME

A planner should exercise caution when liquidating a client's assets over a specified period of time. Many planners mistakenly rely on the figures given in mortality tables to determine the liquidation period. The problem with this approach is that one-half of the population lives beyond the tabular life expectancy. For this reason, many planners underestimate the client's life expectancy when determining the liquidation period. Even when extending the liquidation period beyond the tabular life expectancies, planners can encounter trouble. Statistics show that 20 percent of the people who reach age 65 will live to age 95.

One way for a planner to be cautious is by recommending that a client purchase a life annuity with his or her accumulated savings. A life annuity permits clients to continue to receive payments until they die, regardless of how long they live. In those cases when clients live beyond the life expectancy on which the annuity was based, the client experiences what is known as mortality gain. The insurance company does not necessarily lose money when it pays mortality gain, however, because theoretically an equal number of people die before the life expectancy on which the annuity was calculated and experience mortality loss.

The Mathematics

Once the planner has made assumptions about the investment return and the liquidation period, these assumptions as well as the client's retirement-income deficit (RID) and decline in purchasing power (DIPP) are applied in mathematical equations to calculate the client's target accumulation. To simplify the process, let's do two separate calculations, one for the RID fund and one for the DIPP.

Amount Needed to Fund the Retirement-Income-Deficit (RID) Fund. Let's assume that Joe wants to have the inflation-protected income stream last for only a specified period, such as 25 years from the date of his retirement, at which point the fund would be exhausted. In this situation, you need to calculate the stream of payments that Joe would like to receive from an inflation-protected retirement-income deficit and discount the payments to the value at retirement age assuming the principal will be paid out along with the interest. Equation 23-1 is the appropriate equation.

EQUATION 23-1
Funds Needed at the Client's Retirement Date for Total
RID—Liquidating Principal*

$$\begin{array}{c} \text{Funds needed} \\ \text{(RID funds)} \end{array} = \begin{array}{c} \text{Retirement} \\ \text{date RID} \end{array} \times (1+\text{int}) \times \left[\frac{1-\left(\dfrac{1+\text{inf}}{1+\text{int}}\right)^n}{\text{int}-\text{inf}} \right]$$

where n = liquidation period expressed in years
       int = interest rate
       inf = inflation rate

---

*This equation calculates the funds needed to provide an income stream that is inflation protected but will be completely liquidated after a given number of years.

Assuming that inflation stays constant at 4 percent, that Joe retires at age 65 (recall that Joe's retirement-income deficit had risen from $316 to $468 at age 65), that Joe expects to liquidate the fund over 25 years, and that Joe earns an aggressive 8 percent interest after tax, Joe will need $7,717 at retirement according to the following calculation:

$$\begin{array}{c} \text{Funds needed} \\ \text{(RID fund)} \end{array} = \$468 \times (1+.08) \times \left[\frac{1-\left(\dfrac{1.04}{1.08}\right)^{25}}{.08-.04} \right]$$

$$= \$7,717$$

If Joe's desired liquidation period were 35 years with the same inflation and interest rates, he would find, using equation 23-1, that $9,264 would be the sum needed at retirement.

If Joe desires to have income growing but not to have the principal reduced, however, he must use a different equation. Equation 23-2 calculates the stream of payments Joe would like to receive from an inflation-protected retirement income deficit fund and discounts the payments to the value at retirement age assuming the principal will not be liquidated and only interest will be paid out.

EQUATION 23-2
Funds Needed at the Client's Retirement Date for Total
RID—Not Liquidating Principal*

$$\underset{\text{(RID fund)}}{\text{Funds needed}} = \text{RID} + \frac{\text{RID} \, (1 + \text{inf})}{\text{int} - \text{inf}}$$

where int = interest rate
inf = inflation rate

*This equation calculates the funds needed to provide an income stream that is inflation protected and will continue forever (no liquidation of principal). The payments will increase each year by the rate of inflation.

With the same interest and inflation assumptions, this equation becomes

$$\underset{\text{(RID fund)}}{\text{Funds needed}} = \$468 + \frac{\$468 \, (1.04)}{.08 - .04}$$

$$= \$12,636$$

Table 23-3 summarizes Joe's situation for determining the retirement-income-deficit fund.

TABLE 23-3
Retirement-Income-Deficit Fund

Liquidation Method	Sum Needed at Age 65
25-year liquidation	$ 7,717
35-year liquidation	$ 9,264
Income only	$12,636

Amount Needed to Fund the Decline in Purchasing Power (DIPP). In addition to funding the retirement-income deficit, Joe needs to set aside additional funds to maintain the purchasing power of his pension. In this case, you need to first calculate the present value of the stream of payments that Joe should be receiving from an inflation-proof pension and then determine the present value of a stream of level payments for the same period. The difference between these present values represents the supplemental funds Joe needs to make his pension benefits inflation proof. Equation 23-3 is the appropriate equation for solving this problem.

EQUATION 23-3
Funds Needed at the Client's Retirement Date for Total DIPP—Liquidating Principal*

$$
\text{DIPP} = \begin{array}{c}\text{income}\\\text{needing}\\\text{inflation}\\\text{protection}\end{array} \times (1 + \text{int}) \times \left[\frac{1 - \left(\dfrac{1 + \text{inf}}{1 + \text{int}}\right)^n}{\text{int} - \text{inf}}\right] -
$$

$$
\begin{array}{c}\text{income}\\\text{needing}\\\text{inflation}\\\text{protection}\end{array} \times (1 + \text{int}) \times \left[\frac{1 - \left(\dfrac{1}{1 + \text{int}}\right)^n}{\text{int}}\right]
$$

where n = liquidation period expressed in years
       int = interest rate
       inf = inflation rate

---

*This equation calculates the funds needed to provide an inflation-protected supplement to a level or fixed-income stream for a given number of years. This provides increasing payments to supplement the fixed-payment stream.

The income to be protected in this case is only the pension income.

Note that it is projected that Joe's pension at age 65 will have grown from $20,000 (at age 55) to $29,605, assuming a 4 percent inflation rate. Therefore, Joe will need $146,877 at retirement determined as follows:

$$
\text{DIPP} = \$29,605\,(1.08)\left[\frac{1 - \left(\dfrac{1.04}{1.08}\right)^{25}}{.08 - .04}\right] - \$29,605\,(1.08)\left[\frac{1 - \left(\dfrac{1}{1.08}\right)^{25}}{.08}\right]
$$

$$
= \$29,605\,(1.08)\,(15.26850409) - \$29,605\,(1.08)\,(10.67477619)
$$

$$
= \$488,186 - \$341,309
$$

$$
= \$146,877
$$

Using the same formula for a 35-year liquidation, the amount needed will be $213,363. If Joe desires, however, to have income growing but not have the principal reduced, he must use a different equation that will not liquidate the principal. Equation 23-4 should be used.

EQUATION 23-4
Funds Needed at the Client's Retirement Date for Total DIPP—Not Liquidating Principal*

$$\text{DIPP} = \begin{matrix} \text{income} \\ \text{needing} \\ \text{inflation} \\ \text{protection} \end{matrix} \times \left[1 + \left(\frac{1 + \text{inf}}{\text{int} - \text{inf}} \right) \right] -$$

$$\begin{matrix} \text{income} \\ \text{needing} \\ \text{inflation} \\ \text{protection} \end{matrix} \times (1 + \text{int}) \left(\frac{1}{\text{int}} \right)$$

where int = interest rate
    inf = inflation rate

*This equation calculates the funds needed to provide an inflation-protected supplement to a level or fixed-income stream for an unlimited number of years. This provides increasing payments to supplement the fixed-payment stream.

Using the same interest and inflation rate assumptions, Joe would need

$$\text{DIPP} = \$29,605 \times 1 + \left(\frac{1.04}{.04} \right) - \$29,605 \times 1.08 \times \frac{1}{.08}$$

$$= \$29,605 \times 27 - \$29,605 \times 13.5$$

$$= \$399,667$$

Table 23-4 summarizes Joe's situation for determining the decline in the purchasing power fund.

TABLE 23-4 Decline in Purchasing Power Fund	
Liquidation Method	Sum Needed at Age 65
25-year liquidation 35-year liquidation Income only	$146,877 $213,363 $399,667

Adding Up the Total Funds Needed. To determine exactly how much he will need at retirement, Joe must add together the amount necessary to fund the RID and the amount necessary to fund the DIPP. Note that Joe could choose different liquidation methods for the retirement-income-deficit fund and the decline in the purchasing-power fund. For example, he could use a 25-year liquidation for the RID fund and a 35-year liquidation for the DIPP. This method would be most appropriate if he wanted to hedge on his and Betty's life expectancy. Assuming Joe chooses the same liquidation for both, which is the more common choice, table 23-5 indicates the target amount that Joe will need to accumulate in addition to other retirement resources.

TABLE 23-5 Target Accumulation			
Liquidation Method	Retirement Income- Deficit Fund	+ Decline in Purchasing- Power Fund =	Total Target Fund
25-year 35-year Income only	$ 7,717 $ 9,264 $ 12,636	$146,877 $213,363 $399,667	$154,594 $222,627 $412,303

IMPLEMENTING A SAVINGS SCHEDULE TO FUND THE TARGET AMOUNT

Once a target has been calculated, the planner's focus turns toward using this data to set up a savings schedule. Joe could use a variety of techniques to fund his retirement target, including making a lump-sum payment from gain realized on the sale of his home and/or the liquidation of his stock portfolio. (If the portfolio is liquidated, a new target must be calculated because the old target included dividends from the portfolio as a source of retirement income.) In addition to making a lump-sum payment, Joe could fund the payments in the remaining years until retirement. The two most popular methods of doing this are (1) funding the payments on a level basis until retirement or (2) using the annual-funding method that increases payments annually to coordinate payments with increasing income (the stepped-up method).

Level Annual Funding

If Joe wanted to use level annual funding until retirement at age 65, equation 23-5 should be used. This equation essentially calculates the amount of annual payments (based on the fact that the payments made are earning compound interest) so that a level amount is saved annually.

EQUATION 23-5
Level Annual Funding*

$$\text{Annual funding} = \frac{\text{Target amount (from table 23-5)}}{\left[\dfrac{(1+\text{int})^n - 1}{\text{int}}\right] \times (1+\text{int})}$$

$$\text{where int} = \text{interest rate}$$
$$n = \text{number of years in accumulation period}$$

*This equation provides a way to calculate the level investment (savings) payment necessary to accumulate the target amount over a given number of years (n) if those funds earn interest at the assumed interest rate throughout the n-year accumulation period. (If the funds are producing taxable income, the interest rate should be an aftertax rate.) Any target amount can be used, and it should represent the dollar amount desired at the end of the n-year period.

For example, if Joe wanted to have a 25-year liquidation (target amount $154,594), he would need to make $9,881 payments at the beginning of each year until retirement, determined as follows:

$$\text{Annual funding} = \frac{\$154,594}{\left[\dfrac{(1+.08)^{10} - 1}{.08}\right] \times (1+.08)}$$

$$= \$9,881$$

Using this same formula, the level annual amount needed to fund for a 35-year liquidation target ($222,627) would be $14,229 and to fund the income-only target ($412,303) would be $26,353. Table 23-6 summarizes the level annual payments needed.

TABLE 23-6 Level Annual Funding	
Liquidation Method	Level Annual Payment
25-year liquidation	$ 9,881
35-year liquidation	$14,229
Income only	$26,353

Stepped-Up Annual Funding

If Joe wanted to use stepped-up annual funding, equation 23-6 should be used. This equation calculates an increasing scale of payments that Joe would need to fund the target amount. Equation 23-6 only gives you the first year's annual payment. To determine payments in the subsequent years of the accumulation, multiply the prior year's payment by one plus the inflation rate.

For example, if Joe wants to use a stepped-up annual funding method to coordinate savings increases with increases in salary and have a 25-year liquidation (target amount $154,594), he would need to make a first payment of $8,437, determined as follows:

$$\text{Annual funding} = \frac{\$154,594 \times (.08 - .04)}{1 - \left[\frac{1.04^{10}}{1.08}\right] \times (1.08)^{11}}$$

$$= \$8,437$$

Joe's second-year payment would be $8,774.48 ($8,437 x 1.04), and his third-year payment would be $9,125.46 ($8,774 x 1.04). Table 23-7 shows all ten of Joe's payments.

EQUATION 23-6
Stepped-Up Annual Funding*

$$\text{First-year funding} = \frac{\text{Target amount} \times (\text{int} - \text{inf})}{\left[1 - \left(\dfrac{1 + \text{inf}}{1 + \text{int}}\right)^{n}\right] \times \left[(1 + \text{int})^{(n+1)}\right]}$$

where int = interest rate

inf = inflation rate

n = number of years in accumulation period

*This equation calculates the level of first-year investment (saving) contribution to an accumulation fund that will accumulate a target amount by the end of a given period of years (n) if the fund earns the assumed interest rate throughout the n-year period and the contributions to the fund increase at the assumed inflation rate. Note that what we call inflation rate is really the growth rate of the funding contribution each year. It could be any rate the client is capable of contributing to the accumulation fund.

TABLE 23-7
25-Year Liquidation Target/Stepped-Up Payments

Age	Year	Payment
55	1	$ 8,437
56	2	8,775
57	3	9,125
58	4	9,490
59	5	9,870
60	6	10,265
61	7	10,675
62	8	11,103
63	9	11,547
64	10	12,008

**YOUR FINANCIAL SERVICES PRACTICE:
CALCULATING YOUR CLIENT'S TARGET**

When calculating your client's target, you should keep in mind the following:

- Equations 23-1 and 23-2 are applicable to the retirement-income deficit and calculate an annuity due (payments start immediately). Equations 23-3 and 23-4 are applicable to the decline in purchasing power and calculate an immediate annuity that delays the start of payments for one period (in this case one year).
- The decline in purchasing power (DIPP) is not just for pensions. The DIPP calculation also applies to any other sources of income that will not be adjusted for inflation after retirement. For example, a cash value life insurance policy that will be converted to level annuity payments at retirement to use as a retirement resource is not inflation protected after retirement and will be added to the pension income to get the income needing inflation protection in equations 23-3 and 23-4.

For the 35-year target ($222,627), an initial payment of $12,149 is required. Table 23-8 illustrates payments under this system.

**TABLE 23-8
35-Year Liquidation Target/Stepped-Up Payments**

Age	Year	Payment
55	1	$12,149
56	2	12,635
57	3	13,140
58	4	13,666
59	5	14,213
60	6	14,781
61	7	15,372
62	8	15,987
63	9	16,627
64	10	17,291

For the income-only target ($412,303), an initial payment of $22,500 is necessary. Table 23-9 illustrates the payments under this system.

TABLE 23-9
Retirement-Income-Only Target/Stepped-Up Payments

Age	Year	Payment
55	1	$22,500
56	2	23,400
57	3	24,336
58	4	25,309
59	5	26,322
60	6	27,375
61	7	28,470
62	8	29,608
63	9	30,793
64	10	32,025

SOURCES OF FUNDING

Joe will probably decide to use savings from his current income to meet whatever payment schedule he chooses. If Joe can manage to save 22.5 percent of his salary (note that this becomes increasingly feasible after mortgage payments cease), he can meet the 35-year stepped-up annual funding schedule (table 23-8). This strategy is illustrated in table 23-10.

TABLE 23-10
Joe's Savings Strategy

Age	Salary	22.5 Percent Savings	35-year Liquidation (from table 23-8)
55	$54,000	$12,150	$12,149
56	56,160	12,636	12,635
57	58,406	13,141	13,140
58	60,743	13,667	13,666
59	63,172	14,214	14,213
60	65,699	14,782	14,781
61	68,327	15,374	15,372
62	71,060	15,989	15,987
63	73,903	16,628	16,627
64	76,859	17,293	17,291

In addition to a 22.5 percent savings from Joe's current salary, Betty could become employed in an effort to earn additional savings. (Note that if this is the case, a recalculation might be necessary to account for an increased Social Security benefit as a retirement resource.) Another option is for Joe to delay retirement until beyond 65, thereby increasing the amount of time to save and decreasing the target amount.

Regardless of the method Joe and Betty choose, they will be faced with making additional investments of the funds being used to provide for the targeted amount. Planners should give advice concerning these investments and should make investment-return assumptions that are consistent with expected investment results. (See the next chapter for in-depth coverage.)

Determining Retirement Needs Using a Consumer Work Sheet

We now have the methodology, let's apply it in a worksheet.

The worksheet that follows can be used to illustrate the percentage of salary a person needs to save each year. Conceptually, this work sheet makes most of the assumptions for you—for example, an 80 percent replacement ratio (step 2) and a 25-year life expectancy (see line 8 explanation). While this simplicity can be a limitation for a planner (as discussed earlier), it can be a blessing for the weary client. For this reason, planners may want to use this type of work sheet as an informational piece in a client mailer (with strong comments about its limitations).

Example: The financial information for Bob and Donna:

- They are 15 years from retirement.
- Their current combined salary is $100,000.
- They have a defined-benefit plan of $2,000 a month ($24,000 annually).
- Their combined Social Security benefits are estimated to be $18,000.
- They have $130,000 in IRAs, 401(k) plans, and mutual funds.

Using the work sheet in table 23-11, Bob and Donna can see that they need to save 25 percent of their current salary.

Determining Retirement Needs Using a Planner's Work Sheet

The work sheets in tables 23-12, 23-13, 23-14, and 23-15 allow the planner to focus on tailoring a retirement needs analysis to a particular client. The first step is to list a variety of assumptions (these are discussed with the clients prior to filling out the work sheets). The second step is to list factors generated from time-value-of-money tables. An explanation of how each factor was determined follows the work sheets in the commentary for tables 23-16 through 23-23. The third step is to calculate the amount the clients need to save in the initial year.

Case Study Facts

Ann (aged 44) and Robert Stack (aged 46) are married and have two children. Ann and Robert both plan to retire in 19 years unless their planner counsels otherwise. Robert will be 65 and Ann will be 63 when they retire. Pertinent financial data includes the following:

- Ann earns $35,000 as a school teacher.
- Robert earns $140,000 as an engineer.
- Ann has $64,000 in her 403(b) retirement plan.
- Ann will receive a pension of $1,400 a month at age 63.
- Robert has a 401(k) plan with $120,000 in it.
- Robert has no defined-benefit plan at work.
- Robert will receive $1,100 a month from Social Security when he retires at age 65.
- Ann will receive $800 a month from Social Security when she retires at age 63.
- Both Social Security amounts are in today's dollars and, where applicable, reflect early retirement reductions.
- They have joint savings of $50,000 earmarked for retirement.
- They have sufficient savings to meet their other long-term financial goals, including sending their children to college.

After an initial interview with the planner, it was decided that the following assumptions will be used:

- an inflation rate of 4 percent
- an expected duration of retirement of 25 years. (Note that the Stacks have decided to set aside the potential gain from the sale of their home and vacation home to cover them should they live longer than the 25-year period—if not, this will be part of the legacy they leave their children.)
- an aftertax rate of return of 8 percent prior to retirement
- an aftertax rate of return of 7 percent after retirement
- an 80 percent replacement ratio
- a savings step-up rate of 6 percent. (This means that the annual allocation to savings will increase by 6 percent each year until retirement.)

TABLE 23-11
Work Sheet: Calculation of Retirement Expenses—Alternative 2[*]

	Your Circumstances	Example
1. Current annual gross salary	$_____	$ 100,000
2. Retirement-income target (multiply line 1 by 0.80 percent target)	$_____	80,000
3. Estimated annual benefit from pension plan, not including IRAs, 401(k)s, 403(b)s, or profit-sharing plans[1]	$_____	24,000
4. Estimated annual Social Security benefits[1]	$_____	18,000
5. Total retirement benefits (add lines 3 and 4)	$_____	42,000
6. Income gap (subtract line 5 from line 2)[2]	$_____	38,000
7. Adjust gap to reflect inflation (multiply line 6 by factor A, below)	$_____	68,400
8. Capital needed to generate additional income and close gap (multiply line 7 by 16.3)[3]	$_____	1,114,920
9. Extra capital needed to offset inflation's impact on pension (multiply line 3 by factor B, below)	$_____	204,000
10. Total capital needed (add lines 8 and 9)	$_____	1,318,920
11. Total current retirement savings (includes balances in IRAs, 401(k)s, profit-sharing plans, mutual funds, CDs)	$_____	130,000
12. Value of savings at retirement (multiply line 11 by factor C, below)	$_____	416,000
13. Net capital gap (subtract line 12 from line 10)	$_____	902,920
14. Annual amount in current dollars to start saving now to cover the gap (divide line 13 by factor D, below)[4]	$_____	25, 578
15. Percentage of salary to be saved each year (divide line 14 by line 1)[5]	_____ %	25%

Years to Retirement	Factor A	Factor B	Factor C	Factor D
10	1.5	7.0	2.2	17.5
15	1.8	8.5	3.2	35.3
20	2.2	10.3	4.7	63.3
25	2.7	12.6	6.9	107.0
30	3.2	15.3	10.1	174.0

[1] Lines 3 and 4: Employers can provide annual estimates of your projected retirement pay; estimates of Social Security benefits are available from the Social Security Administration at (800) 937-2000. Both figures will be stated in current dollars, not in the high amounts that you will receive if your wages keep up with inflation. The work sheet takes this into consideration.

[2] Line 6: Even if a large pension lets you avoid an income gap, proceed to line 9 to determine the assets you may need to make up for the erosion of a fixed pension payment by inflation.

(Continued on following page)

TABLE 23-11 (Continued)
Factors for Work Sheet Calculations Assuming 4 Percent Inflation and 8 Percent Rate of Return

[3] Line 8: This calculation includes a determination of how much capital you will need to keep up with inflation after retirement and assumes that you will *deplete the capital over a 25-year period.*

[4] Line 14: Amount includes investments earmarked for retirement and payments by employee and employer to defined-contribution retirement plans such as 401(k)s and 403(b)s. The formula assumes you will increase annual savings at the same rate as inflation.

[5] Line 15: Assuming earnings rise with inflation, you can save a set percentage of gross pay each year, and the actual amount you stash away will increase annually.

* Reprinted with permission from *U.S. News & World Report*, August 14, 1989, page 62.

TABLE 23-12—Planner's Work Sheet
Step 1: List Assumptions

	ASSUMPTIONS	
A1.	Inflation rate prior to retirement	4%
A2.	Inflation rate after retirement	4%
A3.	Number of years until retirement	19 years
A4.	Expected duration of retirement	25 years
A5.	Rate of return prior to retirement	8%
A6.	Rate of return after retirement	7%
A7.	Savings step-up rate	6%

TABLE 23-13
Planner's Work Sheet—Step 2: Calculate Factors

The following factors were calculated using tables 23-16 through 23-23, which follow your blank work sheet in this book. Each table has a detailed explanation (and example) of how to extract the appropriate factor.

	Factors		Assumptions (from table 5-3)
F1.	Preretirement inflation factor	2.11	Table 23-16; years = A3, rate = A1
F2.	Retirement needs present value factor	17.936	Table 23-17; years = A4, rate = A6 minus A2
F3.	Current assets future value factor	4.32	Table 23-16; years = A3, rate = A5
F4.	Defined-benefit income present value factor	12.469	Table 23-17; years = A4, rate = A6
F5.	Savings rate factor	0.01435	Table 23-21; years = A3, rate = A5; use A7 to find appropriate table

Table 23-14
Planners Work Sheet
Step 3: Computation of Retirement Need and Amount to Be Saved

		COMPUTATIONS		
L1.		Projected annual retirement budget	$140,000	(80% of $175,000)
L2.	–	Social Security benefit	22,800	(Ann & Robert annual total)
L3.	=	Net annual need in current dollars	$117,200	
L4.	X	F1 factor	2.11	
L5.	=	Inflation-adjusted annual need	$247,292	
L6.	X	F2 factor	17.936	
L7.	=	Total resources needed for retirement		$4,435,429
L8.	=	Total in defined-contribution plans	$184,000	
L9.	+	Total private savings ear marked for retirement	50,000	
L10.		Current assets available for retirement	$234,000	
L11.	X	F3 factor	4.32	
L12.	=	Future value of current assets		$1,010,880
L13.		Annual income from defined benefit plan	$16,800	(Ann's annual pension)
L14.	X	F1 factor	2.11	
L15.	=	Inflation-adjusted annual income from defined-benefit plan	$35,448	
L16	X	F4 Factor	12.469	
L17.	=	Lump-sum value of defined-benefit plan		$442,001
L18.		Total resources available for retirement (line 12 and line 17)		$1,452,881
L19.		Addition amount you need to accumulate by retirement		$2,982,548
L20.	X	F5 factor		0.01435
L21.	=	Amount you need to save—first year		$42,800
				((24% of salary)

(Savings in each subsequent year must increase by the savings step-up rate, 6%)

TABLE 23-15
Retirement Planning Work Sheet

ASSUMPTIONS

A1.	Inflation rate prior to retirement	_____
A2.	Inflation rate after retirement	_____
A3.	Number of years until retirement	_____
A4.	Expected duration of retirement	_____
A5.	Rate of return prior to retirement	_____
A6.	Rate of return after retirement	_____
A7.	Savings step-up rate	_____

FACTORS

F1.	Pre-retirement inflation factor	_____
F2.	Retirement needs present value factor	_____
F3.	Current assets future value factor	_____
F4.	Defined-benefit present value factor	_____
F5.	Savings rate factor	_____

COMPUTATIONS

L1.		Projected annual retirement budget	_____
L2.	−	Social Security benefit	_____
L3.	=	Net annual need in current dollars	_____
L4.	X	F1 factor	_____
L5.	=	Inflation-adjusted annual retirement need	_____
L6.	X	F2 factor	_____
L7.	=	Total resources needed for retirement	_____
L8.		Total in defined-contribution plans	_____
L9.	+	Total private savings earmarked for retirement	_____
L10.	=	Current assets available for retirement	_____
L11.	X	F3 factor	_____
L12.	=	Future value of current assets	_____
L13.		Annual income from defined-benefit plan	_____
L14.	X	F1 factor	_____
L15.	=	Inflation-adjusted annual income from defined-benefit plan	_____
L16.	X	F4 factor	
L17.	=	Lump-sum value of defined-benefit plan	_____
L18.		Total resources available for retirement (line 12 and line 17)	_____
L19.		Additional amount you need to accumulate by retirement	_____
L20.	X	F5 factor	_____
L21.	=	Amount you need to save—first year	_____

THE INFLATION AND FUTURE VALUE FACTORS

Table 23-16 is used to select the appropriate Preretirement Inflation Factor (F1) and Current Assets Future Value Factor (F3) for use in the Retirement Planning Work Sheet. An explanation of the use of the table follows.

TABLE 23-16
Future Value Factors

Yrs	Rate						
	0%	1%	2%	3%	4%	5%	6%
1	1.00	1.01	1.02	1.03	1.04	1.05	1.06
2	1.00	1.02	1.04	1.06	1.08	1.10	1.12
3	1.00	1.03	1.06	1.09	1.12	1.16	1.19
4	1.00	1.04	1.08	1.13	1.17	1.22	1.26
5	1.00	1.05	1.10	1.16	1.22	1.28	1.34
6	1.00	1.06	1.13	1.19	1.27	1.34	1.42
7	1.00	1.07	1.15	1.23	1.32	1.41	1.50
8	1.00	1.08	1.17	1.27	1.37	1.48	1.59
9	1.00	1.09	1.20	1.30	1.42	1.55	1.69
10	1.00	1.10	1.22	1.34	1.48	1.63	1.79
11	1.00	1.12	1.24	1.38	1.54	1.71	1.90
12	1.00	1.13	1.27	1.43	1.60	1.80	2.01
13	1.00	1.14	1.29	1.47	1.67	1.89	2.13
14	1.00	1.15	1.32	1.51	1.73	1.98	2.26
15	1.00	1.16	1.35	1.56	1.80	2.08	2.40
16	1.00	1.17	1.37	1.60	1.87	2.18	2.54
17	1.00	1.18	1.40	1.65	1.95	2.29	2.69
18	1.00	1.20	1.43	1.70	2.03	2.41	2.85
19	1.00	1.21	1.46	1.75	2.11	2.53	3.03
20	1.00	1.22	1.49	1.81	2.19	2.65	3.21
21	1.00	1.23	1.52	1.86	2.28	2.79	3.40
22	1.00	1.24	1.55	1.92	2.37	2.93	3.60
23	1.00	1.26	1.58	1.97	2.46	3.07	3.82
24	1.00	1.27	1.61	2.03	2.56	3.23	4.05
25	1.00	1.28	1.64	2.09	2.67	3.39	4.29
26	1.00	1.30	1.67	2.16	2.77	3.56	4.55
27	1.00	1.31	1.71	2.22	2.88	3.73	4.82
28	1.00	1.32	1.74	2.29	3.00	3.92	5.11
29	1.00	1.33	1.78	2.36	3.12	4.12	5.42
30	1.00	1.35	1.81	2.43	3.24	4.32	5.74
31	1.00	1.36	1.85	2.50	3.37	4.54	6.09
32	1.00	1.37	1.88	2.58	3.51	4.76	6.45
33	1.00	1.39	1.92	2.65	3.65	5.00	6.84
34	1.00	1.40	1.96	2.73	3.79	5.25	7.25
35	1.00	1.42	2.00	2.81	3.95	5.52	7.69
36	1.00	1.43	2.04	2.90	4.10	5.79	8.15
37	1.00	1.45	2.08	2.99	4.27	6.08	8.64
38	1.00	1.46	2.12	3.07	4.44	6.39	9.15
39	1.00	1.47	2.16	3.17	4.62	6.70	9.70
40	1.00	1.49	2.21	3.26	4.80	7.04	10.29
41	1.00	1.50	2.25	3.36	4.99	7.39	10.90
42	1.00	1.52	2.30	3.46	5.19	7.76	11.56
43	1.00	1.53	2.34	3.56	5.40	8.15	12.25
44	1.00	1.55	2.39	3.67	5.62	8.56	12.99
45	1.00	1.56	2.44	3.78	5.84	8.99	13.76

TABLE 23-16 (Continued)
Future Value Factors

Yrs	7%	8%	9%	10%	11%	12%	15%	20%
							Rate	
1	1.07	1.08	1.09	1.10	1.11	1.12	1.15	1.20
2	1.14	1.17	1.19	1.21	1.23	1.25	1.32	1.44
3	1.23	1.26	1.30	1.33	1.37	1.40	1.52	1.73
4	1.31	1.36	1.41	1.46	1.52	1.57	1.75	2.07
5	1.40	1.47	1.54	1.61	1.69	1.76	2.01	2.49
6	1.50	1.59	1.68	1.77	1.87	1.97	2.31	2.99
7	1.61	1.71	1.83	1.95	2.08	2.21	2.66	3.58
8	1.72	1.85	1.99	2.14	2.30	2.48	3.06	4.30
9	1.84	2.00	2.17	2.36	2.56	2.77	3.52	5.16
10	1.97	2.16	2.37	2.59	2.84	3.11	4.05	6.19
11	2.10	2.33	2.58	2.85	3.15	3.48	4.65	7.43
12	2.25	2.52	**2.81**	3.14	3.50	3.90	5.35	8.92
13	2.41	2.72	3.07	3.45	3.88	4.36	6.15	10.70
14	2.58	2.94	3.34	3.80	4.31	4.89	7.08	12.84
15	2.76	3.17	3.64	4.18	4.78	5.47	8.14	15.41
16	2.95	3.43	3.97	4.59	5.31	6.13	9.36	18.49
17	3.16	3.70	4.33	5.05	5.90	6.87	10.76	22.19
18	3.38	4.00	4.72	5.56	6.54	7.69	12.38	26.62
19	3.62	4.32	5.14	6.12	7.26	8.61	14.23	31.95
20	3.87	4.66	5.60	6.73	8.06	9.65	16.37	38.34
21	4.14	5.03	6.11	7.40	8.95	10.80	18.82	46.01
22	4.43	5.44	6.66	8.14	9.93	12.10	21.64	55.21
23	4.74	5.87	7.26	8.95	11.03	13.55	24.89	66.25
24	5.07	6.34	7.91	9.85	12.24	15.18	28.63	79.50
25	5.43	6.85	8.62	10.83	13.59	17.00	32.92	95.40
26	5.81	7.40	9.40	11.92	15.08	19.04	37.86	114.48
27	6.21	7.99	10.25	13.11	16.74	21.32	43.54	137.37
28	6.65	8.63	11.17	14.42	18.58	23.88	50.07	164.84
29	7.11	9.32	12.17	15.86	20.62	26.75	57.58	197.81
30	7.61	10.06	13.27	17.45	22.89	29.96	66.21	237.38
31	8.15	10.87	14.46	19.19	25.41	33.56	76.14	284.85
32	8.72	11.74	15.76	21.11	28.21	37.58	87.57	341.82
33	9.33	12.68	17.18	23.23	31.31	42.09	100.70	410.19
34	9.98	13.69	18.73	25.55	34.75	47.14	115.80	492.22
35	10.68	14.79	20.41	28.10	38.57	52.80	133.18	590.67
36	11.42	15.97	22.25	30.91	42.82	59.14	153.15	708.80
37	12.22	17.25	24.25	34.00	47.53	66.23	176.12	850.56
38	13.08	18.63	26.44	37.40	52.76	74.18	202.54	1020.67
39	13.99	20.12	28.82	41.14	58.56	83.08	232.92	1224.81
40	14.97	21.72	31.41	45.26	65.00	93.05	267.86	1469.77
41	16.02	23.46	34.24	49.79	72.15	104.22	308.04	1763.73
42	17.14	25.34	37.32	54.76	80.09	116.72	354.25	2116.47
43	18.34	27.37	40.68	60.24	88.90	130.73	407.39	2539.77
44	19.63	29.56	44.34	66.26	98.68	146.42	468.50	3047.72
45	21.00	31.92	48.33	72.89	109.53	163.99	538.77	3657.26

ANNUITY FACTORS

Table 23-17 is used to select the appropriate Retirement Needs Present Value Factor (F2) and Defined-Benefit Present Value Factor (F4) for use in the Retirement Planning Work Sheet presented. An explanation of the use of the table follows.

TABLE 23-17
Present Value of Annuity Factors

Yrs	0%	1%	2%	3%	4%	5%	6%
				Rate			
1	1.000	1.000	1.000	1.000	1.000	1.000	1.000
2	2.000	1.990	1.980	1.971	1.962	1.952	1.943
3	3.000	2.970	2.942	2.913	2.886	2.859	2.833
4	4.000	3.941	3.884	3.829	3.775	3.723	3.673
5	5.000	4.902	4.808	4.717	4.630	4.546	4.465
6	6.000	5.853	5.713	5.580	5.452	5.329	5.212
7	7.000	6.795	6.601	6.417	6.242	6.076	5.917
8	8.000	7.728	7.472	7.230	7.002	6.786	6.582
9	9.000	8.652	8.325	8.020	7.733	7.463	7.210
10	10.000	9.566	9.162	8.786	8.435	8.108	7.802
11	11.000	10.471	9.983	9.530	9.111	8.722	8.360
12	12.000	11.368	10.787	10.253	9.760	9.306	8.887
13	13.000	12.255	11.575	10.954	10.385	9.863	9.384
14	14.000	13.134	12.348	11.635	10.986	10.394	9.853
15	15.000	14.004	13.106	12.296	11.563	10.899	10.295
16	16.000	14.865	13.849	12.938	12.118	11.380	10.712
17	17.000	15.718	14.578	13.561	12.652	11.838	11.106
18	18.000	16.562	15.292	14.166	13.166	12.274	11.477
19	19.000	17.398	15.992	14.754	13.659	12.690	11.828
20	20.000	18.226	16.678	15.324	14.134	13.085	12.158
21	21.000	19.046	17.351	15.877	14.590	13.462	12.470
22	22.000	19.857	18.011	**16.415**	15.029	13.821	12.764
23	23.000	20.660	18.658	16.937	15.451	14.163	13.042
24	24.000	21.456	19.292	17.444	15.857	14.489	13.303
25	25.000	22.243	19.914	17.936	16.247	14.799	13.550
26	26.000	23.023	20.523	18.413	16.622	15.094	13.783
27	27.000	23.795	21.121	18.877	16.983	15.375	14.003
28	28.000	24.560	21.707	19.327	17.330	15.643	14.211
29	29.000	25.316	22.281	19.764	17.663	15.898	14.406
30	30.000	26.066	22.844	20.188	17.984	16.141	14.591
31	31.000	26.808	23.396	20.600	18.292	16.372	14.765
32	32.000	27.542	23.938	21.000	18.588	16.593	14.929
33	33.000	28.270	24.468	21.389	18.874	16.803	15.084
34	34.000	28.990	24.989	21.766	19.148	17.003	15.230
35	35.000	29.703	25.499	22.132	19.411	17.193	15.368
36	36.000	30.409	25.999	22.487	19.665	17.374	15.498
37	37.000	31.108	26.489	22.832	19.908	17.547	15.621
38	38.000	31.800	26.969	23.167	20.143	17.711	15.737
39	39.000	32.485	27.441	23.492	20.368	17.868	15.846
40	40.000	33.163	27.903	23.808	20.584	18.017	15.949
41	41.000	33.835	28.355	24.115	20.793	18.159	16.046
42	42.000	34.500	28.799	24.412	20.993	18.294	16.138
43	43.000	35.158	29.235	24.701	21.186	18.423	16.225
44	44.000	35.810	29.662	24.982	21.371	18.546	16.306
45	45.000	36.455	30.080	25.254	21.549	18.663	16.383

TABLE 23-17 (Continued)
Present Value of Annuity Factors

Yrs	7%	8%	9%	10%	11%	12%	15%	20%
				Rate				
1	1.000	1.000	1.000	1.000	1.000	1.000	1.000	1.000
2	1.935	1.926	1.917	1.909	1.901	1.893	1.870	1.833
3	2.808	2.783	2.759	2.736	2.713	2.690	2.626	2.528
4	3.624	3.577	3.531	3.487	3.444	3.402	3.283	3.106
5	4.387	4.312	4.240	4.170	4.102	4.037	3.855	3.589
6	5.100	4.993	4.890	4.791	4.696	4.605	4.352	3.991
7	5.767	5.623	5.486	5.355	5.231	5.111	4.784	4.326
8	6.389	6.206	6.033	5.868	5.712	5.564	5.160	4.605
9	6.971	6.747	6.535	6.335	6.146	5.968	5.487	4.837
10	7.515	7.247	6.995	6.759	6.537	6.328	5.772	5.031
11	8.024	7.710	7.418	7.145	6.889	6.650	6.019	5.192
12	8.499	8.139	7.805	7.495	7.207	6.938	6.234	5.327
13	8.943	8.536	8.161	7.814	7.492	7.194	6.421	5.439
14	9.358	8.904	8.487	8.103	7.750	7.424	6.583	5.533
15	9.745	9.244	8.786	8.367	7.982	7.628	6.724	5.611
16	10.108	9.559	9.061	8.606	8.191	7.811	6.847	5.675
17	10.447	9.851	9.313	8.824	8.379	7.974	6.954	5.730
18	10.763	10.122	9.544	9.022	8.549	8.120	7.047	5.775
19	11.059	10.372	9.756	9.201	8.702	8.250	7.128	5.812
20	11.336	10.604	9.950	9.365	8.839	8.366	7.198	5.843
21	11.594	10.818	10.129	9.514	8.963	8.469	7.259	5.870
22	11.836	11.017	10.292	9.649	9.075	8.562	7.312	5.891
23	12.061	11.201	10.442	9.772	9.176	8.645	7.359	5.909
24	12.272	11.371	10.580	9.883	9.266	8.718	7.399	5.925
25	12.469	11.529	10.707	9.985	9.348	8.784	7.434	5.937
26	**12.654**	11.675	10.823	10.077	9.422	8.843	7.464	5.948
27	12.826	11.810	10.929	10.161	9.488	8.896	7.491	5.956
28	12.987	11.935	11.027	10.237	9.548	8.943	7.514	5.964
29	13.137	12.051	11.116	10.307	9.602	8.984	7.534	5.970
30	13.278	12.158	11.198	10.370	9.650	9.022	7.551	5.975
31	13.409	12.258	11.274	10.427	9.694	9.055	7.566	5.979
32	13.532	12.350	11.343	10.479	9.733	9.085	7.579	5.982
33	13.647	12.435	11.406	10.526	9.769	9.112	7.591	5.985
34	13.754	12.514	11.464	10.569	9.801	9.135	7.600	5.988
35	13.854	12.587	11.518	10.609	9.829	9.157	7.609	5.990
36	13.948	12.655	11.567	10.644	9.855	9.176	7.617	5.992
37	14.035	12.717	11.612	10.677	9.879	9.192	7.623	5.993
38	14.117	12.775	11.653	10.706	9.900	9.208	7.629	5.994
39	14.193	12.829	11.691	10.733	9.919	9.221	7.634	5.995
40	14.265	12.879	11.726	10.757	9.936	9.233	7.638	5.996
41	14.332	12.925	11.757	10.779	9.951	9.244	7.642	5.997
42	14.394	12.967	11.787	10.799	9.965	9.253	7.645	5.997
43	14.452	13.007	11.813	10.817	9.977	9.262	7.648	5.998
44	14.507	13.043	11.838	10.834	9.989	9.270	7.650	5.998
45	14.558	13.077	11.861	10.849	9.999	9.276	7.652	5.998

Selecting the Preretirement Inflation Factor (F1)

The appropriate F1 factor depends on the assumed annual inflation rate prior to retirement (line A1 of the Retirement Planning Work Sheet) and the number of years until retirement (line A3 of the Retirement Planning Work Sheet). The F1 factor is found in table 23-16 by looking in the column with the interest/inflation rate equal to the inflation rate specified in line A1 and the row with the number of years equal to that specified in line A3 of the Retirement Planning Work Sheet. For example, if you assume inflation will average 6 percent per year until retirement (A1) and you expect to retire in 18 years (A3), the appropriate preretirement inflation factor (F1) is 2.85.

Selecting the Current Assets Future Value Factor (F3)

The appropriate F3 factor depends on the assumed rate of return on investment prior to retirement (line A5 of the Retirement Planning Work Sheet) and the number of years until retirement (line A3 of the Retirement Planning Work Sheet). The F3 factor is found in table 23-16 by looking in the column with the interest/inflation rate equal to the rate of return specified in line A5 and the row with the number of years equal to that specified in line A3 of the Retirement Planning Work Sheet. For example, if you assume you can invest at a rate of 9 percent per year until retirement (A5) and you expect to retire in 12 years (A3), the appropriate current assets future value factor (F3) is 2.81.

Selecting the Retirement Needs Present Value Factor (F2)

The appropriate F2 factor depends on the assumed annual inflation rate after retirement, the expected duration of retirement, and the assumed rate of return on investment after retirement (lines A2, A4, and A6, respectively, of the Retirement Planning Work Sheet [table 23-12]). The F2 factor is found using a two-step process. First, you must determine the inflation-adjusted interest rate. This is estimated by subtracting your assumed inflation rate after retirement (A2) from your assumed investment rate of return after retirement (A6).

Specifically,

Value from A6	–	Value from A2	=	Inflation-Adjusted Rate
_____	–	_____	=	_____

Next, you can find the F2 factor in table 23-17 in the column with the inflation-adjusted interest rate equal to that just computed and the row with the number of years equal to that specified in line A4 of the Retirement Planning Work Sheet. For example, if you assume inflation will average 5 percent per year after retirement (A2) and you expect to earn 8 percent on your investments after retirement (A6), your inflation-adjusted interest rate would be

Value from A6	–	Value from A2		= Inflation-Adjusted Rate
8%	–	5%	=	3%

If your expected duration of retirement is 22 years (A4), the appropriate retirement needs present value factor (F2) is found by looking in the 3 percent column and the 22-year row of table 23-17. In this case, F2 is 16.415.

Selecting the Defined-Benefit Present Value Factor (F4)

The appropriate F4 factor depends on the assumed rate of return on investment after retirement and the expected duration of retirement (lines A6 and A4 of the Retirement Planning Work Sheet, respectively). The F4 factor is found in table 23-17 by looking in the column with the interest rate equal to the rate of return specified in line A6 and the row with the number of years equal to that specified in line A4 of the Retirement Planning Work Sheet. For example, if you assume you can invest at a rate of 7 percent per year after retirement (A6) and you expect your retirement needs to last 26 years (A4), the appropriate defined-benefit present value factor (F4) is 12.654.

THE SAVINGS RATE FACTOR

Tables 23-18 through 23-23 are used to select the appropriate Savings Rate Factor (F5) for use in the Retirement Planning Work Sheet. An explanation of the use of the tables follows.

Selecting the Savings Rate Factor (F5)

The appropriate F5 factor depends on the number of years until you plan to retire, the average annual rate of return you expect to earn on investment until retirement, and your savings step-up rate (lines A3, A5, and A7 of table 23-15, the Retirement Planning Work Sheet, respectively). To find the appropriate F5 factor, you must first select the table corresponding to your savings step-up rate (A7). The tables correspond to step-up rates ranging from 0 percent to 10 percent, with the step-up rate increased by 2 percentage points in each successive table.

The savings step-up rate is the rate at which you plan to increase or step up the amount you save each year. Frequently, the step-up rate is set equal to the rate at which a person expects his or her annual earnings to grow. If the step-up rate is set equal to the earnings growth rate, the amount that must be saved each year remains a fixed proportion of those growing earnings. Therefore, the "burden" of saving for retirement remains the same each year relative to your growing income. For example, if you expect your earnings to grow at an average annual rate of 6 percent per year and want your required savings each year to be constant relative to your earnings, you would use the table showing a 6 percent savings step-up rate.

Once you have selected the table corresponding to your desired step-up rate, you would find your savings rate factor (F5) in the appropriate column and row. For example, if you expect your earnings to grow at an average annual rate of 6 percent per year and want your required savings each year to be constant relative to your earnings, you would use the table showing a 6 percent savings step-up rate corresponding to your assumed investment rate of return prior to retirement (A5) and the number of years until you plan to retire (A3), respectively. For example, if your step-up rate is 6 percent (A7), your assumed rate of return is 8 percent (A5), and you plan to retire in 10 years, your savings rate factor (F5) is 0.05031 (table 23-21).

Remember, line 21 of the Retirement Planning Work Sheet (table 23-15) calculates the amount you need to save the first year. In each subsequent year, you must increase the amount you save by your assumed savings step-up rate if you are to reach your goal. For example, assume your savings step-up rate is 5 percent and the amount calculated in line 21 of the Retirement Planning Work Sheet is $1,000. In the second year, you would have to save $1,050; in the third year, $1,102.50; in the fourth year, $1,157.62; and so on.

The amount you must save each year is calculated by multiplying the prior year's savings amount by (1 + the step-up rate). For example, if your savings step-up rate is 6 percent, you would compute each subsequent year's savings amount by multiplying the previous year's savings amount by 1.06.

TABLE 23-18
Yearly Savings Rate Factors
0% Savings Step-up Rate (A7)

Yrs	\multicolumn{6}{c	}{Assumed Rate of Return (A5)}
	1%	2%	3%	4%	5%	6%
1	0.99010	0.98039	0.97087	0.96154	0.95238	0.94340
2	0.49259	0.48534	0.47826	0.47134	0.46458	0.45796
3	0.32675	0.32035	0.31411	0.30803	0.30210	0.29633
4	0.24384	0.23787	0.23207	0.22643	0.22096	0.21565
5	0.19410	0.18839	0.18287	0.17753	0.17236	0.16736
6	0.16094	0.15542	0.15009	0.14496	0.14002	0.13525
7	0.13726	0.13187	0.12671	0.12174	0.11697	0.11239
8	0.11950	0.11423	0.10918	0.10435	0.09974	0.09532
9	0.10568	0.10051	0.09557	0.09086	0.08637	0.08210
10	0.09464	0.08954	0.08469	0.08009	0.07572	0.07157
11	0.08560	0.08057	0.07580	0.07130	0.06704	0.06301
12	0.07807	0.07310	0.06841	0.06399	0.05983	0.05592
13	0.07170	0.06678	0.06216	0.05783	0.05377	0.04996
14	0.06624	0.06137	0.05682	0.05257	0.04859	0.04489
15	0.06151	0.05669	0.05220	0.04802	0.04414	0.04053
16	0.05737	0.05260	0.04817	0.04406	0.04026	0.03675
17	0.05372	0.04899	0.04461	0.04058	0.03686	0.03344
18	0.05048	0.04579	0.04146	0.03749	0.03385	0.03053
19	0.04758	0.04292	0.03865	0.03475	0.03119	0.02794
20	0.04497	0.04035	0.03613	0.03229	0.02880	0.02565
21	0.04260	0.03802	0.03386	0.03008	0.02666	0.02359
22	0.04046	0.03591	0.03179	0.02808	0.02473	0.02174
23	0.03850	0.03399	0.02992	0.02626	0.02299	0.02007
24	0.03671	0.03223	0.02820	0.02460	0.02140	0.01857
25	0.03506	0.03061	0.02663	0.02309	0.01995	0.01720
26	0.03353	0.02912	0.02518	0.02170	0.01863	0.01595
27	0.03212	0.02774	0.02385	0.02042	0.01742	0.01481
28	0.03082	0.02646	0.02261	0.01924	0.01631	0.01377
29	0.02960	0.02527	0.02147	0.01815	0.01528	0.01281
30	0.02846	0.02417	0.02041	0.01714	0.01433	0.01193
31	0.02740	0.02313	0.01942	0.01621	0.01346	0.01112
32	0.02641	0.02217	0.01849	0.01534	0.01265	0.01038
33	0.02547	0.02126	0.01763	0.01452	0.01190	0.00969
34	0.02459	0.02041	0.01682	0.01376	0.01120	0.00906
35	0.02377	0.01961	0.01606	0.01306	0.01054	0.00847
36	0.02298	0.01886	0.01534	0.01239	0.00994	0.00792
37	0.02225	0.01814	0.01467	0.01177	0.00937	0.00741
38	0.02155	0.01747	0.01404	0.01118	0.00884	0.00694
39	0.02088	0.01683	0.01344	0.01064	0.00835	0.00650
40	0.02025	0.01623	0.01288	0.01012	0.00788	0.00610
41	0.01965	0.01566	0.01234	0.00963	0.00745	0.00572
42	0.01908	0.01511	0.01184	0.00917	0.00704	0.00536
43	0.01854	0.01460	0.01136	0.00874	0.00666	0.00503
44	0.01802	0.01411	0.01090	0.00833	0.00630	0.00472
45	0.01753	0.01364	0.01047	0.00794	0.00596	0.00443

TABLE 23-18 (Continued)
Yearly Savings Rate Factors
0% Savings Step-up Rate (A7)

Yrs	\multicolumn{8}{c}{Assumed Rate of Return (A5)}
	7%	8%	9%	10%	11%	12%	15%	20%
1	0.93458	0.92593	0.91743	0.90909	0.90090	0.89286	0.86957	0.83333
2	0.45149	0.44516	0.43896	0.43290	0.42697	0.42116	0.40445	0.37879
3	0.29070	0.28522	0.27987	0.27465	0.26956	0.26460	0.25041	0.22894
4	0.21049	0.20548	0.20061	0.19588	0.19129	0.18682	0.17414	0.15524
5	0.16251	0.15783	0.15330	0.14891	0.14466	0.14054	0.12897	0.11198
6	0.13065	0.12622	0.12194	0.11782	0.11385	0.11002	0.09934	0.08392
7	0.10799	0.10377	0.09972	0.09582	0.09209	0.08850	0.07857	0.06452
8	0.09109	0.08705	0.08319	0.07949	0.07596	0.07259	0.06335	0.05051
9	0.07802	0.07415	0.07046	0.06695	0.06361	0.06043	0.05180	0.04007
10	0.06764	0.06392	0.06039	0.05704	0.05388	0.05088	0.04283	0.03210
11	0.05921	0.05563	0.05224	0.04906	0.04605	0.04323	0.03571	0.02592
12	0.05224	0.04879	0.04555	0.04251	0.03966	0.03700	0.02998	0.02105
13	0.04640	0.04308	0.03997	0.03707	0.03437	0.03185	0.02531	0.01718
14	0.04144	0.03824	0.03526	0.03250	0.02994	0.02756	0.02147	0.01408
15	0.03719	0.03410	0.03125	0.02861	0.02618	0.02395	0.01828	0.01157
16	0.03351	0.03053	0.02780	0.02529	0.02299	0.02088	0.01561	0.00953
17	0.03030	0.02743	0.02481	0.02242	0.02024	0.01826	0.01336	0.00787
18	0.02749	0.02472	0.02221	0.01994	0.01788	0.01602	0.01147	0.00650
19	0.02500	0.02234	0.01994	0.01777	0.01582	0.01407	0.00986	0.00539
20	0.02280	0.02023	0.01793	0.01587	0.01403	0.01239	0.00849	0.00446
21	0.02083	0.01836	0.01616	0.01420	0.01247	0.01093	0.00732	0.00370
22	0.01907	0.01670	0.01459	0.01273	0.01109	0.00965	0.00632	0.00307
23	0.01749	0.01521	0.01319	0.01143	0.00988	0.00854	0.00546	0.00255
24	0.01606	0.01387	0.01195	0.01027	0.00882	0.00756	0.00472	0.00212
25	0.01478	0.01267	0.01083	0.00924	0.00787	0.00670	0.00409	0.00177
26	0.01361	0.01158	0.00983	0.00833	0.00704	0.00594	0.00354	0.00147
27	0.01255	0.01060	0.00893	0.00751	0.00630	0.00527	0.00307	0.00122
28	0.01158	0.00971	0.00812	0.00677	0.00564	0.00468	0.00266	0.00102
29	0.01070	0.00891	0.00739	0.00612	0.00505	0.00416	0.00231	0.00085
30	0.00989	0.00817	0.00673	0.00553	0.00453	0.00370	0.00200	0.00071
31	0.00916	0.00751	0.00613	0.00500	0.00406	0.00329	0.00174	0.00059
32	0.00848	0.00690	0.00559	0.00452	0.00364	0.00293	0.00151	0.00049
33	0.00786	0.00634	0.00510	0.00409	0.00327	0.00261	0.00131	0.00041
34	0.00729	0.00584	0.00466	0.00370	0.00294	0.00232	0.00114	0.00034
35	0.00676	0.00537	0.00425	0.00335	0.00264	0.00207	0.00099	0.00028
36	0.00628	0.00495	0.00389	0.00304	0.00237	0.00184	0.00086	0.00024
37	0.00583	0.00456	0.00355	0.00275	0.00213	0.00164	0.00074	0.00020
38	0.00542	0.00420	0.00325	0.00250	0.00191	0.00146	0.00065	0.00016
39	0.00503	0.00388	0.00297	0.00226	0.00172	0.00131	0.00056	0.00014
40	0.00468	0.00357	0.00272	0.00205	0.00155	0.00116	0.00049	0.00011
41	0.00435	0.00330	0.00248	0.00186	0.00139	0.00104	0.00042	0.00009
42	0.00405	0.00304	0.00227	0.00169	0.00125	0.00093	0.00037	0.00008
43	0.00377	0.00281	0.00208	0.00153	0.00113	0.00083	0.00032	0.00007
44	0.00351	0.00259	0.00191	0.00139	0.00101	0.00074	0.00028	0.00005
45	0.00327	0.00240	0.00174	0.00126	0.00091	0.00066	0.00024	0.00005

TABLE 23-19
Yearly Savings Rate Factors
2% Savings Step-up Rate (A7)

Yrs	Assumed Rate of Return (A5)					
	1%	2%	3%	4%	5%	6%
1	0.99010	0.98039	0.97087	0.96154	0.95238	0.94340
2	0.48773	0.48058	0.47360	0.46677	0.46009	0.45356
3	0.32035	0.31411	0.30803	0.30210	0.29633	0.29071
4	0.23671	0.23096	0.22538	0.21997	0.21470	0.20959
5	0.18656	0.18115	0.17590	0.17083	0.16592	0.16116
6	0.15317	0.14800	0.14301	0.13820	0.13355	0.12907
7	0.12934	0.12437	0.11958	0.11498	0.11056	0.10631
8	0.11149	0.10669	0.10208	0.09766	0.09343	0.08938
9	0.09764	0.09297	0.08852	0.08426	0.08020	0.07633
10	0.08657	0.08203	0.07772	0.07361	0.06970	0.06599
11	0.07753	0.07311	0.06892	0.06495	0.06119	0.05762
12	0.07001	0.06571	0.06164	0.05779	0.05415	0.05072
13	0.06367	0.05946	0.05550	0.05177	0.04826	0.04496
14	0.05824	0.05413	0.05028	0.04665	0.04326	0.04008
15	0.05355	0.04953	0.04577	0.04226	0.03898	0.03592
16	0.04945	0.04553	0.04186	0.03845	0.03527	0.03232
17	0.04585	0.04201	0.03843	0.03511	0.03204	0.02920
18	0.04266	0.03890	0.03541	0.03218	0.02920	0.02646
19	0.03981	0.03613	0.03272	0.02958	0.02670	0.02405
20	0.03726	0.03365	0.03032	0.02727	0.02448	0.02192
21	0.03495	0.03142	0.02817	0.02520	0.02249	0.02003
22	0.03286	0.02940	0.02623	0.02334	0.02071	0.01834
23	0.03097	0.02757	0.02447	0.02166	0.01912	0.01682
24	0.02923	0.02591	0.02288	0.02014	0.01767	0.01546
25	0.02764	0.02438	0.02142	0.01876	0.01637	0.01423
26	0.02618	0.02298	0.02009	0.01750	0.01518	0.01312
27	0.02483	0.02170	0.01887	0.01635	0.01410	0.01211
28	0.02359	0.02051	0.01775	0.01529	0.01311	0.01120
29	0.02243	0.01942	0.01672	0.01432	0.01221	0.01036
30	0.02136	0.01840	0.01576	0.01343	0.01138	0.00960
31	0.02036	0.01746	0.01488	0.01261	0.01062	0.00890
32	0.01943	0.01658	0.01406	0.01185	0.00992	0.00826
33	0.01856	0.01576	0.01330	0.01114	0.00927	0.00767
34	0.01774	0.01500	0.01259	0.01049	0.00868	0.00713
35	0.01697	0.01429	0.01193	0.00988	0.00813	0.00664
36	0.01625	0.01362	0.01131	0.00932	0.00762	0.00618
37	0.01558	0.01299	0.01073	0.00879	0.00714	0.00576
38	0.01494	0.01240	0.01019	0.00830	0.00670	0.00537
39	0.01434	0.01184	0.00969	0.00784	0.00629	0.00501
40	0.01377	0.01132	0.00921	0.00742	0.00591	0.00467
41	0.01323	0.01083	0.00876	0.00702	0.00556	0.00436
42	0.01272	0.01036	0.00834	0.00664	0.00523	0.00408
43	0.01224	0.00992	0.00795	0.00629	0.00492	0.00381
44	0.01178	0.00951	0.00758	0.00596	0.00463	0.00356
45	0.01134	0.00912	0.00723	0.00565	0.00436	0.00333

TABLE 23-19 (Continued)
Yearly Savings Rate Factors
2% Savings Step-up Rate (A7)

	Assumed Rate of Return (A5)							
Yrs	7%	8%	9%	10%	11%	12%	15%	20%
1	0.93458	0.92593	0.91743	0.90909	0.90090	0.89286	0.86957	0.83333
2	0.44717	0.44092	0.43480	0.42882	0.42296	0.41722	0.40072	0.37538
3	0.28522	0.27987	0.27466	0.26957	0.26461	0.25976	0.24592	0.22496
4	0.20463	0.19980	0.19511	0.19055	0.18612	0.18181	0.16959	0.15134
5	0.15656	0.15210	0.14779	0.14361	0.13956	0.13564	0.12460	0.10836
6	0.12475	0.12059	0.11657	0.11269	0.10894	0.10533	0.09524	0.08065
7	0.10223	0.09830	0.09453	0.09091	0.08742	0.08407	0.07480	0.06161
8	0.08550	0.08179	0.07823	0.07483	0.07157	0.06845	0.05989	0.04795
9	0.07263	0.06911	0.06575	0.06254	0.05949	0.05658	0.04867	0.03783
10	0.06246	0.05911	0.05592	0.05290	0.05004	0.04732	0.03999	0.03016
11	0.05424	0.05105	0.04803	0.04518	0.04249	0.03995	0.03316	0.02425
12	0.04749	0.04445	0.04158	0.03889	0.03636	0.03398	0.02769	0.01961
13	0.04186	0.03896	0.03624	0.03369	0.03131	0.02908	0.02326	0.01595
14	0.03711	0.03434	0.03176	0.02935	0.02711	0.02503	0.01964	0.01302
15	0.03307	0.03042	0.02796	0.02569	0.02358	0.02163	0.01665	0.01067
16	0.02959	0.02706	0.02472	0.02257	0.02059	0.01877	0.01416	0.00876
17	0.02657	0.02416	0.02194	0.01990	0.01804	0.01634	0.01208	0.00722
18	0.02394	0.02164	0.01953	0.01760	0.01585	0.01426	0.01033	0.00595
19	0.02164	0.01943	0.01743	0.01561	0.01396	0.01248	0.00885	0.00492
20	0.01960	0.01750	0.01559	0.01388	0.01233	0.01094	0.00760	0.00407
21	0.01780	0.01579	0.01398	0.01236	0.01091	0.00961	0.00653	0.00337
22	0.01620	0.01428	0.01256	0.01103	0.00967	0.00846	0.00562	0.00280
23	0.01477	0.01294	0.01130	0.00986	0.00858	0.00746	0.00485	0.00232
24	0.01349	0.01174	0.01019	0.00882	0.00763	0.00658	0.00418	0.00193
25	0.01234	0.01067	0.00920	0.00791	0.00679	0.00581	0.00361	0.00160
26	0.01130	0.00971	0.00831	0.00710	0.00605	0.00514	0.00312	0.00133
27	0.01037	0.00884	0.00752	0.00638	0.00539	0.00455	0.00270	0.00111
28	0.00952	0.00807	0.00681	0.00574	0.00482	0.00403	0.00234	0.00092
29	0.00875	0.00737	0.00618	0.00516	0.00430	0.00358	0.00203	0.00077
30	0.00806	0.00673	0.00561	0.00465	0.00385	0.00317	0.00176	0.00064
31	0.00742	0.00616	0.00509	0.00419	0.00344	0.00282	0.00152	0.00053
32	0.00684	0.00564	0.00463	0.00378	0.00308	0.00250	0.00132	0.00044
33	0.00631	0.00517	0.00421	0.00341	0.00276	0.00222	0.00114	0.00037
34	0.00583	0.00474	0.00383	0.00308	0.00247	0.00198	0.00099	0.00031
35	0.00539	0.00435	0.00349	0.00279	0.00222	0.00176	0.00086	0.00025
36	0.00498	0.00399	0.00318	0.00252	0.00199	0.00156	0.00075	0.00021
37	0.00461	0.00366	0.00290	0.00228	0.00178	0.00139	0.00065	0.00018
38	0.00426	0.00337	0.00264	0.00206	0.00160	0.00124	0.00056	0.00015
39	0.00395	0.00309	0.00241	0.00187	0.00144	0.00110	0.00049	0.00012
40	0.00366	0.00285	0.00220	0.00169	0.00129	0.00098	0.00043	0.00010
41	0.00339	0.00262	0.00201	0.00153	0.00116	0.00088	0.00037	0.00009
42	0.00315	0.00241	0.00183	0.00139	0.00104	0.00078	0.00032	0.00007
43	0.00292	0.00222	0.00168	0.00126	0.00094	0.00070	0.00028	0.00006
44	0.00271	0.00205	0.00153	0.00114	0.00084	0.00062	0.00024	0.00005
45	0.00252	0.00188	0.00140	0.00103	0.00076	0.00055	0.00021	0.00004

TABLE 23-20
Yearly Savings Rate Factors
4% Savings Step-up Rate (A7)

Yrs	Assumed Rate of Return (A5)					
	1%	2%	3%	4%	5%	6%
1	0.99010	0.98039	0.97087	0.96154	0.95238	0.94340
2	0.48298	0.47592	0.46902	0.46228	0.45568	0.44924
3	0.31411	0.30803	0.30210	0.29633	0.29071	0.28522
4	0.22980	0.22428	0.21891	0.21370	0.20864	0.20372
5	0.17932	0.17418	0.16920	0.16439	0.15972	0.15520
6	0.14575	0.14090	0.13623	0.13172	0.12736	0.12316
7	0.12184	0.11724	0.11282	0.10856	0.10446	0.10052
8	0.10396	0.09958	0.09537	0.09134	0.08747	0.08375
9	0.09011	0.08592	0.08190	0.07807	0.07440	0.07089
10	0.07908	0.07505	0.07122	0.06756	0.06407	0.06075
11	0.07009	0.06622	0.06255	0.05905	0.05573	0.05258
12	0.06264	0.05892	0.05539	0.05205	0.04888	0.04589
13	0.05636	0.05278	0.04940	0.04620	0.04318	0.04033
14	0.05102	0.04757	0.04431	0.04125	0.03836	0.03565
15	0.04641	0.04309	0.03996	0.03702	0.03426	0.03168
16	0.04241	0.03920	0.03619	0.03337	0.03073	0.02827
17	0.03890	0.03580	0.03291	0.03020	0.02768	0.02533
18	0.03580	0.03281	0.03002	0.02742	0.02501	0.02277
19	0.03305	0.03016	0.02748	0.02498	0.02267	0.02054
20	0.03059	0.02781	0.02522	0.02282	0.02061	0.01857
21	0.02839	0.02569	0.02320	0.02090	0.01878	0.01683
22	0.02640	0.02380	0.02139	0.01918	0.01715	0.01529
23	0.02460	0.02209	0.01977	0.01764	0.01569	0.01392
24	0.02296	0.02053	0.01830	0.01626	0.01439	0.01270
25	0.02147	0.01913	0.01697	0.01500	0.01322	0.01160
26	0.02011	0.01784	0.01576	0.01387	0.01216	0.01062
27	0.01886	0.01667	0.01466	0.01285	0.01120	0.00973
28	0.01771	0.01559	0.01366	0.01191	0.01034	0.00893
29	0.01665	0.01460	0.01274	0.01106	0.00955	0.00820
30	0.01567	0.01369	0.01190	0.01028	0.00883	0.00755
31	0.01476	0.01285	0.01112	0.00956	0.00818	0.00695
32	0.01392	0.01208	0.01041	0.00891	0.00758	0.00641
33	0.01314	0.01136	0.00975	0.00831	0.00703	0.00591
34	0.01242	0.01069	0.00914	0.00775	0.00653	0.00546
35	0.01174	0.01007	0.00857	0.00724	0.00607	0.00504
36	0.01111	0.00950	0.00805	0.00677	0.00564	0.00467
37	0.01052	0.00896	0.00757	0.00633	0.00525	0.00432
38	0.00997	0.00846	0.00712	0.00593	0.00489	0.00400
39	0.00945	0.00800	0.00670	0.00555	0.00456	0.00371
40	0.00897	0.00756	0.00631	0.00521	0.00425	0.00344
41	0.00851	0.00715	0.00594	0.00488	0.00397	0.00319
42	0.00808	0.00677	0.00561	0.00459	0.00371	0.00296
43	0.00768	0.00641	0.00529	0.00431	0.00346	0.00275
44	0.00730	0.00608	0.00499	0.00405	0.00324	0.00256
45	0.00695	0.00576	0.00471	0.00380	0.00303	0.00238

TABLE 23-20 (Continued)
Yearly Savings Rate Factors
4% Savings Step-up Rate (A7)

	Assumed Rate of Return (A5)							
Yrs	7%	8%	9%	10%	11%	12%	15%	20%
1	0.93458	0.92593	0.91743	0.90909	0.90090	0.89286	0.86957	0.83333
2	0.44293	0.43676	0.43072	0.42481	0.41902	0.41336	0.39706	0.37202
3	0.27987	0.27466	0.26957	0.26461	0.25977	0.25504	0.24154	0.22107
4	0.19893	0.19429	0.18977	0.18538	0.18111	0.17695	0.16516	0.14753
5	0.15082	0.14658	0.14247	0.13849	0.13463	0.13090	0.12036	0.10485
6	0.11910	0.11518	0.11140	0.10775	0.10422	0.10082	0.09129	0.07749
7	0.09673	0.09308	0.08957	0.08620	0.08295	0.07983	0.07117	0.05881
8	0.08019	0.07678	0.07351	0.07038	0.06738	0.06450	0.05658	0.04549
9	0.06754	0.06433	0.06128	0.05836	0.05558	0.05292	0.04567	0.03568
10	0.05758	0.05457	0.05171	0.04899	0.04640	0.04394	0.03729	0.02830
11	0.04959	0.04675	0.04407	0.04152	0.03911	0.03684	0.03073	0.02263
12	0.04306	0.04038	0.03786	0.03548	0.03324	0.03112	0.02551	0.01823
13	0.03765	0.03512	0.03275	0.03052	0.02843	0.02647	0.02131	0.01476
14	0.03311	0.03072	0.02849	0.02640	0.02445	0.02264	0.01790	0.01200
15	0.02926	0.02701	0.02491	0.02295	0.02114	0.01945	0.01510	0.00980
16	0.02598	0.02385	0.02187	0.02004	0.01834	0.01678	0.01278	0.00802
17	0.02315	0.02114	0.01928	0.01756	0.01598	0.01452	0.01085	0.00659
18	0.02071	0.01880	0.01704	0.01543	0.01396	0.01261	0.00924	0.00542
19	0.01857	0.01677	0.01512	0.01361	0.01223	0.01098	0.00789	0.00447
20	0.01670	0.01500	0.01344	0.01202	0.01074	0.00958	0.00675	0.00369
21	0.01506	0.01344	0.01198	0.01065	0.00945	0.00838	0.00578	0.00305
22	0.01361	0.01208	0.01070	0.00945	0.00834	0.00734	0.00496	0.00252
23	0.01232	0.01087	0.00957	0.00841	0.00737	0.00644	0.00427	0.00209
24	0.01117	0.00980	0.00858	0.00749	0.00652	0.00566	0.00367	0.00173
25	0.01015	0.00885	0.00770	0.00668	0.00578	0.00498	0.00316	0.00144
26	0.00924	0.00801	0.00692	0.00596	0.00512	0.00439	0.00273	0.00119
27	0.00842	0.00726	0.00623	0.00533	0.00455	0.00387	0.00235	0.00099
28	0.00768	0.00658	0.00562	0.00478	0.00405	0.00342	0.00203	0.00082
29	0.00702	0.00598	0.00507	0.00428	0.00360	0.00302	0.00176	0.00068
30	0.00642	0.00543	0.00458	0.00384	0.00321	0.00267	0.00152	0.00057
31	0.00588	0.00494	0.00414	0.00345	0.00286	0.00237	0.00131	0.00047
32	0.00538	0.00450	0.00374	0.00310	0.00255	0.00210	0.00114	0.00039
33	0.00494	0.00410	0.00339	0.00279	0.00228	0.00186	0.00099	0.00033
34	0.00453	0.00374	0.00307	0.00251	0.00204	0.00165	0.00085	0.00027
35	0.00417	0.00342	0.00279	0.00226	0.00182	0.00146	0.00074	0.00023
36	0.00383	0.00312	0.00253	0.00203	0.00163	0.00130	0.00064	0.00019
37	0.00352	0.00285	0.00230	0.00183	0.00146	0.00115	0.00056	0.00016
38	0.00324	0.00261	0.00209	0.00165	0.00131	0.00102	0.00048	0.00013
39	0.00299	0.00239	0.00190	0.00149	0.00117	0.00091	0.00042	0.00011
40	0.00276	0.00219	0.00172	0.00135	0.00105	0.00081	0.00036	0.00009
41	0.00254	0.00201	0.00157	0.00122	0.00094	0.00072	0.00032	0.00008
42	0.00235	0.00184	0.00143	0.00110	0.00084	0.00064	0.00027	0.00006
43	0.00217	0.00169	0.00130	0.00099	0.00076	0.00057	0.00024	0.00005
44	0.00200	0.00155	0.00118	0.00090	0.00068	0.00051	0.00021	0.00004
45	0.00185	0.00142	0.00108	0.00081	0.00061	0.00045	0.00018	0.00004

TABLE 23-21
Yearly Savings Rate Factors
6% Savings Step-up Rate (A7)

Yrs	Assumed Rate of Return (A5)					
	1%	2%	3%	4%	5%	6%
1	0.99010	0.98039	0.97087	0.96154	0.95238	0.94340
2	0.47831	0.47134	0.46453	0.45788	0.45137	0.44500
3	0.30803	0.30211	0.29633	0.29071	0.28522	0.27987
4	0.22312	0.21781	0.21265	0.20763	0.20276	0.19802
5	0.17236	0.16748	0.16276	0.15818	0.15375	0.14945
6	0.13867	0.13414	0.12976	0.12553	0.12144	0.11749
7	0.11473	0.11048	0.10639	0.10246	0.09866	0.09501
8	0.09688	0.09289	0.08905	0.08536	0.08182	0.07843
9	0.08309	0.07932	0.07571	0.07225	0.06894	0.06577
10	0.07214	0.06858	0.06517	0.06191	0.05881	0.05584
11	0.06325	0.05988	0.05666	0.05359	0.05067	0.04789
12	0.05591	0.05271	0.04967	0.04677	0.04402	0.04141
13	0.04976	0.04672	0.04384	0.04110	0.03851	0.03606
14	0.04454	0.04166	0.03892	0.03634	0.03390	0.03159
15	0.04007	0.03732	0.03473	0.03229	0.02998	0.02782
16	0.03619	0.03359	0.03113	0.02882	0.02664	0.02460
17	0.03282	0.03034	0.02801	0.02582	0.02376	0.02184
18	0.02985	0.02750	0.02529	0.02321	0.02127	0.01946
19	0.02724	0.02500	0.02290	0.02093	0.01910	0.01740
20	0.02492	0.02278	0.02079	0.01893	0.01720	0.01559
21	0.02284	0.02082	0.01892	0.01716	0.01552	0.01401
22	0.02099	0.01906	0.01726	0.01559	0.01404	0.01261
23	0.01932	0.01748	0.01578	0.01419	0.01273	0.01138
24	0.01781	0.01607	0.01445	0.01294	0.01156	0.01029
25	0.01645	0.01479	0.01325	0.01183	0.01052	0.00932
26	0.01521	0.01364	0.01217	0.01082	0.00958	0.00845
27	0.01409	0.01259	0.01120	0.00992	0.00875	0.00768
28	0.01306	0.01163	0.01031	0.00910	0.00799	0.00699
29	0.01212	0.01077	0.00951	0.00836	0.00731	0.00636
30	0.01126	0.00997	0.00878	0.00769	0.00670	0.00580
31	0.01047	0.00925	0.00812	0.00708	0.00614	0.00530
32	0.00975	0.00858	0.00751	0.00653	0.00564	0.00484
33	0.00908	0.00797	0.00695	0.00602	0.00518	0.00443
34	0.00846	0.00741	0.00645	0.00556	0.00477	0.00406
35	0.00790	0.00690	0.00598	0.00514	0.00439	0.00372
36	0.00737	0.00642	0.00555	0.00476	0.00404	0.00341
37	0.00688	0.00598	0.00515	0.00440	0.00373	0.00313
38	0.00643	0.00558	0.00479	0.00408	0.00344	0.00287
39	0.00602	0.00520	0.00446	0.00378	0.00318	0.00264
40	0.00563	0.00485	0.00415	0.00351	0.00293	0.00243
41	0.00527	0.00453	0.00386	0.00325	0.00271	0.00224
42	0.00493	0.00424	0.00360	0.00302	0.00251	0.00206
43	0.00462	0.00396	0.00335	0.00281	0.00232	0.00190
44	0.00433	0.00370	0.00313	0.00261	0.00215	0.00175
45	0.00406	0.00346	0.00292	0.00243	0.00199	0.00161

TABLE 23-21 (Continued)
Yearly Savings Rate Factors
6% Savings Step-up Rate (A7)

	Assumed Rate of Return (A5)							
Yrs	7%	8%	9%	10%	11%	12%	15%	20%
1	0.93458	0.92593	0.91743	0.90909	0.90090	0.89286	0.86957	0.83333
2	0.43877	0.43268	0.42671	0.42088	0.41516	0.40957	0.39347	0.36873
3	0.27466	0.26957	0.26461	0.25977	0.25505	0.25044	0.23726	0.21726
4	0.19342	0.18894	0.18459	0.18035	0.17624	0.17223	0.16086	0.14383
5	0.14529	0.14125	0.13734	0.13355	0.12988	0.12631	0.11626	0.10144
6	0.11368	0.11000	0.10644	0.10300	0.09968	0.09647	0.08749	0.07443
7	0.09149	0.08810	0.08484	0.08170	0.07868	0.07577	0.06768	0.05610
8	0.07516	0.07203	0.06903	0.06615	0.06338	0.06073	0.05341	0.04311
9	0.06273	0.05983	0.05705	0.05440	0.05186	0.04944	0.04280	0.03362
10	0.05301	**0.05031**	0.04774	0.04529	0.04296	0.04074	0.03471	0.02651
11	0.04525	0.04273	0.04035	0.03808	0.03594	0.03390	0.02842	0.02109
12	0.03894	0.03660	0.03438	0.03229	0.03031	0.02844	0.02345	0.01690
13	0.03375	0.03156	0.02950	0.02756	0.02573	0.02402	0.01947	0.01362
14	0.02942	0.02738	0.02546	0.02367	0.02198	0.02040	0.01625	0.01103
15	0.02578	0.02388	0.02209	0.02042	0.01886	0.01741	0.01363	0.00897
16	0.02269	0.02091	0.01925	0.01770	0.01626	0.01492	0.01148	0.00732
17	0.02005	0.01839	0.01684	0.01540	0.01407	0.01284	0.00970	0.00598
18	0.01778	0.01622	0.01478	0.01344	0.01221	0.01108	0.00822	0.00491
19	0.01582	0.01435	0.01301	0.01177	0.01063	0.00959	0.00698	0.00403
20	0.01411	0.01274	0.01148	0.01033	0.00928	0.00832	0.00595	0.00332
21	0.01261	0.01133	0.01016	0.00909	0.00812	0.00724	0.00507	0.00274
22	0.01130	0.01010	0.00901	0.00802	0.00712	0.00630	0.00434	0.00226
23	0.01015	0.00903	0.00801	0.00708	0.00625	0.00550	0.00371	0.00187
24	0.00913	0.00808	0.00713	0.00627	0.00550	0.00481	0.00318	0.00155
25	0.00823	0.00724	0.00635	0.00556	0.00485	0.00422	0.00273	0.00128
26	0.00743	0.00650	0.00568	0.00493	0.00428	0.00370	0.00235	0.00106
27	0.00672	0.00585	0.00508	0.00439	0.00378	0.00325	0.00202	0.00088
28	0.00608	0.00527	0.00455	0.00391	0.00334	0.00285	0.00174	0.00073
29	0.00551	0.00475	0.00408	0.00348	0.00296	0.00251	0.00150	0.00061
30	0.00500	0.00429	0.00366	0.00311	0.00263	0.00221	0.00129	0.00050
31	0.00454	0.00387	0.00329	0.00277	0.00233	0.00195	0.00112	0.00042
32	0.00413	0.00350	0.00296	0.00248	0.00207	0.00172	0.00096	0.00035
33	0.00376	0.00317	0.00266	0.00222	0.00184	0.00152	0.00083	0.00029
34	0.00343	0.00288	0.00240	0.00199	0.00164	0.00134	0.00072	0.00024
35	0.00313	0.00261	0.00216	0.00178	0.00146	0.00119	0.00062	0.00020
36	0.00285	0.00237	0.00195	0.00160	0.00130	0.00105	0.00054	0.00017
37	0.00261	0.00215	0.00176	0.00143	0.00116	0.00093	0.00047	0.00014
38	0.00238	0.00196	0.00159	0.00129	0.00103	0.00082	0.00040	0.00012
39	0.00218	0.00178	0.00144	0.00116	0.00092	0.00073	0.00035	0.00010
40	0.00199	0.00162	0.00130	0.00104	0.00082	0.00065	0.00030	0.00008
41	0.00183	0.00147	0.00118	0.00094	0.00074	0.00057	0.00026	0.00007
42	0.00167	0.00134	0.00107	0.00084	0.00066	0.00051	0.00023	0.00006
43	0.00153	0.00123	0.00097	0.00076	0.00059	0.00045	0.00020	0.00005
44	0.00141	0.00112	0.00088	0.00068	0.00053	0.00040	0.00017	0.00004
45	0.00129	0.00102	0.00080	0.00062	0.00047	0.00036	0.00015	0.00003

TABLE 23-22
Yearly Savings Rate Factors
8% Savings Step-up Rate (A7)

	Assumed Rate of Return (A5)					
Yrs	1%	2%	3%	4%	5%	6%
1	0.99010	0.98039	0.97087	0.96154	0.95238	0.94340
2	0.47373	0.46685	0.46013	0.45356	0.44713	0.44084
3	0.30211	0.29633	0.29071	0.28522	0.27987	0.27466
4	0.21666	0.21155	0.20659	0.20176	0.19707	0.19251
5	0.16568	0.16105	0.15657	0.15222	0.14800	0.14392
6	0.13192	0.12768	0.12358	0.11961	0.11578	0.11207
7	0.10801	0.10409	0.10031	0.09666	0.09315	0.08976
8	0.09023	0.08660	0.08310	0.07974	0.07650	0.07339
9	0.07656	0.07317	0.06992	0.06681	0.06382	0.06096
10	0.06574	0.06258	0.05956	0.05667	0.05391	0.05126
11	0.05700	0.05405	0.05124	0.04855	0.04599	0.04354
12	0.04981	0.04706	0.04444	0.04194	0.03956	0.03729
13	0.04382	0.04125	0.03880	0.03647	0.03426	0.03216
14	0.03877	0.03636	0.03408	0.03190	0.02985	0.02790
15	0.03446	0.03221	0.03007	0.02805	0.02613	0.02433
16	0.03076	0.02865	0.02665	0.02477	0.02298	0.02131
17	0.02755	0.02558	0.02371	0.02195	0.02029	0.01873
18	0.02475	0.02291	0.02116	0.01952	0.01798	0.01653
19	0.02230	0.02058	0.01895	0.01741	0.01597	0.01463
20	0.02014	0.01853	0.01700	0.01557	0.01423	0.01298
21	0.01823	0.01672	0.01530	0.01396	0.01271	0.01155
22	0.01653	0.01512	0.01379	0.01254	0.01138	0.01029
23	0.01502	0.01370	0.01245	0.01129	0.01020	0.00920
24	0.01367	0.01243	0.01127	0.01018	0.00917	0.00823
25	0.01245	0.01130	0.01021	0.00920	0.00825	0.00738
26	0.01136	0.01028	0.00926	0.00832	0.00744	0.00663
27	0.01038	0.00937	0.00842	0.00753	0.00672	0.00596
28	0.00949	0.00854	0.00766	0.00683	0.00607	0.00537
29	0.00868	0.00780	0.00697	0.00620	0.00549	0.00484
30	0.00795	0.00713	0.00636	0.00564	0.00498	0.00437
31	0.00729	0.00652	0.00580	0.00513	0.00451	0.00395
32	0.00669	0.00597	0.00530	0.00467	0.00410	0.00357
33	0.00614	0.00547	0.00484	0.00426	0.00372	0.00323
34	0.00564	0.00502	0.00443	0.00389	0.00339	0.00293
35	0.00518	0.00460	0.00405	0.00355	0.00308	0.00266
36	0.00477	0.00422	0.00371	0.00324	0.00281	0.00241
37	0.00439	0.00388	0.00340	0.00296	0.00256	0.00219
38	0.00404	0.00356	0.00312	0.00271	0.00233	0.00199
39	0.00372	0.00328	0.00286	0.00248	0.00213	0.00181
40	0.00342	0.00301	0.00263	0.00227	0.00195	0.00165
41	0.00316	0.00277	0.00241	0.00208	0.00178	0.00150
42	0.00291	0.00255	0.00222	0.00191	0.00163	0.00137
43	0.00268	0.00235	0.00204	0.00175	0.00149	0.00125
44	0.00247	0.00217	0.00188	0.00161	0.00136	0.00114
45	0.00228	0.00200	0.00173	0.00147	0.00125	0.00104

TABLE 23-22 (Continued)
Yearly Savings Rate Factors
8% Savings Step-up Rate (A7)

	Assumed Rate of Return (A5)							
Yrs	7%	8%	9%	10%	11%	12%	15%	20%
1	0.93458	0.92593	0.91743	0.90909	0.90090	0.89286	0.86957	0.83333
2	0.43469	0.42867	0.42278	0.41701	0.41137	0.40584	0.38994	0.36550
3	0.26957	0.26461	0.25977	0.25505	0.25044	0.24594	0.23307	0.21354
4	0.18807	0.18376	0.17956	0.17548	0.17151	0.16765	0.15667	0.14023
5	0.13996	0.13612	0.13239	0.12878	0.12528	0.12189	0.11230	0.09814
6	0.10849	0.10503	0.10168	0.09845	0.09532	0.09230	0.08382	0.07147
7	0.08650	0.08336	0.08033	0.07740	0.07459	0.07188	0.06433	0.05349
8	0.07040	0.06753	0.06478	0.06213	0.05958	0.05714	0.05038	0.04083
9	0.05821	0.05558	0.05306	0.05065	0.04835	0.04614	0.04008	0.03164
10	0.04873	0.04632	0.04401	0.04181	0.03972	0.03772	0.03226	0.02480
11	0.04121	0.03899	0.03688	0.03487	0.03296	0.03114	0.02623	0.01961
12	0.03514	0.03309	0.03115	0.02931	0.02757	0.02592	0.02149	0.01563
13	0.03017	0.02828	0.02650	0.02482	0.02323	0.02173	0.01773	0.01253
14	0.02606	0.02432	0.02268	0.02113	0.01968	0.01832	0.01471	0.01010
15	0.02262	0.02102	0.01951	0.01809	0.01676	0.01552	0.01226	0.00817
16	0.01973	0.01824	0.01685	0.01555	0.01434	0.01321	0.01026	0.00664
17	0.01727	0.01590	0.01462	0.01342	0.01231	0.01128	0.00862	0.00541
18	0.01517	0.01390	0.01272	0.01163	0.01061	0.00967	0.00726	0.00442
19	0.01337	0.01220	0.01111	0.01010	0.00917	0.00831	0.00614	0.00362
20	0.01181	0.01073	0.00972	0.00880	0.00795	0.00716	0.00520	0.00297
21	0.01046	0.00946	0.00853	0.00768	0.00690	0.00619	0.00441	0.00244
22	0.00929	0.00836	0.00751	0.00672	0.00601	0.00536	0.00376	0.00201
23	0.00826	0.00741	0.00662	0.00590	0.00524	0.00465	0.00320	0.00166
24	0.00737	0.00657	0.00584	0.00518	0.00458	0.00404	0.00273	0.00137
25	0.00658	0.00584	0.00517	0.00456	0.00401	0.00352	0.00233	0.00113
26	0.00588	0.00520	0.00458	0.00402	0.00352	0.00307	0.00200	0.00093
27	0.00527	0.00464	0.00406	0.00355	0.00309	0.00268	0.00171	0.00077
28	0.00472	0.00414	0.00361	0.00314	0.00272	0.00234	0.00147	0.00064
29	0.00424	0.00370	0.00321	0.00278	0.00239	0.00205	0.00126	0.00053
30	0.00381	0.00331	0.00286	0.00246	0.00211	0.00179	0.00108	0.00044
31	0.00343	0.00297	0.00255	0.00218	0.00186	0.00157	0.00093	0.00036
32	0.00309	0.00266	0.00228	0.00194	0.00164	0.00138	0.00080	0.00030
33	0.00279	0.00239	0.00204	0.00172	0.00145	0.00121	0.00069	0.00025
34	0.00252	0.00215	0.00182	0.00153	0.00128	0.00107	0.00060	0.00021
35	0.00227	0.00193	0.00163	0.00137	0.00114	0.00094	0.00051	0.00017
36	0.00206	0.00174	0.00146	0.00122	0.00101	0.00083	0.00044	0.00014
37	0.00186	0.00157	0.00131	0.00108	0.00089	0.00073	0.00038	0.00012
38	0.00169	0.00141	0.00117	0.00097	0.00079	0.00064	0.00033	0.00010
39	0.00153	0.00127	0.00105	0.00086	0.00070	0.00057	0.00029	0.00008
40	0.00138	0.00115	0.00095	0.00077	0.00062	0.00050	0.00025	0.00007
41	0.00126	0.00104	0.00085	0.00069	0.00056	0.00044	0.00021	0.00006
42	0.00114	0.00094	0.00077	0.00062	0.00049	0.00039	0.00019	0.00005
43	0.00104	0.00085	0.00069	0.00055	0.00044	0.00035	0.00016	0.00004
44	0.00094	0.00077	0.00062	0.00050	0.00039	0.00031	0.00014	0.00003
45	0.00086	0.00070	0.00056	0.00044	0.00035	0.00027	0.00012	0.00003

TABLE 23-23
Yearly Savings Rate Factors
10% Savings Step-up Rate (A7)

Yrs	Assumed Rate of Return (A5)					
	1%	2%	3%	4%	5%	6%
1	0.99010	0.98039	0.97087	0.96154	0.95238	0.94340
2	0.46924	0.46245	0.45581	0.44932	0.44297	0.43676
3	0.29634	0.29071	0.28522	0.27987	0.27466	0.26957
4	0.21041	0.20550	0.20072	0.19607	0.19155	0.18716
5	0.15927	0.15487	0.15061	0.14648	0.14247	0.13859
6	0.12550	0.12152	0.11768	0.11396	0.11037	0.10689
7	0.10165	0.09804	0.09454	0.09117	0.08792	0.08478
8	0.08401	0.08070	0.07751	0.07444	0.07149	0.06864
9	0.07048	0.06745	0.06453	0.06173	0.05904	0.05645
10	0.05984	0.05705	0.05438	0.05181	0.04935	0.04700
11	0.05129	0.04872	0.04627	0.04392	0.04167	0.03952
12	0.04430	0.04194	0.03968	0.03753	0.03547	0.03351
13	0.03851	0.03633	0.03426	0.03228	0.03040	0.02860
14	0.03365	0.03165	0.02974	0.02793	0.02620	0.02456
15	0.02954	0.02770	0.02595	0.02428	0.02269	0.02119
16	0.02604	0.02434	0.02273	0.02119	0.01974	0.01837
17	0.02302	0.02146	0.01998	0.01857	0.01724	0.01598
18	0.02042	0.01898	0.01762	0.01632	0.01510	0.01395
19	0.01816	0.01683	0.01558	0.01439	0.01327	0.01221
20	0.01618	0.01496	0.01381	0.01272	0.01169	0.01072
21	0.01445	0.01333	0.01227	0.01126	0.01032	0.00943
22	0.01292	0.01189	0.01092	0.01000	0.00913	0.00832
23	0.01158	0.01063	0.00974	0.00889	0.00809	0.00735
24	0.01039	0.00952	0.00869	0.00792	0.00719	0.00651
25	0.00933	0.00853	0.00778	0.00706	0.00639	0.00577
26	0.00839	0.00766	0.00696	0.00631	0.00569	0.00512
27	0.00755	0.00688	0.00624	0.00564	0.00508	0.00455
28	0.00680	0.00619	0.00560	0.00505	0.00453	0.00405
29	0.00613	0.00557	0.00503	0.00453	0.00405	0.00361
30	0.00553	0.00502	0.00452	0.00406	0.00363	0.00322
31	0.00500	0.00452	0.00407	0.00365	0.00325	0.00288
32	0.00451	0.00408	0.00367	0.00328	0.00291	0.00257
33	0.00408	0.00368	0.00330	0.00295	0.00261	0.00230
34	0.00369	0.00333	0.00298	0.00265	0.00235	0.00206
35	0.00334	0.00300	0.00269	0.00239	0.00211	0.00185
36	0.00302	0.00272	0.00243	0.00215	0.00190	0.00166
37	0.00274	0.00246	0.00219	0.00194	0.00171	0.00149
38	0.00248	0.00222	0.00198	0.00175	0.00154	0.00134
39	0.00225	0.00201	0.00179	0.00158	0.00138	0.00120
40	0.00204	0.00182	0.00162	0.00143	0.00125	0.00108
41	0.00185	0.00165	0.00146	0.00129	0.00112	0.00097
42	0.00167	0.00149	0.00132	0.00116	0.00101	0.00087
43	0.00152	0.00135	0.00120	0.00105	0.00091	0.00079
44	0.00138	0.00123	0.00109	0.00095	0.00083	0.00071
45	0.00125	0.00111	0.00098	0.00086	0.00075	0.00064

TABLE 23-23 (Continued)
Yearly Savings Rate Factors
10% Savings Step-up Rate (A7)

Yrs	\multicolumn{8}{c}{Assumed Rate of Return (A5)}

Yrs	7%	8%	9%	10%	11%	12%	15%	20%
1	0.93458	0.92593	0.91743	0.90909	0.90090	0.89286	0.86957	0.83333
2	0.43068	0.42474	0.41892	0.41322	0.40765	0.40219	0.38647	0.36232
3	0.26461	0.25977	0.25505	0.25044	0.24594	0.24155	0.22898	0.20991
4	0.18289	0.17873	0.17469	0.17075	0.16692	0.16320	0.15261	0.13672
5	0.13482	0.13117	0.12762	0.12418	0.12085	0.11761	0.10847	0.09493
6	0.10352	0.10027	0.09712	0.09408	0.09113	0.08829	0.08029	0.06862
7	0.08176	0.07884	0.07602	0.07331	0.07069	0.06817	0.06112	0.05099
8	0.06591	0.06328	0.06075	0.05831	0.05597	0.05373	0.04749	0.03865
9	0.05397	0.05159	0.04931	0.04712	0.04502	0.04302	0.03748	0.02974
10	0.04475	0.04259	0.04053	0.03855	0.03667	0.03487	0.02995	0.02316
11	0.03747	0.03551	0.03364	0.03186	0.03017	0.02855	0.02416	0.01821
12	0.03164	0.02986	0.02816	0.02655	0.02502	0.02357	0.01966	0.01442
13	0.02690	0.02528	0.02374	0.02228	0.02090	0.01960	0.01610	0.01150
14	0.02300	0.02153	0.02013	0.01881	0.01756	0.01639	0.01326	0.00922
15	0.01977	0.01842	0.01716	0.01596	0.01483	0.01378	0.01098	0.00742
16	0.01707	0.01584	0.01469	0.01360	0.01258	0.01163	0.00913	0.00600
17	0.01479	0.01367	0.01262	0.01164	0.01072	0.00986	0.00762	0.00486
18	0.01286	0.01184	0.01089	0.00999	0.00916	0.00838	0.00638	0.00396
19	0.01122	0.01029	0.00942	0.00861	0.00785	0.00715	0.00536	0.00323
20	0.00981	0.00896	0.00817	0.00743	0.00675	0.00612	0.00451	0.00264
21	0.00860	0.00783	0.00710	0.00643	0.00582	0.00525	0.00381	0.00216
22	0.00756	0.00685	0.00619	0.00558	0.00502	0.00451	0.00322	0.00177
23	0.00665	0.00601	0.00541	0.00486	0.00435	0.00388	0.00273	0.00145
24	0.00587	0.00528	0.00473	0.00423	0.00377	0.00335	0.00232	0.00120
25	0.00519	0.00465	0.00415	0.00369	0.00328	0.00290	0.00197	0.00099
26	0.00459	0.00410	0.00364	0.00323	0.00285	0.00251	0.00168	0.00081
27	0.00407	0.00362	0.00320	0.00283	0.00248	0.00217	0.00143	0.00067
28	0.00361	0.00320	0.00282	0.00248	0.00217	0.00189	0.00122	0.00055
29	0.00320	0.00283	0.00249	0.00217	0.00189	0.00164	0.00104	0.00046
30	0.00285	0.00251	0.00219	0.00191	0.00166	0.00143	0.00089	0.00038
31	0.00254	0.00222	0.00194	0.00168	0.00145	0.00124	0.00076	0.00031
32	0.00226	0.00197	0.00171	0.00148	0.00127	0.00108	0.00065	0.00026
33	0.00202	0.00176	0.00152	0.00130	0.00111	0.00095	0.00056	0.00022
34	0.00180	0.00156	0.00135	0.00115	0.00098	0.00083	0.00048	0.00018
35	0.00161	0.00139	0.00119	0.00102	0.00086	0.00072	0.00041	0.00015
36	0.00144	0.00124	0.00106	0.00090	0.00076	0.00063	0.00036	0.00012
37	0.00129	0.00111	0.00094	0.00079	0.00067	0.00055	0.00031	0.00010
38	0.00115	0.00099	0.00084	0.00070	0.00059	0.00049	0.00026	0.00008
39	0.00103	0.00088	0.00074	0.00062	0.00052	0.00043	0.00023	0.00007
40	0.00093	0.00079	0.00066	0.00055	0.00046	0.00037	0.00020	0.00006
41	0.00083	0.00070	0.00059	0.00049	0.00040	0.00033	0.00017	0.00005
42	0.00075	0.00063	0.00053	0.00043	0.00036	0.00029	0.00015	0.00004
43	0.00067	0.00056	0.00047	0.00039	0.00031	0.00025	0.00013	0.00003
44	0.00060	0.00050	0.00042	0.00034	0.00028	0.00022	0.00011	0.00003
45	0.00054	0.00045	0.00037	0.00030	0.00025	0.00020	0.00009	0.00002

If you specify a zero percent savings step-up rate, you will reach your retirement accumulation goal by saving the same level amount each year as determined in line 21 of the Retirement Planning Work Sheet (table 23-15), assuming your actual investment rate of return matches your assumed rate of return.

CONCLUSION

The planner's work sheet that you have just reviewed, as well as the other material in this chapter, will help you and your client to set goals and to better understand the retirement needs analysis. Properly utilizing the tools provided and properly analyzing the assumptions needed will assist clients immeasurably. We feel it bears repetition, however, that this is an art form, not a science. The numbers are not absolute. Your best judgment should be used in conjunction with what this chapter has given you to achieve the best results for your client.

CHAPTER REVIEW

Answers to the review questions and self-test questions start on page 673.

Review Questions

23-1. Using the replacement-ratio method, find the amount of income needed (in today's dollars) to fund the desired retirement lifestyle for the following clients:
   a. Jane is 63 years old, earns $100,000, and anticipates no increase in standard of living between now and retirement at age 65. Jane is comfortable assuming an 80 percent replacement ratio.
   b. Keith is 45 years old, earns $50,000, and anticipates a 2 percent growth rate in lifestyle until retirement at age 65. Keith would be comfortable with a 90 percent replacement ratio.

23-2. Explain how to determine a client's retirement income status.

23-3. Discuss which of the following retirement resources need inflation protection from the client:
   a. Social Security benefits
   b. pension benefits
   c. dividend income from a stock portfolio
   d. the client's retirement income deficit

23-4. Tom has a taxable investment that earns 10 percent interest. Tom pays taxes at a marginal rate of 28 percent. What is the after-tax rate of return that Tom will receive?

23-5. Discuss the methods that can be used to liquidate retirement funds.

23-6. What method can be used to help keep clients from outliving their retirement savings?

23-7. What amount of money would it take to have a retirement income that provides $16,000 worth of purchasing power throughout a 35-year retirement period (assuming the fund earns 7 percent interest and the benefits increase by 3 percent each year)?

23-8. How much money does your client have to accumulate by retirement in order to protect against the inflation-related loss of purchasing power on a $33,000 level annual pension (assuming the fund assets earn 6 percent interest, inflation will be 2 percent, and the funds will be payable for 30 years)?

23-9. Your client (aged 48) would like to use level annual funding to accumulate $350,000 at retirement (at age 65). Determine the amount of the level annual contribution assuming contributed funds earn 7 percent interest.

23-10. Your client (aged 60), would like to use stepped-up annual funding to accumulate $150,000 by retirement (at age 65). Assume (1) an 8 percent interest rate and (2) an increase in contributions each year by a 4 percent inflation rate.
   a. Determine the amount of the first annual contribution.
   b. Determine the amounts of contributions for the remaining 4 years.

23-11. Kevin and Julie (both aged 45) are married and have a combined income of $80,000. In addition, they have $300,000 set aside for retirement in Kevin's 401(k) plan, and are expecting no money from a defined-benefit pension from Julie's employment. Both will receive $10,000 (totaling $20,000) from Social Security. They make the following assumptions:
   a. inflation rate prior to retirement: 4 percent
   b. inflation rate after retirement: 4 percent
   c. number of years until retirement: 19
   d. expected duration of retirement years: 25
   e. rate of return prior to retirement: 8 percent
   f. rate of return after retirement: 7 percent
   g. savings step-up with rate: 6 percent
   Using the retirement planning worksheet from the text, calculate the amount they need to save next year.

Self-Test Questions

T   F   23-1. The process of calculating the amount of the client's retirement need is complicated by time-value-of-money and inflation considerations.

T   F   23-2. To find the amount of income needed to achieve the desired retirement lifestyle under the replacement-ratio method, the planner in all cases needs only to apply the desired replacement ratio to the client's salary and adjust for inflation.

T   F   23-3. In order to estimate the client's retirement-income status (RIS), the planner must subtract the amount of the annual target for retirement income from the estimated annual retirement income.

T   F   23-4. The retirement income status (RIS) will always be a positive number.

T   F   23-5. Social Security is generally considered to be protected from a decline in purchasing power due to increases in inflation.

T   F   23-6. Pension income is generally considered to be protected from a decline in purchasing power due to increases in inflation.

T   F   23-7. Dividend income from a stock portfolio is generally considered to be protected from a decline in purchasing power due to increases in inflation.

T   F   23-8. The longer the liquidation period assumed for depleting assets, the greater the amount of funds needed for the retirement target.

T   F   23-9. One way to protect a client from outliving retirement savings is to have the client purchase a life annuity with his or her accumulated savings.

T   F   23-10. The decline in purchasing power only affects a person's pension income.

T   F   23-11. Under a level annual funding method, the amount saved each year increases to coordinate salary increases with savings increases.

24

Investing for Retirement

Learning Objectives

An understanding of the material in this chapter should enable the student to

24-1. Identify the considerations that apply to retirement investing.

24-2. Discuss the long-term accumulation period.

24-3. Discuss the portfolio restructuring period.

24-4. Discuss the preservation and current income period.

Chapter Outline

RISK-RETURN CONSIDERATIONS

In order to properly advise clients about investing for their retirement, planners must first understand the relationship between risk and return. In general, the higher the risk of any investment, the higher must be the expected return in the long run. Conversely, the lower the risk of an investment means the lower the expected return. Risk includes the variation in the amount of the annual income as well as the potential for gain or loss of all or some of the assets' value. From this perspective, investing for retirement can be seen as a trade-off between what is acceptable to the client and what is appropriate for the client. For example, despite the fact that high-risk investment vehicles might enhance the client's ability to accumulate the needed funds for retirement, if the client is unwilling to accept that degree of risk, then the high-risk, high-return investment will not be a viable alternative for retirement accumulation purposes. Thus, a willingness to accept or not accept a high degree of investment risk can have a large effect on the amount of assets that a client will need to accumulate to fund his or her retirement income target. In addition, that choice will affect the annual saving required to accumulate that fund.

> *Example*: Recall (in chapter 23) that we used an 8 percent after-tax investment assumption, a 4 percent inflation rate, and a 25-year liquidation period for Joe Brown when figuring his retirement target was $154,594. If we change only the after-tax interest rate for the 10-year accumulation period to a 5 percent after-tax return, Joe will need to accumulate $233,747, which is an additional $79,153 to reach the same retirement standard-of-living objective.

A second consideration is not what level of risk a client can withstand, but what level of risk is appropriate for retirement planning purposes. For example, as a client nears his or her retirement date, the amount of risk that can be taken must be reduced as a means of preserving the funds needed for retirement. This shift to lower-risk, lower-return investments will reduce the total amount of funds accumulated for retirement. To offset this reduced return, additional annual saving will be needed during all, or at least the last few years, of the accumulation period.

> *Example*: If Joe Brown reduced his after-tax return from 8 percent to 5 percent after he attained age 60 and had been contributing $14,940 per year to achieve his objective, Joe would need to save an additional $4,525 during each of the remaining 5 years to meet his objective.

LIFE-CYCLE CONSIDERATIONS

In addition to accommodating the client's risk profile, retirement planners also need to be aware of the unique characteristics of retirement investing at each stage of a client's life cycle. When planning for a client's retirement, the following three time periods are important:

1. the long-term accumulation period
2. the portfolio restructuring period
3. the preservation and current-income period

LONG-TERM ACCUMULATION PERIOD

long-term accumulation period

The *long-term accumulation period* starts when the client first begins to accumulate funds for retirement purposes and continues until the client is within 5 to 15 years of retirement. During the long-term accumulation period, the planner·must

- recognize the client's preference for risk and choose investment vehicles that correspond to the client's "zone of acceptance"
- monitor the portfolio's performance
- revise the portfolio to correspond with changes in the client's personal finances, the client's attitude toward risk, and the economy
- account for inflation's influence on the client's need for retirement funds

Regardless of an individual's willingness to bear investment risk, the long-term accumulation period is the time when a client can take on the highest tolerable risks to strive for the largest possible accumulation of assets. A greater risk can be taken during this period because clients still have many years of employment remaining and are in a position to alter their saving habits should investment losses occur.

Thus, the client who can be categorized as a risk-taker would build a high-risk, high-return portfolio that would include some high-risk investments such as stocks of newly formed publicly traded businesses, master limited partnership units, or other investments near the peak of the risk-return triangle shown in figure 24-1. The risk-blender would prefer a medium-risk, medium-return portfolio that would hold some investments such as common stocks, mutual funds, and other vehicles from the middle of the risk-return triangle. The risk-avoider, on the other hand, has a preference for a low-risk, low-return portfolio and would want investments largely selected from the bottom portions of the risk-return triangle.

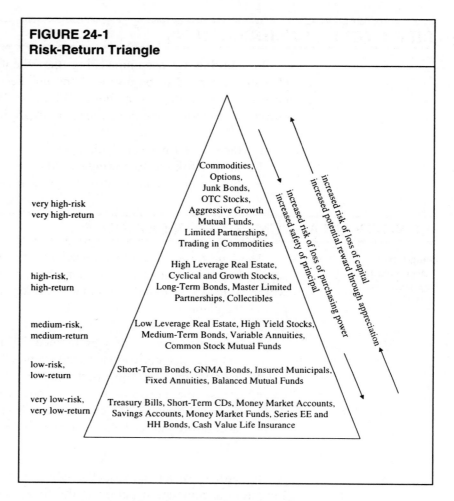

FIGURE 24-1
Risk-Return Triangle

An appropriate portfolio for the long-term accumulation period includes a mix of investments that are both consistent with the client's attitude toward risk and appropriate for meeting the client's long-term objectives. These objectives may not be met, for example, if a risk-avoider chooses an extremely conservative portfolio, because in addition to the investment risk, retirement investing faces the risk that long-term inflation will reduce the buying power of the monies placed into the investment vehicle. (This is referred to as "inflation risk" or "purchasing power" risk.) Therefore, during the long-term accumulation period, even the risk-avoider should consider some investments that will have as two of their characteristics a higher return and a potential for appreciation. Such investments provide a means of offsetting some of the purchasing power risk even though risk of capital loss is increased. Without some investment returns that will counterbalance the effects of inflation, the task of accumulating sufficient retirement funds becomes even more formidable.

However, there is not one best portfolio for any one client-risk profile that will achieve these objectives. Figure 24-2 shows three widely different portfolios that offer similar degrees of risk and approximately the same opportunity for long-term gain for each of the three different client-risk attitudes. (Other portfolio configurations could also be developed.) For example, the risk-avoider could construct a portfolio consisting of 80 percent very low-risk, very low-return investments and 20 percent very high-risk, very high-return investments. And, although this particular portfolio would have results similar to the two other portfolios for this risk preference, the presence of 20 percent of the investable monies in a high-risk, high-return investment might be inappropriate for some clients within this profile. Therefore, a portfolio configuration that is consistent with risk and return objectives for the general risk category might be unacceptable for a client within that profile.

(*Planning Note*: The retirement planner must exercise caution when recommending investment vehicles during the long-term accumulation period. The portfolio must fall within the client's "zone of acceptance." Otherwise, the client may reject the full set of recommendations and either do nothing, which would be detrimental to the client, or, worse yet from the planner's standpoint, look for someone else to do his or her retirement planning.)

Other Investment-Related Issues

In addition to the client's risk profile, there are other elements of the portfolio building and long-term accumulation phase that apply to virtually all clients. The first of these elements is that investors are planning for a long-term objective. Portfolio design should not be swayed by short-term impulsive changes in conventional wisdom as to what is the right investment for the moment. Unless fundamental, long-term changes are occurring that will affect the investment portfolio path chosen by the client, long-term goals are more likely to be achieved by using a buy-and-hold strategy that includes periodic monitoring and selective repositioning. (*Planning Note: Dollar-cost averaging* [DCA]), an approach in which a fixed-dollar amount is invested in a security in each period, is consistent with a buy-and-hold strategy. Clients who use this approach will purchase more units of a security when its price is low and fewer units of the security when its price is high. Over a long period of time, the investor ends up with a lower average cost for the security than was the average acquisition price for each transaction. For example, dollar cost averaging occurs when an individual makes monthly contributions to a specific mutual fund in a 401(k) plan.)

dollar-cost averaging

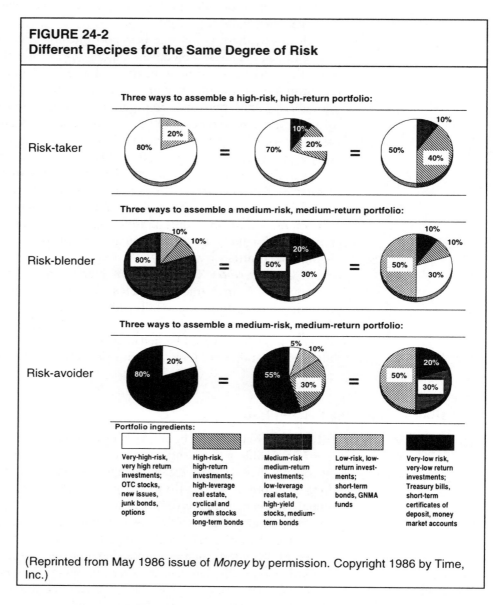

FIGURE 24-2
Different Recipes for the Same Degree of Risk

Three ways to assemble a high-risk, high-return portfolio:

Risk-taker

Three ways to assemble a medium-risk, medium-return portfolio:

Risk-blender

Three ways to assemble a medium-risk, medium-return portfolio:

Risk-avoider

Portfolio ingredients:

| Very-high-risk, very high return investments; OTC stocks, new issues, junk bonds, options | High-risk, high-return investments; high-leverage real estate, cyclical and growth stocks long-term bonds | Medium-risk, medium-return investments; low-leverage real estate, high-yield stocks, medium-term bonds | Low-risk, low-return investments; short-term bonds, GNMA funds | Very-low risk, very-low return investments; Treasury bills, short-term certificates of deposit, money market accounts |

(Reprinted from May 1986 issue of *Money* by permission. Copyright 1986 by Time, Inc.)

A second common issue, alluded to in the last planning note, is the importance of regularly putting aside money to invest for retirement. The amount of funds needed to fund a secure retirement is daunting and, for most, the only way to accomplish the goal is to invest funds on a regular basis as part of their routine money management.

The fact that each client's financial affairs will undergo change is another common element. Therefore, an annual review of the client's situation should be an integral part of the retirement planning process. This review is important for the following reasons:

- As the standard of living grows, the need for additional saving to fund the increased standard of living also increases.
- Planners may want to suggest that as real income grows the current standard of living should grow at a somewhat reduced pace. Assume real after-tax income increases by 10 percent. If the client limits any increases in lifestyle expenditures to 5 percent of the increase in income, then there will be a sizable increase, proportionately, in funds available for retirement accumulation purposes.

Example: If a client has income of $100,000 and allocates $80,000 for lifestyle and $20,000 for retirement purposes, a 10 percent increase in real income will provide an additional $10,000. If the increase in lifestyle expenditures can be kept to $4,000 (or 40 percent of the $10,000 increase), then $6,000 is available for retirement. This $6,000 represents a whopping 30 percent increase in annual retirement funding! In addition, the $4,000 increase in lifestyle expenditures raises the current standard of living by 5 percent.

- Planners must consider downward revisions of funding goals because of job-related reversals or other economic reversals.

A fourth factor is that a client's risk propensity changes over time. This can occur for many reasons such as having a poor experience with previous investments. For example, the sharp stock market decline in October 1987 may have been so devastating psychologically to a client that investments in common stocks (or common-stock-based mutual funds or variable annuities), previously within that client's zone of acceptance, may no longer be an acceptable investment choice. Should this occur, the client needs to (1) reevaluate the expected return from the accumulated funds, (2) restructure the portfolio of accumulated funds, (3) change the allocation of new funds regularly being invested, and (4) alter the amount of annual funding to achieve the retirement target.

The widespread opportunity for clients to participate in an employer-sponsored defined-contribution retirement plan is a fifth common element. Many such plans give investment discretion to the employee. When the client has this opportunity, the investment vehicle(s) chosen should be considered a part of the aggregate portfolio mix for the purpose of assessing the match of the portfolio with the client's risk profile. (*Planning Note:* Employer-sponsored plans often permit additional voluntary contributions (typically on an after-tax basis) that can be made through payroll deductions. This option can provide both the forced element of retirement saving that some individuals need as well as the opportunity to purchase securities with little, if any, transaction costs to the plan participant. More importantly, however, all earnings on qualified plan assets are tax deferred.)

A sixth factor for many clients is the direct ownership of common stocks. Many corporations encourage stockholders to increase their ownership interest in the corporation by offering two attractive methods. One method is for corporations to permit stockholders to make contributions, generally not more frequent than quarterly and within minimum and maximum dollar amounts, to purchase additional shares through this stockholder plan. Another method is the automatic reinvestment of dividends into additional shares of the corporation's stock. In addition to the ease of purchasing additional shares, the attractiveness of these two methods is that the transaction costs are subsidized since the corporation either pays that cost or acquires shares in the market in large volume so that the corporation obtains a negotiated and reduced brokerage commission that can be passed on to the shareholders in the form of lower transaction costs.

When this technique is used, the corporation's stock should be evaluated with respect to its risk-return characteristics and be within the acceptable criteria for the overall retirement portfolio. Clients should be advised against relying so heavily on acquiring these stocks that they do not have a diversified portfolio.

PORTFOLIO RESTRUCTURING PERIOD

portfolio restructuring period

The *portfolio-restructuring period,* the time when major restructuring of a retirement portfolio occurs, will vary depending on the client. The restructuring typically begins somewhere between 5 and 15 years prior to the planned retirement date. Therefore, if the client's target retirement age is 65, this phase could begin as early as age 50, but is often delayed until the middle or late 50s or until the early 60s.

As a client approaches retirement, he or she becomes less growth oriented and begins to be more concerned about having enough income from the portfolio for retirement income needs. This change in emphasis occurs for several reasons. First, as the client realizes that since only a few years remain until retirement, he or she has less time in which to recover losses should the higher-risk investments suffer reverses. Therefore, the client is now less willing to bear risk within the portfolio and less willing to invest additional funds in or even retain some or all of the currently owned higher-risk investments. Consequently, annual retirement funding during these years is directed into investment media near the bottom of the risk-return triangle in figure 24-1. Even if the client retains the currently owned, higher-risk investments acquired in the accumulation period, the risk profile of the total portfolio declines.

A second factor influencing the structure of the client's portfolio is the perceived need for an increased level of income during the retirement years. Assets whose main attraction was that of long-term appreciation during the accumulation period lose their appeal as clients become increasingly concerned about having sufficient current income to maintain the desired standard of living during retirement. This increased focus on income combined with the downward risk profile of the portfolio has the effect of generating more current annual income but less total return each year from the portfolio. As a consequence, until retirement actually takes place, the reinvestment of the portfolio's annual income stream becomes an ever-increasing segment of total portfolio management.

This process of redirecting the portfolio composition continues as the client ages, leading to a portfolio mix at or around retirement that contains significantly less risk than the one held at the beginning of this period. Accompanying this risk reduction is the portfolio's production of a much larger current income stream. The planner and the client must both keep in mind that a higher current income stream does not necessarily equal a higher annual return. The form of the return will change. Investments that produce high current income streams may realize little or no appreciation. The total return from the portfolio will most likely decrease over time. If the return does decrease during this period, the client may not, in the absence of increased annual funding, have accumulated the desired amount of assets at retirement. Fortunately, this shift in portfolio emphasis and performance typically coincides with a reduction in the client's other personal financial responsibilities. The client might have finished funding his or her children's education and largely paid off homes and personal assets. These reduced demands make available savings that can be used to supplement amounts already being set aside for retirement.

Other Investment-Related Issues

Many clients in this phase of their retirement accumulation planning and investing are nearing the peak years of their earning power, therefore, their employers' contributions (or their own contributions if self-employed) to a qualified pension plan approach the largest amounts that will be set aside on their behalf. As a consequence, the importance of integrating pension plan accumulation with personal retirement accumulation becomes more crucial. Each client needs to assess his or her situation and then make the necessary allocations in the personal plan segment to most effectively combine the two components to achieve the final phases of accumulation and to provide the appropriate sources, stability, level, and growth of income during the retirement years.

***Example*:**   If it is a defined-benefit pension plan and a lump-sum distribution from the plan is not permissible, then the retirement income will take the form of a fixed-pension income. With this constraint, the client could certainly consider placing a portion of the personal assets, both before and during retirement, into investments having some opportunity for growth to supplement the fixed pension plan income and provide inflation protection. However, if a defined-contribution plan or profit-sharing plan is the employer's primary retirement plan and if the funds being set aside are placed primarily in the employer's stock, then a more conservative investment policy may be needed to provide the appropriate balance and diversification during the later years of retirement asset accumulation.

No single solution or mix of portfolio assets can be prescribed as the only one acceptable, but guidelines such as those shown in figure 24-2 that are adjusted to fit the particular client provide the starting point for making the portfolio selections.

A second issue arises for clients who are at or near the peak of their earning power. Their accumulation objective would be achieved more easily if the setting aside of investments outside of qualified plans could be done in a tax-advantageous manner. Ideally, the annual funding contributions would be deductible, and the income earnings of the fund would have tax-deferred status. Unfortunately, recent changes in the income tax laws reduced the tax-advantaged opportunities and eliminated most of the opportunities to deduct contributions. Some tax-deferral opportunities still remain and planners should use them when appropriate for the client's accumulation objectives. For example, both fixed and variable-deferred annuities retain their tax deferral on income earned during the accumulation period. Thus, these investment vehicles can fit the needs of either a low- or medium-risk portfolio. Even if a tax-deductible contribution cannot be converted to an IRA, the opportunity to accumulate earnings on a tax-deferred basis until the monies are withdrawn without penalties also provides a meaningful tax saving during the accumulation period. Of course, seeking the capital appreciation with medium- or high-risk investment provides additional tax deferral since gain is not taxed until the securities are sold. Unless these contributions can be made directly to a qualified plan, as discussed earlier in this chapter, this avenue of tax-deductible investment contributions is essentially extinct.

A third common factor that will affect many clients in this accumulation period is the reinvestment. Reinvestment is a recurring event for personally managed portfolios. In addition, clients who take a lump-sum distribution from a qualified pension plan will have to reinvest a large amount at one time. If such distributions are likely, the client should be developing plans for their eventual reinvestment at the time of their distribution or maturity. In addition to developing the primary plan for investing these funds, contingent alternatives must be developed should investment conditions change drastically just prior to the receipt of the plan distribution. Consider for a moment the dilemma of a client who received a plan distribution on October 19, 1987, the day the market lost more than 20 percent of its value. Without contingent plans, a faulty investment program might have been instituted.

PRESERVATION AND CURRENT-INCOME PERIOD

preservation and current-income period

The time that begins just prior to the retirement date and continues throughout the retirement period is the *preservation and current-income period*. The portfolio design now focuses on preserving the assets. The opportunity to rebuild the stock of assets no longer exists since retirement is at hand. The client wants to keep what he or she has and utilize these investment assets as one source of planned retirement income. Therefore, some further restructuring of the portfolio will take place as the client seeks to both reduce the portfolio's risk profile and provide the desired current income to supplement Social Security and pension plan benefits. However, a portion of the invested assets must be devoted to protecting the client from the effects of inflation during the retirement years. The relative size of this portfolio portion will be influenced by factors such as the client's risk profile, health of self and spouse, financial obligations other than personal maintenance, and expected stability of pension plan income.

Portfolio shifting can generate income tax gains and losses. A successful buy-and-hold strategy generally produces significant gains over a long period of years. Careful planning and scheduling can reduce the tax consequences of the portfolio repositioning. Obviously, using losses to offset gains is one effective technique to reduce tax consequences. Another strategy involves carefully assessing, prior to the end of the year, one's income level and tax liability for the year and then carefully shifting enough assets to realize an amount of gain from the sale of assets that will not push the client into a higher tax bracket. Further, the taking of capital losses to offset gains made earlier in the year can reduce the tax burden as well as prune the portfolio of problem investments.

Common Elements

In addition to shifting the portfolio to meet the retirement objectives, a common consideration among clients is how to manage the portfolio with minimum care and effort. The design of the portfolio should include such factors as an easy system of record keeping for personal and tax purposes and relative stability of the income flow among the months (or perhaps quarters) of the year. For clients who travel extensively or spend extended periods at a vacation home, the ability to have direct deposit of income into income-earning accounts prevents the accumulation of idle, nonincome-producing money. (*Planning Note:* It is possible that the flow of retire-ment income, particularly if a large portion is portfolio income, will not be level during the year. The use of a money market account or mutual fund provides an easily accessible repository for temporarily accumulated funds and will earn a competitive short-term interest rate.)

Frequently, only one spouse actively manages the family finances. If this spouse is the first to die or become disabled, the surviving spouse faces what may appear to be insurmountable problems. Many advisers suggest that the financially inexperienced spouse be given the opportunity to manage the family finances in case the task later becomes his or her responsibility.

Lastly, the potential for a major expenditure, such as buying into a retirement life-care community, is a common concern for many retirees and spouses. Often the financing comes from the sale of the residence. The current prices of these life-care facilities and the average prices of residences indicate that a transaction of this form may generate some additional investable assets for income-producing purposes. Retirees can always find uses for any additional income, such as increasing their standard of living or making gifts to relatives.

CHAPTER REVIEW

Answers to the review questions and self-test questions start on page 673.

Key Terms

long-term accumulation period
dollar-cost averaging
portfolio restructuring period

preservation and current-income
period

Review Questions

24-1. Discuss the risk-return considerations that should be deliberated when investing for retirement.

24-2. What role does the planner play with regard to his or her client's investments during the long-term accumulation period?

24-3. a. List seven very high-risk investments.
      b. List five high-risk investments.
      c. List five medium-risk investments.
      d. List five low-risk investments.
      e. List seven very low-risk investments.

24-4. a. Explain dollar-cost averaging.
      b. Why is dollar-cost averaging an effective investment strategy for retirement savings?

24-5. Why is an annual review of the client's retirement plan important?

24-6. Discuss the portfolio restructuring period.

24-7. Discuss the preservation and current-income period.

Self-Test Questions

T   F   24-1. In general, the higher the potential risk with any investment, the higher the potential return in the long run.

T   F   24-2. As the client gets closer to his or her retirement date, the amount of risk that can be taken must be reduced in order to preserve the amount of funds needed for retirement.

T   F   24-3. The long-term accumulation period is the part of the client's life cycle that is closest to his or her retirement date.

T   F   24-4. Regardless of an individual's willingness to bear investment risk, the long-term accumulation period is the period in which the client can take on the highest possible tolerable risks because losses can be made up.

T   F   24-5. Commodities are considered low-risk investments.

T   F   24-6. Cash value life insurance is generally considered a low-risk investment.

T   F   24-7. Variable annuities are considered a low-risk investment.

T   F   24-8. Purchasing power risk is the variation in the amount of the annual return and the potential for the loss of all or some of the amount paid for the investment.

T   F   24-9.   Portfolio design during the long-term accumulation period is best achieved through a buy-and-hold strategy.

T   F   24-10. The technique of making periodic contributions of funds used to purchase a deferred variable annuity is considered a dollar-cost-averaging technique.

T   F   24-11. One way to enhance retirement savings and to reduce retirement needs is to suggest that as real income grows the client's standard of living should grow at a somewhat reduced pace

T   F   24-12. A planner should ignore a change in a client's risk propensity.

T   F   24-13. When the client has the opportunity to direct investments in an employer-sponsored retirement plan, the client's plan investments should be considered separately from the aggregate portfolio mix when assessing whether the client's risk profile is achieved.

T   F   24-14. The portfolio restructuring period typically begins somewhere between 5 and 15 years prior to the planned retirement date.

T   F   24-15. A client approaching retirement typically becomes more concerned about the appreciation possibilities for his or her portfolio.

T   F   24-16. The client's portfolio typically undergoes risk reduction during the portfolio restructuring period.

T   F   24-17. Participants whose employer-sponsored retirement plan provides a fixed pension benefit, and not a lump-sum distribution, should consider investing their private savings in income-oriented investments.

T   F   24-18. Clients in the portfolio restructuring period typically seek tax-sheltered investments.

T   F   24-19. Even though preservation of capital is an important objective for the retired investor, a portion of the invested assets must be devoted to protecting the client from the effects of inflation during the retirement years.

25

Distributions from Retirement Plans—Part I

Learning Objectives
An understanding of the material in this chapter should enable the student to

25-1. Discuss the tax treatment of qualified plans, 403(b) annuities, and IRAs.

25-2. Identify when distributions can be rolled over into other tax-advantaged retirement plans.

25-3. Discuss the special tax rules that may apply to lump-sum distributions from qualified plans.

25-4. Describe the two basic minimum-distribution rules.

Chapter Outline

Planning for the distribution of funds from employer-sponsored retirement plans and IRAs can be one of the most challenging aspects of retirement planning. Any strategy selected must account for the following factors:

- the client's needs and goals
- the variety of distribution options that are available in your client's particular situation
- the implications of choosing one option over another from a tax perspective
- the implications of choosing one option over another from a cash-flow perspective
- the implications of choosing one option over another from a death benefit and estate tax perspective
- the ability to delay the receipt and taxation of a distribution by rolling the distribution over into an IRA or another qualified plan

This chapter examines the tax implications of the withdrawal. The following chapter will discuss the nontax rules, typical distribution options, and planning considerations for selecting the appropriate distribution option.

TAX TREATMENT

General

From the employee's perspective, the advantage of tax-sheltered retirement plans (qualified plans, 403(b) plans, IRAs, SEPs, and SIMPLEs) is that taxes are deferred until benefits are distributed—the day of reckoning. Generally, the entire value of a distribution is included as ordinary income in the year of the distribution. If the individual has made after-tax contributions or receives an insurance policy and has paid PS 58 costs, he or she will have a "cost basis" that can generally be recovered. Taxable distributions from tax-sheltered retirement plans made prior to age 59 1/2 are also subject to the 10 percent Sec. 72(t) penalty tax, unless the distribution satisfies one of several exceptions.

If the benefit is distributed in a single sum, the taxable portion may be eligible for one of several special tax benefits, but only if the distribution is from a qualified plan and satisfies certain lump-sum distribution requirements. Persons born before 1936 may be eligible for 10-year forward averaging or special capital-gains treatment. Any participant that receives employer securities as part of a lump-sum distribution can defer tax on the unrealized appreciation until the stock is later sold.

In many cases, all taxes, including the Sec. 72(t) penalty tax, can be avoided by rolling—or directly transferring—the benefit into an IRA or other qualified plan. Today, most distributions are eligible for rollover treatment. Taxes cannot be deferred indefinitely, however, under the minimum-distribution rules, distributions generally have to begin at age 70 1/2.

Estate Taxation of Pension Accumulations

Qualified plan and other tax-sheltered benefits payable to a beneficiary at the death of the participant are included in the participant's taxable estate. Benefits payable to beneficiaries are still subject to income tax, although the benefit amount is treated as income with respect to the decedent, meaning the income taxes are reduced by the estate taxes paid as a result of the pension benefit.

Sec. 72(t) Penalty Tax

Sec. 72(t) penalty tax

Distributions prior to age 59 1/2 from all types of tax advantaged retirement plans are subject to the 10 percent *Sec. 72(t) penalty tax* (unless an exception applies). The 10 percent penalty applies to distributions that are made from a qualified plan, a Sec. 403(b) plan, an IRA, or a SEP. The rule also applies to SIMPLEs, with a modification. During the first 2 years of plan participation, the early withdrawal penalty is 25 percent instead of 10 percent.

The 10 percent tax applies only to the portion of the distribution subject to income tax. This means that the tax does not apply when a benefit is rolled over from one tax-deferred plan into another. It also does not apply to the nontaxable portion of a distribution (which may occur with a distribution of after-tax contributions).

However, a distribution made prior to age 59 1/2 can escape the 10 percent penalty if it qualifies under one of several exceptions. To avoid the 10 percent penalty, the distributions must be

- to a beneficiary or to an employee's estate on or after the employee's death
- attributable to disability
- part of a series of *substantially equal periodic payments* made at least annually over the life or life expectancy of the employee or the joint lives or life expectancies of the employee and beneficiary. (If the distribution is from a qualified plan, the employee must separate from service.)
- after a separation from service for early retirement after age 55 (not applicable to IRAs, SEPs or SIMPLEs)
- made to cover medical expenses deductible for the year under Sec. 213 (medical expenses that exceed 7.5 percent of adjusted gross income)

Several additional exceptions apply to IRAs (which include SEPs and SIMPLEs). Distributions from IRAs escape the penalty if the distribution is for

- the purpose of paying health insurance premiums by an individual who is collecting unemployment insurance
- the payment of acquisition costs (paid within 120 days of the distribution) of a first home for the participant, spouse, or any child, grandchild, or ancestor of the participant or spouse (with a lifetime limit of $10,000 per IRA participant)
- the payment for qualified higher education expenses for education furnished to the taxpayer, the taxpayer's spouse, or any child or grandchild of the taxpayer or taxpayer's spouse at an eligible postsecondary educational institution

Qualified home acquisition expenses are those used to buy, build, or rebuild a first home. To be a first-time homebuyer, the individual (and spouse, if married) must not have had an ownership interest in a principal residence during a 2-year period ending on the date that the new home is acquired. Qualified education expenses include tuition, fees, books, supplies, and equipment required for enrollment in a postsecondary education institution.

The following examples should help to illustrate when the 10 percent penalty applies and when it does not.

Example 1:	Greg Murphy, aged 55, takes a $50,000 lump-sum distribution from his profit-sharing plan. The $50,000 lump-sum distribution will be subject to a $5,000 (10 percent) penalty unless Greg has taken early retirement pursuant to an early retirement provision in his plan.
Example 2:	Jane Goodall, aged 45, takes a life annuity from Biological Researchers, Inc., when she quits and goes to work for The Primate Institute. Jane's distribution is not subject to penalty because of the periodic payments exception.
Example 3:	Ed Miller, aged 35, takes a distribution from his 401(k) plan to meet an extreme financial hardship. Ed's distribution is subject to the 10 percent penalty.
Example 4:	Sandra Smalley, aged 45, takes a distribution from her IRA to pay for her child's college education. Sandra's distribution is not subject to the 10 percent penalty.
Example 5:	Cathrine Thegrate withdraws $10,000 from her IRA to make the downpayment on her first home. The distribution is exempt from the 10 percent penalty, however, no additional withdrawals from any of Cathrine's IRAs (or Roth IRAs) can qualify for the exception.

Avoiding the Sec. 72(t) Penalty Tax

In some cases, a client might need to make withdrawals prior to age 59 1/2 to pay personal or business expenses or to make an investment. When a company downsizes, middle-aged workers are often forced to take early retirement. Many of these individuals look for other employment, but may have a period in which they have to tap their nest eggs. Within the list of exceptions to the Sec. 72(t) penalty tax, some planning opportunities do exist. Of limited use is the age 55 exemption. To be eligible for this exemption, the individual must actually terminate employment on or after attaining age 55. The exception applies to qualified plans and 403(b) plans, but not to IRAs. Therefore, if IRA money is needed, even losing a job does not qualify for an automatic exemption from the tax.

For IRA participants (this includes SEPs and SIMPLEs too), the exceptions for educational expenses and first-time home buying expenses can also be quite useful. This is a fact that sponsors should keep in mind when choosing the appropriate type of plan.

Still the most useful exception for planning purposes is the substantially equal periodic payment exception. Under this exception, payments can begin at any age, as long as payments are set up to last for the life of the participant or the joint lives of the participant and his or her beneficiary. The exception applies to all types of plans, but note that with a qualified plan the participant must have separated from service before distributions begin. For the individual who needs the withdrawals for ongoing financial needs, periodic distributions may be just right. If, on the other hand, a large single-sum amount is needed, this strategy could still work. The individual can borrow the sum needed and repay the loan from the periodic distributions.

Under this exception, there is quite a bit of flexibility in calculating the annual withdrawal amount. The withdrawals must be calculated under one of three IRS-approved methods: (1) life expectancy, (2) amortization, or (3) annuitization. Under the life expectancy method, the distribution is calculated using any of the methods of calculating a minimum distribution under IRC Sec. 401(a)(9). Unlike the other methods, with the life expectancy method the amount of withdrawals will increase each year. The amortization method works the same as amortizing a loan—the loan payments are amortized over the life expectancy of the individual. With the annuitization method, the account balance is divided by a life annuity factor.

Payments can be made monthly, quarterly, or annually, and a range of interest rates and mortality tables can be used under any of the methods. These three methods provide for a great deal of flexibility in calculating a desired withdrawal amount. IRS guidance has also indicated that a range of reasonable interest rates and mortality tables can be used. Also, IRS rulings have allowed the calculation to be made for each separate IRA (or qualified plan) meaning that a participant could divide funds into separate accounts in order to better accommodate the appropriate distribution amount. The flexibility allowed is demonstrated with the following example.

***Example*:**   Assume Sara, aged 50, has an IRA account of $200,000. All the following represent withdrawal amounts that satisfy one of the calculation methods described by the IRS:

Life expectancy (33.1 years)	$ 6,042
Annuitization (33.1 years, 5% interest)	$11,888
Amortization (33.1 years, 8% interest)	$16,073

Even though the distribution amount is calculated based on lifetime payments, fortunately the rules do not actually require that payments continue for life. Payments can be stopped without penalty after the later of 5 years after the first payment or age 59 1/2. For example, an individual who began distributions in substantially equal payments at age 56 in January 1995 must continue taking the distributions until January 2000. Or, in the case of an individual beginning withdrawals at age 47, the payments must continue until he or she attains age 59 1/2, which is a period of 12 1/2 years.

A client using the substantially equal payment exception needs to be aware of potential potholes. The largest is that once payments have begun, they must continue for the minimum period in order to avoid the tax. Failure to make the required number of payments means the 10 percent penalty will be due on all distributions made before age 59 1/2, as well as interest on the tax obligation that was avoided during the years that distributions were made. Second, once the payment amount is determined, the amount cannot vary from the prescribed number each year or, again, the excise tax could apply.

Nontaxable Distributions

Most distributions made from qualified plans, IRA accounts, and 403(b) annuities are fully taxable as ordinary income. However, if some of the participant's benefit under the plan is attributable to dollars in the plan that have already been subject to taxation—for example, employee after-tax contributions and amounts attributable to term insurance premiums (PS 58 costs)—then a portion of a distribution may be exempt from tax until the total nontaxable amount has been distributed.

Calculating the appropriate tax treatment for periodic payments can become quite complex. The rules are different depending upon the type of plan and type of distribution involved. At the same time, fewer and fewer participant benefits contain nontaxable basis. This is true in part because of law changes that almost eliminated all new after-tax contributions to qualified plans beginning in 1987 (with the exception of a few large 401(k) plans that still allow after-tax contributions). Also, life insurance benefits in qualified plans have become more and more uncommon, reducing the amount of recoverable PS 58 costs. One new complicating factor is that beginning in 2002, participants are allowed to roll nontaxable contributions into an IRA. The tax treatment of withdrawals from the IRA are different than from a qualified plan. Even though these situations are not that common, they still come up and the financial services professional does need to have a basic understanding of the rules. A summary of the rules follows.

IRA Distributions

Let's begin with the simplest case, the traditional IRA. A participant can accumulate nontaxable amounts (referred to as cost basis) from either nondeductible contributions to the IRA or nontaxable amounts that have been rolled over from qualified plans. The rule is simply that if an individual has unrecovered cost basis, then a portion of each IRA distribution is tax free. The amount excluded from income is

$$\frac{\text{Unrecovered cost basis}}{\text{Total IRA}\atop\text{account}+{\text{Current year's}\atop\text{distribution}}} \times {\text{Distribution}\atop\text{amount}} = {\text{Tax-free}\atop\text{portion}}$$

This calculation is made looking at all of the IRAs an individual owns—which can have quite a negative impact on the recovery of cost basis if the participant has both nondeductible and deductible IRA contributions. This method applies until the individual has recovered all of his or her nondeductible contributions. After that, any distribution is fully taxable. If the IRA owner dies prior to recovering all nondeductible contributions, the remaining amount can be deducted on the individual's final income tax return.

PS 58 Costs

When a participant has had a life insurance policy as part of his or her benefit in a qualified plan or 403(b) annuity, there is generally an accumulation of PS 58 costs over the years. Note, however, that self-employed persons (sole proprietors and partners) do not technically accumulate PS 58 costs and are, therefore, not allowed to recover them upon distribution. PS 58 costs constitute cost basis, which can be recovered, but only in limited circumstances. If the participant receives a distribution to recover the PS 58 costs, the policy must be distributed to the participant. So, if a participant does not want to continue the policy, the trustee can strip the cash value of the policy (by borrowing) to reduce the cash value to the accumulated PS 58 costs and then distribute the contract and the cash.

If the participant dies and the policy proceeds are paid out to a beneficiary, then the PS 58 costs can again reduce the taxable portion of the distribution to the death beneficiary.

Rollovers from Qualified Plans

When a participant receives a distribution from a qualified plan that is eligible to be rolled into an IRA, beginning in 2002, the whole distribution may be rolled into an IRA. However, if the amount is rolled over, it is subject to the IRA recovery rules. As described above, these rules are not very favorable, especially with large rollover accounts. A participant may want to choose instead to roll over all but the nontaxable amount. Under old law, it was clear that this transaction would not result in any income tax consequences. Unfortunately, it is not that clear under the new law how this transaction will be treated.

As mentioned above, when a participant receives a life insurance policy from a qualified plan, the PS 58 costs may be recovered tax free if the policy is distributed. Special consideration must be made when the participant wants to receive the policy but minimize the tax consequences by rolling over as much of the benefit into an IRA as possible. Because a life insurance policy may not be rolled into an IRA, the tax consequences of this transaction can be minimized by having the trustee strip the cash value of the policy (by borrowing) to reduce the cash value to the accumulated PS 58 costs. Then the extra cash is distributed as part of the benefit and may be rolled over.

Single-Sum Distributions

If a participant receives the entire benefit and does not roll it into an IRA or other tax-sheltered retirement plan, recovery of basis occurs at the time of the distribution.

Distribution of After-tax Contributions Prior to the Annuity Starting Date

Prior to 1987, an amount up to the participant's cash basis could be withdrawn prior to the annuity starting date (the time periodic retirement benefits begin) without income tax consequences. The Tax Reform Act of 1986 changed this rule significantly. A grandfather provision still allows a participant to withdraw an amount equal to the pre-1987 cash basis as long as the plan provided for in-service distributions on May 5, 1986. Post-1986 amounts attributable to the cash basis, however, are now subject to a pro rata rule. The general rule is that the amount of the distribution that is excluded from tax is based on a ratio, with the numerator being cash basis and the denominator being the total account balance at the time of the distribution. However, when determining the ratio, an individual may treat employee after-tax contributions and the investment experience thereon separately from the rest of the participant's benefit. This rule still allows a participant to withdraw after-tax contributions with limited tax liability. This principle can be best illustrated with an example.

***Example*:**   Joe has an account balance of $1,000, $200 of which is attributable to post-1986 employee contributions and $50 of which is attributable to investment earnings on $200. Joe takes an in-service distribution of $100. The exclusion ratio is $200/$250 or 80 percent. Therefore, Joe will receive $80 income tax free and will owe tax on $20.

YOUR FINANCIAL SERVICES PRACTICE:
AFTER-TAX CONTRIBUTIONS

It is not uncommon for a business owner to have made after-tax contributions prior to 1987. These amounts can be withdrawn tax free, making them an excellent source of funds if the owner has a life insurance need or some other reason to need cash. After 1986, 401(k) plans are typically the only plans that may still have an after-tax contribution feature.

Periodic Distributions from Qualified Plans and 403(b) Annuities

Again, the rules have changed significantly over time. Today (any distributions that began after November 18, 1996), the amount is determined by dividing the cash basis by the number of expected monthly annuity payments. When the annuity is on the life of the participant only, the number of months are as described in table 25-1. For a joint and survivor annuity, use the number of months described in table 25-2.

The cash basis is the aggregate amount of after-tax contributions to the plan (plus other after-tax amounts such as PS 58 costs and repayments of loans previously taxed as distributions) minus the aggregate amount received before the annuity starting date that was excluded from income.

TABLE 25-1
Number of Months—Single Life Annuity

Age of Distributee	Number of Payments
55 and under	360
56–60	310
61–65	260
66–70	210
71 and over	160

TABLE 25-2	
Number of Months—Joint Annuity	
Combined Age of Annuitants	Number of Payments
Not more than 110	410
More than 110 but not more than 120	360
More than 120 but not more than 130	310
More than 130 but not more than 140	260
More than 140	210

The distributee recovers his or her cash basis in level amounts over the number of monthly payments determined in the tables above. The amount excluded from each payment is calculated by dividing the investment by the set number of monthly payments determined as follows:

$$\frac{\text{Investment}}{\text{Number of monthly payments}} = \begin{array}{c}\text{Tax-free portion}\\ \text{of monthly annuity}\end{array}$$

The dollar amount determined will be excluded from each monthly annuity payment, even where the amount of the annuity payments changes. For example, the amount to be excluded as determined at the annuity starting date remains constant, even if the amount of the annuity payments rises due to cost-of-living increases or decreases (in the case of a reduced survivor benefit annuity). If the amount to be excluded from each monthly payment is greater than the amount of the monthly annuity (as might be the case with decreased survivor payments), then each monthly annuity payment will be completely excluded from gross income until the entire investment is recovered. Once the entire investment is recovered, each monthly payment is fully taxable.

Example: John Thomas is about to begin a retirement benefit in the form of a single life annuity. His investment in the contract is $40,000. John is aged 65 at the time benefit payments begin. The set number of months used to compute the exclusion amount is 260 (for age 65 from table 25-1). Because his cash basis is $40,000, the amount excluded from each payment is $154 ($40,000 ÷ 260).

ROLLOVERS AND TRANSFERS

Most distributions from qualified plans, IRAs, SEPs, SIMPLEs, Sec. 403(b) plans, and 457 plans can be rolled over tax free to an IRA account as long as the rollover is made within 60 days of the receipt of the distribution. In addition, beginning in 2002, distributions from any of these plans can be rolled over into any of the other types of plans. For example a distribution from an IRA can now be rolled over into a qualified plan, or a distribution from a 403(b) plan can be rolled into a qualified plan.

The term *rollover* is used to describe the situation in which the participant physically receives the distribution and subsequently deposits the amount into an appropriate plan. Failure to roll the distribution over within 60 days from its receipt subjects the participant to income tax and, if applicable, the 10 percent Sec. 72(t) penalty on the entire taxable portion of the distribution. With a rollover, a participant has the opportunity to take a short-term loan for 60 days. Because of this possibility, the rules only allow one rollover per year for each plan. Otherwise, participants could continuously borrow from the plan. The once-a-year rule does not apply when assets are transferred directly from the plan's trustee (or custodian) directly to another.

direct rollover rule   Today, a *direct rollover rule* requires that qualified plans, Sec. 403(b) tax-sheltered annuities, and 457 plans give participants the option to have eligible benefit distributions transferred directly from one plan trustee to the trustee of an IRA.

The law also encourages direct rollovers (versus regular rollovers) by requiring 20 percent of any distribution that is not directly transferred to be withheld for federal income tax purposes. In other words, a participant planning to roll over a distribution will receive only 80 percent of the distribution; 20 percent is withheld for taxes. If an individual wants to roll over the entire distribution, he or she has to come up with the additional cash to deposit into the new plan and must request a tax refund. Because both direct rollovers and regular rollovers defer income tax on the distribution, a participant in a qualified plan or Sec. 403(b) tax-sheltered annuity should take advantage of the direct rollover option—thus avoiding the 20 percent income tax withholding.

Note that distributions from IRAs (that includes distributions from SEPs and SIMPLEs) are not subject to either the requirement that participants be given a direct rollover opportunity or the 20 percent withholding rules. An individual in a SEP or SIMPLE who wants to change service providers should arrange with the new carrier for a direct transfer, to be sure the 60-day rollover rules are not violated.

Also, keep in mind that distributions from a qualified plan can also be rolled over (or rolled directly) into another qualified plan. There are several reasons that a rollover into another qualified plan may be preferable to a rollover into an IRA. First, after-tax contributions and life insurance policies can be rolled into another qualified plan, but not into an IRA. Second, for participants born before 1936, rolling the benefit into another qualified plan may preserve the grandfathered 10-year averaging and capital-gains treatment. Third, there is the ability to borrow from the qualified plan. And fourth, the qualified plan may have lower investment costs (fees) or in/vestment options that are not available in an IRA. If an individual is not immediately eligible for participation into another qualified plan, remember that he or she may roll/transfer the benefit into an IRA and later roll the benefit back into a qualified plan.

Distributions Qualifying for Rollover Treatment

The qualified plan rollover rules and the 20 percent mandatory withholding rules apply to qualified rollover distributions. Almost all distributions are eligible rollover distributions with a few limited exceptions. The only distributions that do not qualify are as follows:

- minimum required distributions
- hardship withdrawals from a 401(k) plan
- distributions of substantially equal periodic payments made
  - over the participant's remaining life (or life expectancy)
  - over the joint lives (or life expectancies) of the participant and a beneficiary
  - over a period of more than 10 years

If a distribution from a qualified plan or 403(b) plan is not an eligible rollover amount, then that distribution is not subject to the 20 percent mandatory withholding requirements. This means that, for example, a hardship distribution from a 401(k) is not subject to mandatory withholding.

Rolling over a benefit from one IRA to another (including IRAs associated with SEPs and SIMPLEs) is, in most cases, even easier. The only limitation on rollovers is that amounts subject to the required minimum-distribution rules cannot be rolled over.

When to Use Direct Rollovers or Regular Rollovers

The direct rollover is an important tool for distribution planning, because a client's plan may not provide a distribution option that meets his or her needs. In such cases, plan balances or the accrued benefits may often be rolled over to another plan or to an IRA designed to provide the distribution option desired. In addition, rollovers are used when

- a participant in a qualified plan, 403(b) annuity plan, or IRA would like to continue to defer taxes on the money in the plan, but wants to change the form of investment or gain greater control over it;
- a participant in a retirement plan receives a large plan distribution upon retirement or termination of employment and wants to defer taxes on part or all of the distribution beyond the normal starting date for the plan or to avoid the 10 percent Sec. 72(t) penalty;
- a participant in a qualified retirement plan or a 403(b) annuity plan that is being terminated by the employer wishes to defer taxes on the distribution from the terminated plan;
- the spouse of a deceased employee wants to defer taxation on a lump-sum distribution of the deceased spouse's benefit or prefers a distribution option that is not provided as a survivor benefit option under the plan.

The entire amount qualifying for a transfer or rollover need not be rolled over. However, any amount not rolled over will be subject to income tax and the 10 percent Sec. 72(t) early withdrawal penalty, if applicable.

Distribution of Annuity Contracts

In some cases, qualified plans may distribute an annuity contract to a participant instead of a cash distribution. Assuming the annuity contract has the desired features, the annuity can serve the same purposes as an IRA rollover, because the participant will not be taxed until distributions are made under the annuity contract. The annuity contract does not have to meet the requirements of an IRA, but the tax implications and the distribution requirements and restrictions (such as the minimum-distribution rules, for example), are generally similar.

LUMP-SUM DISTRIBUTIONS

Instead of taking periodic payments from a qualified plan, employees are frequently permitted to receive their retirement benefit in a lump-sum distribution. In the past, participants who received a lump sum from a qualified plan had the opportunity to take advantage of several special tax rules. Most of these rules have been repealed, but several are still grandfathered for certain taxpayers. One rule that continues to be broadly available is the rule that defers the net unrealized appreciation of distributed employer securities. Grandfather rules include 10-year income averaging and a special capital-gains rate available for distributions attributable to pre-1974 participation. These rules are only available to individuals born before 1936.

Unrealized Appreciation

net unrealized appreciation (NUA)

Whenever a recipient receives a lump-sum distribution from a qualified plan, he or she may elect to defer paying tax on the *net unrealized appreciation (NUA)* in qualifying employer securities. If the distribution is not a lump-sum distribution, NUA is excludible only to the extent that the appreciation is attributable to nondeductible employee contributions.

lump-sum distribution

To qualify as a *lump-sum distribution,* the participant's entire benefit (referred to as balance to the credit) must be distributed in one tax year on account of death, disability, termination of employment, or attainment of age 59 1/2. For purposes of 10-year forward averaging (but not the NUA rules) the participant also needs to have 5 years of plan participation to qualify. Under the balance-to-the-credit rules, all pension plans of a single sponsor (defined-benefit, money-purchase, target-benefit or cash-balance plan) are treated as a single plan; all profit-sharing plans (including 401(k)) are treated as a single plan; and all stock-bonus plans are treated as a single plan. This means, for example, that a participant in both a defined-benefit plan and a money-purchase plan would have to receive both benefits in the same year to receive the balance to the credit.

The NUA in the employer's stock that is included in a lump-sum distribution is excluded when computing the income tax on the distribution. NUA is the difference between the value of the stock when credited to the participant's account and its fair market value on the date of distribution. The plan provides the participant with the cost basis. The plan can choose one of several methods for valuing the cost basis as found in Treas. Reg.1.402(a)-1(b)(2)(i).

This NUA is taxable as long-term capital gain to the recipient when the shares are sold, even if they are sold immediately. If the recipient holds the shares for a period of time after distribution, any additional gain (above the NUA) is taxed as long- or short-term capital gain, depending on the holding period (long term if held for one year or more).

The participant can elect at the time of the distribution to pay tax on the NUA (versus taking advantage of the opportunity to defer taxes). The only reason do this is if the effective tax rate using one of the other special averaging rules is less than the capital-gains rate of 20 percent. However, it is unlikely that this will be the case.

To ensure that the participant's unrealized appreciation is taxed at some point, if the stock is left to an heir, the unrealized appreciation is not entitled to a step up in basis, but is treated as income in respect of a decedent (IRD). As with other IRD, the amount retains its character as long-term capital gain, and the beneficiary is entitled to a deduction for the amount of estate taxes paid on the IRD amount.

Taking Advantage of the NUA Rule

Recently, the NUA rule has been receiving more attention in the press. First, it is one of the only remaining special tax rules that apply to qualified plan distributions. Second, with the proliferation of the 401(k) plan, many plan participants are accumulating large employer stock accounts. Many mid-size and large companies provide employer securities as an investment alternative or even make employer matching contributions in employer stock. Third, the current long-term capital-gains rate of 20 percent is half the top marginal tax rate (39.6 percent) for ordinary income. Participants receiving lump sums that include a distribution of employer securities should seriously consider this rule.

Another reason the NUA rule can be quite useful is that a participant may elect to take advantage of the deferral of income recognition on NUA and roll over the remainder of the lump-sum distribution (see Private Letter Ruling 9721036). This means that a participant in a 401(k) plan with an employer securities account can elect NUA treatment on the employer stock account and roll over any other investments tax free into an IRA.

Example: Joe retires at age 62 and receives a lump-sum distribution with a current market value of $700,000. The market value of employer securities is $200,000, but the cost basis is $50,000. Joe should consider rolling the cash (worth $500,000) into an IRA but not rolling over the $200,000. At the time of the distribution, Joe will have to pay tax on the $50,000 cost basis. When he sells the stock, he will pay long-term capital gains on the $150,000 NUA, and he will pay long-term gain on any subsequent appreciation (as long as he holds the stock for at least one year). If Joe is in the 39 percent federal income tax bracket, he pays 39 percent on the $50,000 distribution, but he pays only 20 percent on the rest of the gain. If he rolls the employer securities into an IRA, all subsequent distributions will be taxed at 39 percent.

This example illustrates the importance of considering NUA tax treatment. Factors in the decision-making process include the following:

- the participant's current and future marginal tax bracket
- how long the stock will be held before it is sold
- how close the cost basis is to the market value at the time of the distribution

In the end, there is probably no right decision for any particular taxpayer. In addition to the above considerations, the participant's attitude about paying taxes and projections about future tax rates are important considerations. The planner's main objective should be to help lay out all of the alternatives clearly, so the participant can make the right election for himself or herself.

Grandfathered Special Tax Rules

Individuals born before 1936 who receive lump-sum distributions from qualified plans may still be eligible for several grandfathered tax rules. (These rules never applied to IRA's, SEPs, SIMPLEs or 403(b) plans.) Because these rules effect only a small portion of the pension population, they are covered here only briefly.

Ten-Year Averaging

10-year averaging

Ten-year averaging may still be available for individuals born prior to January 1, 1936 if the following conditions are met:

- The distribution qualifies as a lump-sum distribution.
- The election for 10-year averaging has not been made before (only one election per taxpayer).

The tax rate on a lump sum eligible for 10-year averaging depends upon the amount of the lump sum. The tax rate is calculated as follows:

- calculate one-tenth of the distribution (after taking into consideration a minimum-distribution allowance on distributions under $70,000)
- calculate the tax on that amount using 1986 tax rates considering the lump-sum distribution as the taxpayer's only income
- multiply the result by 10

Since tax rates in 1986 were highly bracketed, the tax rate is generally favorable only when the distribution amount is relatively low. Table 25-3 can be used to determine the tax on a specific distribution. Assume your client receives a lump-sum distribution of $150,000. For simplicity, assume that the entire distribution is taxable and that there are no plan accumulations attributable to pre-1974 service. Looking at the table, the $150,000 distribution falls in the range between $137,100 and $171,600. Therefore, the tax on the $150,000 distribution is equal to $21,603 plus 23 percent of the excess over $137,100. The excess over $137,100 is $12,900; 23 percent of $12,900 is $2,967. Thus, the total 10-year averaging tax on a $150,000 distribution is equal to $21,603 plus $2,967, or $24,570.

The taxpayer reports the tax on Form 4972, which is filed with the tax return for the year. Form 4972 includes detailed instructions and a worksheet for making the calculation.

Capital-Gains Election

Clients born before January 1, 1936, can elect to treat the portion of a lump-sum distribution attributable to pre-1974 plan participation as capital gain. If this election is made, the amount subject to capital gain is taxed at a special grandfathered rate of 20 percent. A recipient may make only one such election.

If the capital-gain provision is elected, the capital gain portion of a lump-sum distribution is then excluded when the person calculates the 10-year averaging tax. Therefore, the total tax payable on a lump-sum distribution when a person elects capital-gains treatment for pre-1974 plan accruals is equal to 20 percent of the portion of the distribution attributable to the pre-1974 plan accruals plus the averaging tax on the remainder. For example, assume that a lump-sum distribution is equal to $150,000, and the capital-gain portion is $33,000. If your client elects capital gain treatment, only the portion of the distribution not attributable to the capital-gain portion (in this case, $117,000) is included in the adjusted total taxable amount when computing the averaging tax.

Clearly, a client born before January 1, 1936, should elect the capital-gain provision for pre-1974 plan accruals whenever the adjusted total taxable amount after subtracting the capital-gain portion is taxed at an effective rate of more than 20 percent. If we look at table 25-3, we can see that a person who elects 10-year averaging will always benefit by electing the capital-gains treatment for pre-1974 plan accruals if the adjusted total taxable amount after subtracting the capital-gain portion is equal to or greater than $137,100. At that level, each additional dollar of adjusted total taxable amount is taxed at a rate of 23 percent or higher.

Choosing Ten-Year Averaging and the Capital Gains Treatment

When should clients who are still eligible for these grandfathered special tax rules elect to receive lump-sum distributions, rather than periodic payouts from their plans (or from IRA rollover accounts)? First, tax rates in 1986 were quite high and the tax rate with special averaging will not be very attractive unless the distribution is approximately $300,000 or less. If this is the case, it is generally appropriate to explore the decision at least to the point of calculating the tax under the special rules.

Once the special tax rate is determined, then the client needs to consider whether the tax rate looks attractive or not. This will depend upon factors including

TABLE 25-3
10-Year Averaging (Using 1986 Tax Rates)*

If the adjusted total taxable amount is		the separate tax is	plus this %	of the excess over
at least	but not more than			
. . .	$ 20,000	0	5.5	0
$ 20,000	21,583	$ 1,100	13.2	$ 20,000
21,583	30,583	1,309	14.4	21,583
30,583	49,417	2,605	16.8	30,583
49,417	67,417	5,769	18.0	49,417
67,417	70,000	9,009	19.2	67,417
70,000	91,700	9,505	16.0	70,000
91,700	114,400	12,977	18.0	91,700
114,400	137,100	17,063	20.0	114,400
137,100	171,600	21,603	23.0	137,100
171,600	228,800	29,538	26.0	171,600
228,800	286,000	44,410	30.0	228,800
286,000	343,200	61,570	34.0	286,000
343,200	423,000	81,018	38.0	343,200
423,000	571,900	111,342	42.0	423,000
571,900	857,900	173,880	48.0	571,900
857,900	. . .	311,160	50.0	857,900

*Persons electing 10-year averaging must use the 1986 single tax rate schedule regardless of the year in which they actually receive the distribution.

- the length of the potential period of additional tax deferral
- the current investment environment
- expected increases (or decreases) in the income tax rates

Estate planning considerations are also crucial in the equation. Sometimes deferring income taxes as long as possible is the best way to pass on wealth to the next generation (see discussion in the following chapter). Other times, concerns about liquidity will weigh in favor of taking a lump sum. In estate planning, the liquidity can be needed for funding a gifting program, retitling assets in the name of the spouse, or funding the purchase of life insurance.

Even when the special tax rate seems quite low, it is appropriate to begin with a healthy skepticism regarding the advantages to paying tax on the lump sum. Tax deferral is hard to beat, especially when the potential distribution stream is going to be 20 years or more—which is the case for most clients.

Ultimately, the decision generally needs to be made only after a lot of fact finding and consideration of the factors mentioned above. Only then can it be determined whether special averaging treatment makes sense for a specific client.

MINIMUM-DISTRIBUTION RULES

The minimum-distribution rules contained in IRC Sec. 401(a)(9) are designed to limit the deferral of taxation on plan benefits. The primary reason for allowing the deferral of taxes is to encourage savings for retirement. This tax-preferred item comes at a great cost to the government; therefore, the minimum-distribution rules have been designed both to ensure that a significant portion of a participant's benefit is paid out during retirement and to limit the period for benefits paid after death.

Proposed Regulations in 2001

The provisions of Code Sec. 401(a)(9) were first interpreted by proposed regulations in 1987. The 1987 proposed regulations were often criticized because of the complexity. Virtually everything was difficult; determining the life expectancy each year, the complexity of the recalculation decisions, identifying the designated beneficiary, addressing plan default provisions and making appropriate, timely elections. Of most concern was that elections made at 70 1/2 would bind the employee in future years during which financial circumstances could change significantly.

In January of 2001 the IRS replaced the old proposed minimum distribution regulations with new proposed regulations[1] which are much simpler and more logical. The 2001 proposed regulations make it much easier for individuals and plan administrators to understand and apply the minimum-distribution rules. Even though the 2001 proposed regulations are not generally applicable until 2002, IRA participants are allowed to elect to use either the old or new rules for distributions made for 2001 only if the plan adopts a model amendment specifying that the new rules apply. Because the changes are so significant, and in many cases lower the required distribution, the following materials reflect the provisions of 2001 proposed regulations.

The minimum-distribution requirements will have the most impact on those individuals who do not need the tax-sheltered retirement income to live and who wish to defer the payment of tax as long as possible. However, the rules will also impact on a much broader spectrum of the retiring population. The minimum-distribution rules apply on a year-by-year basis, and a minimum distribution is always required once the individual has reached the required beginning date (generally April 1 of the year following the attainment of age 70 1/2). Therefore, the minimum-distribution rules have an ongoing impact on any retiree who has reached the required beginning date.

General

The rules of Sec. 401(a)(9) apply in essentially the same way (with a few exceptions) to all tax-preferred retirement plans including qualified plans, IRAs (including SEPs and SIMPLEs), 403(b) annuity plans, and even IRC Sec. 457 plans. Roth IRAs are not subject to the rules governing lifetime distributions to the participant but are required to make distributions to a death beneficiary.

It is important to understand that there are actually two separate minimum-distribution rules. One rule applies to those individuals who live until the required beginning date and a separate rule that applies when the participant dies before the required beginning date.

Another complicating factor is that Code Sec. 402 allows a participant's spouse the option to roll over a benefit received at the death of the participant into an IRA in his or her own name. The rollover is treated as a complete distribution from the participant's plan, meaning that the minimum-distribution rules will have to be satisfied, treating the spouse as the participant. This rule provides planning opportunities, but can also be confusing.

Failing to satisfy the minimum-distribution rules results in an extremely harsh penalty. Under IRC Sec. 4974, if the minimum distributions are not made in a timely manner, the plan participant is required to pay a 50 percent excise tax on the amount of the shortfall between the amount actually distributed and the amount required to be distributed under the minimum-distribution rules. In addition, if the plan is a qualified plan, it may lose its tax-favored status if the minimum-distribution rules are not satisfied. Beginning in 2002, IRA trustees are required to report the amount of the required distribution to both the participant and the IRS, which means the IRS will have a much easier time enforcing compliance.

Minimum Distributions at the Required Beginning Date

The next several pages describe the minimum-distribution rules that apply when the individual has lived until the required beginning date (generally April 1 of the year following attainment of age 70 1/2). The rules for determining the minimum distribution are different depending upon whether the distribution is from an individual account plan or is payable as an annuity—either from a defined-benefit plan or from a commercial annuity. The account plan rules apply to all IRAs, 403(b) plans, SEPs, SIMPLEs, Sec. 457 plans, and qualified plans of the defined-contribution type, unless a commercial annuity is purchased prior to the required beginning date. The account plan rules are reviewed below, followed by a discussion of the annuity distribution rules.

Required Beginning Date

required beginning date

The date benefit payments must begin is called the *required beginning date*. This date is generally April 1 of the year following the calendar year in which the participant attains age 70 1/2. However, there are two important exceptions:

- Any participant in a government or church plan who remains an employee after reaching age 70 1/2 will not have to begin distributions until the April 1 following the later of either the calendar year in which the participant reaches age 70 1/2 or the calendar year in which he or she retires.
- Any qualified plan participant who reaches 70 1/2 and who is not considered a 5-percent owner of the entity sponsoring the plan will not have to begin distributions until the April 1 following the later of either the year of attainment of age 70 1/2 or the year in which the participant retires. This exception also applies to 403(b) plans without regard to the 5-percent-owner rule.

Note that there are no exceptions to the required beginning date for IRAs—which also includes SEPs and SIMPLEs. For these plans, the required beginning date is always the April 1 of the year following the calendar year in which the covered participant attains age 70 1/2.

The required beginning date is somewhat of a misnomer because a minimum distribution is required for the year in which the participant attains

**first distribution
year**

age 70 1/2 or, if one of the exceptions applies, the year in which the participant retires. Because a distribution must be made for this year, it is referred to as the *first distribution year*. The distribution for the first distribution year can be delayed until the following April 1, but required distributions for all subsequent distribution years must be made by December 31 of the applicable year.

Example: Shelley, who has an IRA, turned age 70 on March 15, 2000. On September 15, 2000, she turned 70 1/2. The first required distribution from Shelley's IRA is for the year ending December 31, 2000, but she has the option to take the distribution any time in 2000 or delay it up to the required beginning date of April 1, 2001. However, if she delays the distribution into 2001, she will still have to take a minimum distribution for the second distribution year by December 31, 2001.

As you can see, delaying the first distribution into the second year doubles up the required distribution for that year and increases taxes for that year—not a desirable result in some cases.

Account Plan Distributions During the Participant's Life

Once the participant attains the required beginning date, a minimum distribution is required for each and every distribution year (and no credit is given for larger distributions in prior years) through the year of the participant's death. Under the 2001 proposed regulations, the calculation is quite simple. The required distribution is calculated by dividing the account balance by the applicable distribution period. The participant's benefit in a defined-contribution plan, 403(b) plan, or IRA is based on the participant's account balance. In an IRA account, the benefit for a distribution year is the IRA account balance at the end of the previous calendar year. For qualified plans and 403(b) plans, the employee's benefit is his or her individual account balance as of the last valuation date in the calendar year immediately preceding the distribution year.

The distribution period comes from a table (see table 25-4) and is determined based on the age of the participant at the end of the distribution year. The same methodology is used for every year that the participant is alive. Each year the applicable distribution period is determined by simply looking at the uniform table based on the age of the participant during that year.

Example: Sally, an IRA participant is age 71 at the last day of the first distribution year (the year she attains age 70 1/2). Her IRA balance at the end of the preceding year is $200,000. The first year's required distribution is $200,000/25.3 = $7,905 (table 10-1). This is the required minimum regardless of the beneficiary unless Sally's sole beneficiary for the entire year is her spouse and he is more than 10 years younger than she. For the second distribution year the applicable distribution period is 24.4 (table amount for a 72 year-old participant).

TABLE 25-4
Applicable Distribution Period

Age of Participant	Distribution Period	Age of Participant	Distribution Period
70	26.2	93	8.8
71	25.3	94	8.3
72	24.4	95	7.8
73	23.5	96	7.3
74	22.7	97	6.9
75	21.8	98	6.5
76	20.9	99	6.1
77	20.1	100	5.7
78	19.2	101	5.3
79	18.4	102	5.0
80	17.6	103	4.7
81	16.8	104	4.4
82	16.0	105	4.1
83	15.3	106	3.8
84	14.5	107	3.6
85	13.8	108	3.3
86	13.1	109	3.1
87	12.4	110	2.8
88	11.8	111	2.6
89	11.1	112	2.4
90	10.5	113	2.2
91	9.9	114	2.0
92	9.4	115 and older	1.8

An exception applies if the employee's sole beneficiary is the employee's spouse and the spouse is more than 10 years younger than the employee. In that case, the employee is permitted to use the longer distribution period measured by the joint life and last survivor life expectancy of the employee and spouse (calculated using IRS Table VI [table 25-5]). This exception applies for any distribution year in which the spouse (who is more than 10 years younger than the participant) is the sole beneficiary for the entire year.

Example:	If Sally's beneficiary (in the previous example) was her 51-year-old spouse, the minimum distribution would be $200,000/33.0 = $6,060 (table 25-5). In this case, for the second distribution year, the applicable distribution period is 32.1, which is their joint life expectancy calculated at the end of that distribution year.

TABLE 25-5
Table VI—Ordinary Joint Life and Last Survivor Annuities;
Two Lives—Expected Return Multiples*

Ages	45	46	47	48	49	50	51	52	53	54
68	38.4	37.6	36.7	35.8	35.0	34.2	33.4	32.5	31.8	31.0
69	38.4	37.5	36.6	35.7	34.9	34.1	33.2	32.4	31.6	30.8
70	38.3	37.4	36.5	35.7	34.8	34.0	33.1	32.3	31.5	30.7
71	38.2	37.3	36.5	35.6	34.7	33.9	33.0	32.2	31.4	30.5
72	38.2	37.3	36.4	35.5	34.6	33.8	32.9	32.1	31.2	30.4
73	38.1	37.2	36.3	35.4	34.5	33.7	32.8	32.0	31.1	30.3
74	38.1	37.2	36.3	35.4	34.4	33.6	32.8	31.9	31.1	30.2
75	38.1	37.1	36.2	35.3	34.4	33.6	32.7	31.8	31.0	30.1
76	38.0	37.1	36.2	35.3	34.3	33.5	32.6	31.8	30.9	30.1
77	38.0	37.1	36.2	35.3	34.3	33.5	32.6	31.7	30.8	30.0
78	38.0	37.0	36.1	35.2	34.3	33.9	32.5	31.7	30.8	29.9

*Source: A portion of Table VI from Reg. Sec. 1.72-9.

Death of the Participant after the Required Beginning Date

For the participant that dies after the required beginning date, distributions must continue to satisfy the required minimum-distribution rules. In the year of death, the heirs must take the decedent's required distribution (if this distribution was not taken before death) based on the method under which the decedent had been taking distributions.

In subsequent years, the required distributions will depend upon the chosen beneficiary. When the beneficiary is an individual who is not the spouse, the applicable distribution period is that individual's life expectancy (using IRS Table V [table 25-6]) as of the end of the year following death. In subsequent years, the applicable distribution period is the life expectancy from the previous year less one. This means that remaining distributions are now made over a fixed period. This is true even if the beneficiary at the time of death subsequently dies and leaves the benefit to another heir.

TABLE 25-6
Table V—Ordinary Life Annuities;
One Life—Expected Return Multiples*

Age	Multiple	Age	Multiple
40	42.5	66	19.2
41	41.5	67	18.4
42	40.6	68	17.6
43	39.6	69	16.8
44	38.7	70	16.0
45	37.7	71	15.3
46	36.8	72	14.6
47	35.9	73	13.9
48	34.9	74	13.2
49	34.0	75	12.5
50	33.1	76	11.9
51	32.2	77	11.2
52	31.3	78	10.6
53	30.4	79	10.0
54	29.5	80	9.5
55	28.6	81	8.9
56	27.7	82	8.4
57	26.8	83	7.9
58	25.9	84	7.4
59	25.0	85	6.9
60	24.2	86	6.5
61	23.3	87	6.1
62	22.5	88	5.7
63	21.6	89	5.3
64	20.8	90	5.0
65	20.0		

*Source: A portion of Table V from Reg. Sec. 1.72-9.

Example: John dies at age 82 with an $800,000 IRA account (at the end of the previous year). For the year of death, the required minimum distribution is $800,000/16.0 = $50,000. Assuming that at the end of the year of death the value of the account is $840,000 and, at the end of the following year, the sole beneficiary is Sarah, his daughter, who is aged 54 at the end of that year. The minimum distribution is $840,000/29.5 =

$28,475. The remaining distribution period is now fixed. In the next year, the applicable distribution period is 28.5 (29.5 − 1) and so on in future years. In total, distributions can continue for 29.5 years after the death of the participant. This would be true even if Sarah dies before the end of the period and left the benefit to her heirs.

If there is no designated beneficiary as of the end of the year after the employee's death (which would be the case if a nonperson such as a charity or the estate was the chosen beneficiary), the distribution period is the employee's life expectancy calculated in the year of death, reduced by one for each subsequent year.

Example:	Sandra, aged 80, dies with her estate as the beneficiary. Her account balance at the end of the year of her death is $240,00; her life expectancy is 8.5 (9.5–1) in the year after death. The required distribution in the year after death is $28,239 ($240,000/8.5. In each following year, the applicable distribution period is reduced by one, until all amounts are distributed after 9 years.

If the participant's spouse is the chosen beneficiary, there are a number of options. In most cases, the spouse will elect to roll the benefit into his or her own IRA (or in some cases treat the account as his or her own.) In this case, subsequent distributions (in the year following death) are calculated using the same methodology as when the participant was alive—with the spouse now treated as the participant.

Example:	Rollo dies at age 80 with his spouse Cassandra, age 75, as the beneficiary. Cassandra rolls the benefit into her own IRA and names their only child as beneficiary. During Cassandra's life, the uniform table is used to calculate the minimum required distribution. For example, in the year following Rollo's death, the applicable distribution period is 20.9 (see table 25-4). After Cassandra's death, subsequent distributions are required based on the life expectancy of their child, assuming she is still the beneficiary at that time.

If the employee's spouse is the employee's sole beneficiary at the end of the year following the year of death, and the distribution is not rolled over, the distribution period during the spouse's life is the spouse's single life expectancy. For years after the year of the spouse's death, the distribution period is the spouse's life expectancy calculated in the year of death, reduced by one for each subsequent year.

Annuity Payments

When a defined-benefit pension plan pays out a benefit in the form of an annuity, or if a commercial annuity is purchased to satisfy benefit payments, a separate minimum-distribution rule applies. These rules are quite straightforward and, unlike the account plan rules, the determination only has to be made one time—when the distribution begins.

In most cases, life annuities and joint and survivor annuities satisfy the minimum-distribution rules. In order to satisfy the rules, both of the following requirements must be met:

- Payments must be made at intervals that occur at least annually.
- The stream of payments must be "nonincreasing."

The term *nonincreasing* is defined broadly in the regulations, and variable annuities and annuities that increase due to cost-of-living increases fit within the definition. An annuity with a cash-refund feature also qualifies.

Joint and survivor annuities with a survivor benefit of up to 100 percent are generally allowed. The only exception is for nonspousal beneficiaries who are more than 10 years younger than the participant. In this case, the maximum survivor benefit will be something less than 100 percent. To determine the applicable survivor percentage, see the IRS Table reproduced in table 25-7. The example below explains how this works.

***Example*:**   Sandra wants to elect a 100 percent joint and survivor benefit from her company's defined-benefit plan beginning at age 70. She is considering her son, Albert, aged 45, as the contingent beneficiary. Looking at table 25-7, notice that the maximum survivor benefit for a beneficiary who is 25 years younger than the participant $(70 - 45 = 25)$ is 66 percent.

TABLE 25-7
Table for Determining the Maximum Applicable Survivor Annuity Percentage

Excess of Age of Employee over Age of Beneficiary	Applicable Percentage	Excess of Age of Employee over Age of Beneficiary	Applicable Percentage
10 years or less	100%	28	62%
11	96	29	61
12	93	30	60
13	90	31	59
14	87	32	59
15	84	33	58
16	82	34	57
17	79	35	56
18	77	36	56
19	75	37	55
20	73	38	55
21	72	39	54
22	70	40	54
23	68	41	53
24	67	42	53
25	66	43	53
26	64	44 years and more	52
27	63		

Source: Proposed Treas. Reg. Sec. 1.401(a)(9)-2

The annuity can have a period certain as long as it does not exceed the joint life expectancy of the participant and beneficiary using the uniform table (or joint and survivor table in the case of a spouse more than 10 years younger than the participant).

***Example*:** Suppose Herb, aged 70 (at the end of the first distribution year), chooses a joint and survivor annuity with Sally, aged 80, as the contingent beneficiary. Herb wants to have a period-certain feature and wants to know if there are limitations on the length of the period certain. Because the joint life expectancy under the uniform table for Herb (age 70) is 26.2, this is the maximum length for period-certain payments for an annuity beginning at age 70.

Preretirement Death Benefits

When the participant dies after the required beginning date, distributions must continue in the manner described in the section above. However, when the participant dies prior to the required beginning date, then a separate rule applies for determining the maximum length of the distribution period.

To satisfy the rules, either the 5-year rule or one of the lifetime exceptions must be satisfied. Under the 5-year rule, the participant's entire interest must be distributed by December 31 of the calendar year that contains the fifth anniversary of the date the participant dies. Under this rule, the entire interest could be distributed at the end of the 5-year period.

There are actually two different lifetime exceptions, one that applies to spousal beneficiaries and one that applies with nonspousal beneficiaries. For nonspousal beneficiaries, the minimum-distribution rule is also satisfied if the distribution is made over the lifetime or expected lifetime of the beneficiary, as long as the benefit begins by December 31 of the year following the year of death. The calculation of each required distribution is determined using the same methodology as with a nonspousal beneficiary when the participant dies after the required beginning date.

***Example*:**	Suppose Gilligan dies at age 65 and his daughter, Ginger, is the beneficiary of his IRA. In the year following his death, Ginger is aged 40 and her life expectancy is 42.5. If the lifetime exception is used and the account balance is $300,000 at the end of the year in which Gilligan dies, the required distribution in the following year is $300,000/42.5 = $7,059. Note that as long as distributions begin by the end of the year following the year Gilligan died, distributions can continue for 43 years. If this deadline is not met, the entire distribution must be made within 5 years.

When the beneficiary is the participant's spouse, the distribution may be made over the life of the spouse, as long as payments begin on or before the later of (1) December 31 of the calendar year immediately after the calendar year in which the participant dies or (2) December 31 of the calendar year immediately after the year in which the participant would have reached age 70 1/2. However, if the spouse dies prior to the commencement of benefit payments, then benefits may be distributed to his or her beneficiary under the same rules that would apply to the participant. Note that the spousal exception is generally not utilized because the spouse will typically elect to roll the benefit into his or her own account.

If the participant does not have a designated beneficiary (chooses a nonperson such as a charity or estate), then distributions must be made over a 5-year period. The lifetime exceptions are not an option.

Beneficiary Issues

All the minimum-distribution rules involve identification of the participant's beneficiary. Under the proposed regulations of 2001, the beneficiary used to determine the required distribution is the beneficiary that actually inherits the benefit. Technically, it is the beneficiary identified as of the end of the year following death. (See discussion of post-death planning below.)

The 2001 proposed regulations retain the requirement for a "designated beneficiary" who is an individual (that is, not a charity or the participant's estate) if minimum distributions are to be based on the life expectancy of the beneficiary. A trust is also treated as not having a designated beneficiary unless the trust satisfies the following requirements:

- the trust is irrevocable at death
- the beneficiaries under the trust are identifiable
- the trust document or a statement identifying the distribution provisions is provided to the plan's administrator

In the case of a trust that conforms with the rules, the beneficiaries of the trust will be treated as the beneficiaries for purposes of the minimum-distribution rules. In most cases, the requirement of notifying the plan administrator does not have to occur until the time the beneficiaries have to be identified.

If there are multiple designated beneficiaries at the end of the year following death (and separate accounts for each participant have not been established) the life expectancy of the oldest beneficiary (with the shortest life expectancy) is used for determining the required distributions. If one of those beneficiaries is a nonperson, then the participant is deemed to have no designated beneficiary. If there are multiple designated beneficiaries and separate accounts exist, the minimum distributions of his or her separate share are taken by each beneficiary over the fixed-term life expectancy of each respective beneficiary.

Additional Rules

Multiple Plans

With qualified retirement plans required minimum distributions must be calculated—and distributed—separately for each plan subject to the rules. The rules are more liberal with multiple IRAs or 403(b) plans. With IRAs, the minimum distribution must be calculated separately for each IRA, but then the actual distributions can come from any of the IRA accounts. If, however, an individual has accounts in their own name as well as inherited IRAs, they cannot aggregate the two groups for determining the required minimum 403(b) plans to be aggregated in a similar way (although IRAs and 403(b) plans may not be aggregated).

Rollovers and Transfers

As we have discussed, liberal rules allow participants the right to roll or transfer benefits from one type of tax-sheltered plan to another. This transaction is relatively simple except in the case of the individual rolling over the benefit after attainment of age 70 1/2. In order to ensure that the minimum distributions are made, the rules clarify what to do in this special situation.

Special rules apply to amounts rolled (or transferred) from one tax-sheltered retirement plan to another. From the perspective of the distributing plan, the amount distributed (to be rolled over or transferred) is credited toward determining the minimum distribution from the plan. However, if a portion of the distribution is necessary to satisfy the minimum-distribution requirements, that portion may not be rolled (or transferred) into another plan.

Example:	Shirley, aged 71 1/2, receives a single-sum distribution from a qualified retirement plan. She intends to roll the distribution into an IRA. She may not roll the portion of the lump-sum distribution that represents the minimum distribution for the current distribution year into the IRA.

Once the amount is rolled into the second plan, it will count toward determining the participant's benefit for determining the minimum distribution. However, because the minimum distribution is based on the benefit in the previous year, the amount rolled over does not affect the minimum until the following year.

Spousal Rollovers

When the spouse is the beneficiary of the participant's retirement plan benefit, the spouse has a unique opportunity—to roll the benefit into an IRA in his or her own name. Under the minimum-distribution rules, the rollover is treated as a complete distribution of the participant's benefit, satisfying the minimum-distribution rules from the perspective of the participant's plan. Once the benefit is in the spouse's name, the minimum-distribution rules have to be satisfied with the spouse treated as the participant. The spouse has the opportunity to name a beneficiary and calculate future minimum distributions based upon the joint life expectancy of the spouse and the beneficiary.

Grandfather Provisions for Qualified Plans and 403(b) Plans

There are two situations in which the current distribution rules do not apply. In a qualified plan, participants with accrued benefits as of December 31, 1983, were allowed to sign an election form (prior to January 1, 1984) indicating the time and method of distribution of their plan benefit. The benefit election form had to be specific and had to conform to pre-TEFRA rules, which allowed distributions to be deferred much later than age 70 1/2. These grandfather provisions were contained in Sec. 242(b) of TEFRA and

TEFRA 242(b) elections are generally referred to as *TEFRA 242(b) elections.*

These Sec. 242(b) elections continue to be valid if benefits are being paid from the original plan in which the election is made, and if the plan distributions follow the Sec. 242(b) distribution election. If it is not followed exactly with regard to the form and timing of the payments, the election is considered revoked. A substitution or addition of a beneficiary generally does not result in the revocation of the election. If the benefit election is changed or revoked after the individual has reached the required beginning date under the current rules, the participant will be forced to "make up" distributions that would otherwise (absent the Sec. 242(b) election) have been required under the current rules.

Sec. 242(b) elections can delay the timing of required distributions substantially. The retirement planner should be sure to ask if the client has retained an election form in his or her files. As noted above, the election has to be followed exactly in order to a void having to take a potentially large distribution at some later date.

The other grandfather rule applies to 403(b) plans. As long as a participant's pre-1987 account balances are accounted for, such amounts until the participant attains age 75. There are no exceptions that apply to IRA distributions, which includes distributions from SEPs and SIMPLEs.

Differences from the Old Rules

The 2001 proposed regulations are a tremendous improvement over the old rules. The new rules solve many problems created under the old rules including

- Elections that had been previously made regarding recalculation of life expectancies are no longer relevant.
- The beneficiary identified at the required beginning date is no longer relevant in determining the required minimum distribution.
- The calculation for lifetime and post-death distributions is much simpler in all cases.
- No participants are required to distribute their entire account during their lifetime. All death beneficiaries will receive some period after the participant's death to make distributions.

Even more important than these other changes is that the actual required minimum distributions will be lower in many situations. This is true for lifetime distributions when the beneficiary is not more than 10 years younger than the participant. Or when the beneficiary is a nonperson.

Example: John, an IRA participant, is aged 78 and his 74-year-old spouse, Cindy, is the beneficiary at the end of the current distribution year. They currently use the recalculation method. Under the old rules, the applicable life expectancy (ALE) was 15.9 while under the new rules the life expectancy is 19.1. This results in more than a 15 percent reduction in the required minimum distribution for the year. With an older spousal beneficiary, the impact will be even greater.

The post-death distribution period can also be substantially longer under new rules. This will be most profound in the case of a spousal beneficiary where the spouse died first.

Example: Ralph was aged 70 and his spouse, Susan, was aged 65 at the end of the first distribution year. Under the old rules, they elected not to recalculate either life expectancy. Under the old rules, if Susan died suddenly several years later before Ralph, the spousal rollover election would not be available and the distributions would not be made over a fixed 23-year period. Under the new rules, assume that after Susan's death, Ralph named their only daughter, Karin, as the beneficiary. If Ralph died at age 80, and Karin was aged 50 in the year following death, the length of the total distribution period would be 43 years instead of 23 years (10 years while Ralph was alive and an additional 33 years, Susan's life expectancy in the year following death.)

The post-death distribution period is almost the same in the case of a nonspousal beneficiary. The post-death distribution period can be longer for those who elected a fixed distribution period.

If the rules look too good to be true, is there any upside for the Internal Revenue Service? The answer is yes. The proposed regulations require the trustee of each IRA to report the amount of the required minimum distribution from the IRA to the IRA owner or beneficiary and to the IRS (beginning in 2002). This reporting would be required regardless of whether the IRA owner is planning to take the required minimum distribution from that IRA or from another IRA. For the first time, the IRS will be able to match up required distributions and taxable income reported on the individual's tax return. The proposed regulations indicate that the reporting requirement may also be expanded to 403(b) plans as well.

Planning

Post-Mortem Planning

Under the new rules, the designated beneficiary does not have to be determined until December 31 of the year following the year of the participant's death. This permits some flexibility for determining the postdeath minimum required distributions from the retirement plan or IRA. Of course, the decedent's potential beneficiaries are "carved in stone" at the time of his or her death, since the decedent can no longer make new choices. However, the use of a qualified disclaimer or early distribution of a beneficiary's share could be effective in changing the designated beneficiary to contingent beneficiaries by the time specified to determine such beneficiary.

Example:	Suppose that Helen dies at age 80. At the time of her death, her son, Bud, from her first marriage, her second husband, Saul, and The American College, are each beneficiaries of one-third of the benefit. Before the end of the year following death, Saul rolls his benefit into a spousal IRA, benefits are paid out to The American College, and Bud is the sole beneficiary. This means that subsequent required distributions will be based on Bud's life expectancy. If Helen had also named a contingent beneficiary for Bud's benefit, for example, Bud's child, Kelly, Bud could disclaim his benefit in favor of Kelly and the distribution could continue over Kelly's longer life expectancy.

Another way to limit problems that could arise with multiple beneficiaries is to divide benefits into separate accounts. The regulations define acceptable separate accounting to include allocating investment gains and losses, and contributions and forfeitures, on a pro rata basis in a reasonable and consistent manner between such separate portion and any other benefits. If these rules are followed, the separate beneficiary of each share determines his or her minimum required distribution based on his or her life expectancy according to his or her age on the birthday that occurs in the year following the year of the decedent's death. The 2001 proposed regulations clearly state that if the participant dies before the required beginning date, the regulations clearly indicate that the account can be divided into separate accounts up to the year following the death of the participant. Unfortunately it is not entirely clear under the 2001 rules whether a division can take place after the required beginning date. If not, separate accounts would have to be established at the required beginning date.

Because the beneficiary for purposes of fixing the payout period is the beneficiary as of the year following death, post-mortem planning becomes an important part of the planning process. However, a participant's beneficiaries will be set in stone at the time of death, the beneficiary form becomes an extremely important planning tool. Many participants may choose to have multiple layers of contingent beneficiaries in order to maximize planning opportunities.

YOUR FINANCIAL SERVICES PRACTICE:
BENEFICIARY ELECTIONS

Under the 2001 proposed regulations, taking advantage of maximum deferral is an option that remains open even after the death of the participant, but only if the beneficiary election contains the appropriate list of contingent beneficiaries and qualified disclaimers are made. For a married person with children, the following beneficiary elections may be appropriate:

- payable to the spouse
- payable to a credit shelter trust with the spouse as income beneficiary and the children as remainder beneficiaries
- payable directly to the children
- payable to a trust with the grandchildren as beneficiaries

CHAPTER REVIEW

Answers to the review and self-test questions start on page 673.
For additional review, see case studies in Appendix 11.

Key Terms

Sec. 72(t) penalty tax   lump-sum distribution
substantially equal periodic   10-year averaging
  payments   required beginning date
direct rollover rule   first distribution year
net unrealized appreciation (NUA)   TEFRA 242(b) elections

Review Questions

25-1. Describe the federal income tax treatment of benefit distributions to a participant from a tax advantaged retirement plan.

25-2. Describe the estate tax treatment of an accumulated qualified plan or IRA account and how this affects the income tax treatment of a distribution to a death beneficiary.

25-3. Which of the following plan distributions is subject to the 10 percent Sec. 72(t) penalty?
    a. a death benefit from a defined-benefit plan payable to a beneficiary upon the death of an employee aged 52
    b. a lump-sum benefit from a money-purchase pension plan payable to a disabled employee aged 57

    c. a distribution from a 401(k) plan to an employee aged 52 who qualifies under the plan's "extreme hardship" distribution provision

    d. a lump-sum distribution made to an employee aged 63 from a profit-sharing plan after the funds have been in the plan for 2 years

    e. a $10,000 distribution from a SIMPLE to pay for qualifying acquisition costs of a first home for the participant

25-4. Which method for avoiding the 10 percent early-withdrawal penalty is the most useful and flexible for planning purposes?

25-5. What are the potential potholes with taking early withdrawals under the substantially equal payment exception?

25-6. Ralph has two IRAs, one created with nondeductible contributions (contributions total $12,000 and current value is $43,000) and one IRA created by a rollover from a qualified plan ($357,000). He has not taken any previous withdrawals. Now, Ralph withdraws $12,000 from the nondeductible IRA thinking this transaction will have no income tax ramifications. In reality, how much of the distribution is taxable?

25-7. Your client, Cherie Reisenberg, is single and plans to retire at age 62. Payments from her employer's qualified plan will start at the end of the first month after her 62nd birthday. The monthly retirement benefit that will be paid to Cherie in the form of a single life annuity without any guaranteed payments is $1,000. Her cost basis in the plan is $72,900. What portion of her first distribution will be nontaxable?

25-8. Why is it preferable to elect a direct rollover from a qualified plan to an IRA, instead of receiving the distribution directly and later rolling it into the IRA?

25-9. Why may a rollover into another qualified plan be preferable to a rollover to an IRA?

25-10. When are benefits taxed if the plan distributes an annuity contract to the participant?

25-11. When does the rule that allows deferral of net unrealized appreciation apply?

25-12. What conditions must a lump-sum distribution meet in order to qualify for special tax treatment?

25-13. How is the net unrealized appreciation in the employer's stock that is included in a lump-sum distribution taxed?

25-14. What special tax treatment is available for qualifying lump-sum distributions if the client was born before January 1, 1936?

25-15. What happened in 2001 that impacts the minimum distribution rules?

25-16.   What types of plans are subject to the required minimum distribution rules?

25-17.   Sara Stewart is required to take a minimum distribution of $2,000 from a qualified retirement plan by April 1, 2002. The distribution does not occur. What penalties arise from this failure?

25-18.   James Daniel was born on July 15, 1930. State his required beginning date in the following situations:
a.   He is a participant in an IRA.
b.   He is an employee of Alpha Corp. (and is not a 5-percent owner). He terminates employment on June 1, 2003.

25-19.   Distributions for the first two distribution years have to be made by when?

25-20.   Joe is age 70 at the end of the first distribution year. His IRA account balance was $250,000 at the end of the previous year. His beneficiary is his 65-year-old spouse, Jenny. What is the required minimum distribution for the first distribution year?

25-21.   Taking the facts from the previous question, what is the required distribution for the second distribution year if the account balance is $265,000.

25-22.   Joe is aged 70 at the end of the first distribution year. His IRA account balance was $250,000 at the end of the previous year. His beneficiary is his 52-year-old spouse, Jenny. What is the required minimum distribution for the first distribution year?

25-23.   Sally dies at age 75 and leaves her benefit to her 48-year-old son. How is the required minimum distribution calculated in the year of death and for subsequent years?

25-24.   If a participant dies at age 55 and has named a 30-year-old child as beneficiary, what must happen in order to ensure that distributions can be made over the child's life expectancy?

25-25.   May an individual with two IRA accounts satisfy the minimum-distribution rules by taking a distribution from only one plan?

Self-Test Questions

T   F   25-1.   Reducing the taxation on a client's retirement distribution is the only consideration when making a distribution decision.

T   F   25-2.   Distributions to death beneficiaries are subject to income tax, which may be offset somewhat by a deduction for estate taxes paid because of the pension.

T   F   25-3.   The Sec. 72(t) penalty applies to both the taxable and nontaxable portions of a distribution.

T   F   25-4. An in-service distribution of a life annuity from a qualified plan to a 50-year-old employee is not subject to the 10 percent Sec. 72(t) penalty.

T   F   25-5. A hardship withdrawal from a 401(k) plan to a 40-year-old participant is not subject to the 10 percent Sec. 72(t) penalty.

T   F   25-6. A withdrawal from an IRA to pay for the qualified educational expenses for the participant's child is not subject to the 10 percent Sec. 72(t) penalty.

T   F   25-7. A withdrawal of $50,000 from an IRA by a participant to purchase his first home is not subject to the 10 percent Sec. 72(t) penalty tax.

T   F   25-8. To satisfy the substantially equal periodic payment exception to Sec. 72(t), distributions must continue for the participant's entire life.

T   F   25-9. Sole proprietors that receive a distribution or a life insurance policy from a qualified plan may recover cost basis due to accumulated PS 58 costs.

T   F   25-10. A participant with $8,000 of nondeductible IRA contributions can generally withdraw $8,000 without any income tax consequences.

T   F   25-11. A profit-sharing participant that receives his or her entire benefit of $320,000 can roll the entire amount into an IRA, even if $25,000 represents after-tax contributions (cash basis).

T   F   25-12. A profit-sharing participant that contributed $25,000 of voluntary after-tax contributions prior to 1987 can generally withdraw this amount in-service without any income tax consequences.

T   F   25-13. If a participant elects a direct rollover from a qualified plan to an IRA, then no income tax is required to be withheld.

T   F   25-14. A distribution from a qualified plan can generally be rolled over into a 403(b) tax-sheltered annuity.

T   F   25-15. Failure to complete a regular rollover within 60 days will generally subject the participant to income taxation on the taxable amount of the distribution and, if applicable, the 10 percent early-withdrawal penalty.

T   F   25-16. A single distribution that is part of a life annuity payout will not be a qualified rollover distribution.

T   F   25-17. To qualify for special tax treatment, a lump-sum distribution must come from a pension, profit-sharing, 401(k), stock bonus, employee stock ownership plan, or SEP.

T   F   25-18. With 10-year forward averaging, taxes are paid over a 10-year period.

T   F   25-19.   Persons born before January 1, 1936, may elect to treat the portion of a lump-sum distribution that is attributable to plan participation before 1974 as capital gains taxable at a flat 20 percent rate.

T   F   25-20.   The minimum-distribution rules apply to qualified plans, 403(b) plans, traditional IRAs, SIMPLEs, and SEPs.

T   F   25-21.   Under the minimum-distribution rules, benefits always have to be distributed within 5 years after the death of the participant.

T   F   25-22.   The minimum-distribution rules impose a 10 percent excise tax on the amount by which a distribution in a given year falls short of the minimum required distribution.

T   F   25-23.   The required beginning date for distributions is always the April 1 of the year following the calendar year in which the covered individual attains the age of 70 1/2.

T   F   25-24.   Under the account plan rules, while the participant is alive, the required minimum distribution is determined by dividing the participant's benefit at the end of the previous year divided by the applicable distribution period.

T   F   25-25.   If the beneficiary in the year following death is a person who is not the spouse, the remaining distribution period is fixed based on the beneficiary's age at the end of that year.

T   F   25-26.   A 50 percent joint and survivor annuity purchased before the required beginning date will generally fail to satisfy the required minimum distribution rules.

Note

1   Prop. Reg. Sec. 1.401(a)(9)-1–8, 1.403(b)-2, 1.408-8.

Distributions from Retirement Plans—Part II

26-1. Review the types of benefit distribution options that are available in qualified plans, IRAs, and 403(b) plans.

26-2. Summarize the rules that apply to the different types of pension distributions.

26-3. Identify the key distribution issues for the middle-class client who is concerned about financing retirement needs.

26-4. Identify the key distribution issues for the wealthier client who is concerned about both financing retirement needs and building an estate for his or her heirs.

Chapter Outline

CHOOSING A DISTRIBUTION OPTION

Choosing the best distribution at retirement can be a rather complex decision that involves personal preferences, financial considerations, and an interplay between tax incentives and tax penalties. Planners must keep a myriad of factors in mind in order to render effective advice.

For example, typical considerations include whether

- the periodic distribution will be used to provide income necessary for sustaining the retiree or whether the distribution will supplement already adequate sources of retirement income
- the client has properly coordinated distributions from several different qualified plans and IRAs
- the retiree will have satisfactory diversification of his or her retirement resources after the distribution occurs
- the client has complied with the rules for minimum distributions from a qualified plan

The first step in making a choice is to fully understand the available options. Below is a discussion of the options that are available from qualified plans, SEPs, SIMPLEs and 403(b) plans. Of course, the only way to understand the options for a plan is to read the appropriate documents.

Benefits Available From the Plan

When discussing the options available in tax-advantaged retirement plans, it's important to distinguish qualified plans from those that are funded with IRAs (SEPs and SIMPLEs) and 403(b) plans. Qualified plans are subject to a significant number of limitations while the others are more open ended.

Qualified Plans

Every qualified retirement plan specifies when payments may be made and the benefit options available. Each plan also has a default option if the participant fails to make an election. In pension language, the default is referred to as the *normal form of benefit*. The distribution options are generally quite limited in a qualified plan. This is because any option that is available must be available to all participants. Also, under the anti-cut back rules, options generally cannot be taken away once they are in the plan. To find out when benefits are payable and what the optional forms of benefit are requires a careful review of the plan's summary plan description and, in some cases, a review of the actual plan document.

A qualified plan has a range of options with regard to the timing of payments. Under law, distributions can be deferred until attainment of normal retirement age, but much more typically, the plan will also allow payment at attainment of early retirement age, death, or disability. Today, most plans also make distributions available to employees who terminate employment (prior to retirement age) with vested benefits. This is almost always the case in defined-contribution plans, but also is increasingly common in defined-benefit plans as well.

involuntary cash-out option

When the participant terminates employment with a vested benefit of less than $5,000, the plan can provide that such small benefits will be cashed out in a lump sum—without giving the participant any choice in the timing or form of benefit. Most plans choose this *involuntary cash-out option* to simplify plan administration. When the benefit exceeds $5,000, participants must be given all the benefit options allowed under the plan as well as the right to defer receipt of payment until normal retirement age. (*Planning Note:* Most participants will choose the immediate payout and roll the benefit to an IRA or a new employer's retirement plan. Reasons to stay in the old plan include lower investment costs, favorable investment options such as guaranteed investment contracts or employer stock, or financial penalties for early withdrawal of the benefit.)

In some cases, a plan will also allow withdrawals prior to termination of service. As discussed in chapter 3, this type of provision is not allowed from plans in the pension category, which includes defined-benefit, cash-balance, target-benefit, and money-purchase pension plans. The option is, however allowed in profit-sharing-type plans including profit-sharing, 401(k), stock bonus and ESOP plans. A special rule applies to the salary deferral account in a 401(k) plan— the withdrawals cannot be made unless the participant has a financial hardship (see chapter 5). Because in-service withdrawals result in taxable income, some plans (especially 401(k) plans) also provide for participant loan programs (see chapter 9).

The normal form of benefit for a married individual—in qualified plans that are subject to the qualified joint and survivor annuity rules—must be a joint and survivor benefit of not less than 50 percent or greater than 100 percent and a life annuity for a single participant (see chapter 10). In qualified plans, not subject to the rules (generally profit-sharing, 401(k) and stock bonus plans), the normal form of payment is generally a single-sum payment. Regardless of the plan's normal-form-of-benefit payment, participants frequently choose one of the alternative forms of distribution allowed under the plan. Options for distributions may include

- annuity payments
- installment payments
- lump-sum distributions

Let's take a closer look at some of the more common options available.

Life Annuity. A life annuity provides monthly payments to the participant for his or her lifetime. Payments from a life annuity completely stop when your client dies and no other benefit is paid to any beneficiary. A life annuity can be an appropriate option for individuals who want the guarantee of lifetime payments but who have no need to provide retirement income to a spouse or other dependent.

Joint and Survivor Annuity. A joint and survivor annuity provides monthly payments to the participant during his or her lifetime and if, at the participant's death, the beneficiary is still living, a specified percentage of the participant's benefit continues to be paid to the beneficiary for the remainder of his or her lifetime. The plan will specify the survivor portion and may allow the participant to chose from a 50 percent to a 100 percent survivor portion. Joint and survivor annuities can be appropriate if there is a need to provide for the continuation of retirement income to a spouse or other beneficiary that outlives the participant.

Life Annuity with Guaranteed Payments. A life annuity with guaranteed payments (sometimes referred to as a life annuity with a period-certain guarantee) provides monthly benefit payments to the participant during his or her lifetime. Payments are made for the longer of the life of the participant or some specified period of time. The plan may offer a 5-year, 10-year, or other specified guarantee period.

Example: | Sandy has elected a life annuity with a 10-year certain in the amount of $1,000 a month. If Sandy dies after 8 years, her designated beneficiary will continue to receive a $1,000 a month for 2 years. If instead, Sandy dies 12 years after payments begin, there are no additional payments.

Participants with no real income concern for a beneficiary may still elect guaranteed payments to ensure that, at least, minimum payments are made in case of an untimely death. (*Planning Note:* If a client outlives the guarantee period, he or she has, in effect, gambled and lost because lower monthly benefits will be paid under a life annuity with guaranteed payments than under a straight life annuity.) Also, guaranteed payments can be a good option when the spouse (or some other beneficiary) is ill and has a short life expectancy. For example, if a retiring husband expects to outlive his wife who is in relatively poor health, then a life annuity with a minimum guarantee might be purchased to protect against the unlikely case of the husband predeceasing the wife. The period chosen should reflect, to some extent, the planner's best estimate of the wife's maximum life expectancy and, if applicable, the client's desire to pass on wealth.

Annuity Certain. This annuity provides the beneficiary with a specified amount of monthly guaranteed payments after which time all payments stop (for example, payments for 20 years). An annuity certain continues to be paid whether the participant survives the annuity period or not. If the client dies prior to 20 years, payments will be made to the client's beneficiary. This type of annuity can be appropriate when the participant's income need has a predictable period, such as for the period prior to beginning Social Security payments.

Lump-sum Distribution. This is what it sounds like—the entire benefit is distributed at once in a single sum. A participant interested in rolling the benefit into an IRA will elect the lump-sum distribution option. Some individuals elect this option from qualified plans in order to take advantage of the special tax treatment—10-year averaging for those born before 1936—and deferral of gain for those who receive a portion of their benefit in qualifying employer securities.

Installments. The installment option is similar to, but definitely different from, a term-certain annuity. With installment payments, the participant elects a payout length and, based on earnings assumptions, a payout amount is also determined. Payments will be from the account, not an insurance carrier, and there are no guaranteed payments. If the funds run out before the period is over, payments will stop. If the assumptions are exceeded, the participant typically gets a refund with the remaining account at the end of period.

Value of the Benefit

To understand the value of the benefit provided by the plan, it is important to discuss defined-contribution plans and defined-benefit plans separately. In a defined-contribution plan, the benefit is always based on the value of the account balance. If the participant elects a lump-sum withdrawal, it will represent the entire value of the vested account balance. If installment options are elected, the account balance (along with continued investment return) is simply liquidated over the specified time period. If the participant elects an annuity option, the plan will purchase the annuity from an insurance company. Depending upon the service providers involved in investment of plan assets, the plan may be able to get a favorable annuity purchase rate.

actuarial equivalent

In a defined-benefit plan, the value of each benefit is almost always the *actuarial equivalent* of a specified form of payment—most typically a single life annuity. This means that if, for example, the participant chooses a lump-sum benefit, the amount of the lump sum is based on the single-sum value of a life annuity using the actuarial assumptions prescribed in the plan. Under current rules, actuarial assumptions must be tied to the PBGC long-term rate, which changes each month. In table 26-1 is an example of the value of a number of benefit options based on a $1,565 monthly benefit. The other annuity options pay less than the life annuity because of the longer guaranteed payout period (also in table 26-1).

subsidized benefits

Occasionally, in a defined-benefit plan, all forms of benefit will not be actuarial equivalent. Sometimes a plan provides an unreduced joint and survivor benefit. For example, if the participant is entitled to a $1,000 life annuity, he or she can also elect a $1,000-a-month 50 percent joint and survivor annuity. Forms of payment that are more valuable than the normal form of payment are referred to as *subsidized benefits* It is also not uncommon to see early retirement benefits that are subsidized. For example, the plan may allow an individual aged 60 with 30 years of service to receive the full normal retirement benefit payable at age 65 at the earlier age of 60.

TABLE 26-1
Comparison of Optional Benefit Forms
(Defined-benefit plan with a monthly life annuity payment of $1,565;
assume both the participant and spouse are aged 65)

Annuity Form	*Monthly Benefit*
Life	$ 1,565
Life annuity/10-year guarantee	$ 1,494
Life annuity/20-year guarantee	$ 1,360
Joint and survivor (50 percent)	$ 1,418
Joint and survivor (66 2/3 percent)	$ 1,375
Joint and survivor (100 percent)	$ 1,296
Lump-sum payment	$ 200,000

IRAs

Typically, form-of-distribution options from IRAs are much more flexible than qualified plans, because the individual is the owner and beneficiary. The withdrawals can be made on a discretionary basis or the participant can purchase any of the types of annuities discussed above. In addition, the participant can purchase an immediate variable annuity contract, which can be a very useful way to guarantee lifetime payments while allowing some potential upswing in monthly payments.

Variable Annuities

Variable-annuity contracts are designed to provide fluctuating benefit payments over the payout period that can provide increasing benefits during periods of inflation. Insurance companies do this by investing the assets that back the contracts in higher-risk investments than are used for fixed-dollar annuity contracts and by allowing the owner to participate in the investment performance. (*Planning Note:* Variable annuities have historically enabled clients to maintain some degree of the purchasing power of their benefits. Clients who can undertake the additional risk should seriously consider a variable annuity.)

The types of benefit arrangements available under variable-annuity contracts are the same as those available under fixed-dollar annuities. The only thing that changes is the fluctuating nature of the actual benefit payments.

Operation of a Variable Annuity

Under a variable-annuity contract, your client has given number of annuity units as of the date the contract is annuitized, and that number of units does not change during the benefit payout period. However, the value of any one annuity unit does change. That value fluctuates in direct relationship to the net asset value of the annuity assets managed by the insurance company. As the value of the invested assets increases, the value of the annuity units also increases. Likewise, decreases in the investment portfolio for the contracts lead to decreases in the value of annuity units. The actual benefit payment each month depends on the current value of the annuity unit multiplied by the number of units owned.

Under most variable-annuity contracts, there is an assumed investment rate (AIR) that the investment portfolio must earn so benefit payments remain level. If the investment performance exceeds that AIR, the level of benefit payments increases. On the other hand, if the investment performance falls below the AIR, the level of benefit payments decreases.

403(b) Annuities

Withdrawal flexibility from 403(b) plans generally falls somewhere between the limited options in a qualified plan and the more open-ended options of the IRA. As discussed in chapter 6, 403(b) plans have some restrictions on withdrawals prior to termination of employment. Also, if the plan contains employer contribution, the plans are subject to ERISA fiduciary rules and can even be subject to the qualified joint and survivor annuity rules.

Still, the participant may have more distribution options than with a qualified plan, especially if the benefit is funded with an annuity. Here, the participant may have virtually any annuity option commercially available from the insurance carrier including an immediate variable annuity.

One item that is different for a 403(b) plan than a qualified plan is that the participant can, in many cases, simply maintain the account after termination of employment without selecting a specific cash-out option. This is similar to an IRA. Of course, the participant could also roll the benefit into an IRA account. There are two good reasons to leave the account in the 403(b) vehicle versus an IRA rollover. First, if the participant has accumulated a significant pre-1987 account balance, these amounts are not subject to the normal minimum-distribution rules (payments generally do not have to begin until the participant attains age 75). Second, many carriers will continue to allow participant loans from the 403(b) plan, even after termination of service.

PUTTING IT ALL TOGETHER

Throughout the text, we have discussed rules that affect pension distributions. Learning this information and integrating it into a cohesive package can be highly difficult. To help with these concerns, we will first review the rules as they apply to qualified plans, IRAs, and 403(b) annuities. After that, we will examine common issues that can arise when you are working with different types of clients.

Qualified Plans

Qualified plans must have clear and precise rules regarding the amount, timing, and form of available benefits. The following discusses the tax treatment of these distributions and summarizes the rules that affect qualified plan distributions:

- Distributions are taxed as ordinary income unless the distribution is a lump sum and one of the special tax rules applies (the deferral of gain on employer securities and the grandfathered 10-year averaging and capital gains rules), or unless the participant has basis. Basis includes after-tax contributions and PS 58 costs.

- The 10 percent premature distribution excise tax applies to the taxable portion of a distribution made prior to age 59 1/2. Exceptions apply if the distribution is made because of death or disability, to pay for certain medical expenses, or if substantially equal periodic payments are withdrawn (after separation from service). Another exception (that does not apply to IRAs) is that of distributions to a terminating participant after attainment of age 55.

- If a participant has a qualified plan balance payable to a beneficiary at his or her death, the value of the benefit is included in the taxable estate. Payments to beneficiaries are treated as income in respect to a decedent—meaning that beneficiaries receiving benefit payments pay income tax but may get a deduction for any estate taxes paid because of the value of the pension.

- In-service distributions are subject to limitations. No in-service withdrawals are allowed from plans categorized as pension plans. Profit-sharing-type plans may allow distributions upon a stated event; 401(k) plans are subject to more limiting hardship withdrawals.

- In lieu of taxable in-service withdrawals, plans may offer participant loan programs. Loans within prescribed limits are not subject to income tax.

- Distributions from most plans are subject to the qualified joint and survivor annuity (QJSA) requirements. A limited exception applies for certain profit-sharing plans.

- Distributions are subject to the minimum-distribution rules. The distribution can be made under the pre-TEFRA (Tax Equity and Fiscal Responsibility Act) distribution rules if the participant made a written election in 1983. Participants (except for 5 percent owners) who continue working until they are past age 70 can defer the required beginning date until April 1 of the year following the year in which they retire.

- Distributions other than certain annuities, hardship withdrawals from 401(k) plans, and required minimum distributions can be rolled over into another qualified plan, 403(b) plan, 457 plan or an IRA.

- Qualified plans are required to give participants the option to directly roll over distributions to an IRA or other qualified plan. Distributions that are not directly rolled over are subject to a 20 percent mandatory income tax withholding.

IRAs

The following is a brief review of the distribution rules that apply to IRAs. With one exception (described below), these rules apply to regular IRAs or IRAs associated with SEPs or SIMPLEs.

- Distributions are always taxed as ordinary income unless the participant has made after-tax contributions. None of the special tax rules that apply to qualified plans apply here.
- The 10 percent premature distribution excise tax applies to the taxable portion of a distribution made prior to age 59 1/2. Exceptions apply if the distribution is made because of death or disability, or to pay for certain medical expenses, or if substantially equal periodic payments are withdrawn (after separation from service). With IRAs, there are three additional exceptions: withdrawals to cover medical insurance premiums for certain unemployed individuals, withdrawals to cover post-secondary education expenses, and withdrawals of up to $10,000 for first-time home buyer expenses.
- With SIMPLE IRAs, the 10 percent penalty tax becomes a 25 percent penalty if withdrawals are made in the first 2 years of participation. So this tax cannot be avoided, SIMPLE IRAs cannot be rolled over, or transferred into a regular IRA in the first 2 years of participation.
- If a participant has an IRA account payable to a beneficiary at his or her death, the value of the benefit is included in the taxable estate. Payments to beneficiaries are treated as income in respect to a decedent—meaning that beneficiaries receiving benefit payments pay income tax but may get a deduction for any estate taxes paid because of the value of the pension.
- Participants can make withdrawals from IRAs (as well as SEPs and SIMPLEs) at any time, without limitation. No participant loans are available, however.
- Distributions are subject to the minimum-distribution rules under which the required beginning date is always the April 1 following the year of attainment of age 70 1/2.
- The QJSA rules do not apply to IRAs.

- The 20 percent mandatory withholding rules do not apply to IRAs.
- Except for amounts satisfying the required minimum-distribution rules, distributions can be rolled over or transferred to another IRA, a qualified plan, 403(b) annuity or 457 plan.

403(b) Plans

The following is a brief review of the distribution rules that apply to 403(b) plans:

- Distributions are generally taxed as ordinary income. Although there are no after-tax contributions, it is possible for the participant to have basis due to the PS 58 costs that may be recovered tax free.
- The 10 percent premature distribution excise tax applies in the same way as it does to qualified retirement plans.
- If a participant has a 403(b) account payable to a beneficiary at his or her death, the value of the benefit is included in the taxable estate. Payments to beneficiaries are treated as income in respect to a decedent—meaning that beneficiaries receiving benefit payments pay income tax but may get a deduction for any estate taxes paid because of the value of the pension.
- In-service distributions are subject to limitations. When a plan (funded with annuity contracts) contains a salary-deferral feature, contributions attributable to the deferral election may not be distributed until the employee attains age 59 1/2, separates from service, becomes disabled, becomes a hardship case, or dies. When the plan is funded with mutual fund shares, the special distribution requirements apply to all contribution amounts. 403(b) plans can have participant loan programs.
- Distributions are subject to the minimum-distribution rules. An exception applies to the portion of the benefit that accrued prior to 1987. That amount can generally be deferred until age 75. In addition, participants (except for 5 percent owners) who continue working past age 70 can defer the required beginning date until the April 1 following the year in which they retire.
- Distributions (other than required minimum distributions and certain annuity payments) can be rolled over into another 403(b) annuity, qualified plan, 457 plan or an IRA.
- A participant can generally keep the 403(b) vehicle even after termination of employment. This may be a better option than rolling the benefit into an IRA because of the pre-87 exception to the

minimum-distribution rules and the ability to continue to take a loan from the 403(b) plan.

- Participants must be given the option to directly rollover distributions to a new trustee or custodian. Distributions that are not directly rolled over are subject to a 20 percent mandatory income tax withholding.

- In some cases, distributions are subject to the qualified joint and survivor annuity (QJSA) requirements.

Working With Clients

Financial services professionals work with a wide variety of clients, and each of their needs is unique. The checklist in table 26-2 identifies some client issues. Generally, the typical issues that need to be addressed can be divided into two client profiles. The first consists of those clients with limited resources whose primary goal is making their limited resources last throughout their retirement years. The second group is made up of the clients who will not need all the pension assets during their own lifetime. This group faces the dual concern of financing retirement and maximizing the after-tax estate that they leave to their heirs. We will address each of these situations.

Primary Concern: Funding Retirement Needs

For most of us, accruing adequate retirement resources is a daunting task. In many cases, the most significant retirement asset is the company pension. For this reason, it is imperative that the distribution decisions result in maximization of the family's available after-tax dollars. The following materials address the vital issues that apply to clients whose primary concern is affording retirement.

Preretirement Distributions. The major concern for the individual who receives a pension distribution prior to retirement is ensuring that pension accumulations are used to finance retirement and are not spent beforehand. In this regard, participants want to be sure to satisfy rollover rules so inadvertent taxes do not have to be paid. Meeting the rollover requirements has become much easier now that participants in qualified plans and 403(b) annuities must be given the option to transfer benefits directly to an IRA or other qualified plan. Note that these direct rollover rules do not apply to IRA-funded plans, including SEPs and SIMPLEs. However, when a participant leaves an IRA-funded plan, there is generally no reason for a rollover.

TABLE 26-2
Checklist of Issues and Decisions at Retirement

1. Do you want an annuity for all or part of your funds?

2. What type of annuity is best for your situation?

3. Can you maximize the monthly payment of your annuity by rolling it into an IRA or another qualified plan, in other words, shop your annuity?

4. Should you delay taxation of a distribution by rolling it into an IRA or another tax-deferred plan?

5. Is a rollover possible from a cash-flow perspective?

6. Is a direct rollover to the new trustee preferable to a rollover?

7. Do you want a lump-sum distribution for part or all of your funds?

8. Can you elect the grandfathered 10-year averaging or capital-gains treatment for pre-'74 income?

9. Should you elect 10-year averaging or the capital-gains treatment?

10. What is the best tax strategy for dealing with the distribution of employer stock?

11. Has the client complied with the rules for minimum distributions from the qualified plan?

12. When do distributions have to begin?

13. Have the beneficiary forms been carefully selected?

14. In what order should assets be cashed in order to maintain optimum tax-shelter and proper asset allocation ratios?

15. Has there been proper coordination of distributions from qualified plans and IRAs?

16. Will the distributions be used to provide necessary income for sustaining your client, or will it supplement already adequate sources of retirement income?

17. Did you meet the need to provide for surviving dependents?

18. Has your client integrated their retirement planning with proper estate planning?

Still, some clients are tempted to spend preretirement pension distributions. If you have clients in this position, showing them the power of the compounding return sometimes convinces them otherwise.

Example: Sonny Shortview, aged 40, is changing jobs. He will
be receiving a much higher salary in his new job and
he is feeling quite well off. Sonny has the
opportunity to receive a pension distribution from his
old company in the amount of $35,000. Even though
he does not really need the funds, the amount seems
small enough to Sonny that he is considering paying
taxes and using the after-tax proceeds for an auto
upgrade. Sonny may change his mind when he learns
that with a 10 percent rate of return, his $35,000
distribution would grow to $367,687 by the time he
reaches age 65.

Another difficult situation arises in the case of involuntary dismissal. An employee who is terminated due to downsizing or other reasons may experience a prolonged period of unemployment. In this case, the individual may need to tap into his or her pension. If the participant is younger than age 59 1/2, he or she must pay the 10 percent premature distribution excise tax unless one of the exceptions applies. The substantially equal periodic payment exception is one way to avoid this tax, but the problem is that distributions must be made for the longer of 5 years or until attainment of age 59 1/2, and this period will probably be much longer than the period of unemployment. This problem can be mitigated somewhat by dividing assets into a number of IRAs. For example, part of the need can be met by using a periodic payment from one IRA and simply paying the excise tax for certain short-term needs from another IRA. If a lump sum is needed, the individual could consider borrowing from another source and repaying the loan with periodic distributions.

Form of Retirement Distribution. For the client living on his or her pension distribution, the two most important decisions are usually when to retire and the form of payment that should be received. In chapter 3, we looked at the effect of retiring at different times—especially retiring early. As we discussed, the effect of early retirement can be quite profound, especially in defined-benefit plans. Even if the plan subsidizes some part of the early retirement penalty, there is always a cost for early retirement. Other timing issues that need to be understood are the consequences of delaying payments to some time after retirement and of retiring after the plan's normal retirement age. Spend time with your clients to make sure they understand these important timing issues—it is rare that a plan participant will fully understand them without your help. Of course, the answers always depend upon the specific terms of the plan, so also be sure to review the summary plan description.

Once the client has a full understanding of the timing issues, the next decision is choosing the form of retirement benefits. Almost all individual account-type plans (including qualified plans of the defined-contribution type, SEPs, SIMPLEs, and 403(b) annuities) give the participant the option to receive a lump-sum distribution, which can be rolled into an IRA without tax consequences. This benefit option affords the participant the most flexibility because he or she can take money out as slowly or as quickly as it is needed.

Defined-benefit plans may or may not have a lump-sum option, depending upon the terms of the plan. Also note that a lump sum from a defined-benefit plan is based on the actuarial equivalent of a normal form of payment, usually a life annuity. If the lump sum is calculated with unfavorable assumptions, this option may not be advisable. One way to test the value of the lump sum is to compare the amount payable as a life annuity from the plan to the amount that would result from taking a lump sum, rolling it into an IRA, and then buying a life annuity at commercially available prices.

Many participants will be satisfied with the IRA rollover approach because it provides both investment and withdrawal flexibility. However, this method does not ensure that the participant will not outlive pension distributions. Even with careful distribution planning, investment performance may not meet expectations, or the individual may live too long. To protect against this contingency, retirees should consider having at least a portion of their retirement income payable as some form of life annuity. We reviewed the advantages and disadvantages of various annuity options in the earlier part of this chapter. Participants can generally receive the type of annuity that they want, even if it is a not offered by the particular plan involved. They can accomplish this by electing a lump-sum option, rolling the benefit into an IRA, and then purchasing the annuity. Variable annuities should be considered because they can combine the promise of lifetime benefits with the possibility of increasing payments over time to offset the impact of inflation.

Qualified Joint and Survivor Considerations. A married participant receiving a pension distribution in a form other than a qualified joint and survivor annuity generally must have his or her spouse sign a waiver. Unless there is marital discord, receiving an alternate form of benefit generally poses no special concerns. In fact, the disclosure and paperwork involved probably ensure that the participant is carefully considering all the available distribution options. Still, this is a matter that retirees may not understand.

Explaining the effect of the joint and survivor form of payment is an excellent way to provide service to the client and solidify the advisory relationship.

Tax Issues

For the individual who receives a distribution from a qualified plan and qualifies for special tax treatment, a major issue will be the decision of whether or not to elect special averaging treatment. With smaller distribution amounts, the tax rate using special averaging treatment can look quite attractive; it is possible that the effective rate can be 20 percent or less. Even though this rate is low, remember it must be compared to the individual's marginal tax rate. The effect of deferring taxes is quite powerful, and taking the benefit as a lump sum has to be examined thoroughly.

If the client receives a lump-sum distribution but does not elect special averaging treatment, then the lump sum should be transferred directly into an IRA (to avoid any income tax withholding). Then, to maximize the benefit of tax deferral, amounts should be distributed only when needed, unless, of course, the minimum-distribution rules require a larger distribution.

Fortunately, beginning in 2002, the minimum-distribution rules no longer require the same level of planning as was required previously. Now the middle-income person does not have to make special elections; the calculation of the minimum is virtually the same for everyone during the individual's lifetime. The beneficiary election does, however, affect the length of the distribution period after death. Also, as a matter of sound estate planning, the benefit will pass based on the beneficiary election and not the individual's will. This means the beneficiary form should be reviewed periodically to see if the right person will inherit the plan asset.

Another issue that has become a concern is whether the retiree should elect to convert his or her pension distribution to a Roth IRA. To do this, the distribution first must be rolled or transferred to an IRA and then converted to the Roth IRA. Only single individuals or marrieds filing jointly who have an adjusted gross income of under $100,000 for the year are allowed to convert. As discussed in chapter 18, conversion results in taxable ordinary income in the amount of the conversion. Once in the Roth IRA, growth is tax free as long as the distribution meets certain eligibility requirements. Determining whether to convert is a complex issue that requires a full understanding of the participant's retirement and estate planning concerns. However, there are some general considerations that will affect the participant's decision.

- The Roth IRA conversion becomes more appropriate the longer the period of distributions is stretched out. The individual who is struggling to meet retirement needs will probably require early withdrawals, which means the Roth IRA will not have time to generate substantial tax-free accumulations.

- The Roth IRA conversion is more appropriate when the income tax rate is the same or higher at the time of distribution than at the time of conversion. For the average person struggling to meet retirement needs, the post-retirement income tax rate is probably lower than at the time of distribution. This factor weighs against conversion.

- Any portion of an IRA can be converted to a Roth IRA. This means that the retiree who has all of his or her retirement income may still want to convert some of it as a hedge against future tax-rate increases.

- For many retirees who are struggling to meet their retirement needs, converting and paying taxes does not seem like an appropriate choice. For this group, it may be more appropriate to put away the maximum amount in a Roth IRA each year ($3,000—or $3,500 for a person over age 50—for 2002) (or less), accumulating amounts in this vehicle prior to their retirement years.

Primary Objective: Maximizing the Estate

When examining the needs of your clients, you will find there is a distinct difference between those who will probably spend most of their assets over retirement and those who can afford to leave an estate to their heirs. Nonetheless, it is impossible to divide the world into two distinct client groups, and the issues will certainly be different for the individual with a $20 million estate than for the person with a $2 million estate. Even for the wealthier clients, the first and foremost concern is retirement security, with estate planning as a secondary objective.

However, simply having significant assets in a tax-preferred retirement plan can pose serious problems. As we have learned in the last two chapters, lifetime distributions can be subject to income tax and the 10 percent premature distribution excise tax. If money that is still in the plan is left to heirs, the amount is included in the taxable estate, and distributions are still subject to federal income taxes. If assets are distributed at death, a large portion of the pension asset can be confiscated by taxes. Let's look at an example of the devastating effect that these taxes can have.

***Example*:**

Oliver, aged 80, dies (without a surviving spouse) with $2 million in his IRA account. Assume that Oliver's other assets are large enough that his pension is taxed at the highest marginal estate tax rate of 55 percent. After Oliver's death, the entire IRA is distributed to his beneficiary, who is in the 28 percent tax bracket. Looking just at federal taxes, the benefit will be taxed as follows:

Federal estate tax	$ 1,100,000
(55% of ($2,000,000)	
Income tax on IRA	$ 252,000
(28% of ($2,000,000 – $1,100,000)	
Total reduction	$ 1,352,000
Net value of IRA for heirs	$ 648,000

Percentage of IRA passing to heirs

This tax threat is still quite frightening, even after the elimination of the excise tax on large pension accumulations. Appropriate planning is necessary to minimize the threat. However, it is also important to keep the situation in perspective. Even with the taxes, saving through a tax-sheltered retirement plan will result in larger accumulations than saving on an after-tax basis.

For example, Daniel, a self-employed individual, is considering whether or not to establish a Keogh plan. He is aged 43 and can afford to contribute $30,000 a year to the plan until he retires at age 65. Daniel wants to compare the effect of saving with a Keogh to saving on an after-tax basis. Because his marginal federal and state income tax rate is 40 percent, his annual after-tax savings would be $18,000. In preparing the illustration, we assumed that plan assets would grow at 10 percent, that inflation would remain at 3 percent, and that the participant would remain in the 40 percent income tax bracket. In both the pretax and after-tax examples, we assumed that none of the accumulated amounts were distributed during Daniel's lifetime (except as required under the minimum-distribution rules). We looked at the value (at death) of the amount that would pass to heirs after all income taxes were paid, and we used the worst-case scenario, meaning that all taxes are paid at the time of death. In this case, we did not subtract out estate taxes. Note, as illustrated in table 26-4, that even with the taxes, Daniel's heirs will end up much better off if Daniel saves using the Keogh plan.

TABLE 26-4 **Comparison of Pretax and After-Tax Savings**		
Client's Age at Death	Net to Heirs Pretax Savings	Net to HeirsPost-tax Savings
70	$1,005,830	$ 539,987
75	$1,431,273	$ 722,625
80	$1,975,211	$ 967,036
85	$2,672,980	$ 1,294,112

This information is important because it shows that individuals who are faced with income and estate taxes have not made a mistake in funding their pension plans. However, knowing this is still not that comforting to someone faced with a tax rate of 67 percent or more. Fortunately, there are a number of ways to minimize the tax threat at the time of the participant's death. Under the minimum-distribution rules, it is possible to distribute assets over the remaining life expectancy of the beneficiary after the death of the participant. This strategy spreads out the payment of income taxes, meaning that the pension asset can continue to generate significant income for the beneficiaries. However, in order to take advantage of the extra deferral period, the pension plan assets cannot be used to pay estate taxes. Readers familiar with estate planning know the pension asset problem is similar to problems that can arise with other illiquid assets. In many cases, the solution to the illiquid asset problem is to purchase life insurance—usually using an irrevocable life insurance trust—because the insurance proceeds will not be subject to estate taxes. This approach generates capital for paying estate taxes. In fact, the pension problem is often less difficult to solve than the problem of illiquid assets because distributions from the plan can function as a source of insurance premiums. In many cases, the premiums are simply paid out of distributions that are already required under the minimum-distribution rules.

When the participant is uninsurable or unwilling to purchase insurance, the problem becomes more difficult to solve. One option is to use pension distributions to fund a family gifting program—taking advantage of the ability to give away $10,000 a year to a beneficiary without estate or gift tax consequences. Another solution for the charitably inclined is to leave the benefit to charity. When the charity receives the benefit, it pays no income taxes and the estate receives an estate tax deduction for the amount of the contribution.

This type of client also needs to consider whether or not to convert some or all of their pension assets to a Roth IRA. The major conversion impediment for wealthier clients is that they will earn more than the $100,000 cap. Some advisers are so enthusiastic about the conversion idea that they are looking for ways to reduce the individual's income for a year so the conversion can occur. The reason conversion can be so valuable for the wealthier client is that there are no required minimum distributions during the participant's lifetime. If the spouse is the beneficiary, no distributions have to be made over the spouse's lifetime either. After the spouse's death, distributions must be made over the life expectancy of the beneficiaries at that time. This may mean that even if the conversion occurs at age 65, the Roth IRA will grow income tax free for possibly 25 or more years, followed by distributions that can be spread over the next 30 to 40 years (the life expectancy of the beneficiaries). Similar to planning for distributions from traditional IRAs, the Roth IRA conversion works best when estate taxes are not withdrawn from the Roth IRA. Once again, life insurance can be the appropriate means for preparing for this contingency.

Form of Distribution Option. For the client with substantial assets, the IRA rollover option is generally the appropriate choice. This type of client can afford to self-insure against the contingency of living a long life and, therefore, will generally not want to annuitize the benefit. With the IRA, the participant has both investment and distribution flexibility. This strategy is also necessary if the individual wants to convert some or all of the distribution to a Roth IRA.

As discussed in the previous chapter, individuals with large pension benefits generally will not elect lump sum averaging treatment. The effective tax rate is not that attractive for large distributions. Sometimes electing lump sum averaging is appropriate when an individual is a participant in multiple plans. If, for example, an individual has accumulated benefits of $250,000 in a profit-sharing plan and $1 million in a pension plan, choosing lump sum tax treatment for the profit-sharing distribution may be appropriate. This strategy should be evaluated carefully because there are a number of traps regarding the aggregation of multiple distributions. Also remember that averaging will be available only to those born before 1936.

CHAPTER REVIEW

Answers to the review questions and self-test questions start on page 673.
For additional review, see case studies in Appendix 11.

Key Terms

involuntary cash-out option   subsidized benefits
actuarial equivalent

Review Questions

26-1. What are types of considerations that impact on an individual's decision the concerning appropriate form of pension distribution?

26-2. When do qualified plans typically allow for benefit payments?

26-3. When is an involuntary cash-out allowed, and when does a qualified plan have to give participants the option as to the timing and form of payment?

26-4. Why can a life annuity with guaranteed payments be used to provide for the income needs of a beneficiary?

26-5. In a defined-benefit plan, what does it mean that a life annuity with 10-years-certain payments is the actuarial equivalent to a life annuity?

26-6. In a defined-benefit plan, what does it mean to say that a benefit is subsidized?

26-7. Margo Henning has purchased a variable annuity contract that was issued with a 6 percent assumed investment return (AIR) and a beginning unit value of $100.
   a. What is the effect on Margo's unit value if the actual amount of interest that is earned drops to 3 percent in the first month?
   b. What is the effect on Margo's unit value if the actual amount of interest that is earned increases to 12 percent in the first month?

26-8. Explain the following:
   a. Are distributions from qualified plans always taxed as ordinary income?
   b. What exception to the 10 percent Sec. 72(t) excise tax applies to qualified plans and 403(b) plans, but does not apply to IRAs?
   c. What is the exception that applies to the minimum-distribution rules for qualified plans?

      d.   Do the 20 percent mandatory income tax withholding rules apply to distributions from IRAs?

      e.   In an IRA, is the required beginning date ever later than the April 1 following the year in which the participant attained age 70 1/2?

26-9.   Why is choosing the right distribution option for someone with a relatively small account balance so important?

26-10. Explain the estate tax threat facing those with significant retirement plan balances and the strategies to minimize its effect.

Self-Test Questions

T   F   26-1.   A qualified plan should clearly specify the optional forms of distribution and when benefits are payable.

T   F   26-2.   If a terminating participant is entitled to a lump-sum benefit of $3,000, the plan can force out the payment in a lump sum and forgo giving participants the right to optional forms of distributions.

T   F   26-3.   With a joint and survivor benefit after the death of the participant, a monthly benefit continues to be paid to a surviving beneficiary.

T   F   26-4.   Installment payments and an annuity certain are two names for the same option.

T   F   26-5.   In a defined-benefit plan, an annuity is purchased with the participant's account balance.

T   F   26-6.   A subsidized early retirement benefit generally means that a benefit payable at normal retirement age can begin earlier without an actuarial reduction.

T   F   26-7.   With a variable annuity, if the actual interest rate is higher than the AIR, the annuity payments will decrease.

T   F   26-8.   For the client whose primary objective is funding retirement needs, the most important pension distribution issues are when to begin receiving benefits and what form the distributions should take.

T   F   26-9.   For the client concerned about outliving his or her assets, a rollover into an IRA (not invested in an annuity contract) is always the best distribution option.

T   F   26-10. A client concerned about maximizing his or her estate may want to consider distributing assets as slowly as allowed under the minimum-distribution rules.

T   F   26-11.   A client at or after normal retirement age should never consider converting a traditional IRA to a Roth IRA.

Appendix 1

Post-ERISA Legislation

Below is description, law by law, of legislation affecting the pension field. Following that is a table identifying the laws for those interested in researching them further.

In 1981 the ***Economic Recovery Tax Act*** expanded the retirement market by breathing new life into old retirement products. ERTA lifted the prohibition against employees who were active participants in employer-sponsored plans having an individual retirement account (IRA) and opened the door for widespread sales of IRAs. The public response was tremendous as millions flocked to save for retirement. ERTA also contributed to the success of stock option plans by liberalizing the rules for deducting leveraged employee stock ownership plans (ESOPs) and creating payroll-based stock option plans (PAYSOPs). PAYSOPs, phased out in 1987, allowed for an income tax credit that benefited certain corporations. Finally, ERTA started the trend of making the rules for retirement plans for the self-employed (Keogh plans) similar to those for corporate plans.

The Tax Equity and Fiscal Responsibility Act of 1982 created plan parity between Keogh plans and corporate plans, finishing the job started by ERTA. The major emphasis of TEFRA, however, was on stopping tax abuses, primarily loopholes used by small-employer plans. TEFRA created special rules for plans that unduly benefit key employees—if a plan inordinately favors the privileged few, restrictive "top-heavy" rules take effect. The top-heavy rules guarantee minimum benefits for rank-and-file employees and restrict benefits available for key employees. Other loopholes were closed by TEFRA: it stopped plan loan abuses, limited contributions to the plan and distributions from the plan by reducing the maximum contributions or distributions allowed, and forced plan distributions to be used for retirement purposes, as opposed to sheltering the money for the beneficiary.

The Retirement Equity Act of 1984 shifted Congress's focus from tax abuses by small employers to the perceived mistreatment of women under the pension rules. REA helps people (male or female) who do not fit the standard work pattern, especially those who interrupt or stop their career for children, by reducing the age required to participate in a retirement plan. In addition, REA makes it harder to lose pension benefits because of career interruptions. REA also protects the rights of the spouse or ex-spouse of a plan participant by assuring that the spouse has some say in how retirement money is distributed and by allowing retirement funds to be part of a divorce settlement.

The Tax Reform Act of 1986 represented the biggest shake-up since ERISA. A need for revenue was the motivation for TRA '86 rules that cut back salary reduction contributions previously allowed under some types of plans (401(k), tax-sheltered annuities) and restricted the deductibility of contributions made to individual retirement accounts. A second target of TRA '86 was the discrimination in favor of officers and key employees. Existing discrimination restrictions were tightened, and some plans that had previously escaped nondiscrimination coverage were brought under a new, tougher nondiscrimination umbrella. Other tax reform changes were also included:

- modifications to the profit-sharing rules, which permit profit-sharing contributions when the employer has no profits (this was a response to the trend of using profit-sharing plans as a major source of pension benefits)
- amendments liberalizing ERISA's vesting schedules
- creation of a 10 percent premature distribution penalty tax for most plan distributions prior to age 59 1/2
- minimum distribution requirements and restrictive changes in the taxation of retirement distributions

The Omnibus Budget Reconciliation Act of 1987 (OBRA '87)) focused on yet another legislative target—the underfunded pension plan. OBRA '87 tightened ERISA's funding requirements in an effort to prevent plans from being inadequately funded and consequently reneging on the pension-benefit promises that they have made. OBRA '87 took away some of the leeway actuaries had concerning the amount and timing of plan contributions and forced employers to meet stricter funding requirements. In addition to tightening funding standards the Revenue Act of 1987 also increased insurance premiums that are owed the PBGC from $8.50 to $16 per participant per year. Under the higher premium schedules that were imposed underfunded plans were subject to a variable rate greater than $16, depending on the amount they were underfunded.

The Revenue Reconciliation Act of 1989 represented yet another legislative change to pension law. This act focused on, among other things, restructuring the rules governing employee stock ownership plans (ESOPs). Specifically the act abolished many of the special tax advantages that an ESOP had, such as the estate tax reduction brought about by selling employer stock back to the ESOP after an employee's death.

The Revenue Reconciliation Act of 1990 dramatically changed the rules governing an employer's ability to acquire an asset reversion from a terminating defined-benefit plan (see chapter 13). In addition, the new law enhanced an employer's ability to prefund retiree health benefits in a so-called 401(h) account by allowing excess pension assets to be transferred to the 401(h) account without the employer having to pay either regular income tax or a pension reversion excise tax on the amount transferred. Finally, the new law increased annual PBGC premiums for covered defined-benefit plans from $16 to $19 per participant.

The Emergency Unemployment Act of 1992 changed several of the rules governing distributions from qualified plans. Apparently the policy behind the changes was to encourage employees to save preretirement distributions for their retirement needs. The new rules, effective for distributions after December 31, 1992, liberalize the rollover rules (allowing most preretirement distributions to be rolled into a tax-sheltered IRA or qualified plan); require mandatory 20 percent federal income tax withholding on most distributions made directly to participants; and require qualified plans to allow participants the option to have distributions transferred directly to another tax-sheltered vehicle. (Transferred amounts are not subject to the 20 percent withholding requirements.)

The Omnibus Budget Reconciliation Act of 1993 targeted the benefits of the highly compensated by capping the amount of compensation that could be taken into account for determining contributions or benefits to $150,000.

The Retirement Protection Act of 1994 (RPA '94) made significant changes in the funding rules for single-employer defined-benefit plans, the cash-out provisions for lump sums, and the PBGC premium structure for underfunded defined-benefit plans. The primary focus of the legislation was to give employers added incentive to fund underfunded defined-benefit plans and to put the PBGC in a better financial position.

The Small Business Job Opportunities Act of 1996 was the most sweeping legislation in the pension area in years. Believe it or not, the new law actually simplifies the pension rules. For example, the law creates a less complicated definition of highly compensated employees, simplifies the nondiscrimination testing in a 401(k) plan, and even eliminates nondiscrimination testing in 401(k) plans that comply with certain safe harbors. In the distribution area, the law simplifies the annuity taxation rules and eliminates special 5-year averaging. To provide a 401(k) look-alike savings plan for small employers, the law establishes a "SIMPLE."

The Economic Growth and Tax Relief Reconciliation Act of 2001 is the most positive pension law in years. Many of the pension limits were increased. For example, the $35,000 limit on annual additions in a defined- contribution plan for each participant increased to $40,000 in 2002 and the defined-benefit annual benefit limit increased from $140,000 a year in 2001 to $160,000 in 2002. All the maximum salary deferral limits increased as well, with the limit for Sec. 401(k) plans and Sec. 403(b) plans increasing over the next several years to $15,000 (up from $10,500) and the SIMPLE limit is increasing from $6,500 to $10,000 over the next several years as well.

Even the IRA limits were increased, going from $2,000 in 2001 up to $5,000 in 2008. Participants over age 50 can also now make additional catch-up contributions to 401(k), 403(b), and even to IRA plans.

Many other changes in the law were intended to help encourage small business owners to establish plans. This was done in a number of ways, from eliminating IRS user fees for new plan sponsors to tax credit, to eliminating some of the complexity of maintaining a plan. For example, the top-heavy rules were simplified and the prohibition against certain owners borrowing from the plan was removed. Also, the maximum deductible contribution to a profit-sharing plan went up to 25 percent of compensation, so a sponsor can now maximize contributions to a defined-contribution plan with just one plan.

Other provisions provided simplification for both plan sponsors and plan participants. The most important change was that now participants can roll pension benefits between qualified plans, IRAs, 403(b) plans, and Sec. 457 plans.

Appendix 2

Pension Acronyms

ADP test	actual deferral percentage test
AGI	adjusted gross income
AIR	assumed investment return
Automatic J & S	automatic joint and survivor annuity
CODA	cash or deferred arrangement
COLA	cost-of-living adjustment
DA contract	deposit-administration contract
DAM contract	discretionary asset management contract
DB	defined benefit
DBO Plan	death benefit only plan
DC	defined contribution
DOL	Department of Labor
ERIC	ERISA Industry Committee
ERISA	Employee Retirement Income Security Act of 1974
ESOP	employee stock ownership plan
FASB	Financial Accounting Standards Board
FSA	flexible spending account
GIC	guaranteed-investment contract
IG contract	investment-guarantee contract
IPG contract	immediate-participation-guarantee contract

IRA	individual retirement account
IRC	Internal Revenue Code
IRD	income in respect of a decedent
IRS	Internal Revenue Service
ISO	incentive stock option
LSD	lump-sum distribution
MPPAA	Multiemployer Pension Plan Amendments Act
NRA	normal retirement age
NRD	normal retirement date
PAYSOP	payroll-based stock option plan
PBGC	Pension Benefit Guaranty Corporation
PC	professional corporation
PLR	private-letter ruling
PTE	prohibited-transaction exemption
QDRO	qualified domestic relations order
QPAM	qualified professional asset manager
QPSA	qualified preretirement survivor annuity
QVEC	qualified voluntary employee contribution
SAR	summary of annual reports
SARSEP	salary reduction simplified employee pension
SEP	simplified employee pension plan
SERP	supplemental executive retirement plan

SIMPLE	savings incentive match plan for employees
SMM	summary of material modifications
SPAC	single-premium annuity contract
SPD	summary plan description
TDA	tax-deferred annuity
TPA	third-party administrator
TSA	tax-sheltered annuity
VDEC	voluntary deductible employee contribution
VEBA	Voluntary Employee's Beneficiary Association
401(a)(4)	discrimination rule
401(k) plan	cash or deferred arrangement
403(b) plan	tax-deferred annuity
410(b)(1)	discrimination rule
457 plan	state or local government plan
501(c)(3)	charitable organizations
5500s	pension forms filed with IRS

Appendix 3

Average Life Expectancies

1983 Individual Annuity Table (1971–1976)*				
	Male		Female	
Age	Deaths per 1,000	Expectation of Life (Years)	Deaths per 1,000	Expectation of Life (Years)
30	.76	49.83	.44	54.75
31	.79	48.87	.46	53.77
32	.81	47.91	.48	52.80
33	.84	46.95	.50	51.82
34	.88	45.99	.52	50.85
35	.92	45.03	.55	49.87
36	.97	44.07	.57	48.90
37	1.03	43.11	.61	47.93
38	1.11	42.15	.65	46.96
39	1.22	41.20	.69	45.99
40	1.34	40.25	.74	45.02
41	1.49	39.30	.80	44.05
42	1.67	38.36	.87	43.09
43	1.89	37.43	.94	42.12
44	2.13	36.50	1.03	41.16
45	2.40	35.57	1.12	40.20
46	2.69	34.66	1.23	39.25
47	3.01	33.75	1.36	38.30
48	3.34	32.85	1.50	37.35
49	3.69	31.96	1.66	36.40
50	4.06	31.07	1.83	35.46
51	4.43	30.20	2.02	34.53
52	4.81	29.33	2.22	33.59
53	5.20	28.47	2.43	32.67
54	5.59	27.62	2.65	31.75
55	5.99	26.77	2.89	30.83
56	6.41	25.93	3.15	29.92
57	6.84	25.09	3.43	29.01
58	7.29	24.26	3.74	28.11
59	7.78	23.44	4.08	27.21
60	8.34	22.62	4.47	26.32

1983 Individual Annuity Table (1971–1976) (Continued)*				
	Male		Female	
Age	Deaths per 1,000	Expectation of Life (Years)	Deaths per 1,000	Expectation of Life (Years)
61	8.98	21.80	4.91	25.44
62	9.74	20.99	5.41	24.56
63	10.63	20.20	5.99	23.69
64	11.66	19.41	6.63	22.83
65	12.85	18.63	7.34	21.98
66	14.20	17.87	8.09	21.14
67	15.72	17.12	8.89	20.31
68	17.41	16.38	9.73	19.49
69	19.30	15.66	10.65	18.67
70	21.37	14.96	11.70	17.87
71	23.65	14.28	12.91	17.07
72	26.13	13.61	14.32	16.29
73	28.84	12.96	15.98	15.52
74	31.79	12.33	17.91	14.76
75	35.05	11.72	20.13	14.02
76	38.63	11.13	22.65	13.30
77	42.59	10.56	25.51	12.60
78	46.95	10.00	28.72	11.91
79	51.76	9.47	32.33	11.25
80	57.03	8.96	36.40	10.61
81	62.79	8.47	40.98	9.99
82	69.08	8.01	46.12	9.40
83	75.91	7.57	51.89	8.83
84	83.23	7.15	58.34	8.28
85	90.99	6.75	65.52	7.77
86	99.12	6.37	73.49	7.28
87	107.58	6.02	82.32	6.81
88	116.32	5.69	92.02	6.38
89	125.39	5.37	102.49	5.98
90	134.89	5.07	113.61	5.60
91	144.87	4.78	125.23	5.26
92	155.43	4.50	137.22	4.94
93	166.63	4.24	149.46	4.64
94	178.54	3.99	161.83	4.37
95	191.21	3.75	174.23	4.12
96	204.72	3.51	186.54	3.88
97	219.12	3.29	198.65	3.65
98	234.74	3.07	211.10	3.44
99	251.89	2.86	224.45	3.22
100	270.91	2.66	239.22	3.01

| 1983 Individual Annuity Table (1971–1976) (Continued)* | | | | |
| Age | Male | | Female | |
	Deaths per 1,000	Expectation of Life (Years)	Deaths per 1,000	Expectation of Life (Years)
101	292.11	2.46	255.95	2.80
102	315.83	2.26	275.20	2.59
103	342.38	2.08	297.50	2.38
104	372.09	1.90	323.39	2.18
105	405.28	1.73	353.41	1.98
106	442.28	1.57	388.11	1.79
107	483.41	1.41	428.02	1.60
108	528.99	1.27	473.69	1.43
109	579.35	1.13	525.66	1.26
110	634.81	1.01	584.46	1.11
111	695.70	.89	650.65	.97
112	762.34	.78	724.75	.83
113	835.06	.70	807.32	.71
114	914.17	.67	898.89	.60
115	1,000.00	.50	1,000.00	.50

*These figures come from annuity tables which typically assume a longer life expectancy than other tables that can be used.

Appendix 4

Request for Social Security Earnings Information

SOCIAL SECURITY ADMINISTRATION

Request for Earnings and Benefit Estimate Statement

Thank you for requesting this statement.

After you complete and return this form, we will--within 4 to 6 weeks--send you:

- a record of your earnings history and an estimate of how much you have paid in Social Security taxes, and
- estimates of benefits you (and your family) may be eligible for now and in the future.

We're pleased to furnish you with this information and we hope you'll find it useful in planning your financial future.

Social Security is more than just a program for retired people. It helps people of all ages in many ways. Whether you're young or old, male or female, single or with a family--Social Security can help you when you need it most. It can help support your family in the event of your death and pay you benefits if you become severly disabled.

If you have questions about Social Security or this form, please call our toll-free number, 1-800-772-1213.

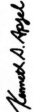 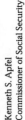

Kenneth D. Appel

Kenneth S. Apfel
Commissioner of Social Security

Mailing Address

Social Security Administration
Wilkes Barre Data Operations Center
PO Box 7004
Wilkes Barre PA 18767-7004

About The Privacy Act

Social Security is allowed to collect the facts on this form under Section 205 of the Social Security Act. We need them to quickly identify your record and prepare the earnings statement you asked us for. Giving us these facts is voluntary. However, without them we may not be able to give you an earnings and benefit estimate statement. Neither the Social Security Administration nor its contractor will use the information for any other purpose.

Paperwork Reduction Act Notice and Time It Takes Statement

The Paperwork Reduction Act of 1995 requires us to notify you that this information collection is in accordance with the clearance requirements of section 3507 of the Paperwork Reduction Act of 1995. We may not conduct or sponsor, and you are not required to respond to, a collection of information unless it displays a valid OMB control number. We estimate that it will take you about 5 minutes to complete this form. This includes the time it will take to read the instructions, gather the necessary facts and fill out the form.

Form Approved
OMB No. 0960-0466

[ ] SP

Request for Earnings and Benefit Estimate Statement

[ ] Please check this box if you want to get your statement in Spanish instead of English.

Please print or type your answers. When you have completed the form, fold it and mail it to us. (If you prefer to send your request using the Internet, contact us at http://www.ssa.gov)

1. Name shown on your Social Security card:

_____ / _____
First Name / Middle Initial

_____
Last Name Only

2. Your Social Security number as shown on your card:

☐☐☐ - ☐☐ - ☐☐☐☐

3. Your date of birth (Mo.-Day-Yr.)

☐☐ - ☐☐ - ☐☐☐☐

4. Other Social Security numbers you have used:

☐☐☐ - ☐☐ - ☐☐☐☐

☐☐☐ - ☐☐ - ☐☐☐☐

5. Your sex: [ ] Male   [ ] Female

For items 6 and 8 show only earnings covered by Social Security. Do NOT include wages from State, local or Federal Government employment that are NOT covered for Social Security or that are covered ONLY by Medicare.

6. Show your actual earnings (wages and/or net self-employment income) for last year and your estimated earnings for this year.

A. Last year's actual earnings: *(Dollars Only)*

$ ☐☐☐ , ☐☐☐ . ☐ 0

B. This year's estimated earnings: *(Dollars Only)*

$ ☐☐☐ , ☐☐☐ . ☐ 0

7. Show the age at which you plan to stop working.

☐☐ *(Show only one age)*

8. Below, show the average yearly amount (not your total future lifetime earnings) that you think you will earn between now and when you plan to stop working. Include performance or scheduled pay increases or bonuses, but not cost-of-living increases.

If you expect to earn significantly more or less in the future due to promotions, job changes, part-time work, or an absence from the work force, enter the amount that most closely reflects your future average yearly earnings.

If you don't expect any significant changes, show the same amount you are earning now (the amount in 6B).

Future average yearly earnings: *(Dollars Only)*

$ ☐☐☐ , ☐☐☐ . ☐ 0

9. Do you want us to send the statement:
- To you? Enter your name and mailing address.
- To someone else (your accountant, pension plan, etc.)? Enter your name with "c/o" and the name and address of that person or organization.

_____
Name

_____
Street Address (Include Apt. No., P.O. Box, or Rural Route)

_____
City   State   Zip Code

Notice:
I am asking for information about my own Social Security record or the record of a person I am authorized to represent. I understand that if I deliberately request information under false pretenses, I may be guilty of a Federal crime and could be fined and/or imprisoned. I authorize you to use a contractor to send the statement of earnings and benefit estimates to the person named in item 9.

▲

Please sign your name (Do Not Print)

_____
Date   (Area Code) Daytime Telephone No.

Appendix 5
Annuity Tables

TABLE V
Ordinary Life Annuities
One Life-Expected Return Multiples

Age	Multiple	Age	Multiple	Age	Multiple
5	76.6	42	40.6	79	10.0
6	75.6	43	39.6	80	9.5
7	74.7	44	38.7	81	8.9
8	73.7	45	37.7	82	8.4
9	72.7	46	36.8	83	7.9
10	71.7	47	35.9	84	7.4
11	70.7	48	34.9	85	6.9
12	69.7	49	34.0	86	6.5
13	68.8	50	33.1	87	6.1
14	67.8	51	32.2	88	5.7
15	66.8	52	31.3	89	5.3
16	65.8	53	30.4	90	5.0
17	64.8	54	29.5	91	4.7
18	63.9	55	28.6	92	4.4
19	62.9	56	27.7	93	4.1
20	61.9	57	26.8	94	3.9
21	60.9	58	25.9	95	3.7
22	59.9	59	25.0	96	3.4
23	59.0	60	24.2	97	3.2
24	58.0	61	23.3	98	3.0
25	57.0	62	22.5	99	2.8
26	56.0	63	21.6	100	2.7
27	55.1	64	20.8	101	2.5
28	54.1	65	20.0	102	2.3
29	53.1	66	19.2	103	2.1
30	52.2	67	18.4	104	1.9
31	51.2	68	17.6	105	1.8
32	50.2	69	16.8	106	1.6
33	49.3	70	16.0	107	1.4
34	48.3	71	14.3	108	1.3
35	47.3	72	14.6	109	1.1
36	46.4	73	13.9	110	1.0
37	45.4	74	13.2	111	.9
38	44.4	75	12.5	112	.8
39	43.5	76	11.9	113	.7
40	42.5	77	11.2	114	.6
41	41.5	78	10.6	115	.5

TABLE VI
Ordinary Joint Life and Last Survivor Annuities
Two Lives—Expected Return Multiples

AGES	51	52	53	54	55	56	57	58	59	60	61	62	63	64	65	66
51	38.2	–	–	–	–	–	–	–	–	–	–	–	–	–	–	–
52	37.8	37.3	–	–	–	–	–	–	–	–	–	–	–	–	–	–
53	37.3	36.8	36.3	–	–	–	–	–	–	–	–	–	–	–	–	–
54	36.9	36.4	35.8	35.3	–	–	–	–	–	–	–	–	–	–	–	–
55	36.5	35.9	35.4	34.9	34.4	–	–	–	–	–	–	–	–	–	–	–
56	36.1	35.6	35.0	34.4	33.9	33.4	–	–	–	–	–	–	–	–	–	–
57	35.8	35.2	34.6	34.0	33.5	33.0	32.5	–	–	–	–	–	–	–	–	–
58	35.5	34.8	34.2	33.6	33.1	32.5	32.0	31.5	–	–	–	–	–	–	–	–
59	35.2	34.5	33.9	33.3	32.7	32.1	31.6	31.1	30.6	–	–	–	–	–	–	–
60	34.9	34.2	33.6	32.9	32.3	31.7	31.2	30.6	30.1	29.7	–	–	–	–	–	–
61	34.6	33.9	33.3	32.6	32.0	31.4	30.8	30.2	29.7	29.2	28.7	–	–	–	–	–
62	34.4	33.7	33.0	32.3	31.7	31.0	30.4	29.9	29.3	28.8	28.3	27.8	–	–	–	–
63	34.2	33.5	32.7	32.0	31.4	30.7	30.1	29.5	28.9	28.4	27.8	27.3	26.9	–	–	–
64	34.0	33.2	32.5	31.8	31.1	30.4	29.8	29.2	28.6	28.0	27.4	26.9	26.4	25.9	–	–
65	33.8	33.0	32.3	31.6	30.9	30.2	29.5	28.9	28.2	27.6	27.1	26.5	26.0	25.5	25.0	–
66	33.6	32.9	32.1	31.4	30.6	29.9	29.2	28.6	27.9	27.3	26.7	26.1	25.6	25.1	24.6	24.1
67	33.5	32.7	31.9	31.2	30.4	29.7	29.0	28.3	27.6	27.0	26.4	25.8	25.2	24.7	24.2	23.7
68	33.4	32.5	31.8	31.0	30.2	29.5	28.8	28.1	27.4	26.7	26.1	25.5	24.9	24.3	23.8	23.3
69	33.2	32.4	31.6	30.8	30.1	29.3	28.6	27.8	27.1	26.5	25.8	25.2	24.6	24.0	23.4	22.9
70	33.1	32.3	31.5	30.7	29.9	29.1	28.4	27.6	26.9	26.2	25.6	24.9	24.3	23.7	23.1	22.5
71	33.0	32.2	31.4	30.5	29.7	29.0	28.2	27.5	26.7	26.0	25.3	24.7	24.0	23.4	22.8	22.2
72	32.9	32.1	31.2	30.4	29.6	28.8	28.1	27.3	26.5	25.8	25.1	24.4	23.8	23.1	22.5	21.9
73	32.8	32.0	31.1	30.3	29.5	28.7	27.9	27.1	26.4	25.6	24.9	24.2	23.5	22.9	22.2	21.6
74	32.8	31.9	31.1	30.2	29.4	28.6	27.8	27.0	26.2	25.5	24.7	24.0	23.3	22.7	22.0	21.4
75	32.7	31.8	31.0	30.1	29.3	28.5	27.7	26.9	26.1	25.3	24.6	23.8	23.1	22.4	21.8	21.1
76	32.6	31.8	30.9	30.1	29.2	28.4	27.6	26.8	26.0	25.2	24.4	23.7	23.0	22.3	21.6	20.9
77	32.6	31.7	30.8	30.0	29.1	28.3	27.5	26.7	25.9	25.1	24.3	23.6	22.8	22.1	21.4	20.7
78	32.5	31.7	30.8	29.9	29.1	28.2	27.4	26.6	25.8	25.0	24.2	23.4	22.7	21.9	21.2	20.5
79	32.5	31.6	30.7	29.9	29.0	28.2	27.3	26.5	25.7	24.9	24.1	23.3	22.6	21.8	21.1	20.4
80	32.5	31.6	30.7	29.8	29.0	28.1	27.3	26.4	25.6	24.8	24.0	23.2	22.4	21.7	21.0	20.2
81	32.4	31.5	30.7	29.8	28.9	28.1	27.2	26.4	25.5	24.7	23.9	23.1	22.3	21.6	20.8	20.1
82	32.4	31.5	30.6	29.7	28.9	28.0	27.2	26.3	25.5	24.6	23.8	23.0	22.3	21.5	20.7	20.0
83	32.4	31.5	30.6	29.7	28.8	28.0	27.1	26.3	25.4	24.6	23.8	23.0	22.2	21.4	20.6	19.9
84	32.3	31.4	30.6	29.7	28.8	27.9	27.1	26.2	25.4	24.5	23.7	22.9	22.1	21.3	20.5	19.8
85	32.3	31.4	30.5	29.6	28.8	27.9	27.0	26.2	25.3	24.5	23.7	22.8	22.0	21.3	20.5	19.7
86	32.3	31.4	30.5	29.6	28.7	27.9	27.0	26.1	25.3	24.5	23.6	22.8	22.0	21.2	20.4	19.6
87	32.3	31.4	30.5	29.6	28.7	27.8	27.0	26.1	25.3	24.4	23.6	22.8	21.9	21.1	20.4	19.6
88	32.3	31.4	30.5	29.6	28.7	27.8	27.0	26.1	25.2	24.4	23.6	22.7	21.9	21.1	20.3	19.5
89	32.3	31.4	30.5	29.6	28.7	27.8	26.9	26.1	25.2	24.4	23.5	22.7	21.9	21.1	20.3	19.5
90	32.3	31.3	30.5	28.5	28.7	27.8	26.9	26.1	25.2	24.3	23.5	22.7	21.8	21.0	20.2	19.4

AGES	67	68	69	70	71	72	73	74	75	76	77	78	79	80	81	82
67	23.2	–	–	–	–	–	–	–	–	–	–	–	–	–	–	–
68	22.8	22.3	–	–	–	–	–	–	–	–	–	–	–	–	–	–
69	22.4	21.9	21.5	–	–	–	–	–	–	–	–	–	–	–	–	–
70	22.0	21.5	21.1	20.6	–	–	–	–	–	–	–	–	–	–	–	–
71	21.7	21.2	20.7	20.2	19.8	–	–	–	–	–	–	–	–	–	–	–
72	21.3	20.8	20.3	19.8	19.4	18.9	–	–	–	–	–	–	–	–	–	–
73	21.0	20.5	20.0	19.4	19.0	18.5	18.1	–	–	–	–	–	–	–	–	–
74	20.8	20.2	19.6	19.1	18.6	18.2	17.7	17.3	–	–	–	–	–	–	–	–
75	20.5	19.9	19.3	18.8	18.3	17.8	17.3	16.9	16.5	–	–	–	–	–	–	–
76	20.3	19.7	19.1	18.5	18.0	17.5	17.0	16.5	16.1	15.7	–	–	–	–	–	–
77	20.1	19.4	18.8	18.3	17.7	17.2	16.7	16.2	15.8	15.4	15.0	–	–	–	–	–
78	19.9	19.2	18.6	18.0	17.5	16.9	16.4	15.9	15.4	15.0	14.6	14.2	–	–	–	–
79	19.7	19.0	18.4	17.8	17.2	16.7	16.1	15.6	15.1	14.7	14.3	13.9	13.5	–	–	–
80	19.5	18.9	18.2	17.6	17.0	16.4	15.9	15.4	14.9	14.4	14.0	13.5	13.2	12.8	–	–
81	19.4	18.7	18.1	17.4	16.8	16.2	15.7	15.1	14.6	14.1	13.7	13.2	12.8	12.5	12.1	–
82	19.3	18.6	17.9	17.3	16.6	16.0	15.5	14.9	14.4	13.9	13.4	13.0	12.5	12.2	11.8	11.5
83	19.2	18.5	17.8	17.1	16.5	15.9	15.3	14.7	14.2	13.7	13.2	12.7	12.3	11.9	11.5	11.1
84	19.1	18.4	17.7	17.0	16.3	15.7	15.1	14.5	14.0	13.5	13.0	12.5	12.0	11.6	11.2	10.9
85	19.0	18.3	17.6	16.9	16.2	15.6	15.0	14.4	13.8	13.3	12.8	12.3	11.8	11.4	11.0	10.6
86	18.9	18.2	17.5	16.8	16.1	15.5	14.8	14.2	13.7	13.1	12.6	12.1	11.6	11.2	10.8	10.4
87	18.8	18.1	17.4	16.7	16.0	15.4	14.7	14.1	13.5	13.0	12.4	11.9	11.4	11.0	10.6	10.1
88	18.8	18.0	17.3	16.6	15.9	15.3	14.6	14.0	13.4	12.8	12.3	11.8	11.3	10.8	10.4	10.0
89	18.7	18.0	17.2	16.5	15.8	15.2	14.5	13.9	13.3	12.7	12.2	11.6	11.1	10.7	10.2	9.8
90	18.7	17.9	17.2	16.5	15.8	15.1	14.5	13.8	13.2	12.6	12.1	11.5	11.0	10.5	10.1	9.6

AGES	83	84	85	86	87	88	89	90
83	10.8	–	–	–	–	–	–	–
84	10.5	10.2	–	–	–	–	–	–
85	10.2	9.9	9.6	–	–	–	–	–
86	10.0	9.7	9.3	9.1	–	–	–	–
87	9.8	9.4	9.1	8.8	8.5	–	–	–
88	9.6	9.2	8.9	8.6	8.3	8.0	–	–
89	9.4	9.0	8.7	8.3	8.1	7.8	7.5	–
90	9.2	8.8	8.5	8.2	7.9	7.6	7.3	7.1

(Reprinted from *Tax Facts on Life Insurance I* by permission. Copyright 2001.)

TABLE VI
Annuities for Joint Life Only
Two Lives—Expected Return Multiples

AGES	51	52	53	54	55	56	57	58	59	60	61	62	63	64	65	66
51	26.1	–	–	–	–	–	–	–	–	–	–	–	–	–	–	–
52	25.7	25.3	–	–	–	–	–	–	–	–	–	–	–	–	–	–
53	25.2	24.8	24.4	–	–	–	–	–	–	–	–	–	–	–	–	–
54	24.7	24.4	24.0	23.6	–	–	–	–	–	–	–	–	–	–	–	–
55	24.2	23.9	23.5	23.2	22.7	–	–	–	–	–	–	–	–	–	–	–
56	23.7	23.4	23.1	22.7	22.3	21.9	–	–	–	–	–	–	–	–	–	–
57	23.2	22.9	22.6	22.2	21.9	21.5	21.1	–	–	–	–	–	–	–	–	–
58	22.6	22.4	22.1	21.7	21.4	21.1	20.7	20.3	–	–	–	–	–	–	–	–
59	22.1	21.8	21.5	21.2	20.9	20.6	20.3	19.9	19.5	–	–	–	–	–	–	–
60	21.5	21.2	21.0	20.7	20.4	20.1	19.8	19.5	19.1	18.7	–	–	–	–	–	–
61	20.9	20.6	20.4	20.2	19.9	19.6	19.3	19.0	18.7	18.3	17.9	–	–	–	–	–
62	20.2	20.0	19.8	19.6	19.4	19.1	18.8	18.5	18.2	17.9	17.5	17.1	–	–	–	–
63	19.6	19.4	19.2	19.0	18.8	18.6	18.3	18.0	17.7	17.4	17.1	16.8	16.4	–	–	–
64	19.0	18.8	18.6	18.5	18.3	18.0	17.8	17.5	17.3	17.0	16.7	16.3	16.0	15.6	–	–
65	18.3	18.2	18.0	17.9	17.7	17.5	17.3	17.0	16.8	16.5	16.2	15.9	15.6	15.3	14.9	–
66	17.7	17.6	17.4	17.3	17.1	16.9	16.7	16.5	16.3	16.0	15.8	15.5	15.2	14.9	14.5	14.2
67	17.1	16.9	16.8	16.7	16.5	16.3	16.2	16.0	15.8	15.5	15.3	15.0	14.7	14.5	14.1	13.8
68	16.4	16.3	16.2	16.1	15.9	15.8	15.6	15.4	15.2	15.0	14.8	14.6	14.3	14.0	13.7	13.4
69	15.8	15.7	15.6	15.4	15.3	15.2	15.0	14.9	14.7	14.5	14.3	14.1	13.9	13.6	13.3	13.1
70	15.1	15.0	14.9	14.8	14.7	14.6	14.5	14.3	14.2	14.0	13.8	13.6	13.4	13.2	12.9	12.6
71	14.5	14.4	14.3	14.2	14.1	14.0	13.9	13.8	13.6	13.5	13.3	13.1	12.9	12.7	12.5	12.2
72	13.8	13.8	13.7	13.6	13.5	13.4	13.3	13.2	13.1	12.9	12.8	12.6	12.4	12.3	12.0	11.8
73	13.2	13.2	13.1	13.0	13.0	12.9	12.8	12.7	12.5	12.4	12.3	12.1	12.0	11.8	11.6	11.4
74	12.6	12.6	12.5	12.4	12.4	12.3	12.2	12.1	12.0	11.9	11.8	11.6	11.5	11.3	11.2	11.0
75	12.0	12.0	11.9	11.9	11.8	11.7	11.7	11.6	11.5	11.4	11.3	11.1	11.0	10.9	10.7	10.5
76	11.4	11.4	11.3	11.3	11.2	11.2	11.1	11.0	10.9	10.9	10.8	10.6	10.5	10.4	10.3	10.1
77	10.8	10.8	10.8	10.7	10.7	10.6	10.6	10.5	10.4	10.3	10.3	10.2	10.0	9.9	9.8	9.7
78	10.3	10.2	10.2	10.2	10.1	10.1	10.0	10.0	9.9	9.8	9.8	9.7	9.6	9.5	9.4	9.2
79	9.7	9.7	9.7	9.6	9.6	9.6	9.5	9.5	9.4	9.3	9.3	9.2	9.1	9.0	8.9	8.8
80	9.2	9.2	9.1	9.1	9.1	9.0	9.0	9.0	8.9	8.9	8.8	8.7	8.7	8.6	8.5	8.4
81	8.7	8.7	8.6	8.6	8.6	8.5	8.5	8.5	8.4	8.4	8.3	8.3	8.2	8.1	8.0	8.0
82	8.2	8.2	8.1	8.1	8.1	8.1	8.0	8.0	8.0	7.9	7.9	7.8	7.8	7.7	7.6	7.5
83	7.7	7.7	7.7	7.6	7.6	7.6	7.6	7.5	7.5	7.5	7.4	7.4	7.3	7.3	7.2	7.1
84	7.2	7.2	7.2	7.2	7.2	7.1	7.1	7.1	7.1	7.0	7.0	7.0	6.9	6.9	6.8	6.7
85	6.8	6.8	6.8	6.7	6.7	6.7	6.7	6.7	6.6	6.6	6.6	6.5	6.5	6.5	6.4	6.4
86	6.4	6.4	6.3	6.3	6.3	6.3	6.3	6.3	6.2	6.2	6.2	6.2	6.1	6.1	6.0	6.0
87	6.0	6.0	6.0	5.9	5.9	5.9	5.9	5.9	5.9	5.8	5.8	5.8	5.8	5.7	5.7	5.6
88	5.6	5.6	5.6	5.6	5.6	5.5	5.5	5.5	5.5	5.5	5.5	5.5	5.4	5.4	5.3	5.3
89	5.2	5.2	5.2	5.2	5.2	5.2	5.2	5.2	5.2	5.1	5.1	5.1	5.1	5.1	5.0	5.0
90	4.9	4.9	4.9	4.9	4.9	4.9	4.9	4.9	4.9	4.8	4.8	4.8	4.8	4.8	4.7	4.7

AGES	67	68	69	70	71	72	73	74	75	76	77	78	79	80	81	82
67	13.5	–	–	–	–	–	–	–	–	–	–	–	–	–	–	–
68	13.1	12.8	–	–	–	–	–	–	–	–	–	–	–	–	–	–
69	12.8	12.5	12.1	–	–	–	–	–	–	–	–	–	–	–	–	–
70	12.4	12.1	11.8	11.5	–	–	–	–	–	–	–	–	–	–	–	–
71	12.0	11.7	11.4	11.2	10.9	–	–	–	–	–	–	–	–	–	–	–
72	11.6	11.4	11.1	10.8	10.5	10.2	–	–	–	–	–	–	–	–	–	–
73	11.2	11.0	10.7	10.5	10.2	9.9	9.7	–	–	–	–	–	–	–	–	–
74	10.8	10.6	10.4	10.1	9.9	9.6	9.4	9.1	–	–	–	–	–	–	–	–
75	10.4	10.2	10.0	9.8	9.5	9.3	9.1	8.8	8.6	–	–	–	–	–	–	–
76	9.9	9.8	9.6	9.4	9.2	9.0	8.8	8.5	8.3	8.0	–	–	–	–	–	–
77	9.5	9.4	9.2	9.0	8.8	8.6	8.4	8.2	8.0	7.8	7.5	–	–	–	–	–
78	9.1	9.0	8.8	8.7	8.5	8.3	8.1	7.9	7.7	7.5	7.3	7.0	–	–	–	–
79	8.7	8.6	8.4	8.3	8.1	8.0	7.8	7.6	7.4	7.2	7.0	6.8	6.6	–	–	–
80	8.3	8.2	8.0	7.9	7.8	7.6	7.5	7.3	7.1	6.9	6.8	6.6	6.3	6.1	–	–
81	7.9	7.9	7.7	7.5	7.4	7.3	7.1	7.0	6.8	6.7	6.5	6.3	6.1	5.9	5.7	–
82	7.5	7.4	7.3	7.2	7.1	6.9	6.8	6.7	6.5	6.4	6.2	6.0	5.9	5.7	5.5	5.3
83	7.1	7.0	6.9	6.8	6.7	6.6	6.5	6.4	6.2	6.1	5.9	5.8	5.6	5.5	5.3	5.1
84	6.7	6.6	6.5	6.4	6.4	6.3	6.2	6.0	5.9	5.8	5.7	5.5	5.4	5.2	5.1	4.9
85	6.3	6.2	6.2	6.1	6.0	5.9	5.8	5.7	5.6	5.5	5.4	5.3	5.2	5.0	4.9	4.7
86	5.9	5.9	5.8	5.8	5.7	5.6	5.5	5.4	5.4	5.3	5.1	5.0	4.9	4.8	4.7	4.5
87	5.6	5.6	5.5	5.4	5.4	5.3	5.2	5.2	5.1	5.0	4.9	4.9	4.8	4.7	4.6	4.3
88	5.3	5.2	5.2	5.1	5.1	5.0	5.0	4.9	4.8	4.7	4.6	4.5	4.4	4.3	4.2	4.1
89	5.0	4.9	4.9	4.8	4.8	4.7	4.7	4.6	4.5	4.5	4.4	4.3	4.2	4.1	4.0	3.9
90	4.7	4.6	4.6	4.6	4.5	4.5	4.4	4.4	4.3	4.2	4.2	4.1	4.0	3.9	3.8	3.8

AGES	83	84	85	86	87	88	89	90
83	4.9	–	–	–	–	–	–	–
84	4.7	4.6	–	–	–	–	–	–
85	4.6	4.4	4.2	–	–	–	–	–
86	4.4	4.2	4.1	3.9	–	–	–	–
87	4.2	4.1	3.9	3.8	3.6	–	–	–
88	4.0	3.9	3.8	3.6	3.5	3.4	–	–
89	3.8	3.7	3.6	3.5	3.4	3.2	3.1	–
90	3.7	3.5	3.4	3.3	3.2	3.1	3.0	2.9

(Reprinted from *Tax Facts on Life Insurance I* by permission. Copyright 2001.)

Appendix 6

Determining the Applicable Divisor for Installment Payments and Maximum Period Certain for Term Annuities

Determining the Applicable Divisor for Installment Payments and Maximum Period Certain for Term Annuities			
Age of the Employee	Applicable Divisor	Age of the Employee	Applicable Divisor
70	26.2	93	8.8
71	25.3	94	8.3
72	24.4	95	7.8
73	23.5	96	7.3
74	22.7	97	6.9
75	21.8	98	6.5
76	20.9	99	6.1
77	20.1	100	5.7
78	19.2	101	5.3
79	18.4	102	5.0
80	17.8	103	4.7
81	16.8	104	4.4
82	16.0	105	4.1
83	15.3	106	3.8
84	14.5	107	3.6
85	13.8	108	3.3
86	13.1	109	3.1
87	12.4	110	2.8
88	11.8	111	2.6
89	11.1	112	2.4
90	10.5	113	2.2
91	9.9	114	2.0
92	9.4	115 and older	1.8

Appendix 7

Determining the Applicable Percentage for Joint and Survivor Annuities

Determining the Applicable Percentage for Joint and Survivor Annuities	
Excess of Age of Employee over Age of Beneficiary	Applicable Percentage
10 years or less	100
11	96
12	93
13	90
14	87
15	84
16	82
17	79
18	77
19	75
20	73
21	72
22	70
23	68
24	67
25	66
26	64
27	63
28	62
29	61
30	60
31	59
32	59
33	58
34	57
35	56
36	56
37	55
38	55
39	54
40	54
41	53
42	53
43	53
44 and greater	52

Appendix 8

Scheduled IRA Increases 2003 and Later

Increasing IRA Contribution Limits			
Year	General Limit	Catch-up for those over age 50	Total for Those Over 50
2003	$3,500	$500	$4,000
2004	$4,000	$500	$4,500
2005	$4,500	$500	$5,000
2006	$5,000	$1,000	$6,000

Active Participant AGI Phaseout Ranges for Years 2003 and Late			
Year	Single	Married filing jointly	Married filing separately
2003	40,000–50,000	60,000–70,000	No change
2004	45,000–55,000	65,000–75,000	No change
2005	50,000–60,000	70,000–80,000	No change
2006	50,000–60,000	75,000–85,000	No change
2007 and later	50,000–60,000	80,000–100,000	No change

Appendix 9

Choosing a Plan Case Studies

After studying tax-advantaged retirement plans, let's look at some common situations and discuss what type of plan is most appropriate, given the company's goals and objectives.

CASE STUDY ONE

Facts

Survey, Inc. wishes to establish a qualified plan for its employees. The company is relatively new, and profits fluctuate wildly. The employer would like to reward employees when the company does well and is somewhat concerned that the company has no retirement plan at all, which might make it difficult to attract experienced people to work there. The company is also concerned about the costs of maintaining the plan.

Solutions

Survey, Inc. clearly sees the value of maintaining a retirement plan. Because its profits vary, the company would probably not want a plan that has a significant fixed cost. Because of this, it would want to choose a plan that provides for discretionary contributions, such as a profit-sharing plan or a SEP. Since the company wants to minimize administrative costs, the SEP is a logical choice. However, some employers do not like that SEP benefits must be fully vested at all times and that employees have access to withdrawals.

If the company is concerned about having a plan that is competitive with other employers, it should also consider a 401(k) plan. Remember that a 401(k) is not required to have a fixed employer matching contribution, although such a feature is quite common. The matching contribution could be discretionary or quite modest. To minimize the cost, the administrative burden can be shared with the plan participants. Also, administrative costs have been coming down with increased competition and "cookie cutter" products. If the employer is willing to make the 3 percent matching contribution each year, then the SIMPLE IRA plan should also be considered.

This company is not a good candidate for any of the pension plans, since they have required annual contributions.

633

CASE STUDY TWO

Facts

Near Retirement, Inc. is a closely held company whose original owners are about to retire. The company has a defined-benefit pension plan, which has already served the purpose of providing benefits for the current owners. Assume that the owners do not have family members interested in the business, that the employees have worked for the company for a long time, and that the employees are potential buyers of the company.

Solutions

This is an interesting case study. One solution really stands out: to establish an ESOP as a mechanism to sell the company to the current employees. The ESOP can borrow to purchase the stock of the retiring owners. If the current owners meet certain rules, they may even be able to delay the payment of capital gains on the sale. The company can make regular payments to the ESOP, which can be used to pay back the loan, at which time stock held in a suspense account can be allocated to the participants. As the loan is retired, the participants of the plan earn more and more shares of stock.

Even though the ESOP is a good choice for a new plan, what should happen to the current defined-benefit plan? Since the company will have to make contributions to the ESOP to retire the loan, the company will be concerned about also having to make required contributions to the defined-benefit plan. One alternative is to simply terminate the defined-benefit plan. If the plan is well funded and currently has excess assets, another alternative is to amend the plan into a cash-balance plan. It is quite possible in this way to use up the excess assets to fund the future benefit accruals under the cash-balance arrangement.

CASE STUDY THREE

Facts

Stable, Inc. has had a modest money-purchase pension plan for a long time. Participation in the plan precludes employees from participating in a tax-deferred IRA. The company realizes that the plan is not adequate but has little additional money to provide retirement benefits.

Solutions

This is a classic case for terminating the money-purchase plan and establishing a 401(k) plan. The modest benefits of participation in the money-purchase plan are offset by the potential loss of the deductible IRA contribution. If an individual is an "active participant" in an employer-sponsored retirement plan, that may preclude the participant's ability to save on a pretax basis (with deductible IRA contributions). With a 401(k) plan, employees can save up to $11,000 (as indexed in 2002) each year (much more than with a $3,000 IRA contribution). The employer can continue to make the same type of contributions to the 401(k) plan or may choose instead to spend its budget on matching contributions for only those employees who choose to contribute.

When the employer's budget is small, the 401(k) plan should always be compared to the SIMPLE IRA. The SIMPLE IRA has many more design limitations, but it is less expensive and easier to administer. Even though employees can contribute only up to $7,000 (for 2002), that is still a lot more than in an IRA.

CASE STUDY FOUR

Facts

Teeny-tiny Corp. has four employees. The owner realizes that competing employers are sponsoring 401(k) plans. To compete with the other employers, the owner would like a similar plan but is not willing to pay the administrative expenses associated with that type of plan.

Solutions

This company is the perfect candidate for the SIMPLE IRA. From the employee's perspective, this plan looks like a 401(k) plan, but from the employer's perspective, it is less expensive to maintain. Remember, with the SIMPLE, the basic employer contribution is a dollar-for-dollar matching contribution (up to 3 percent of pay) for employees who elect to make salary deferrals.

Appendix 10

Plan Design Case Studies

After discussing plan design in Chapters 7-10, let's discuss the design of specific plan features, using three case studies.

CASE STUDY ONE

Facts

Fast Fun, Inc. is a growing company that manufactures go-carts. The company has decided to adopt a 401(k) plan as its only qualified plan. Fast Fun has 150 employees, and the turnover in the shop is significant. A large number of employees have relatively low wages, and making salary-deferral contributions will be somewhat of a hardship for them. Since this is the company's only plan, the sponsor is prepared to contribute a minimum of 3 percent of compensation each year and possibly, in a good year, a lot more.

Solutions

Contributions

In a 401(k) plan, the sponsor will have to decide whether to make matching contributions and/or profit-sharing contributions (for all eligible employees). Since there is a large group of lower-paid employees who will need incentives to make salary-deferral contributions, the employer will probably want to make a generous matching contribution. One option is a fifty cent matching contribution for each dollar that the participant contributes up to 6 percent of salary contributed. This means that the maximum contribution that the employer will make is 3 percent of compensation. If lower-paid employees simply cannot afford a 6 percent deferral (to obtain the 3 percent match), the employer could consider a dollar-for-dollar match on the first 3 percent of salary deferred. One determinative issue here is how much will the highly compensated employees want to defer and what rank-and-file deferral percentage is necessary to support that level of participation.

Any additional employer contributions should probably be made as profit-sharing contributions (as opposed to additional matching contributions). The profit-sharing contributions are totally discretionary, and lower-paid employees who cannot afford to make salary-deferral contributions will still be eligible to earn a baseline pension benefit. In this

637

way, the plan can both act as a more traditional pension plan and provide a profit-sharing incentive (assuming that the employer really does make larger contributions in good years). The plan would probably adopt a compensation-to-compensation allocation formula so that all employees will receive the same percentage of compensation.

Two other contribution decisions also need to be made. First, how much will employees be allowed to defer? Here, the concern is the various pension limits that can apply. It is typical to limit contributions to 10 percent of compensation to ensure that the deductible contribution and the maximum annual allocation limits are satisfied. The other issue is whether or not to allow employee after-tax contributions. Here, the questions are whether employees want this feature and whether the plan can satisfy the nondiscrimination tests if the feature is included. This feature is uncommon in new plans. It is more common in older plans that have had after-tax contributions for many years.

Eligibility

The considerations for determining the appropriate eligibility provisions for a 401(k) plan are somewhat different than for other plans. With the 401(k) plan, nonhighly compensated employees who are eligible but do not contribute bring down the amount that highly compensated employees can contribute under the ADP test. In this case, with a large number of lower-paid employees and a high turnover rate, the employer will probably want to limit eligibility in a number of ways. First, the employer will want to eliminate employees who are allowed to be excluded by law. This includes short-term employees (by requiring a full year of service for eligibility), part-time employees (by requiring 1,000 hours of service), and employees who have not yet attained age 21. Second, the employer may want to identify and exclude a class of employees that is unlikely to make salary-deferral contributions. This is allowed as long as the plan can still pass the coverage requirements (remember that up to 30 percent of the nonhighly compensated employees can generally be excluded).

Vesting

In a 401(k) plan, employee salary-deferral contributions must be fully vested, but employer matching contributions and profit-sharing contributions can be subject to a vesting schedule. Since this employer has a high turnover rate, a vesting schedule, such as 5-year cliff vesting, could encourage employees to stay at least that long to be eligible for that benefit. (Remember, however, the new rule that requires that matching contributions must be subject to the more accelerated 3-year cliff vesting.) Second, even if the vesting schedule does not change employee behavior, it will save the employer some money. Forfeited matching contributions are typically used toward meeting the employer's matching contribution requirement for the remaining employees. Forfeited profit-sharing contributions are typically allocated among remaining employees, which does not reduce costs but does boost benefits for the longer-service employees.

Benefit Payouts and Forms of Benefit

In a 401(k) plan, vested benefits are typically available for distribution within a short time after termination of employment. It is not uncommon for a plan to offer only a lump-sum payment option. Some employers also offer installment payments. A new plan will typically not offer annuities, since this will mean that the plan will have to allow for qualified joint and survivor benefits.

Because terminated employees have immediate access to benefits, the concepts of normal retirement, early retirement, or death benefits become somewhat less important. Here, the primary reason to include such benefits is to fully vest those who otherwise have not satisfied the vesting schedule. The law requires that benefits become fully vested at normal retirement age; the most common age is 65. The sponsor may also want to fully vest participants who die or become disabled before completing the 5 years of service.

CASE STUDY TWO

Facts

Professional Corp. is a group of three owner-physicians and six other support staff. The doctors have decided to establish a profit-sharing plan. They want a plan that has flexible contributions and skews contributions as much toward the doctors as possible. Review plan design options for these doctors.

Solutions

Contributions

This employer wants the option to vary contributions but will most likely make significant contributions each year. The doctors will want an allocation formula that allocates a large percentage of the contribution to themselves. Assuming that the doctors as a group are somewhat older than the other employees, a cross-tested allocation formula can quite possibly result in the doctors' receiving 70 percent or more of the total contribution. The design process here will be to determine the objectives and then to test the formula (using software) under the general nondiscrimination test.

Note that if there are some employees that the doctors want to reward more than others, the allocation formula can be designed with a number of different allocation groups. For example, one group can receive a maximum of 5 percent of compensation, another can receive 8 percent, and the doctors can receive $40,000 (as indexed for 2002). The minimum contribution for any participant is likely to be the top-heavy minimum contribution.

Eligibility

Because this employer is interested in limiting the costs of benefits for employees, the first inclination is to create eligibility requirements that eliminate as many employees as possible. However, when a plan is using a cross-tested allocation formula, there are advantages to bringing in young, less highly paid employees. Under cross-testing, any contributions for young employees convert to significant retirement benefits (because of the length of the accumulation period). These high benefits support a higher level of benefits for the doctors. For this reason, all employees in this case will become eligible immediately.

Vesting

Because this plan will probably be top-heavy, the vesting schedule must satisfy the top-heavy rules. Since one main goal in this case is limiting costs, either 3-year cliff vesting or 6-year graded vesting is appropriate, depending on employee turnover patterns.

Other Considerations

The benefit considerations here are similar to those in the 401(k) plan. In a small defined-contribution plan of any type, most sponsors will want to give participants the opportunity to withdraw benefits shortly after termination of employment. In addition, the doctors will definitely want benefits to vest upon a premature disability and/or a preretirement death. As with the 401(k) plan, forms of distribution will probably be limited to lump-sum payments and installments to avoid the impact of the qualified joint and survivor annuity rules.

One more important issue in a small profit-sharing plan like this is whether the plan allows for individual investment direction. In 401(k) plans, employee investment direction has become almost universal. In defined-contribution plans funded solely by the employer, on the other hand, employee investment direction is less common. The three doctors in this plan, however, may have extremely different financial goals. This case looks like a good candidate for self-directed accounts, similar to a self-directed IRA, in which the participant can choose essentially from among any legal investment choice.

CASE STUDY THREE

Facts

New Nonprofit, Inc. has been in existence for 4 years. The company has 12 employees and has decided to set up its first pension plan. Since New Nonprofit wants a plan that allows employees to make pretax contributions and creates a retirement savings partnership between the employee and employer, the company considered the 403(b) plan, the 401(k) plan, and the SIMPLE. It chose the SIMPLE because it had the lowest cost and administrative burden, and it met the company's benefit budget (3 percent of payroll). New Nonprofit wants its plan to satisfy its current employees and to keep the company competitive when hiring new employees.

Solutions

The SIMPLE has rigid design constraints and the employer has only a few options. A SIMPLE must cover all employees who have earned at least $5,000 in any 2 prior years. The employer can choose to cover employees sooner or lower the $5,000 requirement. New Nonprofit, Inc. is choosing to cover all employees to make the company better able to compete for good employees.

The next decision is the employer contribution—a matching contribution or a nonelective contribution. Since New Nonprofit wants to create a partnership with the participants, the matching approach is better.

In most other respects, the plan design is fixed. Benefits must be fully vested. Participants can withdraw benefits (subject to income tax) or move plan assets to another investment adviser (maintaining either a SIMPLE IRA or other IRA). Employees can contribute up to $7,000 (as indexed for 2002) without regard to the other benefit limitations that apply to qualified plans.

One final interesting issue is communication with employees. In a SIMPLE, participants must be given notice of their rights to make salary deferrals, but unlike in a 401(k) plan, there are no extensive ERISA education requirements. Since New Nonprofit, Inc. wants to get as much value for its plan as possible, it will want to communicate it fully and may want to provide more generic retirement planning education in conjunction with the rollout of the plan. Even for this small organization with a small budget, there are still options, such as buying video educational programs, accessing information from the Internet, and obtaining free information from the IRS and Department of Labor.

Appendix 11

Distribution Planning Case Studies

Now that we've reviewed the issues involved in distributions from tax-advantaged retirement plans (chapters 25-26), let's look at several case studies.

CASE STUDY ONE

Facts

Jerry Jobchanger, aged 32, terminated employment with Midsize Corporation in order to take a job with Mega Corporation as a systems analyst. He was in a defined-benefit plan at Midsize Corporation and a 401(k) plan. The present value of his accrued benefit in the defined-benefit plan is $4,200 and the 401(k) account balance is $9,500. He has come to you to discuss what he should do with his pension distributions from Midsize. He also has told you that he will not be eligible for the Mega Corporation's pension plans for one year. He's thinking about withdrawing both benefits and buying a car better suited for his position as a young executive. Discuss his options with him.

Solutions

The first step is to clarify Jerry's distribution options. To learn about this, review the summary plan descriptions for both plans, any benefit statements that have been distributed, and any benefit paperwork that has been given to Jerry from the company regarding the distributions. If there is still any ambiguity, remember that Jerry has the right to receive a copy of the entire plan document. After that, Jerry may still have to ask the plan administrator a number of questions.

In the past, defined-benefit plans typically required that terminating participants wait until retirement age to begin receiving benefits. More and more plans allow immediate lump-sum distributions to terminating employees. Also, most plans take advantage of the option to cash out those participants with benefits worth less than $5,000. Since Jerry's benefit is less than $5,000, let's assume that Jerry will be cashed out, meaning that he will receive the single sum within a reasonable time after termination of employment. Even with the cashout, the plan is required to give him the option of having the benefit transferred directly to an IRA or other qualified

643

plan or have the benefit distributed directly, in which case 20 percent of the distribution must be withheld for taxes.

Like most other 401(k) plans Jerry's 401(k) plan allows for distributions as soon as administratively feasible after termination of employment. Jerry can choose from a lump sum or installment payments over a period not to exceed 10 years. As required by law, Jerry can also defer receipt of his benefit until age 55, early retirement age.

Jerry's decision to cash out his benefit and buy a car is not a good one. First many people do not understand the tax implications of such a withdrawal. They think that the distribution is taxed at 20 percent, the amount withheld for taxes. The reality is that the distribution is subject to tax as ordinary income, (let's assume that Jerry's marginal tax rate is 28 percent) and the 10 percent early withdrawal excise tax. If there are also state and local taxes Jerry's tax rate could be above 40 percent. More important is Jerry can probably not afford to spend the retirement benefits that he has earned with Midsize Corporation. He's thinking that he's giving up $13,700 in benefits (about $8,000 after taxes), but he's wrong. He's giving up the $147,000 that this amount will be worth at age 60 (growing at 9 percent) or $347,000 if he doesn't begin spending the amount until age 70.

Now that you've convinced Jerry not to spend the benefits, what should he do with them? Remember that he has few choices with the defined-benefit amount, the plan calls for a cash out. He should elect to transfer (also referred to as a direct rollover) from the defined-benefit plan to an IRA or the new company's qualified plan, if it is allowed. If instead he were to receive the check directly, the plan administrator would have to withhold 20 percent of the distribution. The only reason to consider the new company's plan is if either the fees are much lower than if he maintains a separate IRA or if there is some investment option (like a guaranteed investment contract that promises an excellent rate) that would not be available in the IRA. This is rarely the case, and most will choose to establish an IRA.

Similarly, he will most likely choose to have a direct rollover of his lump-sum benefit into an IRA. He could choose to leave benefits in Midsize's plan, and, in some cases, may choose to do so because of fees or investment options. In this case these are not in issue and Jerry chooses to have both benefits transferred to a new IRA account. If this IRA is kept separate from other IRA contributions (a conduit IRA), he could later choose to roll the benefit over into another qualified plan.

Once in the IRA, Jerry has several more choices. First, if his adjusted gross income is under $100,000, he will have the option to convert any portion of the IRA into a Roth IRA. Since he is only 32, this is an attractive option. Even though he would have to pay income taxes, he would not have to pay the 10 percent excise taxes and any future growth would be tax free (assuming the distributions were made after 59 1/2). The conversion also makes sense for Jerry since he will probably be in a higher tax bracket later and may also begin to earn more than $100,000 and not be eligible for the conversion later. If he doesn't want to pay taxes on the whole $14,200, it would still be beneficial for him to convert part of the benefit.

The final consideration is how to invest either the IRA (or converted Roth IRA). With a 30-year investment horizon, Jerry would probably be best suited with all or most of his holdings in common stock. With only $14,200 to invest, he should probably choose mutual funds or some other pooled investment to get professional management and proper diversification.

CASE STUDY TWO

Facts

Joseph Business Owner is 55 years old and has accumulated $1,300,000 in his company profit-sharing plan. That's good news, but the trouble is that this asset represents 80 percent of his net worth. He is a dentist and doesn't expect to be able to sell his practice for a large sum. He has a house, some other personal property, and little other savings. Joseph is married and his wife is 52. He has two children, ages 24 and 27. He is first concerned about his retirement security, but is also concerned about passing on wealth to his children. He enjoys his work and intends to continue working until age 70. After he retires, he anticipates withdrawing his current salary, $150,000 a year, from the IRA (in today's dollars).

Solutions

This is a common situation these days. More and more people are accumulating a large portion of their wealth in tax-sheltered retirement plans. This doesn't mean that these people have made a mistake, they have most likely accumulated a lot more this way than if they had saved on an after-tax basis. However, there are certain tax problems that need to be addressed when planning for the liquidation of the pension assets.

The first tax concern, of course, is that any withdrawals are ordinary income subject to income tax. Therefore, it is generally appropriate to defer withdrawals until they are needed or as required under the minimum-distribution rules. Deferral also allows the continued tax-deferred growth on the entire principal. The second tax issue is that any assets remaining in the retirement plans at death will be subject to estate taxes. If, to pay estate taxes, funds have to be withdrawn from the pension to pay the estate taxes, the distributions are also subject to income tax. If, instead, there is another source from which to pay estate taxes, then the pension distributions can continue as long as allowed under the minimum-distribution rules. This period could easily be an additional 20 years or more and an extremely large amount can be paid out to heirs.

When most of the couple's assets are in the profit-sharing plan in Joseph's name, several other estate planning techniques become more difficult. First, to lower estate taxes, it is generally a good idea for both the husband and wife to each have significant assets in their own name. This often means retitling assets from one spouse to the other. When the asset is in a profit-sharing plan (or other tax-advantaged plan), the asset cannot be retitled without a distribution that would trigger income taxes.

Another useful estate planning technique is the credit-shelter trust. This device allows the individual to minimize estate taxes and still take care of the remaining spouse. Without going into detail here, just note that using a tax-sheltered plan asset to fund the trust is not as tax efficient as using an asset that will not be subject to additional income tax to the recipient.

A good way to begin to get a feel of how these issues affect Joseph is to use a pension distribution software program to see whether Joseph's pension is sufficient to meet his needs. This example was run on Brentmark Software's Pension and Roth IRA Analyzer. The results of the illustration were quite eye opening. The first thing that became clear was that since Joseph will wait until age 70 to begin withdrawals, his $1,300,000 profit-sharing benefit will grow (without any additional contributions) to more than $4,500,000 (assuming a 9 percent annual return). If he withdraws the equivalent of $150,000 in today's dollars he will withdraw $270,000 the first year (assuming a 3.5 percent inflation rate). Assuming that Joseph dies at age 88 and his wife dies at age 90, they will have been able to generate an inflation adjusted stream of income of $270,000 a year ($550,000 in the final year) and still have $4,000,000 left in the plan for the children. Given these assumptions, distributions can continue for approximately 10 more years to the children, generating more than $5,000,0000 of distributions to them.

Joseph and his family are in great shape as long as the pension asset does not have to be liquidated to pay estate taxes. What this means from the planning perspective is that Joseph needs to create a source to pay the estate taxes. Those familiar with estate planning know that the pension asset problem is similar to those that arise with other illiquid assets. In many cases, the solution to the illiquid asset problem is to purchase life insurance—often a second-to-die policy using an irrevocable life insurance trust. If the trust is designed properly, the insurance proceeds will not be subject to estate taxes. This approach generates capital for paying estate taxes. Since Joseph is continuing to work until age 70, he may be able to afford the premiums out of current income. If he is unwilling to do so, he may choose to make withdrawals from the pension plan to pay the premium. Since Joseph is under age 59 1/2, if he chooses to make withdrawals, he needs to be sure to meet the "substantially equal periodic payment exception" from the 10 percent early withdrawal excise tax. Many clients like the idea of paying the premium from the pension asset, because it feels like the problem is being solved with the asset that is causing the estate planning problem.

We also learned from running the software program that Joseph does not need to make additional contributions to his plan to be financially secure in his retirement. If he can afford additional savings, this should be done outside the plan and probably in his wife's name. They might want to consider investments that payoff primarily in capital gains (such as stock or stock mutual funds) to lower their income taxes and to take advantage of the step up in basis that occurs to capital investments at death. They may also want to consider making their more aggressive, higher return investments outside the plan where growth is taxed at a capital gains rate instead of inside the pension plan where distributions are all taxed as ordinary income.

One final thought is a Roth IRA conversion. In this case, Joseph is not eligible because his adjusted gross income exceeds $100,000. However, some advisers are so enthusiastic about the conversion idea that they actively look for ways to reduce income to under $100,000 so that the conversion can occur. The reason that a conversion can be so valuable for the wealthier client is that there are no required minimum distributions during the participant's lifetime. If the spouse is the beneficiary, no distributions have to be made over the spouse's lifetime either. After the spouse's death, distributions must be made over the life expectancy of the beneficiaries at that time. This may mean that if the conversion occurs at age 55, the Roth IRA will grow income tax free for possibly 25 or more years, followed by distributions that can be spread over the next 30 to 40 years. If Joseph could qualify, a conversion of several hundred thousand dollars could be very beneficial for his heirs.

CASE STUDY THREE

Facts

Mary Middle Class is single (divorced) and works for ABCD University as an administrator. Her current income is $42,000. She is aged 62 and is thinking of retiring in the near future. The University has a defined-benefit pension plan and a 401(k) plan. The benefit formula in the defined-benefit plan is one and one-half percent of final average compensation times years of service (limited to 30 years). Mary currently has 12 years of service. She has an account balance of $95,000 in her 401(k) plan.

Mary has come to you to help her determine whether she can afford to retire and, if so, how she should take her distributions from her qualified plans. Identify the process that needs to occur, relevant facts, and possible answers.

Solutions

This is also not an uncommon scenario. If you work with teachers or other middle class professionals, you might have many clients like Mary.

Let's first discuss the process and relevant facts. To determine whether Mary can afford to retire requires that you determine her retirement planning goals and objectives and determine what financial resources she needs to meet these goals and objectives. Since she is so close to retirement, it is appropriate to inventory her specific expenses to determine an appropriate budget.

You find out that Mary was married for 15 years (to a well-paid lawyer) and several years ago she got the large house in the divorce settlement . The house has a small mortgage payment, high taxes, and a significant amount of equity buildup. Other than the house, she has no significant investments. You also find that she would like to live closer to her adult children so that she can spend more time with the grandchildren. She has little interest in travel, but would like to get additional education. You also learn that Mary has been in and out of the workforce over the years.

The next step is to inventory her traditional retirement assets. This includes Social Security, the company pensions, and any income that can be generated from her savings. First, Mary will need to get a benefit estimate from Social Security. Because of what you learned, Mary's divorced spousal benefit may be higher (50 percent of her ex-spouse's PIA) than the benefit earned on her own wages. You need to let Social Security know about her divorce benefit to make sure that they calculate her benefit both ways. Since she is thinking of retiring early, be sure to identify a retirement age under 65 to show the impact of the earlier payments.

To understand her company pension benefits, review her benefit statements and summary plan description. With this fact pattern, it is really crucial that the advisor fully understand Mary's pension benefits. Without knowing all the facts, it appears that Mary is going to have a difficult time affording retirement. With no substantial investment income, she will be extremely dependent on her pension income. In the discussion of the pension plan, especially in the defined-benefit plan, Mary's early retirement will penalize her three ways: she'll have shorter service, lower salary, and the benefit will be reduced for payment beginning before age 65. Waiting until 65 or even later gives her a chance to earn a significantly larger benefit. With the 401(k) plan, retiring now means 3 more years of contributions that won't be made and also earnings will be reduced as distributions are made. These timing-of-payment issues are complex and need to be reviewed and discussed carefully with the client who is unlikely to fully appreciate the impact of the deferral decision.

One other factor in Mary's favor is another less obvious asset—the equity in her home. Since she is predisposed to moving, she may want to choose to purchase a condominium or smaller home. Better yet, she may want to rent for a while to be assured that she likes her new location. Under the current Sec. 121 tax rules, she can exclude up to $250,000 of gain without having to purchase a replacement home. If she decides to stay in the home, she could look into a reverse annuity mortgage to free up some of that equity.

Now that you've gathered the facts you can begin to help Mary form a retirement planning strategy. At first blush, it looks like Mary will have to defer retirement. In addition to the penalties on her pension and Social Security benefits for retiring early, it also turns out that her company does not have any post-retirement medical benefits and, if she retires before 65, she'll have to purchase individual medical insurance. Before sending Mary away disappointed though, it's time for some serious brainstorming. Maybe Mary can still meet some of her goals and still keep working. Simply by thinking through what she wants, she has decided to sit for her grandchildren more and have her grandchildren stay with her over their summer vacations on her own vacation time. It turns out under the company's flexible benefit program that Mary can buy additional vacation time and still be a full-time employee entitled to medical benefits and additional pension accruals.

This fact pattern really illustrates the importance of the expertise and skill of the advisor. Mary's situation could not be adequately understood simply by taking out a retirement planning software package and running the numbers. There are many nuances here, the equity in the home, the divorce spouse Social Security benefit, the complicated pension calculations, and an understanding of her medical insurance coverage.

After successfully formulating a plan and picking a retirement date, there's one more important issue to consider. That is choosing the best form of distribution from her retirement plans.

Let's assume that her defined-benefit plan has a lump-sum option. The amount payable will be based on the "actuarial equivalent" of the normal form of payment—usually a life annuity. If the lump sum is calculated with unfavorable assumptions, this option may not be advisable. One way to test the value of the lump sum is to compare the amount payable as a life annuity from the plan to the amount that would result from taking a lump sum, rolling it into an IRA, and then buying a life annuity at commercially available prices.

Many participants will be satisfied with the IRA rollover approach because it provides both investment and withdrawal flexibility. However, this method does not ensure that the participant won't outlive pension distributions. Even with careful distribution planning, investment performance may not meet expectations, or the individual may live too long. To protect against this contingency, Mary should consider having at least a portion of her retirement income payable as a life annuity. Since Mary is single and does not have any dependents, a single life annuity will provide her with the largest payment and adequate protection. She can do either by electing the life annuity in the plan or rolling over the benefit into an IRA then purchasing an annuity. In this way, she could purchase a variable annuity that ensures lifetime payments and addresses the effect of inflation. So that Mary has the security of a base income for life and the flexibility of an IRA, she might choose to annuitize her defined benefit and roll over the 401(k).

One final point is that Mary is exactly the kind of client that is not a good candidate for a Roth IRA conversion. Since she is near retirement, has a low tax rate, and will be living on her pension benefits, she really can not afford to take the chance of reducing her pension benefits by paying taxes up-front—in exchange for tax-free growth.

CASE STUDY FOUR

Facts

Mr. Barney Businesowner, turns 70 1/2 this year. He has a profit-sharing benefit of $250,000 and a money-purchase pension benefit of $900,000. He is retiring and his daughter has purchased the business. The plans only allow for distributions in the form of a lump sum or in installments, and plan assets are invested by the trustees (no participant investment direction). Barney has a lot of additional income, including installment payments from the sale of the business for the next 20 years. He sees the pension benefits as assets that he doesn't need to live on and that he wants to leave to his family. His first concern is his wife, then his adult children and grandchildren.

Solutions

Without having more comprehensive facts, several issues should be obvious. First, Barney is probably eligible for 10-year averaging and possibly the special capital gains election. He was born prior to 1936 and is likely to be receiving qualifying lump-sum distributions from his qualified plans. If he could take the profit sharing benefit into income using 10-year averaging, his effective tax rate would be 18 percent.

At first glance, it looks like Barney is eligible to take the $250,000 profit sharing amount into income—tax it using special 10-year averaging—and roll the money-purchase benefit into an IRA (or leave it in the original plan). He is eligible for 10-year averaging because he can receive the entire profit-sharing benefit in one tax year, and he certainly has at least 5 years of plan participation. Also, he is receiving the benefit after attaining age 70 1/2. Remember that when determining whether a participant is receiving the "balance to the credit," certain plans must be aggregated. Since profit-sharing plans and money-purchase plans are not required to be aggregated, he does not have to receive the money-purchase benefit to qualify.

Even taxed at 18 percent, Barney is hesitating to paying income tax. Deferring even at this rate, may still work out for Barney, but there are a number of reasons to consider paying taxes now. First, when you quiz Barney, it turns out that he really anticipates higher tax rates in the future. Also, when looking at his estate planning, it turns out that he has a significant life insurance need. Freeing these funds allows them to be used to fund the life insurance policy. There are other advantages to having the profit-sharing funds outside the plan. Assets could be retitled in his wife's name, or he could use the funds to finance a gifting program for his children and grandchildren. As discussed in the case studies above, Barney could also invest these funds in stock, and either have gains taxed as long-term capital gains or avoid income tax altogether under the step-up-in-basis rules if he leaves the stock to his family.

The other issue that should be apparent is that Barney will be impacted by the minimum-distribution rules. Generally, the required beginning date that distributions must begin is the April 1 following the year in which Barney attains 70 1/2. In qualified plans, the date can be later if the participant retires later than age 70 1/2, but that exception does not apply to 5-percent owners. It turns out that Barney has decided not to take advantage of 10-year averaging and will roll both his benefits into an IRA this year (the year that he attains age 70 1/2). He decided not to leave benefits in the qualified plans since those plans do not have participant-directed investments and have limited withdrawal restrictions.

Even though distributions must begin by the following April 1, a distribution must be made for the year in which the participant attains age 70 1/2. When a person rolls a benefit from a plan in a year that a minimum distribution is required, technically the required minimum must be withdrawn as the rollover is made. Also, many individuals who have the opportunity to wait to the following April 1 choose not to wait because a second distribution must be withdrawn by that same December 31.

Since Barney won't need his IRA rollover benefits to fund his retirement, he will want to stretch out payments as long as possible. Because his spouse is in good health, she probably makes the most appropriate beneficiary. If she outlives him, she can roll the benefit into her own IRA and choose new beneficiaries. This will lengthen the distribution period for many years. If his wife predeceases him, he can name his children as beneficiaries and distributions can be made over their lifetimes after his death. Barney may need some life insurance to make sure there is a source outside the plan to pay for any estate taxes due.

Glossary

accrued benefit • the amount of benefit earned as of a given date

accumulated earnings tax • penalty tax for C corporations that attempt to reduce shareholders' tax burden by accumulating earnings instead of paying them out to shareholders

active participant • an individual who is covered by an employer plan and actually receives a benefit or contribution from the employer under the plan. An active participant cannot have a deductible IRA unless he or she has an adjusted gross income below prescribed limits.

actual contribution percentage (ACP) test • a test applied to salary reduction 401(k) plans that operates in essentially the same manner as the ADP test. However, under the ACP test, instead of comparing the salary deferrals—as a percentage of compensation—the matching and after-tax contributions as a percentage of compensation is applied.

actual deferral percentage (ADP) test • a test applied to salary reduction 401(k) plans that ensures that salary reductions taken by highly compensated employees are in line with salary reductions taken by other employees. In order to pass the ADP test one of two requirements must be satisfied:

> (1) *the 1.25 requirement*—The actual deferral percentage for highly compensated employees for the current year cannot be more than 125 percent of the actual deferral percentage for nonhighly compensated employees for the previous year.
>
> (2) *the 200 percent/2 percent difference requirement*—The actual deferral percentage for highly compensated employees for the current year cannot be more than 200 percent of the actual deferral percentage for nonhighly compensated employees for the previous year, and the spread between the two cannot be more than 2 percent.

actuarial assumptions • assumptions that are made about investment return, mortality, turnover, and other factors concerning the employee group to determine the annual funding required in a defined-benefit plan

actuarial cost methods • methods used to determine the annual employer contribution to a defined-benefit plan

actuarial equivalent • a term that means that one form of payment is equivalent to another, based on a specified set of actuarial assumptions

adoption agreement • the vehicle used for choosing among the various optional provisions provided in a master or prototype plan. The adoption agreement lists the various design choices that are available, and employers then pick from the menu of provided options.

advance-determination letter • a letter from the IRS stating that a plan meets the qualification standards. A request for an advance-determination letter is made on IRS Form 5300 or 5307 (master plan, prototype plan or volume submitter).

advisory opinion • an opinion, issued by the Department of Labor, regarding the legality of a given situation. An advisory opinion can be sought before a client enters a transaction in which the ERISA consequences are unknown.

affiliated service group • two or more organizations that are aggregated for purposes of the qualified plan requirements. There are actually several different affiliation rules—all were promulgated to ensure that employees who worked together to produce a single product could not be divided into separate entities to avoid the qualified plan coverage requirements.

age-weighted formula • a defined-contribution method that allocates contributions to participants in such a way that when contributions are converted to equivalent benefit accruals (stated as a percentage of compensation), each participant receives the same rate of benefit accrual

aggregation rules • rules that determine whether affiliated companies will be considered the same entity for purposes of conducting qualified pension plan tests such as the nondiscrimination test

allocated • when contributions are assigned to provide benefits for specific employees, such as individual insurance or annuity contracts

allocation formula • a formula used to determine the amount of profits distributed to each participant in a profit-sharing plan. Allocation formulas can divide the profit-sharing "pie" to favor employees with higher salaries and longer service.

annuity • the distribution or liquidation of a sum of money on an actuarial basis. The amount paid to an annuitant is typically paid monthly and is determined by such factors as the annuity purchase price, the client's age, the number of lives covered by the annuity, the number of guarantees that are offered, and the interest assumption used.

annuity certain • provides an annuitant or his or her beneficiary with a specified number of monthly guaranteed payments after which time all payments stop

anticutback rules • rules that state that once a participant has accrued a benefit or has received a contribution, the benefit or contribution cannot be reduced. Future reductions in accruals or contributions (prospective reductions), however, can be made.

assumed investment rate • the rate assumed in a variable annuity that the investment portfolio must earn in order for benefit payments to remain level. If the experience rate or actual investment rate is higher than the assumed investment rate, then annuity payouts will be higher. Conversely, if the experience or actual investment rate is lower than the assumed rate, annuity payouts will be lower.

average-benefit-percentage test • one of the nondiscrimination rules set out under Code Sec. 410(b). The average benefit of nonhighly compensated employees must be 70 percent of the average benefit of highly compensated employees, and a fair cross section of employees must be covered.

baby-boom generation • reference to the generation of Americans born from 1946 to 1964

backloading • the prohibited practice of excessively accruing benefits in later years. The accrued-benefit rules make backloading impossible in a qualified plan.

blue book • books published after a tax law change by the joint committee on taxation that help to explain the legislative history behind a the tax law. The blue book can be quite informative, but is not considered a primary source of law.

break in service • a technical pension term used to describe a measured absence from employment for vesting and eligibility purposes. A break in service occurs when the individual has fewer than 500 hours in a year.

business risk • the type of investment risk that is the result of consumer preference, ineffective management, law changes, or foreign competition that affect the performance of a particular business

buy-and-hold strategy • a retirement planning strategy under which the client buys securities, bonds, mutual funds, and so on, and holds them until restructuring is required—the opposite of market timing

cafeteria plan • a plan that provides flexible benefit dollars that an employee can allocate to pay for certain benefits from a menu of benefit choices (such as life insurance, health insurance, or child care) and/or place in a 401(k) plan

capital-gains election • a portion of a participant's benefit earned prior to 1974 that may be entitled to capital-gains treatment. The amount subject to capital-gains tax is determined by dividing the amount of months prior to 1974 into the total months that the participant worked under the plan. The subsequent ratio is then multiplied by the amount of distribution to determine the portion that is subject to the favorable capital-gains tax rate.

career-average compensation • a definition of average compensation in defined-benefit plans that either uses the entire salary history in the definition of average compensation or accrues a benefit each year based on that year's compensation

cash-balance plan • a defined-benefit plan that promises a benefit based on a hypothetical account balance versus a traditional plan, which promises a monthly retirement benefit for life

cash equivalents • an investment such as a Treasury bill that either has no specified maturity date or one that is one year or less in the future

cash or deferred arrangement (CODA) • a feature of a profit-sharing or stock bonus plan that allows participants to defer a portion of their compensation on a pretax basis

catch-up provision • a provision that allows employees covered by a 403(b) plan to make larger than typically permitted contributions to the plan

cliff vesting • a vesting schedule under which an employee is not entitled to any percentage of his or her retirement benefit until he or she is fully vested after the attainment of a specific amount of years of service. The maximum amount of years of service that an employee can be forced to wait in a qualified plan is 5 years.

collectibles • items such as antique cars, precious metals, stamps, coins, and Persian rugs. Individual retirement accounts cannot invest in collectibles.

common trust fund • a commingled trust fund that combines assets from a number of trusts

conduit IRA • a rollover from a qualified plan into a new separate IRA. By making a conduit rollover, the benefit can later be rolled into another qualified plan

constructive receipt • when an employee has the opportunity to control the timing of the receipt of a payment from the employer (can take it now or later) the employee is deemed to be in "constructive receipt" and will incur current taxation

controlled group rules • rules that require companies with a sufficient amount of common control to be tested as a single employer for purposes of the qualified plan requirements

controlled groups • aggregations of employers who share a sufficient amount of common ownership. There are three types of controlled groups: parent-subsidiary, brother-sister, and combined.

covered compensation • the average of the maximum Social Security wage bases for the number of years of earnings used to calculate the Social Security benefit for the 35-year period ending with the year the employee reaches the Social Security retirement age. Covered compensation is the integration level used in most defined-benefit plans.

cross-testing • a qualified plan that tests whether its contribution formula discriminates in favor of the highly compensated employees by converting contributions made for each participant into equivalent benefit accruals

deferred compensation • an agreement that states that compensation for services rendered is postponed until sometime after the services in question have been performed

deferred retirement age • any retirement age beyond the normal retirement age. In a defined-contribution plan, contributions will continue to be made after the normal retirement age until the deferred retirement age. In a defined-benefit plan, unless there's a years-of-service cap on the benefit formula, benefit accruals will continue until the deferred retirement age.

defined-benefit plan • a retirement plan that specifies the benefits that each employee receives at retirement. The maximum yearly benefit allowed is the lesser of 100 percent of the high 3-year average compensation or $140,000 (2001 indexed number).

defined-contribution plan • a retirement plan that specifies the contributions that each employee receives. The maximum contribution allowed (called an annual addition) is the lesser of 25 percent of salary or $35,000 (as indexed in 2001) for each year of employment. These contributions are made to an individual's account during the employment years.

direct rollover rule • a rollover directly from the trustee of a qualified plan to an IRA or other qualified plan. Qualified plans are required to offer direct rollovers, and these transactions avoid the 20 percent income tax withholding that generally applies to distributions from qualified plans

discretionary contributions • profit-sharing-type plans that provide the employer with discretion as to how much of a contribution will be made each year

distress termination • a plan termination that is allowed because the employer is experiencing financial difficulties

diversification requirement • an affirmative fiduciary duty that requires the fiduciary to diversify assets to guard against large losses

dividend reinvestment plan • a shareholder's option to have cash dividends automatically reinvested in additional shares of the company's common stock

dollar-cost averaging • a system for timing investment transactions that has a fixed dollar amount being invested in a particular security in each time period

double bonus plan • a Sec. 162 life insurance program where the employer pays both the life insurance premium and a bonus to the executive to cover the taxes resulting from the employer paying the life insurance premium

early-retirement age • the age at which, if the plan permits, employees are permitted to retire and receive benefits prior to the normal retirement age. Typical early-retirement ages are 55, 60, and 62.

economic benefit • a tax concept that states that employment income is subject to income tax at the time the employee is deemed to receive an economic benefit

elapsed-time method • the computation of credit for plan service that is measured from date of employment to date of severance

Employee Retirement Income Security Act (ERISA) • the act that laid the foundation for modern pension law. ERISA established the nondiscrimination requirements, reporting and disclosure requirements, plan funding standards, vesting and participation requirements, and fiduciary responsibilities.

employee stock ownership plan (ESOP) • a profit-sharing type plan that invests primarily in employer stock. ESOPs are usually leveraged by borrowing from a bank to fund the plan.

enrollment meeting • a meeting during which employees may sign up to be covered by the employer's plan. An enrollment meeting is typically held to get proper enrollments in salary reduction plans, such as 401(k) and 403(b) plans, and also to get the adequate participation in a contributory plan.

entry date • a sign-up time at which an employee becomes a participant under the plan. An employee must first satisfy the plan's eligibility requirements to be admitted as a participant on the next plan entry date.

ERISA 404(c) (individual account plan exception) • a provision of ERISA that relieves fiduciaries from liability for the investment decisions of plan participants

excess contribution • a contribution to an IRA or Roth IRA that exceed the allowable limits

exclusion for the sale of a home • an exclusion from federal income taxation of up to $250,000 ($500,000 for married taxpayers filing jointly) of any capital gain realized from the sale of an individual's primary residence. This exclusion applies to individuals who have owned and used the property as a personal residence for at least two years.

exclusive-benefit rule • a rule that prevents misuse of the retirement plan. A fiduciary is required to discharge all duties solely in the interest of plan participants and their beneficiaries.

fiduciary • a person or corporation that exercises any discretionary authority or control over the management of the plan or plan assets, renders investment advice for a fee, or has any discretionary authority or responsibility in the administration of the plan

final-average compensation • a definition of average compensation used in many defined-benefit plans. Final-average compensation generally means the highest 3 to 5 years of a participant's compensation. It may also be limited to the final years of participation, for example, the average of the highest 3 years of compensation earned during the final 5 years of participation.

final regulations • regulations that explain and interpret the various sections of the Internal Revenue Code. Final regulations are legally enforceable, and the Internal Revenue Service is bound by them.

financial hardship • a financial need that is "necessary in light of immediate and heavy financial needs of an employee" and no other resources can be reasonably available to meet this end

first distribution year • under the minimum-distribution rules, the first year for which a distribution is required. For example, when the required beginning date is the April 1 following the year of attainment of age 70 1/2 the first distribution year is the year that the participant attained age 70 1/2.

501(c)(3) organizations • certain tax-exempt organizations as specified in the Internal Revenue Code section that can have a 403(b) plan. A corporation, community chest, fund, or foundation that is organized and operated exclusively for religious, charitable, scientific, testing for public safety, literary, or educational purposes; for fostering national or international amateur sports competition; or for the prevention of cruelty to children or animals will probably qualify for 501(c)(3) status.

flat-amount formula • a formula for determining benefits that does not take into account an employee's service or salary

flat-amount-per-year-of-service formula • a benefit formula that relates the pension benefit solely to service and does not reflect an employee's salary

flat-percentage-of-earnings formula • a benefit formula that is related solely to salary and does not reflect an employee's service

forfeitures • amounts that are lost when a participant terminates employment before being fully vested under the plan's vesting schedule

401(a)(4) rule • a rule that forbids disparity in the amount of contributions or benefits that can be provided for highly compensated employees as compared with those provided for the rank-and-file employees

401(a)(26) minimum-participation rule • a rule that requires that defined benefit plans cover the lesser of 50 employees or 40 percent of the workforce.

401(k) plan • a defined-contribution profit-sharing plan that gives participants the option of reducing their taxable salary and contributing the salary reduction on a tax-deferred basis to an individual account for retirement purposes

403(b) plan • a retirement plan similar to a 401(k) plan that is available to certain tax-exempt organizations and to public schools

457 plan • all nonqualified salary reduction plans sponsored by a governmental or non-church-controlled tax-exempt organization are subject to the rules in Code Sec. 457

full cash-refund annuity • an annuity under which payments are made to the annuitant until the annuitant's death. If, however, at the time of the annuitant's death the full amount of the annuity purchase price has not been returned to the annuitant, then any remainder will be returned to the annuitant's beneficiary

full-funding limit • a funding limitation that applies to defined-benefit plans that requires that limits the deductible contribution if the plan's assets exceed the lesser of 160 percent (for 2001) of the plan's current liability or 100 percent of the plan's projected liability

fully insured • a qualified plan that is completely funded with life insurance or annuity contracts

funding instrument • the type of legal entity used to fund a retirement plan, including trusts, insurance contracts, and annuities

funding policy • a stated strategy for ensuring that the plan has sufficient assets to pay promised benefits

funding standard account • the account used to determine if the minimum funding standards are being satisfied

general-counsel memorandum • a legal memorandum that is relied on by IRS personnel in deciding disputes with taxpayers

golden handshakes • additional benefits paid to employees to induce early retirement

golden parachutes • substantial payments made to corporate executives who are terminated upon change of ownership or corporate control

graded vesting • a vesting schedule under which the participant gradually becomes fully vested over time. The statutory 3-through-7 graded schedule requires 20 percent vesting after 3 years of service and an additional 20 percent for each additional year of service.

group-deposit administration contract • an unallocated group pension contract funded by a series of employer contributions made throughout the year. Contributions are accounted for under two different systems—one that reflects investment guarantees that are given (the active-life fund) and one that reflects the actual investment experience.

guaranteed-investment contract (GIC) • a group insurance investment product in which the insurance company guarantees both principal and rate of return

hardship withdrawal • a withdrawal permitted under a 401(k) plan or 403(b) plan if the participant has a hardship and no other resources available to meet the financial hardship. Under regulations, a hardship has been described as payments for a college education, for a residence, and for medical bills.

highly compensated employees (HCEs) • persons who are more-than-5-percent owners of the business in the previous or current year, and any persons who earned over $85,000 (as indexed for 2001) in the previous year. The employer can elect to limit the second category to only those individuals in the top 20 percent of the employer pay group.

holistic retirement planning • a way of looking at retirement planning that considers all aspects of the person, not just their financial picture

hour of service • any hour for which a participant is paid or entitled to be paid

hours-worked-excluding-overtime method • a method for counting hours of service that looks only at actual hours worked excluding overtime, vacations, holidays, and sick time. If this method is used, an employee needs to work only 750 hours to earn a year of service.

hours-worked-including-overtime method • a method for counting hours of service that looks at actual hours worked including overtime but excluding nonworked hours such as vacation, holidays, and sick time. If this method is used, an employee needs to work only 870 hours to earn a year of service.

immediate-participation-guarantee contract. • an unallocated funding instrument that holds benefit amounts in a commingled fund. At retirement, either the fund is charged directly with benefit payments or the fund is charged with a single annuity premium.

incentive stock options (ISOs) • options to purchase shares of company stock at a stated price over a specified period of time. Different from nonqualified stock options in that the rules governing ISOs are quite strict and the tax treatment is more favorable to the executive. The executive pays no tax at the time options are exercised, only when shares of stock are sold.

incidental-death-benefit rules • ERISA rules that limit the amount of life insurance that can be used in a qualified plan

income-replacement ratio • the amount of gross income that is replaced by the retirement plan

individual retirement annuity • an individual retirement account that is funded with an annuity contract

inflation • an increase in the general (average) level of prices

in-service withdrawals • withdrawals taken from the qualified plan while the participant is still employed. No in-service withdrawals are permitted from a pension plan.

installment payout • the periodic payout of funds from a qualified plan

integration with Social Security • a method of dovetailing a qualified plan with Social Security benefits. Because Social Security discriminates in favor of low-paid employees, an integrated plan is allowed to discriminate in favor of highly paid employees to the extent permitted under the integration rules.

integration level • the dividing line between the base and excess percentages in an integrated plan. The integration level for a defined-benefit plan is typically covered compensation; the integration level for a defined-contribution plan is typically the taxable wage base.

interest-rate risk • the type of investment risk that results from changes in interest rates in the market

investment-guarantee contract (IG) • a group insurance investment product similar to a GIC. The major difference is that contributions are received over a number of years and the guarantee rate for the later years is only a floor with the investor receiving the actual rate if higher.

investment guidelines • a set of principles to help focus the fiduciaries investing plan assets

investment policy • a statement concerning the investment of plan assets that addresses the appropriate degree of risk and yield for the trust and the importance of yield in relation to safety of principal and the plan's cash flow needs

investment risk • the variability in the value of an investment

involuntary cash-out option • a rule that gives the plan administrator the option to distribute benefits valued at less than $5,000 from a qualified plan without giving the participant an election with regard to the timing or form of payment

involuntary terminations • terminations that are called for by the PBGC when a plan is seriously unfunded and the PBGC would be liable for continuation of unfunded benefits. (An involuntary termination can also be called for by the IRS if plan contributions cease and no provision is made for plan continuance.)

IRA (individual retirement account) • a trust or custodial account established by an individual that allows for saving for retirement in a tax-advantaged manner

IRS news releases • announcements about forthcoming regulations and information about statistical and survey results

IRS publications • general reviews of retirement topics provided by the IRS to aid individuals in filing their tax returns

joint and survivor annuity • an annuity for a participant's life that terminates at the participant's death. If, however, at the participant's death his or her spouse is still alive, annuity payments in a predetermined amount will continue for the life of the surviving spouse.

A joint and survivor annuity is the normal form of benefit for married individuals in a qualified plan.

Keogh plan • a qualified plan for unincorporated businesses

key employee • an employee who owns more than 5 percent of the business, an officer who earns over one-half of the Sec. 415 defined-benefit limit, an employee who owns one of the 10 largest shares of the company, or a one percent owner who earns over $150,000

leased employee • a term, under the pension rules, that describes an individual who is leased on a full-time, ongoing basis. The rules require that such leased employees be generally treated as employees for purposes of the qualified plan coverage requirements.

level annual funding • a schedule to save funds for a specific dollar retirement goal where the same level investment is made each year until retirement age

leveraged ESOP • in order to have the funds to purchase large blocks of stock, an ESOP can borrow the funds and repay the loan with the contributions (deductible) that the employer makes to the plan each year

life annuity • an annuity that pays income for the participant's life and stops payments at the participant's death. No survivor or additional death benefits are payable. It will yield the largest monthly payment per given purchase price of all the annuity types, since there are no residual benefits.

life annuity with guaranteed payments • an annuity that pays benefits for a participant's life and stops when a participant dies. If, however, a participant dies before the guaranteed payments are made, payments are made to the participant's beneficiary for the remainder of that period. The longer the stipulation or guaranteed period, the smaller the monthly amount for a given dollar figure. Conversely, the shorter the stipulated or guaranteed period, the larger the monthly amount for a given dollar figure.

life-care retirement communities • organizations that provide housing and services to retired parties in exchange for up-front and/or monthly fees

long-term accumulation period • the stage in an individual's investment program that begins when funds are first accumulated for retirement and is phased out with the onset of the portfolio restructuring period

loose-leaf services • publications that describe the legal and administrative framework of pensions in an up-to-date manner

lump-sum distribution • a distribution from a qualified plan that represents the participant's entire account balance. In order to be considered a qualified lump-sum distribution, the distribution must meet the following conditions:

- – The client must have been a plan participant for at least 5 years.
- – The funds must be distributed to the client within one taxable year.
- – The distribution must represent the entire account balance or benefit.
- – The amount distributed must be payable only upon death, attainment of age 59 1/2, separation from service, or disability.

market risk • the type of investment risk due to changes in political, economic, demographic, or social events that have an impact on the market as a whole

master and prototype plans • standardized plans approved and qualified in concept by the Internal Revenue Service that the insurance companies make available for their agents. Although these plans must go through qualification procedures, a favorable result is more predictable. The master or prototype plan offers an employer fewer choices in plan design and thus can be installed very easily.

matching contribution • a plan feature in which the plan sponsor agrees to match employee savings to a certain extent. For example, the sponsor might agree to contribute 50 cents to the plan for each dollar that the employee saves, up to the first 6 percent of compensation that the participant saves.

maximum insured benefits • the maximum amount that the PBGC will insure. This amount is approximately $3,200 per month.

Medicare, part A • the hospital portion of Medicare. It provides benefits for expenses incurred in hospitals, skilled nursing facilities, and hospices with various limits and restrictions, and for home health care for a condition treated in a hospital or skilled nursing facility. It is available at no monthly cost to any person aged 65 or older who is entitled to monthly retirement benefits under Social Security.

Medicare, part B • the supplementary medical insurance portion of Medicare. It provides benefits for physicians' and surgeons' fees, diagnostic tests, certain drugs and medical supplies, rental of certain medical equipment, and home health service when prior hospitalization has not occurred. With some exceptions, part B pays 80 percent of the approved charges for covered medical expenses after the satisfaction of an annual deductible. Any person eligible for part A is eligible for part B and is automatically enrolled. A monthly premium is charged for part B, which is adjusted annually to reflect the cost of the benefits provided.

minimum-distribution rules • set procedures for determining the minimum required distributions from qualified plans, 403(b) plans, SEPs, and IRAs once a person reaches age 70 1/2

modified cash-refund annuity • an annuity that provides payments for a person's life and stops payment at a person's death. If, however, a stipulated amount of the annuity purchase price has not been received by the annuitant, then that portion will be refunded to the annuitant's beneficiary. It is typically the normal form of benefit for single individuals in a contributory pension plan, thus returning any contributions they made to the plan.

money-purchase pension plan • a defined-contribution plan that specifies a level of contribution (for example, 10 percent of salary) to each participant's account each year

net unrealized appreciation (NUA) • the name given to the rule that allows deferral of the tax on the unrealized gain when a lump-sum distribution from a qualified plan includes employer securities

nonqualified plans • flexible retirement plans that can be established for executives only, but are not eligible for the special tax benefits available for qualified or other tax-advantaged retirement plans

nonqualified stock options • options granted by the company to the executive to purchase shares of company stock at a stated price over a specified period of time. The employee pays tax (as ordinary income) on the difference between the market value and the option price at the time the options are exercised.

normal form of benefit • a distribution from a qualified plan that for a married individual is a joint and survivor annuity of at least 50 percent. For a single individual, the normal form of benefit is typically a life annuity, or in a contributory plan, a modified cash-refund annuity.

normal retirement age • the age at which a participant can retire and receive the full, specified retirement benefit

notice to interested parties • part of the process of applying to the IRS for an advance determination letter is to notify participants of that submission

Office of Pension and Welfare Benefit Plans (OPWBP) • the branch of the Department of Labor responsible for overseeing retirement plans

offset integration • a method of integrating defined-benefit plans by subtracting out a specified amount from the benefit formula that represents a percentage of the participant's Social Security benefits

partial plan termination • a termination in which part of the plan continues for a smaller group of participants and part of the plan ceases to exist

party-in-interest • a person who has a relationship to the qualified plan. Parties-in-interest include plan fiduciaries, plan counsels, persons providing services to the plan, employers connected with the plan, employees in the plan, employee organizations whose members are covered by the plan, relatives of any of the above, and shareholders, officers, and directors who have a 10-percent-or-more ownership interest in any of the above.

past service • service prior to the inception of the plan. In a defined-benefit plan, the employer has the option of funding for past service.

Pension Benefit Guaranty Corporation (PBGC) • an organization that oversees defined-benefit plans and provides insureds protection in case a defined-benefit plan cannot pay promised benefits to participants

pension-funding contract • an unallocated group insurance product that evolved from the IPG contract but which contains no guarantees, no annuity purchases are made, and no funds are earmarked for retired employees

pension plan category • four of the qualified plans (defined-benefit, cash-balance, money-purchase, and target-benefit) are categorized as pension plans. Pension plans are subject to an annual funding requirement, a prohibition from distributing assets prior to termination of employment, and a limitation on investments to 10 percent of employer stock.

percentage match • a situation in which the employee can contribute up to a specified percent of pay per year, and the employer will match up to a specified percent of the employee's contribution

percentage test • one of the nondiscrimination tests set out under Code Sec. 410(b). Under this test, the plan must benefit at least 70 percent of employees who are not highly compensated employees.

permanency requirement • a requirement that all qualified plans must be intended to be permanent

piggybacking • a method that combines a money-purchase and profit-sharing plan. Piggybacking is also used when referring to combining a qualified and nonqualified plan.

plan administrator • the person who administrates the plan

plan termination • the means by which the employer can discontinue his or her obligation to make contributions to participant accounts in a defined-contribution plan or to fund a promised benefit in a defined-benefit plan

portfolio restructuring period • the investment stage during which an individual's portfolio composition shifts from growth orientation to income orientation prior to retirement

preservation and current income period • the retirement period when portfolio management objectives focus most heavily on the preservation of capital and high current income and only to a limited degree on long-term growth

primary sources • the actual text of statutory and regulatory law, when discussing legal research

private-letter rulings • IRS interpretations of the law in light of a specific set of circumstances that face a taxpayer; also, a method by which a taxpayer can inquire about the acceptability of a specific transaction in which he or she is engaged

profit-sharing plan • a defined-contribution plan structured to offer an employee participation in company profits that he or she may use for retirement purposes

profit-sharing plan category • four of the qualified plans (profit-sharing, 401(k), ESOP, and stock-bonus) are categorized as profit-sharing plans. In contrast to plans categorized as pension plans, these plans can have discretionary employer contributions, in-service withdrawals and can invest up to 100 percent of the plan's assets in employer stock.

prohibited transactions • prohibited dealings between the plan and a party-in-interest

prohibited-transaction exemptions • exemptions from the prohibited-transaction rules that allow a transaction that would otherwise be prohibited

proposed regulations • regulations issued right after major legislation so that practitioners can receive guidance on complex provisions of new laws. Unlike final regulations, proposed regulations have no legal force or effect (unless specifically stated in the proposed regulations).

projected benefit • the participant's benefit projected to normal retirement age, assuming that the individual will continue working until that date

provisional income • a technical term to describe the income counted when determining whether Social Security benefits are taxed or not. Provisional income includes adjusted gross income, tax-free municipal bond earnings and one-half of the Social Security benefits received.

prudent-fiduciary rule • a rule that states a plan fiduciary must perform his or her functions as a prudent person would perform them under like circumstances or else legal liability will be incurred. A prudent fiduciary must use the care, skill, prudence, and diligence under the circumstances then prevailing that a prudent fiduciary acting in like capacity would use.

PS 58 rule • a present benefit received by a participant in the form of current life insurance protection that must be included in taxable gross income for that year. The cost attributable to this pure life protection will be the lower of the actual cost as provided by the carrier or the rates supplied by the so-called PS 58 table.

purchasing power risk (inflation risk) • the investment risk associated with the loss of purchasing power due to inflation

qualified domestic relations order (QDRO) • a decree under state law that assigns a participant's plan benefits to a spouse or other designated party

qualified joint and survivor annuity (QJSA) • the normal form of benefit distribution offered to a married participant at retirement

qualified plans • retirement plans that are rewarded with favorable tax status for meeting Internal Revenue Code Sec. 401(a) restrictions. There are eight types of qualified plans including; defined-benefit pension plans, cash-balance plans, money-purchase pension plans, target-benefit plans, profit-sharing plans, 401(k) plans, stock bonus plans, and ESOPs.

qualified preretirement survivor annuity (QPSA) • death benefit given to a surviving spouse following the death of a participant prior to retirement. For a defined-benefit plan, the amount of the survivor annuity is basically equal to the amount that would have been paid under the qualified joint and survivor annuity. To determine this amount, the plan administrator assumes the participant had retired the day before death. Or, if the participant was not yet able to retire, he or she had left the company the day prior to death, survived until the plan's earliest retirement age, and then retired with an immediate joint and survivor annuity. For a defined-contribution plan, the qualified preretirement survivor annuity is an annuity for the life of the surviving spouse that is at least actuarially equivalent to 50 percent of the vested account balance of the participant as of the date of death.

rabbi trust • a trust established and funded by the employer that is subject to the claims of the employer's creditors (thus avoiding current taxation for the employee), but the funds in the trust cannot be used by, or revert back to, the employer

ratio test • one of the nondiscrimination tests set out under Code Sec. 410(b). A plan must benefit a percentage of nonhighly compensated employees that is at least 70 percent of the percentage of highly compensated employees benefited under the plan.

reallocated forfeitures • amounts forfeited by employees leaving prior to full vesting that are distributed to the remaining plan participants

replacement ratio method • the percentage of preretirement income replaced in the postretirement period. For example, a qualified defined-benefit plan will typically replace between 40 and 60 percent of a person's final-average salary.

required beginning date • the date when distributions from qualified plans, 403(b) TDAs, SEPs, and IRAs must commence under the uniform minimum-distribution rules. In most cases, this date is April 1 of the year after a person becomes aged 70 1/2.

revenue procedures • statements concerning the internal practices and procedures of the IRS

revenue rulings • the IRS's interpretations of the provisions of the Internal Revenue Code and regulations as they apply to factual situations presented by taxpayers. Revenue rulings may be used as precedents.

reverse annuity mortgage • a life or term annuity in the form of a loan, paid to an individual and secured by the individual's ownership of his or her residence

risk tolerance • the degree to which an investor can accept risk and uncertainty in either the performance and/or the value of his or her investments

rollover • a way to delay taxation by transferring funds from one IRA or qualified plan to a second IRA or qualified plan

Roth IRA • an individual retirement account in which contributions are made on an after-tax basis and qualifying distributions are made tax free

salary reduction agreement • the form that authorizes the employer to reduce an employee's salary and make plan contributions to a 401(k) or a 403(b) plan in the amount of the reduction

salary reduction plans • nonqualified plans that give executives the opportunity to defer compensation until termination of retirement as a way to lower current income and to save for retirement

sale-leaseback agreement • the sale of a property ownership interest in real estate (or other asset) and the immediate leasing of the property by the seller for either a specified or an indefinite term

savings incentive match plan for employees (SIMPLE) • a simplified retirement plan that allows employees to save on a pretax basis, with limited employer contributions

Sec. 72(t) penalty • Section 72(t) imposes a 10 percent penalty tax on premature withdrawals from qualified plans, 403(b) TDAs, SEPs, and IRAs. Certain Roth IRA distributions are subject to this rule as well. All distributions will incur these penalties except distributions that are
- made on or after the attainment of age 59 1/2, or, if made from a qualified plan, after separation from service for early retirement after age 55
- made to a beneficiary or to an employee's estate on or after the employee's death
- attributable to disability
- made to an alternate payee under a qualified domestic relations order
- part of a series of substantially equal periodic payments made at least annually over the life or life expectancy of the employee or the joint lives or life expectancies of

the employee and beneficiary. (If the distribution is from a qualified plan, the employee must also be separated from service.)

- made to cover medical expenses deductible for the year under Code Sec. 213 whether or not actually deductible
- made to pay health insurance premiums by an individual who is collecting unemployment insurance (applies only to IRAs)
- made to cover medical expenses deductible for the year under Code Sec. 213, whether or not actually deductible
- the payment of acquisition costs (with a lifetime limit of $10,000 per IRA participant) of a first home for the participant, spouse, or any child, grandchild, or ancestor of the participant or spouse (applies only to IRAs)
- the payment for qualified higher education expenses for education furnished to the taxpayer, the taxpayer's spouse, or any child or grandchild of the taxpayer or taxpayer's spouse at an eligible educational institution (applies only to IRAs)

Sec. 501(3)(c) organizations • employers that are exempt from tax under Code Sec. 501(3)(c) or educational institutions of a state or political subdivision of a state

Sec. 401(a)(4) nondiscrimination rule • a qualified plan cannot discriminate in favor of highly compensated employees (HCEs) with regard to benefits or contributions

secular trust • a funding instrument for nonqualified plans in which the assets typically are irrevocable, meaning that they can only be used to pay benefits for participants and can not revert to the employer or be accessed by the employer's creditors

self-directed IRAs • an IRA in which the taxpayer is able to shift investments between general investment vehicles offered by the trustee

separate-investment accounts contract • under the separate-investment accounts contract, the plan fund manager can either invest in one of several separate accounts (similar to mutual funds) offered by the insurance company

separate lines of business • a term used under the minimum-coverage rules that allows a company that operates a separate line of business, and has at least 50 employees, to treat that entity as a separate company under the qualified plan rules

simplified employee pension (SEP) • a retirement plan that uses an individual retirement account (IRA) as the receptacle for contributions. A SEP is a simplified alternative to a profit-sharing or 401(k) plan.

single-premium annuity contract (SPAC) • a product sold when a plan terminates that transfers the employer's liability under the plan to an insurer. SPACs require the payment of a single premium by the employer in return for which the life insurance company issues paid-up annuities to all former participants.

split-funded plan • a term that describes a retirement plan that is funded with both a trust fund and life insurance contracts

split-interest purchase • the acquisition of property by two parties whereby one party owns certain rights to the property, such as lifetime use, and the other party owns the remaining rights, such as full ownership upon the death of the lifetime-use owner

spousal consent • the protection generally afforded by qualified plans for a spouse's interest in a participant's qualified plans by automatic provision of a qualified preretirement survivor annuity (QPSA) in the event the participant dies before retirement and a qualified joint and survivor annuity (QJSA) as the normal benefit when the participant retires. Elections to waive QPSA or QJSA benefits and to elect some other form of benefit or to designate some other beneficiary are not valid unless the spouse of the participant consents in writing in the election.

spousal IRA • a traditional IRA or a Roth IRA for a nonworking spouse that can be up to $2,000 in any given year

stand-alone plan • a 401(k) plan that only provides for employee pretax contributions. The employer does not make any matching contributions or profit-sharing contributions.

standard-hours counting method • a way to compute the hours of service an employee has for plan purposes by counting each hour the employee works and each hour for which the employee is entitled to be paid

standard termination • a voluntary termination of a qualified defined-benefit plan in which the plan sponsor has sufficient assets to pay its benefit commitments

stepped-up annual funding • a schedule to save funds for a specific dollar retirement goal in which the level of contributions is increased (stepped up) each year

stipulated annuity • *See* life annuity with guaranteed payments.

stock bonus plans • defined-contribution profit-sharing-type plans in which the participants have the right to receive distributions in the form of employer stock

subsidized benefits • a term used to describe benefits (such as an early retirement benefit) that is actuarially more valuable than the normal form of payments

substantially equal periodic payments • an exception to the Sec. 72(t) penalty tax

summary annual report (SAR) • a summary of the 5500 forms filed with the IRS that is provided to plan participants every year

summary of material modification (SMM) • an explanation given to plan participants that informs them about major changes in their plan

summary plan description (SPD) • an easy-to-read booklet that explains the retirement plan to participants

superannuated employees • older employees whose productivity levels are lower than their salary levels

supplemental executive retirement plan (SERP)) • a nonqualified plan providing additional (paid for by the employer) retirement benefits for executives and used to attract and retain management personnel

surety bond • a third-party promise guaranteeing that a nonqualified plan benefit will be paid

target-benefit pension plan • a hybrid retirement plan that uses a benefit formula like that of a defined-benefit plan and the individual accounts like that of a defined-contribution plan. The contribution is derived from the benefit formula in a target-benefit plan, but once determined, the plan resembles a money-purchase plan in all other ways.

tax-advantaged retirement plans • employer-sponsored retirement plans that are eligible for special tax treatment. These plans include qualified plans, SEPs, SIMPLEs, and 403(b) plans.

technical-advice memorandum • a private ruling on a completed transaction issued by the national office of the IRS

TEFRA 242(b) elections • grandfather elections made before 1984 that allowed participants to elect out of the current minimum-distribution rules

temporary annuity • a life annuity that expires after a given period of time

temporary regulations • regulations issued right after major legislation so that practitioners can receive guidance on complex provisions of new laws. Temporary regulations have legal force and effect until withdrawn.

10-year averaging • a preferential method for computing the tax on a qualifying lump-sum distribution from a qualified plan that has been grandfathered for certain taxpayers born before January 1, 1936

1099-R Forms • the IRS forms that reports distributions from pension plans

terminal funding approach • funding a plan as benefits are due instead of putting money aside over time. Qualified plans must be funded over time (prefunded) but nonqualified plans can still use the terminal funding approach.

third-party administrators (TPAs) • organizations that offer design consulting, record-keeping, legal, and actuarial services either to support plan administrators (the sponsors or employees of the sponsor) or stand in as the plan administrator

title IV plan • a plan that is covered by PBGC insurance

top-hat exemption • An ERISA exemption for unfunded, nonqualified plans maintained by an employer, primarily for the purpose of providing deferred compensation for a select group of management and/or highly compensated employees

top-heavy plan • a plan that unduly favors key employees by providing 60 percent or more of the benefits or contributions to these employees. These plans are subject to additional restrictions.

21-and-one rule • a rule that states that to be eligible for participation in the plan, an employee must have one year of service and be at least age 21

2-year/100 percent rule • a term used to describe a special qualified plan participation rule that allows the sponsor to exclude employees who have earned less than 2 years of service as long as the participants are 100 percent immediately vested

unallocated group pension contract • a method by which contributions are assigned to a general pool and specifically allocated to employees only at retirement—for example, deposit-administration contracts and immediate-participation-guarantee contracts

unit-benefit formula • a formula that accounts for both service and salary in determining the participant's benefit in a defined-benefit plan

valuation date • the date when investment earnings, gains, and losses are allocated to participant's accounts

variable annuity • an annuity with an equity-based component to it. It is designed to provide fluctuating benefit payments over the payout period that may provide increasing benefits during periods of inflation.

vesting • the acquisition by an employee of his or her right to receive a present or future pension benefit

vesting schedules • methods of determining the portion of the accrued benefit that a participant will receive if he or she terminates from employment prior to normal retirement age

voluntary after-tax employee contribution • a contribution that does not result in matching employer contributions

year of service • a 12-month period in which the participant has 1,000 hours of service

Answers to Review Questions and Self-Test Questions

Chapter 1

Answers to Review Questions

1-1. Opportunities to serve business and the business owner include setting up qualified plans or other tax-advantaged retirement plans for corporations and other for-profit business entities; setting up retirement programs for nonprofit organizations; modifying existing retirement programs to maximize tax-shelter potential; updating existing plans to conform with legislative changes; updating existing plans to conform with changing organizational needs; advising clients about investment strategies that are appropriate for retirement programs; selling investment products that are appropriate for retirement programs (chapters 11–12); planning for the purchase of life insurance in tax-sheltered plans; setting up nonqualified plans for executives; selling IRAs and Roth IRAs to clients; planning for a client's retirement; and, planning for the best disposition of a client's retirement benefits.

1-2. As the pension field has matured, selling retirement plans as tax shelters or as employee benefits is not enough. With the popularity of 401(k) and 403(b) plans, which allow for employee pretax contributions, employees are more involved than ever in ensuring their own retirement security and employers are often looking to their pension advisers to help educate their employees about retirement planning.

1-3. Tax-advantaged retirement plans include eight kinds of qualified plans—defined-benefit pension plans, cash-balance plans, money-purchase pension plans, target-benefit plans, profit-sharing plans, 401(k) plans, stock-bonus plans, and ESOPs—as well as SEPs (simplified employee pensions) and SIMPLEs (savings incentive match plans for employees). Public school systems and those nonprofit organizations qualifying for Code Sec. 501(c)(3) tax-exempt status can also sponsor 403(b) plans that are also referred to as tax-sheltered annuities.

1-4. In all tax-advantaged plans, the employer receives a deduction for contributions while employees do not have to pay income taxes until benefits are distributed. Furthermore, plan assets that accumulate in a trust or an insurance product are not subject to tax, even though such earnings are taxed as distributed to employees. Also, benefits can generally be rolled over to an IRA or other tax-deferred plan until benefits are needed. What makes qualified plans different from the other plans is the special tax treatment available upon distribution. This includes the grandfathered 10-year forward averaging rule and capital gains election as well as the special tax treatment of certain employer securities.

1-5. By deferring taxes until the time of distribution, in most situations, the employee will end up with a much higher accumulation than if amounts were saved on an after-tax basis.

1-6. a. Scopes will save more for retirement under the qualified plan than under the individual savings approach. The qualified plan is entitled to all the tax-saving advantages as outlined in the chapter. The individual savings approach is not as lucrative, however, because the retirement funds are saved after paying personal income taxes at 36 percent, and the earnings on retirement savings can be invested only after they, too, are taxed (unless a tax-sheltered vehicle is used). With the individual savings approach, the amount accumulated will not be taxed at retirement. With the qualified plan, amounts are taxed at distribution. However, the deferral of taxes results in a much larger accumulation, which offsets the later tax bite.

b.

	Qualified	Personal Savings
Amount of savings	$15,000	$15,000
Less taxes	0	5,400 (36%)
Amount actually invested	$15,000	$ 9,600
Plus interest earned on amount invested at 10%	1,500	960
Less taxes on interest earned	0	346* (36%)
Amount saved after one year	$16,500	$10,214*

*All figures have been rounded to the nearest dollar.

1-7.   Because the tax burden owed today can be deferred until the benefit is later distributed.

1-8.   A qualified plan will help RAMCO in all the following ways:
   - RAMCO will be able to attract and retain key employees who have valuable technical skills and knowledge of the new generation of computers because high-salaried employees are generally interested in the income tax sheltering that a qualified plan provides.
   - A qualified plan will help RAMCO avoid unionization because the workers will not feel the need to start a union in order to have their retirement needs met.
   - By instituting a qualified plan related to profits or stock ownership, RAMCO can help increase productivity and employee enthusiasm for its upcoming project.
   - Even though its current concern may not be to promote a graceful transition in the workforce, RAMCO will eventually want younger employees. When the now-younger employees are approaching retirement, RAMCO will be glad that these high-salaried employees can move out and be replaced by lower-paid younger employees who grew up using computers.
   - RAMCO will establish a reputation in the community as a good place to work. In addition, RAMCO will meet its social responsibility of providing a comfortable retirement for long-service employees.
   - RAMCO will provide employees with the most effective compensation package possible.

1-9.   In addition to the reasons that larger businesses establish retirement plans, owners of small businesses have several other reasons for establishing plans including creating a tax shelter, building a liquid asset, building retirement security, and, for C corporations, avoiding the impact of the accumulated earnings test.

Answers to Self-Test Questions

1-1.   True.

1-2.   False. A SEP is not a qualified plan, even though it is eligible for many of the same tax advantages. The distinction is important when learning about the retirement field, because qualified plans are subject to one set of rules, while other plans, such as the SEP, SIMPLE and 403(b) plans are each subject to a unique set of rules.

1-3.   False. Only distributions from qualified plans are eligible for special 5-year and 10-year forward averaging; 403(b) plans, as well as SEPs and SIMPLEs, are not eligible for this special tax treatment.

1-4.   False. Plan funds invested in either tax-advantaged or non-tax-advantaged investments are accumulated on a tax-deferred basis in a qualified plan or other tax-advantaged retirement plans. This gives qualified plans the advantage (over nonqualified plans) of being able to invest in higher-yield taxable investments.

1-5.   True.

1-6.   False. One trait that all tax-advantaged retirement plans share is that in order for the owners and managers to participate in the tax benefits, the plan must cover a significant number of rank-and-file employees.

1-7. True.

1-8. True.

1-9. True.

1-10. False. Retirement plans play a key role in attracting and retaining older and highly marketable employees because these employees are interested in retirement savings and tax shelter. Younger employees, however, are more apt not to care about a retirement program but would, instead, prefer increased wages over deferred compensation.

1-11. True.

1-12. True.

1-13. True.

1-14. True.

1-15. True.

1-16. True.

Chapter 2

Answers to Review Questions

2-1. ERISA has four distinct Titles. The first protects an employee's right to collect benefits. Title II amended the Internal Revenue Code, setting forth the necessary requirements for special tax treatment. Title III created the regulatory and administrative framework necessary for ERISA's ongoing implementation. Title IV established the Pension Benefit Guaranty Corporation, an agency that insures pension benefits.

2-2. a. Maximum deductible contributions—Throughout the 1980's and 1990's the trend was to lower the maximum deductible contribution for highly compensated employees. However, the 2001 tax law changed direction allowing larger contributions for individual employees. This new direction is intended to encourage small businesses to establish plans and to encourage a higher level of qualified plan savings.

   b. Limiting tax deferral—Code Section 401(a)(9) was introduced in 1986, requiring that distributions from all tax-sheltered plans begin at age 70 1/2 (or, in some cases at actual retirement, if later). These minimum-distribution rules have an impact on any retiree receiving qualified plan, 403(b), or IRA distributions.

   c. Parity—Over the years, the trend has been toward giving all types of business entities equal access to retirement plan vehicles. With a few minor exceptions, today C corporations, S corporations, sole proprietorships, partnerships, and even limited liability companies (LLCs) are all on the same footing.

   d. Funding—Over the years, a number of law changes increased required employer contributions and PBGC insurance premiums to shore up the financial status of the PBGC.

   e. Simplification—After years of more and more complexity, in 1996 there was true pension simplification. Administration of 401(k) plans became easier after this law change. The simplification trend continued in 2001 with the several rules that simplified administration of 401(k) plans.

2-3. Legislative changes require a lot of effort by the financial services professional. After studying the new law, clients have to be informed of the changes and notified of the impact of the new law on their particular plan design. Many law changes also require plan amendments. Even though new laws require a lot of work, they can also provide for new opportunities to help clients meet their particular needs.

2-4. The IRS plays the most prominent role of all the bureaucratic agencies: (1) It supervises the creation of new retirement plans (in pension parlance, initial plan qualification). (2) It monitors and audits the operation of existing plans. (3) It interprets federal legislation, especially with regard to the tax consequences of certain pension plan designs.

2-5. The case as stated is an accurate interpretation of the law. At the time of this writing, the benefits community adheres to the informal statement limiting universal life insurance to 25 percent of the account balance. If Dr. Scalpel wanted to pursue the issue, the financial services professional involved could secure a private letter ruling from the IRS asking that the IRS resolve the apparent conflict and allow 50 percent funding with universal life insurance. If the IRS acquiesced in Dr. Scalpel's case, the private letter ruling would be binding on the IRS in only that situation; theoretically, it could not be used by others in deciding the same issue (although this is often done).

2-6. Through its office of Pension and Welfare Benefit Plans (PWBP), the DOL (1) ensures that plan participants are adequately informed through enforcement of some of the reporting and disclosure rules, (2) polices the investment of plan assets, (3) polices the actions of those in charge of the pension plans (fiduciaries), and (4) interprets legislation.

2-7.   The organizations that provide plan services include consulting houses, actuarial firms, insurance companies, administrative consultants, and software companies. In the financial market, there are trust companies, commercial banks, investment houses, asset-management groups, and insurance companies.

2-8.   The most important sources are the primary ones, that is, the Internal Revenue Code, ERISA and other statutory law as well as regulations and other regulatory guidance. Books and periodicals can shed light on the meaning of the rules and so can loose leaf services that are updated regularly. Today, many commercial sources of information are also available on the Internet, and the primary sources have never been easier to access for free, as they are posted on governmental websites.

Answers to Self-Test Questions

2-1.   False. Title IV of ERISA established the Pension Benefit Guaranty Corporation and deals with insuring plan benefits. In fact, sometimes plans are categorized as Title IV plans (most defined-benefit plans) and other plans. The information described in the statement pertains to Title I of ERISA.

2-2.   True.

2-3.   True.

2-4.   False. Employers are not required to secure an advance-determination letter. They can take deductions and wait for an IRS audit to determine whether the plan is qualified, but because of the risk of disqualification this is seldom attempted.

2-5.   False. The item described in the question is a revenue ruling, not a regulation. Regulations (whether they are final, temporary, or proposed) explain and interpret the various sections of the Internal Revenue Code and deal with the finer points of the law. Regulations apply to all taxpayers.

2-6.   True.

2-7.   True.

2-8.   True.

2.9.   True.

2-10.   False. Most defined-benefit plans must be covered by PBGC insurance. There is, however, an exception for professional-service employers with 25 or fewer active participants.

2-11.   False. The qualified-plan rules for Keogh plans and regular corporate plans are similar.

2-12.   False. Master and prototype plans are easier to use than individually designed plans.

2-13.   True.

2-14.   False. Many loose-leaf services are updated weekly. The term *loose-leaf* refers to the fact that individual pages can be constantly revised to reflect recent happenings and then mailed to subscribers in a loose-leaf binder to replace current pages. In this manner, information about the legal and administrative framework can be kept current.

2-15.   True.

Chapter 3

Answers to Review Questions

3-1.   The financial adviser should sit down with June and walk her through a pension planning fact finder. The fact finder will contain a list of the most common retirement concerns that face people like her. This list includes questions that ask June to prioritize her personal tax needs, her desires to underwrite benefits for other employees, and other typical retirement issues. Once the issues have been prioritized, June will be asked to discuss the interplay among each of the factors. For example, do June's tax and retirement needs outweigh the need to avoid the cost of including rank-and-file employees in a qualified plan? After this comparative analysis, June will once again be asked to prioritize her retirement concerns, this time in list form. She will be concerned with costs, and at this juncture, cost concerns will be addressed. The adviser will then distinguish between June's personal needs that the plan will satisfy and the organizational goals that will be accomplished. This is especially important if other principals are involved, because the adviser can begin to see what issues will ultimately be considered important by all principals, not just by June. Finally, the adviser will analyze the flower shop's employee data.

After taking all these steps and garnering as much information as possible, the adviser will be in a position to make insightful recommendations.

3-2. Frequently, the person you speak with will not correctly represent the desires of the entire body of authority within the organization. Also, the company's attorney or accountant may resent playing the subordinate role (even though he or she may know little about pension plans). For both problems, the solution is diplomacy.

3-3. Doyle's Furniture, Inc., should use a defined-benefit retirement plan. Under a defined-benefit approach, the company, not the employees, would run the risk of investing contributions. This would allow Doyle's employees to have a benefit that would not be subject to the stock market; but it would mean that if investment performance is poor, the company will have to come up with extra funding to provide the promised benefit.

A second reason a defined-benefit approach is preferable is because defined-benefit plans can fund for past service, whereas defined-contribution plans cannot. This enables Doyle to take care of employees who have been with him for a long time because service worked for the employer prior to the inception of the plan can be counted.

A third reason for using a defined-benefit approach is because defined-benefit plans can gear retirement payments to salary levels used just prior to retirement. Defined-contribution plans, on the other hand, can only provide benefits based on the entire career earnings, which are less than the final years' earnings of an employee. In addition, salary levels at retirement will account for any inflation that took place during the employee's career, whereas a career-average salary will not fully account for preretirement inflation.

A final reason that a defined-benefit plan would be preferable is that long-service employees will lose benefits if they change employers. Under a defined-benefit plan, the benefit builds more quickly at the end of the person's career when they have many years of service and the highest salary. Changing jobs means that benefits are calculated based on a lower salary.

3-4. Defined-contribution plans have more easily determinable costs, participants more easily appreciate the value of the benefits, the benefits are more portable and participants generally have the option to receive a lump-sum distribution. These factors are appealing to both the employer and the employee, and for these reasons most new plans set up today are of the defined-contribution type.

3-5. a. defined-contribution plan
b. defined-benefit plan
c. defined-contribution plan
d. defined-contribution plan
e. defined-contribution plan
f. defined-benefit plan

3-6. Combination defined-benefit and defined-contribution plans are most commonly used by larger employers looking for a very comprehensive retirement package.

3-7. The three differences are: (1) In a pension plan, the employer is committed to annual funding while in a profit-sharing plan the employer is not. (2) A profit-sharing-type plan can allow for in-service distributions while a pension plan cannot. (3) In a pension plan, only 10 percent of the plan's assets can be invested in employer securities, while in a profit-sharing plan up to 100 percent of the plan's assets can be invested in employer securities.

3-8. To determine Faye's maximum deduction, you must first determine her contribution rate as follows:

(1) List the plan contribution as a decimal   0.25
(2) Add 1 to the rate in line 1 and show this as a decimal   1.25
(3) Divide line 1 by line 2.   .20

Once you know what percentage Faye can contribute, you can then determine her maximum deduction.

(1) Self-employment contribution rate   .20
(2) Net earning from Schedule C $100,000.00

(3)	Deduction for self-employment tax		
	(for 2002)		$ 6,434.00
(4)	Subtract step 3 from step 2.		$ 93,566.00
(5)	Multiply step 4 by step l.		$ 18,713.20

Thus, we have determined that Faye's deduction will be $18,713.20.

Answers to Self-Test Questions

3-1. True.
3-2. False. Small organizations, such as closely held businesses, are particularly concerned with providing maximum benefits for owners and other key employees and tend to want to minimize benefits for rank-and-file employees as a cost-saving measure.
3-3. True.
3-4. True.
3-5. True.
3-6. False. 403(b) plans are a unique type of plan because only 501(c)(3) tax-exempt organizations and public school systems can maintain this type of plan.
3-7. True.
3-8. False. The maximum yearly benefit allowed under a defined-benefit plan is the lesser of 100 percent of the high 3-year average compensation or $160,000 (as indexed for 2002). The lesser of 100 percent of salary or $40,000 (indexed for 2002) limit used in the statement is the maximum yearly contribution allowed under a defined-contribution plan for any particular employee.
3-9. True.
3-10. True.
3-11. False. It is defined-benefit plans that can gear their retirement payments to final salaries. Defined-contribution plans are limited to career-average salaries.
3-12. True.
3-13. False. The employee bears the risk of preretirement inflation in a defined-contribution plan because some contributions are geared to salaries in the early years of employment.
3-14. True.
3-15. True.
3-16. False. Under a profit-sharing plan the organization retains the flexibility to avoid annually funding the plan.
3-17. False. Plans from the pension category can only invest up to 10 percent of their assets in employer stock.
3-18. True.
3-19. False. Keogh plans cannot be structured to include loan provisions for owner employees.

Chapter 4

Answers to Review Questions

4-1. a. Ralph should use a unit-benefit formula. The unit-benefit formula accommodates Ralph's objective to retain and reward experienced personnel because a unit benefit is based in part on the years an employee works for the employer. The unit-benefit formula also meets Ralph's goal of rewarding owner-employees and key employees who have high salaries because the pension benefit is based, in part, on salary. Finally, the unit-benefit formula meets Ralph's need to provide a specific income-replacement ratio for employees (see b).
      b. A formula that meets Ralph's needs reads: Each plan participant will receive a monthly pension commencing at the normal retirement date and paid in the form of a life annuity equal to 2 percent of final-average monthly salary multiplied by years of service. Service is limited to a maximum of 30 years. (*Note:* Ralph would probably want to integrate this formula with Social Security in order to limit the costs of providing benefits to lower-paid employees. Integration is discussed later in the course.)
4-2. A flat-amount-per-year-of-service formula is most typically found in a union setting.

4-3. With a flat-amount formula, all participants receive the same benefit regardless of their salary or years of service.

4-4. a. In any benefit formula that is tied to compensation, participants must read the definitions of compensation and final-average compensation carefully. Defining compensation as base salary may result in a much different benefit than if all taxable compensation is considered. Similarly, if final-average salary is the highest 3 years, the benefit will be larger than if it is the highest 5 years of compensation.

b. No a life annuity with 10 years certain is a more valuable benefit than the life annuity only.

c. No a life annuity payable at 65 is less valuable than a life annuity payable at 62.

4-5. Using past service is a way to provide larger benefits for long-service employees. It can also be used in small tax-sheltered plans to increase the benefit (and deductible contribution) for the business owner.

4-6. Bill can provide a different formula for future service than he has for past service. If Bill provides a downgraded benefit for past service and a lucrative benefit for future service, he will accomplish his objective. A second alternative he has is to use the same formula for past service as for future service, but to fund the past-service benefit over a longer period of time. The law allows the past-service benefit to be funded over a 30-year period. This option is discussed later in the course.

4-7. a. The cash-balance plan is a defined-benefit plan that looks like a defined-contribution plan to employees. As a defined-benefit plan, it is subject to the flexible contribution requirements that apply to such plans, and it is subject to the PBGC insurance program.

b. In a traditional defined-benefit formula, the benefit is stated as a life annuity in an amount that is generally expressed as a percentage of the participant's final salary. In a cash-balance plan, the plan still promises a benefit, but in this case, the promise is stated as a single sum, which is the total of employer contributions and earnings (using a stated rate in the plan).

c. If the employer currently maintains a well-funded defined-benefit plan and perceives that employees would prefer a defined-contribution-type plan, the employer will consider the cash-balance option. The plan is simply amended so that participants have an opening "account balance" based on the old benefit, then future additions are added each year. In this way, the employer can use up extra funds in the plan to fund the future account additions.

4-8. A money-purchase pension plan may be the right choice for a company with a steady cash flow, relatively young employees, and a need to have a fixed contribution level that is easily communicated to employees. Drawbacks include the inability to protect against preretirement inflation and the inability to accumulate adequate benefits for older participants only in the plan for a short time.

4-9. Dr. Dwyer should adopt a target-benefit plan. A target-benefit plan is uniquely suited to Dr. Dwyer's needs because it permits a speedy accumulation of substantial retirement benefits for her, while at the same time minimizing costs for lower-paid employees. This occurs because there is less time to "fund" Dr. Dwyer's benefit than there is to fund the younger employees' benefits. Therefore, contributions will be high for Dr. Dwyer and low for other employees. A second factor in Dr. Dwyer's choice is that she can only contribute $20,000 per year to the plan. If she could have contributed a larger amount on her own behalf (for example, $50,000 a year), a defined-benefit plan would have best served her needs because the plan would have allowed annual funding for her in excess of the 100 percent of salary/$40,000 defined-contribution limit. However, Dr. Dwyer's ideal contribution does not conflict with this limit and the target-benefit plan suits her needs. Also note that the question asks what type of pension plan would be appropriate. An age-weighted or cross-tested profit-sharing plan (discussed in the next chapter) might even be more appropriate since she would not be required to make annual contributions.

4-10. a. money-purchase plan

b. cash-balance plan

c. defined-benefit plan

Answers to Self-Test Questions

4-1. False. Employers generally do not believe there is any need to replace 100 percent of final-average salary because Social Security benefits, private savings, and lower postretirement costs indicate that the same standard of living can be maintained on less income.

4-2. True.

4-3. False. A flat-percentage-of-earnings formula relates the benefit solely to salary and does not reflect an employee's service. A formula that relates the benefit solely to service is a flat-amount-per-year-of-service formula.

4-4. True.

4-5. False. This is exactly the type of situation where this definition of compensation would be discriminatory. In this company, benefits for highly compensated employees are based on total compensation, while some earnings are excluded for the other employees.

4-6. True.

4-7. False. Past service is usually accounted for in the small-plan market because the decision makers within the organization have large amounts of past service themselves and their personal interests will override any corporate objectives.

4-8. False. The situation is exactly the opposite. Receiving a $2,000 life annuity beginning at age 62 is more valuable than having the $2,000 benefit begin at age 65, because the benefit payments will be made for a longer period.

4-9. True.

4-10. False. Defined-benefit candidates typically do not have predictable costs because funding is subject to an annual actuarial determination.

4-11. True.

4-12. False. Cash-balance plans are a form of defined-benefit plan. This is important because even though the plan looks like a defined-contribution plan, it is subject to the rules that affect defined-benefit plans, including coverage under the PBGC insurance program.

4-13. True.

4-14. True.

4-15. False. The maximum annual contribution for a particular employee to a money-purchase plan is the lesser of 100 percent of compensation and $40,000 (as indexed for 2002).

4-16. True.

4-17. True.

4-18. True.

4-19. False. Under a target-benefit plan, the employee bears the investment risk and gets the benefit of the investment return.

4-20. False. An employer hopes to provide the targeted benefit at retirement, but there are no guarantees that the targeted benefit will be paid.

4-21. False. Target-benefit plans are uniquely suited for older owner-employees who are initiating a retirement program late in their careers.

4-22. True.

Chapter 5

Answers to Review Questions

5-1. Umbrella, Inc. should adopt a profit-sharing plan. A profit-sharing plan suits the company's needs because it can be designed to work around the cash-flow problem by structuring the plan's contribution formula so the company makes contributions only in the year it has substantial profits. For example, a portion of profits in excess of $50,000 will be contributed to the plan.

  A second advantage that a profit-sharing plan holds for Umbrella, Inc., is the ability for participants to withdraw funds from their accounts as early as 2 years after they were contributed by the employer. By adopting this feature in the plan, the owners of Umbrella, Inc. will have access to most of their retirement funds when it comes time to expand the business.

5-2. Because of the discretionary nature of a profit-sharing plan, it may be difficult to get employees to appreciate the value of the plan. To get the most out of the plan, the employer should clearly communicate the amount of the contribution and how it was derived; identify circumstances that would result in larger employer contributions; and be sure to provide clear and regular benefit statements to participants.

5-3. The allocation formula is the method for determining how much of the total contribution is allocated to specific participants.

5-4. To calculate how much will be allocated to each participant, you must calculate the percentage for each employee multiplied by the total contribution of $20,000 ($30,000 less $10,000) as follows:

Step 1. Find the percentage of contributions to which each participant is entitled.

Anne $\dfrac{\$\,100,000}{\$\,200,000}$ = 50% of total

Bob $\dfrac{\$\,70,000}{\$\,200,000}$ = 35% of total

Cassie $\dfrac{\$\,30,000}{\$\,200,000}$ = 15% of total

Step 2. Multiply the percentage of the allocation by the amount of profits to determine the amount allocated to each participant's account. In this case, the amount of profits is $20,000 ($30,000 profit less the $10,000 of profit that is not to be allocated).

Anne	50%	of	$20,000	=	$10,000
Bob	35%	of	$20,000	=	$ 7,000
Cassie	15%	of	$20,000	=	$ 3,000
					$20,000

5-5. Prior to 2002, John would probably been interested in adopting a profit-sharing plan and a money-purchase pension plan. However, with the maximum deduction limit increasing to 25 percent in a profit-sharing plan, he can accomplish his goal with just a profit-sharing plan and retain maximum flexibility.

5-6. A profit-sharing plan can invest a portion of the plan's assets in key person life insurance. If the key person dies, the plan receives the proceeds of the policy, which is then allocated to the participants.

5-7. For 2002, the maximum salary deferral is $11,000 for those under 50 and $12,000 for individuals who are aged 50 or older. Also, note that the contribution limit is scheduled to continue to increase through 2006.

5-8. The four types of 401(k) contributions are employee salary deferrals, employee after-tax contributions, employer matching contributions, and employer profit-sharing type contributions.

5-9. Salary deferral contributions can only be withdrawn upon termination of employment, attainment of age 59 1/2, or a financial hardship. The plan could provide for more liberal in-service withdrawals for other types of employer contributions.

5-10. The first step toward determining whether ABCO will pass the actual deferred percentage test is to determine who falls into the highly compensated group.

- Abner Anderson is a highly compensated employee because he is both (1) a 5-percent owner and (2) he receives compensation in excess of $85,000.
- Barbara Bellows is also a highly compensated employee. Barbara falls into both the highly compensated employee categories.
- The rest of the employees are not highly compensated employees because they do not meet any one of the definitions. Note that for a company this size, the top 20 percent election is not meaningful. Under that rule, if, for example, there were 10 employees and four made more than $85,000, only the two highest paid employees would be considered highly compensated if the company makes the election.

The second step necessary to perform the ADP test is to determine the average deferral percentage for the nonhighly compensated group for 2001.

Highly Compensated	Percentage	Nonhighly Compensated	Percentage
Abner Anderson	8%	Cindy Clark	5%
Barbara Bellows	8%	Don Davidson	5%
		Ellen Ewer	9%
		Frank Fern	5%
		Gary Grant	5%
average deferral	8%	average deferral	5.8%

The final step is to calculate the maximum salary deferral for the highly compensated employees for 2002. This will be based on the higher of the two numbers from performing the two tests.

Test 1: Under the first test, the maximum deferral percentage for the nonhighly compensated employees is

$$5.8\% \times 1.25 = 7.25\%.$$

Test 2: Under the second test, the maximum deferral percentage for the highly compensated employees cannot be more than the lesser of (a) 200 percent of the deferral percentage for nonhighly compensated employees ($5.8\% \times 2 = 11.6\%$) or (b) the deferral percentage for all nonhighly compensated employees plus 2 percentage points ($5.8\% + 2\% = 7.8\%$).

Therefore, the maximum deferral percentage for the highly compensated group for 2002 will be 7.8%. Looking at the deferral percentage for the highly compensated group for 2001 (8%), the plan administrator will have to require that the highly compensated group lower their contribution rates for 2002.

5-11. Today, there are a number of alternatives for helping to satisfy the ADP test. The test can be avoided altogether if the plan adopts the 401(k) SIMPLE provisions, or elects to make the safe harbor contribution. The sponsor gets to choose to test for nondiscrimination using either prior year or current year testing. Finally, if the plan does not satisfy the rules by the end of the year, the sponsor has a number of methods to go back and correct the situation.

5-12. An ESOP can borrow to purchase a large block of stock at one time and the employer pays the loan off with the employer's tax-deductible contributions to the ESOP.

5-13. Life insurance on the lives of the key employees gives the plan a source of funding to purchase stock from terminating or deceased employees.

Answers to Self-Test Questions

5-1. True.

5-2. True.

5-3. True.

5-4. True.

5-5. True.

5-6. False. The employer does not need to have profits in order to make contributions to a profit-sharing plan.

5-7. True.

5-8. True

5-9. False. The maximum salary reduction that can be taken under a 401(k) plan is $11,000 (as indexed for 2002). The limit described in the question applies in total to all types of contributions to the 401(k) plan, including salary deferrals, employer matching contributions, profit-sharing-type contributions, and after-tax contributions.

5-10. False. The maximum amount that can be saved in on a pretax basis in a 401(k) plan is $11,000 (for 2002) while the maximum deductible contribution to an IRA is only $3,000. As we will see in assignment 8, many individuals are not allowed to make deductible IRA contributions at all. Because of this, the 401(k) plan is almost always a better pretax savings vehicle.

5-11. True.

5-12. True.

5-13. True.

5-14. False. Withdrawals from a 401(k) plan are restricted to retirement, death, disability, separation from service, attainment of age 59 1/2, or financial hardship. The general 2-year distribution rule for plans that fall into the profit-sharing category does not apply to 401(k) plans.

5-15. True.

5-16. False. For purposes of the actual deferral percentage test, a highly compensated employee must be a more-than-5-percent owner of the company for the current or prior year. Because Sally has only 2 percent ownership in both the current and prior year, she is not a highly compensated employee. Because in the prior year (2001), she earns less than $85,000 (indexed for 2001), she is not a highly compensated employee for 2002.

5-17. True.

5-18. False. Social Security FICA taxes are based on the employee's unreduced salary regardless of whether a salary reduction is taken.

5-19. True.

5-20. True.

5-21. False. Under the technique known as *leveraging,* the plan trustee acquires a loan from the bank and uses the borrowed funds to purchase employer stock. Shares of this purchased stock are allocated to participant accounts when contributions are made to the plan. The employer is entitled to a deduction when contributions are made, as is the case for contributions to any qualified plan. Concurrently, the money that would normally be used to make contributions is used to pay off the bank loan. The result is that the employer receives the full proceeds of the bank loan immediately and pays the loan off through tax-deductible contributions to the ESOP.

5-22. True.

5-23. True.

Chapter 6

Answers to Review Questions

6-1. A SEP is similar to a profit-sharing plan in that contributions are discretionary and the maximum deductible contribution is 25 percent of compensation. It is similar to other qualified plans because the annual additions limit applies and the plan is subject to the top-heavy limitations. Since SEPs are funded with IRA accounts, they are subject to the full and immediate vesting rules, investment restrictions, withdrawal limitations and tax treatment that applies to other IRAs. The eligibility rules are unique to SEPs as is the requirement that contributions can only be allocated on a compensation-to-compensation or integrated basis.

6-2. A SEP has many of the same advantages of a discretionary profit-sharing plan with less administrative hassle. If the employer has many part-time, long-service employees, or wants to limit the plan to one group of employees then the profit-sharing eligibility rules may be preferred. Also, many employers do not want to give participants full and immediate vesting or immediate access to the retirement account.

6-3. a. Either a profit-sharing plan or a SEP look like appropriate choices. What is chosen will depend upon the coverage, vesting and withdrawal issues.

  b. Because of the interest in administrative ease, the SEP seems preferable in this case to a profit-sharing plan.

  c. Because of the employer's interest in a salary deferral option a SEP is not a good choice. Here the employer will consider either a 401(k) plan or a SIMPLE.

  d. Because of the interest in purchasing stock using leveraging, an ESOP is the right choice.

6-4. Both Sally and Rich are eligible. Each earns more than $450 in three of the five calendar years prior to the year in question.

6-5. A SIMPLE can only be sponsored by an employer that does not sponsor another type of retirement plan and does not have more than 100 employees. It has to be available to those employees who earn at least $5,000 in two calendar years and eligible employees must be given the right to defer up to $7,000 (2002 limit) of compensation. The employer has to either make a 2 percent nonelective contribution for all eligible contribution or a dollar for dollar matching contribution up to 3 percent of compensation. No other contributions are allowed. All contributions must be fully vested and SIMPLEs are funded with IRAs so that the investment restrictions, access to funds and other considerations that apply to SEPs also apply to the SIMPLE.

6-6. An employer is required to make a contribution every year. The contribution can be a 2 percent contribution for all eligible employees or a matching contribution. The matching contribution must be a dollar-for-dollar match, with a maximum contribution of 3 percent of compensation. With the matching contribution, the employer does have some flexibility. The match can be reduced to as low as one percent of compensation in any 2 of 5 years.

6-7. The SIMPLE is especially effective for employers looking for their first retirement plan that offers participants the option to make pretax salary deferrals. The plan can work much better than a 401(k) plan if only a small percentage of the workforce is intending to make salary deferral contributions.

6-8. 403(b) plans can be used in public school districts and 501(c)(3) nonprofit organizations

6-9. a. Dr. Smith is eligible because he would be considered a hospital employee and not an independent contractor.

  b. Dr. Jones is an independent contractor and as such is not an employee of the hospital; therefore, he is not eligible for the plan.

  c. Gary Green would also be considered ineligible because of independent contractor status.

  d. Joy Cheerful is eligible even though she is a part-time employee because part-time employees are eligible for inclusion in 403(b) plans.

6-10. a. 403(b) plans can only be funded with annuity contracts or mutual fund custodial accounts.
       b. Contributions to annuity contracts can be used to provide insurance protection as long as the insurance protection is incidental and the value of the insurance is taxable to the employee each year. Contributions to mutual fund custodial accounts can be used to purchase insurance if (1) the insurance has no cash value, (2) the insurance is incidental, and (3) the cost of the insurance is included in the employee's gross income.

6-11. A plan that only contains employee salary deferrals is a very simple arrangement. The employer does have to give the opportunity to defer salary to essentially all employees willing to contribute $200 or more, but the actual operation of the plan is quite simple. This type of plan is not subject to ERISA and has few compliance requirements. With this type of plan, vendors solicit employee participation directly and the employer is generally involved only to the extent of administering the salary deferral elections. In a plan that does contain employer contributions, the situation is quite different. Now, the plan will be subject to ERISA, meaning that certain fiduciary and reporting requirements apply and the plan has to satisfy the 410(b) coverage rule, along with several other requirements.

Answers to Self-Test Questions

6-1.   True.
6-2.   False. Even though a simplified employee pension plan is not technically a qualified plan, SEPs are still required to follow a number of the qualification rules, including the rule regarding nondiscriminatory contributions.
6-3.   False. Large corporations usually do not choose SEPs because of the rigid coverage requirements.
6-4.   True.
6-5.   False. New salary reduction SEPs cannot be established after December 31, 1996. However, old plans can continue under the old rules.
6-6.   True.
6-7.   False. A part-time employee with $450 (as indexed in 2001) or more in earnings must be covered under a simplified employee pension plan.
6-8.   False. SIMPLEs are funded with IRAs. Like SEPs, such plans cannot provide for participant loans. Other IRA rules apply as well, such as immediate vesting and no investments in life insurance or collectibles.
6-9.   False. What makes the SIMPLE different from all other types of retirement plans is that a sponsor cannot maintain any other type of tax-advantaged plan at the same time that it sponsors the SIMPLE.
6-10. False. The contribution requirements for the SIMPLE are quite rigid. The employer can make either the 3 percent matching contribution or the 2 percent nonelective contribution, but not both.
6-11. True.
6-12. False. Full-time and part-time employees of a qualified employer will be eligible employees if they are so-called common-law employees. However, if they are independent contractors instead of common-law employees, they cannot be covered by the organization's 403(b) plan.
6-13. True.
6-14. True.
6-15. True.
6-16. True.
6-17. False. A 403(b) plan can be designed to permit participant loans.
6-18. True.
6-19. True.

Chapter 7

Answers to Review Questions

7-1.   The design process is facilitated with the use of a detailed fact finder and the adoption agreement that makes up the optional part of a prototype plan.
7-2.   Highly compensated employees include individuals who are 5 percent owners during the current or previous year and individuals who earned $85,000 (as indexed in 2001) in the preceding year. Moreover, under the $85,000

rule, the employer can—and generally will—elect to limit the group to only those individuals whose earnings put them in the top 20 percent of all employees. In this example, the employer should make the election because it will affect how many employees fall into the highly compensated category.

- Al Abernathy is a highly compensated employee because he is a more-than-5-percent owner.
- Becky Brooks is a highly compensated employee because she earns over $85,000 in annual compensation from the employer and her earnings put her in the top 20 percent group.
- Charlie Carr is not a highly compensated employee because even he does not earn more than $85,000. It does not matter that he is an officer.
- The rest of the employees do not fit the definition of a highly compensated employee.

7-3.   The percentage test, ratio test, and average-benefits test.

7-4.   If an employer has qualifying separate lines of business, the 410(b) test performed is counting only the employees of the separate line of business. To qualify, the line of business must be operated for bona fide business reasons and must have at least 50 employees.

7-5.   Every defined-benefit plan must cover the lesser of 50 employees or 40 percent of the entire workforce. However, if there are only two employees, both must be covered.

7-6.   The employees of both companies are counted when performing the coverage requirements—even if the plan only covers one of the companies.

7-7.   Under the leased employee rules, the leased employee will generally have to be counted as an employee when determining whether the plan satisfies the coverage requirements. The leased employees do not actually need to be covered unless they are needed to satisfy the coverage requirements. Leased employees can be disregarded entirely if no more than 20 percent of the recipient company's nonhighly compensated employees are leased and the leasing entity maintains a safe-harbor plan.

7-8.   a.   All businesses under common control are treated as a single employer in determining whether the proper number of employees are covered under the plan. Off the Books and By the Numbers would be considered under common control because they are a brother-sister group. This is because Al and Becky each have ownership interests in both companies— together they own 100 percent of both companies (satisfying the 80 percent test), and they have an identical ownership interest of 54 percent (satisfying the 50 percent test). Remember, under the 50 percent test Al's identical ownership is 50 percent (the lesser of his 95 percent ownership in Off the Books and his 50 percent ownership interest in By the Numbers), and Becky's identical ownership interest is 4 percent (the lesser of her 50 percent interest in By the Numbers and her 4 percent interest in Off the Books). Because both ownership tests are satisfied, the companies have to be aggregated (considered together) for determining whether the coverage tests are satisfied.

   b.   The Off the Books plan will satisfy the 410(b) nondiscrimination requirement, even though it is aggregated with the By the Numbers Company because it passes the percentage test. To pass the percentage test, at least 70 percent of the nonhighly compensated employees have to be covered. In fact, because all Off the Books employees are covered and none of the By the Numbers employees are nonhighly compensated, 100 percent of the nonhighly compensated employees are covered (more than the 70 percent required). Because the plan is a defined-contribution plan, it is not required to satisfy the 401(a)(26) minimum-participation test. Therefore, all the coverage requirements have been met.

   c.   The By the Numbers plan will not satisfy the 410(b) nondiscrimination requirements. Because the two plans must be aggregated, the seven nonhighly compensated employees from the Off the Books Company must be counted. This means zero percent of the nonhighly compensated employees are covered, so that neither the percentage nor the ratio test is satisfied. Finally, the average-benefit-percentage test is not satisfied; because the nonhighly compensated employees receive no benefits, the average-benefit percentage for nonhighly compensated employees cannot be at least 70 percent of the average-benefit percentage of highly compensated employees.

   d.   The separate-line-of-business exception does not apply because a separate line of business must have at least 50 employees. Therefore, this escape route is closed to small businesses such as those involved in this case.

7-9.   Even though the law allows an employer to exclude some employees from a qualified plan, the decision to include or exclude employees is more of a business decision. Exclusion could result in dissatisfied employees who do not stay employed for long.

7-10. The law provides that short-term employees, part-time employees, and HCEs can be excluded from the plan. Also, up to an additional 30 percent of the nonhighly compensated workforce can be excluded as long as the Age Discrimination in Employment law is not violated.

7-11. a. The benefits to the architectural firm of delaying participation are (1) to save retirement dollars attributable to turnover, (2) to save administrative and record-keeping costs, (3) to save front-end load costs if insurance policies are used to fund the plan, and (4) to help the firm's plan pass nondiscrimination tests because employees who have not met the minimum age and service requirements are not required to be counted for nondiscrimination purposes.

The architectural firm may want to avoid delay in plan participation because immediate participation allows employees to maximize retirement benefits, and it helps to attract key employees by making the plan highly competitive. In this case, B&W should consider what is best for the firm, keeping in mind these factors, as well as its hiring practices and objectives.

b. If an annual entry date is chosen, the age requirement cannot be more than 20 1/2, and the service requirement cannot be more than 6 months.

7-12. a. In addition to counting actual hours worked, there is the elapsed-time method, hours-worked-excluding-overtime and a number of pay-period methods.

b. When picking a counting method, the employer will be concerned about administrative convenience as well as choosing a method that does not have the impact of including part-time employees that could have been excluded under another counting method.

7-13. SEPs must cover employees who have attained age 21 and who have earned $450 (as indexed in 2001) in 3 of the 5 previous calendar years. SIMPLEs must cover any employee who earned $5,000 in 2 previous calendar years and is reasonably expected to earn $5,000 in the current year. If a 403(b) plan includes employer contributions, the plan must satisfy 410(b). In addition, the ability to make salary deferrals must be given to any employee willing to contribute $200 or more to the plan.

Answers to Self-Test Questions

7-1. True.

7-2. False. An adoption agreement is a planning tool issued by insurance companies and other sponsoring organizations in conjunction with a master or prototype plan. It is the vehicle used for choosing among the various optional provisions found in the master or prototype plan. The adoption agreement lists the sections of plans and the design choices that are available under each section and asks the employer to select from the menu of options provided.

7-3. True.

7-4. True.

7-5. False. In order to satisfy the 410(b) nondiscrimination requirement, an employer is required to pass only one of the three named tests.

7-6. False. The percentage is 70 percent, not 56 percent.

7-7. True.

7-8. True.

7-9. True.

7-10. True.

7-11. True.

7-12. False. Segregating management into a separate entity will probably result in a management services affiliated service group. If this is the case, the employees under both sets of corporations will be aggregated for purposes of the 410(b) test.

7-13. False. Leased employees must be counted when determining if the recipient's plan satisfies the coverage tests. If the plan can pass the tests without the leased employees, they do not have to be included as plan participants.

7-14. True.

7-15. False. Under the 410(b) coverage requirements, a highly compensated employee can be excluded from the plan without having an impact on the coverage test. The only exception is that under the 401(a)(26) requirement that applies to defined-benefit plans, highly compensated employees are counted for determining whether the 40-percent or 50-employee rule has been satisfied.

7-16. True.

7-17. False. The maximum age to which plan participation can be delayed is 21.

7-18. False. The maximum service requirement is typically one year. However, a 2-year maximum service requirement may be implemented if the participant is fully vested when he or she enters the plan.

7-19. True.

7-20. False. A year of service is a 12-consecutive-month period for which an employee works 1,000 hours. An employee does not receive a year of service after he or she has worked 1,000 hours, but rather on completion of a 12-month period in which the employee has worked 1,000 hours.

7-21. True.

7-22. True.

7-23. False. Because the controlled-group rules apply when determining whether a SEP satisfies the coverage rules, a SEP cannot be used in this case. SEPs must cover all eligible employees of the entire controlled group.

7-24. True.

Chapter 8

Answers to Review Questions

8-1. Yes, providing a level percentage of compensation for each participant is considered nondiscriminatory under 401(a)(4).

8-2. a. In a defined-contribution plan, the accrued benefit is the participant's account balance.

b. In a defined-benefit plan, the accrued benefit is the participant's currently earned benefit using compensation and years of service to date.

c. In a defined-benefit plan, the projected benefit is the benefit expected at normal retirement age assuming that the individual continues in service until that time. The projected benefit is generally calculated using current salaries.

8-3. As long as the average work year is at least 2,000 hours, an employer can require 2,000 hours of service before a participant is credited with a full year of service for benefit purposes. If this is done, participants with 1,000 hours of service must be given credit for one-half year of service.

8-4. The compensation cap limits the compensation that can be used under the plan's benefit or allocation formula. It has the impact of limiting benefits for those earning more than the cap ($200,000 for 2002).

8-5. a. When the integration level is the taxable wage base and the contribution based on total compensation is 5.7 percent or more, the maximum contribution for wages earned in excess of the taxable wage base is 5.7 percent.

b. When the integration level is the taxable wage base and the contribution based on total compensation is 3 percent, the maximum contribution for wages earned in excess of the taxable wage base is 3 percent.

c. When the integration level is set under the taxable wage base, the maximum contribution in excess of the taxable wage base has to be reduced. In 2001, the taxable wage base is $80,400. A $70,000 integration level is more than 80 percent of the taxable wage base, meaning that the maximum contribution on wages in excess of the integration level is 5.4 percent.

8-6 Cross testing in a defined-contribution plan means converting the contributions to equivalent annuity benefits at retirement. This method results in larger allowable contributions for older participants because they have a shorter time to retirement and the annuity purchase price would be higher than for a younger participant.

8-7. Even one older nonhighly compensated employee can disrupt the plan design.

8-8. The strength is its flexibility and the ability to make larger contributions for the older business owners. The limitations are all related to administrative complexity and cost.

8-9. A profit-sharing plan, because of the ability to make discretionary contributions.

8-10. A 401(k) plan is subject to three possible nondiscrimination tests. The salary deferrals must satisfy the ADP test, the employer matching contributions and after-tax contributions must satisfy the ACP test, and profit-sharing contributions must satisfy the 401(a)(4) nondiscrimination test.

8-11. A SEP must either allocate contributions as a level percentage of compensation or allocate with a formula that is integrated with Social Security.

8-12. The plan satisfies the integration rules because the excess benefit percentage does not exceed either limit. The excess benefit is .75 percent and the maximum total excess benefit equals 26.25 percent. Furthermore, the benefit based on total compensation is one percent, greater than the .75 percent excess amount. Weese's benefit is $13,900, calculated as follows:

.01	x	$50,000	x	20	=	$ 10,000
.0075	x	$26,000	x	20	=	$ 3,900
						$ 13,900

18-13. Plans with voluntary contributions must perform the ACP nondiscrimination test, which is quite similar to the ADP nondiscrimination test that applies to salary reduction contributions in a 401(k) plan. If the plan also calls for employer matching contributions, the voluntary after-tax contributions and matching contributions both get counted in the nondiscrimination test.

Answers to Self-Test Questions

8-1. True.

8-2. False. Today's regulations provide clear objective tests for determining whether the plan satisfies the rules. The plan can satisfy a design safe harbor, or actual contributions or benefits can be tested each year for nondiscrimination.

8-3. True.

8-4. True.

8-5. False. The annual compensation considered in the contribution formula is limited to $200,000 (in 2002) for any participant. Therefore, in this case, Able's benefit will be $20,000 (or 10 percent of $200,000) and not $30,000.

8-6. False. A plan's benefit formula can be amended by the employer as long as it does not cut back on existing benefit accruals. In fact, a common plan-design strategy, known as updating, is to gradually increase the amount of benefits provided under the plan.

8-7. False. This formula fails because the integrated portion cannot exceed the contribution based on total compensation. In this case, the maximum excess contribution is 4 percent. Note also that satisfying the integration rules means that the plan satisfies the design safe harbor. It is actually possible to choose a different integration method, as long as the plan satisfies the general nondiscrimination test on an annual basis.

8-8. True.

8-9. False. With the compensation cap (which is $200,000 in 2002), the integrated plan formula does not result in a significant amount of skewing to the owner. The small business owner who wants to receive the lion's share of the contribution should look to the cross-tested and not the integrated formula.

8-10. False. The allocation formula in a SEP has to either allocate contributions as a level percentage of compensation or be integrated with Social Security.

8-11. True.

8-12. True.

Chapter 9

Answers to Review Questions

9-1. a. The advantages of including a loan provision are that (1) it allows the best of both worlds—tax shelter for plan contributors and immediate access to sheltered funds, (2) business owners in a C corporation can have plan loans, and (3) there are mechanisms to minimize administrative problems.

b. The disadvantages of including a loan provision include the fact that (1) the loan provision may be inconsistent with the employee's objective of providing retirement security, (2) the loan may default, which would put additional administrative responsibilities on the administrator, and (3) owners in S corporations, partnerships, sole proprietorships, LLC's, and sole proprietorships cannot have a plan loan.

9-2. Loans are quite common to 401(k) and 403(b) plans, because they provide tax-free access to participants' salary deferral contributions. Loans are less common in plans funded totally with employer contributions. Still, they may be available simply as an additional benefit or as an alternative to in-service withdrawals. Defined-benefit plans rarely have loan provisions, because there are no participant accounts. Neither do ESOPs because of the investment restrictions. SEPs and SIMPLEs are not allowed to have participant loans.

9-3. Plan loans unlock funds by making them currently available to employees. Plan sponsors who are hesitant to set up a plan because they are reluctant to "put money away" may find the loan provision mitigates against this fear.

9-4. The maximum loan limit is the lesser of $50,000 or one-half of the vested account balance. Although the tax rules allow a participant to borrow up to $10,000 even if this exceeds one-half of the vested account balance, most plans do not allow such loans due to labor regulations.
   a. The maximum loan for Woods under most plans is $8,500. If the plan were to allow Woods to take $10,000, it would have to have the loan secured with property in addition to Woods's account balance.
   b. The maximum loan for Muhlenberg is $50,000 (which equals the lesser of $50,000 or one-half of his account balance).
   c. The maximum loan for Dickenson is $50,000. Prior to 2002, loans could not be made to owners of S corporations. This restriction no longer applies.

9-5. An employer is required to choose a vesting schedule that is equal or more liberal than one of two statutory vesting schedules. The first statutory vesting schedule is a 5-year cliff vesting schedule under which the employee is zero percent vested until 5 years of service are completed, at which time the employee becomes 100 percent vested. The second statutory vesting schedule is a 3-through-7-year graded vesting schedule, under which the participant becomes 20 percent vested after 3 years of service and receives an additional 20 percent vesting for each subsequent year of service.
   a. The first schedule cannot be used in a qualified plan because it exceeds the maximum cliff period of 5 years.
   b. The second schedule can be used in a qualified plan because it is at least as "liberal" as the 3-through-7-year graded schedule. Note that in each year of service an employee is as well off, or better off, under the graded schedule presented.
   c. The third schedule cannot be used in a qualified plan even though the participant becomes 100 percent vested more quickly than in the 3-through-7-year graded vesting schedule. The reason the third schedule is not as liberal as the 3-through-7-year schedule is that a participant with 3, 4, and 5 years of service is "worse off" than is statutorily permitted under a graded schedule.

9-6. A special rule requires that employer matching contributions in a 401(k) plan must be subject to a vesting schedule that satisfies the top-heavy rules. That is a schedule as favorable as either 3-year cliff vesting or 6-year graded vesting.

9-7. a. Restrictive vesting schedules may reduce benefit costs if a significant number of employees terminate employment before becoming fully vested. Also, a restrictive vesting schedule acts as a "golden handcuff," tying the employee to the company until benefits become vested.
   b. More liberal vesting schedules are often used to create a competitive advantage by providing a better plan than a competitor.

9-8. a. Service prior to eligibility earned by a 20-year-old participant must be counted for vesting purposes.
   b. Service earned by a 16-year-old employee need not be counted for vesting purposes.
   c. Service for a subsidiary of the employer, even though the subsidiary did not have a qualified plan, must be counted for vesting purposes.
   d. Service with a predecessor—employer, if the successor—employer maintains the predecessor's plan, must be counted for vesting purposes.
   e. Years of service in which the employee did not make mandatory contributions to the plan need not be counted for vesting purposes.

9-9. Prior vesting service can be disregarded under three break-in-service (a year with fewer than 500 hours of service) rules. First, prebreak service can be disregarded until an individual is reemployed and completes a full year of service. Second, in a defined-contribution plan, if a participant has five consecutive breaks in service, the nonvested portion of the benefit earned prior to the breaks can be permanently forfeited. The third, but less useful, rule applies only to participants who are zero percent vested. If such a participant has five consecutive breaks in service, prebreak service can be disregarded entirely.

9-10. A post-65 normal retirement age should be considered in a new defined-benefit plan that has a number of older employees or in an existing plan that frequently hires people 55 or older. This is because, absent a "later" normal retirement age, the start-up funding cost will be prohibitive.

9-11.   a. The advantages of putting an early retirement provision in the plan is that it enables employees who are superannuated or physically worn out to gracefully retire.

        b. The disadvantages of putting an early retirement provision in the plan is that certain key employees will leave and take a job with a competitor.

9-12.   Deferred retirement provisions are important because the Age Discrimination in Employment Act prohibits involuntary retirement. In addition, it will help to encourage productive employees to remain on the team.

Answers to Self-Test Questions

9-1.   True.

9-2.   False. Owner-employees in S corporations are ineligible to have plan loans. Business owners in C corporations can have plan loans.

9-3.   False. A 401(k) plan can have a loan provision. In fact, by putting a loan provision in a 401(k) plan, the employer will enhance its chance of passing the actual deferral percentage test because this gives employees access to the retirement funds, thereby enticing the required plan participation.

9-4.   True.

9-5.   False. A fair market rate of interest must be charged on plan loans. No sweetheart rates can be given to any participant.

9-6.   True.

9-7.   True.

9-8.   True.

9-9.   False. Over the years, changes in the law have decreased the period an employee must wait before becoming fully vested under his or her plan.

9-10. False. Under a 5-year cliff vesting schedule, an employee is not vested until 5 years of service have been completed.

9-11. True.

9-12. True.

9-13. False. 401(k) salary-deferred contributions are not subject to the plan's vesting schedule. Instead, they are considered to be 100 percent vested immediately. In fact, an employee must be 100 percent vested in his or her own contribution to the plan at all times, regardless of whether the contribution is made on a voluntary, or salary reduction basis.

9-14. False. Reallocated forfeitures are forfeitures that are used as an additional contribution to employees who remain in the plan. When reallocated forfeitures are used, employer costs are not reduced.

9-15. False. Forfeitures that are reallocated to employees are added to other contributions, and the aggregate amount cannot exceed the 100 percent or $40,000 limit.

9-16. False. Usually the inclusion of one of the required vesting schedules (or a less restrictive schedule) guarantees that the plan will meet IRS standards. There is, however, a general exception: a plan cannot, in practice, have a pattern of abuse that discriminates in favor of highly compensated employees. For example, a plan could not have a discriminatory turnover rate if the company made a practice of firing employees before their benefits were vested.

9-17. True.

9-18. False. A one-year break in service will occur if an employee has fewer than 501 hours of service in a year.

9-19. True.

9-20. True.

9-21. True.

9-22. False. A plan's normal retirement age can be greater than 65. The amount of delay depends upon the participant's age at hire. For example, the normal retirement age for a participant hired at age 69 could be age 74, not 65.

9-23. False. An employer can use the service requirement when determining early retirement. A typical early retirement requirement is age 65 and 10 years of service. There is no rule, however, limiting the employer to 10 years of service.

9-24. True.

9-25. False. The Federal Age Discrimination in Employment Act prohibits involuntary retirement except in very limited circumstances.

9-26. True.

Chapter 10

Answers to Review Questions

10-1. The incidental benefits tests are intended to ensure that the plan is being used primarily to provide retirement benefits. In a defined-contribution plan, the basic rule is that only 25 percent (in aggregate) of the participant's benefit can be used to pay life insurance premiums. However, if the policy is a whole life policy, the 25 percent limit becomes 50 percent. In a defined-benefit plan, an alternative rule can be used; the life insurance benefit can not exceed 100 times the expected monthly retirement benefit.

10-2. When designing a plan for the small employer of the professional corporation, the insurance needs of the principal individuals will control the death benefit design. In medium and large companies, the retirement plan's insurance benefits will be decided by competition and other market factors.

10-3. The advantages of including death benefits in a qualified plan are (1) competitiveness, (2) attraction and retention of employees, and (3) the ability of the business owner to receive group rates, shift a personal expense to the company, and gain favorable underwriting.

10-4. If disability benefits are provided in the retirement plan, benefits can take on several forms:
   a. They can be a distribution of a 100-percent-vested accrued benefit or account balance.
   b. They can be a distribution from a defined-benefit plan plus a plan-paid subsidy.
   c. They can be provided by disability insurance purchased under the plan.

10-5. The definition of disability can be restrictive (in which it mirrors the Social Security definition) or liberal (in which separate standards for verification are outlined).

10-6. a. The purpose of the top-heavy rules is to strictly scrutinize small organizations from making the plan exclusively a tax shelter for the business owners
   b. Top-heavy rules typically affect small businesses.

10-7. a. An individual is a key employee if at any time during the prior year he or she has been any of the following:
   - an officer receiving annual compensation in excess of $130,000 (as indexed for 2002)
   - a person who owns more than 5 percent of the company
   - a person who is more than a one-percent owner with annual compensation of more than $150,000
   Allen is a key employee because she was a 5-percent owner at the end of the previous year. In addition, McFadden is also a key employee because she is an officer earning more than $130,000. McGill, Melone, and Rosenbloom, however, are not key employees because they do not meet any of the definitions.
   b. To determine whether the Trophy Shop plan is top-heavy, we must check whether more than 60 percent of the aggregate account balances belong to key employees. The key employees are Allen ($100,000) and McFadden ($60,000), and combined they hold $160,000 of the plan's assets. The nonkey employees are McGill ($40,000), Melone ($12,000), and Rosenbloom ($8,000); combined they hold $60,000 of the plan's assets. Because the $160,000 in assets held by key employees is 72 percent of the total plan assets ($220,000), the plan is top-heavy.

10-8. If a plan is top-heavy, special accelerated vesting schedules apply. The top-heavy version of the 5-year cliff schedule is a 3-year cliff schedule. The top-heavy version of the 3-through-7-year graded schedule is a 2-through 6-year graded schedule.
   A second consequence of being top-heavy is that a minimum benefit must be supplied to nonkey employees. In a defined-benefit plan, the benefit for each nonkey employee must be at least 2 percent of compensation multiplied by the number of the employee's years of service in which the plan is top-heavy up to a maximum of

10 years. In a defined-contribution plan, the minimum employer contribution for nonkey employees must be at least 3 percent.

Finally, a plan that is top-heavy will have a special limit for situations where both a defined-benefit and defined-contribution are present.

Answers to Self-Test Questions

10-1. False. If universal life insurance is used to fund the plan, the aggregate premiums paid for the policy cannot exceed 25 percent of the participant's total benefit.

10-2. True.

10-3. True.

10-4. False. Plans need only contain a qualified preretirement survivor annuity for married participants.

10-5. True.

10-6. True.

10-7. False. Small business owners may want life insurance in a plan for a number of reasons including administrative convenience, the ability to use tax-deferred amounts to purchase insurance, and the need for insurance for estate planning purposes.

10-8. True.

10-9. True.

10-10. False. A defined-benefit plan is top-heavy if more than 60 percent of the present value of the entire amount of the plan's accrued benefits is set aside for key employees.

10-11. False. A key employee is not a so-called highly compensated employee. The definitions are different, and both terms are used in a number of contexts in the pension area.

10-12. False. If a plan is top-heavy, a special top-heavy vesting schedule is applied. The top-heavy version of the 5-year cliff schedule is a 3-year, 100-percent cliff schedule. The top-heavy version of the 3-through-7-year graded schedule is a 6-year graded schedule. Employees, however, need not be 100 percent immediately vested in a top-heavy plan.

10-13. True.

Chapter 11

Answers to Review Questions

11-1. The objective of the minimum funding requirements that apply to qualified plans is to ensure the plans have sufficient assets to pay promised benefits.

11-2. The actuary must use reasonable actuarial assumptions in determining the annual required contribution. However, the actuary can select from among several actuarial methods, choosing the method that best suits the employer's needs.

11-3. An irrevocable trust, valid under state law, is established that clarifies the investment powers of the trustees, the allocation of fiduciary responsibility, the payment of benefits and plan expenses, and the rights and duties upon plan termination.

11-4. Life insurance and annuity contracts can also act as the plan's funding instrument.

11-5. a. If an individual has discretionary authority over the disposition of plan assets or provides investment advice for a fee, he or she will be considered a plan fiduciary.

b. Service providers, such as accountants and lawyers, are generally not fiduciaries, and even those selling investments are often not considered investment advisers.

11-6. The four affirmative fiduciary obligations are (1) to maintain the plan for the exclusive benefit of the participants, (2) to discharge fiduciary duties with the prudence of a knowledgeable investment professional, (3) to diversify plan assets, and (4) to invest plan assets in accordance with the plan's documents.

11-7. To satisfy the individual account plan exception, participants must be given at least three core investment options and have the right to have the opportunity to make changes at least quarterly. Participants must be given information about each investment option and must have the right to request more detailed information. Employer stock can be an option, but it must be in addition to the three core options.

11-8. Even if the plan conforms with the 404(c) regulations, the fiduciaries are still responsible for ensuring that participants do not engage in prohibited transactions. Also, the fiduciaries are never given relief from the responsibility of prudently selecting the investment alternatives.

11-9. a. The sale of real estate owned by the ABC plan to the wife of the treasurer of the ABC Company is a prohibited transaction. It is considered an excluded dealing to sell, exchange, or lease property between the plan and a party in interest. Because the treasurer's wife is a relative of an employee, she is considered to be a party in interest.

b Loaning money from the plan to an officer of the company is not a prohibited transaction. Loaning money or extending credit to a party in interest is generally a prohibited transaction. However, if the plan has a loan provision and loans are made available on a nondiscriminatory basis (as in this case), then there is no prohibited transaction.

c. The acquisition of 25 percent of employer stock by a defined-benefit plan is a prohibited transaction. A defined-benefit plan cannot acquire employer securities in excess of the 10 percent allowable limit. Profit-sharing plans, stock-bonus plans, and employee stock ownership plans, however, are exempt from the 10 percent limitation.

d. The acquisition of real estate from the plan for less than its market value is a prohibited transaction because it constitutes self-dealing with plan assets by a fiduciary.

11-10. Your client should obtain a prohibited transaction exemption (PTE) from the Department of Labor. A PTE exempts the sale of the land from the plan to the company from the prohibited transaction rules. The willingness to pay a market price for the land will weigh in favor of granting the PTE. However, the DOL will be skeptical of the transaction because of the possibility that employees will be cheated through self-dealing. The DOL will expect assurances that the participants' interests are being protected.

Answers to Self-Test Questions

11-1. False. The terminal funding approach may not be used to fund a qualified plan. Instead, retirement benefits must be prefunded according to the minimum funding standards prescribed in ERISA.

11-2. True.

11-3. False. The minimum funding requirements are intended to fund projected benefits over a number of years. This means that, especially in the early years, the plan may satisfy the funding requirements but not have assets sufficient to pay promised benefits earned to date. This would mean that if the company were to have financial difficulty and the plan were terminated, assets would not be able to pay for all promised benefits.

11-4. False. The projected-benefit cost method will provide for relatively level costs from year to year. It is the accrued-benefit cost method that provides for a lower liability at first, which steadily increases until the plan reaches maturity.

11-5. True.

11-6. False. The choice of an actuarial cost method does not affect the ultimate cost of the plan.

11-7. True.

11-8. False. The higher the investment assumption is, the lower the annual cost of the plan.

11-9. True.

11-10. True.

11-11. True.

11-12. True.

11-13. True.

11-14. True.

11-15. True.

11-16. False. Split funding is a method under which the employer places part of the funds in a life insurance contract and part of the funds in a side fund or trust.

11-17. False. A financial services professional who has discretionary control over plan investment purchases is a fiduciary to the plan. Similarly, the adviser will also be a fiduciary if he or she regularly gives investment advice for a fee and that advice is the primary basis for the investment decisions.

11-18. False. There are no facts presented that indicate the investment is imprudent. However, this could be a violation of the exclusive-benefit rule. Here, the motivation for the investment appears to be to gain the goodwill of the client, not concern for the benefit of plan participants. Investments like this need to be analyzed carefully and pursued cautiously.

11-19. True.

11-20. False. Participants have to be able to select from only three investment options for the fiduciaries to be eligible for relief under the ERISA 404(c) rules.

11-21. True.

11-22. True.

11-23. True.

11-24. True.

11-25. False. Small business owners sometimes forget that plan assets cannot be used for the benefit of the company and/or as personal assets. The entrepreneurial owner wants to put the pension assets to work. It is important, therefore, for knowledgeable advisers to look for prohibited transaction problems.

11-26. True.

Chapter 12

Answers to Review Questions

12-1. Investment guidelines help to establish the fiduciaries' obligations. They are also the appropriate first step in making investment decisions—that is, determining the goals and objectives of the fund. They can also provide protection for the fiduciaries when their actions are questioned.

12-2. The common objectives of a defined-benefit investment strategy usually include accumulating sufficient assets to pay benefits and minimizing the long-term cost and variability in annual costs. Sometimes these objectives are at odds with each other.

12-3. The single investment objective in a defined-contribution plan is to invest for the long-term retirement needs of the plan participants.

12-4. With self-directed defined-contribution plans, the primary objective is to provide investment alternatives appropriate to meet the diverse needs of participants with different ages, risk tolerances, and investment goals.

12-5. When establishing investment guidelines, it is helpful to ask such questions as: What is the minimum level of return necessary to accomplish the goal? What is an acceptable level of risk in relation to the whole portfolio? What is the appropriate time horizon?

12-6. Considerations when identifying investment goals should include permissible categories of investments, limits on asset quality, asset allocation ranges, diversification concerns, policies on proxy voting of stock, and other limits due to legal restrictions.

12-7. There are four types of risk relevant to investing plan assets: purchasing power or inflation risk, interest rate risk, market risk, and business risk.

12-8. Plans invest in cash equivalents to satisfy the need to make other investment transactions and to have readily accessible money to pay benefits. Bonds are often used to ensure that the plan will have sufficient cash to pay expected benefits as they arise. Also, bonds are used simply because they provide more stable returns than equities and higher returns than the cash equivalents mentioned above. Because investment in equities generally results in higher returns over the long haul, equities typically represent more than half of the assets held by the plan.

12-9. An IPG (immediate participation guarantee) contract is an unallocated funding instrument that holds benefit amounts in a commingled fund. At retirement, either the fund is charged directly with benefit payments or the fund is charged with a single annuity premium. The IPG contract contains no interest guarantees, but allows a plan sponsor to have an immediate reflection of the actual investment and mortality experience under the plan.

12-10. Like a mutual fund, a separate-investment account is generally pooled and is always participating. A second similarity to mutual funds is that the separate-investment account has preestablished types of investments—for example, a bond or equity fund can be chosen. A third similarity to mutual funds is that each fund has a directed-investment philosophy and certain investment goals. And a fourth similarity to mutual funds is that the sales appeal of any separate-investment account is based on its competitive market history.

12-11.   Unlike assets held in an insurance company's general account, assets in separate accounts are not subject to the claims of the insurance company's creditors.

12-12.   Like a CD, a GIC offers a predetermined rate of return. It also guarantees the principal and limits the timing of withdrawals. Unlike a CD, GICs sometimes offer some withdrawal flexibility, because GICs can be structured to pay out interest annually or to distribute the principal investment piecemeal.

12-13.   a.   GICs provide both the guarantees and safety of principal that Gillman desires. In addition, Gillman can use the GIC-invested portion of his defined-benefit plan to protect against downside risk, while at the same time becoming less risk averse with the other portion of his portfolio.

  b.   To avoid making interest-rate bets, the Gillman Company should place its business by making annual GIC contributions for the same stated period (for example, each year invest the plan's contribution in a 5-year GIC). By using this hedging philosophy, the company avoids the negative consequences of incorrectly guessing the direction of interest rates.

  c.   Gillman will probably choose a bullet GIC for his defined-benefit plan because he suspects that interest rates are going to drop, and he will want to lock in up front with a single large contribution.

12-14.   The major selling point of an IG (investment guarantee) contract is that it allows plan funds to receive the experience account or the guarantee, whichever is better, thus, limiting the downside risk to the plan. Another selling point for IGs is their pension orientation. Like GICs, IGs uniquely meet the investment concern of pension managers because they maximize long-term rates of return and generate cash flows to match the required benefit payments while preserving safety of principal. They are most suitable when an upswing in the market is expected.

12-15.   a.   The IG is the best contract for those who expect interest rates to increase.

  b.   A window GIC is the recommended choice because (1) the window period helps to accommodate the stream of contributions under the plan and (2) a window GIC investment is good if interest rates are expected to drop.

  c.   The recommended choice is a separate-accounts contract because (1) investment discretion is retained, (2) ongoing contributions are possible, and (3) no guarantees are provided.

  d.   The recommended choice is a bullet GIC because (1) the bullet GIC meshes well with the defined-benefit plan and (2) a bullet GIC is a smart investment if interest rates are expected to drop.

12-16.   Annuities are sometimes used to fund plans in situations where life insurance is not available because of underwriting considerations. Although life insurance underwriting requirements are not typically stringent in the retirement arena, there are times when a prospect is uninsurable and the "guaranteed issue" or graded death benefit amount is not sufficient. In these cases, annuities are suitable substitutes for life insurance in filling the funding need. A second reason annuities are used to fund plans is because of the guaranteed payout rates they sometimes offer. If this is the case, the same annuity that is used for funding purposes is also used for payout purposes.

Answers to Self-Test Questions

12-1.   False. Investment guidelines are most important when the fiduciary's actions have been questioned. The fiduciary cannot defend a course of action unless the investment objectives are clear. Guidelines also provide a structure that the fiduciary can follow.

12-2.   True.

12-3.   False. As a premium for the tax-exempt status, these investments pay a lower rate of return than investments subject to tax. Because qualified trusts are not subject to tax, it is generally not a good idea to invest in tax-free investments.

12-4.   True.

12-5.   True.

12-6.   False. The percentage is over 50 percent for both defined-benefit and defined-contribution plans.

12-7.   False. The immediate-participation-guarantee contract contains no guarantees but instead allows the plan sponsor to have an immediate reflection of the actual investment experience under the plan.

12-8.   True.

12-9.   False. Separate-investment-accounts contracts are generally pooled but are sometimes segregated for larger plans.

12-10.   True.

12-11.   True.

12-12.   False. A precise dollar contribution is not stipulated under a GIC. It is more likely that the amount contributed will be linked to a percentage of contributions.

12-13.   True.

12-14.   True.

12-15.   True.

Chapter 13

Answers to Review Questions

13-1.   Typically, the financial services advisor involves other professionals to set up and administer the plan. The advisor stays involved in plan design and troubleshooting when problems arise.

13-2.   The steps include adopting the plan with a board resolution and plan document, obtaining an advance-determination letter from the IRS, giving notice to interested parties, explaining the plan to the employees and, in some cases (if employees have the option to contribute or are given investment options), conducting an enrollment meeting.

13-3.   a.   The plan administrator is typically the company.

   b.   Specified employees carry out the administrative duties with the help of outside service providers such as consultants, insurance companies, or accountants.

13-4.   The summary plan description is uniquely suited for this task because it bridges the gap between the legalese of the pension plan and the understanding of the layperson. In any case, the employer is required to provide a summary plan description (SPD), so the use of such a description proves cost effective because a second document need not be created.

   The easy-to-read SPD also serves as a method for an employer to tout the fact that a significant employee benefit is being provided to employees and that the retirement benefit should be considered as an important part of the employee's overall compensation package.

13-5.   a.   The summary plan description is a legal document required by ERISA that explains but does not "sell" the plan.

   b.   Essentially, the summary plan description must clearly explain eligibility for the plan's benefits and describe how to apply for benefits. It must also describe the plan's appeal procedures if the participant is denied benefits.

13-6.   a.   Form 5500 is the annual report required for all pension plans except "one-person" plans.

   b.   Schedule A is attached to the appropriate annual report when benefits are provided (in whole or in part) by an insurance company.

   c.   Schedule SSA is filed for terminated employees who are entitled to deferred benefits (it is not required for employees who are paid out at termination of employment).

   d.   Form 5500EZ is the annual report filed for one-participant plans.

   e.   Form PBGC-1 is filed with the PBGC for covered defined-benefit plans.

13-7.   a.   Summary annual reports containing some basic information about the financial status of the plan must be distributed to all participants each year.

   b.   Although personal benefit statements are not required (unless specifically requested by the participants), most sponsors distribute them to ensure that participants both understand and appreciate their benefits.

   c.   Whenever the plan allows for employee contributions or investments, there is quite a bit of ongoing interaction between the administrator and the participants. New election forms, educational materials, investment seminars and retirement planning seminars, and software are part of the retirement planning landscape today.

   d.   Plan documents are amended when the sponsor wants to change the plan design or when a law change requires an amendment. In either case, the plan is typically filed for another IRS determination letter whenever a significant amendment has been adopted.

13-8. Plans sponsored by sole proprietors or partnerships may be exempt from Filing form 5500 (or be required to file Form 5500 EZ instead of Form 5500). They may also be exempt from the ERISA reporting requirements. As mentioned in chapter 3, special rules apply to calculating the maximum allowable contribution and to plan loans.

Answers to Self-Test Questions

13-1. True.

13-2. True.

13-3. True.

13-4. False. Plans that only contain employer contributions are typically set up at the end of the tax year when the employer knows that it can afford a contribution to a plan. Plans with employee contributions (401(k) and 403(b) are established prior to the effective date of the plan so election forms can be completed.

13-5. False. There is no requirement that the employer receive an advance-determination letter—although it is generally a good idea to do so.

13-6. True.

13-7. False. A summary plan description must be fair and evenhanded; it cannot be used to persuade employees to join the plan, rather it must explain the plan.

13-8. True.

13-9. True.

13-10. True.

13-11. False. The plan administrator is not prohibited from delegating responsibility. In fact, the trustee, a third-party administrator, or an insurance company may take over a significant number of the plan administrator's duties.

13-12. True.

13-13. True.

13-14. False. This plan is probably exempt from any reporting requirements—as long as the plan has always had less than $100,000 of assets and the sponsor does not also sponsor another plan (and assets in total exceed $100,000).

13-15. True.

13-16. True.

13-17. False. The plan administrator must issue a personal benefits statement to an employee if the employee requests it. The employee cannot demand a statement more than once in any 12-month period.

13-18. True.

13-19. True.

Chapter 14

Answers to Review Questions

14-1. Employers choose to terminate qualified plans for a number or reasons. The sponsor may no longer be in a financial position to make further plan contributions. Or the sponsor wants to change plan design to another type of plan. Changes may also occur if the business is sold or merged, or there are other substantial changes in business operations.

14-2. If an employer wants to cease additional benefits but does not want to distribute benefits, the plan can be "frozen." If a defined-benefit plan does not have sufficient assets to pay promised benefits, freezing benefit accruals is quite common. Also, if the employer wants to change the nature of the plan, in some cases, the plan can be amended instead of terminated. For example, a traditional defined-benefit plan can be amended into a cash-balance plan.

14-3. If an employer is considering the termination of a qualified plan, the following issues should be considered: First, if the plan is less than 10-years old, the IRS may require a valid business reason for the plan's termination. Second, if the plan is a defined-benefit plan covered by the PBGC, it can be terminated only under certain circumstances. Third, if the plan has had any compliance problems, they should be addressed before completing the plan termination.

14-4. Terminating a defined-contribution plan will require a corporate resolution and plan amendments terminating further accruals. In some cases, plans also need amendments for retroactive law changes. Participants must be notified 15 days prior to the termination date. The employer must make any remaining required contributions and liquidate plan assets in preparation for distribution. Benefit distribution paperwork must be prepared and in the year that benefits are distributed, when the annual IRS Form 5500 is filed, it is marked as the "final form."

14-5. A plan that is not submitted raises a "red flag" and may be audited.

14-6. Unlike plans covered by the PBGC program, a non-PBGC plan can be terminated even if it does not have sufficient assets to pay all plan benefits. Also, the administrative burden is not as great with the non-PBGC plan although the plan does have to take all of the steps required for terminating a defined-contribution plan.

14-7. To be eligible for the lower 20 percent excise tax, the employer must share a portion of the excess with the plan participants. Either 20 percent of the excess must be allocated to the participants in the terminating plan or 25 percent of the excess must be transferred to a replacement plan.

14-8. With SPACs (single-premium annuity contracts), the insurance company issues annuity certificates in the amount promised to participants under the plan. The law requires that the SPAC distribution options match the original plan distribution options and, at the time of distribution, the insurer provides election forms, qualified joint and survivor notices, and so on.

14-9. A termination can occur without action by the employer if (1) there has been a partial termination, (2) the plan is a profit-sharing plan and there is a complete discontinuance of contributions, and (3) the plan is a defined-benefit plan and the PBGC initiates a termination because one of a number of events threatening the financial status of the plan has occurred.

Answers to Self-Test Questions

14-1. False. A qualified plan can be terminated within 10 years of adoption. If the reasons for termination are not valid, however, the IRS might retroactively disqualify the plan.

14-2. False. PBGC coverage is limited to defined-benefit plans only.

14-3. True.

14-4. True.

14-5. True.

14-6. False. To qualify for the 20 percent tax rate, the employer must either (1) establish a qualified replacement plan to which it transfers assets equal to the excess of 25 percent of the reversion or (2) provide pro rata increases in benefits for qualified participants in connection with the plan termination equal to at least 20 percent of the reversion.

14-7. True.

14-8. False. Single-premium annuity contracts are not risk free from the insurer's point of view. In fact, SPACs are difficult for an insurer to price because of the long-term nature of the guarantees and their one-time expense charge.

14-9. False. Whether a partial termination has occurred is determined on a facts and circumstances basis. However, with 20 percent being the litmus test, 5 percent probably does not result in a partial termination. The impact of partial termination is full and immediate vesting.

14-10. True.

Chapter 15

Answers to Review Questions

15-1. Financial services professionals working in the pension area may want to offer nonqualified plans for a number of reasons: (1) to provide comprehensive services, (2) to gain access to an upscale market, and (3) to find a good market for significant life insurance sales (for funding the nonqualified plans).

15-2. The course materials identify many objectives that a nonqualified plan can meet. These objectives fall into three general categories. Nonqualified plans can be used as an alternative to qualified plans, as supplemental benefits for executives, or as a tax-sheltering device for a business owner.

15-3. One of the first concerns the advisor should have is whether Rhonda would be better served by a nonqualified plan or some other form of executive compensation, such as an incentive stock option plan, incentive pay, salary increases, executive bonuses, or some form of noncash reward (a company car or a country club membership). Rhonda should be made aware of the various executive-compensation techniques available, and the advisor should discuss the advantages and disadvantages that each technique holds in Rhonda's situation.

If Rhonda feels that a nonqualified deferred-compensation plan is appropriate, the advisor should help her fill out a nonqualified plan fact finder. The fact finder will help Rhonda to prioritize her objectives and it will enable the agent to gather the information necessary for making insightful suggestions and rendering accurate advice.

15-4.   a. The term *golden handshakes* implies any type of plan that encourages retirement through the use of a financial reward.

        b. The term *golden parachutes* denotes benefit plans provided to soften the financial hardship if an executive is terminated upon change in the company's ownership.

        c. The term *incentive pay* refers to bonuses given for accomplishing short-term goals that can be used by the executive for retirement purposes.

15-5.   A salary reduction plan gives participants the option to defer compensation as a way for them to lower their current income taxes and build retirement income.

15-6.   A SERP provides additional employer-provided retirement benefits to executives. The objective is typically to complement an existing qualified plan.

15-7.   Think of Code Sec. 457 as a provision that limits and controls the taxation of any nonqualified plan sponsored by a nonprofit organization or government entity. Unless the plan qualifies for a special exception (referred to as 457(f)), any nonqualified salary reduction agreement must satisfy the dollar limitations of Sec. 457.

15-8.   Because JTE is dependent on Sue to bring in business through her personal contacts, JTE should strive to secure her unique talents beyond her retirement. The firm can protect against a drop in revenue when Sue retires by setting up a nonqualified plan that provides retirement benefits and requires her to continue working on a part-time consulting basis.

15-9.   a. The Rayco Nonqualified Plan can be designed to include a golden-handcuffs provision, which discourages executives from leaving the employment of your client by providing for the forfeiture of substantial benefits if service is voluntarily terminated prior to normal retirement age.

        b. The law firm's nonqualified plan can be designed to include a covenant-not-to-compete provision, which calls for the forfeiture of nonqualified benefits if the employee enters into competition with the employer, either by opening a competing business herself or by working for a competitor. In order to be considered valid, the covenant-not-to-compete provision must be carefully drafted. The provision should be reasonable in terms of the geographical area and the time period over which it applies.

15-10.   An executive may want benefits to accelerate in case of a change in control or the financial condition of the company. He or she may also want the ability to access benefits prior to retirement in case of a financial hardship.

15-11.   a. Salary reduction plans are usually designed as defined-contribution plans while salary continuation nonqualified plans (SERPs) can be either defined-contribution or defined-benefit plans.

        b. Participation generally needs to be restricted to "a select group of management or highly compensated employees" in order to avoid ERISA coverage.

        c. The plan can provide for full vesting, distribution and or additional retirement accruals when the participant goes out on disability. Of course, it is crucial to coordinate benefits between the nonqualified plan and other employer plans.

        d. With no legal limitations choosing the plan's retirement age is strictly a matter of meeting the plan's benefit objectives, at a cost that is affordable to the employer.

        e. Nonqualified plans can provide preretirement and/or postretirement death benefits. The choice of a death benefit should, therefore, be closely coordinated with the life insurance product used in the plan.

15-12.   At the time the options are granted, there are no income tax consequences. At the time of exercise, the participant has ordinary income in the amount of the difference between the option price and the current market price. The employer receives a deduction of this same amount. When the stock is later sold, it is taxed as short-term or long-term capital gains, depending upon the holding period.

15-13.   There are no income tax consequences to the participant either at the time the options are granted or at the time the options are exercised. However, at the time of exercise, there could be an alternative minimum tax. The employer gets no deduction At the time the stock is sold, the whole taxable amount (difference between the sale price and option price) is taxed as long-term gains if certain holding period requirements are satisfied.

Answers to Self-Test Questions

15-1.   True.

15-2.   True.

15-3.   False. Nonqualified plans are not subject to any nondiscrimination requirements.

15-4.   True.

15-5.   True.

15-6.   False. A golden handshake is an additional benefit paid to induce early retirement. A golden parachute, however, is a substantial payment made to corporate executives who are terminated upon change of ownership or corporate control.

15-7.   False. Salary reduction plans are salary deferral plans without monetary restrictions.

15-8.   True.

15-9.   True.

15-10. True.

15-11. True.

15-12. True.

15-13. True.

15-14. False. A covenant-not-to-compete provision calls for the forfeiture of nonqualified benefits if the employee enters into competition with the employer. In order to be considered valid, the covenant-not-to-compete provision must be reasonable in terms of the geographical area and the time period over which it applies. Therefore, a covenant that says a former employee cannot compete in a certain region for his or her lifetime would definitely not be considered valid.

15-15. True.

15-16. False. Nonqualified plans can contain both death and disability benefits. There is no such ERISA restriction.

15-17. False. An incentive stock option program has more restrictions than a nonqualified stock option program. The ISO has more favorable tax consequences, at least from the participant's point of view.

Chapter 16

Answers to Review Questions

16-1.   With a qualified plan, the sponsor is given tax advantages in exchange for covering a wide group of employees and meeting a large number of "qualification requirements." With a nonqualified plan, the employer is subject to the normal rules that apply to the taxation of compensation, but in exchange has much more design freedom.

16-2.   Under the concept of constructive receipt, deferred compensation may be taxed currently if the individual has the option to take the payment now or later.

16-3.   Under the concept of economic benefit, deferred compensation may be taxed currently if the amount is set aside irrevocably for an executive, even if the benefit is not available currently.

16-4.   Under Sec. 83 of the Internal Revenue Code, the executive is not taxed until his or her rights in the property become transferable or are no longer subject to a substantial risk of forfeiture. A substantial risk of forfeiture is deemed to occur if the plan contains forfeiture provisions, that is, if the rights to deferred compensation are conditional on the performance—or nonperformance—of substantial services.

16-5.   a. The ABC transaction would not be considered a taxable event. In effect, ABC has informally funded its nonqualified plan. The informal funding does not fall into a constructive receipt/economic benefit/Sec. 83 trap because the employer has not made the funds available to the employee nor transferred the funds in such a way as to provide the executives with an economic benefit. Finally, for Sec. 83 purposes, the executives are not taxed because their rights in the property are not transferable (no "valued" interest has been exchanged), and the rights are subject to a substantial risk of forfeiture—the golden-handcuff clause.

        b. The DEF officers are subject to immediate taxation on the amount of the bonus they could have taken in cash. The fact that these officers turned their backs on the compensation means that they constructively received the bonus. In addition, the transfer of funds to a trust for the employees leaves the officers open to economic benefit and Sec. 83 claims.

c. As long as the GHI Corporation has met the requirements for a rabbi trust, the key executive is not subject to taxation on the funds placed with the trustee.

16-6. With a rabbi trust, assets contributed to the trust are typically irrevocable to the extent that they cannot be returned to the employer, protecting the participants in case of a change in management. However, to avoid current taxation to the participants (at the time contributions are made to the trust), assets must continue to be available for the claims of the creditors.

16-7. In contrast, a secular trust can protect against both change in control and insolvency, but with the adverse consequence that assets are taxable at the time they are contributed (or when the participant's benefits become nonforfeitable.

16-8. Almost all executive nonqualified deferred-compensation plans are drafted to satisfy the top-hat exemption of ERISA. Without an exemption, the plan would have to satisfy certain vesting, participation, and funding requirements. To satisfy the top-hat exemption, the plan must be unfunded and be maintained by an employer primarily for the purpose of providing deferred compensation for a select group of management and/or highly compensated employees. A final requirement of the exemption is that the plan sponsor send a one-page notice of the plan to the Department of Labor.

16-9. Life insurance as a funding vehicle for nonqualified plans has the following strengths: (1) it has tax-free inside buildup, (2) the company receives tax-free death benefits, (3) pre-retirement death benefits can protect the employer from financial losses or can be used to fund the participant's benefit, (4) it has funding flexibility, and (5) there are supplemental disability benefits.

16-10. In order to install a nonqualified plan, the employer should adopt a corporate resolution adopting the plan and authorizing the funding mechanism (typically purchasing life insurance). The sponsor must also create a plan document and, if a rabbi trust is used, a trust document. Finally, a one-page ERISA notice should be completed and sent to the Department of Labor.

Answers to Self-Test Questions

16-1. False. The statement as written describes a qualified plan, not a nonqualified plan.

16-2. True.

16-3. True.

16-4. False. The doctrine of constructive receipt is triggered if an executive has the ability to control the time and the actual receipt of his or her income. The doctrine described is the doctrine of economic benefit.

16-5. True.

16-6. False. The plan is considered funded when the company, in order to meet its promise of providing benefits under the nonqualified plan, contributes specific assets to an escrow or trustee account in which the employee has a current beneficial interest. The plan, as described, is considered informally funded, which means that it is unfunded for tax and ERISA purposes.

16-7. False. Unsecured promises pose major problems for executives because benefit payments hinge on the fiscal health of an employer at the time benefits become payable. Many employees remain skeptical about enjoying their current favored status when it comes time to collect. A change in management, business buyout, or decrease in rank due to performance problems or office politics may put an employee in an untenable position when he or she approaches the time to collect benefits.

16-8. False. Funds placed in a rabbi trust are subject to the claims of an employer's creditors.

16-9. False. Under the model trust, a rabbi trust cannot contain an insolvency trigger.

16-10. True.

16-11. False. Secular trusts differ from rabbi trusts in that employer contributions to a secular trust and any trust earnings are currently taxable to the employee. Money held in a secular trust cannot, however, be reached by any of the employer's creditors and, therefore, provides absolute security for executives against the company's insolvency.

16-12. False. In order to prevent the purchase of a surety bond from triggering a constructive receipt, economic benefit, or Sec. 83 problem, the executive must bear the cost of the surety bond, and the employer should not be involved with the bonding company.

16-13. True.

16-14. True.

16-15. True.

16-16.   True.
16-17.   True.

· **17**

Answers to Review Questions

17-1.   Both qualified plans and traditional IRAs are tax-favored savings plans that encourage the accumulation of savings for retirement because they allow contributions to be made with pretax dollars (if the taxpayer is eligible) and earnings to be tax deferred until retirement.

17-2.   Contributions are not deductible in a Roth IRA, but qualifying distributions are tax free.

17-3.   a.   The maximum annual contribution is $3,000 for 2002 and increasing for future years.
     b.   For 2002, a $500 additional contribution can be made for an individual who has attained age 50 (or older) by the end of 2002.
     c.   A spousal IRA can be established, in most cases, when the couple is married and filing jointly.
     d.   IRA contributions must be made by the due date of the individual's tax return for the year (April 15 for most taxpayers).
     e.   Contributions made in excess of the limits are referred to as excess contributions and are subject to a 6 percent excise tax.

17-4.   Single taxpayers who are not active participants in an employer-sponsored retirement plan may make a deductible contribution to an IRA regardless of their income level. If the single taxpayer is an active participant, then a deductible contribution is only allowed if adjusted gross income is below a specified limit. The rules are similar for married taxpayers filing jointly, with one exception. If a married person is not an active participant but their spouse is an active participant, then a deductible contribution can only be made (for the nonparticipant) if the couple's adjusted gross income is below $160,000.

17-5.   a.   John is considered an active participant. In general, anyone covered by a qualified plan is considered an active participant, and a Keogh plan is considered a qualified plan.
     b.   Barb is not considered an active participant even though her employer has a qualified plan because Barb is not covered by the plan.
     c.   Patty is an active participant because salary reductions to a 401(k) plan trigger active participant status.
     d.   Bob is not an active participant because he will not actually receive any contributions under his employer's profit-sharing plan.
     e.   Tim is considered an active participant because Tim's spouse is an active participant in a qualified plan.

17-6.   a.   For 2002, the deduction is phased out for adjusted gross income between $34,000 and $44,000.
     b.   For 2002, the deduction is phased out for adjusted gross income between $54,000 and $64,000.

17-7.   George Barke can deduct $2,010, determined as follows:

$$\text{Deductible amount} = \$3,000 - \left(\$3,000 \times \frac{\text{adjusted gross income - filing status floor}}{\text{phaseout amount}}\right)$$

$$\text{Deductible amount} = \$3,000 - \left(\$3,000 \times \frac{\$57,317 - \$54,000}{\$10,000}\right)$$

$$\text{Deductible amount} = \$3,000 - \$995.10$$

$$\text{Deductible amount} = \$2,004.90$$

$$\text{Rounding up} = \$2,010$$

Mary can deduct $3,000, because she is not an active participant and the couple's AGI is less than $150,000.

17-8.   a.   Eligibility to make Roth IRA contributions depends solely on an individual's adjusted gross income. The ability to make contributions is phased out for single taxpayers with AGI between $95,000 and $110,000 and for married taxpayers filing jointly with AGI between $150,000 and $160,000.

      b. Unlike in traditional IRAs, contributions can continue for participants after age 70 1/2.

      c. Qualified tax-free withdrawals can be made after the plan has been in existence for 5 years and the participant attains age 59 1/2, dies, becomes disabled, or withdraws up to $10,000 for first-time homeowner expenses.

17-9. The common types of rollovers are those from one IRA to another and rollovers from qualified plans, 403(b) annuities, and 457 plans to an IRA.

17-10. The taxpayer must be single or married filing jointly and have less than $100,000 of AGI for the year of the conversion.

17-11. Upon the conversion, the taxpayer must pay ordinary income tax but does not pay the 10 percent early withdrawal penalty.

17-12. a. Unless the participant has made nondeductible contributions, distributions from IRAs are treated as ordinary income and are subject to federal income tax. Nondeductible contributions are withdrawn tax free on a pro rata basis. If the participant dies, payments to beneficiaries are still subject to income tax. However, the income is treated as "income in respect to a decedent," which means that income taxes are reduced by the amount of estate taxes paid as a result of the IRA. If distributions are made prior to age 591/2, the premature distribution rule imposes an additional 10 percent excise tax unless an exception applies.

      b. Qualifying distributions from a Roth IRA are withdrawn tax free. If a nonqualifying withdrawal is made, an individual can withdraw his or her Roth IRA contributions (or converted contributions) without income tax consequences. Once all contributions have been withdrawn, amounts representing earnings are subject to both income tax and the 10 percent premature distributions penalty. A special rule applies to converted Roth IRAs. The 10 percent premature distribution penalty continues to apply for 5 years after the conversion—even if no income tax is due.

Answers to Self-Test Questions

17-1. False. No contribution, deductible, nondeductible, or Roth IRA can be made by a taxpayer whose only compensation is passive income.

17-2. False. Self-employeds who have a net loss from self-employment can make IRA or IRA annuity contributions if they have salary or wage income. They do not have to reduce the amount of the salary income by the net loss.

17-3. True.

17-4. False. Spousal IRAs can be set up even if the taxpayer does not contribute to his or her own account.

17-5. False. An excess contribution is subject to a 6 percent excise tax.

17-6. True.

17-7. True.

17-8. False. A participant in a nonqualified plan is not considered an active participant.

17-9. False. In a profit-sharing plan where employer contributions are discretionary, the participant must actually receive some contribution for active-participant status to be triggered.

17-10. False. A partially reduced IRA deduction is always rounded up to the nearest $10 increment.

17-11. True.

17-12. False. Contributions to a Roth IRA are never deductible.

17-13. False. Active participant status has no bearing on the ability to contribute to a Roth IRA. Because this individual has earned less than $95,000, he or she can contribute $3,000 to a Roth IRA for the year.

17-14. False. Qualifying withdrawals from a Roth IRA are always income tax free. However, this distribution is not "qualified" because the account has only been open for 3 years. Nonqualifying withdrawals may be tax free but only if to the extent that the participant is only withdrawing contributions. Because this question said the withdrawal is always tax free, the answer is false.

17-15. False. A rollover must be made within 60 days of the distribution.

17-16. True.

17-17. True.

17-18. False. Amounts converted from an IRA to a Roth IRA are taxed as ordinary income. However, the 10 percent premature penalty tax will not apply.

17-19. True.

Chapter 18

Answers to Review Questions

18-1.   a.   An individual retirement account is a trust or a custodial account whose trustee or custodian must be a bank, a federally insured credit union, a savings and loan association, or a person or organization that receives IRS permission to act as the trustee or custodian.

      b.   An individual retirement annuity is an annuity contract issued by an insurance company. It is not transferable and has no fixed premiums.

18-2.   Life insurance and collectibles (antiques) are prohibited investments. Gold bullion is allowed if it meets the exception to the collectible prohibition. Real estate owned by the participant would most likely be prohibited under the prohibited transaction rules.

18-3.   An annuity can be used to reduce exposure to the risk of "living too long." The annuity will also typically have a waiver-of-premium feature if the individual becomes disabled.

18-4.   A SIMPLE IRA is different from a traditional IRA in one regard: Distributions from SIMPLE IRAs in the first 2 years of participation are subject to a 25 percent early withdrawal penalty tax. Because of this tax, there is a prohibition on the transfer out of a SIMPLE IRA and into a regular IRA in the first 2 years of participation.

18-5.   a.   Carlos can make either a $3,000 deductible IRA contribution or a $3,000 Roth contribution for 2002 (or he could divide the $3,000 contribution up into both).

      b.   Anthony cannot make a deductible IRA contribution or a Roth IRA contribution. He could make a nondeductible IRA contribution.

      c.   Sam cannot make a deductible IRA contribution (AGI over $64,000) but Sally can (AGI less than $150,000). Both can make Roth IRA contributions (AGI less than $150,000).

      d.   Neither can make a deductible IRA contribution or a Roth IRA contribution. Of course, both can make a nondeductible IRA contribution.

18-6.   Investing directly in stock or mutual funds may be a better alternative to nondeductible IRA contributions because of the disparity in the tax rate. Long-term capital gains are taxed at a 20 percent rate while IRA withdrawals will always be ordinary income.

18-7.   Determining when the Roth makes economic sense is a complicated analysis that involves a review of the individual's entire retirement and estate planning picture. The Roth can be quite valuable to young persons, those with estate planning problems and individuals with a large percentage of their assets already in tax-sheltered retirement plans.

18-8.   An employer-sponsored IRA is a very simple alternative (or supplement to) an employer-sponsored tax-advantaged plan. The program can include (or exclude) any employees (no nondiscrimination requirements) and contributions may be made as additional compensation or as a salary reduction.

Answers to Self-Test Questions

18-1.   True.

18-2.   False. IRAs cannot be invested in life insurance.

18-3.   False. IRAs, generally, cannot invest in collectibles, but they can be invested in precious metals and certain coins.

18-4.   True.

18-5.   True.

18-6.   True.

18-7.   True.

18-8.   True.

18-9.   False. Individuals who are concerned about maximizing the estate left to their heirs may find that a Roth IRA conversion can help accomplish this goal.

18-10.   False. There is no requirement that the employer-sponsored IRA be available to all employees or be nondiscriminatory with respect to coverage.

Chapter 19

Answers to Review Questions

19-1. a. Four goals Kathy should have as a retirement planner are (1) to make clients aware of the financial requirements facing them during retirement, (2) to educate clients about the effect inflation has on retirement savings, (3) to help clients understand the effect financial well-being has on the quality of life, and (4) to lay out the available alternatives for developing a plan that leads to financial self-sufficiency.

      b. Kathy should point out the consequences of not saving for retirement. These consequences can range from making cutbacks in the standard of living to becoming impoverished. Kathy should also point out that the combination of an employer-sponsored pension plan and Social Security will not provide adequate funds during retirement to maintain a preretirement standard of living. In addition, Kathy should make her clients aware that Social Security may not provide the same help toward retirement in the future that it provides today. Finally, Kathy should also make her clients aware of the health and inflation issues facing retirees.

19-2. Baby boomers will make a significant impact on retirement when their turn comes. Surveys suggest that they may not be as prepared as they need to be. This is especially true for boomers who are employed at firms with less than 25 employees.

19-3. a. The seven roadblocks to retirement savings are:
        (1) improper spending/saving ratios
        (2) unexpected expenses
        (3) inadequate insurance coverage
        (4) divorce
        (5) lack of a retirement plan at work/spending preretirement distributions
        (6) lack of financial literacy
        (7) other savings objectives

      b. Strategies to overcome these roadblocks might be
        (1) a 90/10 spending/saving ratio
        (2) an emergency fund
        (3) an insurance check-up
        (4) the use of qualified domestic relations orders
        (5) rolling over premature distributions
        (6) financial education
        (7) Making retirement saving supplemental to, not subordinate to, other savings objectives.

19-4. Client retirement objectives are influenced by health, age, marital status, children, differences in ages between the husband and wife, and personal preferences.

19-5. Retirement objectives may include
    1. maintaining preretirement standard of living
    2. maintaining economic self-sufficiency
    3. minimizing taxes
    4. retiring early
    5. adapting to noneconomic aspects of retirement
    6. passing on wealth to others
    7. improving lifestyle in retirement
    8. caring for dependents

19-6. a. The topics covered include
      • employer-provided retirement plans
      • Social Security
      • personal saving and investments
      • IRAs and Roth IRAs
      • income tax issues
      • distribution issues
      • insurance coverage

- asset allocation and risk
- long-term care options
- retirement communities
- relocation possibilities
- wellness
- nutrition
- lifestyle choices

   b. Five elements of a retirement planning practice are:
1. incorporating retirement planning as a segment of comprehensive financial planning
2. dealing with other professionals
3. dealing with relatively young clients
4. monitoring and updating the client's plan
5. conducting seminars

19-7. A variety of resources are available to aid the retirement planner including membership organizations, seminars, AARP, and websites.

Answers to Self-Test Questions

19-1. True.

19-2. False. The proper spending ratio is 90/10. This ratio approaches an 80/20 split as clients draw closer to retirement.

19-3. False. If a client's income is primarily from commissions, 6 months' worth of income should be held in an emergency fund.

19-4. True.

19-5. True.

19-6. True.

19-7. False. Most clients are not as acquainted with financial products and services as they need to be in order to retire successfully.

19-8. False. Minimizing taxes does not always maximize wealth. For example, low yielding tax-advantaged investments may not be as profitable as some taxed investments.

19-9. True.

19-10. True.

19-11. True.

19-12. False. Retirement planning is best if clients start saving for retirement at a relatively young age.

Chapter 20

Answers to Review Questions

20-1. Deferring retirement means continuing to live on salary and not savings. It also means continuing with employer-paid benefits, such as medical, life, and accident insurance. It could also have an impact on the individual's self-esteem.

20-2. Health impacts a client's retirement in three major ways:
1. Poor health may force the client to cease work earlier than expected; good health may mean continued employment after normal retirement age.
2. Caregiving may be required for a family member in poor health.
3. Clients may retire early based on the fear of poor health in their retirement years and a desire to "get out while they can still enjoy retirement."

20-3. The longevity assumption has a major impact on the amount needed to be saved. If the individual expects a short life, then the financial picture will seem quite rosy. In the end, a reasonable assumption that takes into consideration both statistics and the individual's feelings about his or her life expectancy is appropriate.

20-4.   They both have the advantage of
   - forced savings
   - cash-value buildup
   - ability to beat inflation, and
   - provision of benefits for a surviving spouse

20-5.   Portfolio recommendations will not be followed if they are beyond the client's understanding. In addition, the client's risk tolerance will impact on recommendations the planner may make.

20-6.   The qualified plan gives the owner the opportunity to save pretax dollars and to protect assets from creditors. It also gives the owner the ability to build some equity and not be so dependent upon the sale of the business as the sole retirement asset.

20-7.   (1) They statistically have lower earnings.
   (2) They statistically experience higher turnover.
   (3) They historically tend to be employed in industries without pensions.
   (4) They tend to outlive their spouses.
   (5) They are more likely to be caregivers.

20-8.   If a plan is terminated, the participant automatically becomes 100 percent vested. In addition, the client must be kept informed by the employer. Finally, PBGC protection might apply.

20-9.   Retirement planning and estate planning at first blush seem incongruous. However, careful coordination is required.

20-10. a. Reverse annuity mortgages come in several forms. With one type, the homeowner stays in the home until some specified time and the buyer buys a remainder interest. The more common form today is a loan, in which each homeowner receives a stream of income while remaining in the home. When the homeowner moves out or dies, the loans are repaid with the sale of the proceeds from the house.
   b. A good reverse annuity program may not be available, or the homeowner may not have enough equity in the home to make it worthwhile. Also, the homeowner may lose some control over subsequent changes to the home.

20-11. a. Moving to a smaller home can free up assets for retirement. In addition, lower heating, cooling, and maintenance costs may ensue.
   b. It is difficult to reverse a wrong relocation decision without severe financial consequences.

20-12. Because Jane is under age 65 in 2001, her Social Security will be reduced $1 for every $2 in earnings in excess of $10,680 (as indexed in 2001). To determine Jane's Social Security reduction, subtract the earnings limit of $10,680 from her actual salary of $15,680. The $5,000 difference is then divided by 2. The result is a $2,500 reduction in Jane's Social Security benefit of $10,000.

Answers to Self-Test Questions

20-1.   True.
20-2.   False. With some exceptions, the Age Discrimination in Employment Act prohibits involuntary retirement at any age.
20-3.   True.
20-4.   True.
20-5.   False. Planners typically take into account a client's family history for life expectancy. In addition, planners typically add 5 to 10 years to a life expectancy because the effect of underestimating an actual life expectancy by using a projected life expectancy table can be disastrous.
20-6.   True.
20-7.   False. If there is no need for additional life insurance protection, a deferred-annuity contract should be used instead of a cash value life insurance policy.
20-8.   True.
20-9.   True.
20-10. False. Funds saved in a qualified plan are *not* subject to the reach of a business's general creditors in cases such as bankruptcy or corporate liability.

20-11. False. Retirement planners must account for a business owner's ability to receive payment for business interests sold at retirement.

20-12. True.

20-13. False. Assets passed to a surviving spouse are typically free of transfer (estate and gift) taxes because of a federally permitted 100 percent marital deduction.

20-14. True.

20-15. True.

20-16. True.

20-17. False. Under a sale-leaseback arrangement, the house is sold to an investor and rented back by the seller for the remainder of his or her life.

20-18. True.

20-19. False. Planners typically advise only a temporary and partial commitment to a relocating client (such as retaining a current home or renting in a new area).

20-20. True.

20-21. False. Becoming reemployed after starting to receive Social Security benefits will reduce a client's Social Security benefit if the amount earned exceeds a certain threshold amount.

Chapter 21

Answers to Review Questions

21-1. Late-career clients are the most interested in retirement planning and they have a better view of their retirement needs. Middle-career clients will have to account for inflation and real growth when projecting income needs for retirement. Finally, early-career clients should focus on "financial independence planning" to help motivate them for retirement.

21-2. The materials indicate that the percentage is 60–80 percent.

21-3. There are tax breaks spreading reductions and saving reductions. These include
- FICA tax cessation
- increased standard deduction
- beneficial taxation of Social Security income
- state and local tax breaks
- increased use of the medical expense deduction
- lower work-related expenses
- lower home ownership expenses
- lower payments for dependent children
- lower savings because the client is no longer saving for retirement
- age-related reductions in spending

21-4. The general rule that applies to James is that a married taxpayer can exclude all Social Security benefits from his or her income for tax purposes if the taxpayer's modified adjusted gross income plus one-half of the Social Security benefit does not exceed the base amount of $32,000. If the base amount is exceeded (but does not exceed $44,000), the taxable amount of Social Security benefits will be the lesser of one-half of the Social Security benefit or one-half of the combined income (one-half of the Social Security benefit plus the entire amount of modified adjusted gross income) in excess of $32,000.

James's combined income is derived by adding his $29,000 pension to one-half of his $9,000 Social Security benefit ($4,500). Because $33,500 ($29,000 + $4,500) exceeds the base amount of $32,000 by $1,500, James will be taxed on one-half of this amount, or $750. Thus, James will pay taxes on $750 of his Social Security benefit.

21-5. a. A client's living expenses will be reduced by many of the factors cited in the answer to 21-3. In addition, certain budget items decline in retirement (mortgage, food, clothing, and so on).

b. Items that increase in retirement include medical expenses, travel, vacations and other life style changes, utilities and telephone and house maintenance.

21-6. There are a variety of unknown variables that must be reasonably estimated, but can never be known until retirement plays itself out.

21-7. The expense method is the preferred approach to estimating the needs in the first year of retirement. It relies on predicting a client's budget.

21-8. The factors to be considered when estimating a client's expected starting date for retirement include
- the national trend toward early retirement
- changes in Social Security law
- the size of the client's organizations
- the probability of "forced retirement"

21-9. Because it represents a moderate view of long-term inflation

21-10. The higher the rate-of-inflation and standard-of-living increases, the more savings a client will need for retirement.

Answers to Self-Test Questions

21-1. True.

21-2. True.

21-3. False. A replacement ratio of between 60 and 80 percent of a client's final-average salary should be used when planning for the income needed in the first year of an individual's retirement. In addition, a higher replacement ratio may be defined if the client wants to be conservative.

21-4. False. Social Security taxes are eliminated for retirees.

21-5. False. Single taxpayers are entitled to add $1,100 (as indexed for 2001) to the standard deduction. Marrieds filing jointly can add $900 for each spouse over 65.

21-6. True.

21-7. True.

21-8. True.

21-9. True.

21-10. True.

21-11. False. If the planned retirement date occurs after the actual retirement date, the retirement need will be underestimated.

21-12. True.

21-13. True.

Chapter 22

Answers to Review Questions

22-1. First, the client must be in a group that is covered. One of the largest groups of employees not covered are employees of the federal government hired prior to 1984. Also, railroad retirement workers and other selected groups may not be covered. However, most people are covered by Social Security. Second, the client must have credit for 40 quarters of coverage.

22-2. Dependents include
- a spouse aged 62 or older
- a spouse of any age if the spouse is caring for at least one child or a retired worker
- dependent, unmarried children under 18 (full-time students up to age 19, disabled children of any age so long as they were disabled before age 22)

22-3. Cost-of-living adjustments are typically made each January based on the increase in the consumer price index (CPI).

22-4. Robert Rose's benefit will be reduced 5/9 of one percent for every month that early retirement precedes age 65. Because Robert's benefit will start at age 63, 24 months before age 65, Robert's benefit will be 86.67 percent of the benefit he would have received at age 65, determined as follows:

Percentage of benefit reduction = 5/9 x months prior to age 65

Percentage of benefit reduction = 5/9 x 24

Percentage of benefit reduction = 13.33

100% minus 13.33% = 86.67%

22-5.   Jane Maple's benefit will be increased 3 percent for each year she delays retirement beyond 65. Because Jane is delaying her retirement for 36 months, her benefit will be 109 percent of the benefit she would have received at age 65.

22-6.   Medicare part A is available at no cost to anyone aged 65 or older who is eligible for a monthly retirement benefit under Social Security or the railroad retirement program. If aged 65 and not eligible, the individual may generally purchase part A. Medicare is not available to retirees who retire before age 65. Those eligible for part A are also eligible for part B but must pay a monthly premium for part B coverage.

22-7.   Part A, the hospital portion of Medicare, provides
- benefits for expenses incurred in hospitals for 90 days in each benefit period
- skilled-nursing facility benefits
- hospice benefits
- some home health care
- 60 lifetime reserve days of coverage

22-8.   a.   Part B, the doctor's portion of Medicare, provides
- physicians' and surgeons' fees
- diagnostic tests
- physical therapy
- some home health care
- drugs administered by a physician at the hospital
- radiation therapy
- medical supplies
- prosthetic devices
- ambulance services
- some vaccines
- mammograms

  b.   What part B, the doctor's portion of Medicare, does not provide
- drugs that are self-administered
- routine physicals
- routine foot care
- some immunizations
- most cosmetic surgery
- most dental care
- custodial care
- eyeglasses
- hearing aids
- orthopedic shoes

22-9.   To gather information about employer-sponsored pension benefits, review annual benefit statements, the summary plan description, and the 1099R form that is generally distributed along with the check.

22-10. The replacement ratios under each are not set up to provide enough income. Retirement is a three-legged stool of economic security that requires private savings.

22-11. For the client who is not adequately prepared for retirement, planning strategies may include postponing the retirement date, moving to a less expensive region, using the home as a financial asset, or even adjusting expectations for retirement living.

22-12. The list includes, IRAs, Roth IRAs, retirement community plans, personally owned life insurance, stocks, bonds and other financial assets, and tangible assets.

Answers to Self-Test Questions

22-1.   True.

22-2.   False. Credit for Social Security eligibility purposes is based on quarters of coverage.

22-3.   True.

22-4. True.

22-5. False. The age is 62, not 55.

22-6. False. Although a spouse is entitled to Social Security benefits based on the other spouse's eligibility, the benefits will be reduced if taken prior to age 65.

22-7. True.

22-8. False. A worker who retires at age 62 and elects Social Security coverage will receive 80 percent of the benefit that he or she would have received at age 65.

22-9. False. Workers who delay applying for Social Security retirement benefits until after age 65 are eligible for an increased benefit.

22-10. False. Most civilian employees of the federal government who were employed by the government prior to 1984 are covered under the civil service retirement system, not the Social Security system.

22-11. False. The book refers to this as a stepped-up savings approach.

22-12. False. In order to be covered by part B of Medicare, a monthly premium must be paid.

22-13. True.

22-14. True.

22-15. True.

22-16. False. An integrated defined-benefit plan typically provides a replacement ratio to rank-and-file employees that is much lower than 60 percent of final-average salary.

22-17. False. Defined-contribution plans are not protected against preretirement inflation because they provide benefits based on a client's career-average salary.

22-18. True.

22-19. False. The combination of a pension benefit and a Social Security benefit is typically inadequate to provide the proper amount of retirement income.

22-20. True.

22-21. False. If your client makes both deductible and nondeductible IRA contributions, separate IRAs should be established for each type to simplify recordkeeping.

Chapter 23

Answers to Review Questions

23-1. a. In order to determine the amount of income needed to fund Jane's desired retirement lifestyle, multiply the desired replacement ratio by her current salary, as follows:

80% x $100,000 = $80,000

Jane will need $80,000 a year in today's dollars in order to achieve her lifestyle in her retirement years.

   b. Keith must first apply a growth factor to his salary in order to determine the amount of income needed to fund his desired retirement. He will use the following future-value formula:

$$FV = PV(1 + r)^n$$

where PV = Keith's current salary

r = Keith's 2 percent growth rate

n = number of years until Keith retires (20)

FV = $50,000 (1 + .02)^{20}$

FV = $74,297

Once Keith has determined a salary that reflects growth, the replacement ratio is then applied as follows:

90% x $74,297 = $66,867

Keith will need $66,867 a year in today's dollars in order to achieve his desired lifestyle in his retirement years.

23-2. To determine a client's retirement income status, the client must subtract his annual target for retirement income from his estimated amount of annual retirement income.

23-3. a. Social Security benefits do not need inflation protection because they are already subject to a cost-of-living adjustment (COLA) by the government.

   b. Most private pensions are not subject to a COLA and, therefore, the client must save an additional amount in order to protect the pension's purchasing power.

    c. Dividend income is protected from inflation if the principal is left intact.

    d. The client's retirement income deficit is not protected from inflation. (The deficit will grow each year based on inflation).

23-4. In order to determine a client's after-tax rate of return (ROR), use the following formula:

After-tax ROR $= r(1-t)$

       where r = before-tax rate of return

           t = marginal tax rate

In this case, Tom's after-tax rate of return will be

After-tax ROR $= 10(1-.28)$

After-tax ROR $= 7.2$

23-5. Clients can choose to liquidate all assets over the retirement period. They can also choose to partially liquidate assets or not to liquidate assets at all.

23-6. Life annuity products can be used to help a client not to outlive their income.

23-7. In order to determine the amount of money it would take to furnish a retirement income that provides \$16,000 worth of purchasing power for 35 years, use equation 23-1 from the text.

$$\frac{\text{Funds needed}}{\text{(RID fund)}} = \text{desired purchasing power} \times (1+\text{int}) \times \left[\frac{1-\left(\frac{1+\text{inf}}{1+\text{int}}\right)^n}{\text{int}-\text{inf}}\right]$$

$$\frac{\text{Funds needed}}{\text{(RID fund)}} = \$16,000 \times (1+.07) \times \left[\frac{1-\left(\frac{1+.03}{1+.07}\right)^{35}}{.07-.03}\right]$$

$$\frac{\text{Funds needed}}{\text{(RID fund)}} = \$17,120 \times \left(\frac{1-0.263554}{.04}\right)$$

$$\frac{\text{Funds needed}}{\text{(RID fund)}} = \$17,120 \times 18.41115$$

$$\frac{\text{Funds needed}}{\text{(RID fund)}} = \$315,198.88$$

23-8. In order to determine the amount of money it would take at retirement to provide inflation protection for level annual pension benefits of \$33,000, use equation 23-3.

$$\text{Funds needed} = \begin{array}{c}\text{income}\\\text{needing}\\\text{inflation}\\\text{protection}\end{array} \times (1+\text{int}) \times \left[\frac{1-\left(\frac{1+\text{inf}}{1+\text{int}}\right)^n}{\text{int}-\text{inf}}\right] - \begin{array}{c}\text{income}\\\text{needing}\\\text{inflation}\\\text{protection}\end{array} \times (1+\text{int}) \times \left[\frac{1-\left(\frac{1}{1+\text{int}}\right)^n}{\text{int}}\right]$$

$$\text{Funds needed} = \$33,000 \times (1+.06) \times \left[\frac{1-\left(\frac{1+.02}{1+.06}\right)^{30}}{.06-.02}\right] - \$33,000 \times (1+.06) \times \left[\frac{1-\left(\frac{1}{1+.06}\right)^{30}}{.06}\right]$$

$$\text{Funds needed} = \$34,980 \times \frac{1-.315376}{.04} - \$34,980 \times \left(\frac{1-.17411}{.06}\right)$$

$$\text{Funds needed} = \$34,980 \times 17.1156 - (\$34,980 \times 13.76483)$$

Funds needed = $598,703.69 − $481,493.75

Funds needed = $117,209.94

23-9.　In order to calculate the amount of level annual funding it takes to accumulate $350,000 over 17 years (age 48 to age 65), use equation 23-5.

$$\text{Annual funding} = \frac{\text{Target amount}}{\left[\frac{(1+int)^n - 1}{int}\right] \times (1+int)}$$

$$\text{Annual funding} = \frac{\$350,000}{\left[\frac{(1+.07)^{17} - 1}{.07}\right] \times (1+.07)}$$

$$\text{Annual funding} = \frac{\$350,000}{\left(\frac{3.1588 - 1}{.07}\right) \times 1.07}$$

$$\text{Annual funding} = \frac{\$350,000}{32.9988}$$

Annual funding = $10,606

23-10.　a.　In order to calculate the amount of the first-year contribution needed to accumulate $150,000 using stepped-up funding, equation 23-6 should be used.

$$\text{First-year funding} = \frac{\text{Target amount} \times (int - inf)}{\left[1 - \left(\frac{1+inf}{1+int}\right)^n\right] \times (1+int)^{(n+1)}}$$

$$\text{First-year funding} = \frac{\$150,000 \times (.08-.04)}{\left[1 - \left(\frac{1+.04}{1+.08}\right)^{5n}\right] \times (1+.08)^{(5+1)}}$$

$$\text{First-year funding} = \frac{\$150,000 \times .04}{(1-.82803) \times 1.58687}$$

$$\text{First-year funding} = \frac{\$6,000}{.17197 \times 1.58687}$$

$$\text{First-year funding} = \frac{\$6,000}{0.27289}$$

First-year funding = $21,986.88

b.　To determine the remaining 4 years' contribution, multiply the prior year's contribution by 1.04 (1 plus the inflation rate).

Year 2 = $21,986.88 × 1.04 = $22,866.36
Year 3 = $22,866.36 × 1.04 = $23,781.01
Year 4 = $23,781.01 × 1.04 = $24,732.25
Year 5 = $24,732.25 × 1.04 = $25,721.54

23-11.

Retirement Planning Work Sheet		
ASSUMPTIONS		
A1.	Inflation rate prior to retirement	4
A2.	Inflation rate after retirement	4
A3.	Number of years until retirement	19
A4.	Expected duration of retirement	25
A5.	Rate of return prior to retirement	8
A6.	Rate of return after retirement	7
A7.	Savings step-up rate	6
FACTORS		
F1.	Pre-retirement inflation factor	2.11
F2.	Retirement needs present value factor	17.936
F3.	Current assets future value factor	4.32
F4.	Defined-benefit present value factor	12.469
F5.	Savings rate factor	0.01435
COMPUTATIONS		
L1.	Projected annual retirement budget	64,000 (80% of $80,000)
L2. −	Social Security benefit	20,000
L3. =	Net annual need in current dollars	44,000
L4. X	F1 factor	2.11
L5. =	Inflation-adjusted annual retirement need	92,840
L6. X	F2 factor	17.936
L7. =	Total resources needed for retirement	1,665,178.24
L8.	Total in defined-contribution plans	300,000
L9. +	Total private savings earmarked for retirement	0
L10. =	Current assets available for retirement	300,000
L11. X	F3 factor	4.32
L12. =	Future value of current assets	1,296,000
L13.	Annual income from defined-benefit plan	0
L14. X	F1 factor	2.11
L15. =	Inflation-adjusted annual income from defined-benefit plan	0
L16. X	F4 factor	12.469
L17. =	Lump-sum value of defined-benefit plan	0
L18.	Total resources available for retirement (line 12 and line 17)	1,296,000
L19.	Additional amount you need to accumulate by retirement	369,178.24
L20. X	F5 factor	0.01435
L21. =	Amount you need to save—first year	5,297.70
(Savings in each subsequent year must increase by the savings step-up rate, 6%)		

Answers to Self-Test Questions

23-1.   True.
23-2.   False. In addition to applying a replacement ratio to current salary and adjusting for inflation, the planner must also adjust for a growth factor in the client's lifestyle if it is applicable.
23-3.   True.

23-4. False. A client's RIS can either be a positive or a negative amount. A positive RIS indicates a surplus because current sources exceed the target amount. A negative RIS indicates a deficit and suggests the need for additional accumulations.

23-5. True.

23-6. False. Pension income is generally not considered to be protected from a decline in purchasing power due to increases in inflation. The effects of preretirement inflation may be avoided if the client is in a final-average salary defined-benefit plan, but the pension benefit is not typically protected from inflation after retirement.

23-7. True.

23-8. True.

23-9. True.

23-10. False. A decline in purchasing power applies to any asset that is not inflation protected after retirement. For example, a cash value life insurance policy that will be converted to level annuity payments at retirement is subject to a decline in purchasing power.

23-11. True.

Chapter 24

Answers to Review Questions

24-1. Planners and clients alike know that the higher the risk, the greater the potential return. Risk includes the variation in the amount of annual income as well as the potential for gain or loss of some or all of the asset's value. Risk/return considerations fall into two major considerations: the appropriate amount of risk for the goal and life cycle and the client's ability to tolerate risk.

24-2. During the long-term accumulation period the planner must
- recognize the client's preference for risk and choose investment vehicles that correspond to the client's "zone of acceptance"
- monitor the portfolio's performance
- revise the portfolio to correspond with changes in the client's personal finances, the client's attitude toward risk, and the economy
- account for inflation's influence on the client's need for retirement funds

24-3. a. (1) commodities
   (2) options
   (3) junk bonds
   (4) OTC stocks
   (5) aggressive-growth mutual funds
   (6) limited partnerships
   (7) commodities trading
   b. (1) high-leverage real estate
   (2) cyclical + growth stocks
   (3) long-term bonds
   (4) master limited partnerships
   (5) collectibles
   c. (1) low-leverage real estate
   (2) high-yield stocks
   (3) medium-term bonds
   (4) variable annuities
   (5) common stock mutual funds
   d. (1) short-term bonds
   (2) GNMA bonds
   (3) insured municipals
   (4) fixed annuities
   (5) balanced mutual funds

    e.   (1) Treasury bills
        (2) short-term CDs
        (3) money market accounts
        (4) savings accounts
        (5) money market funds
        (6) Series EE and HH bonds
        (7) cash value life insurance

24-4. a. Dollar-cost averaging is an approach in which the fixed-dollar amount is invested in a security in each period.

        b. The concept of regularly putting money aside meshes well with retirement planning.

24-5. A review is important because

- as the standard of living grows, the need for additional saving to fund the increased standard of living also increases.

- planners may want to suggest that as real income grows, the current standard of living should grow at a somewhat reduced pace. Assume real after-tax income increases by 10 percent. If the client limits any increase in income, then there will be a sizable increase, proportionately, in funds available for retirement accumulation purposes. For example, if a client has income of $100,000 and allocates $80,000 for lifestyle and $20,000 for retirement purposes, a 10 percent increase in real income will provide an additional $10,000. If the increase in lifestyle expenditures can be kept to $4,000 (or 40 percent of the $10,000 increase), then $6,000 is available for retirement. This $6,000 represents a whooping 30 percent increase in annual retirement funding. In addition, the $4,000 increase in lifestyle expenditures raises the current standard of living by 5 percent.

- planners must consider downward revisions of funding goals because of job-related or other economic reversals.

24-6. The portfolio restructuring period begins somewhere between 5 and 15 years prior to retirement. The investment emphasis changes from growth to preservation of income.

24-7. This period encompasses the time period beginning just prior to the retirement date and lasts through retirement. Portfolio shifting and tax consequences are more heightened during this period.

Answers to Self-Test Questions

24-1. True.

24-2. True.

24-3. False. The long-term accumulation period starts when the client is young and continues until between 5 to 15 years prior to retirement.

24-4. True.

24-5. False. Commodities are considered very high-risk investments.

24-6. True.

24-7. False. Variable annuities are generally considered a medium-risk investment.

24-8. False. Purchasing power risk is the risk that inflation will reduce the buying power of the monies placed into the investment vehicle.

24-9. True.

24-10. True.

24-11. True.

24-12. False. If a client's risk propensity changes, the planner needs to (1) reevaluate the expected return from accumulated funds, (2) restructure the existing portfolio, (3) change the allocation of new funds, and (4) alter the amount of annual funding.

24-13. False. When the client has the opportunity to direct investments in an employer-sponsored retirement plan, the client's investments should be considered as part of the aggregate portfolio mix for the purpose of assessing whether the client's risk profile is achieved.

24-14. True.

24-15. False. A client approaching retirement typically becomes less concerned about the appreciation possibilities for his or her portfolio and more concerned about the income possibilities.

24-16. True.

24-17. False. Participants whose employer-sponsored retirement plan provides a fixed pension benefit and not a lump-sum distribution should consider investing their private savings in growth-oriented investments to counteract the effects of inflation.

24-18. True.

24-19. True.

Chapter 25

Answers to Review Questions

25-1. Generally, the entire value of a distribution will be included as ordinary income in the year of the distribution except if a portion of the distribution is deemed to be recoverable cost basis. Taxable distributions made prior to age 59 1/2 will also be subject to the 10 percent Sec. 72(t) excise tax—unless the distribution satisfies one of several exceptions. Taxation may be avoided if the benefit is rolled over into another tax-sheltered plan.

25-2. At death, any remaining benefits will be included in the participant's taxable estate. Distributions to a death beneficiary are subject to income tax, although the benefit amount is treated as income in respect of the decedent, meaning that the income taxes will be reduced by the estate taxes paid as a result of the pension benefit.

25-3. a. A death benefit payable from a defined-benefit plan to a beneficiary upon the death of a 52-year-old employee is not subject to the Sec. 72(t) 10 percent penalty because distributions as a result of death are exempt from the penalty.

   b. A lump-sum benefit payable from a money-purchase pension plan to a 57-year-old disabled employee is not subject to the Sec. 72(t) penalty because distributions made due to disability are exempt from the penalty.

   c. A distribution from a 401(k) plan to a 52-year-old participant because of extreme hardship is subject to a Sec. 72(t) penalty—there is no applicable exception to the tax.

   d. Normally, the in-service distribution from a profit-sharing plan would be subject to a 10 percent Sec. 72(t) penalty. Because the employee is 63, however, the exclusion from penalty tax for employees over age 59 1/2 applies.

   e. Because a SIMPLE plan is funded with IRAs, distributions are eligible for the educational expense and first-time home buyer exceptions to the 10 percent penalty tax.

25-4. The most useful exception to the Sec. 72(t) penalty tax is the substantially equal payment exception. The rules provide a significant amount of flexibility for calculating the amount of the distribution; distributions can stop after the later of 5 years or attainment of age 59 1/2 and benefits can be divided into separate accounts to meet the required income goal. If a lump sum is needed, the participant can borrow from another source (possibly a deductible home equity loan) and repay the loan with the periodic distributions.

25-5. If substantially equal periodic payments do not continue for the prescribed period or they stray from the calculated amount, the participant could be required to pay the 10 percent penalty (including past due interest) on all previous nonconforming distributions.

25-6. The answer is that only $360 is excluded from tax and $11,640 is taxable. The calculation of the amount excluded from tax is $12,000/$400,000 (the total value of both IRA accounts) multiplied by $12,000.

25-7. The answer is $280. The amount of the first distribution that is excluded from tax is calculated by dividing Cherie's investment in the plan (cost basis = $72,900) by 260, the number used for an individual who is aged 62.

25-8. When the direct rollover is elected, no income tax is required. Also, a participant may intend to roll plan proceeds into the IRA within 60 days, then fail to actually make the transaction.

25-9. Because of the ability to attain participant loans, the possibility of lower investment costs or fees, the ability to rollover after-tax contributions, and life insurance contracts, and, for those born before 1936, the ability to retain the option to use 10-year forward averaging.

25-10. At the time, actual annuity payments are made to the participant.

25-11. When the participant receives a lump-sum distribution, or has purchased the employer securities with after-tax contributions.

25-12. The participant must receive the balance to the credit within one taxable year and receive the distribution upon death, disability, termination of employment, or attainment of age 59 1/2. For 10-year averaging the participant also needs 5 years of participation.

25-13. When the stock is taken into income, the participant pays ordinary income tax (and possibly the 10 percent Sec. 72(t) penalty tax) on the cost of the stock as it was allocated to the participant's account. Net unrealized appreciation (the difference between the cost and current market value) is taxed as long-term capital gain when the stock is sold. Additional gain is taxed as long-term or short-term capital gain depending upon the holding period.

25-14. Individuals born before 1936 who receive a lump-sum distribution from a qualified plan may be eligible for the grandfathered 10-year averaging and the gain on unrealized appreciation.

25-15. The rules were greatly simplified under new proposed regulations. In some cases, the required minimum distribution was reduced, and now participants are not required to make decisions at the required beginning date that will be binding into the future.

25-16. The minimum-distribution rules apply to IRAs (including SEPs and SIMPLEs), qualified plans, 403(b) plans and even 457 plans. Roth IRAs are not subject to the rules governing lifetime distributions to the participant but are required to make distributions to a death beneficiary.

25-17. Sara is subject to a 50 percent excise tax ($1,000), which she (not the plan administrator) is responsible for paying. In the past, the IRS did not always know whether an individual was in compliance with the rules. Beginning in 2002, the IRS will receive notification of the amount required to be distributed meaning that a noncomplying participant is likely to be found out.

25-18. a. James Daniel will reach age 70 on July 15, 2000, and age 70 1/2 on January 15, 2001. His required beginning date is April 1, 2002 (the April 1 following the calendar year in which he becomes 70 1/2).

    b. Because James was a participant in a qualified plan, was not a 5-percent owner, and was still employed when he attained age 70 1/2, his required beginning date will be the April 1 following retirement. In this case, his first distribution year will be 2003 and his required beginning date is April 1, 2004.

25-19. Even though the minimum distribution for the first year isn't due until the following April 1, the distribution for the second (and all subsequent years) must be made by December 31.

25-20. The required minimum distribution is $9,542 ($250,000/26.2).

25-21. The required minimum distribution is $10,474 ($265,000/25.3).

25-22. The required minimum distribution is $7,739 ($250,000/32.3).

25-23. In the year of death, the minimum distribution is calculated using the uniform table. In the year following death, the remaining distribution period is fixed based on the age of the beneficiary at the end of that distribution year.

25-24. Distributions must begin by the end of the year following the year of death. Otherwise, distributions must be made over a 5-year period.

25-25. Yes, however, the first step is to calculate the required minimum distribution from each plan separately. Then the distribution can be made from either or both plans.

Answers to Self-Test Questions

25-1. False. Tax planning is only part of the process when making a retirement decision. The ultimate goal is to maximize wealth while meeting the client's cash flow and other needs, not merely to save taxes.

25-2. True.

25-3. False. The Sec. 72(t) penalty applies only to the taxable portion of a distribution.

25-4. False. An in-service distribution made to a 50-year-old employee in the form of a life annuity is subject to the Sec. 72(t) penalty because the individual has not separated from service.

25-5. False. This question is answered incorrectly fairly often. There is no specific exception from the 10 percent penalty tax for hardship withdrawals from a 401(k) plan.

25-6. True.

25-7. False. There is an exception from the 10 percent penalty tax for IRA distributions for first-time homebuyer expenses. However, the exception is limited to a lifetime maximum of $10,000.

25-8. False. Distributions can cease after the later of 5 years or attainment of age 59 1/2 without penalty.

25-9. False. Even though PS 58 costs can be recovered when the policy is distributed to the participant, sole proprietors and partners in a partnership are not allowed to recover PS 58 costs.

25-10. False. With IRAs, a pro rata recovery rule applies to recovering the cost basis of nondeductible contributions.

25-11. True.

25-12. True.

25-13. True.

25-14. True.

25-15. True.

25-16. True.

25-17. False. Special lump-sum tax treatment is only available from qualified plans. A SEP does not qualify.

25-18. False. The tax is paid in one year, but is calculated using the tax rate that applies to a distribution of 1/10th of the distribution.

25-19. True.

25-20. True.

25-21. False. There are several things wrong with this statement. If the participant dies after attaining the required beginning date, the 5-year rule does not apply at all. Even if the participant dies prior to the RBD, there are several exceptions to the 5-year rule.

25-22. False. The tax is 50 percent of the shortfall.

25-23. False. Non-5 percent owners in qualified plans who are still working at 70 1/2 can wait until they retire until beginning distributions.

25-24. True.

25-25. True.

25-26. False. A 50 percent joint and survivor annuity purchased before the required beginning date will generally fail to satisfy the required minimum-distribution rules.

Chapter 26

Answers to Review Questions

26-1. The types of considerations are the need for retirement income, life expectancy, consideration of the income, and estate tax considerations.

26-2. Qualified plans will pay benefits at normal retirement age. Other payout triggers include, death, disability, termination for other reasons, and, in the case of profit-sharing type plans, in-service withdrawals.

26-3. Qualified plans can force a participant who has a benefit of less than $5,000 to take the benefit in a lump sum at the time of termination of employment. If the benefit exceeds this amount, the participant will be able to choose from all available benefit options, including the right to defer payment until attainment of normal retirement age.

26-4. If the beneficiary has a limited life expectancy, a life annuity with guaranteed payments can provide for continued payments to the beneficiary if the participant were to die prematurely.

26-5. It means that the benefit is more valuable than the normal form of payment. Typical examples are early retirement benefits that are not reduced for earlier payment and qualified joint and survivor annuities that are not reduced to equal the life annuity option.

26-6. It means that payments are reduced to reflect the "cost" of including the 10-year certain payments. For example, table 26-3 in the text shows the actuarial equivalent for a life annuity of $1,565 to be $1,494 a month for a life and 10-year certain option.

26-7. a. When Margo's actual assumed investment rate (AIR) is 3 percent and the assumed AIR is 6 percent, her unit value will drop 3 percent. Because the original unit value was $100, the new unit value will be $97.

  b. When Margo's actual AIR is 12 percent and her assumed AIR is 6 percent, the unit value will increase 6 percent. Because the original unit value was $100, the new unit value will be $106.

26-8. a. There can be amounts that are distributed tax free (after-tax contributions and PS 58 costs) and lump-sum distributions could be eligible for one of several special tax rules.

  b. The separating from service after attainment of age 55 exception.

  c. TEFRA 242 B elections.

  d. No, they do not.

  e. No, there are no exceptions to this date for IRAs.

26-9.   Because the decision may effect whether or not the participant has enough funds throughout retirement.

26-10. At the death of a participant, amounts in tax-sheltered plans are included in the taxable estate. If withdrawals are made at that time to pay the tax, it also triggers income tax—and up to 70 percent of asset goes to pay taxes. The most common strategy is to combine income tax deferral strategy (continue paying out benefits after the participant's death under the minimum-distribution rules) and life insurance planning to address the estate tax liquidity need.

Answers to Self-Test Questions

26-1.   True.

26-2.   True.

26-3.   True.

26-4.   False. An annuity certain pays out a specified benefit for a stated period of time. Installment payments are less certain. Essentially payments continue until the account is depleted.

26-5.   True.

26-6.   False. In a defined-benefit plan, any benefit option is based on the value of the base form of payment (typically a life annuity).

26-7.   False. When interest rates are higher than the AIR, the variable annuity payment will increase.

26-8.   True.

26-9.   False. Not necessarily. The guarantee of lifetime income through an annuity can be of tremendous value to the person concerned about outliving his or her assets.

26-10. True.

26-11. False. Because the minimum-distribution rules do not require Roth IRA distributions during the participant's lifetime, converting at a later age may still be an appropriate option.

Index